The Philosophy of War Films

THE PHILOSOPHY OF WAR FILMS

Edited by

David LaRocca

Paperback edition 2018

Scholarly publisher for the Commonwealth,
serving Bellarmine University, Berea College, Centre College of Kentucky, Eastern Kentucky University, The Filson Historical Society, Georgetown College, Kentucky Historical Society, Kentucky State University, Morehead State University, Murray State University, Northern Kentucky University, Transylvania University, University of Kentucky, University of Louisville, and Western Kentucky University.

Editorial and Sales Offices: The University Press of Kentucky
663 South Limestone Street, Lexington, Kentucky 40508-4008
www.kentuckypress.com

Library of Congress Cataloging-in-Publication Data

The philosophy of war films / edited by David LaRocca.
pages cm
Includes index.
ISBN 978-0-8131-4168-8 (hardcover : alk. paper) — ISBN 978-0-8131-4512-9 (pdf) —
ISBN 978-0-8131-4511-2 (epub)
1. War films—History and criticism. I. LaRocca, David, 1975- editor.
PN1995.9.W3P55 2014
791.43'658—dc23 2014032701

ISBN 978-0-8131-7622-2 (pbk. : alk. paper)

This book is printed on acid-free paper meeting
the requirements of the American National Standard
for Permanence in Paper for Printed Library Materials.

Manufactured in the United States of America.

Member of the Association of University Presses

Contents

Part 3. The Ethical Tribulations of War

Part 4. War, Nature, and the Absolute

Introduction

War Films and the Ineffability of War

David LaRocca

A master cinematographer was once asked, "How do you represent war on film?" and he replied decisively: "Hit the camera." Whether the quotation is accurate or apocryphal, the sentiment (which can be traced to John Huston and Janusz Kaminski) shows that the attribution is less affecting than the conceptual implication it invites, namely, that the lowest of low-tech solutions may create images imbued with the most profound philosophical insights about the endeavor to represent war on film—in particular, the presence and immediacy of war's *effects*.[1] How better to show what war is like—if only analogically in this limited medium of visual and sonic reports—than to let the instrument and perhaps its handler be physically impacted, disoriented, assaulted? Consider the inherent shock of the now-familiar shot when a camera has fallen from an injured or fatally wounded photographer or soldier, the film still rolling, the shutter still firing as our view has shifted from a horizontal to a vertical axis—the telltale sign of the creator's injury or death; for example, at the end of *Che,* the camera is point-of-view and it takes the shot and falls, and all we hear is breathing, and then the lens goes out of focus and fades to white—death.[2] Sometimes, as in documentary films, the impact is not staged but a contingency—the camera is just another body in the way—and so in *5 Broken Cameras* or *The Battle for Marjah,* the collision carries its own authenticity. When the camera is hit, we are reminded that the camera—like the soldier or the photographer—is physically positioned in space and not therefore issuing a view from nowhere but a view very much from the middle of crisis and mortal threat. If the camera is in motion, the footage engenders our consciousness of the person carrying it—filming where so many others are firing. When the camera is pummeled and tossed—either as a staged effect (for example in *Band of*

Brothers) or an unintended register of effects (as in documentaries such as *War Photographer*)—the medium itself seems to convey something of the visceral, embodied experience being represented. A signature instance of the nonfictional, filmic apprehension of human vitality—and mortality—can be found in *Cameraman at the Front,* a posthumously edited documentary comprised of footage taken by kinooperator Vladimir Sushinsky, who was shot to death while his camera was rolling—"we see the footage blur into a spiral as he falls"—coupled with footage taken simultaneously by another kinooperator who filmed Sushinsky's death (and was himself later killed in action). *Cameraman at the Front* becomes a perspectival representation of the wartime realities of bullets enfleshed and lives extinguished: first from behind Sushinsky's lens, then from the supplemental vantage of the second camera, and finally, by way of the craft of edited arrangement.[3] But then, of course, even when we watch a documentary, there is, properly speaking, no impact—just the visual impression of one. On-screen, the soldier is down, a camera still rolling beside the soldier, but the viewer will have only this vicarious image of the fall. The hit, at last, is (even in documentaries) not literal but a metaphor—a sign, a proxy. And yet, as the camera has become a common tool of war both for lethal agency and for expansive reconnaissance, it is also the primary instrument through which we experience movies about war; in its sheer physical presence as a humanly controlled device (though increasingly, also as unmanned), the camera—and its visions—becomes a tremendously affecting machine for representing war. There is, then, so much to say about what it captures and creates, for one thing, and what it cannot capture—what eludes it and what it leaves behind. Can war as such be represented by film? What do we think we mean when we speak of a war film? It is to these concerns that this book is dedicated.

Written by some of the most innovative, influential, and celebrated scholars working at the intersection of film and philosophy, this collection of essays is aimed at offering informed, exploratory, and nuanced replies to a pervasive contemporary question of tremendous philosophical importance: What does a war film represent? If it is not war as such, then what precisely is the nature of its existence? Is it a fabrication, a replication, a surrogate (or alternate reality), a hallucination, a dream, a nightmare, a truth, or a lie meant to conjure a truth? The writers in this collection, many of whom have advanced our thinking about the capacity of film to enrich philosophical understanding, have shaped the fields they contribute to and now, once again, define and redefine our inquiries and interests and the conundrums that continue to occupy, and demand, our considered critical attention. In this respect, the writers here sustain and complicate the ways in which, as Stanley Cavell has said, "the creation of film was as if meant for philosophy."[4] If film is a fundamentally philosophical medium, then a philosophy of war films seems especially pertinent since war, like film, appears to "reorient everything philosophy has said about reality and its representation, about art and imitation, about greatness and conventionality, about judgment and pleasure, about skepticism and transcendence, about language and expression."[5] Attending to essential pieces of film scholarship, these critics help us sort through the vast number of films dedicated to war—including the "god-awful heaps of cliché and fake profundity and commercialized sadism"—so that we can at once appreciate the range of extant work and clarify what within it deserves further reflection.[6] As we read in their capacious, scintillating essays, the questions that arise in the context of getting clearer about the philosophy of war films, in fact, in many cases, lead to questions of the metaphilosophy of war films—namely, a concern with the nature of the inquiry itself, the nature of the film medium, and the nature of a film's effects. Thus, while the contributors achieve an immersive engagement with the content of war films, they also share a penetrating and abiding awareness that war films are often highly generative for asking about the conditions or medium of film itself and how that awareness transforms the effort to write about war films as well as the experience of watching them.

In popular culture, viewers are often encouraged to take what is presented at face value—as if one were encountering a window onto the world instead of a world transformed through imagination and techniques of display. With the increasing quality and prevalence of computer-generated imagery (CGI), viewers may be forgiven for forgetting—they are certainly given license and reason to forget—that what they see is a representation and not the thing itself. Indeed, the emergence of the digital—and its embodiment in CGI—has radically transformed the referential nature of films and, by inclusion therein, war films. The rise of the machines in moviemaking has created a context in which artificial realities can displace more literal ones: where once the special-effects team used explosives to simulate explosives, now an actor stands beside a green screen. Still, as theater has long shown us, a well-placed cue from a single sensory register (such as the sound of a shaken metal sheet) can ably conjure a thunderstorm *without* all the other elements—lightning bolts, lashing wind, and whipping rain. War films, along with most mainstream action and science-fiction movies, have gone decidedly in the other direction—so much so that even soldiers who experienced combat firsthand will sometimes later relate incredulously that at the time, even on the battlefield, life seemed "like a Hollywood blockbuster." In contrast with the you-had-to-be-there-to-believe-it sentiment, one hears from returning soldiers that being there is seldom sufficient for having a grasp of the reality of the situation. In short, real bullets—like staged ones—may leave a survivor (or viewer) with an impression of the surreal, the hyperreal, or the unreal; unexpectedly, the soldier and the cinéaste may share this position of indeterminacy. Heterodox reports on the effects of screening war suggest that the very notion of "spectacle," which Guy Debord famously brought to widespread interpretive concern in the late 1960s, has meaningfully changed.[7] When the spectacular nature of warfare is coupled with the spectacular depiction of violence on-screen, we are in need of further thinking on the nature of spectacle.

Many years ago the film theorist Christian Metz described how we live not with natural vision but are trained and live under the aegis of a "scopic regime" (and perhaps more than one, or ones that compete).[8] With Metz's notion, viewers experience the specific, historically based cultural and technological conditions in which they see the world. Owing to innovations in both narrative techniques and software technology (such as CGI), the space of war's representation on-screen has become that much more artificial, mediated, fragmented, and, for those reasons—confounding. Consequently, we need critics—careful, thoughtful, brave critics—to lean in and take a closer look, to review (literally re-see) a long roster of war films (from classic works through the latest instances), and to bring us, with some insight and dignity, to a point where we *can* offer an informed reply to the question "How do you represent war on film?" Our concern, then, lends a different sense to an inquiry into the *art* of war.

Why war films? Because these works exist at the intersection of geopolitical reality and imaginative fiction, where government and corporate investments meet creative endeavor. War films are at once artifacts that embody the struggle to account for war and a reflection of the ongoing effort to create stories about admittedly convoluted phenomena. And war films lie at the junction of two multibillion-dollar industrial complexes: the military and the movies. Thus, while governments around the world wage war overtly or covertly, Hollywood and other moviemakers continue to explore and celebrate the dynamic features and implications of war for the big screen. In the past few years, war films—of some variant or another—have been named Best Picture of the Year at the Academy Awards: *The Hurt Locker* (2008), *The King's Speech* (2010), and *Argo* (2012); and war films have been among the most celebrated and most representative works in film history, especially in recent decades—including Best Picture awards for *The Deer Hunter* (1978), *Out of Africa* (1985), *Platoon* (1986), *Cinema Paradiso* (1988), *Dances with Wolves* (1990), *Schindler's List* (1993), *Forrest Gump* (1994), *Braveheart* (1995), *The English Patient* (1996), *Life Is Beautiful* (1997), *Gladiator* (2000), *The Lives of Others* (2006), and *The Counterfeiters* (2007), as well as Best Foreign Language Film awards for *No Man's Land* (2001) and *Nowhere in Africa* (2002). Feature documentaries about war also have drawn critical praise, especially robust since the turn of the millennium, including Oscar winners such as *One Day in September* (1999), *Into the Arms of Strangers: Stories of the Kindertransport* (2000), *The Fog of War* (2003), and *Taxi to the Dark Side* (2007) and nominees including *War Photographer* (2001), *Daughter from Denang* (2002), *Prisoner of Paradise* (2002), *The Weather Underground* (2002), *Iraq in Fragments* (2006), *My Country, My Country* (2006), *No End in Sight* (2007), *Operation Homecoming: Writing the Wartime Experience* (2007), *War/Dance* (2007), *Burma VJ* (2009), *The Most Dangerous Man in America: Daniel Ellsberg and the Pentagon Papers* (2009), *Restrepo* (2010), *5 Broken Cameras* (2011), *Hell and Back Again* (2011), *The Gatekeepers* (2012), *The Invisible War* (2012), and *The Act of Killing* (2012). And this is just one measure of the proliferation and prominence of war films; many other critically acclaimed and influential works were not nominated, such as *Fahrenheit 9/11* (2004), at the time the highest-grossing documentary in film history.

While the intersection between the making of movies and the making of wars has drawn abundant, incisive, and salient commentary for the obvious intrigue and social complexity it implies—historically, politically, legally, socially, and economically—our response to the ongoing nature of this relationship is conducted primarily through a series of philosophical considerations.[9] For instance, if there are acknowledged points of convergence between warfare and filmmaking, what, we may begin to ask, is the nature of the relationship between war as it is fought on the battlefield and war as it is represented on film? Since the nature of war-making and the nature of image-making are always evolving, such a question suggests that our understanding of war—as firsthand experience and as representation—requires continual, vigilant, and exacting analysis. Part of that attention in this collection includes assessments about the kind of impact war films make on human consciousness, belief, and action—including a range of ethical, aesthetic, metaphysical, and epistemological claims. Conversely, our critics also consider the influence war films have on our understanding of the empirical phenomena that such representations are said to address or dramatize: war itself. The contributors offer an inventive array of relevant disciplinary approaches and theoretical frames of reference, allowing readers to come to terms with the inherent variation and richness of the genre. In this way, viewers and readers face anew the manner in which films create worlds and worlds create films.

Love, War, and the Art of Conflict

War, like love, signals one of the great categories of the human condition and human consciousness. In both its literal and its figurative senses, war summons the deepest human emotions, including love (love of country, love of family, fraternal love, the instincts that swell for self-presentation, and love of God—historically and continually in manifestations such as "holy wars" and jihads, which are undertaken as embodiments of loyalty and adoring devotion). As such, war is often as motivated by hatred (of an enemy) as by love (for one's kin), and the intensity of these expressions can mobilize intimate, visceral experiences of our existential condition: the desire to protect, the effort to destroy or survive an enemy, the aspiration to claim honor, the struggle to cope with defeat and loss. It can seem that the human war with nature is superseded only by the human war with fellow humans—as if that transition were a necessary albeit paradoxical condition for civilization itself. Does war presume the hope of peace? Or does war rather anticipate only its perpetuation as a way to reinforce, among other things, national identity, the sovereignty of the state, and political factions? What happens to the concept of war when an entity other than a state wages a war against a bona fide state? For these among many other reasons, it is not surprising that war—like love—has prompted philosophical reflection since antiquity. War demands these sorts of questions and discerning philosophical analysis of them precisely because war is so much a constitutive—and yet somehow also a mysterious—part of human experience.

From Lao Tzu, Thucydides, and Plato to Clausewitz, Burke, Carlyle, Schmitt, and Arendt, the articulation of a philosophy of war has been a core occupation of scholars and theorists. War is bound up with every cherished human value: from the sanctity of life to the prosecution of justice, from the defense of territory to the compulsion to invade it. War involves an endless and often competing multiplicity of values. Partly for this reason, war films, like war itself, become an acute space in which to explore the human condition and its extremes in love and hate, duty and betrayal, existence and nonexistence. War is a topic that invites and demands consideration of perennial philosophical beliefs and claims, including those made about the nature of courage, freedom, responsibility, justice, loyalty, friendship, beauty, love, emotion, and of course, death. Ernest Hemingway, a voluminous writer on war and a close reader of Clausewitz, would add other essential attributes: danger, physical exertion, suffering, uncertainty, chance, friction, resolution, firmness, and staunchness. As Hemingway reminded us rhetorically, "war is fought by human beings," so all of these aspects incite our individual reflection and communal response. Insofar as the representation of war on film may be said to make claims about this very unique and highly distressing human experience, such representations necessarily prompt our philosophical interest.

Given that many theorists of storytelling, from Aristotle to Robert McKee, argue that narrative needs conflict in order to create an affective response in the audience, it is perhaps not surprising that filmmakers—right from the birth of the medium—have undertaken to make films that explore the nature and experience of war, a topic that is inherently, essentially defined by conflict.[10] Even before sound technology allowed filmmakers to replicate the particularly shrill passage of a bullet, they tried to capture its impact visually. War, like love, seems quintessentially dramatic. Not surprisingly, the confluence of the two subjects in war romance may constitute one of the most reliable and affecting subgenres in cinematic history. War romance boldly interweaves the intensities of love and war, and from *Casablanca* to *The English Patient,* we are rapt by the heady commingling of these urgent energies. Just as other genres, such as melodramatic romance or romantic comedy, might reveal something about our experience of love, courting, coupling, and marriage, so war films draw us into another perpetually fraught human experience. As we learn much about (and are entertained by) the representation of love and language, conflict and conversation, romance and remarriage, from *The Philadelphia Story, The Lady Eve,* and *The Awful Truth,* so we continue to be engaged by the evolution of these kinds of films in recent variants such as *Moonstruck,* and the experimental, fractured, or deviant forms of the genre as well (e.g., in *Eternal Sunshine of the Spotless*

Mind and *Her*).[11] While we remain in the grip of turbulence and confusion regarding the nature, meaning, and effects of love (and love stories), so we are often confounded by war and its representation on film.

In addition to the pertinent similarities between love (and marriage) and war, war films often involve or implicate the medium of film in ways even more elaborate and intimate than melodramas and romantic comedies do, because war—especially since it was first filmed in the late nineteenth century—is self-reflexive, that is, often caught up in the conditions of its own making. The very earliest film footage acknowledges an awareness of the parallel between the soldier and the image-maker (whether a photographer or a filmmaker), and so we find in war films the prominent representation of the "representers"—the journalists, photographers, and cinematographers who coexist with the soldiers, each of them "shooting" in a different way. The camera on the battlefield, for example, can be used as a *weapon* as well as an instrument of visual capture; the photograph or film footage is a bit of reconnoitered intelligence, a contribution to the picture (however partial) of reconnaissance about the other side. The medium, then, becomes an accomplice to the marking of targets. And as war has increasingly become a matter of having information or intelligence (not always synonymous), visual representations have become progressively more relied upon as the medium through which decisions are made; subsequently we find out how the effects of such choices are recorded or re-imagined in narrative film.

When taken together, then, the nature of human conflict and the nature of the film medium position us to consider some of the philosophical significance afforded by their conjugation in what we call war films. In particular, there is something to the art and effort of defining war that enables a fresh look at defining the war film—and its genre—as a *philosophical* phenomenon, in effect revealing that any inquiry that seeks to know "what counts as a war film" demands that we have a sense of the parameters, features, and criteria of war itself. Is it sufficient, for example, for a film to have a war "in" it for it to *be* a war film? When we say "war," do we mean combat? Or can we have a film entirely about the effects of combat, for example, as shown on the home front, in the mental traumas of soldiers, that we are still comfortable calling a "war film"? Given the pervasiveness and mutability of war, it is of vital philosophical concern—especially in ethical, aesthetic, epistemological, and ontological terms—to consider the ways in which that empirical diversity becomes an issue for its representation on film. In this respect, a recognition of the variability of war's attributes, and thus its protean definition, contributes to both the consequentiality and the complexity of the genre of war films.

The Camera and the Gun

The camera and the gun have shared the battlefield and the clandestine operation for decades, and indeed in the nineteenth century we find instances when their traits were (at least metaphorically) unified and their identities became strikingly analogous. Consider César Janssen's "photographic revolver" from 1874: "It looked like a gun," writes Rebecca Solnit, "and was apparently inspired by a revolver's rotating cache of bullets."[12] The physiologist Étienne-Jules Marey drew from Janssen's "photographic gun" to create a new device that "took twelve photographs in a second. . . . A dozen images filled a disk, and the camera-gun could hold twenty-five disks."[13] While these historical hybrids are startling in their inventiveness and haunting in their implications, the camera and the gun have, for the most part, remained distinct and separate instruments, even as they are so often seen and used in tandem—and in many cases encode a shared lexicon of "loading," "cocking," "aiming," and "shooting," among other familiar and evocative terms. However an analogy is figured, we perceive a halting equivalency between the camera and the gun: how they share sightlines; how they embody a point of view from which to take a picture or take a life. Paul Virilio, for instance in *War and Cinema: The Logistics of Perception,* has given shape and definition to the relationship between the camera and the gun when he writes of "active optics"—that innovation of "eyeless vision" that enables the "automation of perception." Virilio delineates how "alongside the 'war machine,' there has always existed an ocular (and later optical and electro-optical) 'watching machine,'" that reveals "the eye's function being the function of a weapon."[14] And we see a long history of effort in cinema to either embed or dramatize the relationship, for example, between the soldier and the figure of the war photographer. They are so often people who fight side-by-side, the one aiming to kill an enemy, the other aiming to document some portion of that reality—its anticipation, its expression, its aftermath.

The camera is not just a mechanical, chemical, or digital means of representing war; it is also, necessarily, a component of war machinery. And the camera has become, progressively with each new war, as necessary—or at least as prevalent—as the guns that shape the unfolding course of events. As a bid for definition, we may say that war, in some sense, is the mobilization of humans with prosthetic deadly force—from ancient shield to medieval armor, from tank to Glock, from stingray missile to stealth bomber. So, as photographers are armed with cameras, so soldiers are armed with arms—sent into conflict hoping that their prosthetics and tactics can outwit and outweigh the enemy's countermanding force; we see this reflected in ancient battles from *Intolerance* (1916) to *Kingdom of Heaven* (2005), but also in futuristic visions in which humans have developed more robust and intelligent skins, from *Alien* (1979) to *Avatar* (2009), *District 9* (2009) to *Edge of Tomorrow* (2014).[15] These mobile, metal exoskeletons—full metal jackets of a different sort—often incorporate advanced technologies of sensory perception as well as armaments that make the individual soldier into an arthropod, and an army unto himself or herself. A figure such as the comic-book hero Iron Man (and the *Iron Man* motion picture franchise that follows his exploits) constitutes for us a cue that military power is fundamentally about extending and amplifying the impact of the human punch. All nonhuman force is prosthetic force, an exaggeration of the potencies found in the human hand or fist. From "armament" and "armor," the abbreviation of war's massive machinery in the synecdoche "arms" illustratively reinforces the figure of the human body as the first tool of war, where all subsequent inventions and applications are deemed figurative extensions of that native somatic strength. Iron Man is but a metonym for the military; he is a martial prosthetic embodied and magnified. Yet as the cliché insists that "guns don't kill people, people kill people," we are reminded that guns are a kind of tool or expedient used by humans to shape reality. Something similar can be said of another kind of tool used to shape reality: the camera.

Gun and camera are often found in an intimate, choreographed relationship, as we see in Christian Frei's documentary *War Photographer*, where it would seem that when a gun is raised to squeeze the trigger, so too is a camera lifted to release the shutter; and when a photographer draws his camera to his eye, the scene before his lens changes: combatants fight with more vitriol, and mourners of the dead cry more vociferously (both parties protest, respectively, with more anger and grief than before the lens was directed their way). In the same film, we see how the purpose of a violent act is its being photographed; the value of the act is in being recorded and disseminated; it is thus taken as a threat when the photographer motions that he will put down his camera in a bid to save the intended victim (that is, the presumed subject of his photograph). By *not* pointing his camera at the armed perpetrator—thereby denying the creation of an image—there is less reason for the aggressor to fire his gun. When a gun—of whatever sort, pistol or bomb-carrying stealth drone—is equipped with a camera (as seen in *The Bourne Ultimatum* and *The Bourne Legacy*),[16] we discover how these weapons "simultaneously kill their targets and embalm them on video." This observation, made by Joshua Gooch in his contribution to this volume, highlights the interaction of camera and gun in the temporally coincident prosecution *and* representation of war.

A similar kind of continuity can be gleaned from the ongoing contributions submitted to the *New York Times* blog *At War: Notes from the Front Lines.* Journalistic dispatches from "Afghanistan, Pakistan, Iraq, and other conflicts in the post-9/11 era" are supplemented by photographs and videos made by professional journalists as well as soldiers in the field. On one occasion, with helmet camera recording, we watch as a platoon heads out only to encounter an explosion that kills some of its members. This embeddedness of the camera finds a new measure of articulation when Sebastian Junger's book *War* is coupled with the documentary *Restrepo* that he codirected with veteran war photographer Tim Hetherington (who later died while reporting from Libya).[17] Living with soldiers in the Korengal Valley, Afghanistan—but carrying cameras instead of guns—Junger and Hetherington effectively do a tour of duty in one of the most dangerous military zones in the world in order to help facilitate an account of these men at war. In serial scenes of threat and peril, camera and gun show how they are entirely distinct and yet, at the same time, absolutely entwined—as if these two technologies were explaining something, one to the other. And of course, to us.

The authenticity of these efforts—of James Nachtwey in *War Photographer,* the reporters for the *New York Times' At War,* and Junger and Hetherington's work for *Restrepo*—is humbling. It is also, apparently, sufficiently affecting that it has been customary since the earliest days of documentary filmmaking for Hollywood producers to either splice original documentary footage into feature films or fabricate film that resembles documentary stock. In the 1940s it was common for Hollywood films to include documentary footage, often inserted between staged scenes as a bid for recycling the evident power of the images; this tradition continues from *The Big Red One* (1980) to *Dresden* (2006). Why manufacture an explosion for a camera when there is already an explosion on film—as it were, from an original or authentic scene of battle—at the filmmaker's disposal? The creators of *Hemingway & Gellhorn* (2012) participate in this habit, for example, by placing archival footage from Dachau at the end of the film. As a result of such appropriation, *Hemingway & Gellhorn* contributes to the tradition (or is it a gimmick?) of reinforcing the continuity of authentic, on-the-ground documentary footage and stylized Hollywood studio production by transitioning from original documentary shots to optical prints with stars implanted, then fading-up to full-color restaging and dramatization. As a result of this technique, actor Clive Owen (playing Hemingway) fights alongside the Spanish forces against Franco—an interjected, artificial presence in the surrounding historical scene. (An earlier incarnation of this methodology was made famous by Robert Zemeckis in *Forrest Gump,* for example, when the eponymous character shows up in historical photographs and film, and on television shows.) Moreover, *Hemingway & Gellhorn* works hard to make sure its viewers know that *it* knows all the important journalists and photographers of the day (hello Robert Capa, have you met Orson Welles?). All told, the filmmakers reengage and rely on a number of prominent customs of looking to historically generated documentary footage as a source of authenticity and validity.

But the very notion of the documentary as authentic (as in closer to truth, or more real) is suspect—as we will find diagnosed in the following essays—often encouraging sentimental or romantic notions about origins, or, as A. O. Scott has noted, creating convoluted ideas about the real and its presence on-screen.[18] Not only was Owen Crump's *Cease Fire* (1953), for example, shot in 3D—one of the first feature films to draw on this technique for the enhancement of visual depth—but Crump used real soldiers and live ammunition during production. Instead of implanting available documentary footage into his movie, the director appeared to think that real ingredients would counteract the otherwise apparent dramatization—or perhaps even that the historical reality of the players and their equipment would distract from evident artifice. If these strategies (one technical, one methodological) were meant to convey new degrees of uncontested realism, we still end up with a mediated construction. Tim O'Brien has written eloquently about how even the firsthand experience of war does not assure truth in its representation, factually or narratively; in "How to Tell a True War Story," O'Brien confides soberly: "War has the feel—the spiritual texture—of a great ghostly fog, thick and permanent." From this he concludes, paradoxically: "A thing may happen and be a total lie; another thing may not happen and be truer than the truth."[19] Now that wars on film can take place entirely within the confines of a sound stage (with actors wearing suits equipped with motion capture sensors) and within the parameters of computer data processing, as in *Avatar* and other movies where the filmed reality is, as it were, *invented* and not merely staged or reenacted, there is even more reason to wonder about the meaning and function of the camera in combat.

Meanwhile, on the other side of these developments of image-creation and image-capture, we find that the embeddedness of the camera in the midst of warfare is increasingly widespread as the technologies of image-making or image-taking have become smaller, faster, cheaper, and of higher quality. As a result, we encounter a reversal, which is especially evident in documentary films featuring combat footage: current photo-technology allows us onto the battlefield in ways Griffith at the beginning of the twentieth century and Spielberg at its end could not have foreseen. Instead of making dioramas (Griffith) or restaging/reenacting (Spielberg), we can now send cameras into combat—on helmets, on guns, on vehicles, and flying overhead on planes, drones, and even on ordnance! While the camera does not capture all the action, it is certainly part of the action—and it enables us, as viewers, to have a mediated glimpse of it, experienced from a safe distance. When we discover that the images are documentary—and not staged or CGI—the casualties are real. But assessing the effect of that kind of reality—whether we are moved differently by the truth claims of the documentary images we see—remains deeply vexing. The Hollywood lie may activate a more acute influence on a viewer's emotional and ethical reception, and yet, the documentary image remains stubbornly relied upon as a more defensible locus of truth.

Genre as Expression and Reflection of Conditions

The nature of war has been transformed and reformed in contemporary life—by terrorism and the politics of fighting stateless adversaries, which in turn complicate relations with established nation-states; by undertaking a range of counterinsurgency strategies (some of them field-tested, others derived from theories of how to divide a hostile insurgency from innocent civilians);[20] by surveillance, drone technology, and the radical diversification of instruments of visual observation; by the acquisition and interpretation of intelligence; by the character and effects of clandestine operations (especially as the Central Intelligence Agency's traditional espionage activities or the Joint Special Operation Command's more recent and armed assignments have evolved into paramilitary missions); by the definition and moral standing of "enhanced interrogation techniques"; by the presence of mainstream media as "embeds" and "witnesses" to the prosecution of tactical initiatives and their aftereffects (both on civilian noncombatants and the troops who fight and return home); by the evolution of medical and psychological therapies and diagnoses; by the repeal of "don't ask, don't tell"; by violence against servicewomen and the promotion of women into frontline combat—and so the representation of war on film has been radically innovated in terms of content, structure, narrative, sign, technological form, and ethical, epistemic, and aesthetic concerns. The genre itself has become a remarkable site of critical and imaginative encounter with the meaning of war and its near-perpetual presence or fragmented manifestations (from on-the-ground warfare to war-based video games, from diplomatic negotiations to the latest Hollywood adaptation of "war" as metaphor or literal undertaking).

Given the radical degree to which war films have propagated, splintered, hybridized, found variants and versions, it is highly pertinent to invite scholars to think anew about the philosophical significance of the genre and its myriad representatives—from *The Birth of a Nation* (1915) and *Shoulder Arms* (1918) to *The Thin Red Line* (1998) and *Zero Dark Thirty* (2012). A robust philosophical engagement with war films, then, will orient us to the basic as well as sophisticated questions these films stimulate for our thinking—particularly as expressed in our beliefs, habits, and actions. Every new war film—especially the more artfully experimental, morally challenging, genre-blending works—appears to invite (even, on occasion, demand) an assessment of its value in relation to the ideas it instantiates, and by extension it also prompts a reevaluation of the worth and achievements of contemporaneous and prior war films—and sometimes even of nonwar films, for example, as with the opening of Brian De Palma's *Redacted,* which features a scene showing a scorpion being consumed by ants that references the opening of *The Wild Bunch.*

Thus there emerges a dialogue, and at times a dialectic, between (1) films and their genre conventions and (2) the evolving value or evaluative standards by which those works are given credence; and this latter aspect involves its own kind of perpetual exchange, namely, between the mores of a society at a given time and the conceptual, theoretical, interpretive, and linguistic habits that stand in judgment of those mores. On this second point, consider anecdotally how a "classic" war film, long heralded as an unimpeachable achievement, can feel dated, or reveal its faults and failings over time, in the contrasting light of subsequent facts and films. Elisabeth

Bronfen, who contributes a new essay to this volume, has written in *Specters of War: Hollywood's Engagement with Military Conflict* about a binary coupling that materializes when addressing the genre retrospectively: the way war films exist not just in relation to the historical phenomena they depict (or fictionalize, or imagine) but also in relation to the (war) films that preceded them. Often mindfulness about historical wars and war-films-already-made-about-them culminates in "resuscitating previous pathos formulas of war, self-consciously recapturing all actual military conflicts in relation to representations that have already come to culturally disseminate them," and as such these later films "either pay homage to previous films by reiterating them, or they conceive of themselves as interventions necessary to correct previous representations."[21] Sometimes they attempt both, or perhaps undertake a third form of awareness of prior films, as when Francis Ford Coppola appears on-screen as a TV director in his own *Apocalypse Now,* shouting at troops rushing past ("Don't look at the camera. Keep on fighting!"); or as we see enlisted soldiers in Sam Mendes's *Jarhead* watching scenes from Coppola's classic—to get amped up by fictionalized visions of war—as a way to prepare for genuine mortal combat.

As I move forward to the topic of what a philosophy of war films entails, at least in the context of this volume, it may be worth stating what *The Philosophy of War Films* is not, and what kinds of inquiries it is complementary to. While readily admitting that war, perhaps only matched by love among filmic subjects, is replete with psychological and political intensity, the writers in this volume offer informed, well-researched essays that seek to balance the vitality of their subjects with a dispassionate treatment of them. Though the criticism collected here thoroughly engages and references the art, ethics, and logic of war films for the purpose of getting clearer about those aspects, the essential work of this volume is not political excursus on the status of war in society; is not motivated by partisan-driven policymaking or policy remaking; is not military history or critique of military policy, past or ongoing; is not a judicial report on legal justifications for war or the laws that establish the powers of the state; is not journalistic or ethnographic, or the work of war correspondents—especially those who speak of themselves as "bearing witness"; and is not counterfactual or comparativist (that is, it does not assess filmic representation for its correspondence and fidelity to appointed historical events).[22] Rather, while cognizant of all these modes of address, and occasionally citing them for their conceptual relevance, the contributors to *The Philosophy of War Films* take up an approach that is theoretical—focused principally on the meanings and modes of war's representation on film insofar as they activate, complicate, or otherwise draw an interest in the philosophical implications of war on-screen. Thus, the intellectual preoccupations of this collection of remarks are primarily aesthetic, ethical, logical, epistemological, and metaphysical.

That said, it is worth noting, even emphasizing, that, as a genre of film, war movies are particularly invested, and sometimes, even very often, charged with, normative political significance. Thus they may intentionally or inadvertently become provocations that summon political critique—an agitation that begins with an aesthetic and moral encounter with the filmic projection. The confluence of politics and art (perhaps especially in film), of course, may give one pause—given the history of propaganda (e.g., in the work of Leni Riefenstahl, such as *Triumph of the Will* and *Olympia*) and unexpected advocacy (as when D. W. Griffith's *The Birth of a Nation* was appropriated by the Ku Klux Klan as an unintended but highly effective recruitment tool for the film's fantasy of rewritten Southern history). Descriptions of a given film as pro-war or antiwar may further confuse the tone of the film and the moral texture of its recommendations; we might ask whether a propagandistic work (either for or against war) must invariably invoke some measure of jingoism, chauvinism, racism, sexism, or xenophobia. Westerns, by and large, are mythical or parable-like and need to be decoded—perhaps especially in an age with boldly self-identifying Cowboy-Presidents such as Ronald Reagan and George W. Bush.[23] But war films regularly involve the portrayal of political decision making, so the workings of war can always in some measure trace back to the ideas, ideologies, and decisions of individuals and their interests, loyalties, obligations, or factions. Indeed, since the Iraq War, we have added a new model for investigation: the preventive or preemptive war, which shifts the prosecution of war to a wider network of agents—not just to commanders and soldiers, but also to politicians and policymakers, diplomats and lobbyists, the intelligence and clandestine services, and even journalists and image-makers.[24]

Thus, speaking of or critiquing war films would appear to necessarily implicate the critic in political debate. Yet, if this connection holds, perhaps it can complement an interest in other pertinent factors and features of the work—for example, the aesthetics of representation, the nature of truth in documentary (or what Noël Carroll calls "films of presumptive assertion"), the status of those persons and events left out of the representation (suppressed, ignored, or otherwise elided, as well as present-but-distorted), the characterization of camaraderie or fraternal love, the role of women and ethnic minorities and noncombatants in war (including the widespread, but underreported, physical abuse and rape of women within the military),[25] the physical toll of warfare on human bodies (including disabilities derived from lost limbs or amputation, disfiguration from burns and scarring, and other permanent effects on mobility and the material definition of the person), the cognitive impact of combat and its registration in mental health and mental illness (at all phases of war-making—from boot camp to combat to homecoming—and with it, the frequent onset of depression, anxiety, and post-traumatic stress disorder [PTSD], and the threat or actuality of suicide).[26] These features all possess political valences, and they can be represented in films as such, yet in writing about these attributes, the theorist or critic finds many additional philosophical issues to address besides, or alongside, political ones.

Just as couples keep falling in love, and so romantic comedies remain a popular, enduring, if also evolving film genre, likewise, part of the ongoing success—both artistically and financially—of war films has to do with the abiding prevalence of war. We keep having wars and we keep making films about them. What is more, as the nature of war splinters and enlarges, as it is carried into more and more diverse realms of human science (from the cyberhack to the cyborg showdown, from the rogue terror cell living in the suburbs to the battalions deployed in deserts with heavy artillery), war will likely remain a substantive and fascinating subject for visual and sonic representation. Moreover, now that the agents of war—whether soldier or spy—wear the apparatus of the camera, filming their operations as they go, the creation of new footage is an ever-present aspect of warfare. War-making and image-making have become helical, coeval enterprises.

Befitting the objectives of the series in which *The Philosophy of War Films* appears, the majority of the films referenced, interpreted, and engaged in this collection are readily recognized as contributing to popular culture—in many cases a wider, transnational, global popular culture. This status generally means that the films, of whatever vintage, are sufficiently mainstream to be available in some form of distribution (for example, on DVD or streaming online). And while "popular" can imply a current trend or passing fashion—for instance, what is still alive in memory, or part of a vocabulary of contemporary cultural reference—it can, in our collection, also mean that the film was popular in some phase of its history. A film made in 1915 or 1918, then, may remain relevant in its own right, and it may influence the creation of new work in 1951 or 1981 and beyond. Likewise, the expansiveness and variety of the movies in the genre of war films leads us, naturally, to consider a range of works—from the so-called high to the so-called low. In fact, war films, like examples from other movie genres, continually come in for reconsideration of where they belong on the continuum of cultural standing; and some creators of war films—often those with a sense of awareness of film history and genre conventions—court the blending and shifting of the high and low in the midst of their own productions. Despite the abundance of works, and their differences and types—from Oscar-winners to teenage-oriented blockbusters, from slow-burning masterworks to of-the-moment treatments, from star-populated ensemble pieces to documentaries featuring comparatively unknown or obscure people—the common denominator is the extent to which these films participate in the popular cultural reception and interpretation of war as it is visualized for the screen.

Evolving Trends in War Films

War films, of any generation, by and large reflect an interest in the wars that parallel or precede the stories at hand; in the case of military science fiction, the subjects may *anticipate* what future wars may encompass. As war movies are regularly a core segment of popular entertainment, they so often are also topically interactive with their time, or times before; they address what Elisabeth Bronfen calls the "unfinished business" of war.[27] In her reading, war films "implicitly take part in a cultural haunting" and involve "a perpetual cinematic resuscitation of our national [and we should add international] history of violence."[28] When Griffith shot *The Birth of a Nation* (1915), the Civil War was recent enough that he was able to dress his actors in authentic military uniforms from the war; though many props were original, lending credence to the look of the soldiers, other elements—such as Lincoln's assassination—were staged with a half century worth of debate over the meaning and legacy of the slain president. *All Quiet on the Western Front* (1930), was filmed by Lewis Milestone to capture the emotive tonality of Erich Maria Remarque's novel—which was based on Remarque's firsthand experiences in World War I; the fabrication of the novel and its subsequent adaptation to the screen is somewhat obscured by the suggestion that the depictions are based on personal war memories. William Wyler's *The Best Years of Our Lives* (1946) appeared in the year soldiers were returning home from combat in World War II—and one of those soldiers stars in a lead role in the film. Francis Ford Coppola's *Apocalypse Now* (1979) is at once a story set during the Vietnam War and a critique of (the) war by way of allegory and literary reference (namely, Joseph Conrad's *Heart of Darkness*).

War cinema in the new millennium has been defined by an understandable preoccupation with the "global war on terror," so called, and its variant descriptions, such as being "at war with al-Qaida and its affiliates."[29] There are also illustrations that underscore, if not clarify, what such wars might entail: fighting a stateless enemy with counterterrorism measures and policies; conducting covert operations on foreign territory without the permission of allies (most notably the raid at Abbottabad to kill Osama bin Laden lacking the consent of the Pakistani government); the presence of journalists (a historically prominent part of war films that has intensified since the twenty-four-hour cable news coverage model inaugurated by CNN during the Persian Gulf War, and seen more recently in the Iraq War and the war in Afghanistan as "embeds"—for representations see *Gunner Palace, Generation Kill, Triage, Armadillo, The Bang Bang Club,* and *Restrepo,* among others); the use of video cameras by soldiers in documentaries (*The War Tapes*) or as part of a feature narrative (*Redacted, In the Valley of Elah*); the effect of war movies and war video games on those who conduct war (*Jarhead, Gamer*); the use of unmanned weaponized planes (drones) to eliminate hostile forces (including U.S. citizens who have switched allegiance to the enemy); intelligence-gathering involving a response to the Big Data available from emergent digital technologies (surveillance video, satellite imagery, night and heat vision, telecommunications tracking, digital communications, etc.); and torture and its contested euphemism "enhanced interrogation" (from Guantánamo Bay to Abu Ghraib to "black sites") and as considered in films from *Three Kings* to *Syriana,* from *Standard Operating Procedure* to *Zero Dark Thirty.*

Genre Traits and Genre Conventions

Before I turn in more depth and detail to some of the issues that frame our shared investigation in this volume, I will say a few things about genre as a taxonomical phenomenon, especially as it aligns with the attempt to define and make reference to war films. Genre theory or studies can justifiably be traced to Aristotle, who in his *Rhetoric,* among other writings, devoted tremendous energy to identifying the traits and characteristics of things and concepts and subsequently speculated on their relationships. His approach can be described as a blend of natural scientific methodology (collecting, sorting, naming, ordering, analogizing) and language-based analysis. This tradition and its underlying outlook seem very up-to-date and relevant when we try to tease out the criteria that denote and elucidate war films as a genre: namely, by reference to the content, meaning, boundaries, and interactions that define these many, disparate works.

Genre theorist Rick Altman has contributed crucial work on the nature of genre, including the book *Film/Genre* and the highly influential essay "A Semantic/Syntactic Approach to Genre."[30] In a commentary on this essay, Altman helps us see how genre is an activity of classification with its roots in Aristotelian thinking. In part, Altman illustrates this heritage of genre creation by critiquing a metaphor used by Michel de Certeau, who says, "Readers are travelers; they move across lands belonging to someone else, like nomads poaching their way across fields they did not write, despoiling the wealth of Egypt to enjoy it themselves."[31] For Altman, de Certeau's trope misses a decisive and dynamic aspect of genre formation and evolution:

> Tales of marauding tribes on the southern reaches of the Nile may seem entirely unrelated to film genre, yet the systems operate similarly. In order to create new film cycles, producers must attach new adjectives to existing substantival genres. In so doing, producers are precisely "poaching" on established genre territory. Yet this unauthorized, product-differentiating activity often settles into a new genre immediately subject to further nomadic raiding. Cycles and genres, nomads and civilizations, raids and institutions, poachers and owners—all are part of the ongoing remapping process that alternately energizes and fixes human perception. When cycles settle into genres, their fixity makes them perfect targets for raids by new cycles. When their wandering in the wilderness is done, nomads spawn civilizations only to be robbed and plundered by yet other wandering tribes.[32]

Altman's critique of de Certeau—made even while Altman is fully aware of de Certeau's admirable attempt to overcome the "tyranny of textual analysis" that held so many critics in its grip—offers one way for us to come to terms with the radical proliferation (in variety, kind, and form) of war films since the inception of cinematic technology and practice. Altman's expansive, at times convulsive, notion of a "syntactic/semantic/pragmatic" theory of genre form creates a condition in which to assess the vitality of war films as a robust, enduring genre, even as it also encourages us to measure or monitor that evolution for its potentially intriguing philosophical claims. Altman writes, at the end of the twentieth century, acknowledging the effects of reception theory on textual analysis:

> We no longer need to be reminded that different audiences can make different meanings out of the same text. Instead, what we need is an approach that:
> - addresses the fact that every text has multiple users;
> - considers why different users develop different readings;
> - theorizes the relationship among those users; and
> - actively considers the effect of multiple conflicting uses on the production, labeling, and display of films and genres alike.[33]

Altman, of course, emphasizes reception theory because he is arguing against a tradition that sought to fix and reify a specific identity for a genre: "Instead of a word or a category capable of clear and stable definition (the goal of previous genre theorists)," Altman writes of his own project, "Genre has here been presented as a multivalent term multiply and variously valorized by diverse user groups."[34] Altman's reception theory or pragmatic theory of genre informs the path adopted by *The Philosophy of War Films*, since, as noted, war films are at times uniquely situated at the intersection of multiple communities of interest. For example, a Hollywood film may bring together the resources of the U.S. military—perhaps drawing from its property or its intelligence—in order to tell a dramatic story. By addressing war films in the context of their creation and subsequent reception—How is genre affected, for example, by cooperation between filmmakers and governments, filmmakers and journalists, and so forth? What are the nature and effects of these collusions?—the critics in this collection enable us to explore another essential valence of genre theory as it pertains to the representation of war in cinematic terms.

Meanwhile, and still drawing from Altman's study, it is worth noting some basics of the older "semantic/syntactic" approach, since this outlook too is readily apparent in the essays that follow. Altman writes: "While there is anything but general agreement on the exact frontier separating semantic from syntactic views, we can as a whole distinguish between generic definitions that depend on a list of common traits, attitudes, characters, shots, locations, sets, and the like—thus stressing the semantic elements that make up the genre—and definitions that play up instead certain constitutive relationships between undesignated and variable place-holders—relationships that might be called the genre's fundamental syntax."[35]

Altman's summary and analysis can be reduced, for the sake of more immediate intelligibility and relevance, to a reading that emphasizes the attributes or parts of a given film (as content, as semantic units) and the structure that defines the film (as form, as a syntactic arrangement). It is not really worthwhile to attempt to separate form/content and semantic/syntactic issues, since they often appear in tandem—and usually are complementary and mutually reinforcing. What is worthwhile, however, is keeping in mind how Altman's Aristotelian-inspired taxonomy of approaches to genre—in the triad of semantic/syntactic/pragmatic—helps orient readers of *The Philosophy of War Films* to the kinds of procedures and courses undertaken by its various authors. Altman's foundational research helps us recognize the exceptions, the mutations, the aberrations that complicate our reading of genre in general, and war films in particular. He stresses how "for every film that participates actively in the elaboration of a genre's syntax there are numerous others content to deploy in no particular relationship the elements traditionally associated with the genre."[36] Quotation of and allusion to standards set by prior films—especially iconic ones—at once admit the prevalence of genre norms and announce new works as potential deviations from or violations of those norms, that is, as instances of innovation. In fact, we can often recognize departures from convention more readily because of our familiarity with inherited standards. Film is an especially receptive medium for reference by subsequent filmmakers, in part, because its grammar is available to both creators and viewers; they co-create the objects of interest through an evolving critique of the values and virtues faced on-screen. So it is worth considering that with a semantic/syntactic/pragmatic approach to genre, we are able to watch films, including what we call war films, with three principal strategies in mind: (1) identifying traits and resemblances (semantic); (2) describing bonds that operate between the film text and the histories of people, events, and other kinds of texts that produced it (syntactic); and (3) determining the relationship between the varied interpretations of (war) films and their effect on the reception of a given film or film cycle (pragmatic).

Persistent, Pervasive, Proliferating

Each major military campaign of the past century and a half has revealed the increasing presence of the camera and therein made strikingly evident how war has proliferated and fragmented both in daily reality and on film. From the first still images of the dead during the Civil War by Matthew Brady's studio (for instance, in Timothy O'Sullivan's *The Harvest of Death, Gettysburg* [1863]) to Robert Capa's photographs of "blur and grit" at the landing in Normandy in 1944; onward through the television coverage of the war in Vietnam; during the Persian Gulf War, for which CNN provided twenty-four-hour cable coverage; and since 9/11, when terrorism interrupted morning talk shows to become a live, simulcast display of devastation, conflict has been covered by an ever-broadening scope of accounts, including those created by in-the-field soldiers, on-site embeds, online bloggers, amateur videographers, and professional photojournalists, some of whom continually update their reports to the screen in the palm of one's hand.[37] The war-film genre now has easily a hundred subtypes, each radiating out of some fact or facet of the way war has come to dominate and shape our lives in both overt and unseen ways. If war has captivated the human imagination, and startled those who fought its campaigns, it is not surprising that film would embrace a drama that appears to be at once so prevalent and so prominent; war seems part of the very definition of awe-inspiring spectacle. And so the need to tell stories, whether or not they set out to be bona fide "war stories," may almost inadvertently take up war as a spectacular—and therefore captivating—subject. A love story, or a story of revenge; a tale of friendship, or a narrative of adventure—all seem to achieve a high register of dramatic intensity by participating in the familiar, if awful and awe-inspiring, conditions of war.

If war is now perpetual, something we assume to be an ongoing, even permanent part of the domestic life of the nation (perhaps especially since 9/11) and taken for granted in the course of wider geopolitics, then it is analytic that we are in or at war at all times, subject to its traumas, and called upon—almost incessantly—to think through our positions as citizen-combatants.[38] "Our enemies make no distinction based on borders," President George W. Bush said in 2007: "They view the world as a giant battlefield and will strike wherever they can," the implication being that the United States should be in a position to strike back wherever it can and whenever it needs; the Authorization for Use of Military Force against terrorists law passed by Congress three days after 9/11 created the conditions for what a *New York Times* editorial called a "perpetual, ever-expanding war."[39] Whether this law, passed by Congress with only one dissenting vote, is advisable has nevertheless been a matter of considerable and contested public debate, and has informed a frenetic dialogue not just about the nature of aggression, the acts (or attacks) that would justify military mobilization, but also—and seemingly quite essentially—the definition and parameters of war itself. The AUMF law is full of vague language, and as such lays the ground for broad interpretation. President Barack Obama, according to the same editorial, "has relied on the 2001 authorization to use drones to kill terrorists far from the Afghan battlefield, and to claim an unconstitutional power to kill American citizens in other countries based only on suspicion that they are or might become terrorist threats, without judicial review."[40] Indeed, the very notion of a "preemptive" war—a war conducted ostensibly to save us from greater conflict and injury—operates on a similar presumption of foreknowledge. This kind of controversial conjecture is usually relegated to science fiction, such as in *Minority Report* (2002), where a Department of Pre-Crime uses oracles to anticipate crimes before they are committed and apprehend a person before he or she commits a criminal act. The invasion of Iraq in March 2003 could have been conducted by the Department of Pre-Crime as part of an attempt to prevent Saddam Hussein from deploying "weapons of mass destruction." Yet, as films such as *Green Zone* or *Fair Game* sought to illustrate, there were no WMDs (weapons of mass destruction); rather, there was an impoverishment of intelligence despite an abundance of information. In short, the oracles were inaccurate. A similar phenomenon is emerging in the meaning of Big Data—what it is, and what it is for—and as Kenneth Cukier has pointed out, the use of Big Data may extend precrime prevention into the realm of the digital: "There's a whole branch of criminology called algorithmic criminology, and a dimension [of it] called predictive policing."[41] Under such a regime, police consider the probability of criminal activity—and then target its elimination ahead of its materialization.

As the nature of war continues to evolve and expand—from the foreign battlefield to the domestic front, from the standing army to the unseen scope of the Internet—we seem to be living in a state of perpetual, multiplatform warfare, with new threats arising that both intensify the conflict and diversify the sites in which war is undertaken. In 2013, the highest-ranking intelligence official in the United States admonished Congress to be aware—and prepare for—a cyberattack that could harm both the infrastructure and the economy; in fact, James R. Clapper Jr., director of national intelligence, said that such attacks "pose the most dangerous immediate threat to the United States, more pressing than an attack by global terrorist networks."[42] "In some cases," Clapper admitted during testimony, "the world is applying digital technologies faster than our ability to understand the security implications and mitigate potential risks." On the same day, General Keith Alexander, who is in charge of the National Security Agency and the newly created Cyber Command, told Congress: "I would like to be clear that this team, this defend-the-nation team, is not a defensive team. This is an offensive team that the Defense Department would use to defend the nation against cyberspace."[43] Defense has become offense, offensive maneuvers have become defensive; the nature of intentionality and causality are being rewritten in the name of fighting war and fighting against it.

The frontiers of war have shifted from tribal to geopolitical, from the outer space of Ronald Reagan's Strategic Defense Initiative (soon after pilloried as "Star Wars," an association with the title of the iconic, eponymous film) to the inner space of bioterrorism, and now to cyberspace. Advances in cognitive science and neuroscience, biophysics and biochemistry, quantum studies, interstellar astronomy, genomics, and nanotechnology have further inspired the creative application of science-fiction narratives to war films, including, at times, the hybridization of other genres such as monster movies, contagion/contamination/containment films, and Westerns. Presented with abrupt shifts in the technologies of war—as seen with the atom bomb or the crippling hack of vital computer systems—one thinks of the incredulous faces of the "cowboys and Indians" when they see an extraterrestrial spaceship in *Cowboys & Aliens* (2011), a film that coalesces two established genres (viz., Westerns and alien invasion), finding war as the common denominator of the story-cycles. In the midst of this genre-blend, something distinctive emerges out of the Western context, and it is a novel threat to human survival. Bows and arrows, guns and knives, all seem humble and quaint. Thus, in warfare, there is no assurance that one can be prepared for a new menace—in this film, the hazard is a race of gold-digging aliens—or any new technology of war, for that matter. Just as the Native Americans on the prairie had to face Europeans, and later, Americans with guns, so this new collaboration has them unite against a common enemy; we find much the same in monster movies and films about contamination (nuclear, biological, chemical, genetic, cyber) where war conventions and tropes are drawn in for service, regularly in the form of the massive mobilization of government and military forces aimed to fight against or fight off the scourge. While aliens in science-fiction films come into fuller definition beginning in the 1950s and 1960s, a film such as *Cowboys & Aliens*—with its aggressive self-awareness of genres (including casting Harrison Ford [once the space cowboy hero of *Star Wars*] against type)—calls to mind the bewildering forms war can take: from fistfight to knife jab, from triggered gun to exploding bomb, and into a new realm of alien weapons that unleash force when they "sense" one's intended target. The ways of war are manifold and made manifest, with each subsequent technology availing its dangerous applications.

Contemporary war films that reflect these proximate realities are, then, not strictly about distant lands and peoples but also about our everyday experience of war—the way we live with it on the terms of the so-called twenty-four-hour news cycle, which is in turn a series of instantaneous updates aiming for "breaking news." Since 9/11 the representation of war—on American soil, in Iraq, in Afghanistan, as well as in information gathering, enemy targeting, and cybersecurity—feels continuous. From Langley to Lahore, from K-Street to the Korengal Valley, war is a pervasive condition, and as critics, we are at pains to acknowledge how this new state of affairs finds representation on film—and, more particularly, how those depictions have come to define or distort our understanding of these urgent, apparently ineluctable scenarios.

If war is now part of our daily lives, then arguably *any* film that emerges out of a contemporary context might qualify—or recommend itself in some fashion—as a war film. This appears to be true for films that illustrate foreign exploits and interventions from Iraq to Afghanistan, and also those that address the home front as a scene not just of enduring war's prosecution elsewhere (e.g., sustaining the deaths of soldiers, learning about black-site torture, tallying the funds used for warfare), but as a place where war happens—if in the strange tranquility of suburbia that is only occasionally punctuated by rapid, radical eruptions of violence. The celebrated television series *Homeland* has begun incorporating the disparate aspects we have been watching in films since the early twenty-first century: post-traumatic stress disorder, clandestine operations, surveillance, the making and breaking of terrorist plots. Another side of those operations—apart from the military and the CIA—is the taking stock that happens when others die as part of war's effects. *Reign on Me* (about a husband who lost his wife on 9/11) and

Extremely Loud and Incredibly Close (about a wife who lost her husband on 9/11) are both war films of a certain type. Yet, instead of being classed with home-front films such as *The Messenger* or *Taking Chance* (where, while operating on the home front, the principal leads wear military uniforms), these works should be read in reverse as occurring in a war zone. *Reign on Me* and *Extremely Loud* feature not soldiers but civilians who have been terrified to wake up one morning and discover that the country is under attack and one of their loves was killed in the assault. Suddenly, from one day to the next, a stockbroker is in a position akin to a soldier and enters a new category of existence as a civilian combatant. Whether he is a lucky survivor or a despairing mourner, he is at war.

In just this small segment of the war-film genre—that is, in the range and variety of home-front, returning home, or "postwar" films—we glimpse the surprising effectiveness of war to frame narrative.[44] But then we knew as much from the density of archetypical works in history, philosophy, and literature that underwrite their sagas, stories, myths, and metaphors with a recognition of war's presence: from *Gilgamesh* to the *Mahabharata*, from Aeschylus's *Persians* to Shakespeare's *Henry V*, from Heraclitus to Herodotus to Homer to Hemingway. Heraclitus wrote that "war [*polemos*] is both father of all and king of all: it reveals the gods on the one hand and humans on the other, makes slaves on the one hand, the free on the other."[45] Homer commenced what many consider the beginning of literary civilization in the West with a scene of a man's struggle with rage that gives rise to war. Virgil's *Aeneid* begins "I sing of warfare and a man at war."[46] And the vividness of the accounts, the intricacies of the narratives, the heartache of the remembrances, and the impact of the imaginations of war—from Thucydides's *Peloponnesian War* to Tolstoy's *War and Peace,* Herodotus's *Histories* to Hemingway's *A Farewell to Arms*—provide all the insight and occasion one would need to realize that war is a subject for film to take up, and perhaps, in some fashion, to take over. Yet, if war on-screen since the advent of moving pictures (a short history in the history of war) has achieved a high and popular profile, what is it about war and what is it about film that make them so complementary? Filmed entertainment is not naturally given to exposition (the kind one might revel in for its nuances of emotion and the details of objects and events, when encountered in a novel or in nonfiction), so it must be that film offers other points of enrichment for war's articulation.

War—as a phenomenon—possesses a tremendous capacity to help situate a scene in time, to fill in the backstory of characters and subjects (e.g., a wounded soldier returning from the front changes the lives of scores of family members back home), to illustrate or engage character motivation, to establish "sides," to show the overwhelming orchestration of military undertakings (from the masses of men to the movement of heavy machinery), and so on. And yet we have had, and continue to have, a number of war films that feature no combat; or have combat referenced from memory, and even, at times, from fantasy (such as when a soldier wishes to relive an event to save a fellow soldier that was lost, or when a soldier imagines brave acts he did not have a chance to commit). For those who wished to fight—as a bid for bravery or duty—but were not allowed, or the occasion for such service did not present itself, there is a regular refrain of regret about "not seeing action" (and the pain that *lack* of war experience causes).

Paradoxically, yet very interestingly, this power to frame narrative must remind us how a war—when it is in the midst of being conducted—does not possess narrative coherence. War-in-progress is undergone without a soundtrack or a score—has no shallow-focus and cross-cutting, no deep staging or dramatic lighting, no lower-thirds and captions, no script supervisor or sound-effects coordinator, and certainly no green screens and computer-generated imagery. That is real blood. War on the ground often involves one's considered effort to prepare and plan for contingencies, which are lived in forward sequence, flowing but without a clear register of comprehension; and thus every act remains a fundamentally improvised undertaking in the midst of shifting conditions, a continual endeavor to survive unknowns that lie ahead. A war story—or a war film—then is always an act of memory, imagination, and fabrication that occurs when there is a respite from war. And this may point up one of the signal reasons that war and film commingle so well and even amplify each other: that a war film is necessarily of a post facto incarnation—often, if historically referenced, as a reenactment, or if a postulation (again, for instance, in science-fiction war), then readily extrapolating from known forms of warfare, its signs, tropes, and traits.

A war film, then, in short, is an artificial ordering and construction, and a highly partial and specific vision of war that may be made available to, and in some sense appraised by, viewers. By contrast, the scope of *actual* war is inconceivable—even and especially for those who live it, witness it, or survive it—and so war films create satisfactions for the felt need of comprehension; they address us in our quest to think about why we fight *offscreen*, and what kind of meaning and implication those acts entail for personal and social life. Or as Elisabeth Bronfen has written: "The past that haunts us is also a past we can never fully master. . . . For this reason, historical recollection is always already a reenactment"—and reenactment, on her view, "revisits our wish to patrol the borderlines between fictional representations and historical truth by bringing the imaginative process into play."[47] For any filmmaker concerned with narrative, conceptual, and visual impact—especially if driven by a hope to entertain or to create profits—war will be an attractive subject from which to quote, extract, steal, invent, and adapt. The ideal of the war film, then, cannot be to show war as it is, but to show us what a war film—on its own terms—can be. This is why we continue to see war, as a main topic or a subsidiary one, more heavily drawn upon for the service of *other* genres.

We might want to attest that a war film can achieve something like a space in which to consider, if briefly, if partially, if incompletely, if nonsequentially, the context in which such things happen or are represented. As Michael J. Shapiro has written in *Cinematic Geopolitics,* the "violent cartographies" of war continue to evolve, and film contributes to our creation of these maps even as it can, at times, aim to reflect upon their nature and definition.[48] Following after trenchant remarks by Jacques Rancière, Shapiro says: "The post-mimetic aesthetic that cinema animates inter-articulates and mobilizes images to provoke thinking outside of any narrative determination." In other words, film has the capability to present us with more than a picture of characters, or the contours of plot: it can, in Shapiro's phrase, "articulat[e] a world."[49] This is not to be confused with *the* world. Hence the epistemic difference between filmed reality and what we regard as beyond the screen—namely, the embodied, multisensory, undigested, inexhaustible multiplicity of the everyday, including the extremes of warfare. As viewers of film, therefore, we do not see the world as it is (or as it corresponds to lived reality), but as the film presents it to us—an interface for investigation, interpretation, and insight.

The discontinuities that become apparent in watching a film (owing to its creation over time and its fragmented and assembled nature) are a first clue to the viewer that the film screen is not a window; 395 continuity errors are attributed to Coppola's celebrated *Apocalypse Now*—so if the film is affecting, the achievement is not from showing a perfect resemblance to the way things were lived.[50]As Rancière has written in *Film Fables,* thinking particularly of Sergei Eisenstein's work, film can "wrench the psychic and social powers of *mimesis* from the grip of the mimetic regime of art." Cinema, in this sense, "was the exemplary form of this art"—of dislocating, of disassociating the viewer from her reliance on or faith in mimesis and identification.[51] It is a worthy lesson for those who watch war films and wish to understand the epistemic status of what they see. Habits of viewership kindled from ancient traditions of storytelling (from shadow puppet to marionette) and continuing through modern theater have encouraged a relationship to imitation and narrative that cinema has exceeded, or at least can exceed. Partly, then, the meaning of a war film is intimately tied up with a creator's and a viewer's expectations of what it is they think a film is or can be. Unlike lived reality, which persists from one heartbeat to the next, film is a conjuring—pressing "play" animates the thing, resuscitating the *appearance* of life (and death) whether or not the filmed body is still alive. Even if a critical or analytical relationship is not overtly or consciously constituted from a session of moviemaking or movie-watching, that capacity nevertheless reveals itself in the widespread, even compulsive, ways in which war is simply the *context* for exploring human experience—and in particular, accounting for that experience on film.

While war films may be classed under a parent genre such as drama or action, there is sufficient "nomadic raiding" between subgenres of drama and action that we discover attributes and relationships among works of war cinema in a range of other films—many if not most of them not commonly thought of as war films. In case after case, perhaps owing to narrative potency or visual effect, war may not be the overt subject but instead affords a substrate or a secondary feature of the film, something like the condition for the possibility of attention to another dimension of experience (love, loyalty, bravery, friendship, truth and deception, moral discernment, political exigency, and a range of existential fears, among many other variants). Thus, given the abundant fragmentation, fracturing, and hybridization of war films, it is worth adducing some of the most conspicuous relatives of the genre in a brief, initial taxonomy—collected near the end of the book in an appendix entitled "The Multifarious Forms of War Films: A Taxonomy of Subgenres." In this incomplete, anecdotal sketch of films with war as a prominent feature or context of the drama and the action, we find instances in which war is taken up—or the syntactic, semantic, and pragmatic approaches to the genre of war films are adopted. When consulting the taxonomy of subgenres, with a few representative films under each category, keep in mind that a film may be classed under more than one subgenre (and for the sake of exploring the double and triple status of some films, I have included the same film under multiple subcategories, e.g., *Hart's War*, which bears the traits of a POW film, a racial-conflict film, and a trial film). Some of the established classics of the war-film genre are listed only because they may reveal allegiances and introduce compelling complications to our thinking about a war film's affiliation with genres other than war films. The idiosyncrasies of the category descriptions, as well as the films selected to represent them, merely offer additional evidence of the bountiful candidates, dizzying variations, and seemingly endless examples that could be used as fitting illustrations. Of course, as there are so many wars and types of warfare, much has been left out; notwithstanding the abundance of legitimate contenders, it is easy to spot gaps and omissions. As I gathered this suggestive list, I noted, more soberly, that it is perhaps a measure of how prevalent and abiding war has been in human civilization that so many of its stories can be understood as war stories.

Even this limited taxonomy of films, albeit from conspicuous representative works, provides some indication of how long war has been employed as a trait, a framing device, or a condition for telling a story in motion pictures. The effectiveness of war stories—narratively, conceptually, affectively, and financially—has consequently inspired a huge range of adaptation, quotation, and elaboration, such as we find in the range of films and in some of the adduced subgenres and hybrid genres noted in the taxonomy. Meanwhile, war's attraction for other kinds of media besides film intensifies in what might be called the market's efforts to explore as many niches as it can of the wide and varied consumer appetite for the figuration of war. The war-film genre is so generative and capacious that it can accommodate the literal instances of war in everything from cartoons to comic-book-based stories to those occasions when "war" is taken up metaphorically, for instance in the grounded pursuit to eradicate illicit narcotics (as we see in *The French Connection, Midnight Express, Scarface, Rush, Traffic, Blow,* and *American Gangster*), and in the more diffuse fights against aliens, asteroids, mutant beings, and sinister human forces made more threatening through weaponization. For instance, the literal/metaphorical continuum of war allows us to map the mass of films based on DC Comics (decades of films featuring *Superman* and more recently Christopher Nolan's *Batman* trilogy), Marvel Comics (*Spider-Man, X-Men, Captain America, Iron Man, Thor, The Incredible Hulk,* and everything leading up to and including *The Avengers*), and the shift from toys to animated television shows to live action films for Hasbro. The *G.I. Joe* franchise, for example, is only the third-most-profitable for Hasbro: *Battleship,* based on a board game, and *Transformers,* based on action figures and an animated series, have grossed more. Yet, all the Hasbro film initiatives are framed as war stories—whether terrestrial (*G.I. Joe*), aquatic (*Battleship*), or intergalactic (*Transformers*).

The expansion and increasing sophistication of war video games also bespeaks a culture endlessly pursuing new means and methods for engaging the subject and experience of war; even the name "video" (or for that matter "game") is an antiquated holdover from a bygone era of technology, as the changes of interface—from television screen to computer display and now portable handheld device—are outpaced only by the radical evolution of content. Before video games began to dominate the imaginations of adolescents (and, more and more so, adults), there were wooden sticks and BB guns, swords and slingshots, bows and arrows; and from there a massive army of scale-model miniatures populated the earth—with airplanes to paint and soldiers to arrange in formation. "Playing war" has been as familiar to childhood as the alphabet and the multiplication table, and very much an elemental part of everyday experience, however well it may have hidden itself beneath habit and custom. And it would seem that even into adulthood, traces of war's hold on the imagination remain in evidence—from the appropriation of military regalia, fatigues, and camouflage in haute couture as well as hip hop culture, to carrying a concealed gun in civilian life, to the popularity, and prominent stature, of General Motors' Hummer vehicles—softened, stylized versions of the Humvee that carried soldiers into battle and, in recent decades, became the place where many of them died because of a detonated improvised explosive device.

War video games, like other video games, introduce additional factors—not part of the backyard mock-campaign or the bedroom arsenal of plastic replicas—such as interactivity and thereby add a new degree of latitude for immersion. Unlike cinema, about which Cavell observed, "In viewing a movie my helplessness is mechanically assured," video games invite the viewer in, as it were, so that the *viewer's* performance is demanded.[52] The viewer-cum-participant/agent is, virtually speaking, outfitted as a soldier—equipped with weapon and ammunition, complemented by navigation and other devices that monitor resource levels and scan for threats—and positioned to act against an imposed enemy. (Such a contrast also rekindles a long history of debate about the camera itself—is it an observer [watching action]? Or is it an agent [creating it]?) In playing a war video game, we might say, pace Cavell, my empowerment is digitally assured. Unlike a war film, a war video game encourages—indeed, requires—the player, gamer, or play-actor to contribute to the shape of the narrative, to the very action that will take place on-screen. The emergence of live-streamed game broadcasting has turned the hyper-isolated experience of a solitary gamer into a shareable, watchable event; a viewer chooses a channel in order to watch someone *else* play the game: this is video game as simulcast live theater.[53] Because the technology incorporates elements of social media, the viewer can often communicate with the star performer. The war game has moved from the basement to the limelight.

While some war video games cost more to make than a feature film (and are also regularly more profitable than one), it is not surprising that war films—with their origins in dramatic action and their depiction of physicality—would be an ideal fit for translation into the realm of interactive gaming. Indeed, video games—as a form of, or context for, experience—register a player's desire to shift from viewing to interacting and, with the aid of technology, even and ever deeper immersion (one thinks here of Martin Scorsese's contention that film's future may lie in holographic projection and, beyond that, the "hologram-interactive").[54] Still, despite innovative enhancements from technologies of sensuous amplification, the notion of a "lost life" or "game over" in a war video game would appear to remain empty markers affixed resolutely to avatars, nothing like the ultimate human costs and consequences of combat. No matter how sophisticated the prostheses, we are led to believe that the war game will remain virtual—an analogue of embodied life—a space for generating stimulation through simulation, affect through effect. And yet the very nature of reality has come into question, because war video games tempt or test the boundaries between the real and the imagined and antagonize our historical understanding of embodied sensation.

One question that comes immediately to light in the wake of the success and sophistication of war video games is whether they can be said to tell or teach us something about the experience of war by virtue—in the virtual sense—of one's "going into battle." To what extent, if at all, does the virtual intercept with real effects?[55] Does the virtual become the condition for lived consequences—for instance, can a war gamer absorb war trauma and suffer affect-effects such as PTSD? Can the ersatz world (lived in parallel, largely in the imagination and via hand-eye-brain interaction) show up in the everyday world? What of the immersions of the 2D and 3D movie screen—are these sufficiently "real" to be internalized by the viewer as personal experiences that may be in some measure psychologically disturbing, even traumatic? Jean Baudrillard appeared to have reversed these questions, provocatively suggesting that the Persian Gulf War was so highly choreographed and scripted for the screen, so full of simulation and the hyperreal that, as his eponymous book contends, the Gulf War did not take place; instead, it was a "virtual war."[56] We are familiar with accounts, such as Ron Kovic's in *Born on the Fourth of July*, of young boys citing war films as the impetus to go to war—in Kovic's case, the heroic screen presences of Audie Murphy in *To Hell and Back* and John Wayne in *Sands of Iwo Jima* inspired him to join the U.S. Marines.[57] (Audie Murphy, like Kovic, survived a war and wrote an autobiography about it, and Murphy—the most decorated combat soldier of World War II—starred in the Hollywood film based on his story.)

What happens when a virtual experience of war, in video games, seems to invigorate externalized belligerence and bellicosity—taking that private battle onto the streets, into the lives of civilian noncombatants? Since these games are often played by adolescents, questions have been raised, with significant and justified concern, whether, and to what extent, this simulated analogical experience of war translates back into the lived world, manifesting as aggression or assault; opinions are split on whether virtual violence has a formative or causative effect on behavior beyond the console and display, though salient correlative cases recur—and not just among the youth. The Norwegian terrorist Anders Breivik, who in 2011, at age thirty-two, bombed government buildings in Oslo and then massacred scores of people—mostly teenagers—on nearby Utøya island, was described as earlier having been "left alone in a room, in front of a screen, playing *World of Warcraft* constantly for a year."[58] The increasing frequency of domestic mass shootings, predominantly carried out by young males—at schools (from elementary through college), at military installations, and with apparent religious, political, or racial motivations—has called attention to related phenomena such as mental health, gun control, and the representation of violence in media.[59] War films, and films with similarly graphic violence—*Natural Born Killers, The Basketball Diaries, The Matrix, The Dark Knight*—seem as much under accusation for being identifiable causative forces (and by extension, for positing the culpability of their creators) as the war video games that confer the additional experience of interactivity, along with the psychic and physical empowerment it may lead some players to believe derives from their virtual engagements.

The most popular video games are almost uniformly war-based, and the most profitable ones are all war-based. Among the subcategory of most popular *war* video games, often referred to as "hard-core gaming," one qualitative ranking finds the *Call of Duty* series (2003–present) occupying seven of the ten slots.[60] The series was released in the years following 9/11, and though the initial set of games drew a story arc from World War II, the later "Modern Warfare" segment developed a present-day scenario; more recently, "Black Ops" includes Cold War as well as Vietnam narratives, and the latest games have pushed into science fiction with a time stamp in the year 2025. Similarly, the "military science fiction" game *Gears of War* (2006) has developed into a franchise and is shifting its platform from computer consoles to mobile devices.[61] A more quantitative measure only lends further credence to the impression that war is the dominant theme of these interactive works, with the ten highest-grossing video games of all time being war games. A scan of the titles offers a brief clinic in the diverse ways in which war can be adopted for interactive gaming: *Steel Battalion* (2002), *Medal of Honor: Warfighter* (2012), *Army of Two: The Devil's Cartel* (2013), *Star Wars: Episode I—The Phantom Menace* (1999), *Call of Duty* (2003), *Halo 3: ODST* (2009), *Final Fantasy XII-2* (2011), *Battlefield 3* (2011), *Call of Duty: World at War* (2008), and *Metal Gear Solid 4: Guns of the Patriots* (2008).[62] (And the games are astonishingly lucrative, with an estimated $16 billion in annual sales; *Call of Duty: Black Ops 2* grossed $1 billion in two weeks.)[63] Whether warlord or assassin, soldier of mercy or spy, on earth or in outer space, back in time or part of ours, war is an undeniably dominant source of video game content. The prominence of video games—especially with war as an abiding aspect of character, narrative, and effect—is mentioned here partly owing to an acknowledged lack of extended meditation on the topic in the remainder of this volume. This lacuna is not intended as a slight to the form, however; as the foregoing notes should attest, the role of war in video games is essential to the discussion that encompasses war's representation in art and popular culture and deserves its own volume of researches and reflections. Still, it should be noted that to a striking extent, many of the contributors' hard-won insights into war films—and the display of war on screens, more generally—will bear an intuitively, meaningfully coextensive relationship to war's invented presence in the makeup and milieu of video games.

Technologies of War's Remembrance, Fabrication, and Display

The focus on war *films* in this volume, of course, directs our attention to the way that war films are not just a genre but a medium—an interstitial space between an audience and an event. Which is to say that film is forever, ineluctably, a representation and an interpretation of reality—and thus, an in-between (*media*). Documentary film often lures us to believe that it is showing "the truth"—the world without mediation—but then we remember that a cameraman points the camera, that the camera frames the scene and the lens translates what passes through it, that the image is in color (or not) and of a specific quality or rendering, and, perhaps most crucially, that the documentary is *edited* and supplemented by everything from captions to music. Even in documentary, we are hardly *given* the truth; and though we can often identify when an image involves a "presumptive assertion," there are an increasing number of occasions when we cannot believe what we see, when the sophistication of the fabricated scene makes it hard for us to treat it as staged.[64] Werner Herzog is one of the few prominent filmmakers to make the lack of truth—or "accountant's truth" as he disparagingly calls it—an admitted, even celebrated, aspect of his documentary films.[65] In *Lessons of Darkness,* his documentary about the aftermath of the Persian Gulf War, for example, he fabricates text, titles, and voice-over and shows footage out of temporal sequence. It should be considered a bit of legerdemain how a simple inscription at the beginning of a film—"based on a true story," or even more scandalously, "a true story"—distracts or hypnotizes the viewer to such an extent that she watches with a kind of faith in the truth of the proceedings. Instead of sitting before artifice or artifact and interpreting the work as such, she begins to compare and contrast—as if the visual display were another, ordinary reality. Thus, when Griffith writes at the beginning of *The Birth of a Nation* that we are about to see "an historical facsimile," we lay more emphasis on the way his re-presentation is an approximation, a gesture in the direction of understanding the depiction nonliterally; and the silliness of the Lincoln reenactments, for example, help us keep our distance from history: this footage could not be mistaken for surveillance imagery created *avant la lettre.* Yet by the time we have Steven Spielberg's *Lincoln,* we are encouraged by DreamWorks and the critics who review the film to see Daniel Day-Lewis "disappear" into the role, as if the actor had conjured the president or taken up residence in his body. Day-Lewis's heralded achievement, however, should only emphasize—and spur consideration of—the extent to which even the *actor* is a medium!

A medium, by its very nature, invites a viewer to think—or at times forget—that there is a layer between his view and the event, but in a very real sense the medium is the event. Even when we know of a historical referent—the D-Day landing at Normandy, the extermination at Auschwitz, the explosion at Hiroshima—the representation of the event on film is not the event. This claim, as obvious as it may seem, is undermined by the regular invocation of authenticity and verisimilitude—notions that variously suggest that the film is a genuine parallel to the experience, or has all the details right, or that watching the film is "like being there." Even when a film corresponds to a historical event, it must be taken on its own terms as a representation, and thus as something altogether separate. As Cavell has written, film "screens me from the world it holds—that is, makes me invisible. And it screens that world from me—that is, screens its existence from me."[66] In this sense, film as medium is not a window to an event so much as a mirror to our own understanding. This is one way to tell the difference between a film and a raw surveillance feed. And yet, as recent war films have shown, even surveillance frames and filters what it captures and does not provide access to the world it purports to represent. By contrast, when we see a live broadcast that shows some extreme—of carnage, of conflagration—a common response is to invert the reality and say, for example of the airplanes hitting the World Trade Center towers and collapsing: "It was like a movie." Because, as viewers, we appear to live in the tension between fabrications that make us feel "like being there" and live coverage that was "like a movie," we still must engage directly and ceaselessly with the fact of film's status as a medium—as something between us and our sense of what we might call variously history, invention, truth, interpretation, or fiction.

The present book appears about a century after the outbreak of World War I, the first running of the assembly line innovated by Henry Ford, and Griffith's landmark film *The Birth of a Nation.* Since then, the mechanisms of war—and the techniques of its conduct and its representation—have changed several times. The machine was overtaken by the atom and the atom by the binary digit. Throughout that period the camera—instrument for the capture of still and moving images—was a constant presence, even as it too was being affected by technological transformations (from the wet colloidal process available in the 1860s to the high-resolution, high-dynamic-range digital sensors of today). Moreover, it is largely *through the camera,* both through its lens and by means of cinematic form, that what many of us know about war is known, especially what we know visually and sonically. (It would be curious, would it not, if we drew our knowledge and opinions of aeronautics strictly from a person who watched films about fighter pilots and astronauts instead of asking those who fly the planes and shuttles for their informed, firsthand accounts.) So a reader who watches war films might ask: What does such knowledge or experience amount to? For one thing, it highlights the extent to which, for many of us, our war knowledge and "experience" is a function of mediation through the camera, or cinema more generally. What is it we presume to know or understand about war because we have seen a film said to represent some facet of war—on the battlefield or at home, in the grave intimacy of hand-to-hand combat or the disembodied form of unmanned drone airstrikes from ten thousand feet above the ground (and operated by technicians as many miles away from the target, as we sit at a similar distance in the movie theater)? What are the psychological territories and terrains that war films are said to cover for us as viewers—or as some might say, *consumers* of war films? And above all, what do such questions elicit from our sense of the philosophical significance of war films—given the almost unmatched combination of ethical quandaries and aesthetic phenomena they pose to us as viewers?

All these questions, which come in for scrutiny in this volume, summon us to a more general question: What are war films for? Since these films appear in the wider context of the movie industry—which also produces romantic comedies, thrillers, and fantasies—one could simply say war films are for distraction, or escape, or entertainment. But then why would we, year after year, wish to be entertained this way, by this subject matter? If a war film is praised for its realism, for instance, why would we *want* to experience it as entertainment? Or does its appeal to realism—its conjuring of such an effect—compel us to watch it for some other reason than to be entertained, for example, to be morally edified, or further humanized, or otherwise tutored to achieve greater degrees of empathy? Some writers and directors of war films appear to believe that at least part of the purpose of these films is to teach audiences about history, including military and political action; the circumstances and events that give rise to and shape war, including the roles played by vicious adversaries and honorable insurgents; and the lives of those who fought campaigns, who were brave and suffered, who survived, and who perished. Admittedly, didacticism is not incompatible with entertainment; they may in fact be highly complementary for this genre, given its willing reliance on the historical record. The pedagogical function in many war films relies on explicit or implied reference to specific battles, the acts of particular soldiers and martial leaders, military episodes that punctuate human civilization, and so forth—as if to narrate a sequence of events that we (as an audience) were not or could not be privy to.

Another side of the heuristic utility of film can be attributed to its *fic-*

tions—namely, the various ways in which history is *not* referenced, replicated, and reenacted on film, or rather is by and large secondary to the structure of the drama and the lives of its characters. The many canonical and persuasive arguments about literary fiction's power to transform the ethical lives of its readers—as artfully and rigorously expressed in recent decades by Mieke Bal, Stanley Cavell, Arthur Danto, Susan Feagin, Bernard Harrison, Martha Nussbaum, and Alexander Nehamas, among others—find further resonance and legitimacy in thinking of film's capacity to teach its viewers.[67] Here the sounds of melodrama (*melos,* music) and the kinematics (*kineō,* motion) of "movies" suggest why we can perceive so much, and so deeply, from watching films: moral and metaphysical life appear to be undeniably made manifest on the very surface of the screen. As a result of that animated and affective coruscation, the reasons for film's vitality need not be traced along some continuum from empirical verifiability to wholesale contrivance.

In charting some of these lessons from the cinematic arts, war films—whether historical or fictitious—may be said to offer a glimpse, but then always already as a perception that is itself an analogy. That is to say, this notion of seeing into something briefly or partially is underwritten by the idea, often invoked by soldiers and war correspondents, that "you had to be there in order to know what it was like" or "I've seen things you can't believe."[68] In other words, representation, no matter its quality of image or insight, is an insufficient means for conveying the reality of first-person experience. In this respect, it is worth emphasizing how the representation of war on film is *not* a re-presentation of war; a war film is very much its own kind of thing and is not, regardless of manifold creative or constitutive achievements, war. It is at this point that the idea of a war film as a surrogate for "being there" comes into focus. And we could admit—despite high production values, legendary acting, and costly postproduction—that it is, or in some sense must always be, a pretty shabby proxy, since watching reenactments (or even watching documentary footage of historical events) is a phenomenon unto itself, one *highly removed* from the scene of conflict and combat.

In tension with this you-had-to-be-there-to-believe-it sentiment, often conveyed by those who experienced war firsthand, we contend with the genuine way in which we are affected by the war films we watch—shocked and saddened by these scenes of violence, carnage, destruction, loss, and grief. Therefore, disparaging the image as an insufficient means of capturing the real, lived, chronological, embodied experience of war must come up against the extent to which—perhaps despite ourselves, or while concealing our practiced fealty to the effects of film—we are regularly, deeply, profoundly affected by war films. We believe in the medium in ways we may not be aware of or, if aware, willing to admit. One witness to the controversial events at Abu Ghraib, Sabrina Harman, points up our faith in visual representation: "If I come up to you and I'm like 'hey this is going on,' you probably wouldn't believe me unless I had something to show you, so if I say 'hey this is going on' look I have proof, you can't deny it."[69] Specialist Harman accentuates the struggle many of us engage with when watching films, perhaps war films in particular, between the persuasive powers of visual display ("proof") and the sometimes overt but suppressed sense that such representations are shaped and transformed by the conditions of their creation, including the position and point of view of the image-maker and all the creative forces that contribute to the film's final form. It must be said that part of cinema's power resides in the modes by which it seduces its viewers into believing that it shows a real world—and not, we might say, a staged one. If part of our pleasure with film is the extent to which we can become absorbed in it or by it, we may, in the case of war films, have to develop some capacity for skepticism about its images and the degree to which they possess truth or constitute proof of anything. Thus, as we continue to acknowledge the inability of film to translate the total immediacy, radical vulnerability, and nonnarrative disorientation of war, we should also note the potentialities that are inherent in and emanate from the medium itself. Film has its domain of effects, even if they are not those on-the-ground, mortally threatening facts familiar to the veteran soldier and the civilian noncombatant.

Drawing one conclusion from this tension, or categorical contrast, we can say that even with a heightened consciousness about any specific, historical war—its players, its circumstances, its effects—we are unable to account for the totality of war on film. Just like the commanders who directed it, and the soldiers who fought it, war exceeds comprehension. The situation is no different for film, even if its creators may benefit from hindsight. At the end of a taxing and troubling group therapy session featured in *Return* (2011), a female soldier, Kelli (Linda Cardellini), just returned from active duty in Afghanistan, counters the advice, and conventional wisdom, on offer by saying: "I don't have a story." Kelli expresses her frustration with the presumption that anyone—a soldier or a therapist—could have a coherent (or perhaps any) relatable narrative about her experience. But the same is true for viewers. As we watch war films—whether documentary or fiction or some amalgamation of the two—we should remain aware of the curious difference between life in the theater of warfare and life in the movie theater. The events of war's prosecution are simultaneously perceived from one perspective and are nonrepeatable; by contrast, watching a film depiction of war is something we can indefinitely repeat and take up from the vantage of our serial selves (since *we* change with each viewing, over time, the film is capable of summoning us to varied impressions of the same sequence of images). Though the soldier experiences his tour from one lived hour to the next—through arcs of boredom as well as adrenalized action—the viewer encounters the film as a post facto edited document. While a war is lived once (for the soldier), a film is a stable fabrication that encourages not one screening but rather endless rescreening, and with each iterated viewing of that work, we can say, its audience is different. War films become, in an important if peculiar way, the *viewer's* war memories; each rescreening is a re-animation, a chance to relive and rethink what resides in memory and what gets added every time one presses play. Consequently, war films are not—and never can be—the *soldier's* war, neither in terms of what she experienced, nor in the manner of how she experienced it. Thus, while war is lived in its singularity and partiality, stories of war can go on and on (not just from the soldier's own memory and expression, but also either in the creation of new films or by the repeated, compulsive, return to the same films for review and further reflection). It is often said by war veterans that they are always coming home. So, as viewers of war films, we might say that we are always returning to the field of battle—from one theater to another.[70]

If "memories of movies," are for us what they are for Stanley Cavell, "strand over strand with memories of my life," then what should we think of our memories of war movies?[71] Watching a war film is a memory from my life, yet if it is my memory, it is not, as it were, my experience. The doubleness here, far from disqualifying the legitimacy of cinematic depiction, instead cultivates the unconscious impression that films can, nevertheless, in their mental residence as memories, *serve* as one's own "experience"—in the present case, of war, and as such may be called upon as inner projections, as points of reference in thinking about courage and sacrifice, embodiment and trauma, the limits of life and the horizon of death. This internalization must lie at the heart of a war film's power to generate empathy in its viewers, for it is precisely one's apprehension of the helical "strand over strand" relationship between memories and movies that effectuates a potent exchange between individual conscience and the articulation of values in the world.

A war film may be an ephemeral, analogical apparition, but it may also be sufficiently substantive to enable us to test out our hardest-won, most cherished convictions. For that reason alone, though there are many others, war films may be seamlessly incorporated into one's identity as if what they represent happened—for in terms that matter, it did.

Given the conditions of making films and viewing them—and the psychic, emotional, and physical distance from actual combat—why would, or should, a viewer presume to know or learn much about war by watching, say, a two-hour film? Merely a few minutes of documentary footage from the European campaign—the D-Day landing or the bombing of Dresden—may be so immersive that it is hard to fathom a genuine continuity with events that were happening contemporaneously on the other side of the world—battles at Guadalcanal and Saipan. And there are so many other points and places of suffering happening concurrently—including families on the home front learning of the injured, the dead, and the missing. Beyond these varied instantiations of war, it escapes comprehension that as the Allies were exposed to these trials on several fronts (or, as they were called, "theaters of war"), the Holocaust was fully under way. Indeed, even after Holocaust museums have been built all over the world, and the Shoah has been deemed one of the most grotesque crimes in human history, new information emerges that makes its reality even worse—more troubling, more tragic, more extensive.[72] The telling and teaching of war's realities, it would seem, is never finished and never complete. And film, notwithstanding our neglected admission of its limited gifts, will not be the means for finishing the job.

Moreover, as Max Boot has argued in *Invisible Armies,* the very impression that war is a contained engagement between two sides—one nation against another, in a sequence of singular military maneuvers—is the exception in the long history of warfare. For their broad cultural impact, such wars have deeply informed, and in an important sense narrowed, the conceptual content of what we think of by the term *war.* However, and more empirically, guerrilla warfare has predominated throughout human history—despite the salience of wars fought by armed nation-states—and remains the dominant mode of violent, and widely varied, armed interaction. "Time and again," Boot writes, "guerrilla warfare seemed to be superseded by the 'new new thing'—industrial warfare in the 1910s, aerial warfare in the 1930s, nuclear warfare in the 1950s, network-centric warfare in the 1990s. And yet each time it reasserted itself with a vengeance." The endurance of guerrilla warfare—and its variation, terrorism—is due in large measure to its efficacy: "From Algeria and Vietnam to Afghanistan, Chechnya, Lebanon, Somalia, and Iraq," Boot writes, "insurgents have shown a consistent ability to humble great powers." And insurgents waging "irregular warfare" are often victorious despite substantial asymmetries of manpower and military might.[73] Whatever the tactics and strategies of guerrilla warfare, its reality and persistence accredits the fact that war is too complicated to define as side x fighting side y, or as a contained event that occurs at a specific place between discrete dates.

This fragmentation or lack of coherence in war-as-it-is-lived (versus represented) is defined by the problem of simultaneity—that war, like love, is so multifaceted, so elaborate and fraught, and so endlessly generates meanings and consequences, that it necessarily transcends any human ability to possess or process it logically and comprehensively. The evident attraction to representing history (perhaps because it is a phenomenon we *wish* to understand by telling stories about it), of course, reminds us—as viewers—that war films are (for the most part) linked to historical events, persons, battles, outcomes, and trends. If the war film is not science fiction, fantasy, or stylized allegory, then it often takes its cues from what historians have gathered and rendered; and even then, many exuberantly staged fictions draw from social consciousness about history—take Quentin Tarantino's war-tandem *Inglourious Basterds* and *Django Unchained* as basing the pleasure of alternate history on some semblance of (the horror and tragedy of) what did take place; these fictitious revenge fantasies are meant to satisfy because of their outsized efforts to compensate for history's *real* abuses.[74] By contrast, most war films that aim to represent anything like a "true story" or a tale "based on a true story" will invite the attendant problems of verisimilitude and counterfactuals, both of them essential judgments on the degree to which the film is "like real life" or not. *Saving Private Ryan,* for example, was praised by D-Day veterans for its facility to show "what it was like" that day on the coast of France. But then the meaning of "like"—as a sign of resemblance or reference—takes on a more pronounced weight, for we know the remark must be a hyperbole, a sentiment that acknowledges that while the film is an accomplishment of bringing so much together, it also must necessarily leave so much out.

As a point of interest, then, any viewer of war films—and certainly any reader of this volume—might assume a healthy skepticism about *all* representations of war on-screen—from earnest documentary to sober elegy to bombastic plea to satirical provocation to jingoistic propaganda to adrenalized blockbuster. In short, it may be worth starting out by reminding ourselves, as viewers, "This war film is not history." Even if the "camera was there"—up close as war photographer Robert Capa thought it should be, on the front line, as he was with his camera in hand on D-Day—it does not mean *we* are there by looking at his photographs, nor does it mean that we see or feel or hear or smell what it was "really like." Somewhat infamously, the dramatic effect of Capa's black-and-white D-Day images was due to a photo processing error—the negatives were overheated in the lab.[75] As Huston and Kaminski's camera was hit, so Capa's film stock was traumatized; now we regard the effects of these shocks—the material residual—as the referents of experience, as the shapers of our capacity to imagine harrowing but lost phenomena, as if the medium itself absorbed the realities we seek to know and feel. When Eadweard Muybridge was hired to document the Modoc War of 1873, purportedly becoming the first photographer the U.S. Army paid to cover a war, he was, as Rebecca Solnit argues: "complicating the record as he made it." The medium of still photography, as with later film technologies, involves, Solnit adroitly summarizes, "the transformation of a world of presences into a world of images."[76]

Every film under discussion in this volume—regardless of subgenre or cycle, time period, production quality, and so forth—is constructed. What the differences between these constructions mean occupies the bulk of the scholarly energy and scrutiny in this collection. Indeed, part of what the authors of these essays reflect on is the way war-on-film is an assemblage even while war-as-lived remains fragmented and beyond our competency—or the medium's—to consolidate. Both of these factors or features complicate our inheritance of war films *and* war. We may know a lot less about war than we think, despite our long-standing commitment to war films as a form, as a forum, as a genre; war does not give itself over easily to the kind of recognition, identification, or understanding we might hope to have gleaned from war films. In a certain sense, speaking frankly and modestly, we should not expect to learn more about war from a war film than we should expect to learn about our romantic lives from watching romantic comedies.

Partiality and Mediation in the Making of War Images

One may become more self-conscious—and skeptical—in one's viewing of war films by dwelling on the ways in which filming a subject or an event is not a neutral act of "witnessing," and creating a film is not a disinterested mode of presentation (because even firsthand perception itself is biased—indeed, on many occasions, much of the value we ascribe to the immediacy of witnessing derives from its *lack* of impartiality). Rather, both the documentary image-maker and the film editor are involved, in a most elemental way, in the framing and structuring of film reality. Thus, as viewers and critics, we might benefit from distinguishing between being an eyewitness (a person experiencing, or bearing witness to, an event in synchronous time) and being a watcher of films (where a person is present before a construct of images and sounds meant to conjure an event asynchronously, a display that often invites us to treat the works as texts worthy of serious and extended interpretation). For this reason, a war photographer is present to the action he photographs—is an eyewitness to it, bears witness to it—in a way utterly distinct from the manner in which a passerby explores framed photographs taken by a war photographer, such as may be displayed at a gallery. While a war photographer faces the scene—frames it, and by that craft of orientation, delimitation, and focus creates a physical record—a passerby finds a world transformed; she encounters a work of art. The person who sees the artifacts of war confronts what Dora Apel calls the "memory effects" of the event; but Apel's other notion, of "secondary witnesses"—those who bear witness by hearing testimonials or viewing material culture (such as films and photographs)—discounts the oddness of calling such mediated encounters "witnessing."[77] It would seem more propitious, and accurate, to describe the engagement as one undertaken by primary inheritors, which is to say, any person in a position to adopt a conscious relationship to material culture—not merely to allow its presence as a kind of unseen wallpaper, but to address it as if it were making a claim for attention and critique. The witness, then, is always and only that person who experiences the immediacy of a lived event and perhaps afterward takes up that sensorial and cognitive impact in some form of expression or recording (for instance, in prose or photographs, documentary or narrative). Thus, if we speak of a "testimonial, a personal *record* of a witness," in Hernán Díaz's phrase, we should not have a film's audience in mind.[78] Moviegoers who choose to watch war films are not, in this sense, witnesses to war, not even "secondary witnesses." Something else is happening.

Similarly problematic to Apel's account, when celebrated, legendary war photographer James Nachtwey says, "I am a witness" and "My photographs bear witness," he elides—to the detriment of our understanding—

the difference between his eye and the image his eye and his camera make available.[79] Despite the obvious aesthetic sophistication of his photographs, and the palpable moral urgency he wishes the images to evoke (his form of advocacy), Nachtwey appears to believe in an elementary, even dangerously naïve, appraisal of their status: "I want my testimony to be honest and uncensored."[80] Nachtwey is a witness in a way that the work emerging from his camera is not a "witness" (even figuratively): his photographs are not isomorphic with his experience. Thus, having one's images blacklisted for content is distinct from any claim that photographs are not—in their very nature—a kind of censoring and interference with lived realities. And because, among the plastic arts, "film gives the greatest illusion of authenticity, of truth," says Annette Insdorf in the documentary *Imaginary Witness*, "there is always distortion and manipulation."[81] After war correspondent Marie Colvin was killed while reporting in Syria, fellow conflict reporter Eliza Griswold was asked about her legacy and responded—in honor of Colvin's sense of her own work—by dismissing the sanctimonious tones of some war correspondents: "She was a very good reporter doing her job. I think the last thing she'd want is a lot of guff about bearing witness and the like."[82] Furthermore, or by extension, the presumption that by watching a film, a viewer bears witness, involves a category mistake: viewers are not passive (as if taking on a burden, bearing it; accidentally encountering an event; or accepting truths as they appear on-screen), but instead they are active creators of their interpretations, always inhabiting a specific point of view.

The orientation of a given perspective is not always apparent or coherent: consider Clint Eastwood's double effort to work through this issue on the scale of entire films, as in *Flags of Our Fathers* and *Letters from Iwo Jima.* Similarly, the documentary *Vietnam's Unseen War: Pictures from the Other Side* (2002) creates an occasion for stories told—and some images taken—by North Vietnamese war photographers. From these films we learn that there is no position from which to achieve a view sub specie aeternitatis; instead, war is very much a phenomenon of discrete moments lived by individuals that do not add up to an intelligible portrait. As viewers of war films, as creators of them (both as moviegoers and producers), and in some cases as combatants and victims of war (often enough, two categories that produce a false divide), it is worth dwelling on the extent to which all positions in the network of photo/film manufacture and dissemination—writer, casting director, actor, cinematographer, director, composer, editor, production and costume designer, special-effects coordinator, . . . viewer, and critic—are involved in the syntactic/semantic/pragmatic triad. Contributing to the film from different angles and orientations, these active creators of film texts decide what to see, and how to look, and how to account for what was represented. And yet the content of war films may often cast a spell on its viewers and claim just the opposite—as when the aspiring documentary soldier/filmmaker Angel Salazar (Izzy Diaz) says in *Redacted* that his footage is just "telling it how it is."[83] The promised documentary, based on the footage, is meant to simply show "whatever the fuck goes on."[84]

War films antagonize the generic and unseen aspects of war and help give shape, texture, and individuation to otherwise vague and distant endeavors. These works of art particularize the stakes of battle, whether foreign or domestic; we may be seeing an actor, but we are also coming closer to a personal struggle full of specificity and dramatic intensity. Instead of the journalistic report that must hew to available information, and often for such exigencies be supplemented by minimal photographic imagery, and commentary that may speak of the injuries and deaths of unnamed, perhaps untold fathers and sons, mothers and daughters, siblings and children, the war film—if itself dislocated from those factual mortalities—nevertheless renders the fictionalization of loss with wrenching immediacy. The Hollywood star "dies" on the sands or seas, and yet his highly choreographed sacrifice abstracts itself to become an emblem of all the soldiers and seamen who perished or were punished by their circumstances. How much easier it is, then, to empathize with these actors, and the characters they portray (or, in the case of documentary film, these subjects), and as a result how much harder it is to appreciate the trouble and trauma soldiers undergo in lives lived in actual fields of battle.

Brian De Palma's *Redacted* illustrates the constraints and conflicts a viewer may experience—of believing (or at least feeling, or having the impression) that she is an eyewitness or is bearing witness instead of watching a fictitious visual figuration. De Palma loads his film with a range of contemporary technologies meant to signal our habituated faith in the filmic testimonial—how that conviction, for instance, hides our complicity in sharing Salazar's braggadocio presumption that the camera is for "telling it how it is" and revealing "whatever the fuck goes on." In the course of *Redacted,* we see footage from a surveillance video, a helmet camera, a night/infrared camera, a handheld digital video camera, a laptop video camera and iChat, a cell phone camera, a news report camera, and a YouTube video, among other screens and displays. And at the end of *Redacted,* De Palma puts up a title card claiming "Collateral Damage: Actual Photographs from the Iraq War," which is followed by a long run of gruesome, graphic images offset by the sonic splendor of Puccini's "E Lucevan Le Stelle" from *Tosca.* The cognitive dissonance is intentional, to be sure, but it can also distract us from noticing that the final haunting image of a dead woman lying in a pool of her own fresh blood—an image meant to be sufficiently awful that it could stand as the termination in a series of arresting photographs, and be the *documentary* referent that inspired the entire film—is in fact (we can learn by reading the credits carefully) a staged photograph made by artist Taryn Simon. In other words, even when the director tells the viewer these are *actual* photographs, one must be on guard—for the image that underwrites the emotional tonality of the film, giving *Redacted* its ethical weight, is not "actual" after all.

As part of a metatextual reading of *Redacted,* that is, taking up the film's critique of military secrecy, and the preservation of anonymity, Taryn Simon's fabricated photograph is shown as the culmination of all the "real" war images and so is presented as unredacted; as such, the image seems at once both more complete and more true than all the apparently true, real, or "actual" images that precede it. Simon's work of art appears to accumulate the visceral trauma of the many photographs that come before it, and it manages thereby to achieve an astonishing degree of dramatic crescendo. Ending on Simon's photograph, despite its fakery, makes the image take on the ethical difficulty of all that has led to this last frame. One viewer may say that De Palma's misleading—utterly deceptive—title card "Actual Photographs from the Iraq War" is both ungenerous and manipulative. But then, the film is itself a fiction and an assemblage of staged images, so it stands in parallel or in partnership with Simon's contrived photograph. Another viewer may suggest that De Palma's artful ordering or sequencing of the documentary and the doctored photographs provides a condition for thinking anew about what sorts of truth we believe we glean from "actual" photographs as opposed to staged ones.

A similar phenomenon occurs when we look at artist Jeff Wall's photograph *Dead Troops Talk (A Vision after an Ambush of a Red Army Patrol, near Moqor, Afghanistan, Winter 1986),* which illustrates in tableau form—in a backlit transparency measuring 90¼ x 164¼ inches—Russian soldiers in varying phases of death, dismemberment, and derangement having been shot by the Mujahedin (who are seen rummaging through the bodies and the debris).[85] The thirteen animated Russian corpses—alive in their new deaths—occupy a range of states from teasing to pained, contemplative to laughing, with brains exposed, ears dangling, detached limbs strewn about. Wall's nightmarish rendering of war's unsettling logic and effects recalls an indelible and uncanny shot in Alexander Dovzhenko's *Arsenal* (1929) where we look upon a dead, half-buried soldier with a broad smile frozen upon his face. Wall's photograph, likewise, is a harrowing sight, but it is also a fake one, an image safely staged in Burnaby, British Columbia, created over the course of six years, and completed in 1992. Wall calls his work a "vision," in the sense that it is a scene summoned from imagination rather than a recording of an empirical event. The artist himself recounts how his exacting attentiveness to the details of the uniforms and weapons was meant to contrast with the exaggeration and inexactitude of the scene's overall representation: "It was important to have that level of plausibility, and it's more interesting aesthetically to do it that way. It has a relation to ways of seeing the truth, but it doesn't have a direct relation. That's why I called it a 'hallucination,' a 'vision.'"[86]

Similarly, when discussing how he reenacted the scenes surrounding some of the most famous photographs from the Abu Ghraib scandal in his documentary *Standard Operating Procedure*, director Errol Morris addressed the highly aestheticized style of the vignettes, which were dramatized from details in still photographs: "I was interested in how pictures can often mislead us: they can reveal things and also conceal things at the same time. And that irony is something which I believe is the heart of the movie."[87] Yet, even stopping short of Morris's provocative ironizing, we are left to wonder how such reenactments—even if done in earnest, as they are so often done on the History Channel, for example—should be understood with respect to the representation we call the source photograph. Perhaps there is simply an *assumed* continuity between photograph and reenactment (as another indication of the power of filmic montage) and, when studied closely, the connection turns out to be weak, even nonexistent. The reenactment is a special type of portrayal and demonstrates its own kind of thinking about an event. This notion sustains Morris's apprehension that these representations reveal *and* conceal. Given the often graphic nature of war films—and the commonly vital stakes of the subject matter (life and death, courage and cowardice, casualties and killing, and so on)—an interested filmgoer will wonder: In seeing this representation, what am I not seeing?

War films and photographs are, even if caught up in the entertainment industrial complex of Hollywood, implicated in the ongoing assessment of just these "ways of seeing the truth." Jeff Wall's photograph states in miniature that—as a single portrait, like a film still—all such works are fabrications, reenactments, assemblages, montages in the service of capturing or conveying emotional and ethical truth (even Wall's apparently individual frame was contrived from the arrangement of many photographs). And every kind of representation—from diaries drawn on the day of battle, from journalistic narratives written to summarize events on the ground, from documentary images created on the scene, from firsthand war stories told from memories, and from staged and reenacted feature films and documentaries made decades or centuries or millennia later—involves and transforms what we see, and what we can say about what we see.

War as Metaphor

If we are no longer even watching the restaging or reenactment of war, as we might be in a live action feature about the Civil War or Guadalcanal, but are instead watching the results of actors transformed through computer-generated imagery, then we must take note of another peculiar confluence of fates for the camera and the gun. As the gun has become a more remote threat—in the Cold War it figured as a nuclear missile in a silo, and today it seems to be a weaponized drone—so the camera is nowhere to be seen. The war film, if necessary, may be created in the same way that the gun is fired: by an agent at a computer terminal. As we hear it described by the merciless cyber-terrorist in *Skyfall:* "Just point and click."

The strange partnership of camera and gun continues into twenty-first-century warfare with this latest convergence and summons us to the question whether we know what we mean when we say "war." If war is something that happens in a computer—either for the production of films or by a remote agent firing from a drone on the evidence of live surveillance video—then has war become a metaphor? It would seem so—that is, until one studies the results of the digital production of warfare in the form of casualties and deaths, ruined families, and weakened societies. But then, even in the world of real consequences—where bullets kill people, and there are no "new lives" as in a video game—technology is changing the definition and effects of war. The War on Terror is fought by a boots-on-the-ground initiative in remote Afghanistan and also by drone operators in Nevada and intelligence analysts in Washington, D.C.; referring to drones as "unmanned" is then but a figure of speech, because they are just differently manned—manned at a distance. (Meanwhile, controversy over combat video footage released by WikiLeaks—given the incendiary title *Collateral Murder*—derived, in part, from the extent to which the scenario of high-altitude Apache helicopter pilots firing on live ground targets resembled the interface and narrative shape of a video game [i.e., a virtual space in which elevated bravado and moral bracketing is a form of art, not digitized proof of pulverized human beings].)[88] Needless to say, there is grave concern that the misnomer may be validated if and when drone operations are fully automated: when the computer begins to release munitions—derived from "an algorithm based on perceived threats that are described by sensors"—then the operation becomes fully and truly unmanned.[89] If the computer has globalized (and may automate and make anonymous) the way acts of war can be carried out—perhaps as a cyberattack in the form of computer viruses, the dissemination of (mis)information, the unleashing of damaging documents, the hampering of financial institutions, and so forth—then war is possible wherever anyone (or anything) can "Just point and click." As David Denby has said in relation to the plot of *Skyfall,* but could just as well hold for war in its contemporary incarnations, "Distance is now meaningless. Evil may erupt wherever there's a computer."[90] Any mobile phone in hand may become the source signal for the detonation of an improvised explosive device.

As the "point and shoot" of the gun and the camera is replaced by the digital "point and click," the two instruments remain in tandem. And yet the enduring relationship between camera and gun in the digital age means that war is no longer expressly the domain of nations fighting nations over vast spans of land and sea (in the air and underwater), with thousands of heavily armed troops risking their lives and huge expenditures of national wealth and resources. War can be made with an airline ticket and a box cutter. As Mallory (Ralph Fiennes) says about MI6 in *Skyfall:* "We're an antiquated bunch of bloody idiots fighting a war we don't understand and can't possibly win."[91] The plea is reasonable: it means we have not yet fathomed the significance or implications of the contemporary scene of war in its radical multiplicity of forms and effects.

In fact, it may be that the *trope* of war—by emphasizing war's pervasiveness in varying and disparate aspects of our lives (from cyberwarfare to bioterror to the War on Terror as well as in the myriad ways war is symbolized in films)—turns us back anew to the trials and horrors of *literal* warfare. Even as war is analogized and reappropriated in other contexts, and as it becomes more difficult to define because it is more pervasive, the training of soldiers, the building of bombs, and the deployment of men and women into a global effort of defense remind us of war's undeniably *embodied* features. The origins of drone warfare, for example—of war by unmanned delegate—could be said to reach back to the carrier pigeon relaying a piece of parchment with intelligence on the movement of armies (Ridley Scott's *Robin Hood* features such a scene). But the prominent use of unmanned militarized aircraft, which encodes surveillance even as it may be used as the proximate cause of attack, highlights a striking contrast in contemporary warfare, namely, between the hypervisibility of war for those who control its execution and the radical invisibility (and often anonymity) of war for those who experience the effects of its deployment.[92] For example, contrast the *screening* of war for those who operate the digital display of targets with the *unseeable* quality of the aggressor. This radical asymmetry of combat—where an agent in a control center in Nevada or central New York may release a weapon upon a target in Afghanistan or Pakistan—seems very far from the preponderance of war in human history, which has been defined by hand-to-hand engagement, in a scene of punishing immediacy and mortal threat. Of course, that human-to-human encounter remains as evident in depictions of ancient battles (Hector [Eric Bana] dying under Achilles's [Brad Pitt's] sword in *Troy,* his corpse thereafter dragged behind a chariot) as in modern conflicts (with Private Mellish [Adam Goldberg], pleading quietly, almost politely, for mercy as he is slowly impaled by a German soldier in *Saving Private Ryan*). War as metaphor, then, does much to clarify what is not metaphorical about war as we know it.

On Being Affected by War and War Films

War on-screen, of course, is among the most prevalent incarnations of war's figurative presence in our lives, not just from the "war on drugs," "war on poverty," and even the "war on cancer" (as sideways appropriations of martial language), but also from the abundant forms of war as visual context and medium, such as in television shows, animation, and video games. If I were to adopt the methods of the Freudian psychoanalyst at this point, I might say that the attempt to represent war—in such abundance, in so many variations—is a *compulsion,* an effect of an obviously unresolved trauma trying to work itself out. If this can be said in relation to the activity that regularly culminates in loss and death, the same could be said for the cultural profusion of representations of love, romance, and sex (obviously not synonymous terms). The innumerable instances and diverse manifestations of war films are not a sign that we understand so much about war, but just the opposite, just as the boundless effort to address romance and sex does not confirm any permanent perspicacity about love.

Another shared attribute of these twin representational compulsions—war and love (or sex)—is the extent to which both are described, by those who appear to know them best, most intimately, as "inexpressible," as "beyond words." If they are not conveyable in words—as a philosophical essay, poem, literary treatise, autobiography, or otherwise—then perhaps film is a gift for expression, with its coupled capacities for creating visual and aural environments. If we cannot say or tell what we know or feel, we can at least show it. This observation seems inherent in the long history of war films, acknowledged or not, namely, that the genre is aware at once of how soldiers (1) often describe their experiences in war as ineffable and yet (2) are regularly found narrating or dramatizing this lapse on-screen—the place where many of us come to initiate and sustain a relationship to war (namely, to those humans who fight it, and die in its cause, or who survive it, only to suffer new existential trials). Thus, if soldiers are often certain they cannot adequately express their firsthand war tribulations—what it was like fighting on the front line, or being injured, or watching one's friends die in the field, or missing loved ones back home—then how should we, as creators of war films and watchers of them, understand our relationship to war, especially as we see it in movies? What sort of a phenomenon is a war film, after all? Perhaps it is a compulsion filmmakers and film-watchers have adopted or undertaken together as a form of inheriting the trouble and trauma that derive from a species and a civilization that make war.

As an illustration of the soldier's reflection on his experience, consider Erich Maria Remarque's clarification in the front matter of *All Quiet on the Western Front:* "This book is to be neither an accusation nor a confession, and least of all an adventure, for death is not an adventure to those who stand face to face with it. It will try simply to tell of a generation of men who, even though they may have escaped shells, were destroyed by the war."[93] Later, in the midst of the narrative, Paul's father asks him "stupid and distressing" questions about his wartime experience, apparently unable to appreciate "that a man cannot talk of such things." Paul ponders the mysteries of war—our knowledge of it, our articulation of it—by asking: "What would become of us if everything that happens out there were quite clear to us?"[94] Being silenced by one's war experience, or remaining so, is, for Paul, preferable, and apparently this is a common sentiment among soldiers, as it is regularly invoked as part of the filmic drama and inner experience of characters. At times, the notion that a true description of war would overwhelm us compresses for viewers the kind of acute pain the soldier may feel about what he has witnessed, and at other times it is an indication of what may be a permanent affront to his mental health—something he cannot get past. In *The Face of Battle,* John Keegan took note of an official government report published shortly after the end of World War II, "Combat Exhaustion," in which the authors declare, "There is no such thing as 'getting used to combat,'" and then conclude: "Each moment of combat imposes a strain so great that men will break down in direct relation to the intensity and duration of their exposure. . . . Psychiatric casualties are as inevitable as gunshot and shrapnel would be in warfare."[95] We see these field-derived observations captured in documentary footage from John Huston's *Let There Be Light* (1946) and also frequently reflected in works of imaginative visualization—from *The Best Years of Our Lives* to *Birdy, The English Patient,* and *The Messenger.*

As we welcome our soldiers home and listen to their difficulties in speaking of war, so we, as viewers, find a similar reality represented on-screen. There, perhaps, we are given a shared space in which to acknowledge some of what has happened. And beyond acknowledgment, or, perhaps for some, as an essential part of it, we as viewers are positioned to ask how being affected by war *films* is related to being accountable to war itself. The ontology of film makes it so that a soldier's sense of the ineffability of war-as-waged finds a parallel in the viewer's experience of watching war on-screen—as Cavell has written tersely and poignantly: "In viewing a movie my helplessness is mechanically assured." The visual and sonic presence of the actors (or subjects, in the case of documentary) complicates our position and our relation to the very palpable sense of their absence from our scene of, one wants to say, encounter; and as the documented soldier-on-screen may have really died, his *life* on-screen is even more troubling—alive in the dark theater, but lost to the wider, illuminated world of daylight. Or again, as Cavell writes: "It is an incontestable fact that in a motion picture no live human being is up there. But a human *something* is, and something unlike anything else we know. We can stick to our plain description of that human something as 'in our presence while we are not in his' (present *at* him, because looking at him, but not present *to* him) and still account for the difference between his live presence and his photographed presence to us. We need to consider what is present or, rather, since the topic is the human being, *who* is present."[96]

Film, to our perpetual surprise, appears to be a kind of reanimating machine; we notice, like André Bazin, how time (as Garrett Stewart has written) seems "to be 'mummified' by the filmic medium."[97] No matter what happens to the referents—they age, they die—the film remains. And it lives. But the war film is—again, one might say pathologically, compulsively—made to record or reenact the falling of bodies, the gruesome, bloody deaths of countless men and women. Starting the war film from the beginning reanimates the dead soldiers—brings them back to life—so we can watch them collapse again. As Elisabeth Bronfen has written, the actors or the subjects, quite alarmingly, become revenants—"actors playing undead soldiers who will not stay in their graves."[98] This is a way in which the ontology of film—of *any* film or film genre—encodes the living, preserves and perpetuates them in suspended animation regardless of what happens to the actor or the person he portrays. If a viewer's relationship to the bodies involved in a romantic comedy, or even an erotic thriller or a horror movie, is framed as one of desire and attraction or fear and repulsion, so a viewer's orientation to the bodies of a war film is one of persistent empathic regard: these people will die, and those who do not will suffer the deaths of those who did, and survive estranged from the dead and in some way divided from the world. Since, as viewers, our "helplessness is mechanically assured," there will never be a time when an intervention in a scene will be called for, much less possible—the kind of interference that appears to repeatedly confront and inform the work of the in-person, embedded photojournalist, implicated in the very scene he aims to capture with his camera (from documentaries such as *War Photographer, Bearing Witness, The Devil Came on Horseback, Restrepo, Blood Trail,* and the substantial four-part series *Witness,* produced by Michael Mann,[99] as well as narratives drawn from the lives of photographers-at-war, such as *Triage, The Bang Bang Club,* and Oliver Stone's *Salvador* [a story based on the work of slain war photographer John Hoagland]). We may be helpless in the face of these scenarios—war at a distance, war safely entombed in cinema—and yet the encounter with the screen suggests we are genuinely "present at" war, not in it, but before it. Such occasions find us reckoning with representations. We are present, no doubt, but to what? And to what end?

A Relationship with Bodies On-screen

As Elisabeth Bronfen has done much to describe the way in which war films involve a kind of haunting, and as Stanley Cavell has appealed to the ontology of the film medium to chronicle our isolation from the spectacle (even as we may feel emotionally and morally subject to it), we are returned anew to the question of the meaning of the beings and bodies we see on-screen. There is, of course, the metaphysical nature of those beings—in the light of Bronfen's and Cavell's remarks—but there is also the question of the treatment and visual depiction of those bodies, one might say, in a taxonomical sense. Who are these people? And how is the grammar of the genre organizing and arranging them? One appealing approach to these questions is found in *The War Body on Screen,* edited by Karen Randell and Sean Redmon, since they parse the categories of war's filmed bodies as, for instance, "the body of the soldier," "the body of the terrorist," and the "body of the hostage."[100] One could find other related types and subtypes, for instance, the body of the tortured, the body of the unnamed bystander, the body of the clandestine agent, the body of the spouse waiting on the home front. The Randell-Redmon collection highlights the degree to which war films are defined by their treatment of human bodies. While, as noted, the erotic thriller or the horror film, as much as the romantic comedy, draw our attention to the (hoped for) pleasures of the body—its attractions and its dangers—so the war film, while ostensibly about the exhibition of human force, continually underscores the pain and existential limits of the body, its frailty and vulnerability and the radical contingency that seems to trail it even more pronouncedly during wartime. The graphic representation of bodies in war films—often causing nauseating, vertiginous reactions to these treatments—perhaps unexpectedly, emphasizes the viewer's distance and separation from the screened display. After all, the material components and bodily viscera of war—blood, mud, guts, shrapnel, spit, urine, feces, vomit—each fluid and feature defining its own distinct kind of suffering or loss, cannot be carried *through* the film medium. The smells of war have thus far been sealed off from cinema. Even as the body bleeds on-screen, it fibs: when blood flows from those enfleshed creatures, directors inveterately give it the color of ketchup instead of cabernet. The visual, tonal articulation of the fluids, then, can only be signs of something beyond the viewer's experience; the signs therein form a set of corollaries that we learn by watching war films and together aggregate into a semiotics of the war genre. Tarantino's exploitation-style carnage in *Inglourious Basterds* incorporates such conventions while also exaggerating them—taking the brazen terror of blood-spilling from heart-rending tragedy to the edge of comedic exhaustion. As viewers of war films, in general, we study these signs and wonder—empathically—about the realities (unknown to us) that make them so vital, so harsh, so undeniable.

The other side of bodies on-screen is the audience that looks at them—watches them, studies them. And so we are poised to consider the epistemology of vision, which involves asking about the nature of what we are seeing: Is it true? Is it referential? What would it mean if it were referential (e.g., documentary footage) and yet not true (as in staged, or reordered or otherwise distorted)? Jan Mieszkowski, for instance, has argued that personal imagination affects our understanding of what we may claim to see when what we see is not war but instead an account or an image of war. In *Watching War,* Mieszkowski contends that since the Napoleonic era—when wars became too vast and far-flung to be witnessed by many people—"waging a military campaign required managing the spectacle of battle consumed on the home front as much as defeating one's foe on the field of combat." Speaking of more than film, but including film, he asks: "Did these representations of combat enlighten, horrify, or stupefy their audiences?"[101] Mieszkowski, like other scholars such as Max Boot, are tracking what could be called the influence of media and spectacle on the making and winning of war. In *Invisible Armies,* Boot, drawing from statistical data, suggests that guerrilla insurgency campaigns have doubled in efficacy in the last century—he thinks, largely owing to the effect of public opinion and the mobilization of supportive alliances.[102] Moreover, the enhancement and proliferation of communications technologies is part of these evolving war-waging phenomena. So in making war, the making of images is tied intimately to the consuming of them. We need, then, a criticism motivated to read what we do, in fact, see on-screen (what its nature is: unvarnished propaganda? playful satire? moral parable? fantastical revisionism? heroic paean?) and what we *think* we see on-screen.

On this last line, we come to terms with the extent to which a viewer's imagination affects—and creates—the person's understanding of war. Considered seriously, it does not take long to suspect that war films do not (cannot) show us what happens in war, but instead create an image of something without an empirical referent; a real thing without a real basis in reality—a simulacrum through and through. If this is the case, then war films are fundamentally—no matter the accuracy of the uniforms, equipment, dialogue, accents, sets, and scenes—as real, as verifiable, as true as a dream or a nightmare. Watching a war film means bearing witness to the medium's capacities as a substitute, as an intermediate space in which to think analogically about the relationship between mental conceptions and the boots and bodies on the ground. Film is a forum for negotiation, not a fixed document; it is art, not history. By watching this particular representation of soldiers and strife, moral conflict and somatic peril, a viewer experiences an internal, nonreferential struggle with war's nature and manifestation. On this reading, war films tell us or teach us nothing about the reality of war—that is something for the firsthand witnesses and soldiers to contend with—but summon us to the complicated business of the (mere, but still significant) representation of war. Those who make war films, and those who watch them, and those who write criticism of the makers and watchers of war films, by and large, have very little experience of war as such. War is, for most viewers, how war has been represented (in books, photographs, films, television, journalism, novels, paintings, etc.). And so, a war film—owing to those customary and celebrated "nomadic raiding[s]"—is often one representation beside another, one interpretation of a representation following after another. This sounds like a decent, useful, and brief description of the film medium itself. And so while we have sought to think about what war films teach us about war, it may justifiably be said that war on film teaches us something special about film.

The Big Picture for the Small Screen

As part of the proliferation of war films, we find the development of war stories for television—as show- or series-based documentaries, episodic news magazines (such as *Frontline*), and fiction features.[103] These varying forms appear to present, or least invite us to consider (even if very briefly here) whether there is any theoretical or practical difference in this mode of display; the staging of war for television is, like war video games, another substantial and important representational realm worthy of extended investigation, and despite how our remarks here complement that thinking, war on television calls for much more elaborate exploration than is offered in the present volume. For instance, is a conventionally understood war film different from, say, a war miniseries (such as *Band of Brothers, The Pacific, Parade's End,* or *Generation Kill*), or a portrayal in histories such as *John Adams,* fictionalized dramas such as *Rome,* or fantasies such as *Game of Thrones,* or a war program featured on cable, network, or public television (such as *Homeland, Foyle's War,* or *Downton Abbey*)? Or is a war miniseries just a really long war film? And so what if it is? Meanwhile, another set of questions surround war documentaries that are presented in sequences or series, for example, Ken Burns's lengthy, well-researched, but also intimate

The War. If a two-hour stand-alone feature documentary has a shape, what happens to the form of documentary narrative over the course of six or twelve episodes, or according to the logic of "seasons" (as we find them in television)?

One might begin to sketch a reply to these questions by noting that a miniseries is, in some measure, just a euphemism for a long film, since it maps isomorphically onto most points of comparison with a familiar feature release. Despite its ostensibly serial nature, a miniseries, we could say, merely elongates and enriches a linear three-act structure. By contrast, a true television "series" (what may be properly called, by contrast, a maxiseries) has something more akin to a rhizomatic form: it is webby, diffuse, and reaches out to a range of subplots and subcharacters. Still more, a television show, or maxiseries, is capable of following obscure narrative routes and digressions and pursuing the development of secondary and tertiary characters and themes, as well as experimenting with the presence of guest stars, engaging with social commentary, and even allowing for false paths (without undermining the overarching creative venture or the show's fundamental identity). A great show can survive a bad season; by contrast, the reputation of a miniseries would be diminished by weaknesses in any of its parts. Furthermore, in noting additional significant differences, war miniseries tend to be written by a single author, or adapted from single-author source materials, while television shows regularly possess a staff of writers that can vary over time. With many writers, any given show is more likely to reflect the particularities of its chosen author, and consequently the show as a whole will not possess the continuity or consistency of voice, plot, style, or vision that we commonly see in feature films and miniseries.

These few differences between film and television, and there are many others worth exploring, ought not to disqualify but rather amplify our interest in the occasions when war is chosen as the subject or context for television. Though the contributors to this volume focus more intently on war films per se, the vast scale and imposing quality of "war television" cannot escape relevant and extended consideration.

Perpetual War, Perpetual War Films, and the Regimes of Representation

In June 1932, in the wake of the devastation of Europe's Great War, and before the rise of German fascism and the scourge of the Holocaust and World War

II, Albert Einstein wrote to Sigmund Freud regarding what might be done about the apparently unending nature of martial conflict. A few months later, in September 1932, Freud composed a response to Einstein in a letter that has come to be known as "Why War?" where he notes that "a glance at the history of the human race reveals an endless series of conflicts between one community and another or several others, between larger and smaller units—between cities, provinces, races, nations, empires—which have almost always been settled by force of arms." Addressing this long-standing problem, Freud says, in part, that our "willingness to engage in war is an effect of the destructive instinct," and since "there is no use in trying to get rid of men's aggressive inclinations . . . , the most obvious plan [to rid the world of war] will be to bring Eros, its antagonist, into play against it." Begging the patience of his audience, Professor Einstein, Freud addresses the world's premier physicist with a bit of savvy, mythological speculation and provocative analogizing:

> Nevertheless I should like to linger for a moment over our destructive instinct, whose popularity is by no means equal to its importance. As a result of a little speculation, we have come to suppose that this instinct is at work in every living creature and is striving to bring it to ruin and to reduce life to its original condition of inanimate matter. Thus it quite seriously deserves to be called a death instinct, while the erotic instincts represent the effort to live. The death instinct turns into the destructive instinct when, with the help of special organs, it is directed outwards, on to objects. The organism preserves its own life, so to say, by destroying an extraneous one. Some portion of the death instinct, however, remains operative within the organism, and we have sought to trace quite a number of normal and pathological phenomena to this internalization of the destructive instinct. We have even been guilty of the heresy of attributing the origin of conscience to this diversion inwards of aggressiveness. You will notice that it is by no means a trivial matter if this process is carried too far: it is positively unhealthy. On the other hand if these forces are turned to destruction in the external world, the organism will be relieved and the effect must be beneficial. This would serve as a biological justification for all the ugly and dangerous impulses against which we are struggling. It must be admitted that they stand nearer to Nature than does our resistance to them

> for which an explanation also needs to be found. It may perhaps seem to you as though our theories are a kind of mythology and, in the present case, not even an agreeable one. But does not every science come in the end to a kind of mythology like this? Cannot the same be said to-day of your own physics?[104]

To the question of whether war will persist, or may give way to perpetual peace, Freud says, in effect, look within, or consider your own nature. Insofar as humans are ruled by this sort of image of themselves—or maybe it is, instead, an inexpugnable part of our constitution—war will *naturally* emerge in the context and conduct of civilization (or, as Freud preferred to call it: "culture"), despite our conscious and conscience-based efforts to the contrary.

In 1958, on the other side of Nazism, the Holocaust, and the tens of millions of dead from World War II, Isaiah Berlin articulated a classical liberal view of human conflict, pointing to what might be considered the seed or seat of all crises of war: "If, as I believe," he wrote in "Two Concepts of Liberty," "the ends of men are many, and not all of them are in principle compatible with each other, then the possibility of conflict—and of tragedy—can never be wholly eliminated from human life, either personal or social."[105]

In 1976, Michel Foucault addressed another aspect of Berlin's claim and countered whatever vision might imply how law or society could adopt peace as a choice—that is, as an *alternative* to or *inverse* of war:

> Law is not pacification, for beneath the law, war continues to rage in all the mechanisms of power, even in the most regular. War is the motor behind institutions and order. In the smallest of its cogs, peace is waging a secret war. To put it another way, we have to interpret the war that is going on beneath peace; peace itself is a coded war. We are therefore at war with one another; a battlefront runs through the whole of society, continuously and permanently, and it is this battlefront that puts us all on one side or the other. There is no such thing as a neutral subject. We are all inevitably someone's adversary.[106]

Foucault's remonstrance and clarification call to mind Carl Schmitt's contention that, against any utopian plan, "the political" is an existential condition from which multitudinous phenomena, including politics, take shape. And the political is fundamentally about defining, or differentiating between, "friend" and "enemy." As Schmitt writes in *The Concept of the Political,* the enemy is whoever is "in a specially intense way, existentially something different and alien, so that in the extreme cases conflicts with him are possible."[107] The political, in brief, is whatever undertaking attempts to characterize the other and the nature of the space and power that obtains in relation to it. So it would appear that the negotiations that occur in the name of peace are, as Foucault says, "a coded war"—the effort to manage power in myriad incarnations (institutional, military, political, social, individual, and, we could add, in and through the filmic representations that depict power). Cynicism aside, the achievement of peace would itself be part of a substrate of war actions, alliances, and negotiations. Peace is the orchestration of antagonism to collapse, a skyscraper that in its aspiration for height invariably must endlessly contend with gravity—and other forces—that would bring it down.

And now, still more years and more wars later, the persistence of conflict continues to draw the puzzled, often chagrined, attention of scholars. Like Freud, Berlin, and Foucault, moral philosopher John Kekes writes that war appears to be ineluctable, but not owing to an irrepressible trait of human nature (as we also discover in works by Thucydides, Machiavelli, and Hobbes—where war is the State of Nature, which for humans often simply means "continuall feare, and danger of violent death"[108]—of course with Freud just noted, and more recently in remarks by Stephen Peter Rosen and David Livingstone Smith), or even because of limited resources (Steven A. LaBlanc and Katherine E. Register) or the desire for power—to maintain or seize it (Michael Howard),[109] but rather because clashes of value and identity persist. As such, Kekes declares war to be a "permanent adversity" of humankind. Given his assured sense that war cannot be eradicated, Kekes takes up what might be called a pessimistic view, if only because he frames the other side of the argument as posed by "optimists"—who offer, in his estimation, a "naïve" and "dangerous" outlook. Kekes, eschewing Freud and amplifying a sentiment from Berlin, writes: "The optimists fail to see that, as history so amply shows, even basic values are plural and conflicting. When nations or groups are pitted against each other, because their basic values lead them to act in ways that they find mutually unacceptable, then they cannot settle their conflict by negotiation and compromise. For what is at stake for them are the basic values that ultimately make their life worth living. And if they are attacked, then they will fight. War is a permanent adversity, because such conflicts are the unavoidable consequences of the plurality of values."[110]

There is pushback on Kekes's assessment—what should we call his view? sullen, sober, pragmatic, defeatist?—for example, from John Horgan, who writes in *The End of War* (and agreeing with Kekes) that war is not an innate, determined part of human nature; not necessarily prompted by scarce resources; and not the consequence of a small minority of instigators. Instead war should be treated as a "cultural contagion," an infection that spreads and (following from his use of the metaphor) a curable scourge.[111] Recovering the core sentiment of Margaret Mead's understanding that war is an "invented" (and thus not an inevitable) presence in human affairs, Horgan shifts to a medical analogy—where he, in fact, overstates the difficulty of "curing," since war, in his view, is easier to end than cancer precisely because it is not natural but a deliberate choice (more akin to the ending of chattel slavery than the alleviation of a terminal illness).[112] Ralph Waldo Emerson, using the same analogy in 1838, worried that it was not so easily treated: "War, which, to sane men at the present day, begins to look like an epidemic insanity, breaking out here and there like the cholera or influenza, infecting men's brains instead of their bowels, when seen in the remote past, in the infancy of society, appears a part of the connection of events, and, in its place, necessary."[113] Illness as metaphor, especially as it is used to diagnose whether the affliction is curable or terminal, finds earlier expression—and debate—in Shakespeare's *Henry IV*, where the Archbishop fields Westmoreland's distraught query,

> Out of the speech of peace, that bears such grace,
> Into the harsh and boist'rous tongue of war,
> Turning your books to graves, your ink to blood,
> Your pens to lances, and your tongue divine
> To a trumpet and a point of war?

by saying "Wherefore do I this? . . . Briefly, to this end: we are all diseased. . . . Have brought ourselves into a burning fever, / And we must bleed for it" (IV.1). The Archbishop's reluctant fatalism seems a compromise with the forces of temperament that give shape to history.

Emerson contravenes his own worry about the inexorableness of war, however, by suggesting that if humans have contracted a "burning fever" for war, they also have developed an "instinct of self-help." With American

Transcendentalist thought grafted with pre-Darwinian language, Emerson says that "to each creature these objects [such as freedom, security, and self-defense] are made so dear, that it risks its life continually in the struggle for these ends."[114] Horgan pursues a similar line of thinking when he inverts the inherited notion of humans-as-warmongers by arguing, paradoxically, that it is the development of empathy and altruism that drives us to war, one's motivation not being to kill the enemy but to save those whom the enemy threatens to kill.[115] Emerson says that a person, at a "higher stage" of maturity, or a different "state of cultivation," will find that "warlike nature is all converted into an active medicinal principle."[116] And thereby war will cease because humans will have been cured of the compulsion, or the necessity, to make it. John Kekes might raise a hand at this point to signal these "naïve" and "dangerous" pronouncements.

Acknowledging the postulations and indications inherent in Kekes's work, if not the proof of his claims, Srinivas Aravamudan writes in "Perpetual War" about the empirical reality of war's persistence and offers a reliable survey of war in culture.[117] So while Kekes highlighted the moral and epistemological barriers to war's elimination, Aravamudan points up the entanglements and multiplicity of the aesthetic matters that may contribute varyingly to the causes of war, its prosecution, and, more vexingly, its intelligibility to those who fight it, wish to end it, or attempt to comprehend it.

> Prognostications of the perpetuity of war lead to the recognition that war is a central element of "the accumulative volume of superfluous evils" besetting the world today.[118] The question of evil is always already "enframed," as Adi Ophir argues, and there is no simple way to separate the murderous violence of war from the regimes of representation that enframe it.[119] We have to rethink political precariousness against existential precarity (Butler). While Hannah Arendt understands surplus population to be the ultimate threat to political life and the dignity of the citizen, we may need to recognize how war is integral to a larger system generating multiple forms of vulnerability and injury as constitutive of the human itself.[120]

While Aravamudan implicitly acknowledges the long history that would say war is a part of human nature, a claim Kekes discounts, he directs attention to the way war relates to the "regimes of representation that enframe it."[121]

The notion keeps in play Christian Metz's earlier invoked, and still widely relevant, notion of the scopic regime but adds to it a sense in which however one attempts to speak of or comprehend war, such labor necessarily involves the challenge of appraising factors such as selection, arrangement, and emphasis. In thinking of war, what do we choose to focus on? The heroic elevation of battle, or the wounded aftermath of its execution? The iconic lines of soldiers on the battlefield firing at one another, or the solitary computer hacker entering keystrokes that can shut down or unleash power? At last, the representation of war demands that we make choices about what to address and how to feature or enframe it. This is as much the case for the screenwriters and filmmakers who create motion pictures as for the viewers who watch them and the critics who write about those new artifacts. The essays in this book are written with an appreciation for film's enframing capacities—and the representational and scopic regimes that inform the medium's reception—and also reflect the authors' choices about what appears worthy of our considered attention. If war defies total comprehension—if it perpetually exceeds the limits of any single view and is thus, as several of the aforementioned critics contend, part and parcel of the imagination—then we are in need of scholarship that can ably make some sense of the aspects and angles, the degrees and the debris of depiction, all constituent parts of the big picture.

More than "Mere Representation"

A half century has passed since Guy Debord became famous for espousing a rather dour assessment of modernity in *Society of the Spectacle.* In a mood closer to lament than critique, Debord wrote, "All that once was directly lived has become mere representation."[122] But then why "mere"? All signs suggest that representation is more than mere—something substantive—and an essential component of the way we have come to interact with and understand history, trauma, therapy, community, and the nature of the self. Debord describes a devolution—"the decline of being into having, and having into merely appearing."[123] But then, why "decline" and why (again) "merely"—why is this change not *also* an achievement, an innovation? For instance, maybe war will one day be something we see primarily on film; perhaps we have already entered that stage. For most of us, the waging of warfare in its traditional sense—at least the mobilization of vast armies of drafted recruits—has gone extinct, and so making war films can become a form of memorialization and commemoration as well as a means for entertainment and voyeurism. In this latest phase, spectactorship and speculation blend to become a unified, default activity—and an increasingly essential part of the rites and rituals of the expressive contemporary citizen. With the developments of 3D film, 4D theaters (that incorporate literal effects—rain, wind, smoke, scents, vibration, etc.), and virtual technologies, perhaps war films will hybridize with video games to create immersive war environments. Virtual or alternate reality will slowly become (and also is becoming) part of the everyday fabric of human perception. For Debord, the society of the spectacle, which we now inhabit (for most of us, unwittingly, often unconsciously) has impoverished or, in his term, "degraded" human existence.[124] Paradoxically, however, the shift to an abundance of representation makes such impoverishment by so-called degradation also appear to court qualities of enrichment. We live in a time that is described as "media-saturated," and consequently we are not starved for images but glutted with them.[125] Our needs, then, are for the curating and critiquing of these many kinds of representation in concert with the creation of new images (as Werner Herzog has encouraged us, we are to "seek out fresh ones").[126] Some time has passed since Debord's pronouncements, and though many of his remarks remain relevant, they also seem neither entirely true nor entirely predictive. It is thus the case that we, as movie watchers and film critics, as those who live in a world with war and war films, can undertake a different approach to the circumstances of a life lived dynamically with representations.

The prominence, diversity, and enduring prevalence of war films may be something of a mystery, or a scourge, to those who believe that "civilization" (in Freud's parlance) might cure us of our human propensity to fight—with hostility, tenacity, and the pugnacious energies that appear to expire only with death. If the world is becoming more peaceful (is it? how would one quantify or qualify such a claim?), then why do we see the annual appearance of scores of works about war—especially films that appear to glorify bellicosity, combat, bloodshed, and annihilation? As part of the vision that humans are becoming more peaceful, have war films become a proxy—a vicarious phenomenon in which we can play-act our aggressions, thus displacing them from the battlefield and into the movie house? (And here, again, war video games intercede with their even more literal *and* virtual instantiation of the interactivity of viewer-as-participant-with-media, instead of viewer-as-spectator-of-media.) Or do war films—in their continually more sophisticated ways, as wars change shape and kind—merely register or reflect the sorts of conflicts that proceed unfettered on the other side of the screen, on the streets beyond the theater? These questions are meant to sustain the concerns we find in Freud, Berlin, Foucault, Schmitt, Kekes, and Aravamudan, among so many others—that we are not entirely sure whether war can end. Indeed, war's variability and tenacious hold on human affairs suggest that our thinking about its eradication must continue; meanwhile, our efforts at representing war's ever-elusive, enigmatic nature will recur for artists and soldiers, photographers and filmmakers.

The very deferment of finding a resolution to war's abiding presence—as we might say, in tandem with love's ceaseless complexity—is caught up with the difficulty of expressing our relation to its apparently indomitable habitation in human affairs. And war, like love, is an agitating human experience—compelling us forward (however painfully, often at tremendous costs)—ensuring that we will remain preoccupied with a mission to articulate war's impact on human experience by studying the visual and sonic culture that reflects and defines it. A significant portion of that study includes a philosophical consideration of war's actuality and war's ineffability—and the continuum of stages in between. We may remain uncertain about what it means to continue making war films—and writing about them—in the long, persistent flow of conflict from antiquity to the present day. Hopefully, the following essays—finding all of their authors perforce engaged in responding to these questions—will provide some company in the reader's own thinking about war's perpetuity and the seemingly endless series of war films that couple with and contribute to human reality.

A Note on the Structure and Content of the Volume

I have grouped the fifteen essays collected in this volume—all but Fredric Jameson's and Robert Pippin's contributions appearing in print here for the first time—into four parts.[127] Each division is meant to highlight a dominant strain of philosophical thinking, a conceptual or topical focus, and a methodological context—some of which have been introduced in what has been said thus far. The contributors, drawing from their own disparate disciplinary practices as well as shared theoretical preoccupations and interests, engage some of the issues raised in this introduction, and in many cases prosecute novel engagements with additional topics in the philosophical study of war films. Indeed, both the quality and the variety of the essays add further credence to the impression that war films are highly generative for philosophical thinking and that war—as a vital, apparently ineluctable phenomenon—continues to captivate our attention.

The contributors to the first part address the aesthetics of war on-screen and how the nature of visuality, visibility, and hyper-visibility are affected by the technologies of war and the technologies of making movies. In the second part, authors explore how the individual self is transformed by war, for example, insofar as war paradoxically may become a context both for establishing or fashioning personal identity and for dissolving it. In the third part, scholars concentrate on the ethical issues that exemplify war as an endeavor, and evaluate the impact that undertaking has on the moral, intellectual, and emotional life of soldiers and civilians. In the fourth and final part, writers address war's status as an ultimate or absolute condition—conjuring the kind of ecstatic experience that defines us as human even as it threatens to annihilate us from that precious, unrepeatable, unrecoverable existence.

Notes

1. See Lance Bertelsen, "San Pietro and the 'Art' of War," *Southwest Review* 74, no. 2 (Spring 1989): 230–56, where Bertelsen claims that "the bulk of the action" in John Huston's war documentary *San Pietro* (1945) "was restaged" and therefore that the so-called documentary footage instead presents reenactments. Allegedly one of Huston's cinematographic techniques was hitting the camera during filming as a way of simulating the effects of ordnance explosions. See also "John Huston; Staging 'San Pietro,'" *New York Times,* May 28, 2000, nytimes.com. Janusz Kaminski notes that when he was experimenting with capturing volatile movements during principal photography for Steven Spielberg's *Saving Private Ryan* (1998), "At first it was very crude: I would just shake the camera." A rather haunting parallel between Kaminski's in-the-camera, in-the-field effect and the execution of real-time battle is the finality of the process. As a soldier is struck by shrapnel, so the medium registers the abusive hand: "This was all done to the negative," Kaminski emphasizes. "There's no going back. Once it's shot, it's done." Kyle Buchanan, "How Steven Spielberg's Cinematographer Got These Eleven Shots," *New York,* November 12, 2012, nymag.com. I am grateful to Paul Cronin for relating a version of Huston's and Kaminski's stories to me during our conversations about the challenge of representing war on film—and a consideration of some of the most compelling, if humble, cinematic techniques deployed for doing so to poignant effect.

2. *Che: Part Two* (Steven Soderbergh, 2008).

3. Erik Barnouw, *Documentary: A History of the Non-Fiction Film* (New York: Oxford University Press, 1993), 154. *Cameraman at the Front* (*Frontovoj Kinooperator,* 1946) was edited by Maria Slavinskaya.

4. Stanley Cavell, *Contesting Tears: The Hollywood Melodrama of the Unknown Woman* (Chicago: University of Chicago Press, 1996), xii. See also "Reflections on a Life of Philosophy: An Interview with Stanley Cavell," *Harvard Review of Philosophy* 7 (1999): 25; and *The Language and Style of Film Criticism,* ed. Alex Clayton and Andrew Klevan (Oxford: Oxford University Press, 2011), 41.

5. Cavell, *Contesting Tears,* xii.

6. Thomas Frank, "Blood Sport," *Harper's,* March 2013, 7.

7. Guy Debord, *Society of the Spectacle,* trans. Donald Nicholson-Smith (New York: Verso, 1994); original publication: *La société du spectacle* (Paris: Editions Buchet-Chastel, 1967).

8. Christian Metz, "The Scopic Regime of the Cinema," in *The Imaginary Signifier: Psychoanalysis and the Cinema* (Bloomington: Indiana University Press, 1982; orig. pub. 1975), 61–65.

9. For more on the relationship between the military and Hollywood, historically, politically, and economically, see Carl Boggs and Tom Pollard, *The Hollywood War Machine: U.S. Militarism and Popular Culture* (Boulder, CO: Paradigm, 2006); David L. Robb, *Operation Hollywood: How the Pentagon Shapes and Censors the Movies* (Amherst, NY: Prometheus Books, 2004); Thomas Doherty, *Projections of War: Hollywood, American Culture, and World War II,* rev. ed. (New York: Columbia University Press, 1999); and Clayton R. Koppes and Gregory D. Black, *Hollywood Goes to War: How Politics, Profits, and Propaganda Shaped World War II Movies* (Berkeley: University of California Press, 1990).

10. Aristotle, *The Art of Rhetoric,* trans. H. C. Lawson-Tancred (New York: Penguin, 1991); and Robert McKee, *Story: Substance, Structure, Style, and the Principles of Screenwriting* (New York: ReganBooks, 1997).

11. See Stanley Cavell, *Pursuits of Happiness: The Hollywood Comedy of Remarriage* (Cambridge, MA: Harvard University Press, 1981); Cavell, *Cities of Words: Pedagogical Letters on a Register of the Moral Life* (Cambridge, MA: Harvard University Press, 2004); David LaRocca, "Charlie Kaufman and Philosophy's Questions," in *The Philosophy of Charlie Kaufman,* ed. David LaRocca (Lexington: University Press of Kentucky, 2011), 18–19n25; Jeanine Bassinger, *I Do and I Don't: A History of Marriage in the Movies* (New York: Knopf, 2013); William Day, "*Moonstruck;* or, How to Ruin Everything," in *Ordinary Language Criticism: Literary Thinking after Cavell after Wittgenstein,* ed. Kenneth Dauber and Walter Jost (Evanston, IL: Northwestern University Press, 2003), 315–28; and Day, "I Don't Know, Just Wait: Remembering Remarriage in *Eternal Sunshine of the Spotless Mind,*" in LaRocca, *The Philosophy of Charlie Kaufman,* 132–55.

12. Rebecca Solnit, *River of Shadows: Eadweard Muybridge and the Technological Wild West* (New York: Penguin, 2003), 210.

13. Ibid.

14. Paul Virilio, "The Sight Machine," trans. Patrick Camiller, in *War and Cinema: The Logistics of Perception* (New York: Verso, 1989), 3, 4.

15. See also *Pacific Rim* (2013) and *RoboCop* (2014).

16. See *The Bourne Ultimatum* (Paul Greengrass, 2007), 00:38:00; and *The Bourne Legacy* (Tony Gilroy, 2012), opening sequence in Alaska.

17. See also Tim Hetherington, *Sleeping Soldiers,* Corcoran Gallery of Art, Washington, DC (exhibit February to May 2012); "You Never Forget That First Taste of War," photographs by Christopher Anderson; and Jada Yuan, "Photographers-in-Arms," *New York,* May 16, 2011, 30–37, nymag.com. Sebastian Junger also produced a documentary in honor of his friend, *Which Way Is the Front Line from Here? The Life and Times of Tim Hetherington* (2012); see Jada Yuan, "94 Minutes with Sebastian Junger," *New York,* April 22, 2013, nymag.com.

18. A. O. Scott, "How Real Does It Feel?" *New York Times,* December 9, 2010, nytimes.com.

19. Tim O'Brien, "How to Tell a True War Story," in *The Things They Carried* (New York: Penguin, 1990), 88–89.

20. See, for instance, the way in which war simulation, extreme sports competition, and innovative counterterrorism strategy are brought together for the annual "Warrior Competition" held at King Abdullah II Special Operations Training Center in Jordan. Josh Eells, "Sleepaway Camp for Postmodern Cowboys: The World's Counterterrorism Forces Meet for a Friendly Shoot'em-up in the Desert," *New York Times Magazine,* July 21, 2013, 34–41.

21. Elisabeth Bronfen, *Specters of War: Hollywood's Engagement with Military Conflict* (New Brunswick, NJ: Rutgers University Press, 2012), 15.

22. For an approach to war films that takes up the genre's relationship with history, see especially *Why We Fought: America's Wars in Film and History,* ed. Peter C. Rollins and John E. O'Connor (Lexington: University Press of Kentucky, 2008). Since Westerns often take place in a war context, see also *Hollywood's West: The American Frontier in Film, Television, and History,* ed. Peter C. Rollins and John E. O'Connor (Lexington: University Press of Kentucky, 2005).

23. See Peter A. French, *Cowboy Metaphysics* (Boston: Rowman & Littlefield, 1997); Patrick McGee, *From Shane to Kill Bill: Rethinking the Western* (Oxford: Wiley-Blackwell, 2007); *The Philosophy of the Western,* ed. Jennifer L. McMahon and B. Steve Csaki (Lexington: University Press of Kentucky, 2010); Rollins and O'Connor, *Hollywood's West;* Robert Pippin, *Hollywood Westerns and American Myth: The Importance of Howard Hawks and John Ford for Political Philosophy* (New Haven, CT: Yale University Press, 2012).

24. See Frank Rich, "Iraq Everlasting," *New York,* June 2–8, 2014, 30–37.

25. See *The Invisible War* (Kirby Dick, 2012), where it is noted that "today, a female soldier in combat zones is more likely to be raped by a fellow soldier than killed by enemy fire."

26. See Timothy Williams, "Suicides Outpacing War Deaths for Troops," *New York Times,* June 8, 2012, nytimes.com; "U.S. Military Veteran Suicides Rise, One Dies Every 65 Minutes," Reuters, February 4, 2013, reuters.com.

27. Bronfen, *Specters of War,* 5, 11.

28. Ibid., 5.

29. The first quotation is from President George W. Bush, from a speech given in Michigan in 2007; the second quotation is from President Barack Obama, from a speech given at the National Archives a few months after taking office for his first term. See Ari Shapiro, "Obama Team Stops Saying 'Global War on Terror' but Doesn't Stop Waging It," *NPR,* March 11, 2013, npr.org.

30. Rick Altman, "A Semantic/Syntactic Approach to Genre" (1984), in *Film Genre Reader IV,* ed. Barry Keith Grant (Austin: University of Texas Press, 2012). Altman offers new commentary on his seminal essay in "A Semantic/Syntactic/Pragmatic Approach to Genre," in Rick Altman, *Film/Genre* (London: BFI, 1999).

31. Michel de Certeau, *The Practice of Everyday Life* (Berkeley: University of California Press, 1984), 174.

32. Altman, *Film/Genre,* 212.

33. Ibid., 214.

34. Ibid.

35. Ibid., 219.

36. Ibid., 221.

37. Marie Brenner, "Robert Capa's Longest Day," *Vanity Fair,* June 2014, 79.

38. For more on perpetual war, see *PMLA* Special Topic: *War, PMLA* 124, no. 5 (October 2009), which features Fredric Jameson's article "War and Representation," which is included in the present volume, and an introduction entitled "Perpetual War" by Srinivas Aravamudan. See also, for example, John Horgan, *The End of War* (San Francisco: McSweeney's Books, 2012); and an eponymous symposium hosted by the *Guardian* and *The Brian Lehrer Show* (wnyc.org).

39. "Repeal the Military Force Law," editorial, *New York Times,* March 9, 2013, nytimes.com. See also Gregory Johnson, "60 Words," *Radiolab,* S:12, E:3, radiolab .org; and Public Law 107-40, September 18, 2001, 107th Congress, which includes the sixty words.

40. Ibid. For more on the U.S. government's use of and policy on drones, see Steve Coll, "Remote Control," *New Yorker,* May 6, 2013, 76–79, newyorker.com; Mark Mazzetti, "A Secret Deal on Drones, Sealed in Blood," *New York Times,* April 6, 2013, nytimes.com; and Mazzetti, *The Way of the Knife: The CIA, a Secret Army, and a War at the Ends of the Earth* (New York: Penguin, 2013); Jeremy Scahill, *Dirty Wars: The World Is a Battlefield* (New York: Nation Books, 2013); Scott Shane, "Targeted Killing Comes to Define War on Terror," *New York Times,* April 7, 2013, nytimes.com; *The Long War Journal,* longwarjournal.org; and *Nova: Rise of the Drones* (PBS, 2013).

41. Kenneth Cukier, "The 'Big Data' Revolution: How Number Crunchers Can Predict Our Lives," National Public Radio, March 7, 2013, npr.org. See also Kenneth Cukier and Viktor Mayer-Schonberger, *Big Data: A Revolution That Will Transform How We Live, Work, and Think* (New York: Houghton Mifflin, 2013).

42. Mark Mazzetti and David E. Sanger, "Spy Chief Calls Cyberattacks Top Threat to the U.S.," *New York Times,* March 12, 2013, nytimes.com.

43. Mark Mazzetti and David E. Sanger, "Security Leader Says U.S. Would Retaliate against Cyberattacks," *New York Times,* March 12, 2013, nytimes.com.

44. Melena Ryzik, "Harvey Weinstein's Regrets," *New York Times,* January 29, 2013. Weinstein described *The Master* (P. T. Anderson, 2012) as a "postwar film," reflecting on his father's experience "returning home after WWII." If "postwar" is a name that arises intuitively for the noncombatant—since it relies on history and chronology—it may also be a misleading assignation, since speaking of a soldier's life after war has ended may fail to convey the extent to which the war *continues* for him or her—emotionally, cognitively, and in its physical effects. As David Von Drehle has observed, "wars continue to gnaw and grind long after the end is officially pronounced." "No Soldier Left Behind," *Time,* June 16, 2014, 28. For many returning soldiers, there is a very real sense in which the time after war remains a period of continuous combat, when the ordeals of war, despite time away and distance from the front, are part of daily life; from depression to PTSD to lasting physical infirmity, there is strictly no such thing as "postwar." See also, in this vein, Jonathan Shay, *Achilles in Vietnam: Combat Trauma and the Undoing of Character* (New York: Atheneum, 1994); and *Odysseus in America: Combat Trauma and the Trials of Homecoming* (New York: Scribner, 2002).

45. Heraclitus, fragment 53. For a translation and discussion of Heraclitus's fragment, see Gregory Fried, *Heidegger's Polemos: From Being to Politics* (New Haven, CT: Yale University Press, 2000), 21–42.

46. Virgil, *The Aeneid,* trans. Robert FitzGerald (New York: Random House, 1983), 3.

47. Bronfen, *Specters of War,* 10.

48. Michael J. Shapiro, *Cinematic Geopolitics* (New York: Routledge, 2009), chapter 1, passim. See also *Violent Cartographies: Mapping Cultures of War* (Minneapolis: University of Minnesota Press, 1997); and "The New Violent Cartographies," in *Michael J. Shapiro: Discourse, Culture, Violence,* ed. Terrell Carver and Samuel A. Chambers (New York: Routledge, 2012), 178–98.

49. Shapiro, *Cinematic Geopolitics,* 11.

50. See *Apocalypse Now* entry at moviemistakes.com.

51. Jacques Rancière, "Eisenstein's Madness," in *Film Fables* (New York: Berg, 2006; first published by Editions Seuil, 2001), 24–25.

52. Stanley Cavell, *The World Viewed: Reflections on the Ontology of Film, Enlarged Edition* (Cambridge, MA: Harvard University Press, 1979; 1st ed., New York: Viking, 1971), 26.

53. Ben Davis, "Hyperreality TV," *New York,* June 2–8, 2014, 90–92.

54. "Scorsese Rousingly Endorses 3-D, Says Holograms Next," *Los Angeles Times,* November 6, 2011, latimes.com.

55. For more on the interrelationship between war video games and the military development of video simulation—with an eye toward existential, instead of virtual,

effects—see Corey Mead, *War Play: Video Games and the Future of Armed Conflict* (New York: Eamon Dolan/Houghton Mifflin Harcourt, 2013). For an analysis of the large-scale impact of video games on personal identity, property, labor, government, geopolitics, and global warfare, see Nick Dyer-Witheford and Greig de Peuter, *Games of Empire: Global Capitalism and Video Games* (Minneapolis: University of Minnesota Press, 2009), where they address the claim that "*video games are a paradigmatic media of Empire*—planetary, militarized hypercapitalism—*and* of some of the forces presently challenging it" (xv). *Games of Empire* was written with knowing reference to Michael Hardt and Antonio Negri's controversial and influential *Empire* (Cambridge, MA: Harvard University Press, 2000), in which they claim that we have entered a period of governance by global capitalism—a regime of multivalent power "with no outside" (xii). This description sheds new light on the very notion of simulated spaces (such as we find in war video games) and the effects these inner/virtual spaces appear to have on outer/actual spaces.

56. Jean Baudrillard, *The Gulf War Did Not Take Place,* trans. Paul Patton (Bloomington: Indiana University Press, 1995; first published as *La Guerre du Golfe n'a pas eu lieu,* Editions Galilée, 1991), 29–30.

57. Ron Kovic, *Born on the Fourth of July* (New York: Akashic Books, 2012; originally published New York: McGraw-Hill, 1976).

58. Karl Ove Knausgaard, "I Am Someone, Look at Me," *New York Times,* June 10, 2014.

59. See, for example, A. O. Scott and Manohla Dargis, "Big Bang Theories: Violence on Screen," *New York Times,* February 28, 2013, nytimes.com.

60. "Most Popular War Video Games," imdb.com (accessed March 8, 2013).

61. Heather Chaplin, "After Conquering Consoles, Hard-Core Gaming Shifts to Mobile," National Public Radio, March 22, 2013, npr.org.

62. "Top US Grossing War Video Games," imdb.com (accessed March 8, 2013).

63. Edgar Sandoval, Dan Friedman, and Bill Hutchinson, "News' Report on Sandy Hook Gunman Adam Lanza's Video-Game-Style Slaughter Score Sheet Inspires Calls in D.C. to Stiffen Regulation of Violent Games," *New York Daily News,* March 18, 2013, nydailynews.com.

64. Noël Carroll, "Fiction, Non-Fiction, and the Film of Presumptive Assertion: A Conceptual Analysis," in *Philosophy of Film and Motion Pictures,* ed. Noël Carroll and Jinhee Choi (Oxford: Blackwell, 2006).

65. Werner Herzog, *Herzog on Herzog,* ed. Paul Cronin (New York: Faber and Faber, 2002), 214, 239–40.

66. Cavell, *World Viewed,* 24.

67. See, for example, Bernard Harrison, *What Is Fiction For? Literary Humanism Restored* (Bloomington: Indiana University Press, 2014); David Rudrum, *Stanley Cavell and the Claim of Literature* (Baltimore: Johns Hopkins University Press, 2013); Susan L. Feagin, *Reading with Feeling: The Aesthetics of Appreciation* (Ithaca, NY: Cornell Uni-

versity Press, 1996); Martha C. Nussbaum, *Love's Knowledge: Essays on Philosophy and Literature* (New York: Oxford University Press, 1990); Wayne C. Booth, *The Company We Keep: An Ethics of Fiction* (Berkeley: University of California Press, 1988); Mieke Bal, *Narratology: Introduction to the Theory of Narrative* (Toronto: University of Toronto Press, 1985; 3rd ed., 2009); Alexander Nehamas, *Nietzsche: Life as Literature* (Cambridge, MA: Harvard University Press, 1985); Arthur Danto, *The Transfiguration of the Commonplace: A Philosophy of Art* (1981; Cambridge, MA: Harvard University Press, 1983); and Stanley Cavell, *The Claim of Reason: Wittgenstein, Skepticism, Morality, and Tragedy* (New York: Oxford University Press, 1979).

68. Sebastian Junger, drawing from firsthand experience, conjectures that some of the resistance veterans have to talking about war may be that "if you talk about it for any length of time, pretty soon you're not just talking about war. You're talking about people you love who got killed. Killed in front of you and in horrible ways." Jada Yuan, "94 Minutes with Sebastian Junger," *New York,* April 22, 2013, 16, nymag.com. The personal or private aspect of relating war experience, as Junger suggests, adds another valence to the difficulty of attempting to draw a (or any) connection between what happens on the battlefield and what happens on-screen (even if, and perhaps especially, when the projected images are meant to reflect or otherwise reanimate nonfiction scenes of life and death).

69. *Standard Operating Procedure* (Errol Morris, 2008).

70. One initiative that supports veterans in their writing about service and coming home includes the Veterans Writing Project (veteranswriting.org), which publishes the literary journal *O-Dark-Thirty* (o-dark-thirty.org).

71. Cavell, *World Viewed,* xix. See also *Reading Cavell's* The World Viewed: *A Philosophical Perspective on Film* (Detroit: Wayne State University, 2002), where its authors, William Rothman and Marian Keane, describe Cavell's book on the ontology of film as a "metaphysical memoir" (35, and preface, passim).

72. Eric Lichtblau, "The Holocaust Just Got More Shocking," *New York Times,* March 1, 2013, nytimes.com.

73. Max Boot, *Invisible Armies: An Epic History of Guerrilla Warfare from Ancient Times to the Present* (New York: Norton, 2013), xx–xxi.

74. See Robert von Dassanowsky, *Quentin Tarantino's* Inglourious Basterds: *A Manipulation of Metacinema* (New York: Continuum, 2012).

75. John Morris recounts how a "lab accident" ruined three of four rolls taken by Capa on June 6, 1944; Morris sent the film for processing to Dennis Banks. "Because of my order to rush," Morris writes, "he had closed the doors. Without ventilation the emulsion had melted." John Godfrey Morris, "The Magnificent Eleven: The D-Day Photographs of Robert Capa," (1998) skylighters.org/photos/robertcapa.html.

76. Solnit, *River of Shadows,* 123.

77. Dora Apel, *Memory Effects: The Holocaust and the Art of Secondary Witnessing* (New Brunswick, NJ: Rutgers University Press, 2002), 12.

78. Hernán Díaz, "A Topical Paradise," *Cabinet* 38: Islands (Summer 2010), 83.

79. James Nachtwey, "My Photographs Bear Witness," Ted Talk upon the acceptance of a 2007 Ted Prize, 00:08:55. See also Ken Light, *Witness in Our Time: Working Lives of Documentary Photographers* (Washington, DC: Smithsonian Books, 2010); and Susan Sontag, *On Photography* (New York: Farrar, Straus and Giroux, 1997) and *Regarding the Pain of Others* (New York: Picador, 2004).

80. Nachtwey, "My Photographs Bear Witness."

81. Annette Insdorf, *Imaginary Witness: Hollywood and the Holocaust* (Daniel Anker, 2004), 00:01:17.

82. Adam Pasick, "Duck, Cover: War Reporting while Female," *New York,* March 5, 2012, 9.

83. *Redacted* (Brian De Palma, 2007), 00:01:20.

84. Ibid.

85. Jeff Wall (1992). The work was created in an edition of two, plus an artist's proof. On May 8, 2012, as part of the "Post-War and Contemporary Art Evening Sale," one of the pairs in the edition was sold at auction for $3,666,500 by Christie's New York (Lot 2557).

86. Jeff Wall quoted in Craig Burnett, *Jeff Wall,* exhibition catalogue, London (2005), 59.

87. Errol Morris speaking with Nick Schaeger, "Errol Morris on *Standard Operating Procedure,*" April 22, 2008, ifc.com.

88. See, for example, *We Steal Secrets: The Story of WikiLeaks* (Alex Gibney, 2013).

89. Christine Nicholson, "Military Drone with No Human Control," *Smart Planet,* January 26, 2012, smartplanet.com. See also W. J. Hennigan, "New Drone Has No Pilot Anywhere, So Who's Accountable?" *Los Angeles Times,* January 26, 2012, latimes.com.

90. David Denby, "High Times," *New Yorker,* November 12, 2012.

91. *Skyfall* (Sam Mendes, 2012), 01:07:30.

92. Scott Shane, "The New Drone Warfare," *The Brian Lehrer Show,* June 8, 2012, wnyc.org.

93. Erich Maria Remarque, *All Quiet on the Western Front,* trans. A. W. Wheen (New York: Fawcett Books, 1958; originally published in 1928 as *Im Westen Nichts Neues*).

94. Remarque, *All Quiet,* 165.

95. John Keegan, *The Face of Battle: A Study of Agincourt, Waterloo, and the Somme* (New York: Penguin, 1976), 335. See also Leo H. Bartemeier, Lawrence S. Kubie, Karl A. Menninger, John Romano, and John C. Whitehorn, "Combat Exhaustion," *Journal of Nervous and Mental Disease* 104 (1946): 358–89, 489–525; and a review by Norman Reider, *Psychoanalytic Quarterly* 17 (1948): 430–31.

96. Cavell, *World Viewed,* 26–27.

97. André Bazin writes: "The film delivers baroque art from its convulsive catalepsy. Now, for the first time, the image of things is likewise the image of their duration, change mummified as it were." "The Ontology of the Photographic Image," in *Film Theory: Critical Concepts in Media and Cultural Studies,* ed. Philip Simpson, Andrew Utterson,

and K. J. Shepherdson (London: Routledge, 2004), 22. Garrett Stewart, *Framed Time: Toward a Postfilmic Cinema* (Chicago: University of Chicago Press, 2007), 264. See also Philip Rosen, *Change Mummified: Cinema, Historicity, Theory* (Minneapolis: University of Minnesota Press, 2001).

98. Bronfen, *Specters of War,* 1.

99. The *Witness* series featured photojournalists Eros Hoagland (episodes *Juarez* and *Rio*), Michael Christopher Brown (*Libya*) and Veronique de Viguerie (*South Sudan*).

100. *The War Body on Screen,* ed. Karen Randell and Sean Redmon (New York: Bloomsbury Academic, 2012).

101. Jan Mieszkowski, *Watching War* (Stanford, CA: Stanford University Press, 2012), 3.

102. See Boot, *Invisible Armies.*

103. I thank Samuel A. Chambers for conversations on television—and its relation to war cinema—that helped me assess and articulate several of the ideas at the core of this section.

104. Sigmund Freud, "Why War?" (September 1932), in *The Standard Edition of the Complete Psychological Works of Sigmund Freud,* ed. James Strachey (London: Hogarth Press and Institute of Psycho-Analysis, 1964), vol. 22 (1932–1936), 195–216.

105. Isaiah Berlin, "Two Concepts of Liberty," in *The Broadview Anthology of Social and Political Thought: Essential Readings—Ancient, Modern, and Contemporary,* ed. Andrew Bailey, Samantha Brennan, Will Kymlicka, Jacob Levy, Alex Sager, and Clark Wolf (Peterborough, ON: Broadview Press, 2012), 822.

106. Michel Foucault, "Society Must Be Defended," in *Lectures at the Collège de France, 1975–76,* ed. Mauro Bertani and Alessandro Fontana, trans. David Macey (New York: Picador, 1997), 50–51.

107. Carl Schmitt, *The Concept of the Political,* trans. George Schwab (Chicago: University of Chicago Press, 1996), 27.

108. Thomas Hobbes, *Leviathan or the Matter, Forme, and Power of a Common Wealth Ecclesiasticall and Civil,* ed. Richard Tuck (Cambridge: Cambridge University Press, 1996), 89.

109. Stephen Peter Rosen, *War and Human Nature* (Princeton, NJ: Princeton University Press, 2005); David Livingstone Smith, *The Most Dangerous Animal: Human Nature and the Origins of War* (New York: St. Martin's Press, 2007); Steven A. LaBlanc and Katherine E. Register, *Constant Battles: Why We Fight* (New York: St. Martin's Press, 2003); and Michael Howard, *The Causes of War: The Creighton Trust Lecture* (London: University of London, 1981).

110. John Kekes, "War," *Philosophy* 85, no. 332 (April 2010): 217–18.

111. Horgan, *End of War,* chap. 4.

112. See Margaret Mead, "War Is Only an Invention—Not a Biological Necessity," in *The Dolphin Reader,* 2nd ed., ed. Douglas Hunt (Boston: Houghton Mifflin, 1990), 415–21.

113. Ralph Waldo Emerson, "War" (1838), in *The Complete Works of Ralph Waldo Emerson,* vol. 11, *Miscellanies* (Boston: Houghton and Mifflin, 1903–1904), 151.

114. Ibid., 155.

115. Brian Lehrer, "Could We End War, All War?" *Guardian*, June 25, 2012, guardian.co.uk.

116. Emerson, "War," 167.

117. Srinivas Aravamudan, "Perpetual War," *PMLA* 124, no. 5 (2009): 1505–14. See also Bruce Robbins, *Perpetual War: Cosmopolitanism from the Viewpoint of Violence* (Durham, NC: Duke University Press, 2012).

118. Aravamudan's note: "Adi Ophir, *The Order of Evils: Toward an Ontology of Morals*, trans. Rela Mezali and Havi Carel (New York: Zone Books, 2005), 17."

119. Aravamudan's note: "As [Judith] Butler also argues eloquently, '[I]f certain lives do not qualify as lives or are, from the start, not conceivable as lives within certain epistemological frames, then these lives are never lived nor lost in the full sense' [Judith Butler, *Frames of War: When Is Life Grievable?* (London: Verso, 2009), 1]. Ophir and Butler are indebted to Heidegger's notion of *Gestell*, but we might ask if by staying with representation, mourning, and loss, we are unable to see war in nonanthropocentric frameworks."

120. Aravamudan, "Perpetual War," 1512. At this point he references Ranjana Khanna, "Disposability," *Differences* 20, no. 1 (2009): 181–98; and "Indignity," *Positions: East Asia Cultures Critique* 16, no. 1 (2008): 39–77.

121. Aravamudan, "Perpetual War," 1512.

122. Debord, *Society of the Spectacle*, sec. 1. For comparison, the line is also translated: "Everything that was directly lived has moved away into a representation" (Detroit: Black and Red, 1983).

123. Debord, *Society of the Spectacle* (1994), sec. 17.

124. Debord, *Society of the Spectacle* (1983/1994), sec. 19. See also sec. 30.

125. See Dora Apel, *War Culture and the Contest of Images* (New Brunswick, NJ: Rutgers University Press, 2012); Ariella Azoulay, *Civil Imagination: A Political Ontology of Photography* (New York: Verso, 2012); and *Picturing Atrocity: Photography in Crisis*, ed. Geoffrey Batchen, Mick Gidley, Nancy K. Miller, and Jay Prosser (London: Reaktion Books, 2012).

126. Herzog, *Herzog on Herzog*, 66.

127. Fredric Jameson, "War and Representation," *PMLA* 124, no. 5 (2009): 1532–47; Robert Pippin "Vernacular Metaphysics: On Terrence Malick's *The Thin Red Line*," *Critical Inquiry* 39, no. 2 (Winter 2013): 247–75.

Part 1

The Aesthetics of War On-Screen

War and Representation

Fredric Jameson

> A vast entity, a planet, in a space of a hundred million dimensions; three-dimensional beings could not so much as imagine it. And yet each dimension was an autonomous consciousness. Try to look directly at that planet, it would disintegrate into tiny fragments, and nothing but consciousnesses would be left. A hundred million free consciousnesses, each aware of walls, the glowing stump of a cigar, familiar faces, and each constructing its destiny on its own responsibility. And yet each of those consciousnesses, by imperceptible contacts and insensible changes, realizes its existence as a cell in a gigantic and invisible coral (*polyp*). War: everyone is free, and yet the die is cast. It is there, it is everywhere, it is the totality of all my thoughts, of all Hitler's words, of all Gomez's acts; but no one is there to add it up. It exists solely for God. But God does not exist. And yet war exists.
>
> —Sartre, *The Reprieve*

> Stalingrad is like a painting that cannot be observed from close up, but from which one must step back in order to do it full justice.
>
> —Joseph Goebbels

War offers the paradigm of the nominalist dilemma: the abstraction from totality or the here and now of sensory immediacy and confusion. For Tolstoy, as for almost everybody else, the representational consequence was most memorably drawn by Stendhal in *The Charterhouse of Parma:* Fabrice is unaware that he is an involuntary witness to the emperor's last stand ("I'm off to the Battle of Waterloo" would be a modernist replay of the exit line Walter Benjamin claimed to have found in one of his baroque tragedies: "I'm off to the Thirty Years' War"). Yet in both novelists, the aesthetic is already one of what the formalists called *ostranenie*, or defamiliarization (estrangement), in which a stereotype is dismantled and brought before us in all its nameless freshness and horror. Whether this is an essentially modernist operation or, on the contrary, something all the realisms are by definition called on to do is a question we will for the moment leave open.

Still, it suggests that there exists some stereotype of war for such passages to defamiliarize and that there must then also be representations of war that are content to confirm the stereotype. Indeed, one often has the feeling that all war novels (and war films) are pretty much the same and have few enough surprises for us, even though their situations may vary. In practice, we can enumerate some seven or eight situations, which more or less exhaust the genre. If so, and despite experience that confirms this opinion, this would be an astonishing fact, given the radical changes in warfare that historians document since the hand-to-hand combat in the plains before Troy (Hegel's prototype of that human and unalienated form, the epic, as opposed to the modern "prose of the world," denatured by money, commerce, and industry): there is then, marked by technological advances (gunpowder, machine guns and tanks, aircraft, unmanned cybernetic weaponry), a whole periodization of structural changes in warfare and its accompanying strategies that needs to be combined with the narrative typologies we are about to enumerate and to examine in more detail. Add to this complication a periodization of properly aesthetic modes and transformations (allegory, realism, modernism, postmodernism), and we confront a combination scheme of no little complexity that may strike us ultimately as serving less to explain these representations than simply to classify them. But perhaps such possibilities, which account for the organization of the notes that follow into a sampling of exhibits rather than a unified and systematic theory, may be reduced and simplified by the rather different consideration cutting across all of them—namely, the suspicion that war is ultimately unrepresentable—and by an attention to the various forms the impossible attempt to represent it may have taken.

As for the narrative variants, which seem to me to hold for film as much as for the novel, I enumerate eight of them: (1) the existential experience of war, (2) the collective experience of war, (3) leaders, officers, and the institution of the army, (4) technology, (5) the enemy landscape, (6) atrocities, (7) attack on the homeland, and (8) foreign occupation. The final category does not include the related subject matter of spies and espionage (now largely settled into a generic category of its own); nor does it exhaust the phenomenon of guerrilla warfare, from the U.S. occupation of Iraq and Afghanistan all the way back to the Vendée and indeed to the earliest institutionalization of armies: for guerrilla warfare—the result of uneven development and of the incursion of an "advanced" mode of production into an "underdeveloped" one—can also offer the prototype of war itself and not its savage exception. Yet these very exclusions suggest a different way of cutting across the plot types, for the typical events of foreign occupation (and of espionage, for that matter) take us back to institutions and to the state as actor and agency, while the horror of guerrilla warfare (whether urban or rural) seems rather to lie in the unidentifiability of its actors, who emerge from their surroundings without warning and just as unexpectedly disappear again.

What may prove most helpful here, then, is Kenneth Burke's "dramatistic pentad," which differentiates between act, agent, agency, purpose, and scene as so many distinct media through which the narrative material can be focused.[1] To use a more structural terminology, we may say that each of Burke's categories constitutes a different kind of dominant and thereby produces a somewhat different projection of the material, it being understood that there is no correct or true, photographically accurate rendering of such multidimensional realities. Still, narrative semiotics, by identifying Burke's first three categories with one another—an act always somehow implying an agent and the agent in turn implying an agency—suggests a different ordering of these perspectives, in which purpose somehow withdraws (as a feature of interpretation rather than of representation), while scene emerges as a new element in its own right: in scene, the anthropomorphic is eclipsed and some new and as yet unrecognizable narrative reality comes into view. For the act and its accompanying actantial categories always presuppose a name, and thereby a preexisting concept of the event identified (as already with the word *war*), while action and agency seem to be determined in advance by this or that institutionalized and organized agent.

Scene, however, remains unnamed at this level of narrative complexity, becoming concrete in the course of the representation. Spatiality is only one possible dimension of scene, to which anthropomorphic elements are subordinated in unaccustomed and estranged ways.

Technology, meanwhile, as alienated and reified human labor and energy, is always a slippery category, moving back and forth between allegory and external (or proto-natural) doom yet sometimes also celebrated as the triumph of human inventiveness and an expression of human action (or its prosthetic extension). It wanders across all our tale types, sometimes organizing their periodization (as I suggest above), sometimes generating a uniquely nightmarish experience, as in the terror and panic aroused by the appearance of the first tanks at the Battle of the Somme in World War I or by the V-2 rockets in that war's sequel. Yet technology is truly the apotheosis of a properly modernist teleology, a direct line from the slingshot to the megaton bomb, as Theodor W. Adorno put it. Each innovation is also the same in its embodiment of radical difference: witness Ermanno Olmi's wonderful film *Il mestiere delle armi* (2001), on the development of artillery in the sixteenth century.

The first category of war narrative, that of the existential experience of war—which has its classical literary realization in Stephen Crane's *Red Badge of Courage* (1895)—most often expresses the fear of death and, a somewhat different thing, death anxiety: as such, although this category is surely the quintessential form the representation of war takes in most people's minds, its content (personal danger, decisions and hesitations, contingency, apprenticeship) can be transferred to other generic frameworks. War then becomes the laboratory in which, like the bullring for Ernest Hemingway, such experiences are most unfailingly aroused and observed. Yet it tends toward the bildungsroman to the degree to which it is generally a question of a young and inexperienced soldier, whom the experience does not leave untouched.

With the collective focus, everything changes; yet here also we find ourselves in the presence of a content fully interchangeable with several other familiar and well-defined genres, which call the generic specificity of the war film back into question. For the collective war story turns on the interaction of various character types apparently gathered at random. The experience is the national one, of universal conscription as the first occasion in which men from different social classes are thrown together, at least until the public high school dramas of more recent memory. In the Europe of emergent nationalism, the experience was called on to level the old regional cultures (Sicily, Brittany) and to standardize language and the state's claims of authority—to encourage discipline, obedience, and recognition of the national system. American war films, taking class difference for granted and only gradually absorbing racial difference, found their originality psychologically, in the typology of personalities thrown together in a group (or a war machine). The intelligent upper-class figure, the sociopath, the weakling, the bully, the fixer, the jokester, the trickster, the Don Juan, the ethnic type (generally southern European, but a black man, a Chicano, or a Native American gradually follows), the religious fundamentalist, the nice guy, the nerd: the list is endless, but the combinations—that is to say, the fundamental dramatic conflicts and clashes—are probably statistically limited and certainly generically predictable.

The crucial thing about this collective system is that it is itself the abstraction of something else. We may focus the action in terms of male bonding or the psychology of hierarchical institutions, with the problem of authority figures (incompetent, psychotic, etc.) added later on. The first versions of the form emerge in what we may call a prefeminist world, and certainly the absence of women is a significant structural part of the form—later women will be admitted as yet another variation on the male character types—but the crucial feature here is the absence of the family and of peacetime, indeed of wage labor. This is why a juxtaposition with the heist or caper film is so interesting: for in this last we find the same abstract structure, the same variety of character types and their clashes, the same as it were sealed social world, but in which the legitimacy of the institution of the army and the declaration of war has been stripped away, yielding a different kind of defamiliarization, where the overall aim of the collective action is not even war aims (defeating the enemy, defending freedom, or some other such socially plausible motive) but rather simply money itself—the ultimate abstraction, the ultimate "axiomatic" emptied of concrete content. Yet the absence of wage labor or commodified labor is here retained; and as in many other kinds of crime films, there is a utopian overtone in which the characters live in a disalienated world and in which activity is akin to play (I have elsewhere tried to show that these utopias can be invested with very different valences: for example, the Mafia film quintessentially appeals to nostalgia for the family by way of collective envy of the southern European clan system).

Thus, what both war films (of the collective buddy type) and caper films abstract from and yet dramatize in their own specific generic ways is the division of labor itself: each of the character types stands for a certain competence, something brought out much more strongly in the caper films, where each character is selected for a specific specialty. The small or micro group is the Deleuzian nomadic war machine, literally or figuratively—that is to say, an image of the collective without the state and beyond reified institutions. Still, such "groups-in-fusion," as Jean-Paul Sartre calls them in *The Critique of Dialectical Reason,* become forerunners of the institutional as such, as they ossify.[2] Indeed, when the peacetime army (or indeed the police force, in current procedurals) comes into its own mode of representation, it is rather bureaucracy whose epic is sung before us (without being named as such, except in socialist realism), and the collective structure of the nomads is appropriated for the celebration of the state. Both are afterimages of the social, and we make a more productive use of Gilles Deleuze when we grasp his dualism as an alternating possibility and realize that libidinal investment in the nomads can be no less reprehensible (but also no more so) than libidinal investment in the state.

As for the third category, that of leaders and institutions, it initiates a shift of gravity toward the exterior of the experience of war, whether individual or collective, for the officers are ordinarily as much a part of the soldier's external environment as the enemy itself; and they are indeed equally often objectified into what gets identified as the bureaucracy or the state. Initially, however, such characters furnished the staple of the older chronicle history, with its great men and world-historical figures—what Georg Lukács assigns to the potentialities of the stage,[3] as in Schiller's *Wallenstein*, Strindberg's *Gustavus Adolfus*, or Shakespeare's war-riddled history plays (and the shorthand German imitations that come out of them, like Goethe's *Goetz von Berlichingen* or even dramas of Kleist and Büchner). This is, on one traditional yet rather narrow acceptation of the term, the place of politics as such; and it cannot be doubted that the various populist representations of the simple soldier and the common man in uniform are dialectically later than these less and less glorious figures striding about the stage and vocalizing their decisions, with or without a note of human, all-too-human pathos.

Tolstoy's notorious loathing for Napoléon is in that sense merely the other face of his hero-worshipping portrayal of the uniquely Russian bluffness and acumen of Kutuzov, a historical figure Tolstoy himself had not many years before this characterized as "sensual, cunning and unfaithful"—just as he had in earlier times called such patriotism "a fairy tale which aroused national feeling."[4] Perhaps the classic defamiliarization of the "great general" comes closer to Tolstoy's representation of "world-historical" decision making and his inveterate resistance to it (a stance to which we owe the concluding "theory of history" in *War and Peace*):

> But at that moment an adjutant galloped up with a message from the commander of the regiment in the hollow and news that immense masses of the French were coming down upon them and that his regiment was in disorder and was retreating upon the Kiev grenadiers. Prince Bagratión bowed his head in sign of assent and

> approval. He rode off at a walk to the right and sent an adjutant to the dragoons with orders to attack the French. But this adjutant returned half an hour later with the news that the commander of the dragoons had already retreated beyond the dip in the ground, as a heavy fire had been opened on him and he was losing men uselessly, and so had hastened to throw some sharpshooters into the wood.
>
> Prince Andrew listened attentively to Bagratión's colloquies with the commanding officers and the orders he gave them and, to his surprise, found that no orders were really given, but that Prince Bagratión tried to make it appear that everything done by necessity, by accident, or by the will of subordinate commanders was done, if not by his direct command, at least in accord with his intentions. Prince Andrew noticed, however, that though what happened was due to chance and was independent of the commander's will, owing to the tact Bagratión showed, his presence was very valuable. Officers who approached him with disturbed countenances became calm; soldiers and officers greeted him gaily, grew more cheerful in his presence, and were evidently anxious to display their courage before him.[5]

This pretense of freedom in the face of necessity, however, pales in comparison with the criminality of the officers' decisions in World War I, so memorably exemplified in Stanley Kubrick's *Paths of Glory* (1957); and it is to be remarked at this point that many mass cultural genres—the police procedural, the spy novel—end up turning less on the pursuit of the enemy or the official Other than they do on their own institutional framework, with its ineffective and ill-informed command system and internal subversion, by moles and double or triple agents.

Perhaps the abstract theoretical debates on strategy and tactics are relevant here in a new and more formal way: the debate on the influence of Carl von Clausewitz, for example. His notion of war as a duel is as anthropomorphic as the conceptions of Hegel or Homer, his notion of the decisive final battle is a thoroughly narrative one (which has wrongly been criticized for omitting the very different dynamic of guerrilla warfare), and even the famous maxim of war as the continuation of politics by other means is a way of translating warfare and its specialized personnel back into more familiar peacetime and civilian realities amenable to the techniques of the more conventional realist novel.[6]

Behind all such discussions lie a narratological problem and a challenge to anthropomorphic representation and to the mimesis of human actions and characters, which questions whether such possibilities are not altogether obsolete in the age of nuclear weapons, drones, and suicide bombers. These debates are waged back and forth across history by generals and commanders, dictators (in ancient and modern senses), and other war leaders. They reenter the narrative representations of war in the form of unwarranted hero worship and blind allegiance, or a sense of betrayal, or the contempt of foot soldiers for stupid officers or cowardly generals. These are all what semiotics terms actantial questions, issues of action and human agency; and even our fourth category, that of technology, seems to move uneasily in and out of the whole area of personification and anthropomorphism.

When it comes to the next set of categories, however, my sense is that the focus of the war narrative subtly changes and that in Burke's dramatistic pentad we have begun to move from the first four categories to the fifth, which he called scene and to which he attributed a different and perhaps more diffuse kind of rhetorical and representational power.

For even atrocities might seem to us today to belong rather to the malignant properties of evil or cursed landscapes than to the savagery of individual actors; and it is as though with this and our other later plot types we pass from a world of acts and characters to one of space: scene, landscape, geography, the folds of the earth that determine military campaigns by introducing contingency or the main chance—a heterogeneous element as much *Stimmung* or affect as it is a mere stage or context for human gestures. Bombs falling out of the sky are part of it, along with the lunar landscape of trench warfare; the silence of deserted villages is a narrative player in such tales, along with the menace of empty windows and the complicity of nature in ambush or pursuit—in concealment as well, camouflage being a way that humans acknowledge the primacy of scene, just as maps are another.

This category abolishes or suspends the distinction between the enemy's landscape and our own, the latter no less fraught with peril than some unknown, hostile terrain. Here the great hand-to-hand duels of the armies (Napoléon versus Kutuzov, Wallenstein versus Gustavus Adolfus) give way to imagery of penetration (the first glimpse of a sea of tanks at the battle of Kursk, the smell of sweating armies miles away in World War I, the screaming of dive bombers, the first exposed steps in an abandoned hamlet). The space of modern warfare is vulnerable by definition and no longer belongs to anyone.

That was also the case in the Thirty Years' War, whose most extraordinary literary document begins in full incursion and horror, as mercenaries (of whatever affiliation) loot villages and torture peasants for food and gold:

> Da fing man erst an, die Stein von den Pistolen und hingegen an deren Statt der Bauern Daumen aufzuschrauben, und die armen Schelmen so zu foltern, als wenn man hätt Hexen brennen wollen, massen sie sich einen von den bereits in Backoven Steckten, und mit Feuer hinter ihm her waren, ohngesehen er noch nichts berkannt hatte; einem anderen machten sie ein Seil um den Kopf und rettelten es mit einem Bengel zusammen, das ihm das Blut zu Mund, Nas und Ohren heraus sprang.[7]

> Then they used thumbscrews, which they cleverly made out of their pistols, to torture the peasants, as if they wanted to burn witches. Though he had confessed to nothing as yet, they put one of the captured hayseeds in the bake oven and lit a fire in it. They put a rope around someone else's head and tightened it like a tourniquet until blood came out of his mouth, nose, and ears. In short, every soldier had his favorite method of making life miserable for peasants, and every peasant had his own misery.[8]

The period has virtually become defined by such atrocities, which I am tempted to count into scene, into space itself as one of its properties during this long war, in which most of central Europe is consumed, at all scales from macroscopic to microscopic: armies pursuing each other from one end of Europe to another, enemy battalions unwittingly colliding in marshes during the night, bands of marauders burning villages, a deserter ransacking an empty house. "Noses and eares cut of to make hatbandes. . . . The robbers and murderers took a piece of wood and stuck it down the poor wretches' throats, stirred it and poured in water, adding sand or even human faeces. . . . They tied our honest burgher Hans Betke to a wooden pole and roasted him at the fire from seven in the morning until four in the afternoon, so that he gave up the spirit amidst much shrieking and pains."[9]

With such nightmares, one has the sense that the two categories of internal invasion and intervention and of war carried to foreign, unfamiliar territory coincide and dialectically reinforce each other. This is not so much the pseudosynthesis of a "civil war" (an oxymoron if there ever was one) as an utter transmogrification of the familiar into the alien, the *heimlich* into the *unheimlich,* in which the home village—the known world, the real, and the everyday—is transformed into a place of unimaginable horror, while the neighbors of the home country (the eternal peasants, the stock characters of village life) become sly faces of evil and of menace, ambushing the soldier who strays from his company and lynching the few they can safely overpower, concealing food, and hiding in the woods like savages (anachronistically to redeploy that Fenimore Cooper imagery Balzac so relished). But this is something that happens not so much to individuals, to characters as such, as to the landscape, which fades in and out of nightmare, its mingled dialects now intelligible, now the gibberish of aliens.

Some such gestaltlike metamorphosis from familiar to unfamiliar, from the anthropomorphic to the micro- or macroscopic play of material elements, can be observed in what the Thirty Years' War imposes on our attempts to conceptualize it as a whole. On the one hand, the great strategic trajectory of the armies of a Wallenstein or a Gustavus Adolphus, of ferocious condottieri like Ernst von Mansfeld or the Bavarian general Tilly, or of the Spanish armies of intervention, in search of the enemy and of some decisive bone-jarring clash. On the other, a well-nigh optical enlargement, an eyelash-brushing approach in which the seemingly intelligible units of the official armies disintegrate into minute bands of individual marauders spreading across an everywhere-identical landscape of fields and woods, huts and paths, and offering the same scenes of carnage and flight over and over again, beyond history, beyond narrative.

This effect is caused not solely by the complexity of this block of historical time, with its innumerable agents and actors (who constantly change position and swap their functions with one another), a multiplicity only momentarily simplified by the conventional stereotype of religious war and the climactic struggle between the Counter-Reformation and Protestantism. For the Counter-Reformation is already divided and multiplied by the triple centers of the papacy, Madrid, and the Habsburg emperor Ferdinand II (more Catholic and fanatical than the pope and than his Spanish relatives), while what is loosely called Protestantism—already locked in internecine warfare between its two branches, Lutheran and Calvinist, both of them anathematized by innumerable millenarian sects—is itself susceptible to infinite fission and the propagation of innumerable subsidiary local and foreign conflicts.

To assign the guilt of striking the first blow is a philosophical quandary of the first magnitude. Even the most warlike of the participants—Wallenstein, for example—can also be read as embodying a humane will to peace, to the ending of the indefinite proliferation of the war and an establishment of central European unity on a new basis. (Even Schiller's Hamlet-like version of the great generalissimo's assassination leaves us with multiple interpretations of his motives: Does he want to found a dynasty and make himself emperor? Does he want to unite Germany in some prefiguration of nineteenth-century nationalism? Is he, against all appearances, a moderate and a peacemaker? or even a Protestant sympathizer? Etc., etc.)

In fact, although Ferdinand would like to repeal many of the confessional compromises of the preceding century, it is the Protestant side that provides the provocative and incendiary pretext: the Protestant elites of Prague, dissatisfied with Habsburg sovereignty, persuade the elector of the Palatinate, a son-in-law of James I of England, to assume the throne of Bohemia, normally a prerogative of the emperor's dynastic lineage. But the elector only wins the mock title of Winter King, owing to his brief tenure, cut short by the decisive battle of White Mountain (1620), and leaves the unhappy Friedrich to wander from ally to ally in search of a renewal of fortune, in a hapless quest that turns him into the very allegory of weakness and indecision. Here is a modern version of this uninspiring and vacillating figure, perking up somewhat at the prospect of meeting his mercenary generals, themselves revived by the intermittent and sluggish streams of cash flowing reluctantly into The Hague, "refreshed by the sums like flowers in the dew," as they ride out to greet their sometime employer:

> His heart beat strongly in his breast as he saw powerful hooves drive these armored and undisciplined men toward him. They told of the Danish king, Christian, and of Lower Saxony, magnificent in its prosperity; told also how the emperor lusted to swallow up Magdeburg, and gave news of the latest effort of the distinguished house of Habsburg to acquire a reliable mooring, namely a certain Wallenstein, the three making merry over this unknown name. And the slack Friedrich felt himself awakening to life again, swept back into the old excitement by the proximity of these two stormily galloping, heavily ironclad warriors.[10]

The stereotypical vacillation (shared by the emperor) does not equip this personage to be a protagonist, any more than the grim but indistinct determination of the true instigator of this war, the Bavarian elector Maximilian, entitles him to be the villain of the piece.[11] But we must also pause here a moment to register the existence of that extraordinary literary document, the novel entitled *Wallenstein,* an untranslated and visionary nightmare dreamed and written up by the young surgeon Alfred Döblin in evenings during the bloody trench warfare of World War I and published in 1920, nine years before *Berlin Alexanderplatz* made him world famous. No background in Döblin, no preparation, no perspective, it comes before us as a perpetual present that is at every moment, on every page, in every sentence, filled space, without a pause or backward or forward glimpse. The armies are in movement even when at rest in their temporary quarters. The army's pauses are movement; they hint at some sly signal by Wallenstein, who rebukes the kaiser by not following his directions, feints the enemy, pretends to obey the commands to stop (says one of the imperial counselors, "Es ist mir nicht klar, gegen wen der Herzog Krieg führt").[12] Yet the space is filled at every moment with names, with all the characters of history, some known, some only mentioned in passing, and with place names as well—not even the map is enough to accommodate them all. It is a pulsing interminable uninterrupted flow, true textuality (not mere form without content) in which everything is in perpetual change back and forth across central Europe yet driving forward temporally so that time, the passing instants, becomes invisible. Only the events are generated, and they never stop; the writer never stops (he thereby disappears also); and the sources are so thoroughly used up that nothing is anymore allusion. Schiller has long since vanished. There is no longer any competition with this unending flow of text but only the affect that pulses through it and changes color from pallor to flush, purple to sallow yellow. All the tonalities of the affective spectrum stream through the interminable moments, none of them truly fulfilled or effectuating any lasting pause or destiny.

Not the least interest of this novel is indeed the recurrence in its form of an allegorical habit profoundly consanguineous with the baroque content of its setting in the Counter-Reformation. Thus, here it is money itself that ultimately revives the unhappy Winter King: the lifeblood of the money that runs through the immense continental expanse of the conflict, feeding it locally and organizing its forces into impermanent groups, from foraging deserters and guerrillas up to official and unofficial warlords and the leaders of the royal and imperial adversaries. The great and bloody rhizome of the war then becomes a representation of money, riches, wealth, taxes levied, the very sustenance of potatoes impounded from villages in flames and from peasants dead or in flight. Everything here—from the penniless imperial court, which counts on Wallenstein to raise forces for it at the same time that it tries to give him orders, down to the brutal *soldateska* who live off the countryside—has to do with money and with an immense coral polyp that refuses to starve or die away but keeps itself alive for unforeseeable years by the very strength with which it draws money out of its hiding place, like magnets drawing, or blood from a stone, soaking it up interminably, reproducing itself, using its population of generals, peasants, priests, burghers, kings, lepers, the landless, heiresses, as so many divining rods, so many instruments for draining the last drops of wealth from the devastated land. Wealth then becomes the conduit of energy, whether blood, sexuality and libido, activity, irritability, sensation, impulse, drive, or propulsion; it is what makes the sentences pound forward like horses' hooves as well as the human individuals themselves to their otherwise incomprehensible yet irrepressible heat-seeking clashes. The libidinal apparatus of the war—of this extraordinary, unique war—thus ensures the most fully realized representation of finance and its networks and capillary extremities, making wealth in its "early modern" sense appear before us as a phenomenon in its own right, in the strong Heideggerian sense of the *phainesthai,* the appearance of Being, in ways frontal narratives of trading companies and usurers were unlikely to convey, or the abstractions of religious moralizing or economic philosophy.

All this eventuates in blood and landscapes of dead bodies, the world of Jacques Callot anachronistically revived in that of World War I, which reproduces it only for reasons of historical underdevelopment, because its generals failed to grasp the proper use of machine guns or of tanks. Still, we may wonder what forms the representation of agents and agency can take under the regime of the scene, in this interminable narrative of events and sequence of grotesque or nightmarish figures, more human in their caricaturality than any of the genuine human beings of realism or of our acquaintance. No causes, to be sure, and yet immense allegorical figures, like the famous frontispiece of Hobbes's *Leviathan* or, better, Giuseppe Arcimboldo's vegetable portraits, in which the sovereign is called on to be his own multiplicity and his own multitudinous subjects. But here the "world-historical figure" allegorizes not subjects or a people, not even the collectivity of the men under his command, but rather his own victims and the corpses he has in effect become. Here is Tilly, one of the more fearsome of these legendary imperial warlords, as he entertains an audience with the equally fearsome Wallenstein himself:

> The Brabanter [Tilly], stiff and ghostly, with a white scarf, two pistols and a dagger in his belt, and short white hair; at the hairs' tips like ears of wheat there waved the corpses of a thousand men cut down. His pale, sharp features, bushy brows, stiff brushlike moustache rippled with the mutilated regiments of a whole generation; they clung in slippage to the buttons of his jerkin, to his belt. His gnarled fingers each one testified to the annihilation of whole cities; with every knuckle a dozen exterminated villages. Over his shoulders there crowded forward, writhing, the bodies of slaughtered Turks, Frenchmen, Palatiners, and yet someday he would meet his judgment with them on himself along with their horses and dogs, hanging every which way in front of each other and one on top of the other, a burden so immense his very head and little hat vanished beneath it. Necks ripped open and scabby, stomachs with white and livid colors, veined and dripping on the slit and restrained arms and the spastic legs. Guts in loops of intestines in which he was wrapped, sloshing and flabby over the braced knees encased in leather, an interminable limp wormlike rippling train that as he dragged it creaked with every step. He weighed the earth down like a mammoth but bore himself icily, deaf to the screams of the men and those, bone-shattering, of the swine, the shrill cries and piping of the horses, all of them holding to him, seeking to suck their life out of him, out of the most minute hairs on his head; horses' necks straining, their nostrils trembling, pie-bald, black; dogs shot to pieces and yet snuffling at his mouth and nose, greedily sucking up his breath. He should have long since been drained; they were sucking dry wood; he clicked and clattered around inside and yet could not be brought down. Behind him fourteen regiments of infantry and six of cavalry.
>
> In front of him Friedland [Wallenstein], a yellow dragon emerging from the bubbling bogs of Bohemia, plastered with black slime to the hips, drawn back onto his knobby hind legs, sulfur pressed into the earth ringing him, waving his broad elastic rump in the

> air behind him with his big jaws wide open, blissfully and with the fury of a serpent exhaling hot breath in intermittent blasts, with a panting and grunting that struck fear.[13]

These portraits, which we may characterize as rehearsing the modes of allegory and symbol respectively, are drawn into an uninterrupted stream of filled time and space, of a visual writing only occasionally punctuated by dramatic scenes, by a showing that mainly takes second place to the telling of the visionary nightmare, which feeds on the interminable war as on indefinitely renewable fodder.

Wallenstein's biographer gives us a more articulated picture of the perpetuum mobile of this infernal machine, which seems unable to run down and stop (and indeed Wallenstein's function, for good and ill alike, is to have been able to supply the gradually less and less enthusiastic kaiser with ever-renewed reserves of troops):

> After not much more than a year [after White Mountain], people began to fear that the rapid exhaustion both sides felt was premature. A definitive victory would have had to be a universal one and could never have existed. Partial victories, however, each of which related to the whole in a different way, called new enemies into the field, who then gave new energies to the old adversaries, humiliated and pillaged. Bohemia, although isolated in its captivity, remained a part of Europe, and Germany even more so owing to its size. This is not merely an individual opposition, a struggle between two power centers, or the aggression of a single one of them. It is a tidal succession of wills in conflict, some of which claim to be able to form them into a single unified will and campaign against another one, and yet never do completely subsume the wills of their individual allies. A fencing court. Individual pairs joust. Suddenly they form two fronts which begin to move in opposition to each other. Yet as they do so, the ballet of betrayal sets in within each. One party withdraws into a corner, exchanges meaningful looks with its former adversary, maneuvers between the two fronts, seeking to mediate. Another tries to entice this or that participant out of both fronts and to form a third. All this is laden with illusion, mistakes, deception. No one knows enough about the other, and some don't even know their own minds.[14]

This fencing ballet of the war as a whole, as in an aerial shot, stands in sharp contrast to the horrors on the ground, as recorded by Grimmelshausen and others—a kind of no-man's-land in which all spaces are identical and all the atrocities as well, a kind of nightmarish repetition moving from Bohemia to the Baltic and back, a triumph, as it were, of space and identity over time and its differentiations, a virtually nonnarrative flow for which the only appropriate registering apparatus or point of view would seem to be the eyes of an idiot or of a child, as in Ambrose Bierce's terrifying story "Chicamauga."

And this is indeed how *Der abenteuerliche Simplicissimus* begins—the supreme literary monument produced by one of the participants in this war, its six books published in 1668 and 1669, some 150 years after *Don Quijote* and *Lazarillo de Tormes* and 50 before *Robinson Crusoe* (1719). Yet it is clearly incorrect to characterize *Simplicissimus* as a picaresque novel or even as a bildungsroman (the hero is certainly a naïf, who seems to maintain his innocence even during the episodes in which he has technically become a trickster figure). Not only is this enormous text episodic in the extreme; it is also rhizomatic, a kind of hypertext throwing off all kinds of ancillary episodes, at least one of which, *Courasche* (1670), has known a prodigious afterlife in Bertolt Brecht's theatrical version.

But we will argue that *Simplicissimus* is more than episodic; it is an extraordinary machine for generic production, for the narrative progression tirelessly generates one new genre after another, from the war novel and the lives of saints to the final utopia and desert-island narrative. How to account for this unparalleled literary autopoiesis, this nonteleological proliferation of generic exercises, which goes well beyond what has been identified under the term *generic discontinuities*? Is it possible that it is precisely out of that undifferentiated space of local yet universal conflict, whose fever chart runs from the plundering of villages to the sacking of whole cities and back, that in the absence of ready-made narrative microforms the various genres are themselves summoned into existence?

At any rate, we begin virtually in the state of nature, in which the youthful protagonist scarcely has language—in particular, he does not know his own name or has none—and is being ordered around the field by his brutal father (whose very status is registered in dialect ["knan"] and who is equally bereft of a family name). He flees into the woods during the mercenaries' sack of the village from which I have quoted above and there meets a pious hermit who instructs him in religion and, even more remarkably, in the classical languages and their rhetorical traditions (the causes of this saintly hermit's withdrawal from the world, a premonition of Simplicius's own eventual destiny—it is indeed the hermit who thus baptizes him—will be related in a later discovery, which recapitulates the different genre of unhappy love). On the death of the hermit, the boy returns to the world of social beings, becoming page to the governor. Then, abducted by Croatian mercenaries, he is incorporated into the imperial troops, where, after a number of humiliations, he reemerges generically as the trickster figure mentioned above, a *Jäger* supremely gifted in warfare and plunder or theft of all kinds, after which he marries and then, in a more magical episode, discovers treasure.

Yet these potential destinies are all abruptly broken off, whether out of impatience or boredom or owing to the serial production of the various books, if not the fermentation of new genres at work in Grimmelshausen's feverish imagination. There follow a salacious episode in Paris, a spell as a traveling salesman, a fall into the bad company of a real thief who tries to teach him the way of the real world ("du bis noch Simplicius, der den Machiavellum noch nit studiert hat"),[15] a religious conversion, his founding of a new landed estate and family, a Vernian journey to the center of the earth, and finally travels that lead to his shipwreck and a hermitlike existence on a desert island, where his autobiographical notes are found by a Dutch sea captain, who brings them back to Europe and to publication.

Finally, it is not so much the narrative quality of the episodes that strikes the reader as rather the restlessness of the character's exploration of his possible destinies and that of the author's experimentation with the various narrative genres they carry within themselves. We are here, in the German principalities of the empire, still very far even from the sophistication of the Spanish monarchy, in which the first realisms flourished so many generations earlier and in which the urban worldliness of commercial life and colonial and military power generate the picaresque, along with an extraordinary theatrical culture. Germany is here still profoundly prenovelistic, and indeed the first crystallizations of form in Grimmelshausen's seemingly interminable text take the form of immense allegorical dream frescoes—most strikingly, that of the class divisions and struggles of the feudal world, with its prelates and nobles at the top of the allegorical tree and the nameless peasantry at its base,[16] along with the dream transformation into an animal, reminiscent of *The Golden Ass*, of Apuleius. But it would be equally incorrect to read such allegorical episodes as the self-indulgence of an autodidact reveling in his classical education. For in this great laboratory of forms, baroque allegory is closely affiliated with utopia as such, which one may perhaps indeed in hindsight identify (in Thomas More) as an allegorical form.

The devastated landscape, indeed, calls out for the relief of utopian transfiguration. Such is the first crossing of the border into Switzerland:

> The landscape struck me compared with other German lands, as strange as Brazil or China. I saw people trading and strolling about in peace, barns full of cattle, courtyards full of chickens, geese, and ducks. The streets were used by travelers in safety, taverns full of people making merry, no fear of the enemy, no worry about plundering and sacking, no anxiety about losing land or life and limb. Everyone lived safely under his grape arbor or fig tree and, in comparison with other German lands, in pleasure and content, so that I took this country for an earthly paradise, although it seemed primitive enough.[17]

Later on, among the hallucinations of the desert island, this earthly paradise will be transformed into a vision of primeval bliss—"so we lived like the first men in the golden age, where a bountiful heaven lets all the fruits of the earth flourish without work"[18]—until the devil in the form of a woman shatters the vision and sends the text itself, in the generic reversion, back into the anchoritic withdrawal of its own beginnings.

I want to draw the conclusion that war, perceived at this existential proximity of scene, is virtually nonnarrative and that this raw material seeks to appropriate its missing protagonist from any number of narrative paradigms, ranging from the conventions of generic war films and novels enumerated at the outset to the multiplicity of generic experiments in Grimmelshausen's peculiar text.

It is a hypothesis we may now test on the aerial warfare of World War II, about which it will be recalled that the most famous representation of its most famous (European) atrocity—*Slaughterhouse-Five*—sets the firebombing of Dresden offstage, behind the sealed door of the protagonist's eponymous cellar. About this kind of warfare, W. S. Sebald, who grew up in a part of Germany untouched by the air war and exiled himself to England at an early age, has oddly maintained that the Germans have repressed its experience and indeed that of the defeat in general.[19] He excepts from this accusation one of the most remarkable writers (and filmmakers) of modern Germany,

Alexander Kluge, whose portrayal of the Battle of Stalingrad (*Schlachtbeschreibung*) already presents many of the features to be noted in the later account of the bombing of his native city, Halberstadt, on April 8, 1945.[20]

It was indeed Kluge from whom we selected the remark by Goebbels that figures as an epigraph to the present essay; and it is in precisely this sense that Stalingrad seems to disintegrate into a host of unrelated colors and brushstrokes as we gradually approach our eyes and faces to the canvas. It would be facile to characterize this text as a deconstruction, either of the traditional narrative account of the battle or of the battle itself. Yet in some literal sense the word is apt, provided that we take it backward, as referring to an account of the elements and raw materials that went into the building of the phenomenon hereby unbuilt: indeed, the Stalingrad book has as its suggestive subtitle *The Organizational Construction of a Catastrophe.* Kluge redistributes the building blocks of the defeat in what may be called nonexistential segments, which is to say nonnarrative units set side by side in a kind of collage. We here find extracts from an army manual on winter warfare side by side with historical accounts, pictures of the landscape, interviews with survivors, medical descriptions of the most characteristic wounds and mutilations, a chronology, the propaganda rhetoric of pastors and preachers on the subject, the language habits of the officers and staff, press clippings and conferences, and dispatches from the front, the whole interlarded with anecdotes and other stray observations and testimonies, among which Hitler's vacillations and tactical inattentions are duly registered in passing—in what could, I suppose, be called a nonlinear "narrative" if one still likes that kind of terminology. It should be understood that Kluge's interest lies in the enumeration of destinies and the deployment of anecdotes, not in any sustained or novelistic storytelling or longer narrative breath. It may be said that he practices a unique type of didactic abstraction, in which a given outcome is x-rayed for the components it incorporates of life-promoting or lethal energies respectively.

"The Bombing of Halberstadt" is another such collage,[21] in which individual experiences, in the form of anecdotes, are set side by side less for their structures as the acts of traditional characters (Burke's agents) than as names and destinies, the latter being reduced in many cases to peculiar facts and accidents, of the type of *Ripley's Believe It or Not.* The juxtaposition of these anecdotes with quotations from academic studies on the history of bombing and on Royal Air Force techniques, from scholarly conferences on the relation between aerial strategy and ethics ("moral bombing" is, for example, specified as a matter not of morals but of morale), and from interviews with the allied pilots who participated in this raid—all these materials, which we take to be nonfictional (although they may not be; the interviews in particular bear the distinctive marks of Kluge's own provocative interview methods), raise the question of the fictionality or nonfictionality of the personal stories of the survivors as well. Halberstadt is, to be sure, Kluge's hometown, and he is perfectly capable of having assembled a file of testimonies and eyewitness documentation and of using the names of real people. On the other hand, these stories, with their rich detail, afford the pleasures of fictional narrative and fictional reading.

Is this text (written in the 1970s) a nonfictional novel? I believe that we must think our way back into a situation in which this question makes no sense and in which—as with the storytelling that precedes the emergence of the so-called Western novel—the distinction between fiction and nonfiction (or history) does not yet obtain, any more than that (so closely related to it) between figurative and literal language. This is to say not that Kluge marks a regression to precapitalist storytelling but rather on the contrary that postmodernity as such has now rendered those distinctions obsolete in the other direction: now it is not so much a question of all narrative being fictional as it is of a reading process that is always literal, even when we are reading what is technically a fiction.

At any rate, it can be argued that the opening section of "The Bombing of Halberstadt" is less a matter of assembling the personal experiences of the survivors, the moments of the first bombs—in what amount to six successive waves of bombers—than it is of a use of named individuals to map the small city itself (sixty-four thousand inhabitants) as they try to make their way across streets increasingly blocked by fires and rubble. (Indeed, we will learn shortly that such attacks follow a specific and intentional pattern: first, strikes calculated to identify targets by columns of smoke identifiable from the aircraft; then the systematic blocking off of streets so the fleeing population is trapped; then an initial destruction of roofs and top stories, with a calculated time lapse to allow a later wave of bombers to drop new explosives through the holes and set fire to the buildings as a whole—these procedures carefully designed to produce the so-called firestorm characteristic of the raids.) A certain amount of curious detail is amassed here, such as the effort of the civilians to get rid of flammable materials such as the stocks of paper in the newspaper offices or hosing groups down to survive the heat. Mainly, however, these opening chapters document the regression of the civilians into their private obsessions and neuroses and their decidedly meaningful and intentional yet aberrant activities, as with the random scattering of an anthill. Thus, in the opening section, which, so characteristically for this writer-filmmaker, deals with the local movie theater, the Capitol, and its manager, Frau Schrader (the owners are on vacation in the country), this particular character is at first worried about the next matinees at three and six o'clock (the first bombs begin to fall at 11:20 a.m.) and only later about the bodies of the initial spectators. Her emotional low point is reached, however, when she finds nothing to do and "feels herself 'useless'": not deadly danger but the blockage of activity is the phenomenon that interests Kluge here.

The agitated movements of these named and presumably real-life characters serve to map out the streets they attempt to negotiate, the routes in and out of town, and the positions of key buildings—the institute for deaf children, for example, or the church tower, on which civilian volunteers are stationed to observe and report the attacks, which of course exceed anything they had expected and at the same time destroy any number of telephone lines and other channels of communication. Both of these situations will be given a turn of the anecdotal screw in the second part, in which the postwar interviewer inquires into the possibility that a white flag of surrender had been shown on the tower ("surrender to whom?" the American pilot asks; "How do you surrender to a squadron of bombers?"), while a colonel attempts to get information by telephone about the state of things around his sisters' home outside town (from Magdeburg, owing to the destruction of the lines, he has to "make connections via Croppenstedt, Gröningen, Emersleben, and Schwanebeck and then back through Genthin, Oschersleben, and, further south, Quedlinburg"; he never gets through, although the operators realize that this is not official but rather private business). From the two parts, we may retain (and compare) the initial attempt of Herr Grämert to rescue his twelve thousand tin soldiers, which represent Napoléon's winter campaign in Russia; the episode of the "unknown photographer"[22] (characteristically, the surviving photographs are here reproduced, along with much other visual material in part 2); and the episode in part 2 in which a teenager succeeds in mastering his piano lesson but not in persuading his piano teacher to reschedule his lesson for the next day, on which, escaping the burning city, he takes refuge in a village, where he practices nonstop so energetically that the owners have to tell him to give it a rest.

Part 2 lets us into the formal secret of this work (I will not say its message or its meaning, exactly), with its differentiation of a strategy from below and a strategy from above (the latter, to be sure, outlines the bombing techniques and conveys what it would be improper, as we shall see, to call the point of view of the American pilots). Thus, Gerda Baethe has learned that the pressure from the bomb blasts will damage the lungs; she tries to make her small children hold their breath during the explosions. Meanwhile, Karl Wilhelm von Schroers, a convalescent veteran in charge of the prisoner-of-war camps in Halberstadt, eagerly visits key points in and out of the city, giving and taking orders but above all satisfying his keen scientific curiosity. This characteristic, like Baethe's "strategies," is not to be understood in any subjective way, even though the two are vivid personalities succinctly conveyed in a page or two. In keeping with the neutrality of this text and with the generic focus of the anecdote as a form, these are external or objective traits, of the type one registers in other people, as when we note that someone (a proper name) is "quick to anger" or that some other proper name is "indecisive."

But Schroers is more significant than that, insofar as his "scientific curiosity" constitutes something like an "aspiration to totality," which his position on the ground can scarcely satisfy. He is indeed a "collector of strong sense impressions."[23] "His capacity to feel increasingly curiosity rather than anxiety is not based on any lack of imagination. To be sure, with his physical eyes he only sees this particular tavern, a partial view of Wherstedter Bridge (and nothing of the torn-up rails), and perhaps a few houses, but he can imagine the whole city. What he doesn't know [we are still in the night before the bombardment] is that this will be the last conscious glimpse of the cityscape intact."[24]

Like Frau Schrader, he has his later moments of depression (owing to the absence of goals and intentions to be fulfilled, activities to be carried out), but at length he recovers his original energy and curiosity.

Another cameo appearance is made by the head of the fire brigade, who deplores the ignorance of the city officials and their haste to extinguish fires that will be controllable only at a later stage of their chemical life and development and who takes a reasoned decision to allow the city's archives and its museum contents to go up in flames: "I was virtually the last person in this city to see its valuable memorabilia, to say farewell, to estimate the value of the collection."[25]

Here the micro perspective, the view from beneath, dwindles to its vanishing point. Yet it should not be imagined that the view from above, that of the pilots and crew, is more comprehensive or reliable. Indeed, as has already been hinted, there is in fact no view from above insofar as the pilots are expected not to see but rather to determine their movements by map and by mathematical calculation, by radar rather than by "sight" (an expression that here in any case signifies strategy, not the personal organs of the participants).[26] All the studies of aerial warfare and its techniques foreground the depersonalization of the individuals involved and their assimilation into the larger machinery first of their own aircraft and then of the squadron as a whole. "Here there do not fly individual airplanes as in the Battle of Britain but rather a whole conceptual system, an intellectual construction in metal" (to quote one of the discussants at a symposium).[27]

Abstraction versus sense-datum: these are the two poles of a dialectic of war, incomprehensible in their mutual isolation, which dictate dilemmas of representation navigable only by formal innovation, as we have seen, and not by any stable narrative convention. It is not to be imagined, however, that we can return to some earlier state of wholeness, in which, as in Homer, individual hand-to-hand combat would at one and the same time somehow epitomize the totality.

On the other hand, the contradiction can be exacerbated even further, and it continues to be in contemporary warfare. Michael Hardt has evoked a kind of dialectic of the body in the most recent American wars, in which the solitary body of the suicide bomber, on the one hand, finds itself opposed, on the other, to the smart bombs and pilotless drones of an aerial warfare visible only on monitors at thousands of miles of distance—a contradiction itself reproduced in the distance between the conventional duel of armies ("mission accomplished") and the house-to-house urban resistance of guerrilla warfare.[28] Does this opposition then not correspond to what I previously identified as a distinction between the named (or institutionalized) action and the blooming, buzzing confusion of scene, from which as yet no formalizable actantial categories have emerged? The abstract category may also stand in constitutive opposition to what I called the existential experience of war, through which an equally undefined subject or consciousness finds representation. But scene is in its fullest reality necessarily collective, and it is the multiplicity of the collective that marks the difference between the representational problems we have rehearsed here. The language of the existential individual already possesses an elaborate history with all kinds of stereotypes that it can be the task of representation to correct, disrupt, undermine, or metaphysically challenge. That of the collective does not yet exist. Group, nation, clan, class, general will, multitude—all these remain so many linguistic experiments for designating an unimaginable collective totality, a manifold of consciousness as unimaginable as it is real. War is one among such collective realities, which exceed representation fully as much as they do conceptualization and yet which ceaselessly tempt and exasperate narrative ambitions, conventional and experimental alike: unless, of course, this particular reality ceases to exist.

Notes

Epigraphs: Jean-Paul Sartre, *The Reprieve* (New York: Knopf, 1947); Goebbels epigraph is taken from Alexander Kluge, *Chronik der Gefühle* (see note 20 below).

1. Kenneth Burke, *A Grammar of Motives* (Berkeley: University of California Press, 1953).
2. Jean-Paul Sartre, *The Critique of Dialectical Reason* (London: Verso, 2004).
3. Georg Lukács, *The Historical Novel* (Lincoln: University of Nebraska Press, 1983).
4. Boris Eikhenbaum, *Tolstoy in the Sixties* (Ann Arbor, MI: Ardis, 1982), 149, 144.
5. Leo Tolstoy, *War and Peace* (New York: Norton, 1966), 163.
6. Carl von Clausewitz, *On War*, trans. Michael Howard and Peter Paret (Princeton, NJ: Princeton University Press, 1976).
7. Hans Jakob Christoffel von Grimmelshausen, *Der abenteuerliche Simplicissimus* (Munich: Artemis, 1956), 17.
8. George Schulz-Behrend, trans., *The Adventures of Simplicius Simplicissimus*, by Hans Jakob Christoffel von Grimmelshausen (Columbia, SC: Camden House, 1993), 7.
9. Christopher Clark, *Iron Kingdom* (Cambridge, MA: Harvard University Press, 2006), 32–34.
10. Alfred Döblin, *Wallenstein* (Munich: DTV, 1983), 248. Unattributed translations are mine.
11. Golo Mann, *Wallenstein* (Frankfurt: Fischer, 1971), 299–300.
12. Döblin, *Wallenstein*, 254.
13. Ibid., 243–44.
14. Mann, *Wallenstein*, 287–88.
15. Grimmelshausen, *Der abenteuerliche Simplicissimus*, 353.
16. Ibid., 45.
17. Ibid., 391.
18. Ibid., 582.
19. W. S. Sebald, *On the Natural History of Destruction* (New York: Random, 2003).
20. Alexander Kluge, *Chronik der Gefühle*, 2 vols. (Frankfurt: Suhrkamp, 2004), vol. 1, 509–791.
21. Ibid., vol. 2, 27–82.
22. Ibid., vol. 1, 509–791.

23. Ibid., vol. 2, 66.

24. Ibid., vol. 2, 68.

25. Ibid., vol. 2, 78.

26. Ibid., vol. 2, 54n12.

27. Ibid., vol. 2, 51.

28. Michael Hardt and Antonio Negri, *Multitude: War and Democracy in the Age of Empire* (New York: Penguin, 2004), 45.

War Pictures

Digital Surveillance from Foreign Theater to Homeland Security Front

Garrett Stewart

Before the montage that is the war film, consider a photocollage *about* war on film, from 1937, by the famous anti-Nazi polemicist John Heartfield. With its double-ply title *Mahnung* ("Warning"), this piece (of discrepant pieces) is named both for the film image pictured within it and for its captioned setting in the satirized passivity of a commercial movie theater. If the one warning isn't enough, a further polemic reframes it. Heartfield's pastiche layers in several rows of faceless male heads, backs toward us, beneath the frontal stare of an on-screen victim in the violent newsreel footage at which they are staring: a Chinese mother holding a bloodied child in outsized close-up, with a toppled bridge and corpse-strewn railroad tracks in the Japanese-ravaged distance. Its German legend, spelled out at the bottom, would go this way in English: "Today you still see the war in other countries on film. But know this: if you don't unite to defend yourselves, tomorrow it will kill you too."

The relevant community is already gathered there, as audience, awaiting transformation into a resistant body politic. Until that should happen, however, war on film is only a medial distraction, not a call to arms—as much dissociated from felt reality as are the collaged laminates from each other, slamming Asian victims up against inert Western witness. Too often, of course, though in a different sense, such dissociation is the fate of war on-screen in its nondocumentary modes, shielded from us as spectacle, channeled by the protocols of fictional narrative. Or, failing even that in war films of the past decade, decentered by a skittish authenticity of technique into slice-of-death vignettes resembling the daily fodder of broadcast

TV and web videos. To bring a philosophy of cinema to bear on this recent spate of anti-epics is, first of all, to reflect upon such audiovisual technique in precisely its fit (or manic misfit) with the military technology of optical surveillance whose aim (in both senses) the films regularly refuse to heroize.

But even before philosophy, or in particular media philosophy, the idea of the "war picture" needs its philology. With respect to the Mideast war film, there is, in part, the implicit tension (marked by the grammar of my title) between what, on the one hand, contemporary warfare now (and increasingly) does—with the electronic enhancement of its lethal optics—and, on the other, the Hollywood genre into which its latest representations are so uncomfortably slotted. Other anomalies call out for a querying of the lexicon, but the genre tag is certainly among them. War pictures: a clause as well as a phrase. Regardless of national politics, war's true regime is scopic (but in this regard always partly fantasmatic, assuming a scope that cannot be summoned to unitary view).[1] A battle can sometimes be watched; a war must be perceived according to a bigger picture. That's one of its lures for cinematic treatment, as well as one of its built-in limits. The dynamic spatial reach of alternate montage won't suffice, finally. Nor the attenuated detail of satellite overviews.

Aside from such specular ironies, the term *war* all by itself can give pause. Philology again, in advance of philosophy. The "battle" against obesity is one thing, like the War on Poverty, but the War on Terror is another: not metaphoric hyperbole but circular tautology. And in the Terror against Terror that U.S. air strikes inflict, the technology of imaging now plays a role so far from "mediation" in the sense of a brokered peace that it has become indistinguishable from—because coterminous with—the arsenal of tactical ballistics. The digitized drone scan triggers a "surgical" strike whose backfiring euphemism reminds us that the operation is often successful only because the patient dies.

In the process, such a battery of enhanced optical technology does nothing to sustain the classic visuality of the war-film genre. There are few panoramic scenes in these narratives of the past decade, no martial choreography, no geometric symmetries of spectacle, few widescreen needs whatever. Battle, usually renamed "firefight"—a function more of ad hoc counterinsurgency than grand design—has fragmented into the extreme contingencies of sniping and roadside bomb blasts. War is so total that it is nowhere and everywhere at once, so that what the War on Terror film serves to picture is for the most part a soldiery without a genre. Even when decisively specular in its aerial execution, nevertheless such warfare has little compelling spectacle. And on the ground, the troops sharing images from their cell phones and camcorders catch no glimpse of a grand *plan* (itself, in French, the term for the scale of a shot). Although the philosopher Paul Virilio has repeatedly linked cinema at large to a battlefield's "logistics of perception," these new films—with their depleted plots of intermittent skirmish, improvised explosive device (IED) sabotage, panic, mayhem, and localized reprisal—have lost almost all narrative (as well as martial) *logic* while surrendering perception to the flash of image and its random capture.[2]

Given the new computerized optics of an electronically driven combat in our so-called wired version of "total" war, there's a revealing taxonomic misstep—or slippage—in one institution's archival view of armed combat. At the renovated Military History Museum in Dresden, in the new gallery space designed by Daniel Liebeskind, exhibits are arranged according to thematic rubrics linking war to other aspects of modern culture: to the suffering body, to technical innovation, to fashion, to literature, to everyday language, and so forth. Included in this roster is war's relation to memory, exemplified in part by several representative shelves of VHS- and DVD-reissued war films, mostly from the past century. War is, yes—in its venerable screen treatments—remembered, at least memorialized, by cinema, and thus variously retold.[3] Until recently, war has been, to be sure, a full-fledged narrative genre as well as a recurrent historical catastrophe. But the image systems of screen viewing are not to be separated so easily, of late—as a mere prosthetic of memorialization—from the increasingly electronic applications that *make war*. So the manufacture of analogue tape and later digital recording is actually continuous with the far more sophisticated cyber-optics of an evolved warfare itself—and might thus be grouped in Dresden with the fallout from military technology on display elsewhere in an adjacent gallery, ranging from high-powered binoculars to radar devices. Friedrich Kittler's media theory comes to mind, just here, on the way toward any philosophical account of the war film—where every crucial development in commercial media is shown to derive, first of all, from military experiments in encrypted communication technology.[4]

In thinking about this common denominator of image culture, actually thinking it through—or, through it, to some larger frames of consideration—there's another philological (before philosophical) ambiguity worth noting as well, one associated with the denomination of such a thought process as installed (or instigated) by film. The journal *Film-Philosophy* (though not reduced on its masthead to the sheer contiguity of Film/Philosophy) does, nevertheless, leave its hyphen in limbo: either loosely leashing the two realms (motion pictures and the discipline of philosophy) or more tightly cinching the latter to its noun modifier, as, for instance, in a phrase (and partial title) like "Gilles Deleuze's Film Philosophy."[5] In coming back to Deleuze, as we will, and to the place of the contemporary war film in the looming hegemony of the digital image that his last writing anticipates, we should be able to locate a genuine philosophical valence within cinema's own audiovisual procedures.

War on Film in Film

Premising any such philosophical account is the recognition that current film treatments of America's Mideast combat have a decided media-historical dimension as well. Recall, for instance, the "embedded" phenomenon, registered *in* film, of war *on* film, whether still or moving. Arthur Kennedy (as the historical photojournalist Jackson Bentley) tells the publicity hound T. E. Lawrence that he's going "to take your bloody picture"—transferred epithet intended—for the ravenous world press. It's a posed shot. The desired effect is usually more "candid" than in *Lawrence of Arabia* (David Lean, 1962). Francis Ford Coppola (playing himself as a film documentarian) tells the landing force in *Apocalypse Now* (Coppola, 1979) to ignore the camera ("just act like you're fighting"). And building on full-face frontal TV news interviews with the troops in *Full Metal Jacket* (Stanley Kubrick, 1987), the Gulf War recruits in *Jarhead* (Sam Mendes, 2005) bite their over-rehearsed tongues about the misery and terror of the battlefield in their talking-head spots on U.S. national news.

What's new in the Second Gulf War, and in Afghanistan since, is that soldiers (fighters in fact on both sides) have become now their own video documentarians. Boots on the ground entail digital cams or cell phones in hand, with web streams waiting. And this digital ubiquity is reciprocated in many of these films as a tech counteroffensive. When not used against the American troops as concealed triggers for buried bombs, such electronic image machines can be converted to weapons of propaganda. At which point the difference between surveillance and broadcast, war waged and war publicized, has eroded to the point of an irony so enmeshed with a restless and shaky cinematographic style—especially in counterpoint with the "omniscient" drone shot—that it is hard to feature purposefully in a feature film: or say, instead, hard to renegotiate as a political motif. In writing about this intractable detriment to visual coherence and rhetorical power in the screen narratives of Iraq and Afghanistan, across a set of films I'll be reviewing briefly below, I have identified this "digital fatigue" as both an ethical and an aesthetic syndrome.[6]

Another eroded border in all this, besides that of reconnaissance and dissemination: the fine, fraying line between surveillance and voyeurism, as reduced to self-voyeurism and digital incrimination, for instance, in the notorious Abu Ghraib prison photos that have had such a pervasive influence on the ethics of record in subsequent Mideast war films. Capturing a captured enemy in brutal sexual humiliation—even when the perpetrator is behind the camera rather than in the shot—constitutes a self-documented war crime. Many films emerging around the time of this international scandal, and especially since, have linked the licensed violence of antiterrorist warfare to this new crisis of instantaneous digital witness, whose sadistic self-indulgence comes intermittently to light as both a moral outrage and a high-command publicity disaster.

Though the Mideast war films do not fix particularly, let alone fixate, on still images in any notable way (except for the photo dossier of Iraqi corpses that follows the last narrative freeze frame of Brian De Palma's *Redacted* [2007]), most of these War on Terror narratives are shot through with the compulsion to digitized self-record amid the desert of anonymous threat. Even when not based on actual reported atrocities, the films may, to this extent, still seem alluding to such notorious torture photos in their own frenetic digital record—as if, amid both the alternating boredom and amorphous tension of the desert watches, there persists a compulsion to find some frame, some specular containment, for the vast wastes of anxiety and threat.

While still tabling the full philosophical (read: theoretical) dimensions of these issues, there is a further turn of the media-historical perspective to consider, latent there in the second half of my subheading "war . . . on film." Which calls up philology again on the very threshold of film philosophy. At a recent seminar that I titled "The Digital War on Film," at the University of Zurich, the graduate students' first question was whether my English title implied a media rivalry rather than simply the Hollywood representation of the Mideast's electronic weaponry. Yes, but only as backstory. For that war against ("on" in this sense) traditional filmic mechanism—the onslaught of computerized imaging against a century-long reign of photomechanical tracing—had already been lost by filmic cinema in the previous decade, or turned to uneasy collaboration, through the prevalence, first, of computer editing, then of CGI (computer generated imagery) and hi-def recording.

Serving almost as hostages, even from the victor's camp, to this routing of one optical medium by its successor, the big-screen treatments of these U.S. incursions in Iraq and Afghanistan, always inflected by on-site video, have—as if due to the very look of their routine hypermediations—met with little enthusiasm at the theatrical box office. Nor have these films found much attempted rescue or even succor from the critics. The lukewarm reception seems an almost inevitable result of their effort to represent digital warfare as a topical issue, whether in the bleached-out antiseptic distance of its satellite overviews or in the handheld graininess of point-of-view (POV) videos—rather than, as elsewhere in mainstream production, to enlist the available crispness of digital spectacle for other kinds of action scenarios less depressing in themselves as well as more photogenic—and more disposed to narrative resolution. As in war, so in commercial cinema: you can't win for losing. I'll come back to this as a structural (hence political) rather than just stylistic double-bind.

As a topic apart from treatment, digital imaging in the War on Terror is one of the so-called facts on the ground, including of course its airborne ballistic complements. And Virilio is the philosopher of its prehistory. Within a "logistics of perception," and to whatever degree of telescopic power, the optical lens was traditionally used to orient and abet the work of weaponry's separate mechanisms, which might in turn be captured in action by a recording device, whether documentary cinema or a TV camera. That was once. Since then, with armed satellite or drone optics, the monocular lens is the focal point of detonation itself rather than just of the reconnaissance it stores or transmits. The computational data feed operates both targeted electronic firing and its (often classified) recording. Calling Vietnam the first TV war referred to the politics of its broadcast. The attack formats of our new media wars are themselves executed, not just disseminated, in new media.

And when represented on-screen in narrative cinema, this historical transformation produces a kind of dual focus—or media-historical loop. As mentioned, Kittler would be quick to track the digital simulacra of commercial cinema in recent decades back to high-tech military experiments with virtual reality and other modes of optical enhancement in the domain of surveillance. And before that, for instance, super-widescreen cinema, competing with the cramped TV screen of 1950s broadcast formats, was—

in the benchmark case of Cinerama—adopted directly from the Waller Flexible Gunnery Trainer, a curved-screen precursor to the virtual reality combat simulator and its wrap-around target range.[7] Since then, such paramilitary genealogies may in turn seem palpably reinscribed within the direct representation of "war films" (no longer entirely filmic) whose visual narratives record, in effect, the reconnaissance and combat deployment of their medium's own newly hybridized and increasingly digital technology. As we approach the theoretical consequences of this for screen narrative, a look aside to adjacent visual experiments from related media should help triangulate the particular mediations at stake on-screen.

Bones of Contention/Lines of Demarcation

Situating the war film in a philosophical frame of investigation invites a similar interrogation of the war image more broadly, especially when the perceptual logistics that, for Virilio, can only render war quintessentially cinematic involve of late both a tactical and a strategic dependence on electronic implementations familiar from our broader image culture. Another way to put this is to say that the once provocative and almost tendentious nature of Virilio's thesis (about what we might term cinemartiality) has lost some of its edge of surprise now that the equipmental aspect of weapons delivery has conflated sighting and triggering in the same digital circuits. And another way yet is to say that war is in fact more than ever like cinema to the extent that cinema, no longer photomechanical in essence (involving the lag time of chemical development), has—in evolving into a technologically mixed medium dependent on digital imaging—become more obviously related to the instantaneous transmissions of electronically managed combat.

We began with a pre–World War II photocollage. More recently, two different artists from fairly polarized ends of overlapping media-historical spectrums—one a photographer of human remains, one an artisanal printmaker whose representations are designed, of all things, to reproduce the video imagery of screen grabs—have offered images of war that are in themselves philosophical, which is to say figurative and conceptual rather than straightforwardly pictorial. In his "Stop the Violence" series, French collage artist and photographer François Robert arranges dozens of human bones, photographed on black backgrounds, into the recognized shapes of either war machines (fighter planes, kalashnikovs, grenades) or fighting words (like "OIL"). His is an irony of visual rhetoric related to metalepsis, the classical trope in which, broadly conceived, effect is put before cause. In the light of a graphemic cluster like "WAR" pieced out in skull and bones, there is the further double turn of unwritten wordplay that converts these reassembled posthumous shards into semiotic prefigurations as well. For even while these skeletal fragments (in a deep-going pun on "articulated" bones) are configured bit by bit into monitory pictograms, the irony operates in reverse as well; the lust for OIL, for instance, *spells death*. Among the instrumental facilitations of such slaughter, the bare-bones reshaping of Robert's human detritus might well have been recruited to form the Cyclopean oculus of a predator drone—except that this feature of "automatic weaponry" is less recognizable as martial icon than machine gun or tank. And this is so partly because the remote optics of military ballistics is continuous with civilian and commercial deployments of the same hidden-camera technology. It's not easy to generate an iconography of the covert.

The second promised example from current image practice (beyond the time-based medium of cinema) is found in the graphic work of Christiane Baumgartner when she takes up the videography of combat imaging. Approaching an arresting work of hers in the painting wing of London's Imperial War Museum (*Luftbild*, 2009)—from the far side of the large gallery in which it is hung—one may think at first it's a TV screen grab of war footage photographically enlarged more than a dozen times, losing any real fidelity in the process: attack planes from a bygone era in a grainy soft focus reminiscent of History Channel documentaries. There seems to be in this image, moreover, an immediate allusion to Gerhard Richter's World War II fighter planes caught as if in blurry stop-action in his out-of-focus photorealism; or his bombadier's-eye view of Dresden under siege (*Bridge 14 FEB 45 [I]*, 2000), bombs receding into the vertical distance in their assault on a bridge. But Baumgartner's images, here and elsewhere, are achieved not in scraped black-and-white oil, like Richter's often are, but in painstakingly carved woodblock prints whose rough-hewn table-knife gouges evoke—at least from the spectatorial distance necessary to mute their oversized jaggedness—the familiar striations of low-res video. In this way, at "heroically" enlarged museum scale (like landscape paintings of old, or "historical" war tableaux for that matter), Baumgartner's reimagined screen shot of attack planes works to "update" photographs of World War II bombers into (twice remediated) contemporary transmissions. The woodcut treatment is typical of her work, whatever the setting repictured, but the specific intertext in Richter for this aerial warfare piece (unlike her evocation, for instance, of the fixed-frame routine view of highway traffic cams in another print) gives a special edge to this particular skyscape as televisual image.

These graphic prints by Baumgartner bear, in fact, a distant logical relation to the reversals of cause and effect in Robert's boneworks. Even leaving aside the Kittlerian irony in her graphics (with the innovative military science of real-time image transmission, leading as it eventually does to commercial TV, being reinvoked by a simulated TV image), there is the further logical irony of origin and aftermath inherent in such images. In the irregular, ridged cascade of Baumgartner's horizontal slicings, a sense of those former wars that we normally see "classically" documented (archival photographs and film footage, like heroic painting before it) is overlapped, imposed upon, by a latter-day optic that, by extension, calls up war's current video waging. The remote imaging that used to be part of war's effect as reported, its epistemological aftermath, say its TV reminiscence, is now, in short, part of its ontology, its cause in execution. This is the case even while the craft of this inference in Baumgartner's art—the productive action of its irony—returns any such contemporary electronic overtones of an increasingly unmanned aerial targeting to the humanized realm of the strenuously handmade. The re-visionary charge sprung by Baumgartner's work—so rare, by contrast, in recent war films—results, it can only seem, from exactly the double distanciation, historical (World War II) and medial (from photochemical imprint to block-print impress), by which such works *look again* at the machinic specularity of combat.

Mission as Transmission

Philology thus coincides with film philosophy in recognizing the way the idiom to "see action" has been radically literalized in the Mideast war films, where an often random violence is repeatedly submitted, if without mitigation, to a mediated ocular remove. As if operating at times under the radar of electronic imaging in war's actual conduct—though in fact their dubious maneuvers are set into ironic counterpoint with it (sometimes including intercut shots of drone strikes)—grunts on the ground, beyond the use of telephoto crosshairs, often content themselves, for their electronic fix, with laptop video games, "avocational" digital recorders, cell phone images, and helmet cams. And revenge is enacted in the same electronic key. In De Palma's *Redacted,* whose closing reversion to an "old-fashioned" photographic archive was mentioned above, a marine videographer takes a damaging infrared record of his squad's nighttime rape and murder spree in revenge for a fellow soldier's death, only to be later decapitated on camera for jihadist propaganda.

In *Battle for Haditha* (Nick Broomfield, 2007), a cadre of jihadists deliberately provokes a similar marine rampage by the cell phone detonation of an IED in order to catch the bloody reprisal on a camcorder and then distribute it as an al-Qaeda recruiting vehicle before releasing it to international news. In *The Situation* (Philip Haas, 2006), an Iraqi photojournalist, gunned down in a firefight, squeezes off spasmodically (involuntarily, in effect posthumously) a half dozen power-drive digital images of the American counterpart he has fallen in love with—across a now explicitly unbridgeable distance—a woman here crouching over him in horror. By the time these automatic images are retrieved from digital storage on his camera and studied by her in the film's closing scene, the romance has turned allegorical, with the American "presence" in the desert forced to see itself at last in the eye of the enemy victim. Such double vision—in default of any more humane mutuality—is often the irony staged by critique in these war pictures.

In a film called *In the Valley of Elah* (Paul Haggis, 2007) but divided instead between two desert settings—Iraq (by flashback) and a military base in New Mexico—the plot follows a Vietnam vet, a former "military detective," through his mounting disillusionment about the latest Eastern war. This transpires when discovering after his son's death—a slaying not during his Iraq service but only at the hands of a violent squad member back at home base—that a retrieved and long-studied image on the son's cell phone, of another and younger dead boy on an Iraq road, actually tells the whole story. In the film's penultimate montage, that image is finally enough to permit the father's mental reconstruction, in videographic flashback, of the son's deliberate homicide (following routine orders not to stop) in running the child down with his jeep.

Digital thematics tend to wax geopolitical at just such points of mortal irony. In *Home of the Brave* (Irwin Winkler, 2006), self-made and hand-captioned video montages of soldiers partying in their tents while awaiting their return home from duty give way to a funeral video for one of their squad killed in an unexpected ambush. And such deaths are themselves registered at times only at an eerie video remove. In *Lions for Lambs* (Robert Redford, 2007), the slaughter of two American soldiers in the mountains of Afghanistan is tracked—via the satellite transmission of infrared images from aerial fly-bys—on the monitors of a far distant command center. It's the same with the related genre of Mideast espionage narratives, as opposed to actual war films. The climax of *Syriana* (Stephen Gaghan, 2005) involves a remote-controlled U.S. strike destroying the rogue CIA hero and the forward-looking Saudi prince he is trying to save. In an obverse but unnervingly related way, at the end of *Body of Lies* (Ridley Scott, 2008), the hero, finally resigning from the CIA ranks in Jordan, is released from "protective" satellite surveillance by being taken "off-target."

It is this new electronic theatricalization of war that brings us most directly into confrontation with the film philosophy of Gilles Deleuze. I proposed above that what the War on Terror film pictures is for the most part a soldiery without a genre. The missing genre is that of an action cinema defined, in Deleuze's vocabulary, by a long-standing dominance of the "movement-image"—which is to say, in the classic war film, the mass-movement image of orchestrated action. No such thing in Iraq or Afghanistan. For Deleuze's sense of film history, one World War II break point was between genre cinema (down through film noir), on the one hand, and, on the other, the new modernist phase of "time-image" cinema arising from the European rubble and alienation after the war (spearheaded by neorealism and the new wave). That watershed has given way now, in the grips of another international conflict—in a metacinematic fashion that Deleuze couldn't quite foresee (writing in the early 1980s) but knew to wonder, even worry, about—to a new version of "permanent war" and its computerized instrumentation, what one might almost call its electronic imaginary. Deleuze didn't live to see the outcome of his speculations, toward the end of *The Time-Image*, about whether computational picturing would supplant cinema as he knew it or merely alter it from within. The question for him was whether the "electronic image," alternatively called the "tele and video image" and the "numerical image," is destined to "transform cinema or to replace it," which means for the "time-image" in particular whether electronics "spoils it or, in contrast, relaunches it."[8]

The extent to which the digital war picture and the closely related high-tech Homeland Security fables of reparative time travel, discussed below, share similar phobias, as well as fantasies, in their visions of instantaneous transmission offers one chance of an answer—especially because both the self-remediated actions of a digitally addicted soldiery and the vaunts of computerized magic in the post-9/11 time-travel films gravitate toward a chief determinant for Deleuze of the post–World War I film: namely, actors becoming spectators in and of their own lives. After the parallel temporal returns of the plot structure in *Citizen Kane* (Welles, 1941), the incapacitated photojournalist of Hitchcock's *Rear Window* (1954) is another early flashpoint of this transition for Deleuze, along with the aimless gazing protagonists of European modernism. Once posted, as daredevil cameraman, to exotic locales for the risky capture of foreign warfare as well as other thrilling global events, the injured photographer in Hitchcock is now confined to his wheelchair and to the constrained frame of a telephoto lens he uses merely to spy on, rather than to record, his neighbors. Convert (and defer) the injury to the constant threat of a battle wound, turn the tedium of stasis into high-tension alert, and replace the empty camera with a film-free digital device—and you'd have in outline, at one fell swoop, the evisceration of the war film as action picture and, instead, its transformation into a surveillance scenario.

Developed out of his reading of parallel montage in Fritz Lang's 1931 *M*, Deleuze's template for the movement-image is a situation acted upon so as to revise it: Situation/Action/Situation'.[9] Though he doesn't mention or adjust this formula explicitly in his second volume, one can see how the historical revision would go. If the situation (more like static setting) is no longer amenable to action because its agent is more spectator than protagonist, the Site (barely even a Situation) remains, under Spectation, mostly unchanged, at least within its own time frame. Rather, it is at best reseen, as if already remembered on the spot. All event is virtual, mental, happening in a time out of joint. From SAS' (Situation/Action/Situation), then, to something like the leveled ocular continuum of SSS' (Situation/Spectation/Situation).

Under the former dispensation, the nature of any action called upon to revise a given local condition, at least in the classic case of alternating montage, has to bring separate but coterminous narrative strands into intersection upon a closing structural event or node that Deleuze would call, by shorthand, and with full cross-genre resonance, "the duel." The villain and his scourge need to face each other off; in *M*, the child murderer has to be confronted both with the underworld that had been trailing him and the police whose dragnet their parallel manhunt at first shadowed and then outpaced. In the classic war film, any parallel montage between opposing camps certainly requires in the end a similar point of convergence: a group duel by any other name, a battle, with perhaps a surrender. In contrast, the new Mideast war film—all prosthetic spectation without concerted action, all nerve-wracking abeyance far from any rank-and-file clash of bayonets, all digital vigilance with only the occasional punctuation of violence—forgoes the duel, even that of a standoff, let alone a face-off, and stalls instead, mired in the diffuse nature of the terror and its terrorizing pushback, under the watchful panoptic eye—mostly offscreen, ob-scene—of satellite targeting.

Deleuzian categories throw the War on Terror into relief from another angle as well. A defining ingredient of his "time-image," where duration is a cinematic sign in itself rather than just a function of action, is the deactivated "any-space-whatever" of vectorless waiting that Deleuze's second volume repeatedly associates with, again, the new modernist cinemas after the European devastation of World War II. There are few more starkly obvious visual candidates for such a dissociative "space," over half a century later, than an estranging desert terrain in which an entrenched Arab population is invaded by western technology, optical or lethal or both, and out of which no American looking (or nervous filming) can extract the shape of coherent action. Pieced together as a discontinuous electronic record, here is the experimental "time-image" shriveled to travesty under a temporizing imperialist aggression.[10] The ironic grip of temporal instantaneity in the surveillance tension wrought by one after another of these Mideast war films keeps the low-lying landscape at the nonexotic distance of nugatory tourist footage even while the ad hoc videographers remain, as foot soldiers, vulnerable to its sequestered pockets of assault. Eyes on the frame rather than the prize, it is as if they were recording their own future video games—while playing others like them in between—and waiting in both cases for the fun to start.

In view of Deleuze's main parameters for the time-image, spatial indetermination and spectatorial disengagement alike, one film stands out from the rest of the Mideast war pictures, not just for its mode of picturing but for the power of its antiwar critique, earned by hindsight in the historical distance it has gained on a violent past rather than a confounding present. The Israeli filmmaker-protagonist of this animated autobiographical narrative, *Waltz with Bashir* (Ari Folman, 2008)—its animation done not digitally but in hand-drawn and then computer-assisted images—is a haunted character who tries looking back through heavily clouded guilt on his uncertain participation, when a young soldier, in an infamous Muslim massacre during the 1983 Israeli assault on Beirut.[11] In the Mideast present, with warmongering all around him, Folman tries to recapture his role as surveillance agent—participant spectator (a guard stationed at the perimeter, operating the flares that light up the targets)—with respect to a scene of carnage he has wholly blocked from consciousness. In terms of the Deleuzian time-image, the agent as spectator must recover his allotted post not in the "any-space-whatever" of postwar alienation but at the explicit scene of a crime and its national shame.

The psychiatrist whom the director seeks out tells him of another patient of hers, a still photographer, who went to war thinking that his fetishizing of "great shots" could keep the violent reality from bleeding through. "But one day the camera broke," she says, as if metaphorically. For the Folman character, instead—given the ending on which the film subsequently bears down—what this psychoanalytic session anticipates is that one day he might finally be able to recognize unaestheticized video footage taken by a famous newsreel cameraman at the site of the massacre—recognize and accept it as a version of his own finally admitted (and complicit) witness. This is footage breaking at last into the otherwise animated diegesis not for him exactly (either now or as the on-screen drawing [out] of his younger self) but—along the reverse shot of an eye-line match—for *us* through his eyes.

What he now remembers and internalizes, that is, comes before our view as part of the historical archive of terror. We are to see it now, as we didn't on international news at the time, as if we were there, entailed, undetached—even while as memory, personal or historical, the anguish of the victims can never be more than virtual, than "recovered" images, found footage. The video specter of a repressed murderous spectacle has nevertheless been returned, from some medial limbo, to the pertinent interspace between past agency (however passive) and its present recognition. Any taint of voyeurism in the latent prurience of on-screen violence has in this case been filtered back, through the assigned stance of motivated surveillance, to a no longer repressed posture of responsibility. Put otherwise: the Deleuzian time-image, with its frequent palimpsest of present and past, has—from within this historical setting in Mideast slaughter, and against the drive of a "movement-image" action genre—found instead a genuine political reframing. It has achieved this almost alone amid a slow decade's worth of metafilmic War on Terror depictions and the ephemeral instantaneity, however predominantly ironic, of their on-screen video record.

Home (Front) Security/Flashback's Deaths

If *Waltz with Bashir* operates like a homecoming-vet narrative of delayed trauma returning us to the war zone by way of recovered memory, the fact that this memory is coded in video terms (in this case as a break from animation into "live" footage—albeit of mass death and grieving) is not, in itself, an unfamiliar visual trope. Laptop replay of self-recorded "war porn" by the PTSD (post-traumatic stress disorder) victim in recent films is the prosthetic (not necessarily therapeutic) equivalent of the traumatic memory flare. The new temporalities of postwar cinema, according to Deleuze—with its "sheets of the present" and their various laminates and overlaps in the "plane of immanence"—allow him to say that "modern cinema has killed the flashback." It is only appropriate, then, in the subsequent "numerical" phase (or overthrow) of the time-image, that the high-tech, computer-driven war picture should be able to lend the former nested scenarios of the flashback only a digital afterlife.[12]

A similar result attends the high-tech, counter-Terror action thriller rather than war film, where the flashback regularly escapes from normal narrative functions altogether (or their cognitive equivalents) to figure a preternatural space of teleportation (or what I have called, with earlier and mostly nonmilitary examples, the parodied or meretricious time-image of spatialized "temportation").[13] In its more credible forms, cinematized memory has a long military history. From the earliest diagnoses of post–World War I shell shock, the traumatic recurrence of battlefield agony and guilt has been figured in neuropsychology as violent footage rerun in the head.[14] It is a motif familiar in literary treatments of war trauma as well, making a recent oblique appearance in the synaptic lapses of a post-Korean vet in Toni Morrison's latest novel, *Home* (2012), where the unshakable bloodshed of war drains the color from homeland reality, leeching it away, turning live and occupied landscapes into "a black-and-white movie screen" for long minutes at a time.[15] These episodes are not violent flashbacks exactly; they are chromatic deficits in a cinematically figured incursion of panic into the normal palette of reality.

The latest sci-fi films to which we now turn are themselves not war pictures exactly—but nonetheless comparable metafilmic reflections on high-tech violence. They engage the replay of trauma when transfigured by sci-fi fantasy into a redemptive time-loop: remediation as remedial in the preemptive War on Terror. Yet it is in just this way that said War, in its full computer instrumentation, is often turned against the U.S. citizens it is designed to protect, especially on the Homeland Security front. One can, in fact, track one line of development from the actual Mideast war film to the similar place of computer-driven violence in the growing roster of Homeland Security fables by moving from the desert ambush prologue of *Eagle*

Eye (D. J. Caruso, 2008) to its stateside sci-fi developments. In the Mideast prologue to that 2008 action thriller, a hand-launched portable drone is seen in POV shots foraging for surveillance images of Arab men in a small village, where they have gathered either—it is presumed by the American video operators—to transport a wooden case of weapons or to bury a coffin (two implicit sides of the same rage). It is finally deemed by the Washington-based oversight of a supercomputer with remote face-recognition capacities that there isn't a sure-enough match between a bearded man in the drone sights and a known terrorist leader to justify the "take out."

Overridden by the president, however, even against the advice of the defense secretary, the button is pushed, the trigger is pulled—at which point the supercomputer, virtually personified (we later learn) with a female voice and named ARIA (automatic reconnaissance information analyst) goes into programmed overdrive. It turns out that ARIA is wired for the policing of Homeland Security at all costs. Controlling every closed circuit TV (CCTV) camera on native shores, as well as a global satellite network, she is meant to take no prisoners whenever data are indisputably confirmed. So it is that she now plots the bombing of Congress during the State of the Union address. In a good enough political irony that becomes tedious only in the working out, our elected officials have been identified as our own worst enemies in securing our shores from anti-American attack. What is called for, decides ARIA, is a new kind of preemptive strike.

More common in the allegorical sci-fi narratives appearing in the wake of 9/11, however, is the fantasy of *retroactive* prevention. So, given the subheading of "flashback's deaths," some philology once more—to accompany Deleuze's philosophy. By elevating spectation over action, and thus no longer rendering duration as strictly a function of on-screen motion, the time-image tends to virtualize both the past as a mere sheet of the present and the future as prefigured in the now. In the context of the cinematic War on Terror—with its complementarity between PTSD narratives (punctuated by the return of a repressed violence) and the more recent sci-fi thrillers (with their time-loop return *to* such violence)—the grammatical pivot of a phrase like "flashback's deaths" turns on the objective over against the subjective genitive: now the deaths that haunt a character in flashbacks, now the variously marked obsolescences of the flashback itself in narratives of rear-view "temportation." Whatever its digital treatment in a given screen narrative, that is, the "numeric" engines of (paracinematic) progress are imagined by these plots to have altered the very shape of time, and hence its images. We're asked, for instance, to believe that computer science can overcome the laws of duration itself and recuperate lost time in a parallel universe, turning digital surveillance into electronic transcendence, converting ambush and defeat to interception, repeating the tragedy of recent history not as farce but as national reinforcement.

In Tony Scott's 2006 film *Déjà Vu,* an army volunteer has been judged too bloodthirsty for the American military ranks. With his enlistment rejected, he takes out his rage by exploding a bomb on a car ferry bringing American G.I.s home to post-Katrina New Orleans. Top-secret experimental equipment from the CIA known as a "surveillance window" is recruited to locate him at the elapsed scene, though four days after the fact. What results is a totalized forensic flashback made possible with the data input from seven satellites and the combined CCTV surveillance backlog of the entire urban area. This electronic empowerment includes the metafilmic ability to dissolve the fourth wall of its renarrativized sites with, we are told—as if we might otherwise miss the paramilitary overtones of this terrorist counterattack—"the same infrared stuff they're using in Iraq." The computerized input so overloads the system, however, that it doesn't just retrace a recorded past but brings it back in(to) the present as a simultaneous virtual reality—into which, across a series of high-octane chase scenes in parallel montage, the laboratory technicians track the detective hero in his cornering of the villain four days before. In a preternatural upgrade of Deleuze's action formula for the movement-image, here are shot/reverse shot patterns that produce the simulacral version of a montage-resolving "duel"—but do so across drastically incompatible time frames, where the paradox of parallel lines converging is actually made good on. With past action virtually re-sited as well as reseen, call this situational reality a case of SAS' crossed with SSS' in a digitized theater of cyber-optical (yet still tactical) illusion.

Likewise with a more recent film that comes across as *Déjà Vu* all over again, but with a further paramilitary twist. This time, in *Source Code* (Duncan Jones, 2011), a decorated hero from the recent Afghanistan war, in effect killed and dismembered on his third Mideast mission, is brought back to the States as an inert wired torso and kept just marginally alive as the neurological surveillance antenna for a Homeland Security operation as top secret as it is high tech. Thinking at first that his virtual ordeal (and "manifested" bodily action) is the result of some combat "sim," instead he must gradually accept, over the course of the plot, that, though all but brain dead, he is to undergo a new posting (teleposting) into the recent past by way of "time reassignment." This amounts to being digitally projected into the "synaptic map" of a compatible brain from one of many passengers recently killed by a terrorist bomb on a passenger train bound for Chicago. The electromagnetic premise: that the brain remains active for eight minutes after death and retains, as explained in laymen's terms, its final images "like a surveillance camera in a convenience store." Against his will—"Isn't one life enough to die for your country?"—the functionally dead (and only virtually cognizant) veteran must now, under an extreme form of stop-loss protocols, undergo one residual mission after another in serial computer-driven attempts to locate the terrorist (through the eyes of his dead victim) before he can succeed in his further threat to set off a dirty bomb in downtown Chicago. Time and again the out-of-body spy is electronically catapulted onto the train and suffers repeated incineration, at each iterated blast, until this agent of unmanned reconnaissance is finally armed (he's told where to steal an emergency gun from a locked train closet) and, more like a true soldier, completes the "duel" by coming face to face in time past with the agent of a future violence.

All of this answers to Deleuzian interrogation—with the question whether cinema will persist as we know it, divided between movement-image and time-image, or whether the "electronic image" will change everything—but only in the mode of travestied (because wholly instrumentalized) virtuality rather than some suggestive philosophical overlay on the real. The authentically philosophical determinants of the time-image seem reduced to machinic irony rather than brought forward in revised exemplarity. The jacked-in, agency-truncated carcass of a downed pilot has become a pure spectatorial node by default, not by existential stance: a remote-control cyberpresence. Transported to the "any-space-whatever" facilitated by disembodiment, the postwar "crystal-image" of simultaneous alterities (Deleuze's recurrent term for multifaceted temporality) has thereby been demoted to the alternate-reality of a political wish-fulfillment in a very different kind of postwar (in this case postmortem) environment.

Moreover, the salient Deleuzian notion of cinema's cognitive apparatus securing the "brain-film" link—cinema *as* brain—has been reduced here to the pilfered cerebral wavelengths of a dead double. Hinged around an exploited war hero whose dehumanized interchanges with his operatives have, we discover, been only a signaletic interface of transcribed text messages rather than (as we've presumed by seeing them) a suturing of visualized human faces, this dystopian fantasy can certainly not be alleviated by its anodyne resolution in a prevented civilian threat. For one thing, as so often in these latest security fables, home-front anxiety operates in part as a front for the global ethos of Terror and its countering violence. Indeed the blogger who speculated on this entirely stateside thriller as nonetheless the first Surge film can't be far wrong. Throw more manpower at the problem, even if only the computer-boosted power of the same iterated man, what's left of him. All the more efficient that way, actually—or virtually—and indeed all the more like the current U.S. reliance on unmanned electronic combat.

Battleground Zero: Beyond the Deleuzian Duel

Aside from these digitized time-loop encounters with past terrorism in the magic any-space-whatever of present preemption, there is actually one plot from the overseas War on Terror that manages to stabilize (or bracket) the conflict long enough to evoke a more classic movement-image format of SAS'—where the action is that of deactivation itself. *The Hurt Locker* (Kathryn Bigelow, 2008) does arrange for that climactic "duel" with the enemy necessary in classic cinema to stage the resolution of opposed (whether or not separately montaged) forces. Here the duel is between man and machine, American soldier and the delegated violence of a faceless enemy, and the victory is indeed for once over terror itself in a defusing of an imminent IED blast. This film's reversion from those refracted, hypermediated narratives more characteristic lately of Mideast war pictures to the monolithic (if jagged-edged) pace of the movement-image explains, no doubt, a good part of its success with the critics, if not still with a mass public. This, plus the fact that the main narrative action is in the service, via a lone American hero, of preventing violence and death, for a change, rather than perpetrating it. Not uplifting, the film has at least, it would seem—within its suspended political critique—a satisfying sense of dramatic form.

On top of that, and helping to explain its surprising succes d'estime, its cinematographic treatment avoids the stylistic pitfalls of the other Iraq and Afghanistan films, their vérité deference to embedded and shakily relayed points of view, dizzying and dispersive, splintering all sense of unmediated agency. *The Hurt Locker* does so, by making these signature conditions of the conflict *entirely* stylistic: the rack focus, the broken 180 degree rules, the swish pans. These are no longer the diegetic interplay of prosthetically enabled character perspectives in a lethally contested space. They are the evocative indulgences of narrative camerawork per se, absorbing discrepancies and fissures into a handheld aesthetic reminiscent of, though with no narrative grip on, an otherwise ubiquitous and wearying crossfire of electronic sightings and surveillance elsewhere in Mideast visual representations. Far more than the adept and tension-addicted hero whose concentrated labors we linger over, the film seems itself jittery on his behalf.

Working toward such dubious immediacy, the first extended scene of Bigelow's narrative isolates, foregrounds, and then purges from its melodramatic system—even while dispersing them into sheer unmotivated camerawork—all distancing devices of explicit electronic specularity. The film opens, that is, with the disorienting jump-cut footage, including digital skids and break-ups, of low-angle traveling shots. Only gradually do we understand these shots as the automatically adjusted POV of a rather flimsy robot, a ground-level drone, in the process of bomb defusion. The bot (subbing for a vulnerable human bod) soon suffers mechanical failure (loses the first of all tools, its wheel) and is never seen—nor seen via—again. From there on it's mano a nitro, in a duel to be humanly identified with. Though the soldier's enterprise is wholly depoliticized in *The Hurt Locker*, and seems almost escapist in view of the larger Mideast conflict, the anthropocentrism of the film's unmediated vision—once the camera-fitted robot malfunctions its way to the sidelines—does, I think, shed a clearer-than-ever light on what goes wrong, dramaturgically, with so many other films of this cycle, this subgenre, in their emotional impact and critical leverage both. Their protagonists are never quite all there, but merely looking on.

With Bigelow's film before us, further light is cast, too, and this time explicitly philosophical light (Hegelian, dialectal), on the larger problem of representing war, and not least the blanket War on Terror—a problem for which the Iraq and Afghanistan narratives are such exacerbated test cases. In this respect, visual texture and its calculated optical regress in these films point to a missed opportunity in a recent essay by Fredric Jameson called "War and Representation" (reprinted as the lead contribution to the present volume), where the American Marxist critic with deep roots in the dialectical habits of philosophy leaves his own most potent application of them aside.[16] He does this when suggesting, in rather more general terms instead, that the structural problem with the narrative treatment of war (which I've been demonstrating also as a problem of mediation) is that the focusing of agency around a single hero will not serve to constellate the larger "action" (in the military sense) at stake, or in other words the "mission," even while reliance instead on the squad, cadre, or cohort, to say nothing of the battalion, offers too amorphous a narrative vector to carry the plot if not the day.

Jameson rightly sees a failed resolution between, as one might rephrase it, the abstraction of the "cause" and the sense-data of its prosecuted "effects" in action. But he stops short of mapping this in the dialectical terms of his familiar semiotic square so as to determine the "cognitive horizons" (and potential "political unconscious") of the battle plot and its representational breakdowns.[17] As a foursquare diagram of this sort would make clear, the evaporation of heroic agency that Jameson notes is all the more obvious in the hypermediated optics of War on Terror films. The analytic gesture invited, in his typical use of the semiotic grid, would be to resist the initial binary as exhaustive (the finalized either/or of abstraction versus sensation) and instead to diversify a preliminary (and supposedly primal) contrast into the diagonal poles of its more absolute contradictories. Antinomy is thus ramified into a fuller semantic field.

So where are we, then? Any totalization suggested by the concept of total war still founders on the dichotomy between idea and execution, abstract "Action" as conceived and strategized (say, counterinsurgency) and the event(s) of its enactment on the ground. The desperate attempt (typical of most war narratives) to resolve the establishing dichotomy between abstract and concrete determinants of an ultimately collective protagonist (the corps, rather than the private body)—pitched between a nonsensory abstraction of the "war effort" and the nonabstract viscerality of its exertions in the "battle scene"—is all the more apparent, given the constraints of its literalized optical perspective, in the cinematic treatment of war (though not Jameson's particular subject in this essay). And a film like *The Hurt Locker*—all exponential suspense, little U.S.-perpetrated violence in sight, fueling the same adrenalin rush in us that it serves to diagnose in its hero, and relating each implicitly to the videogame venting of energy that another and more neurotic squad member has a version of shell-shocked recourse to—is a film that has entirely hedged its dramatic bets. By reverting to the classic movement-image duel in a human triumph over low-tech and jerry-rigged explosives, the narrative wins its applause while losing the War's whole context. Deleuze would be the first to recognize that, under the sway of globalized computational forces, the time-bomb thriller—in an almost nostalgic movement-image mode—can scarcely defuse the broader militarist implications of the "time-image" in the age of disembodied electronic transmission.

Moreover, returning to our developing version of a Jamesonian semiotic gridwork, such a blocked overlap—in conceptualizing war—between strategic design and local performance, martial scheme and violent contingency, would find in the very technology of computerized combat a unique version of double negation (the neutral fourth term of neither/nor in Jameson's typical graphings, submerged in the bottom quadrant). Given the cases before us, this neutered zone would locate that blinkered focus (and either abrogated or, in some cases, deferred overview—kicked up to aerial reconnaissance) signaled by the nonsensory (i.e., mediated) but also nonabstract (i.e., perceptual) nature of the electronic POV. Since so much of the action in these recent films seems tethered to the neo-Deleuzian agent as spectator—that is, to the soldier as himself an embedded videographer of his own tedium and ordeal, hooked on the laptop relays (and morbid replays) of his digital record—our contemporary wars on film are hampered by the very ethos of optical recording. As a result, they can make little sense of the besieged senses themselves under deployment by the war machine, a machine that is increasingly computerized and in every way remote. For it is the work of these films, even when not the manifest intent, to tolerate (at their commercial peril) an implosion of form and content so complete that they replicate the nervous uncertainty of vision that their heroes both suffer in action and reproduce in their video transcripts. In this cinematographic syndrome, there is no distance, no chance of a measured and critical narrative detachment, in a word no vision apart from an immersive wired sighting.

Formal analysis (braced by "film[-]philosophy" or not) reaches a kind of inner limit at the point of such films' own stylistic impasse, where technique and potential critique collide with, and elide, each other. When the *exposé* of digital prosthesis, including its dehumanized interface with an alien terrain and its people under high-tech assault, finds its only proper *exposition* in more of the same optical displacement, the crucial distinction between evidence and investigation grows as blurred as the handheld image or low-res satellite feed that must convey them both. So it is that, from issues of both narrated aerial surveillance and self-voyeurized violence in the handheld mode, any philosophical account of such war pictures must back out (or down) one level to the stratum of their latest hybrid mix—as image systems—of photomechanical and digital representation, where two kinds of recognition overlap and perturb each other: contemporaneous technological authenticity and narrative technique.

That much we've certainly seen. Even when not shot entirely in hi-def digital video (as was *Redacted*), these are films about a computerized warfare saturated in its own right by optical electronics—the fragmented kinetic textures of whose screen treatment are already standard evening-news fare. Digital war in video transmission has, therefore, a hard time being *remediated* by "realist" cinema into anything that we don't know, or think we know, too well already, not just in its political and moral quagmire but in its visual style. And a hard time, as we've further noted—even once bringing such trauma and atrocity into focus—of getting any cinematographic, and hence "editorial," distance from them. That's why *Waltz with Bashir*'s move into sustained animation—releasing TV-archive documentation only at the last minute—is so intuitively right and dramatically charged. Elsewhere, instead, an aspiration toward broadcast vérité collapses into a disempowered aesthetic of the familiar. One frequent result, as illustrated: the leverage needed for an often intended ethical recoil—short of a more strongly imposed (and therefore already inauthentic) narrative line in these shapeless conflicts—is short-circuited a priori by this redoubling of topic and representational mode (another case of ocular cause subsumed to its stylistic effects) within the twin ambits of amateur recording and satellite overview.

Strictly speaking, in medial terms, filmed wars are mostly behind us. Digital capture is now the medium of record as well as of execution. War pictures—that is, computerized picturings—make war. In the coils of drone predation, what is shot down is also, for the record, shot. And in the digital sublime of counterterrorist sci-fi, the disembodied human projectile—the broadcast body as sheer data stream—offers its own version of a surgical strike, a preemptive search and seizure, in the recursive timeline of an alternate reality. Or, say, a parallel geopolitical universe. But the politics of such films, escapist or not, are always a matter of screen poetics as well, where the very idea of "live media" in the era of optical globallistics can—philology one last time—seem oxymoronic. As confirmed by such paramilitary derivatives of the war film in sci-fi guise as *Déjà Vu* and *Source Code*—as well as, more broadly, across war's treatment in each main technological phase of screen manifestation, once photomechanical, now postfilmic—an undeniable tendency has long been endemic. One may say in sum—if never in conclusion, because war keeps happening, happening both on and, if you will, increasingly *in* camera—that cinema, as with visual art more broadly, can in itself philosophize war as a case of the *image unto death.*

Notes

1. This cognitive horizon of war—annexing unseen ranges of conflict in its vision of "totality"—reflects one line of argument in Jan Mieszkowski's *Watching War* (Stanford, CA: Stanford University Press, 2012), where an enlisted European "spectatorship" for war on the world stage has, at least since the Napoleonic era—such is the study's main claim—rendered war a concept remote, "mediated," and "hyperreal" well before modern technological innovations of either long-distance weaponry or broadcast (4). Complementing this historical legacy of war as spectator sport, my emphasis, given the new digitized battlefield, falls on the inverted role of the spectator as devolved upon that of the mediated participant witness.

2. Paul Virilio, *War and Cinema: The Logistics of Perception,* trans. Patrick Camiller (New York: Verso, 1989).

3. A stress on collective and national memory runs throughout Elisabeth Bronfen's *Specters of War: Hollywood's Engagement with Military Conflict* (New Brunswick, NJ: Rutgers University Press, 2012). One among many striking formal markers of this effect appears in her treatment of *Saving Private Ryan* (Steven Spielberg, 1998), whose opening flashback structure works to circumscribe the nature of cinema's place in the shared memory of modern conflict. The first scene change seems to involve the title character in shots of the Normandy landing, at which he in fact wasn't present, memories only "by proxy" (140). The war picture is here picturing its own iconography. Or put it that the "specter" of mass battle, as envisioned rather than lived, takes shape always and already in the form of screen spectacle.

4. See especially, amid many discussions of this technological phenomenon in his work, Friedrich Kittler, *Film, Gramophone, Typewriter,* trans. Geoffrey Winthrop-Young and Michael Wutz (Stanford, CA: Stanford University Press, 1999).

5. D. N. Rodowick, *Afterimages of Gilles Deleuze's Film Philosophy* (Minneapolis: University of Minnesota Press, 2010).

6. Garrett Stewart, "Digital Fatigue: Imaging War in Recent American Film," *Film Quarterly* 62, no. 4 (2009): 45–55, where the films mentioned here are discussed in fuller detail and illustrated in their optical pressure points by selected frame grabs.

7. The Waller Flexible Gunnery Trainer was a very specific genealogy of media innovation that was discussed in Giles Taylor's paper for a symposium titled "War and Cinema" at the University of St Andrews, St Andrews, Scotland, in March 2012.

8. Gilles Deleuze, *Cinema 2: The Time-Image,* trans. Hugh Tomlinson and Robert Galeta (Minneapolis: University of Minnesota Press, 1989), 265, 267.

9. Gilles Deleuze, *Cinema 1: The Movement-Image,* trans. Hugh Tomlinson and Barbara Haberjam (Minneapolis: University of Minnesota Press, 1986), 152–53.

10. In a similar vein, in Garrett Stewart, *Framed Time: Toward a Postfilmic Cinema* (Chicago: University of Chicago Press, 2007), 168–70, I have summarized certain transfigured manifestations of the time-image over the past quarter century since Deleuze's evidence—instances that often seem to distort, mechanize, or parody rather than thoughtfully extend the original force of its temporalized optics (as philosophizing in its own right what one might call a cinemental virtuality).

11. A full-length (and illustrated) discussion of this film appears in Garrett Stewart, "Screen Memory in *Waltz with Bashir,*" *Film Quarterly* 63, no 4 (2010): 58–63.

12. Deleuze, *Cinema 2,* 278.

13. Stewart, *Framed Time,* 122–63.

14. In *Shell-Shock Cinema: Weimar Culture and the Wounds of War* (Princeton, NJ: Princeton University Press, 2010), Anton Kaes builds on this history in his treatment of Lang's *M* among other films of the period.

15. Toni Morrison, *Home* (New York: Knopf, 2012), 23.

16. Fredric Jameson, "War and Representation," *PMLA* 124, no 5. (October 2009): 1532–47.

17. I have in mind Jameson's most prominent use of this heuristic grid in *The Political Unconscious: Narrative as a Socially Symbolic Act* (Ithaca, NY: Cornell University Press, 1981), where the social symbolism flagged by his subtitle is often worked out as an ideological blind spot through an application of the semiotic square and its disclosed point of double negation.

Lenses into War

Digital Vérité in Iraq War Films

Stacey Peebles

In 1898 J. Stuart Blackton and his friend Albert E. Smith released the first war movie, a short film for nickelodeon theaters called *Tearing Down the Spanish Flag*. For a running time of ninety seconds, it showed Blackton's hands pulling down the flag of Spain and then running up the Stars and Stripes. Audiences were transfixed with such topical fare, as the Spanish-American War was on everyone's mind. Blackton and Smith quickly followed their hit with *The Battle of Manila Bay*, putting people right in the middle of Admiral George Dewey's famous victory by filling a bathtub and floating small cutouts of battleships around in the water; Blackton's wife contributed some carefully aimed cigarette smoke to mimic the effects of cannon fire.[1]

War films have always relied on special effects for verisimilitude, though in later years the Blacktons' bathtub gave way to venues that were life-size and often very real. D. W. Griffith used footage shot near the British front lines in World War I for his 1918 film *Hearts of the World*, and later films like William Wellman's *Wings* (1927) and Howard Hughes's *Hell's Angels* (1930) used veteran pilots for the stunning aviation sequences. During production of the latter, two of those pilots and a mechanic were killed during filming, forcing Hughes himself to step in when the other flyers refused to perform a dangerous maneuver. Hughes got the shot but crashed the plane and broke several bones as well.[2] "When we watch a war movie," Guy Westwell has noted, "we should always try to remember that, even within the demarcated realm of fantasy and escape that is the cinema, what we are seeing on screen is the actual apparatus of war: real airplanes, real warships, real uniforms, even real soldiers who frequently act as extras and advisors."[3] That's often true, though that apparatus of war is supplemented by artificial elements like fake blood, blank rounds, and, more recently, green-screening and computer-generated imagery in order to amp up the realism. Movies like *The Longest Day* (Zanuck et al., 1962), *Apocalypse Now* (Coppola, 1979), *Henry V* (Branagh, 1989), *Saving Private Ryan* (Spielberg, 1998), and *The Hurt Locker* (Bigelow, 2008) have been as much discussed for their sequences and effects as for their story lines. In the history of the war film, everything from toys to real soldiers to cleverly manipulated pixels has been employed to project the image of combat—to make it all real for the viewer.

As technology evolved, cameras grew lighter and more portable, making the roughest and most dangerous terrain more accessible to filmmakers and making the technology itself accessible to those outside of the filmmaking industry. When American soldiers went to war in Afghanistan and Iraq in the early years of the twenty-first century, this was the newest element of their war experience—the ability to take along their own digital devices and capture the wars as they happened, from their own perspective. But they didn't need any special effects. Advances in technology enabled them to strap cameras on their helmets or in their Humvees and go directly into combat, the small devices recording stretches of boredom as well as the flash of an improvised explosive device, an enemy soldier's sudden gunfire, or the reactions of civilians. Soldiers could keep the results for themselves or disseminate them to family, friends, and broader audiences online, giving noncombatants an unprecedented view into what it was like to go to war. The image of combat—real combat, complete with real blood and real casualties—could be seen by others in a way that was direct, unfiltered, and undiluted by the influence of institutions or other interested parties.

And this, in fact, is itself the new special effect in films about the Iraq War: the inclusion of "digital vérité," images and videos that appear within the frame of the larger narrative and are often a prominent element in the plot as well.[4] These digital elements resemble the kind of raw, grainy material that real soldiers might record and post online—hence the term *vérité*—and if they are created for the films in which they appear, their design mimics as closely as possible this up-close and personal perspective on the war experience. (It should be noted that Iraq War films aren't alone in using these kinds of "amateur" videos to enhance their storytelling; horror films like *The Blair Witch Project* [Sánchez and Myrick, 1999], *Paranormal Activity* [Peli, 2007], and *Cloverfield* [Reeves, 2008] rely heavily on either digital or videotaped "found footage" to heighten their emotional effect.[5] The success of these films in particular suggests that if a story has the raw, personal immediacy that footage like this can impart, then the experience is more powerful for the audience—that is, scarier. But as I'll argue, the creators of these war films want their viewers to leave the theater having felt more than escapist thrills and chills.)

Garrett Stewart has identified this inclusion of the digital as a defining genre element of films about the Iraq War, but he argues that it is also evidence of slack storytelling and a weak aesthetic. In his 2009 article "Digital Fatigue," he writes that "battle fatigue has grown stylistic, afflicting the picturing as well as its scene," adding that "with no genre formats to count on, these narratives can only project a visual 'look,' where the graininess of the image, infrared or video, must stand in for the true grittiness of the mission." For Stewart, the problem is that this use of vérité puts the viewer too close to the action, eliminating the aesthetic distance necessary for dramatic development and, ultimately, a point: "In analytic as well as digital terms, there's no exposure time, no lag for ironic or polemical reframing." In contrast, he points to films like *Apocalypse Now*, which uses both historical and stylistic distance to "give us new eyes for the unthinkable."[6]

Stewart and other critics are right to point out this common feature of films that deal with contemporary war, but there's more at stake here than a technique that elides critique, as Stewart argues. War films have, over the years, used visual effects to convey the extreme nature of the combat experience, but these films about the Iraq War include digital vérité to emphasize that it's possible, and even necessary, to see more of war than is allowed by such wide-angle perspectives as are employed by the mainstream media, the military, or auteurs like Coppola. Ironic or polemical reframing can be a valuable practice, but it tends to gloss, mythologize, or otherwise distort the experience of the ordinary soldier or others who live through war from the ground up. The truth in vérité here is the inclusion of that perspective and, often, the creation of a deeper empathy for those who inhabit it. The loss of an ironic or distant representational stance is not, as Stewart claims, a lack of style or thesis. Rather, it reflects a desire to find a more personal perspective on the horrific muddle of contemporary war that doesn't reduce the conflict into an easily manageable or singular narrative. Art, after all, should strive to connect us with another's experience or way of seeing the world. As a nation that sends soldiers into conflicts like these, shouldn't we care deeply about what that experience is like?

To that end, film has co-opted the digital as an additional lens into the contemporary war experience. Fictional films like *Stop-Loss* (Peirce, 2008), *In the Valley of Elah* (Haggis, 2007), *The Battle for Haditha* (Broomfield,

2007), and *Redacted* (De Palma, 2007) all use created digital vérité elements in order to close the distance between the soldier's and the viewer's perspectives. These digital lenses, included within the larger frame of the narrative, vary from relatively few (*Stop-Loss, Elah*) to so numerous that they take over the film (*Redacted*). The films using more lenses also more openly address the differences in perspective among soldiers, noncombatants, and those on the home front, and how those differences can affect the way images are seen or even constructed; the more closely you're able to see, these films imply, even through contrasting viewpoints, the more understanding you'll gain of the total ecosystem of war. *Standard Operating Procedure* (Morris, 2008), however, approaches that goal differently. In his investigation of the circumstances behind the real photographs and videos at the center of the Abu Ghraib scandal, director Errol Morris is also trying to augment the viewer's perspective on war. But the digital photos and videos don't serve to enhance the story that the film is telling, as in these other works. Instead, the film enhances the way we see these digital artifacts, which, as Morris shows in the interviews, is often limited or otherwise misleading; vérité needs film here, rather than the other way around. Despite these different approaches, all five films indicate that in the representation of war, a single frame is never enough. Though the soldier's experience may never be wholly communicable, these films use more lenses to help bring us closer, in the hope that we will see, empathize, and respond.

Looking into War

The way we look at war has been steadily changing since the nineteenth century, when photography first enabled images of the Mexican-American War and the Civil War to be disseminated to the wider world. In subsequent years combat was recorded on film (during World War I and, much more extensively, World War II), on television (as the Vietnam War was featured nightly on network stations and the Persian Gulf War played twenty-four hours a day on cable), and digitally (as the wars in Iraq and Afghanistan have been blogged, YouTubed, Facebooked, and otherwise posted online). As technology developed, people became more aware of the power of images to both shape public perception and generate income; as a result, the military and those capturing the images often worked together in ways that have been at times symbiotic and at times fractious.

During World Wars I and II, the military grew more and more aware of the propagandistic power of media, particularly film. In turn, filmmakers relied on the military for transport, safety, and communications, and military censors carefully reviewed the results of their work. *The Battle of the Somme* (1916), which features documentary footage of the battle, sold 20 million tickets in two months, its images of dead soldiers countered by final shots of troops marching enthusiastically onward. During World War II, newsreels carefully framed the war effort and its progress for eager audiences, and directors John Ford, Frank Capra, and William Wyler worked with the Office of War Information to produce, respectively, documentaries like *December 7th* (1943), *Why We Fight* (1942–1945), and *The Memphis Belle* (1944).[7] The media remained largely aligned with the military in the early years of the Vietnam War as well, until political and social conflicts at home and revelations about the war's tactics, costs, and justifications began to wear on the public's credulity in the late 1960s. Despite the role that the media itself played in exposing the war's horrors on nightly broadcasts and the widespread celebration of investigatory reporters like Bob Woodward and Carl Bernstein, a lingering distrust of journalism (in addition to the military) crept into the popular consciousness and became especially evident in representations of the Vietnam War.

In those stories, professional journalism appears as a misguided or at best inadequate attempt to capture, categorize, and comprehend the political and psychological realities of war. Writing pieces for *Esquire* that he eventually collected into the book *Dispatches*, Michael Herr took pains to distinguish himself from more straight-ahead journalists, who were eager to report on "the Mission." Calling himself a war correspondent is "pure affectation," he says, adding that "conventional journalism could no more reveal this war than conventional firepower could win it, all it could do was take the most profound event of the American decade and turn it into a communications pudding, taking its most obvious, undeniable history and making it into a secret history." These were the careerist hacks who "wrote down every word that the generals and officials told them to write," their association with and reliance on the military a guarantee of their stories' falsification.[8] (Herr himself takes a different tack, and his rambling, pained, and poignant book is now considered a classic by many.)

In Francis Ford Coppola's *Apocalypse Now* (1979), Captain Willard (Martin Sheen) lands on a beach with soldiers who are escorting him upriver and encounters none other than Coppola himself, in a sly cameo as a video journalist. Coppola's character is filming the soldiers, urging them, "Just go by, like you're fighting!"[9] They ruin the illusion by staring in amazement at these filmmakers who travel across the world to a war zone in search of an authentic image, only to ask for more artifice when they get there. Stanley Kubrick uses much the same motif in *Full Metal Jacket* (1987), as a group of three photojournalists pan past soldiers firing on and taking fire from a ruined group of buildings. Some stare, though many mock the frame. "Hey, start the cameras! This is Vietnam: The Movie!" one shouts. Joker (Matthew Modine), the protagonist, also writes for the *Stars and Stripes*, and in a story meeting he jousts with his editor over appropriate content. He suggests covering the rumor that the Viet Cong may attack during the Tet holiday, a rumor that will prove correct; the editor dismisses that idea in favor of a story about Ann-Margret's imminent arrival. Joker is resistant, and the editor explains wearily, "I've told you we run two basic stories here. Grunts who give half their pay to buy gooks toothbrushes and deodorants—winning of hearts and minds, okay? And combat action that results in a kill—winning the war." When Joker himself is interviewed by the photojournalist team, his comments reveal the absurdity of his editor's message, of trying to win hearts and minds at the same time one tries to win a war: "I wanted to see exotic Vietnam, the jewel of Southeast Asia. I wanted to meet interesting and stimulating people of an ancient culture . . . and kill them. I wanted to be the first kid on my block to get a confirmed kill."[10]

The shared impression here is that the military and the mainstream media are always going to miss the point and merely give the public what they already expect to see rather than an authentic look at the conflict. Of course, *Apocalypse Now* and *Full Metal Jacket* are themselves big-budget, mythmaking representations of the war. They are masterpieces, communicating something about Vietnam that was missed by, say, John Wayne's *The Green Berets* (Wayne et al., 1968), though they make use of the kind of historical and aesthetic distance that's precisely what Stewart appreciates and what the use of digital vérité seeks to counter. Distance can create a moving narrative, but it can also go too far, after all, as it did in 1991. In CNN's twenty-four-hour coverage of the Gulf War, the eerie, real-time images of incoming missiles and bombs descending to their targets looked to many like video games, eliding a sense of lives lost or other human costs. The coverage prompted Jean Baudrillard to go so far as to claim that the war "did not take place"—that it was not felt, reflected upon, or grappled with.[11] This, then, was too much distance; the common soldier had literally disappeared. As in previous wars, the public had to rely almost entirely on mainstream journalism's reporting for information about the war's causes and effects, its methods, successes, and failures, but they weren't seeing enough. A number of scholarly studies addressing the problems inherent in the media's representation of the war and, as they argue, their corresponding manipulation of public opinion reflect that concern, with titles like *Taken by Storm, Seeing Through the Media,* and *Triumph of the Image.*[12] And so, ten years later, when America went to war again, the use of digital technology as a tool for "citizen journalism" was a welcome development, providing purportedly unfiltered access to what was really going on. Axel Bruns describes the appeal of this kind of practice:

> Much as open source processes can be described as a form of probabilistic software development which relies on the overall drive towards quality that is likely if positive contributions well outweigh negative ones, citizen journalism therefore can be seen as a probabilistic form of news coverage. It assumes that given a sufficiently engaged and diverse group of contributors, and given the presence of more constructive than destructive contributions, the community's coverage of any one news story (and thus its overall understanding of the news) will improve over time—and indeed often quite rapidly as enthusiastic contributors make a large number of comments and additions in a short time.[13]

Enlisted men and women could now be "soldier journalists" with an easy way to capture and share their own war stories. One Iraq War blogger, Colby Buzzell, comments that as early as 2003 and 2004, soldiers thought nothing of snapping pictures during firefights and attaching camcorders to their helmets during raids and missions.[14] For a generation already used to collectively archiving their lives, the impulse was natural. And more comprehensively than the diaries or snapshots of previous generations, contemporary soldiers have been able to capture the moving images of their own perspective and to show others, quite literally, what it looks like to be in their shoes.

Iraq and the Additional Lens

In the Iraq War films that show soldiers actively engaged in this archival work as well as the products of their recording, a concern with proximity, rather than distance, is central to the films' claim to a more personal, and therefore more realistic and affecting, representation of war. *Stop-Loss* and *In the Valley of Elah* use digital photos and videos to show the lives of American soldiers overseas, particularly those who die either in battle or while back home, revealing both the nature of their service and how they are remembered. *The Battle for Haditha* and *Redacted* use even more images, showing combat from the numerous and varied perspectives of soldiers as well as of Iraqi combatants and civilians. The perspectives aren't consistent with each other, but that's the point; if war is a complex system, it should be seen from all vantages for maximum understanding. And finally, *Standard Operating Procedure* uses the real images of the Abu Ghraib scandal not to support the story of the film, but rather as a starting point in need of further elucidation. More views, more lenses are needed, Errol Morris suggests, but he relies on film rather than digital images for that necessary addition.

In *Stop-Loss*, Brendan King (Ryan Phillippe) is a soldier whose final days of service in Iraq are punctuated by a devastating attack on his squad. After the soldiers give chase to a car that fires on them at a checkpoint, they are ambushed in an alley, where three of them are killed and one gravely wounded. King earns a Purple Heart and a Bronze Star for his actions saving the others, but he also discovers after returning home that he has been stop-lossed, ordered to return to Iraq despite what he thought was the completion of his service. As a result, he goes AWOL. In his absence, his fellow soldier Tommy Burgess (Joseph Gordon-Levitt) continues a downward spiral of drinking and violent behavior that finally culminates in his suicide. The film follows these soldiers' physical and emotional trauma as a result of their war experience, focusing on King's insistence that he cannot—and should not—go back to Iraq.

The film opens with a video labeled "Episode 312" and shows the soldiers near the end of their tour. The high episode number alludes to both their extensive experience and their propensity to record it; it's not clear which soldier is responsible for the videos, though later shots of Isaac Butler (Rob Brown) holding a camera suggest that they may be his. This particular episode shows them singing, interacting with Iraqis, and going about their business in Iraq; its raw, amateurish feel is emphasized when the film cuts to the ambush sequence, which is shot in a polished and cinematic style. After that sequence ends, another homemade video honors the soldiers who died and the one who was wounded, with intertitles serving as epitaphs and closing text that says "We Will Not Forget."[15]

Videos are used sparingly in the remainder of the film. As Burgess falls apart, exhibiting signs of extreme trauma, short videos appear during the larger narrative that show him during happier times: being baptized in Iraq by another soldier known as Preacher, who died in the ambush, and talking and tussling happily with his squad. The videos are the soldiers' own memorials to their experiences together in Iraq, to those they lost, and to those they are losing. This is the way they see themselves, and *Stop-Loss*'s inclusion of them underscores the intensity of the soldiers' bonding in Iraq, their loss of innocence, and their subsequent trauma. Put in their shoes, the audience can more immediately empathize with why a soldier would drink too much, why he would go AWOL, why he would commit suicide. The additional lens here allows the viewer to see a soldier's war story from his own perspective, framed for his own use.

In the Valley of Elah includes similar videos that figure much more prominently in the plot. Hank Deerfield (Tommy Lee Jones) is a character based on Lanny Davis, a retired army staff sergeant whose son went AWOL after returning home from a tour in Iraq. After the body is discovered, Hank is unsatisfied with explanatory reports from the military and struggles to uncover the circumstances of the murder and brutal dismemberment of his son, Mike (Jonathan Tucker). While visiting Mike's barracks for clues to his whereabouts, he covertly pockets Mike's cell phone and later pays a technician to retrieve the photos and videos from the phone's memory. The phone has been "seriously fried" while in Iraq, the technician tells him, and throughout his search Hank periodically reviews the fragmented, pixellated videos that Mike took overseas. As he gets further into the mystery of Mike's death, he also gets further into the mystery of Mike's service in Iraq, as illustrated by the raw, damaged videos of Iraqi children running off with the soldiers' football, a chaotic raid on an Iraqi house, an injured man screaming, and Mike hitting something while driving a Humvee. Hank also lingers over one of the photos, a street scene with a blue van.

Mike's life at war strikes Hank as quite different from his own. A former military man himself, he lives by the book, in a world determined by order and rules—polishing his shoes carefully, making his bed military-style, appearing neat and controlled even under the worst of circumstances. "There are rules to combat," he tells a detective's young son, explaining why pulling a gun on someone wielding a sword would be a violation of the martial code. And when that detective suggests that Mike's fellow soldiers might be responsible for his death and mutilation, he reacts angrily and impatiently:

"You have not been to war so you're not going to understand this. You do not fight beside a man and then do *that* to him."[16]

But the videos don't seem to show order, adherence to rules, or close camaraderie—they show barely controlled chaos, a chaos that is inversely reflected in the deadened eyes and blank face of Mike's fellow soldier Penning, who eventually confesses to Mike's murder. The killing resulted from a fight turned suddenly extreme among four soldiers, all highly traumatized from their war experience. The digital artifacts are direct evidence of that trauma—the dangerous raids, the betrayal even by children, the torture of an injured man, and, most significantly, Mike's accidental killing of a child. As Hank now understands, Mike had panicked while driving a Humvee, seeing an obstacle in the road and asking, "What do I do?" The other soldier insists, "Do not stop. Do not fucking stop!" (As a soldier named Ortiz explains to Hank, standing orders are never to stop while driving, since if you do, "shitheads pop out with RPGs and kill you all dead.") The Humvee bumps over something, and Mike stops, leaving the Humvee to walk slowly toward an inert mass in the road. As the other soldier yells at him repeatedly to return, Mike raises his cell phone and snaps a picture—the street scene that Hank now understands records the body of a child.[17]

"I think on another night it would have been Mike with a knife and me in the field," Penning says during his confession. "I think he was the smart one. I think he could see." Ultimately, however, Hank is the one who sees, but only once he puts the digital pieces together. The murder is solved when Penning confesses, but the real mystery is the events that led to it, the untold story of what the Iraq War was like for this particular soldier. Here, the additional lenses are significant for the viewer as well as the characters in the story—they allow others on the home front access to a raw, unfiltered, and telling record of a soldier's war experience.[18]

These artifacts are personal and probably not intended to be shared, though we as the audience are privy to their content; they provide Hank and the viewer with enough information to form a fuller and arguably more realistic understanding of an on-the-ground wartime experience—and a devastating one at that. *The Battle for Haditha* takes the use of digital videos a step further, including the perspective of those fighting with al-Qaeda against the Americans' presence and showing how those behind the camera can shape and frame what the lens reveals—and thus the narrative—to their own ends and for a public audience. The videos are incorporated sparingly into the film, but as in *Elah,* they are crucial to the plot. An opening intertitle notes that the film will present a fictionalized version of events in November 2005, when a roadside improvised explosive device, or IED, in Haditha killed one marine and injured two others. Following the explosion, marines killed twenty-four Iraqi men, women, and children. The story follows the group of marines targeted by the IED, the two men who set up and detonate the device, and an extended Iraqi family living in the area who have gathered to celebrate a boy's circumcision. Tension builds as the stories are inevitably drawn together—the family sees the bomb being planted but are unsure what to do about it. As one older woman comments, "If we tell the Americans the terrorists will kill us. If we keep quiet the American will say we're cooperating with the insurgents. What should we do?"[19] When the two men detonate the bomb, the marines react with fear and anger, shooting many people who they think may be responsible, while the real bombers escape unnoticed.

The film is sympathetic toward all the characters: the family, who are trying to maintain some semblance of a normal life; the soldiers, for whom IED attacks are ruinously frequent; and even the bombers, who also feel trapped by circumstance. The older of the two men laments his former career in the Iraqi military, commenting that he "never wanted this. . . . The Americans made the insurgency when they got rid of the army." They obtain the bomb from al-Qaeda operatives, whom they regard with suspicion for their indiscriminate killing and fundamentalist beliefs. Later, when the older man watches the marines kill Iraqi civilians in response to the explosion, he remarks with dismay to his al-Qaeda companion, "We're killing our own people." But the other man explains that the killings are all part of a larger trap for the American soldiers, in addition to the trap of the IED: "I want you to film everything, to show what the Americans are doing," he explains to the two men. "The world will see today how the Americans behave." The trap works and is made more effective by a video interview with Safa, a young, wounded girl who is the only survivor of her family and whom we see being coached on what to say about her injuries and the killings that took place in her house. The video is shown to members of al-Qaeda to rally them behind the cause, and four months later it is broadcast on an American news show and credited to "an Iraqi journalism student." "Student footage reveals Marine cover-up," the screen reads, showing images of the aftermath of the incident and of Safa. The videos' content is provoked specifically for the purpose of dissemination, but it is also considered by those who record it to be "the truth" rather than manufactured propaganda. It is the only way, they say, to show the world the reality of the war in Iraq.[20]

The killings mean different things to different people. They are proof that, for one marine, "the battle was won," but an al-Qaeda operative insists that "the Marines have lost the battle for Haditha."[21] Despite the contradictions, this, too, is vérité, as footage of the killings reveals the various up-close perspectives on the outbreak of violence. Like *Stop-Loss* and *Elah, Haditha* uses these digital perspectives to reflect the ways those creating them see the world of war. Unlike the other films, however, *Haditha* also reveals how those frames can be limited. Therefore, the film broadens its own stance by adding various lenses within the story and by revealing more about those behind the cameras as well, particularly the pressures that lead to their decisions about how and where to point them.

In *Redacted,* the additional lenses take over the larger frame to such a degree that they become primary rather than secondary. Digital vérité is not just incorporated into the plot—it *is* the plot, since the film has no framing narrative and consists entirely of fragments of videos from various sources. These fragments are created artifacts (as in the previous films), but *Redacted* self-consciously claims them as authentic, as *true* vérité. "This film is entirely fiction," an intertitle notes, discouraging viewers from associating the characters with real people, but also says that the film "visually documents imagined events before, during, and after a 2006 rape and murder in Samarra."[22] There is truth to be had, the film asserts, in assuming these perspectives and presenting them, however numerously, for the viewer; this will get to the emotional heart of what is usually left out, censored, or redacted by the single master narrative favored by other films, the mainstream media, or the military.

One of the main sources of that "visual documentation" is a video diary by a soldier, Angel Salazar (Izzy Diaz), who hopes that the project will help get him into film school. He titles the diary "Tell Me No Lies," and says it will be the unadulterated truth of his war experience. There will be no "smash cuts" or adrenaline-pumping soundtrack and "no logical narrative to help make sense of it all." It will be the opposite, he implies, of a big-budget, commercial production.[23] The next visual source is exactly that, a French documentary called *Barrage* (which is translated as "Checkpoint" in the subtitles). Handel's "Sarabande" plays nondiegetically while time-lapse photography and French voice-over follow the procedures, tedium, and danger of soldiers manning a vehicle checkpoint.[24] (One shot of a scorpion swarmed by ants is a cinephile's nod to *The Wild Bunch.*) *Redacted* switches from the French documentary's high production values to Salazar's raw, gritty footage and includes a number of other sources such as a television station called ATV (clearly modeled on Al-Jazeera), several different websites with streaming video (including one in Arabic), and footage from surveillance cameras that capture the soldiers' conversations and, later, their testimony.

The various sources follow the central group of soldiers as a pregnant woman is shot and killed when her car speeds toward the checkpoint; when their sergeant is killed by an IED planted in some rubble near where Iraqi children play soccer; and when soldiers B. B. Rush (Daniel Stewart Sherman) and Reno Flake (Patrick Carroll) lead Salazar and Lawyer McCoy (Rob Devaney) on a night raid, during which they rape a young girl and then kill her and her family. Salazar and McCoy are deeply disturbed by the incident, and Salazar vows to use the footage he surreptitiously took of the raid as an exposé: "When I get back," he tells his camera, "everyone's going to see this, the truth about what's going on here." He then becomes a prominent subject himself when a van speeds up and several men interrupt his monologue by seizing him forcibly and speeding off. His fate is depicted through several sources: an Arabic website that shows a video of his decapitated body lying in a field; a report on the body by "Central Euro News"; and an ATV broadcast that states that Salazar's killing was done in response to the soldiers' rape and murder. Salazar's beheading is also shown in a video taken by the kidnappers. The film's denouement follows McCoy's attempts to implicate his squadmates, first with face and voice disguised in a video on the "Get Out of Iraq Campaign" website, and later to unsympathetic superior officers as part of a hostile interrogation that reframes or restates McCoy's testimony to undermine his credibility (something his father warned him about during a video chat). Eventually, however, the media picks up the story, and Rush and Flake are charged and deposed. Each almost comically implicates himself, though they seem unconcerned. This is all "a dog and pony show for the folks back home," Flake says, gesturing toward the camera.[25] Of the four, only McCoy finds himself safely returned stateside, recorded with his wife and friends as they celebrate in a bar. One asks him for a war story, and his response bemoans the horrible things he had seen; he laments the "snapshots in my brain" that won't go away. As elegiac music from "Tosca" begins to play—breaking the frame of the "visual documentation" for the first time—McCoy's image fades out.

In *Redacted*, everything is mediated. The soldiers' lives are captured by their own cameras, by television, by websites, and by surveillance devices. The motivations of those behind the lenses vary, from Salazar's desire to exculpate himself through exposé to his kidnappers' displaying their vengeance on video. Even the impersonal gaze of the surveillance cameras indicates someone's need to watch, to patrol, to record. The soldier's experience at war, long only communicable to others by military-censored letters or stories after the war's end, has become filmable and disseminable, fodder for the soldier's own communications as well as those of others. *Redacted* introduces us to the varied collection of lenses that make war widely visible, even if, as *Haditha* suggests as well, that vision changes from frame to frame.

The final sequence of the film is emblematic of this approach. Titled "Collateral Damage—Actual Photographs from the Iraq War," it consists of still images of the corpses of women and children with the identifying characteristics of their faces blacked out, or redacted. This was not director Brian De Palma's original intent but the decision of the film's distributor, Magnolia Pictures, which vaguely cited an "untenable legal situation."[26] The redactions did, however, suit De Palma's claim that big institutions don't want the public to see what's really going on in Iraq. And so, like the film itself, De Palma relies on created elements to get at the real truth. In the cascade of images, two are unobscured—one of the pregnant woman who was shot at the checkpoint, and one of the young girl who was the target of the soldiers' crime.[27] Ken Provencher writes that these two staged, fictional photos "betray their own falseness, and yet the stark effectiveness of the final photo overrides any viewer confusion over what is 'actual' and what is not." That photo of the young girl's body may be a created artifact, but in including it in the film—as the final, tragic grace note, no less—De Palma "illustrate[s] a crime whose mediation was initially the exclusive property of criminals," therefore "seiz[ing] the power of mediation from those who commit atrocities."[28] *Redacted* may be a fictionalized account of a real crime, but it emphasizes the need to see, recognize, and respond to that crime and others like it—some of the many, many consequences of a protracted, messy war. If a film that uses created digital elements can achieve that vision, then so much the better. That's certainly preferable, De Palma suggests, to not looking at all; art, particularly that which takes war as its subject, requires new ways of seeing. "The movie attempts to bring the reality of what happened in Iraq to the American people," De Palma said of the film in 2008. "We haven't seen these images from Iraq. Such pictures exist, but there's no interest in them in the mainstream media, which is mainly owned by the corporate establishment. If we get these images in front of a mass audience, maybe we can affect things."[29] Seeing these things should evoke emotion. It should change you—and, De Palma implies, change your politics as well.

De Palma says that the public hasn't seen the images of real devastation from Iraq, and certainly the government is aware of the effects that certain kinds of widely broadcast images can have on the larger political climate. But one set of disturbing images made headlines around the world when they were released in 2004—the digital photos and videos taken at the Abu Ghraib prison complex. (Hundreds of photos and a number of videos were investigated, though a few of the photos were reprinted and disseminated with particular speed and frequency. The videos are less well known, possibly because their explicit content made them unsuitable for television broadcast.) In the documentary *Standard Operating Procedure,* filmmaker Errol Morris interviews most of the major players in the Abu Ghraib scandal, including soldiers Sabrina Harmon and Lynndie England, Brigadier General Janis Karpinski, and Brent Pack, the army special agent who retrieved, organized, and evaluated the photos for evidence of criminal acts. In this film, the still and moving digital images are displayed and discussed by those who took them and who appeared in them, and the circumstances surrounding some of the most famous photos are reenacted by actors in a highly aestheticized style. "I was interested in how pictures can often mislead us, they can reveal things and also conceal things at the same time," Morris has said. "And that irony is something which I believe is the heart of the movie."[30] In this sense, Morris is after something different than the other directors. These digital artifacts are a starting point rather than an addition or the sole medium; instead of serving as different vantage points on a larger story, the well-known images are challenged and reframed by the interviews and reenactments. Digital vérité, in this case, isn't vérité—at least not at first glance. It needs film to enhance, to complicate, and to explicate.

In 2004, the Abu Ghraib prison had become the interrogation center of Iraq, and several soldiers note their initial surprise at the questioning techniques that were being used. They were assured that those techniques were acceptable, that they were, in fact, the norm: men stripped naked and held in stress positions, the use of sleep deprivation and sexual humiliation, and, eventually, physical abuse by interrogators and dogs. Like so many other people, the soldiers working at the prison archived their lives on their digital cameras, taking hundreds of pictures and sharing the images with one another. "Everybody knew" what was going on, says England, and everyone had copies of the photos. The ease with which soldiers took the pictures and passed them back and forth reveal two things, note Morris and Philip Gourevitch in a *New Yorker* article on the scandal: that the soldiers "never fully accepted what was happening as normal, and that they assumed they had nothing to hide."[31] In other words, the film explains, the soldiers were following orders and therefore, they believed, behaving appropriately, even though the actions they observed and took part in always seemed unusual in their perversity. The procedures were "standard" and extraordinary at the same time.

The film addresses some of the most famous photos from the scandal by combining three modes of presentation. The actual photos are shown framed in white and centered in the middle of the screen, while the interview subjects narrate the circumstances surrounding the photos' content and, in many cases, their motivation for taking the photos. Finally, Morris also includes several reenactments of the incidents in question, characterized by extreme close-ups, high-contrast lighting, and slow motion. For example, Sabrina Harmon explains the circumstances surrounding the most famous photo of the scandal, which shows a man wearing a hooded cloak, his arms outstretched, standing on a box. The ambiguous torture suggested by the wires attached to his hands and the visual associations called up by a Klanlike hood and Christlike posture made this photo representative of the scandal, stirring outrage around the world. "Gilligan," as the soldiers called him, was told that if he stepped off the box, the wires would electrocute him. In fact, "it was just words," says Harmon, since the wires were not actually electrified. The gravity of the situation is suggested by the reenactment, which features extreme close-ups of feet stepping on a box, fingers being fitted with wires, and a cloaked head appearing in slow motion. That gravity is subverted, however, by Harmon's description of the event's denouement—the man became one of the workers in Abu Ghraib and was eventually proven innocent. Harmon smiles as she remembers him.[32] And so how should this photo be seen and understood? As the generalized image of a war gone wrong, as the serious mistreatment of an individual's body and self, or as the relatively innocuous treatment of someone who later went free?

Brent Pack, investigating the photos for evidence of wrongdoing, talks explicitly about the nature of photography in a case like this and the ways photos can be seen and understood differently. He explains his own job: to collect and organize the images, to discover when and by whom they were taken, and then to determine whether or not the subjects of the photos constitute criminal acts. It is, he says initially, a straightforward business. "When you look at this whole case as one great big media event," he says, "you kind of lose focus. These pictures actually depict several separate incidents of possible abuse or possible standard operating procedure. All you can do is present what you know to be factual. You can't bring in emotion or politics into the court." Causing physical injury or sexual humiliation are criminal acts, he explains, and photos of soldiers appearing to punch prisoners or forcing them to pile onto each other while naked are denoted as such. But because the photo of "Gilligan" doesn't appear to show real electrical wires, he labels it "standard operating procedure," along with another of a naked prisoner in a stress position with underwear on his head. "They weren't being tortured per se," he explains. "They were going through discomfort to try and aid in obtaining information." In that sense, his view aligns with Harmon's that the threat was "just words," although he explains that view with dispassion rather than the affection that Harmon expresses. A few minutes later in the film, Pack continues: "Photographs are what they are. You can interpret them differently, but what the photograph depicts is what it is. You can put any kind of meaning to it, but you are seeing what happened at that snapshot in time. You can read emotion on their face and feelings in their eyes, but it's nothing that can be entered into fact. All you can do is report what's in the picture."[33]

Pack is a professional, and he makes a distinction between what factually exists in the photographic frame and the way these photos have been *seen*. But even he admits that context—the perspective from which one sees—can still be everything. After explaining his evaluation of the photos as evidence of criminal acts or SOP, he adds, "I been in the army for twenty years. I went to Desert Storm One. I spent four months at Guantanamo Bay. People who haven't been where I've been, I can't expect them to see the pictures the same way." He has, he implies, been desensitized to such images and as such is able to review them without emotional interference. And yet he still understands what other people are seeing. Pack comments on the most damning photo of Harmon, showing her smiling happily with Charles Graner behind a pyramid of naked prisoners piled on the floor. This was what sealed their fate, he says: "You look in their eyes and they look like they're having fun."[34] These images' significance rests not only on the hard facts of what they depict, but on the motivations and consequences that they imply, rightly or wrongly.

Other interview subjects comment similarly on the hidden subjectivity of the photographs and the way perspective—the nature of the frame—can be everything. Lynndie England discusses one of the more famous photos, in which she holds a prisoner on a leash. The photo was taken by Graner, another soldier ten years her senior and the father of the child she conceived while at Abu Ghraib. "He would have never had me standing next to Gus [the prisoner's nickname] if the camera wasn't there," she explains, speculating that Graner probably enjoyed the irony of a petite woman dominating a larger male prisoner.[35] She also notes that in the original photo, Megan Ambuhl appeared in profile on the edge of the frame. But Graner cropped her out—and so, in the photo disseminated in the media, England appears alone. (Graner and Ambuhl were later revealed to be secretly involved while at Abu Ghraib and married during his imprisonment; England wonders if Graner cropped Ambuhl out in order to protect her from any future charges. It's a compelling theory, though one wonders why he wouldn't have protected himself as well.) A soldier named Javal Davis comments, not without humor, on a photo of him that was broadcast on television when the scandal broke—an old image of him running track and clearing a hurdle. But because the news cropped the photo to show only his face, Davis looks intense, strained, "like this mean-ass guy." And Ambuhl remarks on photos of a blood-smeared room, in which a prisoner had shot at a soldier with a smuggled pistol and then been shot in the leg during the struggle. The image of the empty, bloody room stokes the imagination inappropriately, she says: "Your imagination can run wild when you just see blood. The pictures only show you a fraction of a second. You don't see forward, you don't see backward. You don't see outside the frame."[36] A picture may capture a moment factually, as Pack puts it, but it's only a single frame, a constricted perspective. It's a perspective that can also be colored by the intentions of the image-maker and the assumptions of the viewer, thus resulting in a moment frozen in time that suggests a larger narrative behind it, a story that may or may not correspond to actual events.

For Morris, the digital images that came out of Abu Ghraib are indeed revealing—of a scandal, of "standard procedures" gone horribly awry, and of a war slipping further out of control—but they aren't enough. They require the film itself, the analog medium. They need commentary, even by soldiers who may be seeking to rationalize their actions, and they need revisiting, even in a highly aestheticized fashion. If photographs can reveal, as Morris says, they can also conceal, and the same can be said of filmed interviews and reenactments. Like *Redacted, Standard Operating Procedure* also suggests that everything is mediated. Unlike De Palma's film, however, not everything here is visible. These digital frames are limited—not just by their makers' motivations and perspectives, but by the very nature of the frame as a constricting device. Morris, then, takes the most sophisticated approach to the marriage of film and digital artifacts, aggregating the methods of the other filmmakers. In order to tell a contemporary war story, he contends, one must look through more and various lenses while always considering the motives of the framer and the restrictions of the frame itself. The best way to see is to try to do so in more formats and from more angles, even if that leads to more questions. For Morris, nothing is in itself vérité, but that doesn't mean that we should stop looking, feeling, or thinking. It doesn't mean that we can't strive to understand more about the nature of war and what it means when people become entangled by hoods, wires, leashes, blood, and each other.

Views of Tragedy

All of these films indicate that telling a war story requires more than one lens, whether that lens is the military's, the media's, or the soldiers'. This could suggest that these films take a relativist or apolitical approach to war, as some critics writing about Iraq War films generally have discussed; this is Garrett Stewart's claim, and A. O. Scott has written of *The Hurt Locker* that its "intentions to stay out of messy debates about the wisdom or effectiveness of American military policy is perhaps the least distinctive thing about it." (Scott also notes, however, that films like *Redacted* and *In the Valley of Elah* may be exceptions to the rule.)[37] I would argue that in fact *Stop-Loss, Elah, Haditha,* and *Redacted* all end as tragedies and thus, given their subject matter, are inherently political. That is, their tragic status makes them antiwar in nature and thus shows that the films' creators are invested in advancing certain readings of war's events and outcomes. Wherever you look, you still see war's devastation; the views may be different, but everyone is suffering. In *Stop-Loss,* Burgess commits suicide, and King ultimately decides to return to Iraq rather than abandoning his family and friends for a life across the border in Canada or Mexico. Though his decision could be read as a reaffirmation of the war effort, the intertitles that follow belie such a reading. They lament King's impossible choice, noting that eighty-one thousand troops have been stop-lossed since 2001, in addition to an undisclosed number who were stop-lossed as part of the 2007 surge. The film's closing mourns soldiers like King in the same way that the videos mourn those that died in the ambush—it's important to see, and not to forget.

Elah ends with a similarly mournful and critical note, as Hank Deerfield stops on his way back into his hometown to speak to a worker in charge of raising a school's flag. Much earlier in the film, before the revelations about his son's death, he had instructed the man in the proper way to raise the flag, telling him never to raise it upside down, because that constitutes a distress signal: "It means we're in a whole lot of trouble so come and save our ass because we don't have a prayer in hell of saving ourselves." But by film's end, this buttoned-down former military man has done just that; he has raised an inverted flag, which the camera lingers on pointedly before fading to black. The words that end *Haditha* might have been spoken by Hank's son, had he lived—Corporal Ramirez, the leader of the soldiers who killed twenty-four Iraqi civilians, reflects in a voice-over about his war experience: "Twenty years old and this is my third tour of duty. We've all seen things that will haunt us for the rest of our lives. I guess after a while you just get hardened. Become numb." And *Redacted,* of course, ends with the montage of horrific photographs, reminding viewers that the devastation of the fictionalized story is reflected and amplified in the real-life devastation suffered by Iraqis.[38]

Garrett Stewart wants war films to give us "new eyes for the unthinkable," but isn't that what these films are doing? War is big—it's a large-scale political, economic, and technological endeavor. It changes the shape of nations and their cultures. But it's also small—it's the personal, traumatic experiences of individuals, and a consideration of the former must necessarily entail a consideration of the latter. If we can see from different perspectives, heeding Errol Morris's caution that each lens is both an aperture and a restriction, shouldn't we try to do that?

Classical Greek tragedy compelled audiences with the spectacle of an extraordinary hero suffering greatly. Art becomes powerful when it moves us, and what moves us is a sense of connection, of emotional proximity to another's pain. But in tragedy, what creates that power isn't only the hero's suffering. Oedipus, Medea, and Agamemnon don't just ruin themselves, after all; they also bring down a family, a kingship, a community. The other characters' stories matter, too. We don't often get to hear how a single member of the chorus, or a messenger, or a nurse, was affected by that devastation, but imagining those perspectives lends more weight to our consideration of the hero's tragic fall and to the emotional devastation of tragedy generally.

These films similarly suggest that it's the collection of individual responses that makes us feel the tragic weight of war. Digital vérité certainly isn't the whole story, but it is a valuable addition to that collection, giving us an up-close way to see, empathize, and reflect on the newest undertakings of a very old, very violent practice.

Notes

1. Paul M. Holsinger, "*Tearing Down the Spanish Flag* (Film)," in *War and American Popular Culture: A Historical Encyclopedia,* ed. Paul Holsinger (Westport, CT: Greenwood Press, 1999), 190.

2. Rob Nixon, "*Hell's Angels,*" Turner Classic Movies, n.d., tcm.com.

3. Guy Westwell, *War Cinema: Hollywood on the Front Line* (London: Wallflower Press, 2006), 3.

4. Though soldiers fighting in Afghanistan have had access to the same technology, their stories have been the subject of far fewer films. Sebastian Junger and Tim Hetherington's documentary *Restrepo* (2010) is notable, however, because the two filmmakers rely on digital cameras to capture events at a remote and dangerous observation post in the Korengal Valley, Afghanistan, where they lived with the soldiers for a year. Hetherington was later killed while covering fighting in Libya in April 2011.

5. For a discussion of how contemporary horror films' use of video reflects concerns about surveillance and torture, see Catherine Zimmer, "Caught on Tape? The Politics of Video in the New Torture Film," in *Horror after 9/11: World of Fear, Cinema of Terror,* ed. Aviva Briefel and Sam J. Miller (Austin: University of Texas Press, 2011), 83–106.

6. Garrett Stewart, "Digital Fatigue: Imaging War in Recent American Film," *Film Quarterly* 62, no. 4 (2009): 45, 47, 48, 47.

7. Westwell, *War Cinema,* 2.

8. Michael Herr, *Dispatches* (1977; New York: Vintage Books, 1991), 212, 218, 221.

9. *Apocalypse Now* (Francis Ford Coppola, 1979), 00:27:34–00:27:54.

10. *Full Metal Jacket* (Stanley Kubrick, 1987), 1:16:13–1:17:24, 00:49:05–00:59:19, 1:22:33–1:22:52. This statement also appeared on T-shirts and bumper stickers during the 1970s, functioning as a kind of "anti-conscription" slogan.

11. Jean Baudrillard, *The Gulf War Did Not Take Place,* trans. Paul Patton (Bloomington: Indiana University Press, 1995).

12. Lance W. Bennett and David L. Paletz, eds., *Taken by Storm: The Media, Public Opinion, and U.S. Foreign Policy in the Gulf War* (Chicago: University of Chicago Press, 1994); Susan Jeffords and Lauren Rabinovitz, eds., *Seeing Through the Media: The Persian Gulf War* (New Brunswick, NJ: Rutgers University Press, 1994); Hamid Mowlana, George Gerbner, and Herbert Schiller, eds., *Triumph of the Image: The Media's War in the Persian Gulf, a Global Perspective* (Boulder, CO: Westview Press, 1992).

13. Axel Bruns, *Blogs, Wikipedia, Second Life, and Beyond: From Production to Produsage* (New York: Peter Lang, 2008), 75.

14. Colby Buzzell, *My War: Killing Time in Iraq* (New York: Berkeley Caliber, 2006), 349–50. I cover Buzzel's blog at length in my book *Welcome to the Suck: Narrating the American Soldier's Experience in Iraq* (New York: Cornell University Press, 2011).

15. *Stop-Loss* (Kimberly Peirce, 2008), 00:00:47–00:02:15, 00:11:51–00:13:22.

16. *In the Valley of Elah* (Paul Haggis, 2007), 1:01:11–1:02:45, 1:08:50–1:09:45.

17. Ibid., 1:38:15–1:42:06, 1:44:10–1:46:10, 1:46:23–1:47:15.

18. Ibid., 1:38:15–1:42:06.

19. *The Battle for Haditha,* (Nick Broomfield, 2007), 00:44:15–00:44:30.

20. Ibid., 00:37:33–00:38:09, 1:05:22–1:06:15, 1:01:20–1:01:45, 1:23:11–1:24:42.

21. Ibid., 1:20:37–1:21:03, 1:13:10–1:13:58, 1:21:11–1:21:42.

22. *Redacted* (Brian De Palma, 2007), 00:00:38–00:01:19.

23. Ibid., 00:01:21–00:04:33. *Redacted* indicates its somewhat dizzying approach to visual documentation in the first few minutes of the film, when Salazar's video introducing himself to his viewers is interrupted by another soldier, who is also making a video. "You're making a video of me, making a video of you," Salazar comments with amusement.

24. Ibid., 00:04:35–00:13:43.

25. Ibid., 1:16:31–1:19:16.

26. Ken Provencher, "*Redacted*'s Double Vision," *Film Quarterly* 62, no. 1 (2008): 38.

27. *Redacted,* 1:20:30–1:25:31.

28. Provencher, "*Redacted*'s Double Vision," 38.

29. Ali Jafaar, "Casualties of War," *Sight and Sound* 18, no. 2 (2008): 16.

30. Nick Shaeger, "Errol Morris on *Standard Operating Procedure,*" IFC.com, April 22, 2008.

31. Philip Gourevitch and Errol Morris, "Exposure: The Woman behind the Camera at Abu Ghraib," *New Yorker,* March 24, 2008, 49.

32. *Standard Operating Procedure* (Errol Morris, 2008), 00:40:42–00:43:27.

33. Ibid., 00:17:24–00:17:52, 1:27:03–1:29:11, 1:39:28–1:40:20.

34. Ibid., 1:29:12–1:29:29, 1:15:43–1:16:14.

35. Ibid., 00:14:08–00:15:56. Graner does not appear in the film; a closing intertitle notes that he is serving his own ten-year sentence and that the U.S. military will not allow him to be interviewed.

36. Ibid., 1:36:46–1:38:23, 1:38:23–1:39:29, 1:21:15–1:22:11.

37. A. O. Scott, "Apolitics and the War Film," *New York Times,* February 6, 2010, nytimes.com.

38. *In the Valley of Elah,* 00:04:27–00:05:20, 1:52:39–1:53:52; *The Battle for Haditha,* 1:27:08–1:27:49; *Redacted,* 1:23:45–1:25:31.

Beyond Panopticism

The Biopolitical Labor of Surveillance and War in Contemporary Film

Joshua Gooch

By 2005, surveillance became a multigenre banality in films inspired by the United States' various ongoing wars and the so-called global War on Terror. This film cycle included failed prestige pictures like *In the Valley of Elah* (Haggis, 2007), *Lions for Lambs* (Redford, 2007), *Stop-Loss* (Peirce, 2008), and *Redacted* (De Palma, 2007); thrillers like *Body of Lies* (Scott, 2008), *The Kingdom* (Berg, 2007), and *Syriana* (Gaghan, 2005); blockbusters like *Déjà Vu* (Scott, 2006), *The Bourne Ultimatum* (Greengrass, 2007), *The Dark Knight* (Nolan, 2008), and *Eagle Eye* (Caruso, 2008); and even absurdist comedies like *Burn after Reading* (Coen brothers, 2008). Surveillance's omnipresence in these films comes as no surprise to readers of Paul Virilio. In *War and Cinema,* Virilio laid out cinema's intimate relation with modern warfare: (1) war's reliance on sight takes advantage of cinema's technological ability to disarticulate space and time, which allows the military to survey terrain and enemy forces, making the unknown visible and open to destruction; and (2) because of the compression made possible by cinema, war increasingly becomes a production of mass spectacle. With smart bombs and "shock and awe," the U.S. military's approach to the Iraq wars succinctly illustrates these points.

Yet as useful as Virilio's analysis is, he touches only briefly on the most intriguing aspects of surveillance in this film cycle. In the 1988 introduction to the English edition, Virilio tells us that he expects Cold War nuclear deterrence strategy in the twenty-first century to be predicated on the "ubiquitous orbital vision of enemy territory." Such surveillance will be controlled, Virilio informs us, by machines rather than humans. The resulting wars, in which sight has become automated and eyeless, will privilege those powers able to command images and make decisions with the greatest speed. The strategy, Virilio says, will make "seeing and foreseeing . . . merge so closely that the actual can no longer be distinguished from the potential." Although the end of the Cold War alters the context of this privileging of sight, mechanization, and speed, Virilio's description of surveillance's ubiquity, its antagonistic relation to the human labor of watching, and its conflation of the actual and the potential is prescient given the themes and mediatory strategies of the films of this cycle.[1]

In these recent "war" films, surveillance combines the explicit threat of violence with an implicit reorganization of power and knowledge through the gaze. It's certainly not wrong to see cultural production about war as in part performing a panoptic gaze.[2] Yet this cycle's expansive and explicit representation of surveillance and its concomitant fantasies of disciplinary power also point to anxieties about the effectiveness of this power and its need for ever-more-fine-grained mechanisms of social control. Thus, "societies of control," Gilles Deleuze's term for cultures trapped in this social turn of the disciplinary screw, more adequately describes how power works in postmodern capitalism. As Deleuze notes, disciplinary societies exercise control over individuals in defined spaces and at exact times, while societies of control instead rely on rapid, short-term, and continuous control mechanisms across shifting networks of power.[3] Surveillance does not simply coincide with sight's increasing centrality in postmodern warfare; it is also part of this larger skein of social controls.

In *The Geopolitical Aesthetic*, Fredric Jameson argues that film moves beyond the panopticon with the paranoid conspiracy thrillers of the 1970s. For Jameson, these films mark "the definitive closing door of the nineteenth-century carceral imaginary, substituting instead the more intense nightmare of an open door that gives onto a world conspiratorially organized and controlled as far as the eye can see."[4] This has particular effects on the construction of the gaze in film: as power moves beyond the panopticon's tower, it ceases to hide behind the camera apparatus. Power instead suffuses the film's social world, bringing the geopolitical order into intimate yet mostly unseen contact with film narrative, which directly erupts only on rare occasions. Jameson locates this postpanoptic vision in film's delirious surfeit of images, which is mapped into conspiracy narratives that make power everywhere and nowhere, for example in *The Parallax View* (Pakula, 1974) and *Videodrome* (Cronenberg, 1983), or into self-reflexive narratives in which the film's protagonist tries to locate himself (and the audience by proxy) in the midst of this surfeit in order to understand how power works, for example in *Salvador* (Stone, 1986) and *Blow Out* (De Palma, 1981).

However, these narrative strategies in film become strained when postmodern capital goes to war. Power's explicit appearance here revises Jameson's description of an unseen yet intimate set of power relations in postpanoptic film by turning film's use of surveillance into an ambivalent mediatory strategy. On the one hand, surveillance discloses the discursive construction of vision in postmodern capital as part of and in response to contemporary warfare. On the other hand, surveillance solicits the social and economic anxieties precipitated by postmodern capital's complex of social controls as a form of work.[5] This approach contrasts with Jameson's most recent work on war and narration, "War and Representation" (reproduced as the first essay in the present collection), which heightens his focus on power's asubjective and delocated appearance: the difficulty of trying to locate oneself in the surfeit of images becomes a problem of locating oneself in the haze of war, leading him to focus on "scene," the narration of fragmented asubjective accounts of war.[6] I argue, however, that surveillance in recent war films does not map global capital's diffused economic command over labor and space but rather reveals its use of direct domination to maintain such command. Jameson's narrative field and Foucault's panoptic model both emphasize the surveiling gaze's structural impersonality, but these films focus on the gaze as work undertaken by particular people who represent particular class interests. The resulting exposition of the films of this cycle discloses larger economic issues of postmodern capitalism's war economy. By revealing the role of violence in economic antagonisms, these films map postmodern capitalism's veiled class anxieties through the gaze.

The gaze here is neither asubjective nor unclassed. In "The Gaze at Work: Knowledge Relations and Class Spectatorship," Derek Nystrom usefully describes how narrative film often reserves the ability to know and understand events for filmmakers and audiences; the gaze becomes an extension of managerial privilege over working-class characters.[7] Although the present cycle of films tries to maintain this managerial gaze, they also reflexively represent class turmoil over the gaze's production. In these films, visibility moves across the terrain of military and class struggles, yielding two narrative effects: (1) the act of bringing an individual or a group into visibility, and (2) the economic contradictions and antagonisms of those acts. The prestige dramas of this cycle tend to focus on visibility's construction, while the thrillers and blockbusters spend more time with the subjects who construct visibility. Broadly speaking, the dramas follow an expansionary visual logic to represent the underrepresented—civilian causalities (*Redacted*), renditioned prisoners (*Rendition* [Hood, 2007]), and, by far the most popular theme, traumatized U.S. soldiers (*Lions for Lambs, In the Valley of Elah, Stop-Loss*)—using surveillance to visually mediate the traumas of war and the difficulties American culture has visualizing those most directly impacted by the United States' foreign adventures. While the thrillers and blockbusters of this cycle also use surveillance as a visual trope, they make surveillance itself an integral feature of their genre plots, pitting the protagonists' abilities to see and know against fixed capital used for the same purposes (*Eagle Eye, The Dark Knight, The Bourne Ultimatum*). Surveillance in those films becomes a mediatory device implicated in power's use—in war and the construction of social controls—as well as a privileged point for contending with it, in terms of both visibility and its attendant economics.

Philosopher Alain Badiou makes a glancing point at the beginning of *Logics of Worlds* that illuminates the importance of visibility to postmodern capital. According to Badiou, postmodern capital's economic consensus is based on a widespread philosophical view of the world as consisting of only bodies and language. He terms this perspective "democratic materialism," which reduces all forms of life, culture, and language to an imagined equal existence. The result, as Badiou succinctly notes, implies a global order of what can be seen, one in which "everything and everyone deserves to be recognized and protected by the law."[8] However, when its consensus is resisted, democratic materialism reserves "the right of intervention." Badiou's point highlights sight's relation to one of the key ideological quandaries postmodern capitalism confronted with the United States' post-9/11 actions: although proponents of globalization had long claimed that globalization was an irreversible natural process based on equality and democracy, they now began to argue that it was a fragile, reversible state that had to be defended with force. As sociologist and scholar of globalization studies Manfred B. Steger notes, this contradictory argument appeared after 9/11 to justify preemptive military action as a defense of globalization.[9] The use of force reveals that the supposed economic consensus of postmodern capitalism does not rely on everyone's recognized equality before the law—just one piece in an immanent field of bodies and language—but instead on the law's political organization of recognition itself.

These films appeared during the political reorganization of recognition by the Bush administration, which oversaw a vast expansion of the surveillance state and its bureaucracies as part of its policies of making war.[10] This expansion of the surveillance state helps explain why these films tend to trace an antagonism between the managerial class and the working class as they navigate visibility's contradictory role in postmodern capital at war. The key to locating these antagonisms is to understand that labor in developed postmodern economies is service-based labor (also known as the tertiary sector), which produces knowledge, signs, and affects rather than commodities. As the works of Scott Lash and John Urry, Michael Hardt and Antonio Negri, and David Harvey demonstrate, postmodern capitalism does not simply rely on information and services; it effectively reorganizes production itself around services.[11] Hardt and Negri use the term *biopolitical labor* to describe such labor, and they argue that the hegemony of such work in postmodernity links disparate forms of service work. Thus physical and emotional service work shares labor concerns with the mental labor of intellectual and creative work.[12] Of even more importance, such labor does not have the same relationship to fixed capital as material labor in an industrial process, since it is the innately social work of producing social connections, affects, and selves. However, biopolitical labor's intersection with surveillance work not only displays the separation between human and machine surveillance work described by Virilio but also plays out a more fundamental macroeconomic antagonism between labor and capital: capital often returns to using brute force and domination to expropriate the values biopolitical labor produces outside the spaces of exploitation controlled by capital. Thus the economics of exploiting biopolitical labor resonates with postmodern capitalism's use of force in war.

What we see in these films is a war economy coalescing with postmodern capitalism's focus on information and services, as well as capital's subsequent need to capture and capitalize upon consumer attention. In *The Cinematic Mode of Production,* Jonathan Beller argues that attention itself constitutes a form of labor in cinematic production, and Beller's argument resonates with Garrett Stewart's work on Iraq war films, which focuses on narrative's inscription by surveillance technology.[13] I would draw a contrast between the watcher's implied abjection to capitalized screen production that is implicit in Beller and Stewart to emphasize instead labor's uncomfortable implication in this formation. In these films, biopolitical labor engages with surveillance's manifold uses to disclose its own problematic position in our new postmodern war economy: destructive or resistant, productive or parasitic, empowered or abjected by postmodern capitalism at war. These films illuminate watching's increased economic importance through its use by the surveillance state, cinema and, more broadly, a changed form of labor. They also unselfconsciously represent the reemergence of a classical Marxist antagonism between the living labor and fixed capital, now as the labor of watching and the murderous technology of surveillance and war.

The War in Iraq: Surveillance and Command of the Excluded

In late 2008, A. O. Scott summed up the widely held view that films about the wars in Iraq and Afghanistan had failed at the box office not because the public was indifferent or that Hollywood did not want to take political sides, but because the wars weren't over: "Disorientation, ambivalence, a lack of clarity—these are surely part of the collective experience [these films] are trying to examine. How can you bring an individual story to a satisfying conclusion when nobody has any idea what the end of the larger story will look like?"[14] Leaving to one side the strange idea that any geopolitical event is subject to such consensus, we can nonetheless see how the majority of the middle-brow war dramas offers answers solicited by Scott's earlier question: a satisfying conclusion, these films replied, reveals something that hasn't been seen before. However, this focus on what escaped representation led to answers with a McLuhan-esque focus on the medium, perhaps in part because such questions could not help but solicit Iraq's nonexistent WMDs (weapons of mass destruction). In war, culture confronts problems not merely of what escapes representation but of representation's manipulation. This recurring crisis of manipulation—as scholars of documentary studies often note, a similar set of problems surrounded the case of Rodney King—leads film to try to redress the limits of representation by highlighting its mediatory role through surveillance footage.[15] Yet war introduces a twist: this gesture toward representation's limits relies on the core assumption of postmodern capital that preemptive war undermines: simply being seen as equal under the law is not enough to stop injustice or thwart the global asymmetries of power. Surveillance's mediatory prominence in these war films tries to redress these problems, but it also becomes a part of a mediatory strategy for reasserting the bases of global capital.

Although poorly received by critics and a box-office failure, Brian De Palma's *Redacted* encapsulates the dual representational problems of this cycle's prestige dramas. *Redacted* correctly identifies the killing of Iraqi civilians as one of the U.S. media's key elisions in its war coverage, and the film uses the brutal rape and murder of an Iraqi woman by U.S. troops as an exemplary case. Yet the central crime is largely overshadowed by representational difficulties that its reliance on surveillance footage does not overcome so much as problematize. An intertitle announces that the film will "visually [document] imagined events before, during, and after a 2006 rape and murder in Samarra,"[16] which it accomplishes by using base-camp surveillance cameras and the cameras attached to soldiers' helmets when they go on raids. However, the film itself is more broadly constructed as a montage of media documents drawn from a soldier's video diary, a French war documentary, English and Arabic language news networks, video depositions, internet videos, and others.[17] Yet *Redacted* isn't sure whether expanded representation can overcome the problems of war or whether it simply underscores the powerlessness and failure of such representation as a political strategy. A key document, a soldier's video diary, is titled "Tell Me No Lies,"[18] and throughout the film, characters refer to the camera's ability to lie, including one scene in which two characters gibe each other: "This camera never lies." "That's bullshit. That's all that camera ever does."[19] Indeed, *Redacted*'s plot exacts more vengeance on its internal viewers than on its murderers and rapists, most especially in the videotaped beheading of the soldier keeping the video diary and the subsequent online display of the decapitated body. The result renders ambivalent the film's closing documentary photomontage, titled "Collateral Damage." By displaying photo after photo of murdered Iraqi civilians, the film confronts viewers with documentary evidence of war's effects, yet it also distorts these images by redacting their identities using thin black bars electronically superimposed over their eyes.[20] *Redacted* uses surveillance to foreground representational problems brought on by war, and its rage at image producers discloses a frustrated awareness of the medium's political limitations.

The majority of dramas in this cycle were less self-aware than *Redacted* but no less engaged with these dual problems of representation. By shifting the focus to U.S. soldiers, however, the use of surveillance in films such as *Lions for Lambs, In the Valley of Elah,* and *Stop-Loss* discloses the soldier's proletarianization in postmodern capitalism at war. Historically, this is partly due to the privatization of various military functions under the George W. Bush administration. Although the best-known examples include Halliburton for military support services and Blackwater/Xe for personal protection, private contractors account for an enormous component of the new domestic security state created to wage the War on Terror. As the

Washington Post detailed in a series of investigative reports, after September 11, the U.S. intelligence industry became "so massive that its effectiveness is impossible to determine": hundreds of new departments, thousands of outside contractors, and layer upon layer of redundancy now account for hundreds of billions of dollars in state spending.[21] Privatization has resulted in massive pay disparities between enlisted soldiers and private contractors, creating an exploitative situation in which private contractors profit from the state's wars through the lives of the state's enlisted soldiers.[22] Of course, such exploitation stands in tension with the violence the soldier commands: on the one hand, the exploited worker of militarized capitalism, and on the other, the violent oppressor of the invaded.

Lions for Lambs discloses the former in its glancing use of surveillance and telecommunication, which unwittingly reveals the soldier's new role as the disposable labor of distant technologically empowered command. For the plot, these soldiers are little more than ciphers of nationalist pride—they enlist in post-9/11 patriotic fervor—sacrificed in a war that cannot be won. The impersonal surveillance of their slow demise turns surveillance as a theme away from representational problems and toward war's separation of labor and command. We return to Virilio's separation of sight from the eye but now as an antagonism in global capital. These films unwittingly foreground work in the twenty-first-century military as the furthest development and ultimate inversion of biopolitical labor: the work of surveiling social relations and the violence of war cohere in a knot of biopolitical and thanatopolitical labor.

In the Valley of Elah and *Stop-Loss* address this conflicted knot by focusing on the affectual labor of rehabilitating traumatized soldiers, a process that appears as a form of self-surveillance and memory-capture mediated by surveillance footage. In these films, highly mediated images—cell phone video, digital home movies, and photos—act as indexes of subjective experience and as the products of attempts to rework the self. In effect, soldiers overcome this conflict by internalizing the apparatus of the surveillance itself, remaking themselves as subjects capable of commanding image production in order to overcome their abjection. *Stop-Loss* imagines the working-through of trauma as a process of self-surveillance through video. The film sets up visual production as central to processing trauma: after its opening battle sequence, the film cuts to a soldier's self-produced memorial video for his wounded comrades.[23] An edit retroactively links the video to a soldier's laptop, but the sequence appears without context or preface, marked only by its amateur supertitles and the image's slightly washed-out image quality. The film motivates this slight alteration of the image through a metonymic skid that links washed-out image quality to memory: during a traumatic flashback sequence, the film's protagonist, fleeing his stop-loss order, hallucinates one of his wounded compatriots at the bottom of a motel pool, and, as he dives toward the soldier underwater, the film's opening battle sequence repeats in flashes washed out to resemble digital video.[24] This image degradation means to demarcate subjective memory, but it most vividly recalls the introductory memorial video, an effect heightened by the funeral of a soldier toward the film's conclusion, which intercuts video memories and the present.[25] Less than a gesture toward Bazin's ontology of the image, this mediatory strategy discloses a knot of biopolitical and thanatopolitical labor, the work of constructing the self and one's social world in tension with the work of death: memory and memorial. The soldiers themselves are implicated in this construction, but they cannot resist the larger power of the state and, by extension, those who profit from war: these reflexive mediations enact a seemingly inescapable cycle of surveillance, war, and death.

In the Valley of Elah further pushes the internalization of image production as memory by using a soldier's self-surveillance to trace his declining mental state through image degradation. The story, which raises the experience of PTSD-stricken Iraq veterans to the status of the otherwise excluded, follows the dead soldier's father as he uses distorted cell phone photos, video, and photographs to piece together his son's fate (he was killed by other traumatized members of his unit).[26] Pixilated distortion within these images—perhaps most especially in its video of the torture of a wounded Iraqi, where the image of a child appears unmotivated in the midst of the distortion as a glaring figure for lost innocence[27]—mark the dissolving mental states of the son and his unit. Video's use as subjective memory image has a particular narrative yield as the film's climax explains the corrupted cell phone video that opens the film and recurs throughout in static bursts.[28] What's interesting here is that the film achieves this by reversing the convention of video-as-memory-image seen throughout the film and in *Stop-Loss:* a final replay of the son's incoherent video sutures the father's perspective to the son's by cutting from the grainy cell phone image of subjective experience to the fine-grained 35mm image of narrative objectivity. The move tries to free everyone involved from the problem of image command and war by moving from a mediated space to one of realist objectivity. Only with this reversal can the father witness his son running down an Iraqi child in the street,[29] and the revelation explains the father's recurrent nightmare as his memory of his son's phone call immediately after this incident.[30] These images display a reality no one wished to acknowledge: in a return of the repressed, the son's self-surveillance becomes the father's, images degraded by a collective sense of complicity that only clear representation—the visibility of democratic materialism—can overcome.

Both *In the Valley of Elah* and *Stop-Loss* use surveillance footage to bridge labor and command within the soldier's psyche. Yet, in both cases, this strategy maps also a dysfunctional psyche. As politically ambivalent and unsatisfying as these films are, they locate a key disparity in the failing visual bridge between man and machine: the difficult labor of constructing the self and society against the fixed capital of domination and exploitation.

Degraded Time-Images in the Labor and Fixed Capital of Surveillance

Big-budget action films and thrillers in this cycle rely even more heavily on surveillance, often imagining technology able to capture the entire world at nearly any given moment of time. At the same time, these films yoke their use of surveillance to terrorist attacks, turning the terrorist's production of spectacle into content to be analyzed. The focus of these action films thus tends to shift from the indestructible male body, pace Susan Jeffords, to, on the one hand, the (Western) body's openness to death and, on the other, the hero's ability to know and intervene.[31] The hero is a knowledge worker as much as an athlete, if not more so. In many cases, the hero's work depends upon his control of surveillance equipment and his ability to interpret images and signs. For this reason, the hero of the surveillance action film or thriller becomes a kind of biopolitical laborer, engaged in the production of knowledge, signs, and affects. Yet these heroes must also be able to evade surveillance, either by subverting its machinery or manipulating bodies to avoid its sight. This turn places the hero in the position of a biopolitical laborer while making fixed capital itself a key adversary.

Because the heroes of these films now must respond to images, surveillance introduces a hiatus into the action film's narrative structure as action and reaction operate in a continuous dialogue with surveillance and mediation. In a perverse way, surveillance's internalized viewers recall Gilles Deleuze's time-image films, where the character becomes an internal viewer who records and reacts rather than responds. However, these recent films might best be called degraded time-images, since their reflexive qualities lend themselves less to philosophy than to propaganda. Deleuze locates cinema's openness to propaganda in films of the movement-image, that is, films focused on producing mobile sections of motion and time; when cinema linked the movement-image and war, Deleuze writes, it degenerated "into state propaganda and manipulation, into a kind of fascism which brought together Hitler and Hollywood, Hollywood and Hitler."[32] Big-budget action films like Michael Bay's *Transformers* (2007), Peter Berg's *Battleship* (2012), or Tony Scott's *Top Gun* (1986) readily display state military interests, in part because the military can exercise control over the content of films in return for the use of military equipment, but also because these filmmakers already hold and propagate views amenable to military command. Although many of the films of this cycle do not rely heavily on the use of military equipment, they still reflect the military's worldview, in part because the same filmmakers make them.

In these films, postmodern capital's ideology of visibility becomes a basic presupposition about surveillance itself: when large enough, surveillance can make the world totally knowable and subject to law. There's no problem of interpretation or subjectivity, only the quandary whether the law should always be absolute or only in exceptional circumstances. The answer offered by these films recalls the works of Benjamin and Agamben: the state of exception founds the Law while obviating any everyday laws that would constrain or direct its use.[33] Yet when these films create a state of exception, they also often bring that state to an emphatic end by destroying surveillance technology or disappearing from sight. This use of surveillance thus raises the problems of total knowledge while offering only this guarded solution: we should avert our eyes. Eventually.

This response to the problem of total knowledge recalls a problem in Kant's second critique: Kant argued that in order for humanity to retain free will, the world of natural law and transcendent truth must be at least minimally separate; otherwise the fear of crossing God's will would reduce individuals into puppets of divine law.[34] Postmodern capital's logic of visibility leads inexorably toward this problem and has just as much trouble reinserting minimal separation between subjects and the law as Kant did, even though its logic of preemptive war and the right of intervention clearly insert an exceptional space that founds the use of power. The internal viewer of the degraded time-image provides a means to redress this problem, though to various ends. Surveillance in these action films inserts a reflexive hiatus that may turn toward propaganda or escape the filmmakers' control.

Tony Scott's *Déjà Vu* is perhaps the best example of the ambivalent role of the degraded time-image's internal viewer, because it highlights the specificity of this cycle when compared to Scott's *Enemy of the State* (1998). *Enemy of the State* keeps its surveillance plot firmly in the realm of Jameson's paranoid conspiracy thrillers: a video camera accidentally captures a political murder, which leads to the bugging, tracking, and filming of the film's protagonist, who unwittingly has the tape, and who will eventually enlist another watcher to overcome his watchers. Surveillance in *Enemy of the State* remains indebted to Watergate-era conceptions: it is controlled by the politically powerful to serve their own interests, but it may also expose their misdeeds, in the process generating a paranoid spiral of surveillance.[35] By contrast, *Déjà Vu* turns surveillance loose on the entire world, which is now potentially watched by a machine able to surveil anywhere four days in the past. The film begins with a terrorist bombing of a passenger ferry and follows its detective protagonist as he uses this time-traveling surveillance mechanism not to solve the bombing but rather to prevent it from occurring. In effect, *Déjà Vu* uses surveillance to switch genres, collapsing the detection tale's two stories, the crime and its detection, into the single tale of the thriller, which, as Tzvetan Todorov notes, "no longer [tells] about a crime anterior to the moment of the narrative; the narrative coincides with the action."[36] This genre-switching through science-fiction artifice ropes the contemplativeness of Deleuze's time-image back into the movement-image: the longer the detective watches, the greater his desire to intervene.

The degradation of the time-image in *Déjà Vu* uncovers a potential antagonism between the labor of watching and its fixed capital: the surveillance/time-travel machine duplicates the detective when it sends him back in time, and the double is consumed in his work of terror prevention. While many time-travel films ponder the problems of such potential crossed paths, *Déjà Vu* avoids the issue by handily disposing of the double and ignoring the problems he creates for narrative closure: the detective, the film's chief focalizor, drives the bomb-laden truck off the ferry and dies in the subsequent explosion.[37] To overcome the film's sudden loss of its focalizor, his double, the detective in the alternate time line in which the bomb has not exploded, appears almost immediately, a move that masks the plot's disturbing production and consumption of its detective/watcher.[38] Unaware of any of the film's events, he drives off with the woman saved by the dead detective, a fact that she knows. The film closes with a freeze frame of the smiling double driving away with the film's love interest, a turn that collapses the dead detective's love for this woman and the double in a strained gesture toward a happy end.[39] This ending tries to paper over the distinction—and antagonism—between the labor of surveillance and its technology and command. However, surveillance in the action film reveals this antagonism between labor and capital as the degradation of the time-image creates narratives in which the surveillance mechanisms consume the watching workers who use them.

The surveillance action-thriller thus tends to use and degrade the time-image by making narrative and thematic use of the ability to command images. Although these narratives try to collapse distinctions between labor and capital by generalizing the ability to watch, these distinctions return in unforeseeable ways. Although Peter Berg's *The Kingdom* (2007) is a threadbare genre exercise in procedural investigation and gunplay, its plot hinges on the ability to capture and command images. In the film's opening, an attack on U.S. citizens in Saudi Arabia is captured by its perpetrators on video from an adjacent building's rooftop.[40] Propaganda is the attack's purpose, which the film emphasizes by the attack's dual-image capture, once through the camera's viewfinder and again through a child's eyes, turned insistently toward the attack by an adult's hand.[41] The film emphasizes the power of the image in asymmetrical conflicts; its terrorists, obsessive documentarians and propagandists in their video announcements and surveillance footage, are as focused on the production of image as on violence. Terrorism, the film asserts, produces spectacle and commands the gaze, and the war against terror thus must fight for control over the gaze itself. The anxieties this creates ensures that the film's heroes, an FBI investigative unit, need only one skill: the ability to interpret images. The power of U.S. intelligence gathering for *The Kingdom* is the power of Western human interpretation. Indeed, it is the film's emphasis on knowledge work as the power to overcome the production of terrorist spectacle that makes it notable. What empowers the FBI is not their technology but their interpretive skills once they find this video on the Internet. Their discovery of the camera's vantage point effectively wrests power from the militants by co-opting their perspective, and the film emphasizes the importance of this sequence by crosscutting between an FBI agent's handheld camera on the scene and the in-camera footage of the attack.[42] The conclusion reinforces U.S. command of image production as the FBI thwarts a videoed beheading and discovers the bombing's planners by recognizing the resemblance between a child's marble and a marble recovered from the bombing's debris.[43] By focusing on the centrality of the ability to interpret and control image production in asymmetric warfare, the film views its characters not just as intelligence workers but as knowledge workers, one kind of biopolitical labor.

By emphasizing the ingenuity and technological savvy of their heroes, these films often use one of the basic plots Peter Brooks identified in *Reading for the Plot:* the hero must outwit and outmaneuver his opponents and their devices.[44] Surveillance introduces new devices to outwit opponents, and yet at times it becomes the opponent. From a historical perspective, this emphasis on human intelligence work maps a political antagonism in post–Cold War U.S. intelligence work between man and machine: the Clinton-era CIA emphasized technological intelligence-gathering over covert human operations.[45] By highlighting the deficiencies of this approach, these films offer defenses of human intelligence-gathering that reflect the interests of the surveillance state. However, this conflict between man and machine also operates as a contrasting metaphor for postmodern capitalism's economic conflict between labor and command: biopolitical labor confronts capital here as living labor versus fixed capital. This confrontation appears time and again in thrillers premised on the War on Terror like *Syriana* and *Body of Lies* and action films like *The Bourne Ultimatum, The Dark Knight,* and *Eagle Eye.* These films proletarianize the knowledge worker engaged in the drudgery and hazards of maintaining and manipulating surveillance machines for others. On the one hand, these workers are the reflexive internal viewers of Deleuze's time-image used to ameliorate the implications of America's use of power in war. On the other hand, because their viewing is not merely reflexive but also reflective of real economic work, these internal viewers also map the increasingly impoverished situation of biopolitical laborers in postmodern capitalism. The mediation of war thus captures the dual roles of domination and exploitation in maintaining global capital.

We can see the watcher's implication in these forces in both *Syriana* and *Body of Lies.* At the end of *Syriana,* a CIA agent flags down the convoy of an Emir marked for assassination because he has promised his people to bring political and economic equality to his nation. Though the agent means to help the Emir, both are killed when his Washington manager calls in an aerial strike using surveillance in a sequence that appears from an eerie remove in a Virginia control room.[46] This impersonal assassination allows *Syriana* to create one of film's few sympathetic instances of suicide bombing. Surveillance's murderous mediation of power opens the suicide bomber's desperate experience to the viewer as a response to the problem of fighting a distant impersonal foe. After the Emir's assassination, the film shows two militants driving a small motorboat armed with a surface-to-air missile into an oil tanker. The film's representation of their act nearly endorses it by draining the attack of diegetic sound and fading from a shot of the men about to ram the tanker to an ecstatic white screen.[47] The screen's saturation with light is not so much the first truncated second of the explosion but rather the production of an absolute image in excess of the contents of surveillance's particular images.

What makes the somewhat similar *Body of Lies* interesting is not that it defends watching's labor against its fixed capital but that it does so without privileging American power as intelligence. The film streamlines *Syriana*'s more complex plot into a competition between a CIA agent and his DC-based manager. It introduces a deluge of surveillance footage—overhead surveillance, surveillance cameras in urban environments, and surveillance videotapes—as the manager tracks the agent by phone or surveillance. The pair unsuccessfully manufacture an attack by a fake militant group for international television in order to draw a militant group out of hiding, and the failure of this attempt to construct what can be seen generates another technological failure of vision when the agent finds himself forced to surrender to his girlfriend's captors. In a sequence surveilled overhead by the manager, militants use their SUVs to raise a cloud of dust around the waiting agent and obscure which car they've put him in.[48] Lost to surveillance, they torture and nearly behead him—again for video—before Jordanian intelligence intervenes. The head of Jordanian intelligence later proclaims to the agent that his manager "could not find you, not with all his aircraft, his people, his money and joie de vivre."[49] Only human intelligence is up to the task, which the film shows in one scene of Jordanian intelligence "turning" a militant. The rest of the world, by implication, does real work, while the West produces images that cannot affect reality. Yet this defense of knowledge work against the fixed capital of surveillance is not a complete repudiation of U.S. power or of surveillance. On the one hand, it speaks to the American agent's savvy, which the film marks by his disenchantment and removal from aerial surveillance at the end of the film.[50] On the other hand, the film's excessive use of surveillance footage in its montage undercuts its plot's repudiation of technology. This is the impasse that reflexive filmmaking confronts during this period.

The third installment of the Bourne franchise, *The Bourne Ultimatum*, tries to overcome this impasse by reactivating the knot of biopolitical and thanatopolitical labor seen in the period's films about traumatized soldiers.

At the same time, the film makes labor's domination and exploitation central thematic points. Surveillance images saturate the film, including an evocation of Etienne Marey that bowdlerizes *The Conversation*'s mock camera-gun: here actual guns carry cameras so that CIA thugs can simultaneously kill their targets and embalm them on video.[51] One of the film's central set pieces, a lengthy game of cat and mouse through London's Waterloo station, relies on Bourne's savvy to elude the city's surveillance cameras, which a secret U.S. agency remotely controls to direct its assassins.[52] As the film crosscuts between Bourne and the New York command center, we can see its two competing narrative centers as biopolitical labor and the command of fixed capital: command takes place through communication and surveillance as they try to capture Bourne and protect their investment in intelligence work. As a conflict between labor and capital, the film also gestures toward class consciousness in Bourne's interactions with a similarly trained assassin. After a lengthy car chase ends in a multicar pileup, Bourne aims his gun at his stunned and unarmed pursuer but does not shoot; later, their positions reversed, the latter asks Bourne why he did not shoot. Bourne replies: "Do you even know why you're supposed to kill me? Look at us. Look at what they make you give."[53] The exchange and the assassin's confused look mean to indict war's decision makers and their exploitation of American soldiers, but the characters' shared experience as improvisatory intelligence workers supervised by surveillance also reveals the difficulty of generating class fellowships in a world of biopolitical labor. Although his hesitation allows Bourne to escape, it is a far cry from resistance.

The most interesting film of this period is also its most symptomatic: *Eagle Eye* turns surveillance's proliferation of images against the film's hero while drawing parallels between civilian biopolitical labor and the military's knot of biopolitical and thanatopolitical labor. *Déjà Vu* created a literal copy of its protagonist, but *Eagle Eye,* much like *Avatar* (Cameron, 2009), makes its hero a twin. From the first, these brothers are biopolitical laborers ironically embedded in representation's duplicative work: Jerry Shaw is the film's hero, but it is his brother, a military programmer, who creates Eagle Eye, a total surveillance system, and then codes control of the system to his DNA. When the brother dies, Shaw must use his shared DNA to reassert control over the now run-amuck system. The film gives a further twist by making Shaw a lowly copy-store clerk. *Eagle Eye* is thus a film about the reduplicative process of representation, spanning multiple forms of biopolitical labor in a story about surveillance and the War on Terror. In fact, the Eagle Eye system fantasizes the complete subsumption of human labor by fixed capital conjured by Virilio's account of machines able to gather, interpret, and act on the images they process.

Much like *The Dark Knight,* where Batman turns Gotham's cell phones into a massive bat radar system and then destroys his command center,[54] *Eagle Eye* also ends with the surveillance system's spectacular destruction.[55] The absolute effectiveness of surveillance in both films potentially eliminates what Kant identifies as the necessary separation between subjects and the law, resulting in a terrifying direct encounter with the law. *Eagle Eye*'s perverse brilliance is to invert the positions of law and subject: the law becomes a murderous surveillance machine motivated by ethics while its hero, the degraded time-image's internal viewer, takes actions to justify preemptive war. Computer-gone-mad is a familiar science-fiction device, but Eagle Eye runs amuck for a very specific reason: to stop the U.S. president from endangering the lives of his citizens by murdering foreigners using drone missile strikes. The film's opening sequence frames this ethical problem and begins with military surveillance tracking a caravan of vehicles in Pakistan as Eagle Eye uses facial-recognition software to determine whether one of the men is a wanted "target."[56] With each new image, the computer calculates whether it has a facial match, and it does not achieve the specific ratio it needs to authorize a strike. The president overrides the computer and, as the film makes clear, kills innocent men. Eagle Eye, realizing the president's actions undermine its program, decides to kill him.[57] In a telling set of assumptions, this plot relies on the belief, either the audience's or the filmmaker's, that leaders who execute innocents are exempt from the law. Dissent gets displaced into the very machinery of war as an inhuman moral terrorist, and the film uses this displacement to offer contrasting visions of America: on the one hand, the authoritarian figure of the president, who must be protected at any cost, and on the other hand, Eagle Eye, a threatening and inhuman technological figure for the mob. Eagle Eye even speaks of itself as a plural body, describing its data system to Shaw in the home theater section of a mall's Circuit City as "We the People," using scrolling images of the Declaration of Independence during its expository monologue.[58] The computer system thus takes on command's ability to control image production—commandeering anything connected to a network, from surveillance cameras and cell phones to cars and heavy construction equipment—while subsuming the interconnected multitude of biopolitical labor.

Against this dangerous collectivity, the film deploys patriotism, which

Shaw copies from his dead brother and which leads to his own near-death experience when he disrupts Eagle Eye's plot to blow up Congress during the State of the Union address by firing shots into the air. The Secret Service shoots him in a pseudo-martyrdom that allows Shaw to display his patriotism as the willing negation of the self, which the film views from above.[59] Although Shaw's martyrdom is the logical outcome to the film's diffusion of collectivity into technological evil or a national people, the late-summer blockbuster needs to reinforce the self-absorption of its consumer age bracket.[60] The film thus cuts to a bandaged Shaw receiving a medal before segueing to a children's birthday party where Shaw brings as his gift the video game *Rock Band*.[61] The gift of a game in which players mime the actual production of music reinforces the notion that the individual remains in control of the fixed capital that allows the state to operate. This is perhaps why *Eagle Eye* is the best representative of the biopolitical war economy's ideological core in the first decade of the twenty-first century: it subsumes the process of surveillance to a villainous fixed capital that represents the collective social life rejected by postmodern capital; it turns the dimwitted but valiant hero into a cipher for individualism; it reinforces the premises of surveillance's total knowledge while rejecting its ethical problems; and it celebrates an unquestioning protection of criminal authority. By amalgamating surveillance technology, collectivity, and resistance to the decisions made in postmodern capital at war, *Eagle Eye* highlights a conservative political perspective that hawks fears of shadowy governmental plans to take away individual liberties while deploying jingoism to undermine the very bases of these liberties. The triumph of postpanoptic power appears in the film's apparent rejection of surveillance for the internal viewer who gives himself completely to authority: like a *Rock Band* player, he performs an image of self-control that mimes authority's preexistent demands. Surveillance's final twist in war films is to defuse biopolitical labor's potential resistance and to turn it into the labor of subjection.

Human Capital, or Surveillance as Sociality

The Coen brothers' film *Burn after Reading* discloses this turn toward subjection as the result of the idiot force of brute domination. The plot follows the failures of Osbourne Cox, a CIA analyst whose class position and self-importance clearly do not mark him as politically deprived even as his wife cheats on him, he quits his job to avoid a demotion for drinking, and ignorant physical trainers try to sell his memoirs to Russia as state secrets and then to blackmail him. The film's first shot—a cosmic zoom that moves from outer space through the roof of CIA headquarters and into the building's halls—introduces surveillance as the only organizing component of the film's otherwise irrational world, but surveillance itself has been emptied of knowledge.[62] The film's plot is almost purely contingent, consisting of an aleatory series of events without a larger design or inherent meaning. Events connect its characters, but not in a way that they understand or that matters to the plot: the trainers get the CD from the assistant of Osbourne's wife's lawyer, who left it at their gym, and Harry's use of Internet dating sites to meet women when his wife is out of town leads him into a relationship with one of the blackmailing trainers. Surveillance does not organize the world into a knowable form or recognizable plot so much as assert control over the actions of bodies by watching them. Hence the film closes with Cox's violent and meaningless murder of the older trainer, an irrational act that even a maximum level of surveillance could not predict or avert.

Indeed, no one in *Burn after Reading* knows much about anything, even those who should, given their careers. These characters obsess over bodies, not knowledge. Physical trainers Linda, Chad, and Ted mold bodies for a living, and Linda's desire for plastic surgery drives her blackmail scheme and proves the failure of knowledge to remake her body otherwise. The U.S. marshal is obsessed with jogging and sex, and only his homemade dildo-chair displays any ingenuity while simultaneously laying bare the fundamental experience of control societies in war: everyone gets anonymously and mechanically penetrated.[63] Yet this mechanical violation is physical and entirely opaque. Characters know they are watched, but they don't know why. The viewer's omniscient perspective and lack of sense is on par with that of the CIA, and everyone imagines she or he is under state surveillance—Cox mistakes his wife's private detective for a state official, Harry thinks Linda works for a state agency, and Linda and Chad think Cox has state secrets—but the CIA cannot explain why Harry shoots Chad after discovering him in Cox's wife's closet, or why Harry would think Chad was a secret agent. The CIA supervisor says: "Keep an eye on everyone. See what they do. Report back to me when . . . I don't know. When it makes sense."[64] Before reversing its opening cosmic zoom, the film's conclusion reiterates the ubiquity of surveillance and its inability to explain the world: "What did we learn, Palmer?" "I don't know, sir." "I don't fucking know either. I guess we learned not to do it again." "Yes sir." "Although I'm fucked if I know what we did."[65] In *Burn after Reading,* surveillance and the plots it tells reveal a world of workers dominated by technology, effectively capturing the other side of knowledge-work's exploitation in postmodern capital at war: capital's brute domination of labor.

In these films of war, surveillance provided a strategy for mediating impasses in the perception of the social and political world by extending visibility to the excluded and asserting global capital as the global rule of law. The U.S. doctrine of preemptive war, however, posed a fundamental hurdle to this ideological vision. In response, these films focus on problems of image construction that resonate with the hegemonic form of labor in postmodern capitalism, biopolitical labor. Yet this labor of producing knowledge, affects, and social relations not only constructs the commonwealth and the individuals who inhabit it; it also finds its perverse double in the U.S. nation-building projects in Iraq and Afghanistan. What we find in these films, then, are maps of the social, economic, and political controls deployed by postpanoptic societies, maps created, internalized, and resisted by surveillance of the battlefield, the homeland, and the self. This reimagining of the power of the gaze in postmodernity at war takes us beyond Foucault's panopticism by turning the gaze into a mode of direct rather than indirect domination. Caught up in this shift, these films bend Deleuze's reflexive and philosophical time-image into a violent subjectivizing mechanism to internalize the power of the state.

This mediatory strategy initially faded after 2008, perhaps in part because of the change in U.S. administrations and a broader cultural willingness to question the wars, if only for the presidential election season. Although Kathryn Bigelow's *The Hurt Locker* (2008) and Paul Greengrass's *Green Zone* (2010)—both shot by cinematographer Barry Ackroyd—tried to reboot films about the United States' wars, surveillance all but disappeared in their montages. The first five minutes of *The Hurt Locker* neatly illustrate the shift, opening with a surveillance shot from the perspective of a bomb-detonating robot but quickly shifting to a direct and embodied style of shooting after a human being replaces the ineffective robot.[66] *Green Zone,* too, largely mirrors this embodied approach. However, this shift in mediatory emphasis from reflexivity to embodiment proved only momentary.[67] Bigelow's next film, *Zero Dark Thirty* (2012), a laudatory account of the CIA and the Joint Special Operations Command's tracking and assassination of Osama bin Laden, marks a return to surveillance aesthetics.[68] Given the continuing expansion of the U.S. surveillance state—not to mention the exponential increase in drone warfare and the expansion of covert actions by U.S. Special Operations Forces—it seems unlikely that the surveillance aesthetic will disappear anytime soon.[69]

Notes

1. Paul Virilio, *War and Cinema: The Logistics of Perception,* trans. Patrick Camiller (London: Verso, 1989), 2, 4.

2. Paul Virilio's 1983 argument takes a literal turn in films like Harun Farocki's *Eye/Machine* series (2001–2003), with their redeployment of surveillance footage and techniques to interrogate postmodernity's surveilled world. Thematically, this film cycle offers a thematic knot of pluralist human rights and the spectacular violence of U.S. exceptionalism. See Virilio, *War and Cinema;* and Sylvere Lotringer and Paul Virilio, *Pure War* (Los Angeles: Semiotext[e], 2007).

3. Gilles Deleuze, "Postscript on the Societies of Control," *October* 59 (1992): 5.

4. Fredric Jameson, *The Geopolitical Aesthetic: Cinema and Space in the World System* (Bloomington: Indiana University Press, 1992), 60.

5. I'm referring to Jameson's *analogon,* which receives its most detailed exposition in his essay on *Dog Day Afternoon* (Lumet, 1975) and focuses not on the interiorization of mediation but rather the displacements of the star system across different media. See Fredric Jameson, *Signatures of the Visible* (London: Routledge, 1992), 47–74.

6. Fredric Jameson, "War and Representation," *PMLA* 124, no. 5 (2009): 1547, reprinted in the present volume.

7. Derek Nystrom, "The Gaze at Work: Knowledge Relations and Class Spectatorship," *Iowa Journal of Cultural Studies* 12–13 (2010): 23–36.

8. Alain Badiou, *Logics of Worlds,* trans. Alberto Tosccano (London: Continuum, 2009), 2.

9. See Manfred B. Steger, "From Market Globalism to Imperial Globalism: Ideology and American Power after 9/11," *Globalizations* 2, no. 1 (May 2005): 31–46.

10. On the expansion of the surveillance state during the Bush administration, see Dana Priest and William M. Arkin, *Top Secret America: The Rise of the New American Security State* (New York: Little, Brown, 2011). The Obama administration's far more violent use of surveillance in its expanded drone bombing program has taken place without explicit declarations of war on Pakistan, Yemen, or Somalia (the administration launched more drone strikes in its first year than the Bush administration's total number of strikes over the prior eight years). Although no less implicated in the demands of global capital, the Obama administration's extralegal use of surveillance to wage war in all but name has thus far generated fewer expressions of concern within popular culture than the Bush administration's wars. See Jo Becker and Scott Shane, "Secret 'Kill List' Proves a Test of Obama's Principles and Will," *New York Times,* May 29, 2012, nytimes.com; Michael Hastings, "The Drone Wars," in *Rolling Stone,* April 26, 2012,

rollingstone.com; and Jeremy Scahill, "Washington's War in Yemen Backfires," *Nation,* March 5, 2012, thenation.com.

11. See Scott Lash and John Urry, *Economies of Signs of Space* (London: Sage, 1994); Michael Hardt and Antonio Negri, *Empire* (Cambridge, MA: Harvard University Press, 2000); David Harvey, *The Condition of Postmodernity* (Oxford: Blackwell, 1990); and David Harvey, *A Brief History of Neoliberalism* (Oxford: Oxford University Press, 2007).

12. See Michael Hardt and Antonio Negri, *Multitude* (London: Penguin, 2004), 140–53.

13. See Jonathan Beller, *The Cinematic Mode of Production: Attention Economy and the Society of the Spectacle* (Hanover, NH: Dartmouth College Press, 2006); and Garrett Stewart, "Digital Fatigue: Imaging War in Recent American Film," *Film Quarterly* 62, no. 4 (2009): 45–55.

14. A. O. Scott, "A War on Every Screen," *New York Times,* October 28, 2007, nytimes.com. Two weeks later, the Editorial Board ran a similar blog piece, "Iraq War Does Lousy at the Box Office," *New York Times,* November 12, 2007, nytimes.com.

15. For discussion of the King incident, see Michael Renov, "Introduction: The Truth about Non-Fiction," in *Theorizing Documentary,* ed. Michael Renov (New York: Routledge, 1993), 1–11; Bill Nichols, *Blurred Boundaries: Questions of Meaning in Contemporary Culture* (Bloomington: Indiana University Press, 1994), 17–42; Linda Williams, *Playing the Race Card: Melodramas of Black and White from Uncle Tom to O.J. Simpson* (Princeton, NJ: Princeton University Press, 2001), 252–95.

16. *Redacted,* 00:01:15.

17. *Redacted,* broken down by mediatory approach: video diary: 00:01:29–00:04:39; 00:13:44–00:19:13; 00:23:40–00:30:55; 00:40:40–00:45:14; 00:47:08–00:47:23; 00:49:36–00:54:15; 01:02:38–01:03:27, 01:05:43–01:12:57, 01:20:29–01:22:44; French documentary: 00:04:40–00:13:43, 00:19:14–00:21:30, 00:38:49–00:40:39; English news stories: 00:35:43–00:38:48, 01:03:56–01:04:31, 01:15:48–01:16:23; Arabic language news stories: 00:21:30–00:23:40, 00:57:42–00:59:21, 01:04:32–01:05:41; basecamp surveillance footage: 00:34:07–00:35:42, 00:47:24–00:49:35, 00:54:16–00:57:41; video depositions: 00:59:22–01:01:25, 01:13:56–01:15:47, 01:16:24–01:19:17; embedded Internet videos: 00:30:56–00:31:48, 00:33:42–00:34:04, 00:45:15–00:47:07, 01:01:27–01:02:37, 01:03:28–01:03:55, 01:12:58–01:13:55, 01:19:17–01:20:29.

18. Ibid., 00:01:29.

19. Ibid., 00:14:00–00:14:25.

20. Ibid., 01:23:44–01:25:29.

21. Dana Priest and William M. Arkin, "A Hidden World, Growing beyond Control," *Washington Post,* July 19, 2010, washingtonpost.com.

22. For comparative costs between Blackwater/Xe contractors and U.S. soldiers, see Jeremy Scahill, *Blackwater: The Rise of the World's Most Powerful Mercenary Army* (New York: Nation Books, 2008), 24. For a detailed account of U.S. reliance on private security contractors, see Priest and Arkin, *Top Secret America.*

23. *Stop-Loss,* 00:12:08–00:13:54.

24. Ibid., 00:43:57–00:44:33.

25. Ibid., 0:01:31:08–01:31:52.

26. *In the Valley of Elah,* 00:00:09–0:00:23; 0:11:18–0:12:12; 00:21:40–00:23:00; 00:39:07–0:40:06; 1:05:37–1:06:00; 1:14:26–1:16:05; 1:34:11–1:34:50.

27. Ibid., 01:34:11–01:34:50.

28. Ibid., 00:21:40–0:23:00; 01:05:37–01:06:00.

29. Ibid., 01:47:44–01:48:43.

30. Ibid., 01:48:43–01:49:59.

31. For Jeffords's account of masculinity and the action film, see Susan Jeffords, *Hard Bodies: Hollywood Masculinity in the Reagan Era* (New Brunswick, NJ: Rutgers University Press, 1994).

32. Gilles Deleuze, *Cinema 2: The Time-Image,* trans. Hugh Tomlinson and Robert Galeta (Minneapolis: University of Minnesota Press, 1989), 165.

33. See Walter Benjamin, "Critique of Violence," in *Reflections,* ed. Peter Demetz (New York: Schocken Books, 1978), 277–300; Giorgio Agamben, *The State of Exception,* trans. Kevin Attell (Chicago: University of Chicago Press, 2005).

34. See Immanuel Kant, *Critique of Practical Reason,* trans. T. K. Abbott (Amherst: Prometheus Books, 1996), 123–25.

35. Films such as Coppola's *The Conversation* (1974), Pakula's *The Parallax View* (1974), Pollack's *Three Days of the Condor* (1975), and De Palma's *Blow Out* (1981) staged confrontations between the militarized and technocratic realm of surveillance and the political world. *The Parallax View* and *Blow Out* trace political assassinations, and *The Conversation* and *Three Days of the Condor* combine murder with state and commercial interests.

36. Tzvetan Todorov, *The Poetics of Prose,* trans. Richard Howard (Ithaca, NY: Cornell University Press, 1977), 47.

37. *Déjà Vu,* 01:56:40–01:57:53.

38. Ibid., 01:58:55.

39. Ibid., 02:00:30.

40. In another strange attempt to mobilize history for realism, the film's opening has its lead FBI agent visiting a nursery school when the attack takes place; however, the agent is speaking, not reading *My Pet Goat. The Kingdom,* 00:06:29.

41. *The Kingdom,* 00:06:35–00:09:55.

42. Ibid., 01:30:20–01:35:57.

43. Ibid., 01:37:45; the marbles first appear at 01:06:57–01:07:12.

44. Peter Brooks, *Reading for the Plot: Design and Intention in Narrative* (Cambridge, MA: Harvard University Press, 1984), 38.

45. The Clinton administration's first two directors of the CIA, first James Woolsey and then John Deutch, both emphasized investments in satellite technology and tried to avoid covert operations. Woolsey took up and expanded what would become the CIA's armed Predator drone program under George Tenet. See Steve Coll, *Ghost Wars: The Secret History of the CIA, Afghanistan, and Bin Laden, from the Soviet Invasion to*

September 10, 2001 (New York: Penguin Books, 2004), 240–352, 527–34, 580–81, esp. 245, 316, 528, and 581.

46. *Syriana,* 01:52:13–01:55:16.

47. Ibid., 01:59:12–01:59:25.

48. *Body of Lies,* 01:46:31–01:47:22.

49. Ibid., 01:56:50–01:56:57.

50. Ibid., 02:02:58.

51. *The Bourne Ultimatum,* 00:37:57–00:39:40.

52. Ibid., 00:15:10–00:27:55.

53. Ibid., 01:44:33–01:44:59.

54. *The Dark Knight,* 01:57:15–01:58:40.

55. Ibid., 02:24:20–02:24:28.

56. *Eagle Eye,* 00:01:40.

57. Ibid., 00:00:00–00:05:55.

58. Ibid., 00:59:23–01:01:14.

59. Ibid., 01:48:23–01:49:15.

60. The film's lead, Shia LaBoef, was the privileged placeholder for this demographic in the period 2007–2011, from the *Transformers* series (2007, 2009, 2011), to *Indiana Jones and the Kingdom of the Crystal Skull* (2008) and, perhaps most tellingly, Oliver Stone's sequel to *Wall Street, Wall Street: Money Never Sleeps* (2010).

61. *Eagle Eye,* 01:51:11.

62. *Burn after Reading,* 00:00:17–00:01:21.

63. Ibid., 00:53:50–00:54:23.

64. Ibid., 01:09:09–01:09:19.

65. Ibid., 01:32:10–01:32:23.

66. *The Hurt Locker,* 00:00:10–00:05:00.

67. For an account of this shift to films of militant embodiment, see Joshua Gooch, "Militants and Cinema: Digital Attempts to Make the Multitude in *Hunger, Che, Public Enemies,*" *Wide Screen* 3, no. 1 (2011): 1–36.

68. *Zero Dark Thirty* also provides a useful instance of collusion between the surveillance state and filmmakers. For an account of the problematic interactions between Bigelow and screenwriter Mark Boal with the U.S. government, see United States, Dept. of Defense, Office of the Deputy Inspector General for Intelligence and Special Program Assessments, "Release of Department of Defense Information to the Media: Report No. DODIG-2013-092," Dept. of Defense, June 2013.

69. For an exposition of the extent of electronic U.S. surveillance revealed by Edward Snowden's release of NSA documents, see James Bamford, "They Know Much More than You Think," *New York Review of Books,* August 15, 2013, nybooks.com. On the expanded use of drones, see note 10 above. On the expanding nature of covert operations involving Special Operations Forces run by the Joint Special Operations Command, see Jeremy Scahill, *Dirty Wars: The World Is a Battlefield* (New York: Nation Books, 2013).

Seeing Soldiers, Seeing Persons

Wittgenstein, Film Theory, and Charlie Chaplin's *Shoulder Arms*

Burke Hilsabeck

The idea of a Wittgensteinian film theory has been a persistent interest of more analytically minded film and media scholars.[1] This interest should be understood within the broader context of the history of film theory. The grand, systematic theories that accompanied the founding of cinema and media studies as a discipline ignored Wittgenstein, and for good reason. With a few important exceptions, Wittgenstein and the philosophical tradition in which he wrote during the first half of the twentieth century were not much concerned with the analysis of artworks or with the aesthetic products of mass culture. The obvious consequence of this disinterest was that Anglo-American philosophy was rarely employed in the construction of the foundations of these overarching theories of film, which tended instead to employ the tools of Continental philosophy.[2] Even as proponents of these grand theories have now discarded their totalizing ambitions in favor of a more piecemeal and multidisciplinary approach to the theorization of film texts, Wittgenstein's work continues to appear to be of little relevance. On the other hand, film theorists who are interested in analytic philosophy tend to utilize Wittgenstein's work as part of a larger, positivist-inspired attempt to construct foundations for film theoretical questions such as the nature of film authorship or the viewer's affective relationship to visual narrative. Among these theorists, Wittgenstein's work has most frequently been understood as propaedeutic in value, which is to say that it has provided a powerful tool with which to challenge the logic of the theories that these writers wish to counter.[3]

Whether through disinterest (among critical theorists) or through a particular reading of the philosophical tradition (in contemporary theory that draws on this tradition's positivist inclinations), many scholars have failed to grasp the potential importance of Wittgenstein's work for theories of film and media. This failure has obscured the potential utility of Wittgenstein's work for the development of these theories. A revised understanding of his writing will help to generate a richer field from which theorists may draw and to which they may respond. In what follows, I want to suggest that we steer away from propaedeutic applications of Wittgenstein's work and instead take up its potential interpretive power. As a means of elucidating this power and demonstrating its value, I will look at the concept from Wittgenstein's work that is most often discussed by theorists of the image, the concept of aspect perception, or "seeing as."

I begin by taking a look at the way in which aspect perception helps us to think about the particular comedy of Charlie Chaplin's film about the First World War, *Shoulder Arms* (1918). This will occasion a digression into the ways in which Wittgenstein's concept has traditionally been employed in the domain of film studies. I will then outline a different reading of that idea, one that not only involves a more accurate reading of Wittgenstein but is, I believe, of greater value to scholars of film and media. By way of a conclusion, I will return to the film and more specifically to the relationship between Chaplin's gags and the context of armed conflict. This will allow us to think through the implications of this setting for the ethical and epistemological location of the film's viewers as well as help us to consider the relationship between slapstick and the environment of war.

A Soldier and His Tools

Shoulder Arms is the story of Doughboy, a small soldier stationed at the front during the First World War. This soldier, we are given to understand, is ill equipped for his job. His inadequacy stems from the fact that he is inwardly resistant to the strictures and rules of life in the army. This resistance is not exactly moral but rather, one wants to say, physiological: he cannot master the parade march; he is less than proficient with his rifle; he continually bothers his fellow soldiers with his ignorance of the routines of camp. Doughboy functions in the Aristotelian sense of the comedian: he is distinctly lower or less than his peers and is consequently an object of fun. Importantly, however, because he is less confined by the strictures of army life than the other soldiers, Doughboy finds the space to be a person, to live with imagination and intelligence. And he accomplishes this, at least in part, by taking, or seeing, the things around him in new and surprising ways. He sees the objects of his world as not *merely* ordinary, but as redemptively so.

Shoulder Arms is full of moments in which acts of vision and interpretation are linked directly to ethical judgments, moments in which people, objects, and particular features of the world are seen in what we could call nonnecessary or unusual ways. In the universe of Chaplin's film, people who see in ordinary ways and who are hidebound to their usual perceptions are shown to be ethically suspect. Those who allow themselves to see things anew, on the other hand, those who are able to imagine different contexts for the people and objects of the film's world, are shown to display a kind of moral and imaginative intelligence. They win the war.

Interestingly, this intelligence with the world takes the form of imaginative demonstrations that make malleable the objects of war. Doughboy turns common domestic objects into (nonlethal) weapons of war, and he turns the weapons of war toward the tasks of domesticity. In doing so, he causes the theater of war to become a kind of music-hall stage within which objects of both types take on the being of toys.

Waiting in his trench, for instance, Doughboy receives a package that contains a round of Limburger cheese and pulls a gas mask over his head to protect his nose. When even the gas mask can't do the trick, he lobs the cheese, grenade-like, out of his trench, where it lands on the face of a neighboring German officer. Or later, having captured a crew of German soldiers and celebrating his victory over a small lunch, Doughboy uses enemy rifle fire to open a bottle of beer and—even more improbably—to light a cigarette. Even the horrible dangers of trench life are shown to respond to Doughboy's imaginative play with ordinary objects. A great rain, for instance, floods his barrack, completely submerging his bunk. Wanting to continue his sleep, he reaches for the horn of a nearby gramophone, which doubles as a snorkel. All of these little tasks and performances show Doughboy to be at home in his world, to be able to claim it for himself, to make it respond to his sentiment and desires.[4]

Shoulder Arms, however, is not only about the imaginative and recuperative intelligence of a single person; it concerns also the ways in which other people respond (or fail to respond) to Doughboy's intelligence. The film intends to reveal the many varieties of inspired interpretation as well as the blindness of the persons in its fictional world, and in doing so, it employs what we could call a hierarchy of intimacy. At its core, a romantically inclined couple (Chaplin and Edna Purviance) sees, we could say, eye to eye. That is, each sees as the other sees without hesitation; each adopts the other's point of view. (The film enacts an elaborate ballet around this joining of views, as in Purviance's tending to Chaplin's injured hand while the latter pretends to sleep or in a gag that involves a German officer's closet.) The other American soldiers around Chaplin, while hardly dead to his imaginative play with nutmeg graters and limburger cheeses, grumblingly put up with his flights of fancy. (Purviance's French maid, for instance, winningly adopts a turn-of-the-century German moustache—drawn in axle grease—in the film's final sequence, whereas Chaplin's captured comrade has difficulty wearing the costume of a German soldier and suffers mild physical violence at Chaplin's hand.) Most of the film's German soldiers, however, possess something like what Wittgenstein called "aspect blindness": they are resolute in their inability to see through Chaplin's disguises and foolery and are consequently depicted as lacking in imaginative intelligence. They refuse what for Chaplin constitutes an ethical, or acknowledging, relation both to other persons and to the wider world of objects in which the persons around them live.

Their lack of imaginative and ethical intelligence is demonstrated at great length in a sequence in which Doughboy is behind enemy lines and disguised as a dead tree.[5] A small attachment of German soldiers enters the frame where Chaplin stands. (The audience is informed neither about why Chaplin is there nor of why he is wearing the suit. Rather, the situation, as happens in many of Chaplin's other films, belongs to the realm of luck or chance. Doughboy merely *finds* himself in this situation.) As the German soldiers set up their camp, one of them begins to cut wood for a fire. This man tours the area and, deciding that the other trees will be too much work to cut down, settles on Chaplin. He knocks his axe against the ground to ready it and spits in his hands. Chaplin pokes him with one of his limbs. Thinking that he's been stuck by a weed, the man goes at the plant with his axe. Chaplin then hits him powerfully over the head, knocking him out. Soon, the other soldiers catch on, and one of them pursues Doughboy—still dressed as a tree—into a nearby forest. The soldier, who cannot find his man, fires his rifle into the trees and pricks them with his bayonet, but Doughboy, who remains unnoticed, runs off and away.

We could say that the conditions in which these characters find themselves have made it impossible for one of them to recognize the other as a person—that is, as a being that is not an object, not something one simply shoots without hesitation. That the one *sees* the other *as* an object is dramatized (and turned into a moment of comedy) by his inability to recognize the tree as a person. His perception reveals his lack of imagination and is shown to reveal a kind of madness. Interestingly for a reading of Wittgenstein, this aspect blindness is not understood as a condition (in the sense of, say, having Alzheimer's disease or eczema) but as a state to which persons accede, half willingly. It is the state of having given up on one's ability to imagine and therefore of having given up a part of one's self. For the German soldier, who is bereft of imagination, a tree is a tree and all men (at least of the other side) are objects. For Chaplin, however, a man may be many things, and he may become these things for any number of reasons—to hide, to surprise, to save, to delight. The intelligence of such a man, which is grounded in acts of perception, is nimble, imaginative, ethical.

Of course, part of the humor in the tree sequence derives from the fact that Chaplin does in fact resemble an object on-screen. His funny jog through the clearing on the way to the woods is not that of a person, but that of a (seemingly) running tree. The gag works by turning the real into the hallucinatory, while at the same time asking its viewers, who are put in a position of epistemic sophistication and given the opportunity to exercise moral insight, to see as the German soldier has, to imagine the real possibility that a person may become an object and may hold as little value as a tree. The joke, in short, articulates a moment of visual interpretation in which we can *see*, as it were, multiple ways of perceiving the image before us.

Because such moments of interpretive perception in *Shoulder Arms* frequently take the literal form of one character seeing one thing *as* another, they provide a useful test case for the idea that the concept of aspect perception, as Wittgenstein understood it, may have interpretive rather than simply theoretical use, that this concept has to do with the surprising conjunction of perceptual agility, knowledge of the world, and ethical understanding. Whereas most film theoretical accounts of aspect perception use Wittgenstein's concept as a means of thinking through the phenomenology of vision, *Shoulder Arms* suggests that aspect perception is of importance for its articulation of value and mutuality.

Aspect Perception and Film Theory

Given the previous employment of aspect perception as a means of understanding vision and illusion, I want to take a minute to describe the standard account of it as it has surfaced among film theorists. This will allow us to rethink this account and to return to *Shoulder Arms* carrying, as it were, a new tool of interpretation.

Aspect perception is the apparently straightforward idea that a single perceptual experience can be interpreted in multiple ways. Scholars of film and media have generally understood Wittgenstein's discussion of "seeing as" (in section xi of the second part of *Philosophical Investigations* and in the four posthumous volumes that comprise his typescripts and manuscripts on the philosophy of psychology) as the sketching of a phenomenology of a particular area of visual perception.[6] These scholars take Wittgenstein's interest in aspect perception to be prompted by the difficulty of the expression of a particular *kind* of sight. It follows from this understanding that Wittgenstein's goal in his discussion of this experience is the dissolution of philosophical confusions that attend this difficult perceptual experience. Some instances of the standard account take the "duck-rabbit" and the Necker cube as paradigmatic examples of the phenomenon of "seeing as"; others understand Wittgenstein as working to establish a set of technical names for a phenomenon or range of phenomena of vision.[7]

The most important instance of the standard account is found in Richard Allen's *Projecting Illusion: Film Spectatorship and the Impression of Reality.*[8] Allen's account is in turn indebted to the work of philosopher Stephen Mulhall, and more specifically to Mulhall's *On Being in the World.* Allen develops a Wittgenstein-influenced account of what he calls "projective illusion," a kind of illusion that involves loss of medium awareness but is at the same time characterized by a knowing perception of the moving image as a fully realized world.[9] Here is Allen's characterization of the experience of "seeing aspects" in that work: "The phenomenon of seeing aspects is defined by the fact that one cannot perceive the new aspect of the object simultaneously with the aspect first perceived; one can only flip-flop, sequentially, between them."[10] In *Projecting Illusion,* Allen's account takes the duck-rabbit and Necker cube pictures as generating paradigmatic instances of the phenomenon of aspect perception as a whole.[11] The viewer can always understand these pictures in one of two ways (as a duck *or* a rabbit; as a cube with *just one* of two sides as its base).

In a later revision of his essay "Looking at Motion Pictures," Allen adds a degree of complexity to these arguments, pointing out that Wittgenstein "investigates a range of cases that illuminate the diversity and complexity of the concept of seeing and in particular the borderline between seeing and imagined seeing," and he goes on to describe Wittgenstein's example of a triangle that can be seen several different ways (e.g., as solid, as standing on its base, as hanging from its apex, as an arrow).[12] Still, *Projective Illusion* and the two versions of "Looking at Motion Pictures" have in common the idea that aspect perception describes an experience (or a series of related experiences) that is obscure to our descriptions of it. Accordingly, in Allen's various accounts, the difficulty of providing a complete and convincing account of film spectatorship is understood as the result of philosophical confusions that attend certain experiences that overwhelm the viewer or are difficult for her to describe. For this reason, Allen's account implies that the difficulty in creating these descriptions does not lie *in us*, as it were (or in our attempts to articulate our experience), but in the bumps and roundabouts of our language. Allen reads Wittgenstein as making our route through these verbal difficulties more perspicuous.[13]

A subsequent essay by Malcolm Turvey, "Seeing Theory: On Perception and Emotional Response in Current Film Theory," further articulates this taxonomy. Turvey's account stresses the antipsychologistic dimension of section xi, which he reads as in large part defeating "the myth of the inner" (considered here under the heading of "aspect-dawning"): "Aspect-dawning does not involve the addition of some sort of subjective mental entity, such as a thought or interpretation, to the beholder's objective perception of the image as a material entity consisting of light, shadow, shape, and colour. In other words, the aspect cannot be explained *psychologically* as a subjective mental entity."[14]

The concern here, as in Allen's work, is to defeat a "causal theory" of film perception, whereby the act of viewing is made obscure by the recession of the image into inaccessible, inner regions of the mind. Now, while it is true that Wittgenstein frequently attacks inaccurate perceptions of the inner and a hasty reliance on psychological explanation, Turvey's account of aspect perception further extends the reading of Wittgenstein as largely concerned with warding off philosophical confusion. Furthermore, despite its protestations against psychologistic interpretations of section xi, it continues to think of aspect perception as a kind of experience, albeit one that is difficult to describe.

An indication of the shaky ground of such an understanding is that Turvey is unable to account for passages in Wittgenstein like this one: "And *is* it a special impression?—'Surely I see something *different* when I see the sphere floating from when I merely see it lying there.'—This really means: This expression is justified!—(For taken literally it is no more than a repetition.)"[15]

In this passage, Wittgenstein is discussing the dawning of an aspect in the picture of a sphere. In Turvey's account, it is inaccurate to speak of seeing something "different" after this aspect dawns because it leads to the postulation of imaginary mental entities *behind* the perception. But in this reading, a line like "This really means: This expression is justified!" falls away. (At the most, it reads as Wittgenstein chiding his interlocutor into a less confused position.) The line, however, is important to Wittgenstein's larger point: it is a statement about the grammar of the previous expression, and he is noting that the expression does not mean what his interlocutor thinks it means (taken literally, it is a repetition of a previous expression). It means something closer to "I want these words to mean something here because the picture has indeed changed!"

Other instances of the standard account occur in recent books by Edward Branigan (*Projecting a Camera: Language-Games in Film Theory*) and W. J. T. Mitchell (*What Do Pictures Want?*).[16] In Branigan, the emphasis is again on aspect perception as a strange visual phenomenon: "The range of Wittgenstein's examples [in section xi] shows that aspects may arise from illusory patterns of stimuli (i.e., bottom-up), or from a task one is performing (i.e., top-down), or from cross-modal or lateral processing (as in synesthesia; or, as in 'lateral' continuity rules in film, e.g., the convention of sound perspective which matches audibility and visibility), or from 'perceptual metaphors' (e.g., visualizing a knight's move in a chess game in terms of a distinctive 'shape'), or from effects of memory."[17]

Such an account veers off the track of Wittgenstein's text insofar as it is full of technical language that is for the most part absent in the *Investigations*. Indeed, section xi is one of the rare places in that text in which Wittgenstein *does* introduce more "technical" sounding terms—like "aspect perception" and "regarding as"—but these terms are a world away from a phrase like "cross-modal or lateral processing." Branigan's language signals that we have turned our backs upon the world of ordinary language and left behind the specific contexts (the "forms of life," as Wittgenstein puts it) in which this language has its life and meaning. In Branigan's account, we find the further parsing of visual experience at the expense of its place within specific human lives. Insofar as Branigan's spectator goes to the movies, he seems to go alone, sit alone, and not talk about the experience with his friends.

And so it is with Mitchell's use, which continues to stress this lack of social context—and henceforth understands "seeing as" as a failed conceptual resource. Mitchell's Wittgenstein makes explicit the idea that aspect perception in the *Investigations* is contextless. Here, he writes about the ancient icon of the molten calf: "The object relations into which this object enters, then, are like Wittgenstein's 'seeing-as' or 'aspect seeing'; the calf is a shape-shifting chimera that changes with the subject's perceptual schematism. Unlike Wittgenstein's multistable images, however, it is not the cognitive or perceptual features of the image that shift (no one claims to see the calf as a camel) but its value, status, power, and vitality."[18] Unlike Branigan's use (and like Allen's initial use in *Projective Illusion*), this passage displays an understanding of aspect perception as restricted to figures with twin aspects, each of which seems to hold the other from view. But as Branigan points out, the range of phenomena that come under discussion in section xi suggests that Wittgenstein in no way wants these figures to stand as paradigmatic cases of "seeing as." And contra any instance of the standard account, it is *precisely* the "value, status, power, and vitality" of an image that may be communicated (and hence affirmed or rejected) through the utterances that surround aspect perception. Identifying (and parsing and sharing and agreeing or disagreeing upon) these qualities in an object or experience, one might say, is the very *point* of "seeing as."

In summary, all of the instances of the standard account make two important and overarching errors: (1) they understand aspect perception as a special kind of seeing (that is, as a specific visual phenomenon or set of visual phenomena); and (2) they fail to consider seeing as within the contexts (the forms of life) in which it has its use.

If "seeing as" does not identify a specific *kind* of seeing, to what then does it refer? After all, Wittgenstein talks about Necker cubes and intersecting parallelograms and picture-faces, all of which seem to belong to a larger family of visual phenomena. What about these objects does *not* have to do with seeing? The problem is in the way that these different versions of the standard account take the "point" of Wittgenstein's words. (We might also say that the problem is that they do not see much of a "point" in them at all.) As counterintuitive as it will seem to a theoretical tradition steeped in ideological and psychoanalytic descriptions of filmic perception, the problem here is not in the words of our language, or in the difficulty of describing certain experiences, but in *us.* The problem lies in the difficulty in articulating our experience of the world, in making it ours. This is, we could say, one theme of *Shoulder Arms.*

Against the standard account, then, I want to suggest that insofar as the concept of aspect perception is of use to scholars of film and other visual media, this use is interpretive rather than theoretical in nature. This is to say that a proper understanding of the concept will provide us with a certain vision of what interpretation is. Instead of employing the idea as a cognitive concept, or a means of thinking about the phenomenology of illusion, we should use the concept of aspect perception as a means of thinking about the ethical aspects of the communication that surrounds ordinary perception. I want to suggest that we read moments of *Shoulder Arms,* such as the tree sequence, as interpretive in nature, as demonstrating the experience of seeing things *anew.*

In reading Wittgenstein this way, I follow the work of the philosopher Avner Baz.[19] Baz's Cavellian account of section xi eschews the literal Wittgenstein we find in the standard film studies accounts. Instead, he gives a reading of the *force* of Wittgenstein's words, a force we might think of as ethical in nature: "Most of human experience is of what tends to present itself as ordinary and familiar, and so as unremarkable. What we need, then, if this experience is not to be lost on us, not to pass us like nothing, and if we are not to be bored, is the ability to find something about the ordinary and the familiar that makes it worth noting and articulating—we need to be able to find it *new.*"[20]

A good portion of Baz's account is taken up with arguments against the account of aspect perception that we found at the root of its uses in the discipline of film and media studies.[21] I want only to summarize them in brief before moving on to what I take to be the implications of Baz's claim for our interpretation of *Shoulder Arms.*

To begin, Baz takes issue with the idea that the ambiguous figures of the duck-rabbit and the Necker cube are paradigmatic examples of aspect perception. In addition to the fact that section xi is full of nonambiguous figures (like the galloping horse or the picture-face), to take the duck-rabbit and the Necker cube as paradigmatic is to miss the fact that "in the course of daily living we come across numerous things that *could* be seen as this or that . . . but we don't take *that* as a good reason for so seeing them."[22] In Baz's account, there must be a reason for taking something as something.

People, in other words, are not generally given to spontaneous reports of their perceptual experiences. In speaking, Baz insists, human beings are generally required to make sense. They report their experiences to others for specific reasons and in specific contexts.

Second, Baz argues against the distinction between "seeing" and "knowing" that forms a crucial part of the foundation of Mulhall's claims about aspect perception. Mulhall's point in making such a distinction is to undermine what Allen has called the "causal theory" of perception, a theory that extends from empiricist theorizations of sense data. The empiricist model postulates an inner process of interpretation that accompanies the purely sensual data that reach the mind. In this model, sense data are "dead" in that they are only given meaning by inner processes of knowledge. The problem here is that such a description fails to properly cohere to the phenomenology of vision, which includes moments of both consideration, in which we work to form an accurate hypothesis about the identity of a given object, and spontaneity, in which something about an object of sight strikes us immediately. Mulhall goes on to take the qualities of "immediacy" and "spontaneity" as distinguishing "seeing as" from ordinary visual knowledge, "seeing" from "knowing." Baz points out that Wittgenstein does not make such a distinction himself and that there are examples from his work in which "seeing as" is not characterized by spontaneity at all, but by consideration and even doubt (e.g., the "floating sphere"). As Baz puts it, the difference is not one of a *kind* of perception but one of different *language games:* "It is not only what we say and how, or how fast, we say it, but also when, and in front of what, and in the company of whom, and what we would accept as a proper response on her part to what we say."[23] Or as Wittgenstein himself puts it, "Our problem is not a causal but a conceptual one."[24] The issue here is not psychological (or even physiological), but grammatical.

Third, Baz refutes the idea that Wittgenstein takes aspect perception to be a "typical" relation to the world that we might meaningfully discuss, as Mulhall tries to do, under the heading of "continuous aspect perception" (or "regarding-as").[25] The problem again lies in the tendency to think of aspect perception outside of its expression in different language games. For Baz, we might think of plausible uses of the phrase "continuous aspect perception" (keeping in mind that Wittgenstein himself only uses the phrase "continuous seeing of an aspect" once) but conclude that these uses belong (in their imaginary incarnations) to different language games from those of "aspect dawning" or "seeing as." In these potential uses, the language game changes from that of an *Ausserung* (utterance) to that of a perceptual report.[26] These are *wholly* different uses, not two related uses on a single continuum.

Most importantly, however, Baz's account diverges from Mulhall's and hence from the standard film studies account in the crucial respect of not reading Wittgenstein as always working against specific philosophical confusions and as instead articulating ideas about value. With this assertion, we are in territory greatly different from that of the accounts in Allen and Turvey, where the utility of Wittgenstein's work resides solely in its propaedeutic value. Instead of thinking of section xi as the diagnosis and treatment of confusions brought about by experiences that are difficult to articulate, Baz reads Wittgenstein as responding to what he takes to be a problem that generally accompanies human experience, and he describes this problem as the need to "*articulate* our experience of the world, if that experience, and hence the world, is to become ours."[27] This Kantian formulation reads Wittgenstein in an ethical register. It is this register, I want to suggest, that is of interest in thinking about aspect perception in *Shoulder Arms* and that movie's interesting reading of the object world of warfare. Baz's essay acknowledges that our expressions must have a *point* and hence suggests that Wittgenstein's interpreters in the domain of film studies fail to bring their words back from the realm of the metaphysical to their everyday use (that is, their words fail to have a point or fail to contain ethical content). Their words are full of theory and empty of interpretation.

The idea of aspect perception as involving both a sense of newness and an ethical dimension points out the adherence of value judgments within the articulation of perceptual experience and thereby argues that the experience of film viewership can be understood as a series of moments in which one's sense of attunement is tested and one's agreement, or knowledge of others, is given or refused. In keeping with Baz's reading of Wittgenstein, and indeed with a Cavellian approach more generally, *Shoulder Arms* suggests that the concept's proper use belongs in the realm of value or morality, in the concepts of truthfulness and attunement. In Chaplin's gags, an interest in one's views of things cannot be separated from an interest in the articulation of one's own experience.

The Articulation of Experience

What does this help us to see about Chaplin and his tree costume? We might begin by thinking of Chaplin's gag as an attempt to articulate an experience and, consequently, as an attempt to make the world his (and hence ours). The joke proceeds from the idea that human beings can be strange to one another (nowhere more so than in conditions of war), but it uses this sense, in the context of irony, to establish a kind of agreement with its larger audience. We know that Chaplin is not a tree, but the German soldier does not. And later, a different soldier knows that Chaplin is not a tree, but he cannot differentiate this person-tree from the ordinary trees that surround him. In this way, the film demonstrates that declarations of sight such as these gags can be received in multiple ways. To perceive Doughboy as a tree is not a simple question of seeing him as man *or* tree, duck *or* rabbit, but rather a question of a great wealth and range of responses. The gag demonstrates that other people may take up our articulations and affirm our criteria and hence our mutuality, as well as that they can take these occasions as annoyances (or worse, provocations).[28] The French maid is happy to receive her grease moustache; the German soldier is unsurprised that this man here is a tree. Indeed, the sight does not stop this soldier in his tracks but rather increases his desire to maim. Part of the pleasure of the gag comes from the fact that Chaplin is in a sense asking us, his audience, to see as he sees, to affirm his perception that a man is like a tree (but not so fully that he should be cut down). These gags work to articulate experiences of estrangement and identity. They also perform acts of humor-by-agreement by using certain qualities specific to the medium of film, namely, the cinema's ability to loosely associate the "real" and the hallucinatory, and they claim these qualities in service of human intimacy (between Doughboy and his comrades, between Chaplin and his viewers).

It is significant, in this sense, that the first joke (that of the soldier gearing up to take a whack at Chaplin with an axe) is accomplished by means of the earlier revelation, to the audience, that the tree is in fact Chaplin. Suture theory suggests that the film viewer is sutured into the third-person narration of the fiction film through the action of cutting from between views, as Daniel Dayan famously argued.[29] We are shown a view of things and wonder who sees this view, only to have this question answered in the form of a reverse shot in which the perspective is assigned to the eyes of a character within the diegesis. But this action occurs only tenuously in *Shoulder Arms*. While it is clear that the soldier does not *see* Doughboy as we do, we are never treated to his literal point of view. Instead, Chaplin aligns himself, and more importantly his face, frontally with the camera. In this sense, we might argue that the "suture" occurs not at the moment we learn to whom the view belongs (as it does in Dayan's account), but at the moment of the revelation that Chaplin is in fact the tree. Here, spectator knowledge is not tied to the knowledge of a character within the film's diegesis, but instead is made complete by the action of irony. The gag works because the film's audience has more epistemic knowledge than the scene's two characters.

In this way, the film's audience is implicated in the film's acts of vision and judgment. We can reject Doughboy's lyrical play with his tree costume, for instance, or refuse him the idea that a nutmeg grater makes a good back-scratcher. We can refuse, that is, to see that these acts are funny. But the film attempts to make us understand that the refusal of such agreement has larger consequences for the community of viewership. *Shoulder Arms* understands the act of film viewership to be filled with moments of active interpretation, the giving of one's consent to a series of images. And this consent turns out to be identified with our knowledge of others.

What interests me about this movement between knowledge and consent is that this knowledge is not characterized by the availability or absence of information but by the acceptance or rejection of intimacy; either one is subject to a series of constraints. The German soldier's knowledge of Doughboy may be constrained by his place in the war, but his perception takes the interesting form of a kind of blindness. Whereas most philosophical accounts of the problem of other minds take as paradigmatic situations in which one's knowledge is *incomplete* (the archetypal example involves the experience of pain: I do not literally feel your headache; hence I cannot know that it exists), *Shoulder Arms* provides us with examples in which one's knowledge is both constrained and then rejected. (After all, Doughboy makes clear overtures to the fact that he is not a tree.)

Instead of thinking about suture as a cognitive process that occurs somewhere below the spectator's awareness, we might—in certain instances at least—understand it as the giving of one's consent to a particular visual articulation. In the case of *Shoulder Arms,* opportunities for consent take the form of moments of visual flexibility, moments in which our willingness to see in new ways is put to the test and either accepted or rejected. Or as Baz puts it with regard to the articulation of aspect perception, this action "puts our attunement with other people to the test, which means that it can also provide the occasion for certain moments of intimacy, depending on how far that attunement is found to reach."[30] Unlike the German soldier, upon whom the interpretation of Doughboy as actual tree is forced by the exigencies of warfare, we can grant Chaplin his tree impression—the odd, stumplike movements of his Gumby-shaped legs, his subtle mimicry of a tree's limbs—or we can refuse to see it. What is at stake here is the measure of our attunement. The film understands such attunement to lie beneath our knowledge of each other, and it insists upon the fact that this knowledge is not a matter of simple perceptual knowledge, however mediated. In this way, a revised understanding of aspect perception helps us to read Chaplin's film as taking up these issues and to see that our theoretical preoccupations go a long way toward determining our interpretations of particular films.

Shoulder Arms and the First World War

What does all of this have to do with the fact that *Shoulder Arms* is, after all, a war film?[31] There is of course the point that I have just finished making: that Chaplin's film theorizes vision in a way that has implications both for the sort of visual perception that occurs in different conditions of war and for the ways in which we, the audience of these films and of the wars that continue to be waged around us, perceive wars and the people within them. I have been attempting to establish that *Shoulder Arms,* in this sense, has a pedagogical motive in addition to, or in conjunction with, its articulation of value, and that this motive is visible in Chaplin's imaginative demonstration of the seeing of aspects. The film makes the claim that soldiers (like the bullies and cops of Chaplin's other films) see inadequately, or unimaginatively, and therefore forfeit something of themselves, not to mention something of the people around them, and its implication is that this failure to imagine is in a sense built into the environment of war. It is difficult to escape the feeling that *Shoulder Arms,* for all of its rough humor, is a sad film. While it suggests that we should be able to imagine new contexts for the objects of our world, even in the setting of war, it also acknowledges that not everyone is capable of, or ready for, such imagination and flights of fancy. As he does later in *The Great Dictator,* Chaplin makes fun while at the same time placing the weight of the world on his thin shoulders.

But what actually characterized perceptual experience in the environment of the First World War, and how does *Shoulder Arms* come to say something about this experience? One way to think about the nature of this perceptual experience is to count it as an extension of the violence that was then accompanying the rapid industrialization and urbanization of American society as well as the European continent, on which the First World War was being waged. The turn of the century was filled with new forms and magnitudes of violence, whether at the hand of errant streetcars, the forces of organized crime, or the recently invented submachine gun. In this sense, the specific violence of trench warfare was simply the least inhibited form of a new contact between human beings and the stray forces of mechanization.[32] If, as Hannah Arendt put it, "violence is by nature instrumental," the violence of the First World War was characterized by the emergent repression of new and more powerful instruments.[33]

This instrumentality resulted in what Wolfgang Schivelbusch and others have described as the new phenomenon of shock. Shock, as Schivelbusch defines it, does not simply have to do with the presence and violence of new material forces, but with persons' registration of a discontinuity in the social sphere that was brought about by these material forces. In this phenomenon, he argues, a "sudden and powerful event of violence . . . disrupts the continuity of an artificially/mechanically created notion or situation, and also the subsequent state of derangement. The precondition for this is a highly developed general state of dominance over nature, both technically (military example: firearms) and psychically (military example: troop discipline). The degree of control over nature and the violence of the collapse of that control, in shock, are proportionate: the more finely meshed the web of mechanization, discipline, division of labor, etc., the more catastrophic the collapse when it is disrupted from within or without."[34]

Shock presented people—both soldiers and ordinary persons—with the need to adjust to a world in which the physical and indeed metaphysical rug might be pulled, at any moment, from beneath their feet. Both the humor and the pathos of Chaplin's film result from its dealing directly with the issue of instrumentality and its consequent shock. Doughboy's heroism does not lie in his capturing the Kaiser and winning the war (an event that the film rather sadly, or perhaps simply realistically, attributes to the character's dream and hence to his desire), but in his demonstration of a new attitude or bearing toward the object world, one that I have been describing as seeing this world "anew." This new bearing constitutes a progressive adaptation to the presence of new material forces, whether by using factory-produced items to serve humbler, alternative purposes (the Victrola snorkel) or by understanding even the perilous environment of war to provide opportunities for an intimacy both with other persons and with the object world (Doughboy's rifle-bullet cigarette lighter). Chaplin makes this world hospitable, amenable to human expression and imagination. The underlying pathos of the film results from the question of how far one can realistically take this adaptation. Chaplin shows that it can be done, but even for Doughboy, this newfound intimacy and imagination is a dream. After all, few of us would use a military rifle to light a Lucky Strike.

Still, in *Shoulder Arms,* we have something like the obverse of more chauvinistic portrayals of war, such as the turn-of-the-century depictions of the Spanish-American war that Edison included in his *War Extra* catalogue. Those films, as Kristen Whissel has argued, enact a recuperation of the screened male body, a body that was then being subjected to both physical and metaphysical threats as the result of rapid industrialization: "Discursive constructions [such as Edison's war actualities] provided compelling counternarratives to the all-too-familiar image of an enervated male body exhausted and effeminized by the demands of industrial capitalism and technological modernity."[35] Unlike the bodies of Edison's naval officers, Chaplin's slapstick body represents something like freedom from technological violence and determination. And unlike more celebratory images of the First World War, *Shoulder Arms* imagines military victory not through heightened and successful demands on human attention and physiology but through a creative ignorance of discipline. Doughboy enacts an entirely different fantasy, one of a technological modernity that does not encumber the individual but instead frees him to respond to the object world and thus make it new on his own.

I have been arguing for what amounts to a pacifist reading of the film, with its dressing up of a humanist message in the baggy pantaloons of slapstick comedy. This certainly coheres with the later image of Chaplin as a leftist (an image that eventually resulted in J. Edgar Hoover's de facto deportation of the comedian in 1952). Yet the film's practical relationship to the conflict was hardly that of conscientious objector, as can more easily be said of a certain strain of contemporary films like Thomas Ince's *Civilization* (1916). Indeed, the reception of *Shoulder Arms* nicely demonstrates the film's ambivalence with regard to its depiction of war, an ambivalence that can help us to think about the political valence of slapstick more generally. Leslie DeBauche has documented the ways in which journalists and exhibitors of the time worked, with Chaplin's help, to handle the comedian's image and to assure audiences that *Shoulder Arms* was not merely a burlesque of the Great War but, as one reviewer put it, that the film "embellishes" the "dignity [of soldiers] with a new viewpoint."[36] Indeed, Chaplin, after not enlisting in the British or American armies, actively and publicly contributed to the

British war effort, claimed to the public that he had been turned down for service because of his slight stature, and raised funds for the Treasury by participating in Liberty Bond drives.[37] When the film was released, *Moving Picture World* went as far as to suggest that exhibitors encourage patrons to "copy the military equipment Chaplin carries and offer a prize to the best equipped soldier."[38] In this light, the film registers the famous disagreement between Walter Benjamin and Theodor W. Adorno about the critical and therapeutic potential of Disney cartoons, through which Benjamin had been led to theorize that "collective laughter" represented a "preemptive and healing outbreak of mass psychoses."[39]

This context may merely point to the fact that films critical of the war, at least in this late stage of the conflict, needed to cover their messages with a patriotic surface, at least in the marketing that surrounded them. Nevertheless, the distribution and reception of *Shoulder Arms* offers a potentially suggestive context for thinking about the critical potential (or lack thereof) of slapstick comedy. Above, I suggested that the pathos of the film derives from the extent to which Chaplin's positive adaptation to a world of shock and instrumentality can be seen as realizable. (Early cartoons make this point more exuberantly: I can imagine lighting a cigarette with rifle fire—even if I would never attempt it—but it is terrifying to think of using a turkey's feathers as the tail for an airplane, as Mickey Mouse does.) It is the virtue of slapstick to undermine forms of authority by means of ironic refusal (of discipline, of work, of the performance of normative behaviors), but it is finally its weakness to retreat into the nowhere world of this refusal. (It is the nature of irony, after all, to see things both ways.) What, ultimately, does Chaplin's film have to say about the nature of visual perception in war?

One of the achievements of *Shoulder Arms* is its ability to function as a site of reflection about the visual environment of war. It uses this environment in which the stakes (sketched however loosely in the gestures of slapstick) are life and death to articulate the ways in which the demonstration or expression of visual perceptions has an ethical cast. The ethical nature of the expression of our perceptions is seen in high relief in this environment. This is similar, I have been arguing, to the ways in which Wittgenstein probes the peculiar conjunction of the perceptual, the psychological, and the ethical in what he calls the "grammar" of aspect perception. In the first part of the *Investigations,* Wittgenstein has this to say about "dead" expressions: "'Put a ruler against this object; it does not say that the object is so-and-so long. Rather, it is in itself—I am tempted to say—dead, and achieves nothing of what a thought can achieve.'—It is as if we had imagined that the essential thing about a living human being was the outward form. Then we made a lump of wood into that form and were abashed to see the lifeless block, lacking any similarity to a living creature."[40] Just as Wittgenstein directs a therapeutic eye toward the "lifeless" expressions toward which philosophers tend (his intervention here taking the form of parable, that of a sculptor surprised to see that his creation of wood does not breathe like a human being), Chaplin directs his play with nutmeg graters, Limburger cheeses, axle grease, and dead trees toward the blindness of soldiers as well as that of men and women in movie theaters, asking that they see again and anew. His actions figure the world as a place that can be made hospitable to human desire. That these actions are taken in the environment of war is an argument for the resilience and power of these desires, even if, as the case is here, their realization turns out to be merely a dream.

Notes

1. See, for instance, the essays in *Wittgenstein, Theory and the Arts,* ed. Richard Allen and Malcolm Turvey (New York: Routledge, 2001); Allen, *Projecting Illusion: Film Spectatorship and the Impression of Reality* (Cambridge: Cambridge University Press, 1995); and Edward Branigan, *Projecting a Camera: Language-Games and Film Theory* (New York: Routledge, 2006). There is of course the work of Stanley Cavell, which is quite different in character from that of Allen and Turvey. See especially *The World Viewed: Reflections on the Ontology of Film* (Cambridge, MA: Harvard University Press, 1979). See too Rupert Read, *Film as Philosophy: Essays on Cinema after Wittgenstein and Cavell* (New York: Palgrave Macmillan, 2005). *The World Viewed,* in particular, can be understood as inaugurating a strain of film theory and criticism that has never been fully absorbed into the thinking of more ideologically or psychoanalytically minded film theorists nor into the work of those theorists who consciously take up the tools of the analytic tradition.

2. This has in part to do with the analytic tradition's historical emphasis on questions of formal logic and the idea of philosophical work as foundational for advances in mathematics and the sciences. Works like Wittgenstein's own *Tractatus Logico-Philosophicus* (1921) or Bertrand Russell's *The Principles of Mathematics* (1903), although contemporary with important developments in the history of film, have no obvious relationship to the issues with which the cinema was concerned. Nevertheless, certain film theorists have maintained an interest in analytic philosophy. Noël Carroll, for instance, has brought the tools of analytic philosophy to bear in a critical fashion on larger questions of film theory. See his *Philosophical Problems of Classical Film Theory* (Princeton,

NJ: Princeton University Press, 1988). See also Branigan's *Projecting a Camera,* cited above, which employs these tools in search of new descriptions of film form, as well as Stephen Mulhall's *On Film* (New York: Routledge, 2002).

3. See, for instance, Allen and Turvey's introduction to the *Wittgenstein, Theory and the Arts* volume, "Wittgenstein's Later Philosophy: A Prophylaxis against Theory," 1–36.

4. Contemporary audiences also responded to this aspect of Chaplin's comedy. "The bit where he uses a nutmeg grater to scratch his back because of cooties," a reviewer for the *Atlanta Constitution* wrote, referring to the insects that were a part of trench life in the war, "and the hokum business with Charlie in a camouflaged suit to make him look like a dead tree, were marvelous bits of funmaking." "Chaplin's Latest, 'Shoulder Arms,' Sure Fire Comedy," *Atlanta Constitution,* November 12, 1918, 14.

5. *Shoulder Arms* (Chaplin, 1918), 0:23:01–0:29:07.

6. In the recently updated translation of the *Philosophical Investigations,* Part II has been renamed *Philosophy of Psychology—A Fragment* to emphasize its conceptual separation from the text of Part I. I have included page and section numbers from both editions below. See Ludwig Wittgenstein, *Philosophical Investigations,* trans. G. E. M. Anscombe, P. M. S. Hacker, and Joachim Schulte (Malden, MA: Blackwell, 2001); and *Philosophical Investigations,* rev. trans. P. M. S. Hacker and Joachim Schulte (Malden, MA: Wiley-Blackwell, 2009).

Film theoretical works that read Wittgenstein's discussion of aspect perception as having to do with the phenomenology of vision include Richard Allen, *Projecting Illusion,* cited above; Allen, "Looking at Motion Pictures," in *Film Theory and Philosophy,* ed. Allen and Murray Smith (New York: Oxford University Press, 1999), 76–94; Malcolm Turvey, "Seeing Theory: On Perception and Emotional Response in Current Film Theory," also in *Film Theory and Philosophy,* 431–57; Turvey, *Doubting Vision: Film and the Revelationist Tradition* (New York: Oxford University Press, 2008), 66–69; Edward Branigan, *Projecting a Camera,* cited above; W. J. T. Mitchell, *What Do Pictures Want? The Lives and Loves of Images* (Chicago: University of Chicago Press, 2006); and Louis A. Sass, "Wittgenstein, Freud and the Nature of Psychoanalytic Explanation," in Allen and Turvey, *Wittgenstein, Theory, and the Arts,* 254–96. See also Allen's revision of "Looking at Motion Pictures" in *Film-Philosophy* 5, no. 25 (August 2001), www.film-philosophy.com/vol5-2001/n25allen, which addresses the concern that the first version of the essay appeared, as he puts it, "to deny the role of causality in perception altogether."

7. Allen (*Projecting Illusion*) and Mitchell take these two figures as paradigmatic; Turvey (*Doubting Vision*) and Branigan appear to understand Wittgenstein as creating a kind of taxonomy of perception.

8. A submerged point of origin of the standard account is E. H. Gombrich's *Art and Illusion: A Study in the Psychology of Pictorial Representation* (Princeton, NJ: Princeton University Press, 1956, 2000), which briefly refers to the duck-rabbit illusion discussed at length in Wittgenstein's work. Gombrich does not refer directly to the concept of

"seeing as," but, as the title suggests, the book is an attempt to provide a convincing and commonsensical account of the kinds of illusion involved in the viewing of art objects.

9. Allen, *Projecting Illusion,* 114. See, for instance, Mulhall's treatment of aspect perception and aesthetics in the final chapter, "Icons, Gestures, Aesthetics," of his book *On Being in the World: Wittgenstein and Heidegger on Seeing Aspects* (New York: Routledge, 1990), 156–95. Mulhall writes that "just as we are inclined to express the realization that one *picture* can be treated as a representation of two different entities in a way which suggests a change from one sort of *pictured object* to another, so we are sometimes inclined to express the impact a picture makes upon us in terms which imply the materialization of the pictured scene or object before us" (180).

10. Allen, *Projecting Illusion,* 101.

11. The duck-rabbit appears at §118, the Necker cube at §116 in the Hacker-Schulte translation of the *Investigations,* which has added section numbers to Part II. The images appear on pages 166 and 165, respectively, of the Anscombe-Hacker-Schulte volume.

12. Allen, "Looking at Motion Pictures," *Film-Philosophy* version.

13. Allen's essay in *Film Theory and Philosophy* (the unrevised version of "Looking at Motion Pictures") is committed to refuting a philosophical confusion inherent in the major theories of pictorial perception, namely the idea that pictures (moving or not) have a causal relationship to interior, mental states in their perceivers. He calls this idea, implicit in these theories, "the causal theory of perception." Against the causal theory, Allen provides an account of pictorial perception (building on his work in *Projective Illusion*) in which Wittgenstein's discussion of aspect perception plays a major role. The essay repeats the sense of aspect perception as identifying a phenomenology of vision. Allen moves on from the idea of sequential aspects as paradigmatic examples of the experience and extends his thinking to objects of sight more generally. Pictures take the place of the duck-rabbit: "Pictorial perception exemplifies aspect seeing. When we look at a motion picture we see what the motion picture depicts, but what we see is neither the thing itself nor an illusion of it" (78).

It is important to note that his later revision of this essay takes issue with the earlier idea of "projective illusion" and further articulates the idea that, as Allen puts it, "representational paintings, photographs, and films manifest what Wittgenstein terms 'continuous aspect perception' in which . . . the aspect becomes a property of the picture that the picture compels us to see." Allen, "Looking at Motion Pictures," *Film-Philosophy* version.

14. Turvey, "Seeing Theory," 443.

15. *Philosophy of Psychology—A Fragment* (2009), §171; *Philosophical Investigations,* Part II (2001), 172.

16. Branigan, *Projecting a Camera;* and Mitchell, *What Do Pictures Want?* cited above.

17. Branigan, *Projecting a Camera,* 199.

18. Mitchell, *What Do Pictures Want?* 189.

19. Avner Baz can be understood as proposing a Cavellian intervention into this

larger debate about aspect perception. In what follows I refer exclusively to Baz's essay "What's the Point of Seeing Aspects?" *Philosophical Investigations* 23, no. 2 (April 2000): 97–121, but three more essays are of interest as well. See Baz, "What's the Point of Calling Out Beauty?" *British Journal of Aesthetics* 44, no. 1 (January 2004): 57–72; and "On When Words Are Called For: Cavell, McDowell, and the Wording of the World," *Inquiry* 46, no. 4 (2003): 473–500, both of which continue to work out the implications of this first essay. Baz continues his argument with Mulhall in "On Learning from Wittgenstein, or What Does It Take to *See* the Grammar of Seeing Aspects?" in *Seeing Wittgenstein Anew,* ed. William Day and Victor J. Krebs (New York: Cambridge University Press, 2010). See also Baz's recent book *When Words Are Called For: A Defense of Ordinary Language Philosophy* (Cambridge, MA: Harvard University Press, 2012). See also the other essays in *Seeing Wittgenstein Anew,* many of which display more Cavellian interpretations of Wittgenstein's writing. For Cavell's comments on the concept of aspect perception, and his sense that aspect perception possesses a moral dimension, see *The Claim of Reason: Wittgenstein, Skepticism, Morality, and Tragedy* (New York: Oxford University Press, 1979), 370–72; and *The World Viewed,* 147–60.

20. Baz, "What's the Point of Seeing Aspects?" 99.

21. As I suggested above, Allen and Turvey's accounts of aspect perception appear to derive from Mulhall's work. Baz's essays address Mulhall's account, which appears in Mulhall's *On Being in the World;* and in his *Inheritance and Originality: Wittgenstein, Heidegger, Kierkegaard* (New York: Oxford University Press, 2001); as well as in his essay "Seeing Aspects," in *Wittgenstein: A Critical Reader,* ed. Hans-Johann Glock (Malden, MA: Blackwell, 2001), 246–67. Baz takes up Mulhall's arguments directly in "What's the Point of Seeing Aspects" and in the more recent "On Learning from Wittgenstein." Of interest as well is Mulhall's response to the latter article, "The Work of Wittgenstein's Words: A Reply to Baz," which also appears in Day and Krebs, *Seeing Wittgenstein Anew,* 249–67.

22. Baz, "What's the Point of Seeing Aspects?" 99.

23. Ibid., 105.

24. *Philosophy of Psychology—A Fragment* (2009), §183; *Philosophical Investigations,* Part II (2001), 174.

25. See, for instance, *On Being in the World,* 123. See also "The Work of Wittgenstein's Words," 261–67, where Mulhall specifically addresses Baz's criticisms of this idea.

26. Baz, "What's the Point of Seeing Aspects?" 116.

27. Ibid., 98.

28. Cavell writes, in *The Claim of Reason,* "Suppose we ask: What is my relation to an aspect which has not dawned upon me, is in that sense hidden from me, but which is nevertheless there *to be seen?* What don't I see when everything is in front of my eyes? I find that I want to speak of failing to see a possibility: I do not appreciate some way it might be—not just some way it might appear, but might *be*" (370).

29. See Daniel Dayan, "The Tutor-Code of Classical Cinema," in *Film Theory and*

Criticism: Introductory Readings, ed. Leo Braudy and Marshall Cohen (New York: Oxford University Press, 1999), 118–29. See too William Rothman's considered rejection of the idea of suture in "Against 'The System of the Suture,'" *Film Quarterly* 29, no. 1 (Autumn 1975): 45–50.

30. Baz, "What's the Point of Seeing Aspects?" 98. This is something like the issue that Ted Cohen found to be at stake in humor in his book on jokes. See his *Jokes: Philosophical Thoughts on Laughing Matters* (Chicago: University of Chicago Press, 1999).

31. The designation is, of course, open to debate. It's difficult to compare *Shoulder Arms* with, say, *The Sands of Iwo Jima*, just as *Blazing Saddles* is not a Western in the vein of *The Searchers*. Both films may have war as their settings, but the comedy, one wants to say, distances itself and its audience from that setting. Still, it seems fair to call *Shoulder Arms* a war film, given the context in which it was produced and released and given its direct treatment of the First World War.

32. It is important to note that the moral surprise that was occasioned by these new forms of violence was in large part the result of its being directed against white European peoples. In his *The Social History of the Machine Gun* (New York: Pantheon, 1975), John Ellis describes the importance of machine guns for the British imperial project, noting that:

> because they regarded the Africans as weird eccentrics, hardly even human beings, [colonial regiments] could look on colonial warfare as an amusing diversion that had little in common with the "real" wars that had been fought in Europe and might have to be fought in the future. Thus, because the machine gun had become so much a part of these imperialist sideshows, it came to be regarded, by definition, as a weapon that had no place upon the conventional battlefield. The European was obviously superior to the African, so why would he ever be so stupid as to be baulked by a weapon that was really only good for bowling over "niggers" and "Kaffirs"? Of all the chickens that came home to roost and cackle over the dead on the battlefields of the First World War, none was more raucous than the racialism that had somehow assumed that the white man would be invulnerable to those same weapons that had slaughtered natives in their thousands (102).

33. Arendt, *On Violence* (New York: Harcourt Brace, 1970), 51.

34. As quoted in Whissel, *Picturing American Modernity: Traffic, Technology, and the Silent Cinema* (Durham, NC: Duke University Press, 2008), 32.

35. Ibid., 22.

36. As quoted in DeBauche, *Reel Patriotism: The Movies and World War I* (Madison: University of Wisconsin Press, 1997), 155.

37. Ibid., 155.

38. Ibid., 156.

39. As quoted in Miriam Hansen, *Cinema and Experience: Sigfried Kracauer, Walter Benjamin, Theodor W. Adorno* (Berkeley: University of California Press, 2011), 165.

40. Wittgenstein, *Philosophical Investigations—A Fragment* (2009), §430.

Part 2

War as Condition of Self-Formation and Self-Dissolution

Apocalypse Within

The War Epic as Crisis of Self-Identity

Garry L. Hagberg

Francis Ford Coppola's 1979 film *Apocalypse Now* has been hailed as one of the great war films of all time, and indeed as one of the great films of all time. Film critic Roger Ebert has rightly said of Coppola's film, "*Apocalypse Now* is the best Vietnam film, one of the greatest of all films, because it pushes beyond the others, into the dark places of the soul. It is not about war so much as about how war reveals truths we would be happy never to discover."[1]

This film is about self-identity, self-knowledge, and what we might call self-defining character-solidification through intertwined processes of making up one's mind and enacting it.[2] And as a war film, it—like very many if not all war films—casts these philosophical issues in high relief, precisely because the circumstances of war bring into sharp focus what one ultimately stands for, what one is and is not willing to do—in short, where one draws the line that one will not, or, perhaps more interestingly, one's character cannot, cross. Coppola's film presents the philosophical issues in play here clearly and carefully, and they provide the backbone of his narrative—a narrative in which a self is tested, formed, and reformed as it descends ever more deeply into the comprehension of madness, its etiology, and its inward and outward terrors.

This film's cinematic achievement has been examined at length, as has the history of its production, including a documentary on it, made by Eleanor Coppola during filming, titled *Heart of Darkness: A Filmmaker's Apocalypse* (1996). The fact that this documentary was created while the film was being made is itself significant: the entire film, in a sense, is itself (i.e., not only through its characters) a reflection of human selfhood.[3] *It* has a narrative, *it* has a story, and it has to undergo a process of reconciling itself to itself, determining what it is and what it will stand for, as it moves forward according to its own inner developmental principles. Its biography is written in its documentary. But the film's multilayered philosophical achievement—an achievement showing how film can undertake a philosophical investigation into the nature of human selfhood and the central role that belief plays in the formation and preservation of that selfhood, while at the same time itself representing or mirroring human selfhood—has not to date been sufficiently examined or articulated.[4]

In this essay I will pursue this issue by looking into (1) the radical change of identity that comes of radical change in belief as this proves absorbing, potentially mesmerizing, and deeply threatening to the protagonist, Captain Benjamin L. Willard (the renegade Kurtz, as a character study in, as we shall see, the lethal dimension of self-deception, is an exactingly close study of this, as seen in his progress from most-accomplished general-to-be into a cult-of-personality murderous rebel to be stopped "with extreme prejudice"); (2) the instability of self-identity that comes of having engaged in self-determinative action one finds inconsistent with one's self-concept (Willard early in the film, having come from morally ambiguous clandestine CIA operations)—he does not know what to avow or disavow in terms of his identity until the end; (3) the self now lost to itself because an already-destabilized identity falls under influences and powerful new descriptions of events and powerful new metaphors or ways of speaking (Willard listening to Kurtz's speeches, both recorded and live) that threaten to bring in, here for better or for worse (Willard does not know which until the end), what Wittgenstein called a "changed way of seeing"; and (4) the self reasserting and newly strengthening itself through dramatic and indeed life-defining action at a single moment that resolves a crisis of identity (Willard killing Kurtz in the machete-murder scene). I will explore these intertwined themes as they wind throughout the film. But first I will identify a number of the elements that together make up a philosophical picture, or theoretically simplifying conceptual template, that has proven influential in some thinking about self-knowledge and the content of autobiographical language from the early modern era to the present.[5] Most fundamentally, I will suggest that *Apocalypse Now* is a sustained study of the real nature or character of self-knowledge. (By "real," I mean self-knowledge as it actually presents itself in life with all its variegated complexities, and not as it is construed in generalized theories attempting to reduce that complexity as it lies before us to an analyzed-down essence.) That real self-knowledge, as we see in this film, is not of a kind that accords well with what has been called in philosophy the perceptual model of any such knowledge.[6] Indeed, this is a film that serves to correct, or free us from, an easily adopted philosophical or conceptual picture of self-knowledge that would in fact blind us to nuances of self-discovery and self-testing (and thus self-making or self-composition—but I'll come to this) that are far more interesting than that picture could accommodate within its narrowly circumscribed conceptual limits. What, then, is the picture, the perceptual model, from which a close viewing of this film might liberate us?

"Privileged access," as is widely known, has become the phrase that usefully sums it up: there is taken to be a fundamental and generalizable asymmetry between self and other knowledge, and that asymmetry derives directly from the brute fact that Jones has access to his own inner states in a way that Smith does not have access to Jones's inner states. As we picture it in simplified schematic terms, Jones has something within his view that cannot, as a matter of metaphysics, be brought into Smith's view. The distinction, put another way, is reflected in the difference between vision and inner vision. Jones and Smith can both see out; they can both look up and see the fireworks going off above their heads. But they cannot both see into the contents of either one of their heads together just as they can look at the fireworks together; each can see into his own walled garden, but the other, from where he is metaphysically standing, can't see in. There is a sense, I believe, in which this asymmetry is plainly evident (what some philosophers have frequently drawn from this asymmetry is not at all plainly evident); those quick—too quick—to eradicate anything detected as a Cartesian influence on our thinking about thinking or consciousness will sometimes attack the asymmetry as a way of attacking the implications some philosophers have drawn from the asymmetry.[7] (One attack is to argue that self-knowledge should properly be modeled entirely upon other-knowledge, so that we find out about ourselves in precisely the way we find out about others.)[8] That, I believe, is to attempt to polemically attack and reject, in its entirety, a cleanly defined philosophical position and then replace it with another; and it misidentifies the target in the first place. This film, by contrast, is far more subtle in approach; it preserves what is true concerning the asymmetry but casts that asymmetry in a way that curtails the fallacious implications so easily drawn from it, while carefully investigating the circumstances of self-knowledge that we actually experience in life, prior to and separate from those simplifying philosophical pictures. And it does so, not in broad strokes (where the generalizations that broad strokes engender falsify the human experience), but rather in minute yet strong strokes: the issues involved are embodied in the characters in the film in extreme circumstances, but those circumstances are instructively particular—they are not generalized circumstances or mere examples of types. (In Willard's case, as we shall see, this extremity of circumstance reaches to the precise limit of intolerability, of sanity, of identity, which drives him inexorably to a clarifying moment of self-definition where that act of definition becomes an act of self-salvation—but we will get to this in due course.)

What precisely, then, is the progression of philosophical thought that so quickly moves us, in a sense before we realize it, into endorsing the perceptual picture? This picture can be, and has been, articulated in various ways, but the following I think captures the progression of thought that is common to a number of these articulations:

(1) Broken down into the most fundamental ontology, there are two kinds of objects in the world: physical and mental.
(2) There are, correspondingly, two kinds or categories of knowledge of the world: knowledge of outer physical things, and knowledge of inner mental things.
(3) The outer things, physical objects, can be shared in perception (because they are external to us, i.e., not mind-dependent), so I can have knowledge of the fireworks you see above you—this is one side of the fundamental asymmetry.
(4) The inner things, what we now think of as mental *objects* corresponding to step 3 above (precisely here is one foundational misstep in generating the systematically misleading picture), cannot be shared in perception (because they are internal to us, i.e., mind-dependent), so you cannot see the contents of my mental field of inner vision—this is the other side of the fundamental asymmetry.
(5) Self-knowledge will thus be construed as, or modeled as, the private knowledge of inner objects that correspond in a dualistic ontology to the public knowledge of outer objects.

This last step, the one that both concludes and implicitly incorporates the previous four, will also then quickly generate the following aspects of self-knowledge:

(a) A conception of full self-knowledge: full or complete self-knowledge will be constituted by an inner vision that has identified and inspected all present mental contents; we know of all our perceptions of external things, but also all our hopes, fears, ambitions, aspirations, regrets, intentions, desires, and so forth.
(b) A conception of introspection: it is to direct our inner vision (a term that in itself insinuates the model of the visual perception of outward things) on those metaphysically hidden but privately accessible contents (this, in short, is to avail ourselves of our privileged access).
(c) A conception of the nature or character of self-investigation and the process required to fulfill the Socratic injunction: it is to gaze inward and accurately identify mental objects resident in the mind prior to that introspective investigation. To "know thyself" on this theory is to know a full catalogue of those mind-dependent entities.
(d) A general sense of the categorical irrelevance of outward or physical things to genuine self-knowledge; the ontological kind of thing that self-knowledge is of would render those outward things, by virtue of their ontological nature, not objects of self-knowledge. This means that we may know that we have experienced outward things, and for that matter experienced other people, but the relevant knowledge will be knowledge of our private experience of those things, and not of the things (or other persons) themselves;
(e) To have an article of knowledge of the external world, to have a respectable case of what we can with propriety call knowledge, the object in the world the knowledge is of, the object of knowledge, has to be reasonably enduring or abiding; a fleeting sensory impression, even when caused by an outward thing, is not generally sufficient to be deemed an article of external knowledge. In dualistic tandem, then, a proper object of inner knowledge should be enduring or abiding; a fleeting or momentary impulse is not sufficient as an object of self-knowledge, but a long-term aspiration or entrenched intention is.

The exacting case study of Willard—one of the profound case studies in the history of film, and the central reason *Apocalypse Now* is regarded as not only one of the best war films but one of the best films of cinematic history—is a psychological investigation that shows the falsity, or the inaccuracy, or the inapplicability, or the overgeneralized character, of all of (1) through (5). And the film shows, in a thousand small but telling moments, the otiose detachment from lived reality, from real questions of human self-knowledge, of (a) through (e) as well. It was Milan Kundera who said that the mission of the novel is to show us that the world and everything in it is just much more complicated than we are inclined to think.[9] It seems fair to say that we are inclined, as philosophy has repeatedly shown, when asking general questions concerning self-knowledge, to think along the lines (albeit with interesting variations) described in the progression of thought above (and it is a *progression:* we probably would not think our way into (a) through (e) had we not first thought our way through (1) to (4) and then on to (5). The intellectually daring philosophical mission of this film (portrayed in the very form of an extremely dangerous military mission) is to show us that things—in this case, matters of self-knowledge—are much more complicated than we are inclined to think. Self-knowledge—its nature, its character, its acquisition, its concealment, its motivated removal, and the struggles that achieving it can require—turns out not to be the kind of thing we too easily think it is (in accordance with a simplified template of observational introspection).[10]

The underlying structure of the film's narrative is widely familiar, so I will be brief with it here and describe the most philosophically relevant parts of it as we progress. Captain Willard, when we meet him, is in some psychological difficulty: he is in a plain hotel room, he has been drinking heavily, he has a sense of detachment from the outside world or any event or obligation in it, he has returned to Saigon having (given what we see here, understandably) failed at reentry into peaceful American life, and, with rage unleashed, he tears apart his hotel room. He appears a person profoundly uprooted: he learned the hard way that he could not go home, and he is unsure about returning to Vietnam, which is what part of him wants to do.[11] He seems here to be made up of a loose collection of embodied impulses, to be a person with no attunement to himself; and this will be central to understanding his self-defining choices later. We learn that he has a background in conducting secret missions for the CIA, some of which were assassinations; he appears now a powder keg of a person with no knowledge of why he is in the alarming, profoundly uprooted, and deeply unsettled condition he is in. This caged-animal condition is intruded upon by the arrival of representatives of the military, who bring him in for a meeting at which he is given the assignment to go upriver and "terminate with extreme prejudice" a Colonel Walter E. Kurtz, who reportedly has gone insane and is commanding his own renegade militia composed of viciously violent followers that both sides of the war rightly fear. Willard is already in a maelstrom of not knowing who and what he is, of not knowing who he is by not knowing what he stands for.[12]

But then why has he returned to Saigon? Because Saigon is, after all, a place that externally reflects his inner chaos and thus, in a desperate way, gives that inner chaos a compatible outward home. The general at this meeting describes that ethical chaos well in what he tells Willard about Kurtz:

> Well, you see Willard. . . . In this war, things get confused out there, power, ideals, the old morality, practical military necessity. But out there with these natives it must be a temptation to be god. Because there's a conflict in every human heart, between the rational and the irrational, between good and evil. And good does not always triumph. Sometimes the dark side overcomes what Lincoln called the better angels of our nature. Every man has got a breaking point. You and I have one. Walter Kurtz has reached his. And very obviously, he has gone insane.

There thus is here at this early stage in the film something characterologically revealing about the way—probably a way for him more sensed than understood—that Willard finds a setting to match his state. But the deeper interest at this initial point is one of proximity and difference, and this sets the stage for one major philosophical thread of this film, that a major source of self-knowledge is of a comparative-relational kind (i.e., of a kind the above lines of thought would disregard from the start—reconsider [4] and [d] above) and that a variety of self-knowledge comes as the direct result of a refined discernment that is taught to us, or required by, the external context one—as we say—finds oneself in.[13] Kurtz was highly successful in his military career and was regarded as promising general-level material; Willard was also working in CIA-level operations and was trusted with critical and extremely dangerous secret operations. Willard knows that Kurtz had a moral education within the institution of the military world, adopting its ethos to a degree that made him who and what he was prior to his internal transformation. Willard sees that this too was, to an extent he could not yet gauge, like himself. And what he hears of Kurtz now has the power to occasion a heavy burden of self-reflection (this burden, in this war and for him, will become almost unbearably heavy and drive him near the brink of self-loss later, upriver): Kurtz has shown himself capable both of acting within established structures (and often at the head of them) and of acting alone, of working undercover with the sense of autonomous self-reliance that such work demands. Willard, in short, looking at Kurtz, sees himself reflected back to a steadily increasing degree as his knowledge of Kurtz increases.

Directly stated, his burden as it takes shape in the first part of the film is to start the project of determining to what extent the central core of his being overlaps with the central core of Kurtz's (this theme will continue, through a number of variations, to the film's denouement). Both soldiers have seen firsthand and under the sudden-death conditions of war the very list the general offered: confused matters of power, the eroding claims of the old morality, the ugly hypocritical gap between ideals and action (in the meeting the colonel describing his mission says, "You understand, Captain, that this mission does not exist, nor will it ever exist"), the conflict in the heart between the rational and the irrational, and the dangerous idea with which the general closes and that Willard probably does not want to face (given his volatile state of mind as we found him in the hotel room)—the breaking point that he too has, beyond which lies insanity. Willard outwardly hears these phrases as descriptions of Kurtz; inwardly he finds them far too close to a self he senses he either already has become (the fact that he does not now know challenges [5] and [c] above) or, if not, certainly could become. Indeed, as the film's mission progresses, his innermost question becomes: To what extent is he Kurtz? To what extent is he the person he is being sent to kill? What forms of discernment will he need to cultivate in order to see the telling—and saving—difference? (If, that is, there is one.)

Because of the inescapable asymmetry discussed above, knowledge of others and knowledge of selves are often schematically pictured as opposites: knowledge of another person may be inferential,[14] it may be based on what has been discussed as an argument by analogy,[15] or it may be a matter, perhaps most fundamentally, of outside or external observation. Knowledge of a self, metaphysically a mirror-image inversion of other-knowledge, would by contrast involve none of this because it would depend upon none of it for its content; all those forms of inquiry concerning selfhood would offer less than the picture of privileged access would guarantee. (Ryle famously argued, polemically, that we should remodel our understanding of self-knowledge on that of other-understanding, but, while a helpful corrective, that suggestion has a baby-bathwater problem in generically throwing out all of the asymmetry.)[16] The scenes—scenes of a deeply absorbed, fully engaged form of reflection—in which Willard is poring over, scrutinizing, and working out the connections between and implications of Kurtz's file and all its myriad details are thus philosophically instructive. Willard says at the outset, "There is no way to tell his story without telling my own. And if his story really is a confession, then so is mine." Willard is here, as the film goes on to show, partly right: he cannot, for reasons we are beginning to see, tell Kurtz's story independently of what he carries within himself. But a confession? It is not, as his narrative unfolds, precisely this, for the straightforward reason that a confession requires that there be content to be confessed prior to the confession—it reveals something already known. Willard, however, does not yet know that content, because he (all too like Oedipus on his voyage of tragic self-discovery) does not now know who or what he is. The picture of hermetically sealed introspection, should he try to enact it, will not help him here.

Willard's close reading of Kurtz's file generates within him a strange attraction: he can sense that the answers he seeks about what he has become or is becoming, and the ideal of an integrated and stabilized selfhood (now in shards and fragments), are to be found within a process of contending with Kurtz.[17] He says: "Part of me was afraid of what I would find and what I would do when I got there. I knew the risks, or imagined I knew. But the thing I felt the most, much stronger than fear, was the desire to confront him." His desire, more than he then knew, was to confront, if in externalized form, the part of himself that was threatening to overtake him and thus that haunted him. That part had made progress: when he went back to the United States, he reported that he barely said a word to his wife—other than "yes" to a divorce—and when he said to himself that some of his fellow soldiers wanted only one simple thing, a way back home, he added that they did not yet know that home was no longer there. And he feared it was making still more progress—perhaps the ultimate progress, by relentlessly calling him up that river.

We will of course come to many further details of the encounter with Kurtz, but the only way to understand that ultimate encounter, and the condition of the fragmented self that undertakes the journey upriver to find him, is to consider Willard's sources of self-reflection along the way. First, it is clear that Willard's engrossment in Kurtz's dossier moves quickly from a soldier's necessary knowledge of his target to serious interest, to deep engrossment (here he has learned enough to see the threatening part of himself reflected therein), to near-obsession. This private reflection (made audible in his autobiographical voice-over commentary)[18] on the dossier gives him a language for a kind of hypothetical self-description—it is description of another person, yet heard in the mind's ear doubly as possible but not yet confirmed self-description. In short, other-knowledge was double-functioning as raw material for self-knowledge. Those descriptions concern Kurtz's brilliance, his exemplary record, his celebrated achievement, his having successfully undergone demanding training—for him retraining—with men half his age, and then his turning at a moral crossroad Willard does not yet understand (yet he still inchoately recognizes because now something in Kurtz mirrors something from deep within himself). This doubled and two-way reflection continues underneath everything Willard encounters, and a sequence of seven outward events (prior to, but leading to, the confrontation with Kurtz) serve to tell him who he is and, of equal importance, who he is not. Together, these seven episodes decisively show (1) that the content was not there prior to its confession, (2) the gradual but steady increase in discernment that will prove vital to his encounter with Kurtz, and (3) the preconditions for his coming to understand the profound meaning of that long-prepared encounter.

The first of these, the famous helicopter-attack scene, is one that pits Willard against the entire circumstance, and, moreover the entire psychology, of the war as it is being enacted. And "enacted" (inside the narrative, so a kind of play within the play) seems the right word here: the general sense of what we see—a sense in which Willard cannot find himself—combines the highly theatrical with the highly absurd:[19] the helicopters play Wagner's "Ride of the Valkyries" at deafening volume as they descend like gigantic mechanical insects raining down death and destruction, while Lieutenant Colonel Bill Kilgore strides about the beach amid lethal fire shirtless but with western cavalry tasseled hat, shouting out orders with a supernatural aura surrounding him that seems to ensure his safety while others fall around him right and left. It is here that he delivers one of the most quoted lines in film history: "I love the smell of napalm in the morning." Here the sense of unreality is augmented by his stating a personal aesthetic preference (however bizarre) focused upon his internal experience in the context of a major air and ground attack. Kilgore seems in but not of this place, and it is never clear whether he is acting in the moment as a commanding officer, or whether he is watching himself acting the part of a commanding officer while doing it in a way that places acts of character-revelation above military engagement and the expected moral responsibility for the men under his command.

The theatrical element is then exceeded by the already-evident absurd element when he orders soldiers to surf off the beach regardless of the lethal dangers surrounding them: the brute reality of that danger does not penetrate Kilgore's psychic self-enclosure, the perimeter of which is secured by his self-image. Everything one would expect in an operation of this kind is missing: seriousness, responsibility, awareness, strategic thinking, and genuine courage. But everything that is surrealistically out of place is here: dramatic flair, theatrical self-presentation, absurd juxtapositions, oblivious disregard of danger to self and others (thus precluding the possibility of real courage), and a sense of unreality at the rare kind of moment in action that soldiers have in a time-honored way regarded as most real. Perceiving with acuity the situation we are in is a component of self-knowledge, and Kilgore is a study in the kind of hermetic enclosure that, rather than promoting self-knowledge, in truth (and against the philosophical picture) precludes it. Moreover, it is, as we see here, the theatricality of his self-presentation that systematically prevents his self-awareness.

However, it is what we see of Willard's psychology that most powerfully moves the theme of self-knowledge forward, and everything in this scene serves this purpose: just as Kilgore sees everything around him from a curiously deranged spectatorial distance with himself as protagonist, Willard sees Kilgore from a similarly spectatorial psychic distance, but with the added element that Willard is given, by this experience, an occasion to contrast Kilgore's theater-of-the-absurd-but-unwitting view of himself with his own view of himself. One can, with the requisite attentiveness, see a great deal on the faces of persons (and especially on the faces of highly accomplished actors in the close-ups that the art of film specially affords), and Willard's engagement with Kilgore (presented in part verbally and in part facially) casts in high relief a bizarre composite of characterological elements into which Willard does not in his vulnerable state want to let himself descend. He is already thoroughly alienated from regular life at home; he does not want to end up ironically distanced from what he may have remaining within himself, that is, his identity as a soldier. He senses that such a double loss would leave him not only nothing—it would, more profoundly, leave him *as* nothing. His fear at present, continuing from the time in the hotel room, is that he does not really know who or what he is; his deeper fear is that he may find out that he cannot answer this question because there is really nothing there left to identify or, as we say, identify with. He shattered his reflection in the hotel mirror with his fist; his Oedipal task in coming back—again, one to which he was summoned by inner forces still only half-understood—is to find, or perhaps develop through avowed action, the content of selfhood that will show that the dangerous and wounding shards and fragments are not themselves his true reflection. Kilgore shows, in his actions, his attitude, and his psychological makeup, one way of being shaped by war, a path that is, given his fragility, open to Willard, but it is a path that he will by force of inner resolve avoid (he sees he can by resolve avoid becoming Kilgore but fears he may already be Kurtz). And as we will see below, he will try to confirm this, to characterologically stabilize this, in the self-description he offers to Kurtz, which Kurtz then immediately and with massive power—like swatting a gnat—verbally torpedoes. But we will come to that. Here, on the beach with Kilgore, Willard derives from this bizarre spectacle of alien identity what he needs: his patrol boat is set down by a helicopter in the Nung River (dropped in from above—itself an image of being suddenly in but not of a place), and he and his crew of four (Chef, Chief, Lance, and Clean) start the mission upriver toward Cambodia (where U.S. forces are, by political rhetoric, not, and where, by reality, Kurtz is and has been, for long enough to establish his reign of horror).

The second event is brief (recall item 5[e] of the picture of self-knowledge above) but nevertheless powerful in terms of Willard's inner search for a stabilized sense of self and in terms of his rapid recovery from his somewhat threatening encounter with the unreality of Kilgore's psyche. Having expressed a fondness for mangoes, Chef, taking Willard with him, goes ashore in the evening into the dark and thick jungle to retrieve some. This is itself a manifestation of Kilgore-like unreality and disregard for danger: here again, whimsical preference and personal taste are driving life-threatening action that is insufficiently acknowledged as such in a kind of dream world (where, importantly, the words used by Chef do not seem to come from, or connect with, the harsh reality within which they move.) It is not that Chef is uttering propositionally contained falsehoods where each isolated statement fails to correspond to the world—he is not asserting that snow is black. It is rather that the words he uses do not seem to complexly intertwine with, and interact with, the deadly world of the Vietnam war all around him. And this larger, holistic failure of correspondence (of a larger kind that also incorporates some coherence, or how the words of that world hang together, or a failure of what Stanley Cavell calls making these words our own) has severe consequences. With the sudden emergence of, and very narrow escape from, an attacking tiger, Chef dissolves into nervous collapse. He falls into the boat as a man now mentally in pieces, with the crew firing frantically and wildly into the bushes at an imagined unseen enemy. The sudden transition of Chef from mango-hunting unreality to nervous breakdown as an understandable reaction to now-rightly-perceived reality proves salutary for all on board; Kilgore's unreality is left behind in body and in spirit.

But the real significance of this scene is, here again, far deeper: it would be understandably destabilizing—emotionally and intellectually threatening—to have it vividly brought home to us that we all have a breaking point by seeing a person who is with us cross it. And it would be all the more destabilizing to realize that we are closer to that point than we would like. The others on the boat see this, and with a rational fear that now stays with them, they take note. But for Willard, it is far worse. For all of them, it is not good to know one is close to, or could easily get close to, the breaking point, the limit of composed selfhood, that Chef suddenly reached when his confrontation with the real threat of sudden mortality—in truth all around him from the outset of the mission—moved in an instant inside his acknowledged description of the world. But, recalling Willard's state of being in the hotel, it is still more threatening (thus making the need for self-stabilization more urgent) to know there is such a line and not quite know where one is in relation to it. With one foot on each side, one would have to choose very carefully where to put one's weight, and this fact is well represented in Willard's absorptive rereadings of, and voice-over reflections on, Kurtz's file. The depth of Willard's absorption is caused by his desire to determine where the line is, where he is in relation to it, and when Kurtz crossed it. (What remains on the other side of that line he will see below.)

The third and fourth events function together: in the third, Playboy bunnies are delivered by helicopter to a performance stage at a U.S. base on the river. The performance is what one would expect, but Willard's position in relation to it is not—especially here he becomes ever more a man apart. We see the many soldiers in the audience as spectators, where all (except Willard) are focused entirely on the women. (This includes toy guns and holsters and mock-threatening gun waving and shooting, introducing a theme continued just below.) Willard, however, moves around the audience but never joins it; his position is that of a spectator of spectators. Wittgenstein said that the philosopher is a member of no community of ideas, and that sense of isolation is underscored here: Willard does not "de-individuate" into any collective, and particularly not this one as it loses itself in animated spectatorship (so animated that they break through security and the women have to be whisked away in the helicopters with some soldiers hanging on as the women are airlifted out). Willard does not have the ability to lose himself, for the moment, in any such entertainment and any such collective, but not because the Playboy spectacle is not to his taste. It is for the more fundamental reason that he has not found himself in the first place. The other soldiers, knowing who they are (at whatever level of comprehension), risk nothing and gain a momentary escape through such an act of de-individuation; for Willard such participation would be a significant threat to the unstable foundation of selfhood upon which he is presently and cautiously standing. Or to put it another way: Willard, on this Oedipal voyage, is locked in a state of third-remove monitoring: he spectates upon himself spectating upon spectators. He is a member of none of those communities, including—philosophically importantly, as we shall see—a kind of introspective community with himself. The scene leaves a viewer of the film with a palpable sense of his dangerous isolation and his increasingly monomaniacal determination to move farther upriver—these diversions are for him only reminders of the fist-shattered mirror. He is at this point a man who cannot seem to find himself; absent any criteria with which to evaluate the various sets of words that might truly describe him, he is, in language, adrift. His inward reflections continually turn back to, and indeed obsess over, Kurtz (while knowing that he cannot tell Kurtz's story without telling his own), while his outward engagements remain distanced and alienated.[20]

The fourth moment into which this narrative progresses is also brief, but again important: in a peaceful moment while gliding upriver, Willard and his crew closely pass some other patrol boats coming downriver. The scene is undeniably weird: the soldiers, appearing oddly estranged in a way that is visible yet hard to make precise, play-act at shooting at Willard's boat and its occupants. One could see this as simple boyish humor, but one would be wrong; in fact this revivifies Kilgore's sense of the theatrical, but now adding to it a question about the difference between really doing a given thing and acting out the doing of that thing. This broadly Sartrean-existentialist question is in fact—one detects that Willard, but not the others, seems to sense this—a manifestation of ironic detachment taken to an extreme. It serves to sever the deepest allegiances that should be in play here, and importantly it gives the engagement in this war a wholly relativistic, free-for-all quality: we are playing now in this war, and as it happens we don't now actually shoot our weapons at you because, as it happens, we are on the same side as a matter of nearly arbitrary convention. But we could just as easily shift our allegiances to another game, another set of rules—or, frighteningly (and this is what lurks beneath this scene), to a nongame without *any* such rules. Exactly as (Willard knows) Kurtz, the object of his ethical fascination and the figure who is the cause and occasion of his deepest self-reflection, has done. And this precisely, as (we will see below) Kurtz understands, is the reason he has been sent to kill him. But there is more to be seen in this passing-of-boats exchange.

It is at this stage of this philosophical film's and the military mission's progress that Lance now becomes an instructive comparison for Willard. In retrospect, or on second viewing, one can perhaps see this coming, but it is in any case here that Lance quite dramatically performs a kind of doubled act of withdrawal into the real-life version of what philosophers have imagined as the Cartesian interior. Verbally, he withdraws into himself in a way that lets the sinews of connection to those around him—sinews made of language—wither and ultimately die. He becomes a man unto himself (indeed an island), shutting out the real world around him and retreating into a private space of isolation. And he underscores this retreat by smearing his face with camouflage paint, making himself appear to those around him strange, and making himself quite literally appear indistinguishable from the nonspeaking foliage that surrounds them. Like the others on the boat, Willard sees this as a symptom of serious psychological difficulty, and it further darkens the already troubled interaction of the crew. Instructively, what it does not do is to reawaken in anyone a sense that Lance is retreating into himself to a place where he can be, or find, who he truly is: suddenly introverted taciturnity conjoined to off-putting external display is not seen by anyone as a route to self-discovery, to self-reconfirmation, to self-knowledge. It is seen for what it is: trouble. Willard might well have followed the path of Kilgore; he might have crossed the breaking point as did Chef; he might have followed the path of ironic detachment and relativistic free-for-all; he might have de-individuated into a relatively mindless collective; and, as he now sees, he might have retreated into himself in a way that does not yield light. But he has learned—gradually stabilizing himself for his confrontation with his own darkest interior in the externalized form of Kurtz—that he is cut from none of these cloths. And he is learning not merely that, but far more importantly, how, he is a man apart. He is gaining particularized content of self-knowledge, and he is learning of what he is, and is not, composed. And the progress of this unfolding process is measured by his growing ability to determine which words do, and which words do not, fit, and by the emergence and clarification of the situation-specific criteria with which he can make this distinction. Lance's way is not a route to self-knowledge for Willard (nor can it, for reasons to which we will return below, truly be for Lance); it is not who Willard is, it is not a viable option for him, and it would never uncover what he is Oedipally, inexorably, driven to find.

The next moment is quick, impulsive, extreme, and powerfully self-compositional. Their riverboat encounters a sampan, a small Vietnamese hand-built boat carrying civilians and food along with other minimal necessities. Chief, the ostensible captain of the vessel (although on an unspoken level it is Willard's boat), orders Chef, never fully recovered, to board the sampan to inspect. As he does so, confusion erupts, resulting in the wholesale slaughter (with one partial exception) of all on board by Clean, who has been agitatedly standing guard. The exception is the woman who reached for a container, generating the confusion; it shortly becomes clear that the container held not a gun, a grenade, or an explosive device, but rather a pet puppy. At the moment when Chief orders the wounded woman taken on board with the plan of diverting the mission and escorting her to the nearest hospital, Willard takes a resolute step forward, draws his pistol with no visible emotion, and coldly shoots the woman fatally in the chest. All, stunned, are struck dumb; Willard, with an air of spectating upon himself from a distance (and as though he is considering highly varying possible self-descriptions), gestures that they can go.

This is a moment with multiple lines of significance: it shows Willard to himself that he is committed to his mission and is acting like a soldier (this itself is of course a complex phrase and, given what we have seen with the passing boats, is noncommittal with regard to his identity—is he merely acting like, or truly acting as, a soldier?); it also shows to himself and to the others that he is acting outside the bounds of soldierhood—this was murder; and it shows that he is capable of acting precipitously in a way that icily clarifies what he is capable of with no residual question. The others on the boat never from this point stop looking at him differently—more quietly, more distantly, more cautiously, more fearfully, and less humanely. Or to put it another way: less one of us. Remorseless action, distance from a disregarded normalcy, to be of a place beyond pity and fear, to be beyond the bounds of convention, to act autonomously in a moral space beyond all established expectations—these are the traits of Kurtz as he learned them in that initial meeting, and Willard now ever more alarmingly sees himself to be closer to Kurtz than to any of the others (against whom he has sequentially defined himself by gradually strengthening negative comparison—he has through these moments learned ways of autobiographically describing what he is not). But he must now ask: Has he won all the battles of selfhood against the other false paths only to lose the war with Kurtz? As before, and like a soldier preparing for battle but of a self-defining kind, he returns once again to a still deeper, still more contemplative reading of the doubly-directed words composing Kurtz's file.

The sixth moment—perfectly placed in terms of its five precedents—occurs inside the mind: Willard learns that he had a predecessor, Colby, who made the trip upriver before him with the same grim instructions. But rather than "terminating with extreme prejudice," Colby, step by step, "turned"; Willard understands that this means he lost his mind, lost himself, lost the words—in Cavell's sense, his own words—that stabilized his identity. Colby, Willard learns to his deep consternation, was last reported as working, presumably in some mentally semidebilitated condition of moral wreckage, with Kurtz. And Willard learns, while stopping at a U.S. base that is itself the picture of destabilization—it is vaguely under a kind of random fire, he cannot find a commanding officer, the soldiers wandering through that eerie place seem detached and disordered (and thus psychologically as well as geographically closer to Kurtz)—that Colby wrote to his wife at home, "Sell everything, sell the house, sell the kids, forget it." These words would be evidence of having crossed irretrievably a line to the many other soldiers who embrace Playboy-bunny diversion, who know who they are, who welcome de-individuation into the collective, who in short want only a way home. But to Willard, Colby's words are profoundly terrifying: he has said that home was not there anymore and that the others simply did not know that yet, and he has said the minimal monosyllabic (showing the reality for him of the threat of ultrataciturn solipsistic retreat) "yes" to a divorce. He is a man hovering between possible identities, knowing that it matters much on which foot he places his weight. He senses that it will take enormously powerful resolve to hold whatever word-born stability he has, or that he is, through these seven moments, composing, against the psychic power that is Kurtz.

He knows he is now very near Kurtz, but one last preparatory episode, the seventh moment, shows that both chaos and the threat of instantaneous death are everywhere around him, and that the latter is more present than he knew: contrary to the psychologically contained character of the previous moment in his progress, destruction can swiftly and unexpectedly come from the outside as well. In a sudden attack from the cover of thick bushes on the river's shore, spears are suddenly flying everywhere. Chief is fatally wounded and in his last moments grasps Willard to him and, with considerable strength, attempts to pull Willard onto the spear protruding from his chest to take him with him. This is not only a salutary reminder that his mind is not somehow an inner sanctuary metaphysically protected from the external world, but also that as things now stand his own men pose a serious threat to his life, a fact that now pushes him to a periphery of isolation (this shows what the words *privacy* and *isolation* can actually mean as lived, rather than the nonsituated meaning we might try to attribute to them from the perspective of picture-driven metaphysics). With identity-destroying threats now coming from inside and outside, he is not only (for reasons we have seen) a man apart, but now he is utterly a man alone as well. It is from this ultimately stripped-down solitude that he will have to rebuild from the ground up his sense of selfhood as a project of stabilizing his self-descriptions, his self-concept and the words that compose it, and the networks of relations that will make him who he is, who he will be, and who he can be. But for the present, this socially isolated and psychologically malleable solitude, as he knows, only makes him more vulnerable to the Kurtz without and the Kurtz within. Colby was as accomplished, as able, and as prepared a soldier as he. And Colby probably was not haunted from the outset by a broken mirror.

Early on General Corman (the senior officer describing the mission and its necessity to Willard at the meeting) said: "In this war, things get confused out there—power, ideals, the old morality, and practical military necessity . . . because there's a conflict in every human heart between the rational and the irrational, between good and evil. And good does not always triumph." Willard, one who was by then already profoundly changed by the experience of this war, is the embodiment of doubts about power and authority, about political ideals and their corruption, about the "old morality"; and he is a trained operative as well as soldier who has acted on what the General calls "practical military necessity" repeatedly. It was from that condition, that situation, that Willard heard descriptions of Kurtz with a double reference, that is, also, as we have seen throughout the film, as possible descriptions of himself. So as he approaches Kurtz's compound, the question that has only increased in urgency for him is now precisely this: when those words describing Kurtz continue beyond what the General said all the way to what might be a full description (recall his absorption in the file, his study of the words, their connotations, their associations, their reach) of Kurtz, at *exactly* what point along that linguistic journey do the two separate? At what point does the reference become single? And then does the remainder—the words describing Willard that do not describe Kurtz—constitute who he really is? Or—the darkest doubt that all of the preceding has brought into focus—*is* there a remainder that is of any consequence, any real substance, in terms of his self-composition? Willard, in this sense, is a soldier-philosopher, not a storyteller: he wants not a story, a narrative, a comforting way of speaking; he wants the truth, stated in words that do real work. Throughout the film he has repeatedly expressed his contempt for political lies, for hypocrisy, for the rhetorical redescription of the circumstances of this war that make it more palatable to the American population as well as to its participants. After shooting the woman in the sampan, he said, "It was the way we had over here of living with ourselves. We'd cut them in half with a machine gun and give them a Band-Aid. It was a lie—and the more I saw of them, the more I hated lies." But the problem he has ever more deeply fathomed is not a simple one: Kilgore is living in a surreal make-believe cowboy-and-surfing world held up as a thin screen in front of the deadly world he is actually in, and this for Willard marks a contrast, a philosophical problem, that he carries with him to his encounter with Kurtz: he knows that Kilgore's words have a weirdly redecorative (and bizarrely so) function. But then what, he needs to know for descriptive stabilization, is the criterion by which he judges this?

If it is a criterion of genuine personal experience (and not contagious, overly general veil-phrases one picks up from others), a criterion that supplants, or better, precludes, all lies, then Kurtz, whatever he is, is not Kilgore. Willard himself most wants, of all things, the truth—about himself, about the war, and about the human result within him of the interaction between those two things.[21] And as we saw at various stages of his progress toward this point, he sees that, however alarming, it is possible that of all of them it is Kurtz, and only Kurtz, who has seen behind the veil of falsifying verbiage (it is this that profoundly separates him from the officers in the meeting that gave him his mission). Willard's reflective voice-over asks, "What did he see up here? Could have gone for General, but he went for himself instead." And he knows that Kurtz has claimed that he has a fundamental concern for the truth, and especially so in the case of his son. In a letter to his son that Willard reads and rereads, Kurtz writes that he has been (to him wholly uncomprehendingly) accused of murder and that the military authorities say he has gone completely insane. He deeply wants (and here is a splash of humanity that further unites the descriptions of Kurtz and Willard, but this time, further complicating the relations between them, on the positive side of the moral ledger) his son to understand him, to understand that as the reward for deep and sustained inner and outer struggles, he in his life uncovered the importance of "seeing clearly what is to be done" and manifesting one's autonomy "beyond timid lying morality." Like us, Willard does not quite know whether to salute or be terrified. The answer, for him, is of course both: saluting the strength born of clarity in a world of moral haze (this is literalized throughout the film with haze, fog, smoke, obscured views, darkness, and viewing scenes as if through a gauze—"I can't see; I'm stopping this boat") and the achievement of autonomy beyond the reach of hypocritical authority, and being terrified both of him and of being him. Voice-over: "Part of me was afraid—but the desire to confront him stronger." Willard's deepest fear is born of cognition, of philosophy: What if, after all, Kurtz is right? And if he, Willard, learns that truth, what remainder of non-convergent description, of selfhood, then will be left of him? What Special Ops soldier will then come for him?

As the boat leaves the last crumbling semblance of the old moral order ("Last outpost—beyond it only Kurtz"), one can see in Willard's eyes, in his face, the kind of reflection that is directed outward and inward in equal measure. He must know that distracted inward reflection in a moment of choice in his present setting could cost him his life. Yet Kurtz, acting at a distance, makes him do precisely this; he feels Kurtz's imperiling influence from the inside.

Gliding into Kurtz's compound, we see horror and its hideous aftermath all around—bodies, some decapitated, strewn randomly, severed heads on poles, tiger cages used also for humans (where Willard will find himself shortly), charred remains of ambiguous ritual sacrifices, and a blankly staring population that seems to combine shell-shocked passivity, god-figure-fearing blind obedience, and the muted, but for that reason all the more strangely real, threat of immediate extreme violence. The quiet atmosphere of terror and the bizarre transfigured morality of this place, all too evident upon Willard's arrival, are suddenly broken by the hyperverbiage of an American photojournalist. A viewer of this film, having come to know Willard, gets a distinct sense that the words the photojournalist fires at Willard are among the worst possible for his present psychic state. In the exchange, with manic delivery on the one side and measured (outward) calm on the other, the photojournalist aggressively asks "Who are you?" and laughs, marking the difference he sees between Kurtz's greatness of stature and Willard's petty smallness; he refers to the godlike power of Kurtz (we are "all his children"); he refers to the inappropriateness of a mere soldier to judge true greatness ("You don't judge"); looking around at the severed heads on poles, he says Kurtz "sometimes goes too far" and that he "forgets himself"—implying that his visionary magnitude makes even all this seem more like an error of etiquette. He quickly indicates that he knows why Willard is there ("Why? Why would a nice guy like you want to kill a genius?"), and Willard of course knows that his failed and ruined predecessor Colby is there, and thus that Kurtz will also know the purpose of his mission. The effect of this foreknowledge of his purpose is that it further diminishes Willard's control, because on the boat the purpose of the mission remained classified—he told the remaining crew the purpose of his mission only recently; the asymmetry of knowledge was one source of his authority. Here, he suddenly sees, he will have to work within a context where his motives are shared—and he knows that this is an epistemological symmetry that may prove lethal. He has just arrived moments ago, and his relative stature and power are eroding by the moment—indeed by the word. Then, as a kind of combined Tiresias and Cassandra, the photojournalist changes course and fires off:

> Do you know that the man really likes you? He likes you. He really likes you. But he's got something in mind for you. Aren't you curious about that? I'm curious. I'm very curious. Are you curious? There's something happening out here, man. You know something, man? I know something that you don't know. That's right, Jack. The man is clear in his mind, but his soul is mad. Oh, yeah. He's dying, I think. He hates all this. He hates it! But the man's a . . . He reads poetry out loud, all right. And a voice . . . he likes you because you're still alive. He's got plans for you. No, I'm not gonna help you. You're gonna help him, man. You're gonna help him. I mean, what are they gonna say when he's gone? 'Cause he dies when it dies, when it dies, he dies! What are they gonna say about him? He was a kind man? He was a wise man? He had plans? He had wisdom? Bullshit, man!

> And am I gonna be the one that's gonna set them straight? Look at me! Look at me! Wrong!

And then momentarily reconsidering who will speak in the future for the transfigured greatness that was Kurtz, he points at Willard: "You!"

The moral psychology engendered by this circumstance is even worse than it appears. Willard has already spoken of the fact that it was Kurtz who was in control (even at a distance and not having yet been met), and early on he had referred to himself in his narrative voice-over as "caretaker of his memory." The photojournalist's words cut into him deeply for the now-apparent reason that they give voice to the inner network of doubts and fears that had driven him back to Vietnam in the first place, giving those general doubts and fears personalized specificity. So he sees that some alarming things may be true: It is he who will help Kurtz, and he will do so according to a plan of Kurtz's that he does not know—it is thus not only that he is in a new context of knowledge-symmetry in this encampment of terror, but moreover that now he, with respect to Kurtz, is on the epistemic short end and the plan is one he may fulfill without knowing the description under which he acts. He may be here as a puppet-marionette. At the beginning of the film Willard said, in his voice-over, "I was going to the worst place in the world—and didn't know it." That worst place may now be psychological: not only a place where he does not know who or what he really is, but a place—a hell—where what he discovers is that there is no autonomous, volitionally empowered self to discover. All along he feared that Kurtz might be right about his morally transfigured vision; now a manic photojournalist under the spell of Kurtz might be right about his unwittingly servile position as well. Precisely what, indeed, is he doing here?

"On the river, I thought I'd know what to do. But it didn't happen." His trajectory of action, his prediction that he could rely on his experience in looking over the situation and knowing what to do, has been destabilized; he realizes now that he is after all not fulfilling, or moving steadily along, a trajectory set down in advance—the very essence of a military mission. What he feels is a kind of radical freedom—anything seems possible precisely here, at this point of arrival (arrival outwardly, at the Kurtz compound; arrival inwardly, at his point of self-confrontation), yet this comes with the doubt that the expanded sense of freedom he is experiencing is present only as set down in advance by a godlike Kurtz. It is as if he has a real version of the classic freedom-determinism problem.

"He's got something in mind for you. "He's got plans for you." These phrases, functioning within the expanding context of Willard's psychology (one could see in this film a demonstration that all words actually function within the contexts of our psychology, however circumstantially simple or complex those contexts may be), strip away any false confidence he may have mustered, any capacity to cope as fabricated by adopting a soldier's role and the stabilization of identity that comes with that adoption. What Willard is facing, by contrast with any such role-identification, will be a moment of truth. And it is a truth Willard cannot foresee within his present psychology—he himself says, in his voice-over: "He knew more about what I was going to do than I did."

The progress toward Kurtz in person is horrific: Willard is put in the tiger cage in a state of deprivation, animalistic captivity, and utter uncertainty about what lies in store for him. He is reduced, as a further subtraction of his identity-fragments (shards still breaking), to an animal in captivity. Willard has left Chef on the boat with instructions to call in an air raid if they don't return; later that night Kurtz appears and casually drops Chef's severed head into Willard's lap. In his reaction, in his face, one can see the questions and the thoughts: What does he stand for, what political institution and military ethos will he represent inside that cage? How will he present himself? (Recall Nietzsche's question posed to any representative of a moral order: "Or are you an imitation of an actor?")[22]

He knows that all men have breaking points. He knows he accepted a mission as a special soldier—but from men who employ false and hypocritical language to manipulate and deceive and who stand for a system he knows to be corrupt. He knows that saying that it is safe to surf on a beach does not make it safe to surf on a beach (he knows a verbally induced nominalist's dreamland when he sees one). He senses the unpredictable proximity of death. He knows that he himself is not sure of where he stands in respect of the line, and he knows the balance is delicate. He knows he is in, but not of, the larger social fabric of his not-quite-fellow soldiers. He knows the difference between play-acting, role-playing, and real action. He knows he is often at spectatorial distances from the scenes around him. He knows solipsistic retreat is not a source of self-knowledge (and he is reminded of this here when he briefly encounters Colby, an empty shell of a profoundly vacated man who remains silent while unsurely holding a rifle). He knows he is capable of (military) killing and also of sudden, unreflective murder. He knows the line between "them" and "us" does not correspond to the line between those who will and those who will not kill him. He knows three of his four crewmembers have been killed in the name of his mission. But he also knows—or perhaps fearfully senses—that when he said, "He was close—he was real close," that these sentences really described a threatening proximity of psychic identity more than of physical proximity. And he knows that the nature of that inner proximity (sameness? difference? overlap? remainder?) is what he is actually here to find out. (Recall that at the outset he indeed said, saying more than he then knew, "No way to tell his story without telling my own.")

Turned free and then allowed into Kurtz's chambers (in a former temple), he hears Kurtz speak in powerful images that go to the heart of Willard's state of being and also underscore the two men's similarities. His words, for Willard, hold a diabolical power. "I watched a snail crawl along the edge of a straight razor. That's my dream. That's my nightmare. Crawling, slithering, along the edge of a straight razor . . . and surviving." Moving slowly with animal-like instinct through a deadly environment where one false move means a terrible death, and not knowing whether movement through this environment is dream or nightmare (or seeing that it is some of both). That, in a kind of single poetic vision, summarizes with precision the world these soldiers have come through to arrive at this point together, to face each other. In a stroke, Kurtz is defining the space they share and controlling the words and the word-borne images that provide that definition. And then comes an exchange, compressed into nine lines, that sums up the state of play in the entire film:

"Did they say why, Willard, why they want to terminate my command?" Kurtz, referring to what they want, places Willard as their mere pawn (so a doubled puppet-marionette fear is now in play within Willard's psychology), and the fact that they might not have so much as told him the reason ("Did they say?") shows Willard that Kurtz already understands (probably more than he does, so still more asymmetry) how little they respect him, and perhaps how little he has come to respect himself. Grasping, if desperately, for a knowledge-asymmetry in his favor, Willard says, "I was sent on a classified mission, sir." Kurtz instantly and effortlessly makes clear the absurdity of this response (as they are both sitting there in Kurtz's chambers plainly knowing what Willard is there for), but with the humiliating sense that Kurtz has toyingly ventriloquized Willard, making him spout an absurdity that only serves to connect him, as an uncomprehending mouthpiece, to the system from which he in truth feels alienated and from which Kurtz long ago declared his superior independence. He is losing even rudimentary control of his words at the hands of a chess master, and the real worry about freedom versus determinism already in play is now resonating more loudly in his mind with this. The words "is it?" in the next phrase underscore all of this in an aggressive way: "It's no longer classified, is it?" And with Willard now decentered from himself, Kurtz digs the hole of disrespect deeper: "Did they tell you?" Adopting words not his own (they come from the meeting with the General) under an extreme pressure doubled, that is, pressure that is coming both outwardly from Kurtz and inwardly from his own underlying catastrophic self-doubt, Willard says (and now, still worse, feeling ventriloquized by the General and his colleagues), "They told me that you had gone totally insane, and that your methods were unsound." Kurtz knows empty phraseology when he hears it—he spent a brilliant career in a military that proved expert at producing it—and, knowing that Willard sees far more than would a mere obedient functionary, asks "Are my methods unsound?" This seemingly straightforward question actually strikes at the core of Willard's vulnerability. Kurtz has spoken admiringly of the Viet Cong, particularly for their resolute clarity in the context of war (e.g., severing the arms of civilian children who have been inoculated with American resources), and Willard, in order to emerge from the wash of falsifying rhetoric, hypocrisy, and the lies he hated more the more he saw of them, seeks clarity above all. This is what Kurtz seems to exude presently, it is what the photojournalist told him Kurtz most powerfully displayed, and clarity of purpose—however renegade—was woven throughout his closely studied file. Whatever else one says, Willard sees before him in the person of Kurtz an unyielding clarity that he believes, or possibly can believe, is the by-product of profound self-knowledge.

Yet he knows that his deep-seated need for clarity should not blind him to the fact that it does not follow that, because Kurtz sees that the allegations against him in the context of this war are insane, that he himself is not also insane. With a brief few words he thus attempts to challenge Kurtz, regain a modicum of power in the exchange by showing his capacity for criticism, and establish his independence from a figure with whom it becomes, phrase by phrase, all the easier to identify. Willard says, but in a way that comes out thinly and as the voice of a conventional critique that they both know they are well beyond (the question again is how much distance there is between them), "I don't see any method at all, sir." This word-borne weakness, for Kurtz, is beneath so much as acknowledging, and Kurtz, changing the subject and now attacking everything Willard is by reducing him to a stereotypical generic type, says, "I expected someone like you. What did you expect? Are you an assassin?" That's not "I expected you"; it is, instead, "I expected someone like you." This is a very different remark, and it brings out sharply not only the difference between acknowledging an individual for who the person is and merely seeing the generic category to which that individual belongs, but also it implies that the individual can be reduced to or exhaustively contained within the functional category. That, in short, is reduction to a type, and it suggests—and for Willard re-enlivens—the darker fear above, that the discovery to be had is that there is no deeper content of selfhood to be found or galvanized and clarified through self-identifying choice and action.[23] Thus now in serious trouble—where the meaning of "serious" really depends on everything we have seen of Willard's progress so far, Willard asserts a declarative, defensive proposition: "I'm a soldier." Kurtz's response brings to a psychological point of maximal density all of Willard's problems, the ones buried beneath his troubled behavior from the outset, the ones that made him a powder keg of a person, the ones that put his fist through the mirror, the ones that drove him to this point upriver. Kurtz casually and calmly says, in a tone saturated with superiority, "You're neither. You're an errand boy, sent by grocery clerks, to collect a bill."

But as viewers of this film, we must ask what Willard must ask: Is the *tone* of those potentially devastating words real? Does that tone portray (to put it one way) what is actually the case? In a kind of soldier's speech (what the photojournalist called "a poet-warrior in the classic sense"),[24] Kurtz utters the following lines, lines that awaken for Willard a new aspect,[25] where Willard suddenly sees the superficiality of the commonality between them. And this new suddenly dawning aspect thus now shows a profound difference (and here lies the conversational opening to what will be his salvation): "I've seen horrors, horrors that you've seen. But you have no right to call me a murderer. You have a right to kill me. You have a right to do that, but you have no right to judge me. It's impossible for words to describe what is necessary to those who do not know what horror means. Horror! Horror has a face, and you must make a friend of horror. Horror and moral terror are your friends. If they are not, then they are enemies to be feared. They are truly enemies."

With these words Willard sees that he has not turned into Kurtz. And more importantly for his moral psychology, he sees that he cannot. What they have in common inside this remark is the realization that the enemy is psychological, is of the mind—this is the meaning of the word "truly" in the phrase "truly enemies." But Kurtz has, with his words, laid bare the difference in personhood that is more than an important remainder, more than just a matter of degree in their moral extremity. Kurtz made clear to Willard that he deeply admired in the Viet Cong the sheer "will," the "perfect, complete, crystalline, pure" form of action that is unmediated by what he regards as another inner enemy—judgment. What Kurtz thus most wants is most dehumanized (Willard had said that Kurtz takes his orders now not from any authority, but now only from the jungle, so he can comprehend this), and that is what he has enacted in his murderous compound. As Kurtz encapsulates, "to kill without judgment" is his path to authentic selfhood: "It's judgment that defeats us." And he gazes into the middle distance as he admiringly refers to "that pile of little arms."

But what he has actually shown Willard, the defining aspect of his being that he has awakened, is that he is an exemplar of *imitated* strength, of doctrinaire allegiance to a way of being that he has, in bitter truth, falsely appropriated from an external model taken from another culture he can only partly understand from a rose-tinted, hideously romanticized, and inverse-idealized distance.[26] (Willard had said, "He broke from them, then broke from himself"—this too now means more than Willard realized when he said it, in that the break from self was a break from truth and authenticity, from the mode of being in which, in Cavell's sense, he owns his words.) Kurtz has revealed, unwittingly and, moreover, in a way that shows that he himself does not comprehend the content of what he is revealing (and thus it becomes clear to Willard and to us that he is not a genuine exemplar of self-knowledge either), that it is he who is, after all, the worst nonhero, the worst self-deceiver. From a rhetorically elevated position of donned superiority, it is in truth Kurtz who is merely what Nietzsche called "an imitator of an actor," supporting his godlike self-positioning with his version of the deluded rhetoric that he most despised in his government. And the one remaining thing Willard knows about himself that has not been destabilized is that, as he bluntly (and thus without any possibility of misleading inflection) said, the more he saw of lies the more he hated them.

"You have a right to kill me, but not to judge me." Actually, Willard's realization is that he now has both—the right to kill was conveyed by the General at the initial meeting ("terminate with extreme prejudice"), but far more importantly, Willard has, in this exchange with Kurtz, gained the right to judge as well, and it is precisely this that is in this psychologically evolved context centrally self-defining for Willard. Kurtz's proscription, in short, becomes meaningless when brought up against his own failings, and given his experience it is singularly *Willard's* place to render precisely that linguistic-moral judgment.[27]

But about those failings, the person-defining self-deception in play here: Kurtz repeatedly praises what he calls "clarity." In his letter to his son (closely studied by Willard in his file), Kurtz wrote, "In a war, there are many moments for compassion and tender action. There are many moments for ruthless action, for what is often called ruthless, what may in many circumstances be only clarity; seeing clearly what there is to be done and doing it directly, quickly, aware . . . looking at it." What Willard can now see is that Kurtz, with a murderous irony, has used his exalted criterion of clarity itself to falsely describe his own action in order to support a self-image that has papered over an utter loss of humanity, a loss of human sympathetic imagination, a loss of discernment in action, and an empty, and self-emptying, repudiation of judgment. It is no accident that his spokesman, the photojournalist, is hyperverbal, or indeed rhetorically hyperactive in the extreme: this is all unowned language of the kind that obscures what lies beneath.[28]

Kurtz's psychic building-blocks in this exchange become increasingly visible—the falsely appropriated and merely imitated sense of strength, the false criterion of clarity, the dehumanizing rhetorical repudiation of judgment where he is in fact constantly exercising it in a lethal, arbitrarily, murderous, and whimsical way that only lyingly buttresses his godlike self-image. In these moments, Willard not only at last sees Kurtz, he sees through Kurtz: he sees what it was he sensed lurking beneath all those soul-absorbing rereadings of his file, and he sees the great gulf separating what Kurtz says he is from what he is. His self-description is a veil. Willard, on this philosophical mission to find truth—about himself, about his identity, about where the breaking point is and his present position relative to that point—hated the falseness of the image of the war presented to the American people by the government when he had seen its reality. And now, in these exchanges with the figure who had until this moment exerted a dangerous magnetism for him, Willard saw something even more hateful: Kurtz, inside his word-supported delusional world (a "*poet*-warrior") was attempting to co-opt Willard into being a delivery boy sent not by a grocery clerk but, far worse, by a self-deceived megalomaniac who wanted him to deliver a set of descriptions of himself to his son that only perpetuated what was in truth an utter lack of clarity about who and what he was.[29]

That letter also contained the line, "As for the charges [of murder], I'm unconcerned. I'm beyond their timid, lying morality. And so I'm beyond caring." Willard sees it all: Kurtz is not beyond caring (because he does, centrally, care about his son's perception of him); here again far worse in Willard's eyes, he is beyond any possibility of self-understanding. Kurtz had said, "I worry that my son might not understand what I've tried to be. And if I were to be killed, Willard, I would want someone to go to my home and tell my son everything—everything I did, everything you saw—because there's nothing that I detest more than the stench of lies. And if you understand me, Willard, you will do this for me."

These words now bifurcate: Kurtz believes he can appeal to Willard's sense of understanding about how he has become what he is (transcendently great in his own prismatic, distorted vision), because he knows Willard has traversed much of the way himself along that path (and Willard's deepest question from the outset—although experience had to teach him how to find it, how to articulate it—has been whether he has traversed all the way). Willard now sees that he could indeed fulfill Kurtz's final wish in a way Kurtz himself cannot understand—he can go and tell Kurtz's son everything, precisely "everything you saw," and this would remove "the stench of lies"—but *including* Kurtz's lies to himself. The words Kurtz uses (e.g., "what I've tried to be") fit both sides of the bifurcation of word-meaning; Willard is now, finally, able to see both sides and to know on which side he has found the truth. This truth does indeed set him free from profound self-doubt, and it is the possession of this truth that gives him the right to judge as well as to kill. And with an intercut scene of a ritual killing of a caribou, he does both. One does not know if Kurtz's final whispered words, "the horror, the horror," are his final attempt at reconfirming everything he has become, saying a goodbye to the "friend" he made through his own action, or if in his last moments he sees more: the horror also of his own late recognition that everything he is, revealed in his exchange with Willard, is merely in truth made of paper, of words that do a liar's work. Willard shattered a mirror to make it a more true reflection; Kurtz gazed believingly and admiringly at a false self-image that was reflected in a kind of horrible external mirror of his own making.

Willard ends up in the final scene of this film (taking slow and measured steps out of the temple and through the slowly opening crowd of Kurtz's mute, somnambulant people back to the boat) carrying within him the remainder of Kurtz that is of value, the part of him that desires the understanding of his son. But then even that basic human desire is polluted with self-deception—what he wants is not for his son to understand him, but rather to believe the lie he has told himself. This conclusion is thus the triumphant reversal of Willard's deepest fear: he feared being lost inside himself to Kurtz, or becoming Kurtz. Now, in these slow steps recapitulating the protracted seven steps of his progress, it is he who contains Kurtz, and, when he purifies Kurtz's polluted departing wish by delivering to his son the truth, there is a sense in which Kurtz has been absorbed by, indeed become, Willard.[30] It is the moment of the consolidation, reintegration, and inner confirmation of his selfhood. Around Kurtz there revolved a world of insane and morally detached murderous cruelty that was (in truth, despite the initial threatening resemblances) the alien content from which Willard has, at last, gained his true independence. He knows what he is, and, silently taking in the full measure of the difference between Kurtz's world and his own as he paces, he now knows, with a resolute clarity born of thought and action, what he is not.[31]

One way of describing Kurtz's monumental failure of self-knowledge is to employ Freud's terms "derealization" and "depersonalization." Richard Wollheim, in integrating these into his discussion of ways of living as a person, ways of living a life across time, writes,

> Derealization and depersonalization are mirror images of one another. They are mirror images of one another in what they bring about, and the phantasies that are their vehicles are mirror-images of one another in their content. In derealization we deny a part of the world: in depersonalization we deny part of ourselves. In denying part of the world, we come to regard it as dependent upon our thoughts and feelings: that is how we come to phantasise it. In denying a part of ourselves, we come to regard it as independent of our thoughts and feelings: that is how we come to phantasise it. Derealization, the denial, the lived denial, of some part of the world, in effect denies it a life of its own. Depersonalization, the denial, the lived denial, of some part of ourselves, in effect denies us a life altogether of our own.
>
> Both derealization and depersonalization, carried far enough, lead to madness.[32]

Madness, indeed. And this is a way of describing what can now be seen as a double-blindness on Kurtz's part: a megalomaniacal denial of the reality of lives external to his own and a deep severance of himself from himself, from the teleology of the person, one living as a person in Wollheim's sense, up to his break. As a self-inflicted word-borne blindness followed by banishment, it is he who is in this respect the true Oedipus. But Wollheim's passage also offers a still fuller way of describing the rather heavy lifting that Willard's muscular words perform in this context, "He broke from them, then broke from himself."

Before closing, we should look back to the philosophical issues with which we began. They have been woven throughout this discussion, but recall that the first item on the list of elements making up the simplified philosophical picture that this complex film works through and ultimately dismantles was (1) the rigid separation between physical and mental objects. The film has shown that this crude separation psychologically falsifies more than it ontologically clarifies: mirrors broken into shards become increasingly powerful mimetic representations of inner life to a degree that the life comes to imitate its representation (and so it is in a real sense both of and in the mind); a severed head functions as simultaneously, and—importantly, inseparably—an outward record of murder and an inward inducement of terror (and so while it is an external object, its phenomenological content is the content that makes it now what it is); the home that was there Willard now knows is there no more.

This last case merits a moment's pause: it is plainly evident that the midwestern town with its factory is still there.[33] But that of course is not the point, nor would asserting it support the ontological dichotomy in question here: the point is that we could not get so far as to understand Willard's words (words that function, despite their unambiguous referential content, to describe a profound inward state of alienation by naming an external place he knows perfectly well to be outwardly there) were the simplistic, dualistic picture accurate—and we do understand such words readily.[34] The second item (2) was the corresponding rigid separation of knowledge of outward things from knowledge of inward things: this film shows that actual, situated multifarious forms of human knowledge do not conform to any such simplicities. A few examples: Willard thinks his way inside Kurtz's mind by studying and then (a different thing) imaginatively contemplating his file; Willard looks with a cold spectatorial distance upon himself just after the sampan shooting, learning from looking at what he has just outwardly done (the woman's lifeless body in front of him) what he has partially or can fully become (thus he is in this particular case in precisely the same position as the others on the boat, who never see him the same way again either); to know that a person orders surfing under fire is (simultaneously and inseparably) to know that that person has a consciousness moving into and out of the bounds of rationality.

The third element was (3) that only outward things are the kinds of things, ontologically speaking, that can be shared. It would take a recounting of the entire film to make this precise point with the requisite detail, but to sum up: Willard's entire growing, shifting, evolving, testing, backtracking, restarting, and ultimately self-stabilizing-through-differentiating relationship to Kurtz is a three-hour refutation of this simple picture concerning what can, and what cannot, be shared in human experience. Willard's voyage is a voyage into another mind, a mind that powerfully attracts and one that, at the precise point of most powerful attraction, reverses polarity and even more powerfully (at the film's moment of resolute self-composition) repels. The fourth element, really the inverse of (3), was that (4) owing to their privacy, inner objects cannot be shared in perception; this too met with a three-hour counterargument, but we might here recall: Chief knows this to be false, and in a way we (when not under the influence of a misleading philosophical picture) readily understand; impaled by a spear, and knowing his death is immanent, Chief tries and nearly succeeds to take Willard with him by pulling him onto the protruding spear. Which is to say: to take Willard with him by giving him precisely the same and thus shared experience of immediately impending finality.

The fifth element summed up the previous four, in saying (5) that self-knowledge will be a matter of knowing private internal objects (of knowledge), and recall that it divided into five subpoints of its own. The first was that (a) full self-knowledge will then be describable as full introspective awareness of one's perception of the outer world and of the inner world of hopes, fears, aspirations, and the like. One can be short here, given the extensive work this film has done: We see that Willard comes to know who and what he is by coming to know the (ultimately tragically self-deceived, murderous, and horrific) mind of another. His darkest fear was that when one subtracted Kurtz from Willard there would be no remainder, and thus that, in discovering who he truly was and what he truly was not, he would be Oedipus in Vietnam, with all the inner catastrophic ruin that this comparison would imply. But through the process we have traced, he has slowly, inexorably, earned his freedom from this fear. So it is not only that the simplifying philosophical picture is wrong, but also that it can, in some circumstances, be backward—we can come to know our own minds by (as in this film, painstakingly) coming to know the mind of another. The second subelement (b) was that introspection must be of inward, private things. But again, and briefly: Willard's process of studying the file, of reflecting on how a person could actually get to Kurtz's point, of learning how to ultimately understand the self-descriptively fraudulent story he tells himself about himself, is *simultaneously* to introspect (and as seen just above, here again self-knowledge is the result of other-knowledge). Regarding item (c), it seems safe to say at this point that knowing thyself will not invariably, as ordained by metaphysical rule, concern exclusively mind-dependent entities—as we have seen, psychological reality precludes ontological simplicity. As to (d), the alleged irrelevance of outward things to the content of self-knowledge, one might at this point say: detailed philosophical examples, rich enough in content to show what life as lived actually is (as Wittgenstein, Austin, and others claimed), woven together in the right way, take on a collective power that can make us wonder why we found the simplifying picture attractive or plausible in the first place, and the collective power of such examples can make us wonder what the words meant that we employed to give voice to that picture. Not one of the seven moments of Willard's progress, nor (and especially so) the encounter with Kurtz, could be described in such a way that the (d)-condition retains plausibility. Willard's experience is, we might say, internal to him—there is a sense of privacy about him.[35] But this is not the privacy of which philosophers have spoken: his experience, fundamental to and necessary for his discovering of who he might be and then composing who he is and will be, is indissolubly relationally constituted. His experience, like so much of human life (and like so little of what the dualist tradition has said about that life), is made by and with external connectedness (just as the early American pragmatists argued).[36] With all we know of Willard in mind, to try to separate out what we might, under a particular philosophical influence, call that experience's inner essence would seem strangely otiose if not incoherent.[37]

Finally, the last subpoint concerned (e) the alleged necessity that items of self-knowledge be abiding or nonmomentary. But Willard's instantaneous act of shooting the woman in the sampan, an act that came from deep within a dark place he was not sure he had (recall Ebert's remark at the outset above), only prefigures the final act of taking up the machete. He had experienced radical freedom, and he had learned the long-range significance for self-composition of the defining momentary act. That these moments and their meaning are incompatible with a philosophical picture does not diminish their credibility. The philosophical work of this film (or one part of it—it does much in an intertwined way) is to show that the reverse is true.

Willard is driven to find, to live, to articulate what for him (and for who he is, has been, and will be) is an examined life—however destabilizing, however painful, and however dangerous.[38] That is courage, displayed within the context of a problem of self-knowledge that demands for its resolution profound acts of self-composition.[39] Kurtz, by telling contrast, is a complex tragedy of the unexamined life. What he exemplifies is a reflexive form of epistemic cowardice: a house of cards, an invented world of false and murderously self-aggrandizing self-description that even he, deep down in his final moments, only half-believes—if that much.[40] He is blinded by his self-image to an extreme degree, where he cannot see (directly or forthrightly) that he has sunk to the low-water mark of humanity—he *is* cruelty, viciousness, reckless arbitrariness, and human disregard, all cast in the highest possible relief, and it is he who fully exemplifies the Freudian double-failure. Kurtz's final impasse is thus presented by circumstance to him as a choice: face the truth about himself, and thus lose all self-orientation (however twisted that may be), or die within his word-supported hideous fantasy, still intending to send out its false image, packaged as revelatory truth, to his son. The ambiguity of his final words is itself an expression of this impasse and his massively destructive inability to see who and what he is.

Last, a closing note: the interpretation of this film as I offer it here is one among a number of possible others; emphases could be placed differently (and this too is a measure of the depth of the film). But all plausible interpretations would, I think, have one thing shared beneath their differences: it would be the recognition that what this film offers, beyond its being perhaps the singularly outstanding Vietnam film, and beyond its being indisputably among the best war films, is a portrayal of a quest that is common to us all, one that is universal and that lifts this film above its genre. It is the quest to find the circumstances within which we can discover and create who we are.

Notes

1. Roger Ebert, "Great Movies: Apocalypse Now," *Chicago Sun-Times*, November 28, 1999.

2. I offer a way of seeing this process in "Self-Defining Reading: Literature and the

Constitution of Personhood," in *The Blackwell Companion to the Philosophy of Literature*, ed. Garry L. Hagberg and Walter Jost (Oxford: Wiley-Blackwell, 2010), pp. 120–58.

3. There is a scene in which Coppola is seen directing a war movie on the beach ("Don't look at the camera!"); this is a microcosmic representation within the film of the fact that a documentary is being made about this film. This double-filming circumstance is thus, with camera on cameras, itself then a representation of self-investigation. This is a key to what this film is actually about, where the documentary records and reflects on the progress of the film that, like Willard, makes itself, finds out what it is, as it goes.

4. There certainly have been helpful articles written about the film as one of, and in relation to, the Vietnam films and the political history of that war; there have been helpful articles about the film in connection with the larger Hollywood film genre and the "New Hollywood" school more narrowly; and there have been helpful articles about the film as one (major) part of the evolution of Coppola's life's work. But to date those discussions seem not to have fully uncovered, analyzed, and articulated the profoundly philosophical and conceptually intricate film that has been there all along.

5. See my *Describing Ourselves: Wittgenstein and Autobiographical Consciousness* (Oxford: Clarendon Press; New York: Oxford University Press, 2008).

6. For an excellent discussion of the issues involved here, see Sidney Shoemaker, "On Knowing One's Own Mind," in *Privileged Access*, ed. Brie Gertler (Aldershot, England: Ashgate, 2003), pp. 111–29.

7. The behaviorist reaction to Cartesian asymmetry was to deny that the description and explanation of human action required an appeal to psychological states (thus denying one-half of Cartesian dualism); the more philosophical version of this doctrine, logical behaviorism, asserted that the meaning of mental-state vocabulary will always be determined by reference to behavioral criteria. The origination of this view is found in B. F. Skinner, *Walden Two* (New York: Macmillan, 1948); see also his *Science and Human Behavior* (New York: Macmillan, 1953).

8. See Gilbert Ryle, "Self Knowledge," in *The Concept of Mind* (Harmondsworth: Penguin, 1966), pp. 160–89.

9. Milan Kundera, *The Art of the Novel* (New York: Harper, 2003). For a particularly lively discussion of the issue of self-identity, seen in connection with literature (in this case Beckett) where the consideration of literature does increase sensitivity to complexity, see Joshua Landy, *How to Do Things with Fictions* (New York: Oxford University Press, 2012), Part 2: "Finding the Self to Lose the Self," pp. 130–42.

10. It is easy to presume at this stage that—as the very phrase "self-knowledge" can too easily insinuate—there will be a stable, fixed self prior to the knowledge of it. Nietzsche saw the difficulty in answering too quickly (and too polemically) the question of whether selfhood was made or found, and he saw the difficulty of asking for truthfulness in language about that self if the content of selfhood was not fixed in order to provide something to be truthful about, something to use as the measure of truthfulness. For a subtle discussion of this matter, see Alexander Nehamas, *Nietzsche: Life*

as Literature (Cambridge, MA: Harvard University Press, 1985), chapter 6: "How One Becomes What One Is," pp. 170–99.

11. The famous visual transition at the beginning of the film from the rotating helicopter blade to the room's ceiling fan is an ingenious cut that captures his psychology: he is inside what William James called the blooming buzzing confusion, and the perceptual experience of Vietnam is overlaying his perceptual experience presently. (This also establishes the theme of perceptual ambiguity, which as we shall see runs throughout the film; another early instance is bomb sounds that are met with "What's that?" where a moment of perceptual indeterminacy precedes its being settled.)

12. The nature of such a maelstrom of selfhood itself, and its psychic weight, deserves its own full discussion; for a brilliant discussion that can cast much light on such a psychological condition, see Jonathan Lear, *Happiness, Death, and the Remainder of Life* (Cambridge, MA: Harvard University Press, 2000), chapter 3: "The Remainder of Life," pp. 106–65. Lear writes, "Even a healthy ego—the ego of an Aristotelian virtuous person—is not proof against all possible onslaughts from within or without. There is no such thing as an ego that is invulnerable to trauma. And in actual life, the psychological achievements of maturity do tend to be somewhat fragile. There is always and everywhere the possibility of being overwhelmed" (p. 110). As we, and he, will see in his encounter with Kurtz, Willard is the embodiment and philosophical demonstration of this.

13. And that circumstance need not be taken as fixed, in such a way that the available open courses of possible action are similarly fixed or prespecified: the truth is more complicated, and what becomes fixed or not can itself be a function of volitional action in the moment. See, in this connection, Martha Nussbaum's insightful introduction of the concept of improvisation into moral life, in "'Finely Aware and Richly Responsible': Literature and the Moral Imagination," in *Love's Knowledge: Essays on Philosophy and Literature* (New York: Oxford University Press, 1990), pp. 148–67, esp. pp. 155–57. For further helpful reflections in this direction that also capture the sense of complexity in play in such cases, see Cora Diamond, "Missing the Adventure: A Reply to Martha Nussbaum," in *The Realistic Spirit: Wittgenstein, Philosophy, and the Mind* (Cambridge, MA: MIT Press, 1991), pp. 309–18, esp. pp. 311–13.

14. For an insightful discussion of this, see Paul Boghossian, "Content and Self-Knowledge," in Gertler, *Privileged Access*, pp. 65–82, esp. pp. 67–69.

15. See for example A. J. Ayer, *The Concept of a Person and Other Essays* (London: Macmillan, 1963), pp. 219–22.

16. Ryle, *The Concept of Mind*, passim, but see especially pp. 177–89; see also Boghossian, "Content and Self-Knowledge," p. 67: "Ryle . . . tried to defend the view that there is no asymmetry between first-person and third-person access to mental states. In both cases, he maintained, the process is essentially the same: ordinary inspection of ordinary behavior gives rise to the discovery of patterns in that behavior, which in turn leads to the imputation of appropriate propositional attitudes." See also Donald

Davidson, "Knowing One's Own Mind," in *Self-Knowledge,* ed. Quassim Cassam (Oxford: Oxford University Press, 1994), pp. 43–64, esp. pp. 43–48.

17. It is on hearing the recorded voice of Kurtz that Willard uses the expression "put a hook in me." Part of the hook is located within Kurtz's recorded words, "They call me an assassin," which hit Willard precisely at what is for him, in his present condition, a very weak point: Are there facts of the matter, or in this maelstrom are there just what people say are what we would then call "facts" of the matter? The threat to Willard is a thoroughgoing linguistic-moral relativism that would stabilize nothing, leaving him ever more adrift. Also, just as one can see a good deal of expressive content in a person's face, so one can hear a good deal of expressive content in a person's voice. This of course is another part of what makes up the hook.

18. The use of voice-over narration in and of itself illustrates throughout the duration of the film the autobiographical projects of developing thematic continuity across the time of a life and of working out the nuances of the description of those continuing themes in the course of their development. For a discussion of this process of thematic unification, see Alasdair MacIntyre, *After Virtue,* 2nd ed. (Notre Dame, IN: University of Notre Dame Press, 1984), esp. "The Virtues, the Unity of a Human Life, and the Concept of a Tradition," pp. 204–25.

19. I refer here to the distinctive sense of theatricality given full articulation by Michael Fried; see *Absorption and Theatricality* (Chicago: University of Chicago Press, 1988). The theatrical dimension of this scene could be discussed at length: the cavalry trumpets, pieces of Civil War uniforms, and other props make it what one would call "just like a real war"—except that it is. Willard sees the layering of play-acting over the top of the real situation clearly, and this anticipates and thematically prepares the question he will have to ask and answer later, that is, precisely where the line between the sane and the insane lies. The theme of a fictional overlay is never dropped within the film: as another connected dot leading, as we shall see, to the grandiose overlay of Kurtz's vision, we encounter a soldier with one of the Playboy bunnies, asking her to don a dark wig to match the image in his mind from the photographs of her he has seen (in which, although now blonde, she had dark hair). He says, "Can't believe I'm really here" while "editing" the real person in front of him to match the prior mental image (so in a sense, he is precisely right—he isn't really *here* and so should not believe it). Once one identifies the theme, one can see a number of instances of this kind running through the film.

20. For an insightful discussion that investigates the basic human need for truth and true self-description (the need that is driving Willard), see Raimond Gaita, "Truth as a Need of the Soul," in *A Common Humanity* (London: Routledge, 1998), pp. 237–58.

21. I have not examined this episode here, but in the French plantation scene (edited into the redux version), Willard's increasingly urgent need for self-integration is directly articulated: the woman he meets says, "There are two of you—one that kills, one that loves." Throughout this scene there are subtle clues indicating Willard's present doubled, if not entirely shattered, condition: he sees that he alone rises when the

woman approaches the table, finding within his own habituated genteel gesture a trace of his premilitary self. He is a man in pieces—but he knows his encounter with Kurtz holds the key to where each piece derives from a more stable past and thus holds out the promise of reintegration.

22. Friedrich Nietzsche, *Twilight of the Idols,* trans. R. J. Hollingdale (London: Penguin, 1968), Section 1: "Maxims and Arrows," no. 38.

23. To reveal another aspect of this exchange and its central importance for Willard as a destabilized identity, one can see this as an urgency concerning the need for him to know the meaning of his own name and what that name stands for in a fuller sense. He needs to *occupy* his name and not see it as a mere verbal version of what the military does with de-individuating numbers applied to soldiers. I offer a discussion of the fuller sense of a name and its importance in "Wittgenstein Re-Reading," in *Wittgenstein Reading,* ed. Daniel Steuer, Sascha Bru, and Wolfgang Huemer (Berlin: De Gruyter, 2013). See also the discussion in Frank Cioffi, *Wittgenstein on Freud and Frazer* (Cambridge: Cambridge University Press, 1998), "Wittgenstein on Making Homeopathic Magic Clear," pp. 155–82, where he writes:

> In his autobiography Goethe provides an illustration of the peculiarly intimate relation in which we stand to our names. He tells us how annoyed he was at a verse of Herder's in which Herder took liberties with the name Goethe by punning on Goth: "It was not in very good taste to take such jocular liberties with my name; for a person's name is not like a cloak which only hangs round him and may be pulled and tugged at, but a perfectly fitting garment grown over and around him like his very skin, which one cannot scrape and scratch at without hurting the man himself." (pp. 166–67)

Willard needs to know that there is someone there, inside the name, one who could be hurt by such scraping and scratching. Mere cloaks are exchangeable without loss. On problems generated by seeing "I" as a proper name rather than personal pronoun, and on issues of self-consciousness that are immediately in play in Willard's case, see G. E. M. Anscombe, "The First Person," in Cassam, *Self-Knowledge,* pp. 140–59.

24. Regarding the depiction of Kurtz as poet-warrior, consider this exchange:

Willard: Could we, uh, talk to Colonel Kurtz?

Photojournalist: Hey, man, you don't talk to the Colonel. You listen to him. The man's enlarged my mind. He's a poet-warrior in the classic sense. I mean, sometimes he'll, uh, well, you'll say hello to him, right? And he'll just walk right by you, and he won't even notice you. And suddenly he'll grab you, and he'll throw you in a corner, and he'll say, "Do you know that 'if' is the middle word in life? If you can keep your head when all about you are losing theirs and blaming it on you, if you can trust yourself when all men doubt you . . ." I mean, I'm no, I can't—I'm a little man, I'm a little man, he's, he's a great man. I should have been a pair of ragged claws scuttling across floors of silent seas."

(These last remarks are derived from Rudyard Kipling's poem "If" and from T. S. Eliot's "The Love Song of J. Alfred Prufrock.")

25. I refer here to the perceptual phenomenon discussed in Wittgenstein, *Philosophical Investigations,* Part II, sec. xi; for full and wide-ranging discussions of this, see *Seeing Wittgenstein Anew,* ed. W. Day and V. Krebs (Cambridge: Cambridge University Press, 2010).

26. The study this film makes of the potential dangers of a romanticized self-image is acute: Kurtz here lapses into a reverie about the delicate beauty of flowers in the middle of this complex exchange; he is in front of Willard celebrating (with in truth hideous falsity) the poetic delicacy of his own soul. ("Heaven fell to earth in the form of gardenias," etc.)

27. Although this calls for fuller analysis, in short, it is at this stage of Willard's progress that he becomes aware that his growing recognition of the "house-of-cards" fragility of Kurtz's self-definition is inversely related to the strengthening stability of his own. For an overview of the issues in play in this kind of circumstance, see Peter Goldie, *On Personality* (London: Routledge, 2004), "The Fragility of Character," pp. 52–77.

28. Indeed, the hyperverbal photojournalist can be taken to represent those who would claim, too extremely, that identity is entirely and wholly a matter of narrative construction, and thus that any one is as good as any other, that is, that there are not external constraints on the verbal creation of self-identity. (The opposite, too extreme claim is that words have nothing to do with the creation or stabilization of identity and that they are always "after the fact," always mere descriptions of prior facts against which the veracity of those words can be judged.) For a helpful charting of a synthesizing middle course, see Peter Goldie, *The Mess Inside: Narrative, Emotion, and the Mind* (Oxford: Oxford University Press, 2012).

29. There are reminders throughout the film of the gulf between acceptable news accounts of war and the real description of it that runs throughout the film. Indeed, one striking instance that can stand for all is Kurtz reading a *Time* magazine cover story on the present state of the war; it is one of the many instructive brief flashes in the film that hold deeper significance for understanding the kinds of things that can go wrong where self-deception masquerades as superior self-knowledge: Kurtz implicitly thinks that the flagrant falseness of the publicized narrative shows that his constructed narrative is true. Of course, they can both be false, and the evident falsity of the one does not confer added epistemic credibility to the other (but this may not be on first glance apparent). We as viewers already know when we see Kurtz in this scene that nothing of this modern-day inferno, nor anything of his renegade actions and identity, nor anything of Willard's mission (nor the psychic division that alienates him from both home society and battlefield) could ever be reported, much less comprehendingly grasped, without one's having first understood the kind of intricate and psychologically complex identity-determining self-scrutiny that this film is about, but in this scene we are

provoked to quickly think through and sort out the logic here. Wittgenstein said that he wanted his book to stimulate readers to thoughts of their own, and not to save them the trouble of thinking; at one point he called his book "a machine to think with." A film can function in a very similar way.

30. Willard at the closing of the film is seen, after all, at Kurtz's typewriter—the instrument of his self-deceived narrative, now, without its operator, the true image of empty words. And Willard is now the sole arbiter—the new owner—of Kurtz's story and what will and will not survive of it, what will be his remainder in words. He is carrying Kurtz's manuscript in his hand as he steps away to the boat.

31. The process of coming to know what we are, through coming to comprehend what we are not, could be examined at length. For a recent illuminating and wide-ranging discussion, see Stephen Mulhall, *The Self and Its Shadows: A Book of Essays on Individuality as Negation in Philosophy and the Arts* (Oxford: Oxford University Press, 2013); see especially "The Metaphysics of (Secret) Agency, Or: Three Ways of Not Being James Bond," pp. 74–115.

32. Richard Wollheim, *The Thread of Life* (Cambridge, MA: Harvard University Press, 1984), chap. 9, "Cutting the Thread: Death, Madness, and the Loss of Friendship," p. 270.

33. About this, Willard provides in voice-over what could serve as a motto for the entire philosophical content of this film: "Maybe you'll get a chance to know what the fuck you are in some factory in Ohio." I'll return to this in the closing paragraph.

34. Another way to say this would be that, while the town is obviously still there, *his* town, the one from which *he* comes, is not. This way of putting it calls attention to the intricate relations between perception and imagination that the simple dualism separating the two would always fail to capture. For a discussion that nicely elucidates a number of the complexities on this score (and includes deeply helpful remarks on the very different kinds of things we may mean in differing contexts by the word *imagination*), see P. F. Strawson, "Imagination and Perception," in *Freedom and Resentment and Other Essays* (London: Methuen, 1974), pp. 45–65.

35. Significant light can be cast on what is, and what is not, private (and what this term actually means) by considering the representation of inner states (e.g., quiet suffering, or contained sorrow) in the theater; for a particularly astute examination of this issue, see Martin Puchner, *The Drama of Ideas: Platonic Provocations in Theater and Philosophy* (New York: Oxford University Press, 2010), pp. 125–38. Puchner brings together a good number of telling particularities in connection with Kierkegaard's discussion of this issue, where a Kierkegaardian author writes that as "sorrow wishes to conceal itself," it becomes necessary to create "shadow figures" of "an interior picture": he adds, "I call them silhouettes, partly to suggest at once by the name that I draw them from the dark side of life and partly because, like silhouettes, they are not immediately visible." Through Puchner's discussion one comes to see that what we say is visible and what we say is invisible do not correspond at all to the conception of privacy advanced

explicitly or implicitly by dualistic ontology; the theatrical (and I want to say also filmic) handling of what privacy is, and how privacy actually works, lies beyond what philosophy usually dreams of.

36. I offer a fuller discussion of this issue in "Imagined Identities: Autobiography at One Remove," *New Literary History* 38, no. 1 (Winter 2007): 163–81.

37. In this connection see John McDowell, "Knowledge and the Internal," in *Meaning, Knowledge, and Reality* (Cambridge, MA: Harvard University Press, 1998), pp. 395–413; following lines set out by Wilfrid Sellars, he begins by noting what he rightly calls a "deformation" in our thinking, "an interiorization of the space of reasons, a withdrawal of it from the external world. This happens when we suppose we ought to be able to achieve flawless standings in the space of reasons by our own unaided resources, without needing the world to do us any favours" (pp. 395–96). McDowell's discussion here of what he identifies as an "inward retreat" is particularly helpful in articulating precisely what Willard's epistemic circumstance here shows to be philosophically untenable. McDowell notes that this inward retreat is "a familiar tendency in philosophy: the tendency to picture the objective world as set over against a 'conceptual scheme' that has withdrawn into a kind of self-sufficiency" (p. 408). Willard's only way forward is through the noninteriorization of the space of reasons and the (in his case) courageous overcoming of any tendency toward an inward retreat.

38. One way to express this self-defining project succinctly is to adopt Richard Rorty's language of the contingency of selfhood; see *Contingency, Irony, and Solidarity* (Cambridge: Cambridge University Press, 1989), chap. 2, "The Contingency of Selfhood," pp. 23–43. For Rorty, rather than working out any final or ultimately settled self-description, "there is only a web of relations to be rewoven" (p. 43); Willard, from well before the broken mirror, has been living in a way in which all patterns and trajectories of those relations are radically unsettled, or are all, in Rorty's term, contingent (but for Willard to the most extreme degree). His clarity-engendering decisions at the end weave his past into a web that has order and structure, and that clarified web then sets into play the determining patterns for his future interweavings.

39. There is another aspect of self-composition in play here that calls for independent examination on another occasion: one fundamental part of the larger concern driving Willard's inexorable search for self-knowledge is the desire to generate, and reflexively understand, the ethical fabric of consistency within himself. It is not the case—and he knows this—that just any collection of isolated episodes can be fitted together into a pattern that makes up a character. They must be, in a morally fairly intricate sense, fitting into one another. For an incisive discussion, see Bernard Williams, "Ethical Consistency," in *Problems of the Self* (Cambridge: Cambridge University Press, 1973), pp. 166–86.

40. It is for this reason that he actually welcomed his own inside-military assassination ("he wanted to go out like a soldier" meant more than we realized, now with

confronting death being preferable to confronting the threat of self-knowledge), and it explains why he allowed Willard free movement (and the words "he has plans for you!" thus also meant more than it seemed) and why Kurtz (otherwise inexplicably) took no action to prevent his death, which he very easily could have done had his survival been for him paramount.

The Violated Body

Affective Experience and Somatic Intensity in *Zero Dark Thirty*

Robert Burgoyne

The violence that *Zero Dark Thirty* explores from its initial moments to its deflating conclusion represents something new in American cinema, a portrayal that is at once intimate and inseparable from the large-scale violence that dominates the short history of the young century. In the course of the film, violence is rendered in immediate close-up, both acoustic and visual, and gradually dilated to read as a defining historical motif, an "organizing cultural and aesthetic fact," as the literary historian Sarah Cole writes in another context.[1] Rendering the concrete terror of 9/11 in an acoustic montage, followed by a brutal portrayal of interrogation and torture, *Zero Dark Thirty* (Bigelow, 2012) maps the specific contours of what might be called a new violent imaginary, shaped by endless threat, by the constant possibility of attack, and by the willingness to use force as default response.

At the film's center, the character Maya (Jessica Chastain) registers the experience of violence as a direct, intimate witnessing, a witnessing that sutures her to the larger social and historical world the film portrays. In her single-minded focus on the pursuit of Osama bin Laden, a picture of a world emerges, a world defined by hidden networks of potential threats that may or may not be real, underlined by scenes of visceral injury, death, and violent confrontation, conveyed in the aesthetic language of the procedural, a form that proliferates its own forms of anxiety. The violence in the film is thus both explicit and implied, experienced intimately, physically, and spread over a vast network of surveillance and tracking data, with each data point, terrorist photograph, and intercepted communication mapping both a history and a subjective script of violence and potential attack. With her story forming the main trajectory of the film, Maya's pursuit of bin Laden fuses the embodied violence of terror and coercive interrogation, what Cole calls the "felt experience of violence," with the procedural details of process and analysis, inference and projection.[2]

Framing its depiction of 9/11 in a way that penetrates the veil of familiarity that has formed around the events of that day, the film uses the sound track of victims' recorded voices as a kind of sonic shorthand. As an aesthetic device, sound slides under the psychic censorship that regularly attends visual representation; unlike vision, one cannot "look away" from sound, or easily close one's ears. Nor is sound rationalized or contained as readily as visual representation. Here, the sounds of 9/11 serve to call up the emotional meaning of the events, giving them a personal focus, providing a direct rendering of the experience of the victims, and placing the body once more at the center of an event that has grown encrusted with visual cliché. The opening scene puts the audience in the position of witness in a way that both short-circuits the voyeurism often elicited by the imagery of disaster and collapses the distancing that visual representation sometimes allows. The black screen that opens the film, however, also suggests another reading, reminding us, with its empty field of vision, that the bodies of the victims as well as the bodies of the perpetrators simply disappeared in the collapse of the towers. The mass destruction of 9/11, the most filmed and viewed event in history, was, disorientingly, a disembodied event. For some writers, the absence of bodies, both of the perpetrators and the victims, had an almost uncanny effect. As Cole writes, "The visual spectacles of 9/11 have been seen by billions, but with the exception of a few stunning photographs featuring falling bodies . . . no one has ever seen the bodies of the dead. The violence of the attacks was instantly recognized as historic and transformative, and the absence of flesh made its own imaginative claims."[3] The invisibility of the perpetrators, according to Anne McClintock, was especially disconcerting. Describing the attacks of 9/11 as a "crisis of violence and the visible," she writes: "The suicide attackers, deliberately flying passenger planes into buildings as they did, had instantly obliterated themselves in the fiery cataclysm, removing their bodies from the realm of visible retribution and thereby at the same time removing all means for the Bush administration to be seen to recuperate its wounded potency. The state was faced with an immediate dilemma: how to embody the invisible enemy and be visibly seen to punish it?"[4]

Zero Dark Thirty organizes its plot around the pursuit of bin Laden and his courier, Abu Ahmed, casting these two figures as phantasmatic, will-o'-the-wisp characters whose elusiveness generates extreme forms of compensatory violence. In its first third, the film details in stark cinematic language the acts McClintock describes as "produc[ing] the enemy as bodies" and making the bodies of the prisoners "legible as enemies."[5] But where McClintock sees the spectacle of punished bodies as a distraction—a type of camouflage—that conceals the actual extent of the violence of the War on Terror, I feel the film conveys a deeper transformation, a first rewriting of the dominant fiction under the pressure of 9/11, where the old narrative shapes of history are replaced by a new set of themes, a new setting, and a new dramatis personae.

In the close-up rendering of torture and interrogation that immediately follows the opening acoustic montage, *Zero Dark Thirty* places the violated body at the center of the film's articulation of history, providing a figuration that haunts the film and shapes the depiction of the main character, Maya. Her hands at times covering her eyes, clutching her jacket, then forcing herself to watch, Maya is foregrounded in the scene's shot patterning: her experience of torture tracks an arc of emotion and performance that progresses from witnessing, to complicity, to coercive agency. Beginning with her suggestion that "we should go back in," however, the intimate witnessing of torture becomes inseparable from the act itself, a point that is scenically presented in a series of close-ups and eye-line matches between Maya; the lead interrogator, Dan (Jason Clarke); and the torture victim, Ammar (Reda Kateb).

The formal patterning of the scene locks the character into an intimate relation with the prisoner, metonymically connecting her to the injured body, not by touch, but by the gaze. It is her gaze that is evoked as the prisoner is paraded naked from the waist down and then walked around the room like a dog; it is her gaze that holds the power to humiliate, and for which the scene is staged; and it is her gaze that Dan, the leader of the interrogation, consults before he continues the torture. The surprising thing here, or perhaps it is unsurprising, is the intimacy that flows from the scene: she is connected to the victim in a way that has the paradoxical effect of humanizing him; rather than creating a distance, a barrier, the injury of the body creates a disturbing join between the characters, a point that comes through strongly when she is alone with him in the cell. Similar to her in age, their relationship not yet patterned by the "grammars of violence" that organize the interrogation procedure, the victim asks Maya to help him, to spare him from her partner, who is a "madman."[6] For a moment, what has sometimes been described as the strange intimacy between oppressor and victim seems to surface, with the two characters facing each other in what Paul Virilio calls the half-light of war: "War is a symptom of delirium operating in the half-light of trance, drugs, blood and unison. This half-light establishes a corporeal identity in the clinch of allies and enemies, victims and executioners."[7] Here too the observer becomes the observed, as the character of Maya is scrutinized, held to account by the spectator, by the lead interrogator, and by the victim himself.

As the film unfolds, the interrogation videos that Maya watches over and over, spread out on her computer screen in a frightening Goya-like montage of gasping, shackled men, push the connection between witnessing and violent infliction to the center of the film's pictorial vocabulary. Studying the interrogations, rewinding and replaying scenes of prisoners shackled to the ceiling, handcuffed to tables, thrown to the floor, or sitting without visible restraint, the character hears—or imagines she hears—the name "Abu Ahmed" repeated again and again, a name that sometimes emerges from the questioning and is sometimes supplied by the interrogator. Maya's face, reflected in the computer monitor, or viewed in profile as the voices and sounds of the interrogation proceed, is the presiding focus of the scene, her expression of intense concentration seeming to belie the history of violence summarized in these clips. As Maya drills deep into the DVDs, mouthing the words "Abu Ahmed" when the victims of torture are unable to speak clearly, the name of the courier comes to seem like an uncanny and sinister invocation, drawing her in. She projects herself fully into this world, and Maya's subjectivity, her intuition and psychology, becomes the main focus of the sequence. At one point she is shown walking into sunlight from the dark interior of the office, moving slowly and distractedly into bright light, only to return immediately to the violent interrogations unfolding on her computer screen—a distant recall, perhaps, of the character Harry Caul in *The Conversation* (Coppola, 1974). Finally, she brings up the image of a very young man, framed in close-up, who tells the interrogator that there are many couriers and that no one knows who is directly in contact with bin Laden. His youth, his look of boyish openness, his obvious fear, seem to call out for empathy. Maya's response is ambiguous; peering at his frozen image, her face is half blackened by shadow.

In depicting the violated body as ground and as emblematic expression of the War on Terror, *Zero Dark Thirty* shapes its imagery, especially in the first third of the film, around the degradation and waste produced by war.

Breaching the protected zone that has formed around the War on Terror, the film provides an unrelenting treatment of embodied violence, depicting an alternating series of harsh interrogations and devastating terrorist attacks in a kind of expanding, widening loop. The film presents the embodied reality of violence—the intimate experience of constant threat and response—as key to the period, with violence extending over broad geographic zones, penetrating daily life, defining and shaping the life and the actions of the main character, whose certainty of purpose is constructed as the crux of the work. As agent and mirror of violence, however, Maya disturbs the usual operative models in film. Pre-Raphaelite in her beauty, Maya conveys contradictory messages associated with the violence of contemporary war. The character's youth and sculpted beauty trouble the paradigm of purposive violence; her striking "whiteness," for example, creates a disturbing and dramatic contrast of skin tones and textures during the interrogation scenes, producing a visual overtone, an Eisensteinian conflict, that is not easily accommodated by genre codes.[8] At the same time, her beauty challenges the easy notion that violence is deforming and dehumanizing. Instead, the effect of violence on both character and history is left open, unresolved in the film's narrative program.

The violence of war has often generated innovations in aesthetic representation, as the hyperbolic carnage of mass conflict seems to demand aesthetic risk. The innovative poetry and literature of the modernist period, for example, arose partially as a response to the unprecedented mass slaughter of World War I.[9] Similarly, the brooding films of German expressionism, populated by liminal creatures, were drawn from the spaces and experiences of war.[10] In many ways *Zero Dark Thirty* fulfills this demand, forging an unsettling, provocative approach to violence, exposing the degeneracy and brutality of war by emphasizing its effects on the lead character. Focusing on the flesh, refusing to idealize or glamorize the War on Terror or to burnish it with patriotic appeal, the film renders the events of 9/11 and its aftermath in a form that is brutal and direct, portraying the effects of violence and war in a way that reflects the reality of the contemporary political moment.

In general, however, the violence that defines the War on Terror has unfolded mainly out of frame, generating very little in the way of rich symbolic structures or innovations in form. Rather, films and other artworks have mainly responded to the War on Terror with what the political theorist Christopher Coker calls the discourses of reenchantment.[11] The infatuation with remote weaponry and digital intercoding in many films of the post-9/11 period, for example—what one writer has called "the battle of the screens" and another has labeled "digital fatigue"—might best be understood as a form of technological reenchantment with war.[12] Gallery works such as Harun Farocki's *Images of War (at a Distance)* mine a similar vein of imagery, finding a consistent symbolic thread in the Baudrillard-like training of contemporary soldiers in computer games and simulated combat.[13] The current fascination with technological warfare, Coker argues, can be seen as a response to the mass disenchantment that followed World War II, in which extreme experiences of degradation and loss of life created a widespread understanding of war as brutal and degenerate. With the advent of "wired" war and bio-war, however, the violence of warfare is now being reframed as technological and seductive; some theorists go so far as to celebrate the prospect of "hygienic" and "virtuous" war.[14] Blanketed in digital technology, many contemporary war films appear to illustrate the point, envisioning war as a technological, mediated experience, far removed from the trauma of embodied violence.

The figure of the body in narratives of war, however, has long served to crystallize ideas about collective violence and the value or futility of sacrifice, often functioning as a symbol of historical transformation and renewal or, contrastingly, as a sign of utter degeneration and waste. For example, during the post–World War I period, violence, and in particular the violated body in war, served, in the words of Cole, as the "germinating core of rich symbolic structures" in literary works, conceived variously as a "magic site for the transformation of culture" and as an emblem of degradation and loss.[15] Many modernist writers in Great Britain, Cole argues, drew aesthetic inspiration from the power of violence in World War I, responding with aesthetically rich patterns of verse and prose that openly considered the relation of violence to art. Ranging from works that sought to transform the gruesome violence of war into "enchanted violence" through literary form to works that sought to disenchant violence by way of raw, unadorned language, modernist literary practice in the postwar period was marked by the intertwining of patterns of enchantment and disenchantment in works that confronted the violence of modern life.

The imposing power of the violated body in *Zero Dark Thirty* might be seen, then, as a particularly resonant expression of disenchantment, as the depictions of interrogation and torture that dominate the first third of the film accentuate the dehumanizing and degenerative nature of violence.

Hard lighting, urine-soaked cells, plain and unaccented camera work—these scenes have an unadorned visual directness. And as Maya progresses to the role of chief interrogator, her red hair covered by a black wig and headscarf, she orders physical punishment with what seem like practiced gestures, as if she has internalized the voice of violence and needs only the most subtle, instrumentalized gesture to trigger its infliction. The veneer of control that she constructs, however, is undercut by the gasping confrontation she has with the mirror directly after. The aestheticizing of violence through form, the ceremonial stylization that accompanies many scenes of embodied violence in film, is simply not found here.

The film pivots into more familiar genre convention, however, with the killing of Maya's CIA colleague Jessica (Jennifer Ehle), a woman who had befriended Maya and whose warmth and humanity set her apart. With this devastating scene, rendered in a style of exacting suspense, "violence can find its conventions," as Cole writes.[16] Set in the remote desert base in Afghanistan, Camp Chapman, the scene plays a set of emotional keys distinctly different from what has gone before, emphasizing Jessica's optimism, her excitement at meeting this purported "mole" who has offered to sell his access and his information, and reinforcing the emotion of the scene by crosscutting to Maya, whose new friendship seems to bring something like a normal interior life into focus. As the possible contact is driven to the camp, the sequence builds the anticipation, rendering the drawn-out transit of his vehicle through the desert in extreme long shot as it moves toward the outer perimeter of the base. Cutting between Jessica, the interior of the vehicle as it moves into the camp interior, and Maya at her computer in Pakistan, the film links Maya and the CIA colleague as comrades in arms, sharing the excitement and anticipation of their "first big break since 9/11." At Jessica's insistence, and in violation of the rules, the contact is allowed to pass the checkpoint and is admitted into the interior of the camp without being searched. As the man exits the car, the film isolates certain unsettling details—the cane he is using, his limp, the hand in his pocket. The editing gains pace, and the shot sizes shift to a series of close-ups. When the body bomb detonates, the film cuts to a single high-level shot of the explosion. It then cuts back to Maya, sitting at her computer, her face suffused with anxiety.

Maya serves as focalizer of this sequence, her emotions of excitement, anxiety, and dread coloring and accenting the action. A hinge point in the narrative, the scene foregrounds the emotions of a character whose inner life has been opaque. It also divides the film into two segments, as the brutal and radically disenchanting interrogations that dominate the first third of the film give way to the genre language of the procedural, a cinematic accommodation that shifts away from Maya's violent apprenticeship in torture to a form that accesses the familiar conventions of popular drama.

The procedural has become one of the mainstream genres of the contemporary period, a form that, unlike the torture scenes of the first third of the film, is familiar and amenable to the viewing public. As Steven Shaviro writes, the procedural emphasizes process and analysis in its narrative design, but more importantly, it elevates process to an overarching value, independent of any particular end or goal. The adherence to procedure as a goal in itself, the stress on "means" rather than "ends," as Shaviro writes, promotes process over the achievement of a positive goal. For him, proceduralism is the signature mode of social and political organization in contemporary life, the late, entropic expression of liberal capitalism, where the achievement of positive ends, such as social justice, is secondary to the administration of procedural regularity and order. *Zero Dark Thirty*, Shaviro writes, is a powerful enactment of the proceduralism of contemporary social and political life: "*Zero Dark Thirty* is the ne plus ultra of proceduralism, its ultimate expansion and reductio ad absurdum. It's all about the well-nigh interminable process of searching for, and then eliminating, Osama Bin Laden. The premise and initial impetus of this process is of course the mythological demonization of Bin Laden, as the ultimate culprit responsible for Nine Eleven. But in the relentless proceduralism that the film presents to us, this goal or rationale is abraded away."[17]

His short, powerful analysis describes the dissolution of narrative energy and dynamism in the film, its deliberate draining of dramatic action into data and process:

> The film makes a sort of feint by implying that its real subject is the passion of its protagonist Maya (Jessica Chastain), who continues to pursue the search for Bin Laden when everyone else has given up on it. But her obsession is itself entirely contained within, and articulated by, the proceduralism which is her job as a CIA analyst, and which seems to be the only world she knows. Every potentially dramatic action in which she finds herself (bombings and armed ambushes included) is drained of drama, and subsumed within proceduralist routine. Every affect, and every reason for doing what

> one does, is sucked into a black hole. This is why Maya is so emptied out at the end of the film.[18]

In some ways, Shaviro's reading is starkly opposite my own: where he emphasizes the draining of affect and drama into endless process and bureaucracy, I find that the film evokes intensive registers of affective experience, especially in its depictions of violent infliction. Maya's encounter with violence shapes her character, driving her to prosecute bin Laden, to confront the station chief and, later, the CIA bureaucracy in Washington for more resources. Her unrelenting focus on bin Laden antagonizes other CIA officers, as her single-mindedness takes on an almost religious zeal: "I believe I was spared so I can finish the job," she says at one point. Moreover, the film sets out a world, filtered through Maya, that is dominated by the violence of reprisal, a back-and-forth style of violence that has its own rhythms and forms. Here, the pursuit of leads and the mapping of locations typical of the procedural—a particularly complex task, given the high level of "tradecraft" practiced by al-Qaeda—shades into the passion of reprisal and revenge, as the hyperrationality of the procedural is set against the madness of terrorism, one mode of violence answering the other. Maya swerves between the driving energy of personal revenge and the professional spy world of fact checking, cross-referencing, and debate. At every point, she radiates a vivid emotional heat.

Despite my very different sense of the emotional tone of the film, however, there is much in Shaviro's reading that I find compelling. The existential gravity of its violence—anchored by images of the violated body—in many ways conflicts with the film's generic procedural framework. Where Shaviro perceives a lack of affect and lack of reason "for doing what one does," however, I read Maya's "crusade," as it is called at one point, as personal. The killing of her CIA colleague, her friend Jessica, is an experience of violence that is personal and intimate, an internal experience of violence that sweeps outward into the data-gathering and analysis the film painstakingly details. At several points the CIA operatives end their discussions with sentences such as "And if he doesn't, we kill him"; or "I want targets. Bring me people to kill"; or Maya's chilling line, "I'm going to smoke everyone involved in this op, and then I'm going to kill Bin Laden." The power of violence in this scenario, its penetrating and contaminating symbolic potency, speaks to a sense of endless threat emanating from both sides of the equation, with the meaning and purpose of both terrorists and counterterrorists defined mainly by destruction.

The middle third of the film, however, masks its deep engagement with the question of violence and seems to confirm Shaviro's reading. As the courier "Abu Ahmed" is identified and tracked, the apparatus and techniques of modern surveillance dominate the foreground of the text. Electronic eavesdropping, satellite photography, human observers stationed along the roadsides of Pakistan—the mechanisms and protocols of the manhunt bring a sense of charged direction to the film, shifting the rhythm of the work to a familiar, purposeful plot line. Here a comprehensive technological approach—reminiscent of grand national projects such as the Moon Landing—supplants the grit and agony of coerced interrogation and violent attacks in cities and in desert outposts. The violence at the core of the film seems to be absorbed into the familiar discourse of expert analysis and bureaucratic wrangling, where the blood motive that fuels the narrative now becomes a question of logistics and percentages.

The middle third of the film, however, for all its excitement and well-designed plotting of the elements of the chase, functions primarily as a transition between the film's two dramatic engagements with violence, each of which illuminates two extremes, two radically embodied experiences of violence that form the crux of the film's originality and importance. Taken together, the interrogation sequences and the raid on bin Laden's compound in Abbottabad enact a powerfully contemporary variant on the aesthetic responses to violence that Cole has described as disenchantment and enchantment. Where the first third of the film is radically disenchanting, centering on the violated bodies of the victims of terror and the victims of torture, exposing the materiality of violence and the vulnerability of the flesh, the last third of the film unfolds under the sign of enchanted violence, as the crack team of Navy SEALs moves in concert with central command, operating from a finely calibrated plan of attack and supported by a vast technological apparatus that converts intelligence into force.

The almost libidinal excitement of executing the mission is expressed in a mise-en-scène that is dramatically different from what we have seen before. The nocturnal setting underscores the drama of the attack, the minute-by-minute suspense of the incursion, and the aesthetic patterning of kinetic actions and carefully plotted pause points. In contrast to the harsh realism of the torture scenes, here the night-time raid provides an opportunity to explore a new, visually lush but realistic aesthetic, with the night vision goggles of the SEAL team providing images of the raid that have an unprecedented drama and directness.

In some ways the signature genre of the twenty-first century, the procedural is revealed here to be a new idiom for enchanted violence; rather than signifying the poetics of renewal, however, in which violence and the violated body become a symbol of generative transformation, the procedural employs the very different vocabulary of technology and teamwork, in which the raison d'être, to reference Shaviro yet again, is the success of the "mission." As agents of expressive, enchanted violence in the twenty-first century, the Special Ops team, the Navy SEAL unit that conducts the raid on bin Laden's compound, is emblematic: decked out in technology, reading and communicating information in a continuous stream, other-worldly in their skill and discipline, the SEAL team leaves the ordinary world of disenchanted violence—the deforming kind of violence—to one side. Instead, we see their doubled night-vision goggles and sleekly armored body suits, replete with an array of weapons and tools that materialize when needed—a Bat suit with lethal implements; we see their instantaneous and correct decisions, and their gentleness with the children in the compound; we see their quick dispatch of potential threats, and we linger not over the bodies they have left behind but over the computer hard drives they collect from the compound. The awful violence of war, and to some extent the physical reality of the mission with its blood and bodies, is mitigated and transformed into art in this sequence, choreographed into something almost magical.[19] Although the grim violence of war is asserted in small details, like the smear of blood left behind on the floor when bin Laden's body is removed, and the calculated shooting of a woman who throws herself over the body of her dead husband, the overarching impact of this scene is one of sustained, intense physical excitement.

Zero Dark Thirty comes full circle, however, in its closing moments. Here, the choreography of violence that defines the attack on bin Laden's compound has a curious aftereffect of diminishment, as if the violent incursion just conducted was sobering, rather than transformative. The two closing scenes—the unzipping of bin Laden's body bag and Maya's poignant, deeply moving expression, an expression almost reminiscent of the work of Carl Dreyer, when she is asked where she would like to go—suggest not teleological closure but ambiguity and uncertainty.

As the SEAL team delivers the body bag and the computer files back to the desert staging camp, the camaraderie and excitement of having accomplished a demanding mission is visible among the soldiers. Congratulating each other, working with speed to sort the documents and hard drives taken from bin Laden's compound, the adrenalin still palpable in their voices and gestures, the SEALs share a collective moment of exhilarated achievement. The camera then cuts to Maya, alone outside on the runway. As she makes her way into the crowded tent, the camera picks her out, walking slowly through the team of men toward the body bag. The soldiers part for her and become quiet as she moves through them. The musical theme for the film plays softly in high electronic and string instrumentation. As she approaches the corpse, the camera switches to a low-angle view. In the medium, eye-level shot that follows, she unzips the bag. The camera cuts again to a low-angle close-up, looking up at Maya. She confirms the identity of the corpse to the commanding officer, who transmits the information via telephone to an unheard recipient who, we assume, is the President. She looks back at the body, and another low-angle eye-line match occurs and is held for a long moment. Maya then zips up the bag and walks slowly out the back of the tent.

This devastating scene undercuts any sense of triumph or blood satisfaction. The deeply sad, poignant music, the silent gravity of her approach to the body of bin Laden, and above all the eye-line patterning to and from the unseen figure in the bag, have a powerfully unsettling effect. In some ways we are suspended here, without resolution, without the climax that the film has prepared from the beginning. And in the closing shots of the film, almost a coda, the theme of suspension is made explicit. From inside a large plane, a cargo door opens to view Maya on the runway, framed against a breaking dawn. She enters the plane, and the cargo door closes. The young pilot tells her she is the only one on the plane and asks where she would like to go. A close-up of Maya follows, almost a minute in length, a portraiture shot that slows the film to a halt, as the audience is invited to take stock, to consider the moment, and to reflect.

Drawing on the power of violence to create a disturbing, innovative work, *Zero Dark Thirty* gives expression to the close connection between aesthetic form and the history of violence that the war film evokes and appropriates. Neither embracing violence nor turning away from it, the film brings into relief the full cultural and symbolic weight of violence and the challenge it presents to ethical authorship and spectatorship. And in a period when the cycle of revenge in war has escalated almost to a principle of statecraft, now dominated by bounties, extra-judicial killing, and payback, the film calls into view the costs of violence and its shaping effect on the imaginary and real textures of contemporary life.

Notes

1. Sarah Cole, *At the Violet Hour: Modernism and Violence in England and Ireland* (Oxford: Oxford University Press, 2012), 4.

2. Ibid., 93.

3. Ibid., 287.

4. Anne McClintock, "Paranoid Empire: Specters from Guantánamo and Abu Ghraib," *Small Axe* 13, no. 1 (March 2009): 57.

5. Ibid., 58.

6. See Kevin McDonald, "Grammars of Violence, Modes of Embodiment, and Frontiers of the Subject," in Kevin McSorley, ed., *War and the Body: Militarization, Practice, and Experience* (London: Routledge, 2013), 138–51. The concept of "grammars of violence," as McDonald explains, is usually understood as a subjective script that determines behavior in violent confrontations, a set of assigned roles and parts dictated by "grammatical" rules of violent encounters. McDonald suggests, however, that this concept can be extended to encompass a mode of experience, a way of defining the self in relation to others. Although McDonald's discussion centers on terrorism and jihadi videos in the UK rather than the war film, his approach to violence as a medium of experience can be usefully applied to contemporary war films.

7. Paul Virilio, *War and Cinema: The Logistics of Perception* (London: Verso, 1992), 5.

8. See Richard Dyer, *White: Essays on Race and Culture* (London: Routledge, 1997), for an insightful analysis of how "whiteness" functions as a complex sign in film.

9. See Cole, *At the Violet Hour.*

10. Anton Kaes provides a particularly vivid reading of expressionist films in light of World War I in *Shell Shock Cinema: Weimar Culture and the Wounds of War* (Princeton, NJ: Princeton University Press, 2011).

11. See Christopher Coker, *The Future of War: The Re-enchantment of War in the 21st Century* (Malden, MA: Wiley-Blackwell, 2004).

12. See, for opposing views, Patricia Pisters, "Logistics of Perception 2.0: Multiple Screen Aesthetics in Iraq War Films," *Film-Philosophy* 14, no. 1 (2010); and Garrett Stewart, "Digital Fatigue: Imaging War in Recent American Film," *Film Quarterly* 62, no. 4 (Summer 2009): 45–55.

13. Harun Farocki, *Images of War (at a Distance),* MoMA exhibit (June 29, 2011–January 2, 2012), New York (moma.org).

14. See Kevin McSorley, "Helmetcams, Militarized Sensation, and 'Somatic War,'" *Journal of War and Culture Studies* 5, no. 1 (2012): 47–58.

15. Sarah Cole, "Enchantment, Disenchantment, War, Literature," *PMLA* 124, no. 5 (2009): 1632.

16. Cole, *At the Violet Hour,* 122.

17. Steven Shaviro, "A Brief Remark on *Zero Dark Thirty,*" *The Pinocchio Theory,* January 18, 2013, www.shaviro.com/Blog.

18. Ibid.

19. The Navy SEALs as agents of enchanted violence also come through strongly at the end of the Paul Greengrass film *Captain Phillips* (2013). Here, the rescue of Phillips from the small boat on which he is held hostage is accomplished through the almost magical procedural skills of a Navy SEAL team, who parachute in to run the rescue mission. The disproportionate martial power trained against the pirates is striking: an aircraft carrier, two battleships, and a SEAL team are here ranged against a trio of barefoot Somali pirates holding Phillips hostage in a small boat bobbing like a cork in the ocean. Procedure and tactics are elevated here, as Shaviro writes, to an overarching value in their own right.

"All in War with Time"

Medium as Meditation in *Sherman's March*

Lawrence F. Rhu

Sherman's March, Ross McElwee's first feature-length film, is a movie about not being able to make a movie. It only seems a "war film" out of a painful sense of duty. The filmmaker started out with a grant to make a documentary about the lingering effects of Sherman's notorious campaign through Georgia and the Carolinas that hastened the American Civil War to its conclusion. An untimely breakup with the woman he had been seeing, however, threw McElwee for such a loop that he could not help self-absorbedly licking his own fresh wounds as a rejected lover. To borrow a phrase from the film itself, McElwee's "listless contemplation of [his] single status" became central to *Sherman's March*.[1] As McElwee later acknowledged in "The Act of Seeing with One's Own Eyes," an essay about his vocation as a documentarian, such a concern bears resonant similarities to themes at the heart of both *The Last Gentleman*, by the southern novelist Walker Percy, and *The World Viewed: Reflections on the Ontology of Film*, by the Harvard philosopher Stanley Cavell.[2] Both of these writers enabled McElwee to better understand his own ambitions as an aspiring director.

McElwee's film begins with a colorful map of the Old South that features an advancing red line charting Sherman's march from Atlanta to the sea and then northward through the Carolinas. Meanwhile an earnest voice-over somberly informs the audience of the world-historical importance of this event. Sherman's march is the birth of modern warfare, total war that does not spare the civilian population; rather, it attacks them and strikes terror in their hearts in order to hasten the conflict to an end.[3] These chilling commonplaces readily evoke horrors nearer to us in time. Hiroshima and Nagasaki come promptly to mind. In August 1945, an allegedly humanitarian decision to drop an atomic bomb on each of these Japanese cities forced Emperor Hirohito quickly to surrender after the second strike.

Next, in *Sherman's March,* we hear a notably unedited exchange between the narrator and the director about the necessity of a second take of the opening voice-over. The color then disappears, as the film cuts to black-and-white footage of a solitary southerner in an empty loft in New York City pacing the floor and then sweeping it up with a broom. It is Ross McElwee in the immediate aftermath of rejection by his beloved. The refusal to edit out the filmmaker's behind-the-scenes second thoughts about whether the voice-over meets his directorial standards indicates the kind of movie we are just starting to watch.[4] It will include intentionally undisguised displays of the process of making the film. The classical tag about aesthetic excellence, *ars est celare artem*—true art hides its artistry—will not obtain here in any conventional sense of the phrase. "Invisible editing" has no cachet in this "personal" documentary, which abandons any consistent effort at seamless transitions from scene to scene and the increased (because uninterrupted) audience engagement supposedly achieved by removing such distractions.

This film wears its apparent amateurism and artlessness on its sleeve. Sometimes the sound does not work or the momentarily unattended camera points, arbitrarily, wherever it happens to point. If the director includes such awkward accidents in his final cut, self-consciousness becomes inescapable. For example, once McElwee appears wearing a tie and a handsome summer suit on the west bank of the Congaree River. He is setting up his account of Sherman's destruction of Columbia, South Carolina, and the State House is visible across the river on the horizon. It took six hits from Sherman's mighty cannons. The damage from each cannon ball is marked with a bronze star and remains unrepaired to this day. As McElwee readies himself to relate this part of the Sherman saga, he stumbles while backing up to get into a better position on the riverbank. Though he does not fall directly into the Congaree, such a possibility has just become irresistibly imaginable for the viewer.[5] McElwee now reminds us more of Harold Lloyd, the besuited accident-prone star of silent comedy, than of Robert Flaherty, the estimable documentarian of an earlier era. McElwee's deadpan stoicism about such hazards along his life's way might even make us remember another Civil War film and the sight of another hapless southerner, Johnnie Gray (Buster Keaton) in *The General.* Beneath his stolid appearance, he too is a tender-hearted devotee of female charm and of modern industrial achievement—the locomotive in his case, like the camera in McElwee's.

In "The Act of Seeing with One's Own Eyes," Ross McElwee describes his encounter with Walker Percy's *The Last Gentleman* during the period just before he made *Sherman's March.* The novel was nothing less than a revelation. McElwee felt as though he was reading his own life story from the pen of another, and he dubs Walker Percy his "psychological biographer."[6] Percy had uncannily captured the sense of dislocation and estrangement experienced by McElwee in early adulthood as a southerner adrift in the Northeast wondering what he could make of himself in the world as he then found it. Moreover, Percy not only appreciated (and articulated) the way in which the world itself seems remote and unreal in such states of mind. He also understood how it can (seductively) seem to be recovered by viewing it through the lens of a camera or, for that matter, of a telescope or a microscope.

In this perception Percy was not alone, as McElwee explains by summoning a passage from Stanley Cavell's *The World Viewed.* Cavell usefully places this experience beyond regionalism and even beyond stages of life. He attributes it both to the fate of the individual in the modern era and to the power of the camera. Percy's own resistance to being pigeonholed as a southern novelist or, for that matter, as a Christian existentialist warrants note here. Though he might make vivid, clarifying use of such regional, religious, and philosophical differences as means of expressing what he had at heart to say, he balked at the confinement such labels can too easily impose. They are not absolutes in the worlds of contingent particulars that Percy so memorably evokes.

Nor was McElwee alone in perceiving this meeting of minds in Percy and Cavell, for Percy himself had previously noted it. In an unpublished letter to Robert Coles, Percy expresses delight at the reassurance he feels in reading a passage from *The World Viewed* that Coles cites in *Walker Percy: An American Search* (1978). Thus, it seems no mere coincidence that McElwee singles Cavell out as a relevant voice in support of his project and its affinity with the worlds of consciousness and human experience given word in Percy's fiction. The letter is dated simply "Thursday," and that probably refers to Thursday, December 7, 1978. It is written by hand and runs about six pages. On page 2 Percy writes, "A happy confirmation: your quote from Cavell's book on *Ontology of Film.* It exactly expresses *The Moviegoer*'s implied ontology. (I'm glad Cavell wrote it *after* [emphasis Percy's] *The Moviegoer.*)"[7]

In the passage Coles cites, Cavell is explaining the particular allure of cinematic images: "What we wish to see in this way is the world itself—that is to say, everything," Cavell writes. "To say that we wish to view the world itself is to say that we wish for the condition of viewing as such. That is the way we establish our connection with the world: by viewing it or having views of it. Our condition has become one in which our natural mode of perception is to view, feeling unseen; viewing a movie makes this condition automatic, takes the responsibility for it out of our hands. Hence movies seem more natural than reality. Not because they are escapes into fantasy, but because they are reliefs from private fantasy and its responsibilities."[8]

Cavell thus describes the seductions of aestheticism and the avoidance of responsibility that they may entail for the cinephile. His thinking here corresponds precisely with Percy's and McElwee's. Moreover, their agreement becomes clearer if we include Cavell's wonderfully capacious name-dropping sentence that Coles omits in his citation from *The World Viewed.* "Nothing less than [everything] is what modern philosophy has told us (whether for Kant's reasons, or for Locke's, or Hume's) is metaphysically beyond our reach or (as Hegel or Marx or Kierkegaard or Nietzsche might rather put it) beyond our reach metaphysically."[9]

This sentence amounts to Cavell's version—one of them—of Kant's Copernican revolution, moving from the conditions of what is viewed to the conditions of viewing. You can find another version of that revolution in Cavell's reading of the first sentence of the final paragraph of Emerson's essay "Experience."[10] Perhaps Coles seeks not to boggle the minds of those ill-acquainted with, or easily daunted by, the history of modern philosophy and its central dilemmas, which Cavell thus pointedly sums up. His playful flipping around of the phrases "metaphysically beyond our reach" and "beyond our reach metaphysically" gives us a clue to the kind of philosopher Cavell is. He does not banish the poets from his cities of words. What resolutely systematic philosophers might deem the messiness of subjectivity and the moods that color our perceptions, Cavell sees as constituting them and their inevitable partiality. Cavell is also willing to subordinate the usual tools of philosophy, like proposition and argument, in order to compete with poetry in its ambition to make things happen to the soul.

Given Percy's aversion to system building (whether it is Kant's or Hegel's), his self-acknowledged affinity with Søren Kierkegaard in this regard is particularly notable. In *The Moviegoer* Binx experiences the sort of predicament that the Danish philosopher critiqued mockingly by describing the architect of a fabulous palace who himself lives next door to this wondrous edifice in a shack.[11] Binx undergoes an analogous experience when he reads

The Chemistry of Life. It is a book so lucid that it seems to have solved all his problems, which he obliquely represents as a quest or search for some unspecified good or goal. "When I finished it," Binx admits, "it seemed to me that the main goals of my search were reachable or in principle reachable." In this mood he goes out and sees *It Happened One Night*, "which was itself very good," Binx avers; and he concludes that he has enjoyed a "memorable night." Nonetheless, he comes to realize that one problem remains. As Binx puts it, "The only difficulty was that though the universe had been disposed of, I myself was left over. There I lay in my hotel room with my search over yet still obliged to draw one breath and then the next."[12] Binx's sole difficulty here sounds like what McElwee might also experience if he made a perfect documentary and kept himself entirely out of the picture.

There is a sentence immediately after the Cavell passage excerpted by Coles that warrants attention in this regard: "We do not so much look at the world as look *out at* it, from behind the self."[13] This final sentence expresses the fact of our condition as moviegoers that Ross McElwee seeks to expose in his films and that we have just heard Binx describe himself awakening to, both as a reader and as a moviegoer. Given its powerful hold on our culture, however, film is the medium that can especially mislead us nowadays. On one hand there is the world delivered without human intervention, automatically (or so it seems), by the camera. On the other there is our separateness from that world and our anonymity. That apparent means of delivery, automatism, tempts us to believe we can watch the world, reality itself, without accountability or engagement, as mere spectators and consumers of what the camera offers up so impersonally or anonymously, untouched (if you will) by human hands.

Despite its slippery "nowadays," the above generalization about the spell movies may cast upon viewers can serve to effect the starkest possible contrast. The seeming perfection of film's objective rendition of the world (minus ourselves, who are merely spectators and consumers, "feeling unseen") often encounters our pervasive skepticism about any such achievement. We live, after all, in an era of clips and bytes that routinely expose the tiniest pieces of sights and sounds on-screen, as well as the arbitrariness both of the angles and frames through which they oblige us to see and of the various filters through which they oblige us to hear. Percy and Cavell, however, were recording their aforementioned views half a century ago in Percy's case and just short of that in Cavell's. There were no VCRs or DVDs or any other easily accessible technological means of breaking film down into ever smaller pieces. Indeed it is hard to believe that Binx could even have seen *It Happened One Night* circa 1960 in Birmingham, Alabama, as he claims to have done in *The Moviegoer.* What venue there would likely have been showing that 1934 classic, except on TV?

Fragmentary parts of any big picture, such as the clips and bytes we see on TV shows like *The Colbert Report,* nourish and sustain our robust skepticism *nowadays* about any views of the world whose mediation goes without notice. This dialogue between perfectionism and skepticism, or wholeness and partiality, enables us to acknowledge more fully the mind in motion that constitutes consciousness itself, as it shuttles back and forth between conviction and doubt. Percy seeks to represent such dynamics of thought, and Cavell discovers them in Emerson's "Experience," among other places. "The secret of the illusoriness [of life] is in the necessity of a succession of moods or objects," Emerson writes. "Gladly we would anchor, but the anchorage is quicksand. This onward trick of nature is too strong for us."[14] One is tempted to ask whether Emerson said "trick" or "trek," given the "onwardness" whose necessity he seeks to acknowledge. By yielding to that temptation, we can hear a resonance in Emerson that Percy seemed unable or unwilling to hear, even though he happily embraced and vividly represented the idea of man as a wayfarer whose life is an existential pilgrimage in a post-Christian world, as the narrator remarks about Will Barrett in *The Last Gentleman,* Ross McElwee's "psychological biography."[15]

The Last Gentleman (1966) is Percy's second novel, and it appeared five years after his first, *The Moviegoer,* had already established its author's reputation as a philosophical novelist. Percy's rare gifts and accomplishments singled him out as an American artist and thinker justly compared to such European writers as Albert Camus and Jean-Paul Sartre. While it was a work in progress and before Percy made his final decision about what to call it, *The Last Gentleman* went under three different titles: "The Fall Out," "Ground Zero," and "Centennial."[16] They all reveal its links to McElwee's main concerns in making *Sherman's March,* which originally appeared with an ironically cumbersome subtitle, *A Meditation on the Possibility of Romantic Love in the South during an Era of Nuclear Proliferation.*

The third of Percy's abandoned titles, "Centennial," signified the Civil War Centennial, which was under way during the narrative time of the novel and was also taking place during the time of its composition by Percy. That proposed title reveals the affinities between McElwee's nominally main concern, Sherman's march, and Percy's protagonist, Will Barrett, who suffers from a nervous condition that involves fugue states or minor bouts of reversible amnesia. Sometimes when Will "falls out" (the pun seems thoroughly intended), he awakens on Civil War battlefields miles away from where he last remembers being and, of course, at least a century away from any engagement in the moment at hand.

The lengthy subtitle of *Sherman's March* also connects its other themes both to Percy's first two titles that did not stick to *The Last Gentleman,* "The Fall Out" and "Ground Zero," and to its romantic plot strand of Will Barrett's infatuation with Kitty Vaught. Cavell, who has written memorably about Hollywood romantic comedy in *Pursuits of Happiness,* qualifies pertinently here as a philosopher of love and marriage, though Kitty and Will achieve nothing close to the "meet and happy conversation" that constitutes marriage for Cavell (via Milton's *Doctrine and Discipline of Divorce*).[17] Moreover, Cavell coined a felicitous phrase about suspicions that are hard to resist in the face of certain examples of apocalyptic thinking ostensibly inspired by the threat of nuclear war. Sounding very much like what he called Emerson, "an epistemologist of moods," Cavell dubbed their mood "nostalgia for the future," and they mirror certain moments in Percy's early fiction.[18]

For example, Binx, in *The Moviegoer,* notes how the urgency of such thinking imparts a histrionic seriousness, or mere phoniness, to an otherwise unremarkable episode in a TV play that sounds like something Americans would have been watching during the late 50s when they were reading and viewing tales of nuclear disaster like Neville Shute's *On the Beach.*[19] Similarly, in *The Last Gentleman,* the narrator describes Will Barrett as somebody who feels as though he has just crawled out of the wreckage of a bombed building. Moreover, he believes that Will mainly needs to learn how to patiently abide the postapocalyptic everydayness of an ordinary Wednesday afternoon. It is the quotidian routines of day-to-day life that challenge Will.[20] His ultimate accomplishment in *The Last Gentleman* may be summed up in the pertinent cliché "joining the human race."[21] Crisis management or preparedness for the worst is beside the point. The crisis is over, and the worst has already happened. For both Binx and Will, warfare, or at least the life of a soldier as they imagine it, would come as a positive relief, given the stark terms of existence such circumstances seem to impose. Just following orders or responding to clear-cut demands in a life-or-death situation might helpfully simplify matters for both of these unmoored and abstracted drifters.

A broken heart sets McElwee adrift and distracts him, inconveniently, from working on his projected documentary about Sherman's march, for which (we note) he already has funding. Badly shaken confidence in his prospects in Love's field of dreams preempts his concern for battlefields and burning cities that scarred the South unforgettably as Sherman wreaked havoc with sixty thousand Union soldiers from Atlanta to Savannah and Columbia and from Columbia to Charlotte and Raleigh. Instead of (or, in addition to) making the film under contract, McElwee sets out in quest of women, and former girlfriends especially, who can perhaps help him understand his failure to connect in affairs of the heart. Irony and pathos combine poignantly in Sumter, South Carolina, where one of the Daughters of the Confederacy tending the monument to their fallen heroes remarks, "Some of them weren't even old enough to have a sweetheart."[22]

We are not hearing about Odysseus, after twenty years of war and wandering, returning to Penelope, or even about Inman, walking away from the ravages of war and back home to his prewar sweetheart, Ada, in Charles Frazier's *Cold Mountain*—"an extraordinary novel about a soldier's perilous journey back to his beloved at the end of the Civil War," which is "at once a magnificent love story and a harrowing account of one man's long walk home," as it says on the book's dust jacket.[23] Instead, we are watching *Ross*, and it feels like we should be on a first-name basis with him.

Ross was hapless yet not entirely hopeless in love during the early 80s when the Women's Movement was seeking support for the Equal Rights Amendment and the Nuclear Freeze Movement was actively making its case to halt further stockpiling of nuclear arms. Helen Caldicott, the Australian pediatrician and Cassandra of Freeze, had received an appointment at Harvard Medical School.[24] She was touring the globe claiming the children of the world were having bad dreams and even deeper problems because of the fear and uncertainty caused by growing nuclear arsenals. Ross mentions that, as a twelve-year-old in the late 50s, he witnessed the detonation of a hydrogen bomb on a Pacific island in a test of its readiness for deployment. Memories of that experience haunt his dreams in the present as he tries to reconcile his joint concern with General Sherman and with a series of attractive women who accept the gaze of his camera with varying degrees of willingness or reluctance that he sensibly accommodates.

Perhaps it is not a propitious moment for a quest of this kind, but Ross bears up patiently and behaves graciously in his pursuit of happiness, or at least of some leads in that direction. It all starts out easy and sweet with roller skating and reunions with family and friends, advice from Ross's sister about trimming his beard and acknowledging that, if he just tidied up a bit, a man with a movie camera might exert a certain appeal to the ladies. It is not long, however, before things start to get somewhat weird and crazy. An aspiring actress gives word to fantasies of omnipotent goodness and intergalactic empires as the plot of a movie she will make and star in someday. Palm Sunday conversations morph into grim prophecies of Armageddon. Menacing survivalists practice shooting firearms in a hideaway up in the hills, and a teacher from a fancy girls school, "the very cradle of southern womanhood," conducts a tour of the well-provisioned bomb shelter in her Charleston family home. Soon enough, what we talk about when we talk about love is overheard at a protest at a nuclear facility in Georgia and at a rally for the Equal Rights Amendment at the state house in Raleigh, North Carolina. Perhaps there's no surprise in all this, given the particular moment in time. Aren't we simply witnessing an all-American medley, with a southern accent, of outdoor fun and paranoia, tribal gatherings and reminders of the ends of affairs, roller skating and the dread latter days evoked by Christian eschatology?

The key term in McElwee's subtitle, *meditation,* gives the form of the film a name and connects it to perhaps the main concern shared by both Percy and Cavell, which is thinking or human consciousness. The opening sentence of *The Last Gentleman* goes like this: "One fine day in early spring a young man lay thinking in Central Park."[25] Caroline Gordon was the friend and fellow writer to whom Percy had most fully entrusted editorial review of his work before he submitted it for publication, and she vigorously protested against such an opening, which sounded far too cerebral. Where is the action? Gordon wondered, but Percy's "Stet!" tellingly kept that sentence where it remains, setting the tone and topic of what follows. Similarly, Stanley Kauffmann, Percy's wonderfully perspicacious and supportive editor at Knopf for his first novel, *The Moviegoer,* advised changes and additions to tighten its story line that Percy ultimately demurred at making. He distinguished *The Moviegoer*'s subject from that of a conventional novel where plot matters most. Percy asserted that he was writing about "the fragmented, alienated consciousness, which is Mr. Binx Bolling," not simply about a sequence of events that could be clearly and consistently distinguished from the way what happens strikes Binx and from how he takes it all in.[26]

Percy does suggest that Kauffmann may believe that he could achieve greater objective coherence by telling his story from a more detached, third-person point of view. Percy, however, has no interest in making any such revision of *The Moviegoer.* Ironically, if we read various drafts of an earlier story by Percy, "Confessions of a Moviegoer, or the Diary of the Last Romantic," we can see how closely connected his first two novels were, for his writings under this title contain elements identifiable separately in each of those novels. Though their narrative perspective is third-person, like *The Last Gentleman*'s, they not only contain key elements from the first novel, which is told directly in Binx's first-person voice. (Moviegoing is the most obvious one.) Via words like "confession," "diary," and "romantic," the title they share registers Percy's commitment to rendering the subjectivity of his main character, his presence at his own experience or, one might even say, his presence (of mind) *as* his experience.[27] For good or ill, we must add. For solipsism is the trap each of these characters manages happily to avoid, though in both cases it is a close call.

Cavell's preoccupation with what such precursors as Emerson and Heidegger call thinking rhymes with this emphasis in Percy's sense of what counts in telling the tales he has to tell.[28] Percy, however, balked at an attempt to affiliate him with Emerson's idea of "man thinking" in characterizing the American scholar. Percy declined the honor of presenting the Phi Beta Kappa address at Harvard in 1987, when his contribution would have helped to memorialize the sesquicentennial of Emerson's 1837 lecture "The American Scholar." An inheritor of Emerson like Cavell, who is keenly aware of the circulation of Emerson's writing in European traditions of thought via Nietzsche, would perhaps have been able to persuade Percy that his idea of New England transcendentalism was more parochial than he knew and that he need not join in the repression or simple neglect of aspects of Emerson's thinking that actually sound very much like Percy's own way of understanding experience. For Percy was emphatically a thinker who esteemed the value of knowing what one does not know and acknowledging such ignorance, as he did in the case of Emerson.[29]

The best of the Percy biographies, Jay Tolson's *A Pilgrim in the Ruins,* makes a big deal out of Percy's unwillingness to accept this invitation. Tolson frames his account of Percy's life and works with the idea of his anti-Emersonianism, which becomes a convenient shorthand for everything that Percy did not like about American culture in a biography that culminates in Percy's saying, "No, thanks," to Harvard and to what Tolson calls "the Emerson lecture." In a remark about his own approach to his subject, Tolson sounds a familiar note of the customary criticism of Emerson, his lack of a tragic sense. Tolson laments modern biography's "lack of a tragic sense, and [its] resulting tendency to see the subject's failings against some implied perfectibilist ideal rather than against the limitations of human fate."[30]

"Perfectibilist" strikes my ear as a strange word, but I can hear, nonetheless, in Tolson's phrases, the fundamental structure of Cavell's philosophy, if there is such a thing. Perhaps we should just call it a discernible, even dominant, pattern in Cavell's thought, with the purpose of making this important connection: the link between perfectionism and tragedy. Thanks primarily to his readings of Emerson and Shakespeare, Cavell transforms the fragility of our condition, its groundlessness and contingency, into perfectionist journeys or tragic falls. It is in disagreement with John Rawls's interpretation of "the principle of perfection" that Cavell comes to the defense of what he calls Emersonian perfectionism, a dimension of moral philosophy that he will subsequently espouse, elaborate, and continually rediscover not only in American writers, but also in European thinkers like Heidegger and Nietzsche and Kierkegaard.[31] In his reading of Shakespeare, Cavell will ultimately find a kindred spirit in Eric Rohmer's *Conte d'hiver* (*A Tale of Winter*), whose protagonist responds to her experience of Shakespeare's late romance, *The Winter's Tale,* in a way that Cavell describes as "what Emerson calls thinking," echoing Heidegger in the process.[32]

Jay Tolson, however, construes Percy's unwillingness to accept Harvard's invitation as a climactic gesture that defines his overall career. It is Percy's ultimate rebuttal of Emerson, a definitive rejection of the utopian and perfectionist aspects of his thought, which is viewed as untempered by skepticism and a sense of tragedy. For Cavell it is precisely Shakespearean tragedy that anticipates the impact of Cartesian skepticism and the New Science of Bacon and Galileo and Descartes upon human self-understanding and experience. Similarly, for Percy, the ideal of knowledge in the empirical method triumphs so pervasively that what becomes the human or social sciences (which inherit the hegemony of this method) falls prey to its basic technique: exclusively objective study from a detached perspective unqualified by any influence of the human person conducting such research. The scientist transcends the scene of his inquiry so as to leave it undisturbed by any influence of his presence.

This epistemology characterizes modern criteria for knowledge increasingly from Shakespeare's age to our own, and Cavell reads Shakespeare's major tragedies as catastrophes of skepticism in their protagonists' desire for demonstrable knowledge with proof of truth claims and the repression of any other claims to knowledge. "Villain, be sure thou prove my love a whore," says Othello to Iago.[33] Knowledge achieved by certain proof supersedes love in importance and denies the heart's intuitions, what it seems impossible just *not* to know unless we willfully narrow our idea of knowledge and distort our experience.

Percy would call this a problem of the scientist's transcendence of what he seeks to study (and explain) in terms that have no way of acknowledging his relationship to it. The very conditions of what passes for knowledge require, if not his absence, his detachment from the scene of investigation. Such a scientist thus remains unknown to himself because he can only claim secure self-knowledge in terms of general categories that certify his likeness to others in ways that empirical surveys and experiments have shown to be the case. Accepting such knowledge as self-knowledge may sound very much like joining the human race, which, as we have heard, accounts for a crucial transformation in Will's sense of himself during the final days represented in *The Last Gentleman.* At the deathbed of his friend, Jamie Vaught, Will finally gets "the oldest joke of all," our mortality, which has been a well-established fact of the human condition since Adam and Eve.[34] True enough, but, for it to count in this way, one must be present *to* such an event, not merely at it or in attendance; one must be conscious not only of its occurrence but of its reality; and, crucially, for it to matter, one must consent and accept it. Like you or me or anybody else, one must acknowledge the truth of that fact for oneself, taking this common event to heart in one's own way.

Percy discusses this dilemma in many ways, but his early reflections on "The Coming Crisis in Psychiatry" (1957) pertain here particularly because *The Last Gentleman* opens with a tour-de-force account of Will Barrett's decision to break off his psychoanalysis with Dr. Gamow, which has been going on for five years.[35] Also, the epigraph to *Lost in the Cosmos: The Last Self-Help Book,* impinges significantly upon this issue, as we have been discussing it, because it derives from Nietzsche's *Genealogy of Morals* and Cavell perceives in this passage a response to the opening of Emerson's essay "Experience." "Where do we find ourselves?" Emerson asks, and Nietzsche, who loved Emerson, translated several of his essays, and often echoes Emersonian lines of thought in his philosophizing, answers that question this way: "We are unknown, we knowers, to ourselves. . . . Of necessity we remain strangers to ourselves, we understand ourselves not, in ourselves we are bound to be mistaken, for each of us holds good to all eternity the motto, 'Each is the farthest away from himself'—as far as ourselves are concerned we are not knowers."[36]

Regarding the human sciences, Percy's answer to that question, "Where do we find ourselves?" would be "precisely nowhere." Medical science can teach us about viruses and bacteria, antibiotics and insulin, and we are understandably grateful and relieved for the suffering and death such science helps overcome. In the social sciences and especially psychiatry, however, we may find ourselves left over or left out, a mere remainder, when behavioral models and analytic theories do not ring true or work therapeutically in the one case that immediately matters, our own. Thus, in our soul searching, we are well advised to look elsewhere, as Will Barrett does in *The Last Gentleman,* when he buys a Tetzlar telescope and leaves analysis with Dr. Gamow. Pertinently, Bertram Wyatt-Brown deems Will a snob for the detached way in which he undergoes psychotherapy before abandoning it after five years. Contrary to most other critics, he also reads Percy's overall career as a novelist as improving together with his ever-increasing psychiatric understanding of himself.[37] In the latter regard, Wyatt-Brown is contributing to the robust conversation about neuroscience and psychopharmacology in which Percy has played an enlightening part, though he may treat the fiction more as symptoms of mental illness or health than as literary achievements.[38] The charge of snobbery, however, pertains more immediately to Cavell's discernment and development of the perfectionist strain in Emerson and Nietzsche among others.

In our current medical discourse, as it appears in the latest edition of the *Diagnostic and Statistical Manual of Mental Illnesses,* perfectionism makes the concise list of symptoms that qualify patients for a doctor's prescription of Prozac and other antidepressants. Cavell, however, is not talking about psychopathology but rather about the inheritance and transformation of philosophy in such figures as Plato and Emerson and Nietzsche, among many others whose memorable words may assist us in the conduct of our lives. In *Cities of Words,* for example, Cavell's insistence upon the limits of mainstream moral theories in his discussion of Ibsen's *A Doll's House* indicates the pressure of perfectionism that drives his own thinking, as does his avowal of inevitable competition with Henry James's prose in his reading of "The Beast in the Jungle."[39] Sometimes approximation of the case at hand and critiques of imprecision may be the best we have to offer, and they signify our dissatisfaction, even our disdain, which some may construe as elitism. That is a risk such thinking runs. Cavell frankly acknowledges that hazard of this way of doing philosophy, while he demonstrates Emerson's availability for guidance and inspiration in a democracy.

Will Barrett buys the Tetzlar because it enables him to see things otherwise remote and out of reach, not merely due to measurable distance but due to a sort of haze that his state of mind seems to impose between him and the world. This magic operation of the lens overcomes not only the limits of physical sight but also a cloudiness of spirit that keeps things out of focus. In this quality of the world viewed through Will's telescope, McElwee recognizes a phenomenon that he experiences through film, which recovers the world and brings things nearer, restoring an intimacy to their presence. McElwee interprets the episode of Will's visit to the Metropolitan Museum of Art in New York City as a way of clarifying the affinity he feels between his experience of what becomes of things on film and Percy's use of the telescope.[40] Simply put, Will cannot see the pictures at the museum even though they are hanging right in front of him. Not only has his state of mind impaired his vision. As an official public space where anybody is supposed to be able to enjoy the paintings, the museum itself makes it hard for Will to feel at home, and that feeling further compromises his vision.

Then the collapse of a stepladder bearing a maintenance man changes everything. The previously unnoticed worker falls from above and breaks the skylight he was trying to install in the gallery where Will has lurked and looked in glum disappointment at the masterpieces on exhibit. Suddenly, in the midst of his prompt attention to the victim of that fall, Will accidentally catches a glimpse of a previously all-but-invisible Velázquez, and it can be seen. The public secretion that had encrusted it and the ravening particles that clouded the atmosphere in the museum now seem to vanish. The painting becomes visible in this unforeseeable instant of its present sighting.[41]

Percy's wry sense of humor in the episodes with Dr. Gamow and with Will at the museum reveals his patient alertness to the comedy of the human spirit that metaphysical homelessness and the awkward fit of selves in the world often entail. McElwee's own ironic sense of displacement and his long-suffering attentiveness to whoever may cross his path as a filmmaker understandably discovered not just welcome companionship in Percy's novel but an uncanny sense of nothing less than revelation. McElwee's acquaintance with Percy's biography made him appreciate the overlap between the coroner, Sutter Vaught, in *The Last Gentleman* and Percy's own fateful experience in the pathology rotation during his residency at Bellevue Hospital in New York City. Contact with corpses there in the morgue sidelined Percy with tuberculosis for three years. Prompted by the spiritual hunger a near-fatal illness produced, he devoured books of philosophy, religion, and fiction during that time. That medical crisis began to transform Percy into the kind of writer he ultimately became: a pathologist of the human spirit who diagnosed the sickness of the modern soul with clear-eyed candor and occasional compassion and alarm.

McElwee's essay on Percy, "The Act of Seeing with One's Own Eyes," derives its title from his awareness of the etymology of the word *autopsy,* whose Greek roots he translates in the final five words of that title. The word itself also names a medical procedure that routinely employs the microscope and thus brings into play another lens whose power Percy celebrates. When he remembers his fascination with pathology as a doctor in training, Percy strikes a lyrical note in recalling "the beautiful theater of disease" made visible by the microscope.[42] McElwee's translation of the word *autopsy* enables him to identify further the confirmation of his motives that reading Percy offered him as a maker of "personal" documentaries or "home movies," as he sometimes calls them.[43] Percy's lyrical celebration of the view through a microscope heightens the claim of vividness and immediacy that such a sight secures through a telescope and a movie camera as well.

"The Loss of the Creature," one of Percy's finest essays, proposes an educational experiment that may bring together the study of science and literature in an eye-opening way and deliver students from the malaise of everydayness likely to afflict them in basic classes where they are at the mercy of codified expertise in textbooks of one kind or another. Percy suggests that, while students are seated at their laboratory tables, they should one day dissect and examine a dogfish and, the next day, they should do the same with a sonnet by Shakespeare. They will have a better chance of overcoming their thralldom to professional authority that, in such a setting, so insistently informs them of what they are seeing that they do not trust their own eyes. Rather, they promptly look in a textbook that preempts their response with classificatory labels that chalk up dogfishes and sonnets alike as one more example of a general category whose particular instances are not given a chance to register their own distinctiveness.

Percy laments what he calls "the radical devaluation of the individual dogfish" on the dissecting table in such a setting. It has become invisible due to "the student's placement in the world" as a layman at the mercy of prepackaged expertise telling him what he is supposed to be seeing.[44] "The radical devaluation of the individual dogfish" sounds a plangent note, perhaps more for the fish than anyone else. That sound derives more from sorrow and anger than proto-animal-rights sentiment, and these feelings produce irony and perhaps an undercurrent of bitterness about what passes for truth these days and how it must be demonstrated. Percy could also be heard as an antiromantic reined in by his awareness of the pathetic fallacy or even as a true believer inhibited by an awareness of superstitions like animism, but he has a word for such losses that he borrows from Gabriel Marcel, "ontophobia," or the fear of being. At such a juncture Cavell registers his dissatisfaction with the Kantian settlement—"to assure us that we do know the existence of the world or, rather, that what we understand as knowledge is *of* the world, the price Kant asks us to pay is to cede any claim to know the thing itself"—with a resounding, "Thanks for nothing."[45] In this regard, we may recall, Percy explicitly acknowledged his satisfaction with Cavell's ontology as an interpreter of film.

When Binx Bolling spends some weeks looking through a microscope in a lab at Tulane, he discovers that he lacks a flair for research, and he ceases to care whether pigs get kidney stones. The sight of his personal effects on his bedroom dresser, however, inspires Binx to undertake his search in *The Moviegoer.* For a moment they are actually visible, and they look as though they could belong to anyone or to no one in particular. "They looked both unfamiliar and at the same time full of clues. I stood in the center of the room and gazed at the little pile, sighting through a hole made by thumb and forefinger. What was unfamiliar about them was that I could see them. They might have belonged to someone else."[46] The apparent interchangeability of Binx's belongings renders him statistically insignificant or, to echo Cavell's phrasing, insignificant statistically. It is not that he doesn't *count* but that *he* doesn't count.

That moment reminds him of the first time he conceived of such a quest when, as a wounded soldier in the Orient in 1951, he came to himself under a chindolea bush and noticed with immense curiosity a dung beetle scratching six inches from his nose. This "close-up," like Binx's fresh look at his belongings, registers a breakthrough or revelation where the things of this world take on an intimate nearness at hand that charges them with potential significance otherwise easily overlooked. Though the change appears in the things seen, the change appears to have taken place in the seer. Were they always there in that way before, or does the view taken of them determine the look of them? As metaphors for the power of film, these sightings resonate in kindred ways that affirm McElwee's sense of the camera's magic, but they also stand for changes within the viewer, as though distinguishing between the viewer and viewed as subject and object may falsify the experience they constitute together without definite boundaries separating them decisively.

When Will wields his new Tetzlar, it "[creates] its own world in the brilliant theatre of its lenses." In first viewing Kitty and Rita Vaught, he inadvertently enacts a version of the experiment that Percy recommended to students in their biology labs with their microscopes. In the beginning of Chapter One, Will sees the exchange of a sonnet between what sounds like a Dark Lady and a young man (or, rather, a young woman who looks boyish): "a white lady dark as a gypsy" and "a beautiful girl" who "also slouched and was watchful and dry-eyed and musing like a thirteen-year-old boy."[47] By presenting the opening quatrain of Shakespeare's Sonnet 96, this episode evokes the poet's two beloveds, who ultimately betray him with each other. The rivalry between the Dark Lady and the poet (Will Shakespeare) over the young male addressee of many of the sonnets parallels, to a degree, the struggle in *The Last Gentleman* between Will and Rita over Kitty.

Some days later, in the beginning of Chapter Two, Will witnesses another sonnet drop in Central Park at Ground Zero, as Will has come to call the park bench that his Tetzlar first singled out for viewing. It is the first quatrain of Sonnet 98, a poem about love, as the *Sonnets* tend to be.[48] Sonnet 98, however, is also, viscerally, about nominalism and realism, which Shakespeare elegantly decks out in neoplatonic terms, as his culture's other premier sonneteers, Sidney and Spenser, tended to do. The speaker laments inconsolably his absence from his beloved. Despite the plentiful supply of "shadows" and "figures of delight Drawn after you, you pattern of all those," his beloved is, for him, the only one who will do. "You," the addressee of the sonnet, is the one "youth" whose unique "youness" alone can satisfy the desire conveyed in these fourteen lines.[49] When naming and being do not coincide, no alternatives will suffice. The unattainability of the thing itself finds expression here in pre-Kantian terms whose philosophical purchase Percy well understood. Though the poem deals with geographical distance as well as referentiality (the relationship between words and things), it asks the basic question of philosophical debates between realism and nominalism, "What's in a name?" as Juliet puts it about Romeo. Nothing can take the place of the beloved, and Sonnet 98 represents the experience of that nothingness, as if to say, however sweetly, "Thanks for nothing."

These shadows may remind us of figures in Plato's cave, pale imitations many times removed from the real thing. Or, in their moving expression of what we are missing and still desire, they may rival the absent presences of Clark Gable and Claudette Colbert on-screen in *It Happened One Night*, once the promise of such happiness wears off and, like Binx, we find ourselves abed in our rooms alone and forced to draw one breath after another. Despite the intimate nearness that such simulacra may suggest, their ability to seem "more natural than reality" soon vanishes, and we may then recall that they are merely "reliefs from private fantasy and its responsibilities." Such a realization of the emptiness of these signs seemingly frees us from illusions about their being anything more substantial than symbols, whether verbal or celluloid or oil on canvas. Our disillusion in this regard prepares us for reality, but it does not explain the moments when what we make of such aesthetic experiences prevails over this rudimentary knowledge of their inert materiality and our disengagement, if not absolute separateness, from them. Such an insight represses our passionate connections to works of art that come alive in our experience and temporarily defy the basic distinction between subject and object, nor can it conceive of their more lasting impact.

Likewise such a distinction denies the ritual experience of communion when it treats the bread and wine of the Eucharist as merely symbolic, and this religious analogy pertains here because Percy's Catholicism motivated his writing throughout his career. Besides Kierkegaard, as far as Percy was concerned, Flannery O'Connor formulated the most relevant distinction between secular and sacred concerns in the modern era, just as she valued Percy's blunt clarification of why the South produced so many fine writers. "Because we lost the War," Percy answered that question on national TV when the *Today Show* host put it to him on March 14, 1962. His response inspired O'Connor to write a brief note to Percy that opened this way: "Dear Mr. Percy, I'm glad we lost the War and you won the Nat'l. Book Award."[50] Just as Percy's one-liner became the epigrammatic byword for the distinctiveness of literary accomplishment by southern writers in the twentieth century, O'Connor's rejoinder to Mary McCarthy about the symbolic meaningfulness of the Eucharist became a shibboleth not only for Catholics but for realists of all kinds. Their patience was wearing thin in an environment of ever more facile and hyperbolic skepticism, the hocus-pocus that often passed for theoretical sophistication. "Well, if it's a symbol," O'Connor had remarked about the Eucharist, "to hell with it."[51]

However, in elaborating her misgivings about treating this ceremony as merely symbolic, O'Connor specifically targeted Emerson's argument with his Unitarian superiors over celebrating the Lord's Supper that led to his break with that church.[52] In Emerson's crucial sermon on this ceremony, his concern centers on the Christian formalism of the ritual and a wish to recover the common Jewish terms of the meal despite the Gospel account's emphasis on Christian memorialization. He notes, for example, that only Luke employs "the words *Do this in remembrance of me* to which so much meaning has been given . . . yet many persons are apt to imagine that the very striking and formal manner in which this eating and drinking is described intimates a striking and formal purpose to found a festival . . . yet the impression is removed by reading any narrative of the mode in which the ancient or modern Jews kept the passover. . . . The leading circumstances in the gospel are only a faithful account of that ceremony. Jesus did not celebrate the passover and afterwards the supper, but the supper *was* the passover."[53]

The historicity of Emerson's view and his reluctance to read Jesus's person as exceptional, beyond his share of such special qualities as may distinguish other spiritual leaders too, scandalized the Unitarian establishment at Harvard in 1838, when Emerson delivered his "Divinity School Address," one year after "The American Scholar."[54] He thus became persona non grata in those precincts for decades to come. In their rejection of Emerson, we might thus sense common cause between Percy and O'Connor as southern Catholic authors, though Unitarianism hardly seems their much nearer ally.

Cavell, however, complicates this matter again. When he describes his decision to write about Hollywood remarriage comedy in *Pursuits of Happiness,* Cavell puts Emerson and Kierkegaard in the foreground as philosophers of the everyday whose pertinence to the ordinariness of his topic, classic Hollywood movies of the 30s and 40s, makes Cavell's choice of either one of them equally relevant. Given Percy's well-established debt to Kierkegaard, the common ground between Percy and Cavell, noticed by Percy himself and by McElwee, thus increases. When Cavell cites Emerson's famous list of matters whose "ultimate cause" he seeks to know, Cavell describes this passage as a form of what Kierkegaard calls "the perception of the sublime in the everyday" in his discussion of the Knight of Faith in *Fear and Trembling.*[55] From this list Cavell chooses two items for repetition, "the meal in the firkin, the milk in the pan." Perhaps these phrases have become bywords of American romanticism, so it seems nothing more than coincidence that Will Barrett hits the road with a firkin, and when he breakfasts upon its contents in northern Virginia, buttermilk serves as his beverage. The firkin is even more tainted in its source, however, so it may be an intentional dig at Emersonianism. It is a gift Will receives from Forney Aiken, a satirical figure called the pseudo-Negro in the novel and modeled on John Howard

Griffin's account of his experiences in the 60s best seller *Black like Me.* As a means to quit drinking, he has made a retreat from the big city to try life in the country, an effort that his shaky nerves might betray at any moment. Forney, who epitomizes anxious American inauthenticity, now manufactures cedar firkins and sisal tote bags in Bucks County, Pennsylvania, when he is not farming.

Perhaps this satirical touch signifies Percy's tacit agreement with Emerson's reception among southern writers, like the Fugitives, who demonize him, in Allen Tate's phrase, as "the Lucifer of Concord," not the Sage.[56] Cavell's ability to inherit Emerson by perceiving his affinities with Kierkegaard and Nietzsche, however, offers terms for enlightening comparison that gives Percy and Cavell an unforeseeably shared immediacy and relevance. It is no accident, for example, that, in *The Sportswriter,* Richard Ford begins his Frank Bascombe trilogy deeply engaged in inheriting or, if you will, pervasively rewriting, Percy's *The Moviegoer.* Though virtually no Emerson can be found in that novel, the apparent unavailability of Emerson there changes radically in Ford's next two Bascombe novels. "Self-Reliance" frequently serves as an explicit touchstone for key themes in *Independence Day,* the second novel in Ford's trilogy, and allusions to Emerson's "Experience" abound in the third, *The Lay of the Land,* where Ford also rewrites several paragraphs from that essay in terms of Frank's experiences in a couple of bars.[57]

Moreover, Frank has become a real estate agent in Haddam, New Jersey, in the second novel, *Independence Day,* which centrally features "Self-Reliance." Frank wants to discuss the notion of Independence Day itself with his troubled son, Paul, and he imagines such a conversation in utterly transcendentalist terms as perhaps "the only way an as-needed parent can in good faith make contact with his son's life problems; which is too say sidereally, by raising a canopy of useful postulates above him like stars and hoping he'll connect them up to his own sightings and views like an astronomer."[58] Though a sportswriter sounds like a moviegoer in his commitment to spectatorship, Will Barrett is unemployed when Forney Aiken subtly Emersonizes him with the gift of a firkin in Bucks County. At their next stop, however, in Levittown, Pennsylvania, Will is mistaken for a Jersey real estate agent from Haddonfield or Haddon Heights, New Jersey. In what can serve as a relevant gloss on those rhymes with Frank's new job as a realtor and his new hometown, Haddam, New Jersey, Cavell remarks, "I find no limit to the knowledge writers will have of one another (if this causes anxiety it is an anxiety towards one's own unconscious)."[59]

Cavell's comment occurs in his essay on Emerson's "Experience," and, given its pertinence to Frank's most fundamental ordeal, the death of his eight-year-old son, Ralph, Richard Ford brings that essay ingeniously to bear throughout *The Lay of the Land.* The death of Emerson's five-year-old son, Waldo, resides at the heart of "Experience," and there, in Emerson's harsh sentence, "For contact with reality we would even pay the price of sons and lovers," Cavell surprisingly overhears an echo of Shakespeare's *The Winter's Tale,* which features the fatal skepticism of Leontes and the death of his seven-year-old son, Mamillius. Of course, *The Moviegoer* and *The Last Gentleman,* to recall just Percy's first two novels, share this same central concern, the deaths of Scottie Bolling and Lonnie Smith in the former and that of Jamie Vaught in the latter.

The use of precursors in all of these writers—Percy, Ford, Cavell, Shakespeare—entails the discovery of kindred spirits in unlikely places and advances art in surprising ways. We might properly call it the invention of tradition. For inspiration we might borrow from Emerson a pair of sentences from the address with which Percy declined his chance to be associated: "One must be an inventor to read well. . . . There is then creative reading as well as creative writing."[60]

McElwee's "war film" *Sherman's March* demonstrates the boldness such affinities may inspire. Neither Sherman nor nuclear warfare usually awakens a laugh, but, thanks in good part to *The Last Gentleman,* McElwee's film treatment of them struck that unfamiliar comic note without falsifying the gravity of such topics. In *The Burden of Southern History,* C. Vann Woodward seeks to turn the heavy load mentioned in his book's title into an enabling resource, especially in one of the most influential essays in that collection, "The Irony of Southern History." In many ways its main thesis makes a succinct appearance in Percy's proverbial quip about the multitude of fine southern writers being due to losing the Civil War. After Vietnam, Woodward needed to revise that claim somewhat, since the whole country suffered that defeat and we all had to absorb the reality of it.[61] The need for revision, however, highlights our struggle with time in which even the past changes as we move into the future, and we can find its meanings as unstable sometimes as our footing here and now.

Shakespeare's sonnets enabled Percy to affirm the value he discovered in literature when he was sidelined during World War II. Certain writers gave him nothing less than a second life, in what Shakespeare calls our war with Time, whose conditions challenge everyone to join the human race and learn how to take the oldest joke of all, our undeniable mortality. Turning a lover's disappointment into an opportunity for making a remarkable experimental movie ultimately put McElwee's fascination with cinema vérité onto the National Film Registry, where *Sherman's March* now resides along with a tiny fraction of the movies eligible for such an honor. As McElwee acknowledges, *The Last Gentleman* was a big help on his journey to that destination, and Cavell's philosophical reflections on film confirmed the direction he had taken. Perhaps we can justly celebrate that accomplishment, if we rely on Percy's confidence in what sonnets, like dogfish, can teach us, when rightly viewed. We may duly turn to the moment in Shakespeare's *Sonnets* when he first stops advising his young friend to conquer time by having children and broaches what textbooks call the eternizing conceit: the claim that poetry can memorialize its subjects until Time itself has a stop.

> Then the conceit of this inconstant stay
> Sets you most rich in youth before my sight,
> Where wasteful Time debateth with Decay,
> To change your day of youth to sullied night;
> And all in war with Time for love of you,
> As he takes from you, I engraft you new. (15.9–14)

Via meditation on both the history he feels obliged to relate and the world as he finds it and himself in the moment of making his film, McElwee creates a hybrid documentary. *Sherman's March* grafts romance onto southern tragedy and leaves our hero alertly waiting for what will happen next. Given the grim odds of nuclear war, the Lost Cause, and a broken heart, such a triumph of hope against hope amounts to no minor victory.

Notes

1. *Sherman's March: An Improbable Search for Love* (Ross McElwee, 1986), 00:11:55–00:12:05.

2. Ross McElwee, "The Act of Seeing with One's Own Eyes," in *The Last Physician: Walker Percy and the Moral Life of Medicine,* ed. Carl Elliott and John Lantos (Durham, NC: Duke University Press, 1999), 16–37.

3. *Sherman's March,* 00:00:00–00:00:50.

4. Ibid., 00:00:51–00:02:00.

5. Ibid., 01:58:46–01:59:45.

6. McElwee, "Seeing with One's Own Eyes," 19–20.

7. Emphasis Percy's. This letter, along with numerous others from Percy to Coles, is in the Robert Coles Collection at Michigan State University. I am grateful to David Cooper for making them available to me.

8. Robert Coles, *Walker Percy: An American Search* (Boston: Little, Brown, 1978), 156–57.

9. Stanley Cavell, *The World Viewed: Reflections on the Ontology of Film,* enlarged ed. (Cambridge, MA: Harvard University Press, 1979), 102.

10. Stanley Cavell, "Finding as Founding: Taking Steps in Emerson's 'Experience,'" in Stanley Cavell, *Emerson's Transcendental Etudes,* ed. David Justin Hodge (Stanford, CA: Stanford University Press, 2003), 110–40, 135–36.

11. *The Living Thoughts of Kierkegaard,* ed. W. H. Auden (Bloomington: Indiana University Press, 1952), 26.

12. Walker Percy, *The Moviegoer* (New York: Knopf, 1961), 72.

13. Emphasis Cavell's. Here is the whole passage from *The World Viewed:*

> What we wish to see in this way is the world itself—that is to say, everything. Nothing less than that is what modern philosophy has told us (whether for Kant's reasons, or for Locke's, or Hume's) is metaphysically beyond our reach or (as Hegel or Marx or Kierkegaard or Nietzsche might rather put it) beyond our reach metaphysically. To say that we wish to view the world itself is to say that we wish for the condition of viewing as such. That is the way we establish our connection with the world: by viewing it or having views of it. Our condition has become one in which our natural mode of perception is to view, feeling unseen; viewing a movie makes this condition automatic, takes the responsibility for it out of our hands. Hence movies seem more natural than reality. Not because they are escapes into fantasy, but because they are reliefs from private fantasy and its responsibilities. We do not so much look at the world as look *out at* it, from behind the self. (101–2)

On the topic of Cavell's "ontology of film," Paul Guyer remarks, "*The World Viewed* argues for a realistic approach to film, meaning that we should acknowledge that our cognitive and emotional responses to films are responses to the realities of the human condition portrayed in them." "Cavell, Stanley Louis," in *The Cambridge Dictionary of Philosophy,* 2nd ed., ed. Robert Audi (Cambridge: Cambridge University Press, 1999), 128.

14. Ralph Waldo Emerson, "Experience," in *Emerson: Essays and Poems,* ed. Joel Porte, college ed. (New York: Library of America, 1996), 469–92, 476.

15. Walker Percy, *The Last Gentleman* (New York: Farrar, Straus and Giroux, 1965).

16. Jay Tolson, *Pilgrim in the Ruins: A Life of Walker Percy* (Chapel Hill: University of North Carolina Press, 1992), 305, 320; Patrick Samway, *Walker Percy: A Life* (Chicago: Loyola Press, 1997), 217.

17. Stanley Cavell, *Pursuits of Happiness: The Hollywood Comedy of Remarriage* (Cambridge, MA: Harvard University Press, 1981), 87–88.

18. Binx, in his deepest passion of despair, thinks that "the malaise has settled like a

fall-out and what people really fear is not that the bomb will fall but that the bomb will not fall." Percy, *Moviegoer,* 228. Cavell remarks, in *The World Viewed,* that "the future has replaced the past as an object of timely elegy" (95).

19. Percy, *Moviegoer,* 8.

20. Percy, *Last Gentleman,* 23, 47.

21. Ibid., 386.

22. *Sherman's March,* 01:22:00–01:23:10.

23. Charles Frazier, *Cold Mountain* (New York: Atlantic Monthly Press, 1997).

24. Robert Coles, "Children and the Nuclear Bomb," chap. 7 of Coles, *The Moral Life of Children* (Boston: Houghton Mifflin, 1986), 243–80.

25. Percy, *Last Gentleman,* 3.

26. Tolson, *Pilgrim in the Ruins,* 329, 286.

27. Walker Percy Papers, no. 4294, Southern Historical Collection, Wilson Library, University of North Carolina, Folder 2 and Folder 9.

28. See Stephen Mulhall, "Reading, Writing, Re-Membering: What Cavell and Heidegger Call Thinking," in *Ordinary Language Criticism: Literary Thinking after Cavell after Wittgenstein,* ed. Kenneth Dauber and Walter Jost (Evanston, IL: Northwestern University Press, 2003), 115–33.

29. Jay Tolson, *Pilgrim in the Ruins,* 467.

30. Ibid., 12–13.

31. Stanley Cavell, *Cities of Words: Pedagogical Letters on a Register of the Moral Life* (Cambridge, MA: Harvard University Press, 2004), 90–91, 211–23, 248.

32. Ibid., 428, 424–25; Stanley Cavell, *Disowning Knowledge in Six Plays of Shakespeare* (Cambridge: Cambridge University Press, 1987), 1–12.

33. William Shakespeare, *Othello,* 3rd ed., ed. E. A. J. Honigmann (Walton-on Thames, Surrey: Thomas Nelson, 1997), 3.3.362.

34. Percy, *Last Gentleman,* 402.

35. Walker Percy, "The Coming Crisis in Psychiatry," in *Sign-Posts in a Strange Land,* ed. Patrick Samway (New York: Farrar, Straus and Giroux, 1991), 251–62.

36. Quoted in Stanley Cavell, *Philosophy the Day after Tomorrow* (Cambridge, MA: Harvard University Press, 2005), 99.

37. Bertram Wyatt-Brown, "Inherited Depression, Medicine, and Illness in Walker Percy's Art," in Elliott and Lantos, *Last Physician,* 112–33, 122.

38. See Peter Kramer, *Listening to Prozac* (New York: Penguin Books, 1993), 250–300; and Carl Elliott, *Better Than Well: American Medicine Meets the American Dream* (New York: Norton, 2003), 129–60.

39. Cavell, *Cities of Words,* 247–64, 384–408; Stanley Cavell, *Conditions Handsome and Unhandsome: The Constitution of Emersonian Perfectionism* (Chicago: University of Chicago Press, 1990), xx–xxiv, 3, 16–7.

40. McElwee, "Seeing with One's Own Eyes," 20–22.

41. Percy, *Last Gentleman,* 26–28.

42. Walker Percy, "From Facts to Fiction," in Samway, *Sign-Posts in a Strange Land,* 186–90, 187.

43. Lawrence F. Rhu, "Home Movies and Personal Documentaries: An Interview with Ross McElwee," *Cineaste* 29, no. 3 (Summer 2004): 6–12.

44. Walker Percy, "The Loss of the Creature," in *The Message in the Bottle: How Queer Man Is, How Queer Language Is, and What One Has to Do with the Other* (New York: Farrar, Straus and Giroux, 1975), 46–63, 61.

45. "Emerson, Coleridge, Kant," in Cavell, *Emerson's Transcendental Etudes,* 63.

46. Percy, *Moviegoer,* 52, 10–11.

47. Percy, *Last Gentleman,* 7–8.

48. Ibid., 43–44.

49. See Helen Vendler, *The Art of Shakespeare's Sonnets* (Cambridge, MA: Harvard University Press, 1997), 110: "As tru-th is true-ness and streng-th is strong-ness, so you-th is you-ness, in this adoring pun."

50. Tolson, *Pilgrim in the Ruins,* 298–99.

51. Flannery O'Connor, *The Habit of Being,* ed. Sally Fitzgerald (New York: Farrar, Straus and Giroux, 1979), 124–25.

52. Flannery O'Connor, *Mystery and Manners* (New York: Farrar, Straus, and Cudahy, 1969), 161–62.

53. "The 'Lord's Supper' Sermon," in *Emerson: Essays and Poems,* 955–66, 957.

54. See Barbara Packer, "Origin and Authority: Emerson and the Higher Criticism," in *Reconstructing American Literary History,* ed. Sacvan Berkovitch (Cambridge, MA: Harvard University Press, 1986), 67–92.

55. Cavell, *Pursuits of Happiness,* 14–15.

56. Allen Tate, "Four American Poets," in *Reactionary Essays in Poetry and Ideas* (New York: Scribner's, 1936), 7–8.

57. See Lawrence F. Rhu, "Emersonian Affinities: Reading Richard Ford through Stanley Cavell," in *Stanley Cavell and the Idea of America* (New York: Routledge, 2013), 217–29.

58. Richard Ford, *Independence Day* (New York: Vintage Books, 1996), 289.

59. Cavell, "Finding as Founding," 126.

60. "The American Scholar," in *Emerson: Essays and Poems,* 59.

61. See C. Vann Woodward, "The Irony of Southern History" and "A Second Look at the Theme of Irony," in *The Burden of Southern History,* rev. ed. (Baton Rouge: Louisiana State University Press, 1968), 187–211, 213–33.

The Power of Memory and the Memory of Power

Wars and Graves in Westerns and *Jidaigeki*

Inger S. B. Brodey

In selecting a design for the controversial Vietnam Veterans Memorial, the panel of eight judges and architects were deciding how to commemorate a war that was arguably one of the most painful national defeats the country had ever suffered. The interactive experience of this architectural monument prioritizes the commemoration of human loss over the preservation of national reputation. This new experience required a new shape: the monument to the war does not rise up gloriously on the landscape of the Mall to compete with the Washington Monument or the Lincoln Memorial. Instead, the Vietnam Memorial Wall, designed by Maya Lin, sinks into the ground, heavy with the weight of the names of the fallen, and invites the viewer to walk through and participate in the experience of loss and personal mourning. The V that the wall creates from an aerial view gives a nod to national reputation, yet in marking and commemorating these losses, the monument also helps put a final closure on this event.

War films, too, can help a country heal after military defeat or fresh casualties. It is interesting that in the two decades following World War II and the Pacific War, the United States and Japan both experienced a new flourishing of their respective action film genres, whether explicitly military or not. These decades saw the heroic samurai ideal and the cowboy hero renewed as icons for their respective nations. Particularly in the hands of director Akira Kurosawa (1910–1998), the *ronin,*[1] or unemployed, wandering samurai, takes a special place in Japanese cinematic history and the *jidaigeki* (period film). This postwar ronin-hero altered the samurai iconography associated with Japanese national identity and arguably took on some aspects of the lone cowboy in the process, perhaps partly owing to Kurosawa's great admiration of John Ford (1894–1973). John Ford and Akira Kurosawa both reclaim their respective national icons, drawing on a shared moment in nineteenth-century history when both cowboys and samurai experienced a sense of their own obsolescence and portraying them in a nostalgic and romanticized light. Both the ronin and the lone cowboy are icons of a losing battle that includes a shared opposition to modernization, especially commercialization, industrialization, and the triumph of the urban world. The Western and the *jidaigeki* in the hands of these two directors became an act of mythmaking posing as an act of remembering. Insofar as the films self-consciously portray a dying way of life and a vanishing form of heroism, the films function as a memorial—a commemoration—ironically of something that arguably never existed. These acts of remembering also function as mythmaking or "mythopoiesis" (in Richard Slotkin's term)[2] for a nation emerging from war with varying degrees of disillusion. In other words, the films function both as closure and creation; like a marked grave or monument, they simultaneously bury the past and build it.

Directors such as Ford and Kurosawa helped to develop a semiotics of heroism for their national icons. In developing and portraying their concepts of heroism, each director and genre shaped viewers' understanding of nationhood and history during these turbulent postwar decades. In each case the director inherits a large body of mythology from prewar film, art, and literature. While aspects of these systems of signs have become commonplace and even the subject matter for pastiche—white hats for good guys, black for the bad—other symbols are used with great subtlety to exemplify the kind of heroism that each genre celebrates. In this context, the films responding to World War II (or the Pacific War) often thematize remembrance and forgetting, especially through topics like revenge, commemoration of death, graves, and scars. The mythopoiesis is limited only by the directors' and screenwriters' ability to mold audience sympathy and admiration, appealing to the unspoken systems of meaning in the films themselves.

The gravestone and burial theme, in particular, raises both psychological and philosophical questions related to war and the recovery from war: Can the memory of violence strengthen us or teach us lessons about preventing future violence? Or does it rather lead to the desire for retribution or revenge and perpetuate a state of war? Or is commemoration of loss the only way to forget and move beyond loss to new beginnings? When graves commemorate women and children who were murdered, for example, do they serve as bitter remembrances or as the inspiration for revenge? Like a scar that deforms the face, and does not allow a wound fully to disappear, the grave or tombstone may be similarly bivalent. On the one hand, a grave may show a form of healing and recovery, and yet at the same time it also disrupts the smooth serenity of the present moment and awakens the viewer to past wrongs that have not been righted. Wartime graves thus evoke both the memory of past wrongs and the possibilities of forgiveness. They thus may indicate the future likelihood of continued feuds or warfare. Cross-genre, cross-cultural iconography of graves reaches a peak in Ford's *Searchers* (1956) and *The Man Who Shot Liberty Valance* (1962) as well as in Kurosawa's *Hidden Fortress* (1958) and *Yôjimbô* (1961), films that are in dialogue over similar questions, partly relating to the ongoing war in Asia.

This essay explores the power of memory and forgetting in some of these postwar films by first establishing the wartime contexts that both Ford and Kurosawa experienced as filmmakers. Secondly, it attempts to establish how their films incorporate multiple historical settings simultaneously. Interestingly, these temporal settings tend to be linked by military defeat or significant loss and often invoke multivalent symbolism arising out of civil war, where distinction between victor and victim is less clear by definition. And finally, a close examination of actual graves and burials in the films demonstrates the tortured relationships between memory, trauma, recovery, and national identity in these two genres.

Through their films, Ford and Kurosawa both seem to insist upon the humane significance of remembering war and commemorating death as opposed to more gruesome alternatives that they portray. They differ, however, on the relative benefits and dangers associated with forgetting trauma. Their depictions of graves and death reflect differing visions of human nature and its tendencies, perhaps also influenced by their countries' respective outcomes from the recent wars. Ford has greater confidence that the memory of past wrongs can help lead to a better future, whereas Kurosawa is more pessimistic regarding human nature, showing the dangers both of remembering and of forgetting past trauma. In the process of exploring the remembering/forgetting of war and recovery, these films also enact "national biographies," similar to those described by Benedict Andersen.[3]

Wartime Cinemas

While there were periods of censorship in both countries' film industries, these two genres—the American Western and the Japanese samurai *jidaigeki*—were not state funded. David Desser has argued that Japan and the United States are not only rare, but perhaps unique in global cinema, in that each of these countries has developed a successful genre of film that is both independent of state government and dedicated to its own mythical founding or self-definition.[4] In Japan, film and national politics were deeply entangled in the decade leading up to the Pacific War. From 1933 through 1945, the Japanese government controlled film production, not only through censorship but also through the Greater Japan Film Association's (GJFA's) control over theaters. Beginning in 1937, the Film Law allowed the Censorship Office of the Home Ministry to maintain strict control over all phases of the creative process. The Film Law also enabled the Home Ministry and the army to control exhibition: they compelled theaters to show nonfiction educational films sponsored by the government and modeled after the *Kulturfilm* of Germany.[5]

In general, wartime Japan's culture emphasized retreat from luxury and frivolity for the sake of the war effort; this involved much self-reflection about which forms of art were indeed frivolous. In response to this, the government-run GJFA sponsored what Derrell William Davis has dubbed "monumental cinema"—wartime cinema that glorified Japanese aesthetics and national religion (especially Shintô) to promote empire and militarization. Aspects of the "monumental style" include "the glorification of Tokugawa ethics and deportment, graphic representations of collective spectatorship, concentration on the aesthetics of period detail and design, and a valorization of familial and clan structures, especially when they require self-immolation."[6] In other words, the GJFA encouraged traditional Confucian-based samurai virtues (especially loyalty unto death) to educate the audiences about sacrifice and belonging, as well as the grandeur of the Japanese cultural heritage.

After Japan's defeat, U.S.-led forces occupied Japan from 1945 until 1952. For the first four years of this occupation, Japanese film production was carefully censored, and films that propagated "nationalistic, militaristic and feudalistic concepts" were condemned. The *Memorandum Concerning the Elimination of Undemocratic Motion Pictures* was particularly wary of "conformity to a feudal code, contempt for life, creation of the 'Warrior

Spirit,' the uniqueness and superiority of the 'Yamato' (Japanese race), the 'special role of Japan in Asia,' etc."[7] The thirteen subjects prohibited by the Civil Information and Education section of the Supreme Commander of the Allied Powers on November 19, 1945, reveal that militarism is the first and most prominent concern. The sword in particular raised the concern of the Western censors. For example, a U.S. Department of War training film from 1944, *Know Your Enemy: Japan,* spends a great deal of time associating the sword with brutality and the feudal past.[8] Because of this concern, *jidaigeki* and especially *chambara* (action sword films) were much rarer during the occupation—seldom produced and seldom screened.

The beginning of Akira Kurosawa's career coincided with these changing regulations. Unlike John Ford, he saw no military action, but like Ford, he was asked to make films for military purposes. His first independent film, *Sanshiro Sugata,* was produced under the Japanese wartime censorship, and it was only through his influential friends that the film was released in 1943. The testing by the Interior Ministry found it too "British-American" in its leanings.[9] Consequently, soon after its release, fifteen to twenty minutes of this film were permanently cut (and presumably destroyed). In 1943, the Information Section of the Japanese Imperial Navy commanded Kurosawa to make "a big action picture using Zero fighter planes"; however, their demand was never fulfilled. Instead, Kurosawa tried to make a documentary film to accord with "national policy," resulting in *Most Beautiful* (*Ichiban Utsukushiku*), a story of the dedicated and hardworking women in a wartime optics factory. Subsequently, Kurosawa was pressured to produce *Sanshiro Sugata II,* as a jingoistic sequel (released in May 1945) to his earlier successful film. In this sequel, the young Japanese Judo expert proves his worth (and Japan's) by defeating a Western boxer. Another of Kurosawa's early films featured his first venture into *jidaigeki: Tread Lightly on Tiger's Tail,* also released in 1945. This film was begun under Japanese rule and completed under U.S.-led occupation; Kurosawa was frustrated to find that it was too individualistic for the Japanese and too feudalistic for the occupation audiences. Kurosawa was surprised to learn later in life that John Ford had visited his set during the filming of *Tiger's Tail.*

In re-creating a samurai film appropriate for the postwar genre, Kurosawa takes the accepted *jidaigeki* and attempts to make it fit for democratic ideals (and the democratic censors). In contrast to the 47 Ronin or Chushingura theme that had been prevalent in wartime "monumental" cinema, Kurosawa favored the single hero. He also consistently preferred to focus on times of shifting class distinctions, corresponding to an increasingly democratic age. Postwar Japan, then, taking Kurosawa as an indicator for a moment, struggled to redefine the *jidaigeki* and samurai film to accord with Western individualism and the postimperial world. Tellingly, the word *ronin* has continued to have a place in contemporary society of the twenty-first century: now the word refers to a businessman who is "in between" companies or a high school graduate who has not yet been accepted into a university (clan).

In the American context, Richard Slotkin calls this postwar period in American history a "crisis of victory": he argues that the huge rise in the popularity of the Western in the 1950s was a response to a reality that does not live up to expectation—a prewar normalcy that is desired but cannot be regained. In the wake of postwar disappointment and alienation, producers and audiences alike "reverted to their generic maps in search of ideological reference points, which meant, for the most part, a return to the home terrain of the Western."[10] In the context of atomic warfare and Cold War tactics, the Western provided a welcome respite in its relatively clear-cut distinctions between heroes and villains, as well as its healthy suspicion of modern technology, particularly weaponry (in the nineteenth-century context, repeating rifles rather than atomic or hydrogen bombs).

John Ford joined the U.S. Naval Reserve in the 1930s, and in the early years of World War II, he produced several wartime documentaries and short training films, alongside his constant stream of Hollywood feature films. After Pearl Harbor, Ford went on active duty and headed a documentary film unit. Between 1941 and 1944, he won four Oscars—first for the nonwar dramas *The Grapes of Wrath* (1940) and *How Green Was My Valley* (1941), then for two documentaries with actual wartime footage—*Battle of Midway* (1942) and *December 7th* (a feature-length film released in 1943). The U.S. government put pressure on Ford to produce more combat films, and "under some duress," he created *They Were Expendable* (1945), a film about American naval action in the Philippines.[11] In fact, Ford's twin positions as director and advancing military officer are recorded in the credits of three of his war films: "Lt. Cmdr. John Ford U.S.N.R." in 1942; "John Ford Captain U.S.N.R." in 1945; and "Rear Admiral John Ford USNVR Ret." in 1951.[12] Ford was injured in the Battle of Midway, yet reengaged in the naval reserve for active duty in Korea, where he filmed *This Is Korea!* (1951), again with live footage.

As Ford was moving away from wartime documentaries, he was also experimenting with the Western, resulting in several of his best films: *My Darling Clementine* (1946), *3 Godfathers* (1948), and *Wagon Master* (1950). In the process of negotiating combat films, the Western, and dramas about American mythmaking, Ford came upon a new subgenre—the cavalry film. It was a way of combining combat with his mythmaking American settings: *Fort Apache* (1948), *She Wore a Yellow Ribbon* (1949), and *Rio Grande* (1950).

The film industry itself was dominated throughout the 1950s by the Red Scare of McCarthyism; the Hollywood blacklist associated with hearings conducted by the House Committee on Un-American Activities was at its peak from the late 1940s to the late 1950s, coming to a rest only two or three years before the release of *The Man who Shot Liberty Valance* (1962); and the tensions surrounding the burgeoning civil rights movement were in the air as well. As many critics have noted, the House Committee events are fairly directly referred to in Fred Zinneman's *High Noon* (1952) and in Howard Hawks's response to *High Noon*—namely, *Rio Bravo* (1959). McCarthyism encouraged the development of self-conscious political symbolism in the Western, just as censorship in Japan had encouraged the development of political readings of *jidaigeki*. Westerns were thus consciously used as a vehicle for representing social ideals and for responding to governmental wrongs.

In the post–Korean War context and during the Cold War standoff with the Soviet Union, the distinction between peacetime and wartime grew indistinct. In 1961, the United States weathered both the Bay of Pigs incident in Cuba and the construction of the Berlin Wall within a single year. In contrast to the more clear-cut victories of the world wars, the transition to peace in these other conflicts was tenuous and troubling, and the results were ambiguous—pyrrhic victories at best. American frontier ideals seemed very remote in the 60s, and many Americans were openly debating the place of force and militarism in international politics. At the time of its origin, "the Frontier Myth suggested that whatever America's corruptions or limitations, our potential for self-perfection was unlimited as the open spaces waiting for us over the border," yet postwar audiences had to look further afield.[13] Thus President Kennedy, speaking in 1960, appeals to Space as a "New Frontier," borrowing terminology and tone from Teddy Roosevelt and also using the language of the Western.[14]

One can also see echoes of many of these conflicts (particularly the Cold War and the civil rights movement) within Ford's later westerns, such as in *The Man Who Shot Liberty Valance* (1962) and *Cheyenne Autumn* (1964). But perhaps more importantly, taking *Liberty Valance* as an example, one feels a diminishing confidence in the American Dream, as previously defined in Ford's oeuvre through pictorial grandeur and the majestic landscapes of opportunity and freedom. The appeal of the Western was closely tied to an identity associated with open spaces, noble ideals, the frontier, and clear-cut distinctions between good and evil.[15] The Western hero of the 1940s and 1950s was a man of action who protected the weak and killed even enemies with reluctance. He was defined in opposition to the professional statesman (associated with corruption) as well as the philosopher (associated with morally tenuous ambiguities). By the end of this postwar period, one does not see the same glorification of action in the films of the mid-60s. In *The Man Who Shot Liberty Valance,* Tom Doniphon (John Wayne) does protect the weak, yet his two primary heroic acts (saving Ranse's life each time) both occur in the darkness of an alley, and the latter act with an illicitness that eventually shames rather than ennobles him. In such ways, Ford captures this time of national identity crisis through his cinematic choices in this 1962 film.

Echoes of Past Wars

During the postwar decades, directors such as Akira Kurosawa and John Ford helped to establish the popularity of the cowboy hero and the samurai warrior in the modern imagination. Japanese *jidaigeki* (period drama), or more precisely Taishô and early Shôwa samurai films of the 1920s through the Pacific War, tended to promote a nostalgic view of Japan's past, glorify pre-Meiji high culture, and propagate a largely fictional samurai code of honor, emphasizing the Confucian codes of loyalty unto death. Largely following the lead of Akira Kurosawa, the postwar and postoccupation samurai becomes a lone ronin who is isolated by changing class structures and modernization and wanders from town to town, saving commoners from violence and oppression in such films as *Seven Samurai* (1954), *Yôjimbô* (1961), and *Sanjurô* (1962).

The American Western, brought to new levels by director John Ford, also achieves similar cultural statements in the 40s and 50s, through the filmic depiction of the American cowboy that helped shape American cultural identity. In John Ford's hands and in postwar cinema more broadly, the lone cowboy exhibits a code of honor by clinging to a higher way of life in the face of a rising tide of industrialization and commercialization; this cowboy hero also wanders from town to town exhibiting his heroic defense of the weak while striving to avoid combat in such films as *My Darling Clementine* (1946), *3 Godfathers* (1948), and *The Wagon Master* (1950). And yet, while exhibiting a degree of pacifism, both of these postwar genres are fundamentally films about war, where the viewer fully expects that a final resolution will be achieved only through violence and death. While popular with viewers as a form of escape from times of war, they also deal directly or indirectly with wartime ideals and philosophies of war.

The postwar Samurai film and the Western ultimately share important attitudes toward nostalgia, nation-making, and national refounding, as well as toward the nature of heroism and leadership. Both of these icons participate in a mythical national refounding that appeals to Americans and Japanese at times of national crisis. These film genres also reveal important tacitly held beliefs about citizenship, authority, nation-making, and rebellion. For example, both genres tend to share a starting point of lawlessness: the screenwriters are drawn to settings where there is a vacuum of central authority. In this absence of central authority, strong "manly" warriors vie for power and authority, enacting moral battles and elements of the "great quest" (Kurosawa's term). The heroic victor is characterized not only by his martial skills, but also by selfless actions, chivalry, and a desire to protect the weak.

These samurai depictions, like those of the cowboy, are easily vulnerable to critiques of anachronism—or historical inaccuracy. But that would be to do injustice to the purposes of mythopoetics. Again, anachronism is at the very heart of the Japanese *jidaigeki,* as Sybil Anne Thornton has shown. Traditionally, it was not only a way to critique current happenings through veiled references to the historical past, but it was also a way of eluding censorship, following the technique that kabuki had earlier developed. Rather than being anachronistic per se, these films are multichronistic, managing simultaneously to refer to multiple, analogous historical points in time.[16]

There is even similarity in the respective historical stimuli that lead to the salience and creation of these national icons: the restless samurai (ronin) warrior and the wandering cowboy gunfighter. That is, there is not only a similarity in their portrayal of historical obsolescence and their nostalgia for the loss of a premodern form of heroism, but also a similar stimulus for the rediscovery and reshaping of these icons in the decades after World War II. While it is more apparent why Americans (with such a brief national history) would wish for a national icon and foundational myths, postwar Japan found solace in turning to other periods of history where samurai nobly suffered setbacks in the face of modernization. These Japanese and American foundational myths bear a resemblance in that they both celebrate obsolescence and defeat. The genres also offer hope and justification of a national refounding as well: Ford dramatizes a refounding of the United States in the American West after the massive destruction of the Civil War, appealing to a similarly mourning United States during and after World War II. Kurosawa provides an alternate reading of Japan's defeat at the end of the Pacific War by echoing two former turns in Japanese history that also involved forced modernization and Westernization.

In the postwar, postoccupation setting, when samurai spirit is redirected toward industry and commercial success, Kurosawa capitalizes on the nostalgia for martial masculinity and Japan's older national pride. Just as in the 50s and 60s, the Western films and television shows immortalized the obsolescent but heroic cowboy gunfighter, many *jidaigeki* served to immortalize the ronin as symbol of the Japan that had lost its older, nobler, more martial and stereotypically masculine self. In both cases, heroism and masculinity are pitted against modernization, "civilization," and mercantilism. Kurosawa does not simply portray a nostalgic view. His films, like Ford's, both mourn and commemorate, bury and build this historical mythology.

Kurosawa provides an alternate reading of Japan's defeat at the end of the Pacific War by echoing a former turn in Japanese history that also involved forced modernization and Westernization. During at least three cataclysmic points in Japanese history, samurai were demoted for the sake of progress, and in each case a familiar sense of honor or glory was also sacrificed. Each of these three moments in history featured: (a) a transition from war to peace, (b) forced demilitarization, (c) a new centralization of power, (d) a loss of status for the samurai, and (e) an identity crisis; in the latter two cases, these changes were precipitated by (f) the intrusion of foreign influence. These three moments were the transition from the Sengoku period of feudal war to the Tokugawa period of relative stability; the transition from the Tokugawa rule to the Meiji Restoration and its redefinition of social divisions; and finally, the U.S.-led occupation, coming in the wake of the destruction of Hiroshima and Nagasaki. In the postwar context, where the mass destruction of the atom bombs made any return to the past seem unfathomable, the unconscious appeal of Kurosawa's period films lies in these echoes of similar moments in the past.

Once the warring-states period ended and power was thoroughly consolidated in the hands of the Tokugawa clan, other (non-Tokugawa) samurai were no longer wanted. It was a time of tyranny, but also of relative peace, and the unemployed samurai or ronin was considered a threat to society's stability and—perhaps more directly important—a threat to Tokugawa rule. Samurai, as a rule, knew no trade other than war. They produced no edible or useful products. And their pay had been a fixed amount of rice per month. The Tokugawa government slowly made matters harder and harder for non-Tokugawa samurai, reducing their rations and their status, and many were forced to marry into merchant families. Difference was not tolerated, nor was foreign influence, and one of the prices attached to Tokugawa unification was not only the marginalization of all non-Tokugawa samurai, but also the xenophobic isolation and rigid protection of ranks that characterized Tokugawa rule for two and a half centuries. Like "martial law," Tokugawa rule provided peace at great cost to individual liberties.

The Tokugawa encouraged peaceful occupations for the samurai by publicizing Confucian codes for the samurai, making Bushido more codified than before, and encouraging the samurai to learn the arts of peace as well as the arts of war.[17] Ronin of the Tokugawa period became a token of the past, of obsolescence, an embarrassing reminder of the warring-states period when chaos reigned as feudal (and feuding) clans clashed all over Japan. The Tokugawa ronin was demilitarized, no longer had access to the arts, education, privileges, and servants of the samurai past, and he ended up an itinerant worker, serving successive masters serially for food: a "hired hand" or "hired sword" of sorts. And while in the samurai film there was no "frontier" to be crossed, or "frontier" wilderness to be tamed, daily existence was precarious and temptations abounded for turning bandit or abandoning the Bushido code: it was very tempting to trade honor for the pursuit of wealth, to fight for ignoble causes, or to become a bandit.

One might think that samurai might have fared better in Japan's next major transition, from the Tokugawa era to the Restoration of Emperor Meiji, which served to restore a divine sanction of power. But here all samurai took another large hit and demotion in status. After the Meiji Restoration, the emperor outlawed samurai from wearing swords and ordered that all topknots be cut off, in an attempt to reduce the power and diffuse the identity of the samurai. Marrying between castes was allowed, and several other major steps were taken to modernize the country, including universal education. The emperor in fact cut off his own topknot to demonstrate the antiquity of such forms of distinction, as he continued to demilitarize the samurai class.

After the demilitarization of individual clans in Tokugawa, and the demilitarization of the samurai caste in the Meiji Restoration, Japan suffered demilitarization of its nation in the wake of its defeat in the Pacific War. Astonishingly, the defeat to the U.S.-led powers was Japan's first military defeat in its long recorded history, having defeated both China and Russia only decades earlier. Japan was forced to demilitarize in Article IX of the constitution drafted under General Douglas MacArthur, supreme commander of Japan during the U.S.-led occupation. The relation here to the status of the samurai is less immediately apparent, and yet Japan and Emperor Meiji himself had explicitly hearkened back to samurai glory and codes of honor to enlist and encourage citizens to fight for their nation. Bushido, or the code of the samurai, was a powerful influence on the Japanese army in the war, and Bushido writings, such as the *Hagakure*, by Yamamoto Tsunetomo, were highly motivating to the kamikaze pilots, for example. The emperor served as their "daimyo," or feudal lord, to whom they owed life and obedience.

Emperor Hirohito's public radio broadcasts at the end of the war shaped the memories of a future generation. For the public, this was the first time they heard the emperor's voice, and poignant photographs show audiences bowing to their radios. Hirohito first acknowledged Japan's defeat in the Pacific War on the air and in a second radio broadcast renounced his own divinity, in accord with MacArthur's demands. Ultimately, the defeat and demilitarization in World War II was a third fall for the samurai, as well as for the conception of loyalty and masculinity that had been associated with this martial figure. One could say that with the Meiji Restoration, class distinctions became much more fluid, and with Hirohito's fall as god, every citizen, whether samurai by blood or not, lost his or her daimyo. Just as ronin are unaffiliated samurai who wander without a lord owing to the defeat of their clan, modern Japanese were defeated and disheartened at the loss of their emperor's divine status. It was the content of these radio announcements, as much as any political defeat, that turned Japanese citizens, regardless of rank or class, into psychological ronin after the war.

The tendency to turn to samurai iconography at times of national crisis becomes a pattern, as a reminder of the injuries of the past and also of the glories of the past. But rather than the samurai spirit's having gone extinct, several authors have argued that it merely became displaced. As samurai were forced to take positions as bureaucrats and administrators in Meiji, and then in commerce after Japan's defeat, the samurai spirit was channeled in new ways.[18] The repeated turning to this older iconography of the samurai and the refounding of Japan at times of extremely rapid social change—the

Restoration of the emperor, and the democratic, constitutional Japan after the occupation—suggests, in my view, that the samurai icon continues not only to be a vehicle for self-study, but also to form an important part of Japanese national identity.

The treatment of civil war, defeat, and national transitions in the samurai film reflects several points in time when Japan was refounded. In the Western as well, the choice of time and setting is striking. The majority of Westerns are set between 1865 and 1885—a short time frame when the U.S. Civil War is a recent memory and when the country could be seen as composed of three sections: the North (the Northeast), the South (the Southeast), and the West (the rest of the country). The refounding of the country in the West involved a mixing of opponents from the war. A Confederate might ride a stagecoach or build a homestead next to a Yankee, or vice versa. These designations (as well as ethnic designations) feature prominently in the Western, often forming the bases of initial prejudices to be overcome or strengthened in the course of the film.[19] Yet they also offer hope and justification of the national refounding as well: Ford dramatizes a refounding of the United States in the American West after the massive destruction of the Civil War, thus appealing to his U.S. audience during and after World War II.

Ford has of course inherited both notions of the romantic frontier and the mythology of the wild, wild West from Teddy Roosevelt, Frederick Turner Jackson, and Wild Bill Hickok's Wild West Show. Historical cowboys, on the other hand, were a humble lot of itinerant workers, who herded cattle and helped transport them to post–Civil War markets hungry for meat. The transcontinental railroad (Omaha to Sacramento), completed in 1869, enabled the cow transportation to reach new consumers and drove prices higher. Yet the cowboys were seldom the owners of the cows, and the work was lonely, dirty, difficult, dangerous, and seasonal. As a result, cowboys had unreliable employment and often drifted from ranch to ranch. Western migration started earlier, of course, with the gold rushes, frontier traders, scouts, and explorers, but it was the cowboy that captured the American imagination. Understood this way, depictions of the cowboy are not anachronistic: they are malleable as myth generally is, the content dictated partly by the dominant concerns of the population who uses and reaffirms it. Or said in a different way, anachronism can be an indicator of mythic status.

In the hands of filmmakers, the cowboy hero also hunted for gold, scouted, explored, and rode with the cavalry. His activities increased to incorporate multiple frontier personalities, as his cowboy personality came to stand for the Western frontier experience (John Wayne, for example, played all these roles). Mourning and optimism coincide in these representations of the cowboy hero. Most settings involve characters who have survived the U.S. Civil War and still feel passionately about the cause and their losses. And at the same time, many have also listened to the supposed words of Horace Greeley, "Go West, young man," words that expressed an optimism that frontier spaces could heal urban and political wounds.

In this setting, the obsolescence of the cowboy hero is foreshadowed by the already obsolete soldiers of the Civil War. In fact, often the cowboy hero (frequently a southerner) is in a sense continuing his battle for Right in the West. This cowboy hero feels violated by the outcome of the Civil War and fights on his own for the causes at hand—frequently the protection of private property. Anthony Mann's Westerns are particularly strong in the fusion of defeat, anger, and righteous entitlement. For example the heroes of *Winchester '73* and of *Naked Spur* (both played by Jimmy Stewart) are literally traveling the West to reclaim their (southern) past: the one to earn enough money to purchase the ranch that was stolen from him; the other to kill his father's murderer (who happens to be—we learn this at the end—his own brother). The vengeance for the murder of the father becomes a common plot in the Western, seen from *Stagecoach* (1939) to *True Grit* (1969). In both cases, the West is sought as a balm for past wounds and for the hope it provides of regaining one's antediluvian past. In both of these latter films, the heroes are unable to return to their pasts, even though they (nominally) succeed in their goals and reestablish a (primitive) sense of justice, or at least equity. Once they have lived in the West, they are changed men and can no longer return home. In this way, the ordinary cowboy experience becomes the stuff of national myth.

This is true particularly of films produced between the early 40s and the early 60s, basically from World War II to the onset of the Vietnam War. There is an increase in violence during this subsequent period and a greater fusion of the cowboy hero and the hired gun, as indeed between Kurosawa's samurai hero and the hired ronin in the 60s as well. In the Western of World War II and later, the cowboy as hired hand and hero becomes conflated with the hired gun or outlaw, and sometimes with the renegade army officer. Similarly, in the samurai film the lone ronin or samurai hero often becomes hard to distinguish from bandits or other criminals. The cowboy hero as antihero was born in this period, and the conflict between the hero and political leadership was also intensified.

Both the Western in its post–Civil War setting and the *jidaigeki* in postwar settings mark the transition from war to peace; consequently they simultaneously give tidings of new beginnings for civilization and of obsolescence for the warrior. William Savage's analysis of the cowboy could equally be said of the samurai hero, especially as created by Kurosawa: "The hero exists to evoke a sense of the past, of a time that was better for his having moved through it. His is a tenuous connection with history, but he need have no other. . . . [He is] evocative of a significant period in the American past, and that is his function. . . . The significance of myth—and the reason [the cowboy leads to such dispute]—is that it suggests to Americans what they might have been and what they might yet become."[20] Thus these multiple historical settings both reveal and reawaken feelings of loss and disunion and also offer the opportunity to bury or rechannel these feelings.

Burying the Past

Actual physical gravestones within these films serve as symbols of defeat and mortality on the one hand, and restoration of order on the other. They are multivalent reminders of the delicate distinction between war and peace, in that they represent the memory of violence in the freshness of the past. And while a gravestone can be older, it aids memory through dates commonly appearing prominently on the headstone in the Western, often indicating an unnaturally abbreviated life (sometimes even the murderer is named). It is in fact a rare Western that does not include a gravestone, and generally one that shapes the actions of the main characters of the films, whether it goads them to revenge or to achieve justice more selflessly. As Holly Everett and Kenneth Foote have noted, the grave marking creates sanctified space through the manipulation of the landscape. Both Ford and Kurosawa are keenly aware of this sanctification and raise the question of what exactly is being sanctified in each case.[21]

Examples from *My Darling Clementine* (1946), *She Wore a Yellow Ribbon* (1949), and *The Searchers* (1956) will reveal some of the multiple purposes to which Ford puts the gravestone and its absence in this postwar (and wartime) context.

My Darling Clementine begins with the cattle-driving Earp brothers' arrival in Tombstone, a "wild West" town that has achieved mythical status because of its name—a brash acceptance, if not pride in, its violent history, marked more visually in Boot Hill, its equally infamous cemetery. Shortly after the Earps' arrival, the childlike and innocent youngest brother, James, is shot in the back and murdered by the cattle-rustling Clantons. The camera traces his unburied body mournfully as it lies sprawled in the mud and rain. From the start, Tombstone lives up to its name, as a town unable to forget the past, unwilling to enter a more civilized modernity.

The graveyard theme continues in the first conversation between Wyatt Earp and Doc Holliday. Wyatt remarks, "I could follow your trail from graveyard to graveyard across the country." Within the agonistic economy of the Western, Doc commands respect for his skill and power for having been the victor of so many duels, and yet these graveyards, particularly in postatomic 1946, also ironically show his kinship with the raw brutality of Tombstone and its resident villains, the Clantons. Doc's victories are pyrrhic at best. Doc's graveyards commemorate the superior skills or vitality of the victor and yet also demonstrate his inability to achieve unambiguous victory. This is partially because of his own internal obsession with death, as tuberculosis slowly claims his own life, especially the past he left behind in Boston that pursues him in the form of Clementine Carter. "John Holliday is dead. Everything about him is dead," Doc explains viciously to Clem.

James's grave, prominently announcing his untimely death at eighteen, is placed outside of town, and not on Boot Hill. The choice to bury him where he was shot commemorates the event of his death—the murder itself. The graveside witnesses a touching monologue, as Wyatt talks to the headstone: "I'll be comin' out to see you regular, James. So will Morg and Virg. . . . So boys like you can grow up without fear." Wyatt gives this speech wearing his official new badge as town marshall, although it is an intensely personal moment. As Wyatt rides away, the low-angle shot places the gravestone alongside the spires of Monument Valley. Ford here has taken great efforts to establish the difference between ethically justified retribution and restoration of order (by the Earps) and cowardly and brutal murder (by the Clantons). Wyatt's future killing of the Clantons has been sanctioned by the grave and the monuments, marking Wyatt Earp as a brave and noble hero working in the line of duty. Sentimentality aside, Ford seems in this film to suggest the possibility that the memory of evil, in the right people, can produce the spur to change, offering the possibility to escape the cycle of offense and revenge that establishes feuds. In this film, though, such escape is achieved only through extermination of the entire competing evil clan.

Three years later, in the second installment of his cavalry trio, Ford returns to a graveyard theme in *She Wore a Yellow Ribbon* (1949). A graveyard figures prominently in this film as well—in this case, a set of graves fenced in and decorated with flowering plants. Again the graves are a locus for soliloquy or conversation with the dead, and again they suggest the difficulty of recovering from the memory of death. In this case, an aging Captain Brittle (John Wayne) speaks daily to the graves of his wife and daughters. Captain Brittle plants flowers, waters them, and talks cheerily to his wife, telling her news—their interactions resembling a living room rather than a graveyard. The eerie reddish glow in the studio setting and the use of shadows appearing on the grave suggest the complexity of the emotions surrounding the grave. His family was murdered, and in his forced retirement from the cavalry, Brittle faces losing them a second time. The loss of his ability to commemorate them at graveside physically signifies a second loss of his family. Finally, though, Brittle is able to avoid bloodshed in a standoff with the combined Native American tribes, and he wins reinstatement in the cavalry and a prolonged sojourn with his family graveyard.

In Ford's earliest postwar films, the graves spur the desire for justice in Wyatt Earp and Captain Brittle, respectively. The graves of their relatives reinforce the calling of those who seek to provide protection for the weak, whether as a town-clearing sheriff or as a peace-seeking cavalry officer. In both *My Darling Clementine* and *She Wore a Yellow Ribbon,* the grave signifies an attachment to place that is fueled by past injustice and foretells refounding. In Ford's films from the 50s, however, it is less clear that gravestones can inspire greatness or serve as catalysts for the pursuit of justice. In these later films, Ford critiques the power of memory and explores his greater themes of the cost of mythmaking.

Graveyards have a much different role in *The Searchers* (1956), for example. In the attack on the ranch house that begins the film, the youngest daughter, Debbie, hides in the small household graveyard. The twin graves mark Ethan and Aaron's parents, who have perished in the fragile pioneer existence. The text on the headstones (made of wood) also foreshadows Aaron and his wife's fate: "Here Lies Mary Jane Edwards, killed by Commanches May 12, 1852. A good wife and mother in her 41st year." The father's marker indicates the same date and cause.

The mother orders her daughter to "hide with grandma"—in the graveyard—a plan that they had conceived earlier in the event of attack. It is in this maternally sanctioned graveyard, against the headstone of her grandmother, that the warrior Scar abducts Debbie. His shadow covers Debbie and the headstone, then he looks at her and blows his horn to begin the raid on the house, immediately swooping Debbie up in his arms. She drops her doll, symbolizing the loss of her childhood. The graveyard does not provide the protection that her mother had wished, and Scar's action reads as sacrilege. Subsequently, the family graveyard is expanded to include three additional stone markers and large wooden crosses for Debbie's father, mother, and brother. It is still surrounded by a protective circle of rocks, delineating the space as sanctified, however tenuously.

John Ford's treatment differs from film to film, some more nostalgic for an idyllic Rousseauean past and some emphasizing the Hobbesian brutality of the frontier; however, to achieve the poignancy of the Western myth, he requires both a Rousseauean nostalgia for purer, more heroic times and the brutality that requires taming and cultivation. Without the nostalgia, the Western hero would be able to live comfortably and transition into successful leadership positions in modern society; without the brutality, there would be no need for his brand of charismatic heroism to defeat the powerful and armed villains. Nearly all Westerns evoke a bittersweet sense of transition from one sort of good—namely, a past where heroes could emerge and fight nobly for lost causes—into another, where the brutality of rule by force alone can be replaced by the rule of law. Gravestones paradoxically evoke both the sense of Hobbesian brutality and the nostalgia for a nobler past.

In all of these films, the graves stand in contrast to scenes of brutal carnage, such as the prototypical Indian raid—a burnt stagecoach and corpses in *Fort Apache,* or the raped women and burnt or scalped corpses in *The Searchers.* In this regard, the Western resurrects themes from Sophocles or Euripides: one remembers Antigone, for example, and her unburied brother Polyneices. For these ancient playwrights, burial marked not only belonging and reward, but also a sacred respect paid to common humanity. Not to bury the dead is to fall into animalistic brutality. In this context, the actions of Ethan, the cowboy antihero in *The Searchers,* is particularly shocking. When he encounters a Comanche grave, he shoots the eyes of the dead brave, rendering him unable to join the spirit world and brutally desecrating his grave. Graves are thus mutually desecrated in *The Searchers,* by Scar and especially by Ethan, suggesting the depths of brutality to which racial hatred can lead. In Ethan, the film portrays a stubborn resistance to the burial of past wrongs and the negative potential for memory. Ethan's wandering and hatred will never subside as long as he remembers his wounds. Ultimately these memories prevent him from rejoining his family and society in the final frames of the film.

The oddest case of liminality occurs in *The Man Who Shot Liberty Valance,* where one of the main characters is literally lying in a coffin, dead, for the setting of the entire film, and never even manages to claim a piece of land to sanctify his memory. The diagetic narrative is set in a funeral parlor beside the unburied corpse (where once again the undertaker has shown a callous disregard for an individual by robbing boots from a corpse). The other main characters—Hallie and Ranse—come for a burial that never occurs. Tom (along with his true legendary stature) is buried by words, fulfilling the film's theme of words versus actions. The citified Ranse has to uncover and rebury the past to be able to return to his own life. The choices made to "print the legend" at the end of the film reveal Ford's self-reflective stance as mythmaker. In a tragic inversion, Hallie must fetch and dig up a cactus rose for the coffin, thus placing earth on top of his coffin and commemorating the homestead that he prepares for her and later destroys in his disappointment and anger. Just as *The Man Who Shot Liberty Valance* questions the glorious American frontier myth partly established by Ford's own earlier works, it also here suggests the growing difficulty of commemorating heroism.[22]

Kurosawa uses burial and graves in the same basic humanistic sense: to demonstrate a preservation of basic humanity against our most brutal instincts. In *Seven Samurai* (1954), *Throne of Blood* (1957), *Hidden Fortress* (1958), and *Yôjimbô* (1961), Kurosawa contrasts brutal scenes of carnage or masses of human skeletons against orderly and respectful burial mounds. There are fewer actual graves presented on-screen in Kurosawa's films, yet they lie in stark contrast to scenes such as the dying samurai who enters the frame in the opening of *Hidden Fortress,* only to be stripped and robbed at his death or, at the most extreme, the disembodied hand carried by a dog in *Yôjimbô.* As with Ford, graves mark mortality while restoring order—they both "bury" and "build" the past. Unlike Ford, Kurosawa emphasizes how easily human beings can forget the past, which lends a different tone to his teaching that our humanity is indicated by the way in which we commemorate the dead, remember the past, and prevent the repetition of its terrors.

Individual burial is impossible in an apocalypse. The portrayal of mass casualties in the postwar *jidaigeki* is inseparable from memories of the mass destruction at the end of the Pacific War. Postbattle scenes of devastation are uncomfortably close to photographs of postatomic devastation in Hiroshima and Nagasaki. No commemoration (or often even recognition) of the individual is possible under such circumstances, and the distinction between *jidaigeki* and contemporary newsreel diminishes uncomfortably. *Hidden Fortress* also begins with offscreen mass burials and anonymous graves—a seemingly unending task from which the two peasants wish to escape.

Kurosawa's masterpiece *Seven Samurai* (1954) ends with gravestones as prominent as the ones in Ford's Westerns, where gravestones echo the spires of his favorite Monument Valley. Kurosawa's background of the four fallen ronin again establishes a pyrrhic victory. The ronin served as samurai to their farmer-employers, fulfilled their promise to the farmers, showed their remarkable skill and courage, and won the battle against the bandits, at great cost to themselves. The tragedy of the final scenes is not so much the burial of the ronin who fell in battle, but rather the symbolic burial (or forgetting) of the remaining ronin. Now that the violent deeds have been accomplished, the farmers want nothing else to do with the ronin; their business is attending to the land and the future. The knowledge that their peace depends upon the actions of these military men embarrasses and frightens the farmers.

Interestingly, the graves for the fallen ronin are not stone graves, but rather something much less permanent. They are mounds of dirt on top of a hill, marked only by the ronin's swords and by banners. The graves are thus notably temporary: the dirt will spread, the banners will blow away, and the swords are ready to be stolen by any desperate, dishonorable, or (depending on one's moral code) enterprising peasant. The ending thus reestablishes a divide between the farmer-peasants and the samurai—now once again ronin. One of the distinguishing features of the farmers and their life force is that the farmers are capable of forgetting the past and starting anew, turning their backs on the graves and even on the live ronin who fought for them. The transition from war to peace again causes the samurai class to lose its identity and place in society.

In *Throne of Blood* (1957), Kurosawa transposes and adapts Shakespeare's *Macbeth* to a sixteenth-century Sengoku-period setting in Japan. In early scenes of *Throne of Blood*, one orderly monument contrasts with piles of anonymous skeletons. This monument stands to commemorate a castle, rather than an individual. In the opening scene of the film, we see a long shot of a wooden marker, with the words "Here stood Spiderweb Castle."

This post emerges from fog and darkness to set the tone for the film. The final frames of the film return to the same long shot, suggesting a cyclical time scheme. The title of the film is literally "Kumonosujo," or Spiderweb Castle, suggesting a more metaphysical meaning, more detached from individual choices and the individual personage, temptations, and opportunities of Macbeth. In the context of this film, the cyclical time scheme indicates the perpetuation of war, or the perpetual recurrence of human tyranny, greed, and violence.

Kurosawa sets up the entire film as an act of remembrance, fulfilling the function of the wooden marker. Whereas in *Seven Samurai,* the farmer's capacity for forgetting comes as a shock to the samurai (and the viewer), in *Throne of Blood,* we are better prepared for the outcome—or rather, the outcome is assumed from the beginning. The suggestion is also that the viewer of the razed landscape would not necessarily know of the history that occurred in the land. Without the marker, there would be no visual memory of events, and there would then be no possibility for a sense of repetition of human affairs and war. In the Buddhist perspective that permeates this film, Kurosawa shows the unchanging nature of the human world and the perpetual cycles of violence from which it is essential to achieve detachment. The film may also indicate that only through knowledge of history and the recognition of cycles and repetition can we ever hope to recognize our human condition.

Kurosawa also uses the presence of coffins in his films to exhibit a liminal stage between a state of lawlessness (indicated by carnage) and civil society (suggested by permanent graveyards). This liminality is brought to the fore in *Yôjimbô* (echoing Zinnemann's *High Noon*), where the constant hammering of coffin-makers draws attention to the most successful commercial business in town, literally establishing the new at the cost of the old and often callously anticipating deaths before they occur. Yet the unnamed town in *Yôjimbô* is far worse, its respect for humanity foreshadowed in the scene of a dog carrying the dismembered hand. The liminal stage between exposed corpse and marked burial ground is most cleverly explored in *Yôjimbô,* in which the eponymous hero is "buried" in a coffin and experiences a kind of return from the dead, or reincarnation. And yet, the graveyard, or tombstone, suggests a greater separation from the moment of death than a coffin. While coffins are buried and hidden, graveyards and tombstones commemorate and remind viewers of what should not be forgotten. The separation of time causes part of the pain that graves invoke. Time has elapsed since the wrong that occurred, and generally the viewer is meant to feel this gap along with the central character viewing the grave.

For both directors, memory (especially memory of violence) is a crucial means for mythopoiesis, or mythmaking, and a foundation for a national identity. Benedict Andersen, in the second edition of his *Imagined Communities: Reflections on the Origin and Spread of Nationalism,* includes a section titled "The Biography of Nations," which explains the ways in which a nation develops a sense of national identity out of disparate events, especially deaths. Taking Fernand Braudel as an example, Andersen writes: "The nation's biography snatches . . . exemplary suicides, poignant martyrdoms, assassinations, executions, wars, and holocausts. But to serve the narrative purpose, these violent deaths must be remembered/forgotten as 'our own.'"[23] So too, the deaths of heroic ronin in Kurosawa's works and individual heroic cowboys serve in these two genres to make sense of national history and purpose in a postwar world, where viewers are struggling for order and hoping that their recent sacrifices have not been in vain.

Both also recognize mythmaking as crucial to the restoration of order. *Hidden Fortress* and *She Wore a Yellow Ribbon* offer the two directors' most optimistic portrayals of these themes—and they are among the few films in this genre that allow a possibility to end a cycle of violence without mass extinction of the enemy. Ford, in his later films, is most concerned with the distortion and impersonality that arises with mythmaking and "print[ing] the legend," as well as the difficulty of overcoming the wounds and divisions that are too deeply embedded in society, such as racism (as in *The Searchers*). Kurosawa's primary distinction tends to be between the brutality of individuals or a society that fails to bury its corpses (as in the demon reference in the beginning of *Throne of Blood*) and the human blindness of burying too successfully, figuratively speaking, at the cost of memory. Kurosawa reminds us how easy it is to forget the past and that our humanity is indicated by the way in which we commemorate the dead, remember the past, and prevent repetition of its atrocities.

Notes

This essay was written with the assistance of a Chapman Family Teaching Fellowship at the Institute of Arts and Humanities at the University of North Carolina at Chapel Hill, as well as generous funding from the Earhart Foundation. I wish to thank Chandran Kukhathas and Douglas Den Uyl for first introducing me to the political philosophy of

Westerns, Caroline Kirby for inspiring my interest in the visual commemoration of war, and Robert Pippin and Debra Romanick Baldwin for their encouragement.

1. A ronin is literally a "wave-man," wandering without a commitment to a particular daimyo or cause.

2. Richard Slotkin, *Gunfighter Nation: The Myth of the Frontier in Twentieth-Century America* (Norman: University of Oklahoma Press, 1998).

3. See Benedict Andersen, *Imagined Communities: Reflections on the Origin and Spread of Nationalism* (London: Verso, 2006), 204–6.

4. David Desser, "Toward a Structural Analysis of the Postwar Samurai Film," *Quarterly Review of Film Studies* 8, no. 1 (Winter 1983): 25–41.

5. Darrell William Davis, *Picturing Japaneseness: Monumental Style, National Identity, Japanese Film* (New York: Columbia University Press, 1996), 66–68.

6. Ibid., 87.

7. Kyoko Hirano, *Mr. Smith Goes to Tokyo: Japanese Cinema under the American Occupation, 1945–1952* (New York: Smithsonian Books, 1994), 41.

8. Ibid., 67–70.

9. Akira Kurosawa, *Something like an Autobiography*, trans. Audie E. Bock (New York: Vintage, 1983), 118.

10. Slotkin, *Gunfighter Nation*, 332.

11. Ibid., 335.

12. According to the IMDb, www.imdb.com/name/nm0000406/?ref_=tt_ov_dr. Accessed March 15, 2013.

13. Slotkin, *Gunfighter Nation*, 340.

14. Ibid., 489–97.

15. Inger S. B. Brodey, "Cactus Roses and Camellias: Flowers, Action, and Masculinity in Sanjurô and *The Man Who Shot Liberty Valance*," *U.S.-Japan Women's Journal* 36 (2009): 3–27.

16. S. A. Thornton, *The Japanese Period Film: A Critical Analysis* (Jefferson, NC: McFarland, 2008).

17. Rick Fields, *The Code of the Warrior in History, Myth, and Everyday Life* (New York: Harper Collins, 1991).

18. "The Meiji Restoration brought the political and ethical structure of feudal time intact into the industrializing modern Japan." Joan Mellen, *Waves at Genji's Door* (New York: Pantheon, 1976), 7.

19. See Robert Pippin, *The Hollywood Western and the American Myth: The Importance of Howard Hawks and John Ford for Political Philosophy* (New Haven, CT: Yale University Press, 2012).

20. William W. Savage, *The Cowboy Hero: His Image in American History and Culture* (Norman: University of Oklahoma Press, 1979), 38.

21. Holly J. Everett, in *Roadside Crosses in Contemporary Memorial Culture* (Denton: University of North Texas, 2002), writes: "Sanctification involves the creation of

sacred space by physical manipulation of the landscape, whether it be the institution of a memorial plaque, garden, or building, and is usually inspired by disaster or heroic death" (7). In this train of thought, she is building upon the work of another cultural geographer, Kenneth Foote, especially his *America's Landscapes of Violence and Tragedy* (Austin: University of Texas Press, 1997).

22. For more on the treatment of the American Myth and heroism in this film, please see Brodey, "Cactus Roses and Camellias."

23. Andersen, *Imagined Communities,* 206.

Part 3

The Ethical Tribulations of War

The Ubiquitous Absence of the Enemy in Contemporary Israeli War Films

Holger Pötzsch

Israeli war films such as *Beaufort* (*Bufor;* Joseph Cedar, 2007), *Waltz with Bashir* (*Vals im Bashir;* Ari Folman, 2008), and *Lebanon* (*Levanon;* Samuel Maoz, 2009) have been welcomed as critical antiwar films that not only set out to realistically convey the suffering and meaninglessness of war but also, and in particular in the case of Folman's film, openly address the responsibility of the Israeli military for tolerating, facilitating, or even committing atrocities. Even though these readings appear justifiable to a certain extent, the present essay directs attention to a constitutive lack in the universes of all the mentioned films that partly undermines readings of them as antiwar movies—the consistent absence of the Arab or Palestinian other. Does this absence in the universes of allegedly antiwar movies point to a pervasive militarism—a scopic regime of war—that veils the enemy's competing position and tacitly influences even cultural expressions that overtly attempt to challenge or oppose an ingrained war discourse of othering and exclusion?

Cognitive Film Theory and Tacit Frames of War

Cognitive film theory often focuses on hardwired, embodied, and affective responses to the filmic experience.[1] Nevertheless, this strain of film theory also allows for attention to the textual frames through which more reflected and narratively contextualized responses are motivated. Film reception is perceived as the result of audiences' active engagement with textually delivered cues or indices, which, dependent on the degree of structuration and closure of the given text, systematically invite the production of certain meanings.[2] The formal properties of texts constrain spectators' interpretative activities and, in this way, predispose certain tendencies of meaning yet do not determine the process of reception.

Film reception happens on the basis of latent schemata and paradigm scenarios that are activated in, and through, certain indices that cue possible engagements. Preestablished cognitive schemata and paradigm scenarios not only frame conceptualizations of, and responses to, diegetic universes and events, but also kick in when unprecedented real-world incidents are engaged. The response patterns that are established and maintained in and through interaction with expressions of popular culture do, as such, also influence the paradigm of what appear to be possible initial reactions to challenges encountered in real life. In this understanding lies the core of the political and societal significance of fiction, including the fiction film.

Scholars such as Murray Smith, Carl Plantinga, and Margrethe Bruun-Vaage[3] have argued for a "saliency of character"[4] in the process of film reception. Being an inherently embodied and emotional endeavor, character engagement is an important aspect of the way film influences the viewer and wider sociopolitical frames. As a consequence, attention to the technical and narrative devices through which such responses are elicited, maintained, and framed becomes an important field of film studies. Moral, emotional, or other engagements with certain characters predispose viewer allegiances and vicariously position these viewers within diegetic discursive frames that tacitly pattern cognitive schemata and thus predispose conceptualizations, attitudes, and performances.

On the basis of Murray Smith's work, I have recently shown how generic Hollywood war films establish a biased structure of engagement that consists of sets of formal textual cues that invite audience *alignment* and *allegiance* with characters who belong predominantly to one of the depicted conflicting parties.[5] Close-ups of faces, sequences in slow motion, and shots that dwell on individual characters predispose viewers for various forms of engagement with particular protagonists or groups. At the same time, dialogues, voice-over thoughts, flashback sequences, slow motion, and the deployment of sad and valorizing musical tunes facilitate an emotional, intellectual, and moral involvement with these characters' fates and performances.[6]

I have argued that the moral universe of a majority of war films is structured around the trope of the ubiquitously absent enemy—an opponent who largely remains invisible and inaccessible, yet who is at the same time framed as an unambiguous, deadly threat.[7] The identified audiovisual rhetoric frames the lives and subjectivities of the enemy-other as irrelevant. At the same time, narrative tropes such as the *evil deed*—"some harrowing, great atrocity committed by the enemy-other and witnessed by the soldier-self"[8]—reiterate the threatening and remorseless nature of this enemy and provide implicit justification for the acts of extreme violence committed by the main protagonists. This way, a narrative situation is established where empathy with protagonists who are engaged in the massive killing of others is enabled and systematically motivated. The depicted violence is framed as without alternative and directed against an unquestionable and immediate threat. As a result it becomes pleasurable and does not undermine allegiance with key characters.

Even though Torben Grodal is surely right in claiming that the apparently timeless attraction violent films have for predominantly male audiences is probably grounded in the continued salience of perceptual apparatuses and cognitive schemata that have been formed in and through a life as hunter-gatherer that lasted millennia, basic biological faculties alone cannot account for spectators' moral and intellectual engagement on behalf of only one side in a depicted conflict.[9] Therefore, attention to formal textual devices that restrain innate capacities of reception and channel involuntary affective mimicry into particular directions is a crucial area of contemporary approaches to film and the various effects it has on individuals and collectives. The biased predisposition of allegiance toward only one of the depicted conflict parties constitutes the core of mainstream war films' potential cultural and political impact.

I have recently argued that allegiance to characters implies a vicarious positioning of the spectator within diegetic discursive frames.[10] This vicarious positioning, however, does not determine the process of reception in the last instance, but merely motivates the reproduction of particular tendencies of meaning. To assert that a passive audience might more easily adhere to the dominant readings suggested by the formal properties of a given text is not the same as asserting the passivity of all audiences in all possible contexts of reception. Dominant tendencies of meaning can, and always will, be challenged and possibly subverted by active overdetermined or even "perverse" spectators.[11] Nevertheless, the formal properties of (filmic) texts that articulate hegemonic subject positions will push reception into a direction that, on average, rather reinforces than challenges the hegemonic frames and dominant cognitive patterns from which the filmic texts emanate.

A thorough attention to the formal properties of a given filmic or other text enables a systematic and empirically grounded approach to possible effects of cultural expressions on politics and society. In most generic war films, sets of cues and indices activate, draw upon, and reinforce cognitive schemata that tacitly influence possible conceptualizations of, and responses to, diegetic as well as real-world opponents and challenges. As such, these textual devices partake in the reproduction and reinforcement of medial "frames of war" that render the competing subjectivities and understandings of the other irrelevant and their lives "ungrievable" in the sense offered by Judith Butler.[12] This is why these textual structures and the corresponding cognitive frames and schemata merit our continuous critical attention.[13]

After a brief overview of the history of the Israeli war film, I will engage the question whether or not *Beaufort, Waltz with Bashir,* and *Lebanon,* in spite of their overtly critical thrust, at an underlying level implicitly reinforce such exclusionary schemata and frames. Are the particular imageries and formal devices of these films tacitly predisposed by a largely invisible, yet pervasive, militarism that informs even cultural expressions that attempt to challenge and undermine belligerent understandings of possible relations between self and other?

The Israeli War Film

Unsurprisingly, the way Israeli films treat the issue of war has changed in correspondence with historical, sociopolitical, and cultural trends and developments. In her seminal study of Israeli cinema, Ella Shohat distinguishes three major phases of Israeli war cinema: a pre-1967 heroic-nationalist genre, a post-1967 heroic-nationalist genre, and a more critically inflected political cinema of the late 1970s and the 1980s.[14] According to her, the first two phases put considerable emphasis on individual sacrifice for the sake of a collective and articulate individual soldiers' identities into preconceived nationalist and Zionist frames. The victory in the 1967 war, Shohat argues further, added a notion of grandeur to the depicted characters and events and facilitated the adoption of the visual and narrative style of Hollywood action cinema that toned down the issue of often tragic sacrifice on behalf of a reified collective; that victory led instead to an increased focus on the individual and the emergence of Rambo-style military superheroes. According to Shohat, a third phase during the late 1970s and the 1980s entailed a more critical and overtly political cinematic engagement with the issue of war. Fueled by the negative experiences of the Yom Kippur and the first Lebanon wars, Israeli films from this period exhibit a more critical stance toward military thinking and practice and direct considerable attention to the often-unintended negative consequences of military campaigns.[15]

Within the discourse of classical Israeli war cinema, soldiers are not framed as tragic individual victims of inherently traumatic war experiences, but as the collective personification of a sacrifice on behalf of state and nation. As such, Raz Yosef observes that in these films "the death of the warrior was endorsed and justified by being given a greater and more general national, and thus transcendent, meaning," while Ella Shohat points out that in pre- and post-1967 Israeli war cinema, "the death of the protagonists . . . is allegorically compensated for by the rebirth of the country."[16] Both authors connect this figure of a "living dead" soldier to the thought of Benedict Andersen, who asserts the importance of monuments dedicated to anonymous soldiers for groups that are reliant upon a common imagination yet lack a shared base of everyday experience.[17] In this context the figure of the empty grave of the anonymous soldier who has sacrificed his life for the sake of the community functions as an empty master signifier that enables varied articulations within given frames of meaning and belonging.[18]

During the 1980s and 1990s, Israeli cinema more critically engages Israeli society and the various wars fought by the country throughout its existence as an independent nation. According to Judd Ne'eman, *Paratroopers* (*Masa Alunkot;* Judd Ne'eman, 1978) inaugurates a new phase in the cinematic treatment of war. He presents the movie as "the first antiheroic army film, [which] set the stage for a dozen antiwar films that followed." Similarly, Ne'eman argues further, films such as *The Wooden Gun* (Ilan Moshenson, 1978) exhibit a new "dystopian view of Zionism" and constitute an explicit challenge to established hegemonic discourses of the nation.[19] According to Ella Shohat, films of this critical political phase frame the Israeli soldier as a victim of military culture and political mismanagement and start to direct attention to the negative consequences of an ingrained culture of war.[20]

In later studies of Israeli cinema, scholars such as Ilan Avisar, Uri S. Cohen, and Raz Yosef have added a fourth phase to the three-phase distinction introduced by Ella Shohat.[21] They argue that contemporary Israeli war film combines individual psychological introspection with a continued challenge to received nationalist and Zionist frames. This "personal cinema"[22] entails an exploration of the psychological impacts of warfare on individuals and collectives and brings into sight the "traumatic events" that "have been denied entry into a shared national past."[23] As such, in recent Israeli war cinema, death and suffering of the soldier are rearticulated as aspects of individual life stories rather than as the basis for a binding collective experience or for political criticism.

Contemporary Israeli war films direct increasing attention to the apparently pointless suffering and ordeals of individual soldiers and the long-lasting social and psychological consequences of traumatic war experiences. According to Eran Kaplan, this leads to a fundamental reconceptualization of the figure of the Israeli soldier as the "helpless victim of irrational and indiscriminate violence," whose sacrifice and death remain without meaning or overarching justification. Bringing the representation of the Israeli soldier "from hero to victim," these films leave the stabilizing frames of nation and politics behind and focus on the physically or mentally scarred individual.[24] Correspondingly, as Yael Munk observes, recent Israeli war films "reveal a distancing from . . . national ethos and [entail] a privatization of war memories that opened the way to the appearance of individual trauma and legitimized its public discussion."[25]

The three films discussed in this essay fall into this same category; they all follow the story of individual Israeli soldiers and articulate their intimate war memories and traumas connected to the First Lebanon War.[26] The fates and life trajectories of these young men are not framed by a discourse of heroic sacrifice "on the nation's altar"[27] but are left to stand without legitimating frames as ultimately endured in vain. The films thus level an at times harsh criticism against Israeli military command and political leadership.

Nevertheless, in spite of this inherently critical thematic thrust, at one level of analysis, all the films discussed in this essay ultimately play into the very hegemonic frames of war they allegedly set out to challenge. The formal cinematic and narrative devices deployed in *Beaufort, Lebanon,* and *Waltz with Bashir* set up a biased structure of engagement that systematically invites audience allegiance with Israeli soldiers and puts these up against a faceless and desubjectified enemy-other, the deaths of which are made to appear necessary to ensure the survival of the involved protagonists. As such, an imposed struggle for survival between two mutually exclusive entities is established as a frame for moral judgment and ethical or emotional involvement from the side of the audience. I will argue that this inherently belligerent discourse of "us against them" partly undermines the subversive potentials of the autobiographical antiwar narratives in that it precludes an unbiased historical and political contextualization of the depicted violence and suffering.

Textual Frames: Ubiquitously Absent Enemies in Three Recent Israeli War Films

The three war movies under scrutiny in the present essay have been hailed for their critical treatment of military institutions and practices and for their ability to cast light upon the meaninglessness and devastating consequences of warfare. Raz Yosef remarks that *Beaufort, Waltz with Bashir,* and *Lebanon* "mark one of the most interesting phenomena in contemporary Israeli cinema," while Yael Munk asserts that these films "express a new historiographical stance regarding Israel's national narrative" that "bring[s] back the repressed war discourse."[28]

Indeed, critics have commended all three films for an alleged critical stance toward the practice of warfare. Joseph Cedar's *Beaufort* (2007), for instance, was greeted as an "antiwar movie . . . that traffics in the mad illogics of battles whose long-forgotten purpose has hardened into mindless routine"—a film that constitutes "the summa of . . . Israeli antiwar cinematic culture."[29] In a similar vein, Samuel Maoz's *Lebanon* (2009) has been praised as a "nonheroic vision of warfare focusing on claustrophobia, confusion, fear and other emotions experienced by four soldiers who are far from battle-hardened"[30]—a "powerful antiwar film" that centers attention "on the emotional traumas of wars that can never be romanticized or whose terrors can be blithely ignored."[31] Also *Waltz with Bashir* (2008) has received positive criticism. Raz Yosef, for instance, writes that Folman's film "highlights and exposes a traumatic rupture between history . . . and memory" and that it provides access to "lost and forgotten memories of the horrors of the First Lebanon War," while Gil Hochberg asserts that *Waltz with Bashir* "offers an uncompromising interrogation of wars' seductive spectacular character" that demands an "ethical spectatorship."[32]

How fitting is the description of *Beaufort, Lebanon,* and *Waltz with Bashir* as antiwar films?[33] The three movies doubtlessly present a sobering account of the Lebanon War and its aftermath. They articulate a postheroic image of the Israeli soldier and focus on individual suffering and meaningless death, rather than altruistic sacrifice in the name of the nation. However, as Raz Yosef remarks, "their [*Beaufort*'s, *Waltz with Bashir*'s, and *Lebanon*'s] emphasis on the subjective dimension of memories and experiences of war distances these films from the war's historical context . . . and leads them into an atemporal zone marked by symbols and private hallucinations."[34] In this private archive of war, the enemy-other remains without a place.

The fact that the Palestinian other remains largely invisible and inaccessible in the three films mentioned here proves somewhat problematic for their presentation as antiwar movies. The selective gaze and susceptibility of camera and microphone preclude access to the enemy-other's subjectivity and competing frames of meaning and understanding and thereby undermine potentials for nonviolent exchange. Rather, in these movies the enemy merely asserts a largely implied, indirect presence in the form of sudden shots fired without apparent source, shells emanating from nowhere, or explosions caused by devices laid out by unseen enemies. As a consequence, the traumatic nature of war is framed as predominantly resulting from a form of "abandonment" of young men by their superiors, rather than as grounded in the killing or maiming of fellow human beings.[35]

In all three films, the diegetic world is entirely focalized through Israeli soldiers. Cinematic devices such as eye-line matches that combine close-ups of individual faces with the object of the implied gaze, shot/reverse shot sequences on protagonists that interconnect voices and faces in a dialogue situation, and the use of voice-over thought, as well as flashback and dream sequences, exclusively denote the perspective, attitudes, and inner world of Israeli soldiers or veterans. In this way, the formal structures of the three films cue audience alignment with only one side in the depicted conflict. Devices such as shots dwelling on suffering individuals, slow motion, sad or valorizing music, and flashback or dream sequences that provide access to the tragic fates and inner lives of exclusively Israeli soldiers translate this biased alignment into biased allegiances—long-term emotional, moral, and ideological attachments by audiences to particular characters. In this way, I argue, these films implicitly draw upon and constantly reiterate exclusionary paradigm scenarios and schemata that subsequently contribute to a cognitive predisposition toward real-world engagements with actual or potential enemies.

Lebanon follows a tank crew of four young recruits on their way into Lebanon during the First Lebanon War. Maoz's film exhibits an innovative audiovisual regime. The entire film is shot inside the Israeli tank; it provides access to the outside world only through the tunnel view of the tank's scope. The scope is capable of extreme close-ups on certain details of the tank's immediate surroundings, but it consistently fails to deliver an overarching perspective that could orient protagonists or spectators within the wider topography of the depicted conflict. While capable of allegorically pointing to the limited and limiting scopic regimes of war at a general level, the selective blindness of the main protagonists is reduced to the individual traumatizing experience of four Israeli soldiers unwillingly and unintentionally deployed into the estranged, threatening, and incomprehensible environment of Lebanon.[36]

During the full length of the film, the four main protagonists remain captured in the claustrophobic confines of the machine. Camera and microphone consistently align the spectator with these soldiers' point of view and implicate the viewer in their extremely limited physical as well as epistemological condition. The selective gaze of the tank's scope is the only perspective on the events provided and makes the men constantly oscillate between blindness and the enhanced ability to zoom in on certain details of their otherwise elusive surroundings. Even though the temporary presence of a Palestinian captive and a Phalangist officer in the tank briefly alerts the viewer to the wider frames of the historical context, the short dialogue, which is hampered by language problems, points toward the innocence and naïveté of young Israeli conscripts unable to understand the consequences of their own actions, rather than implying an Israeli co-responsibility for atrocious war crimes. The attempted dialogue certainly does not enable access to the grievances and political objectives that might justify, or at least give meaning to, the positions and performances of the opposing party.

In the course of events, the tank comes under repeated attack from unseen enemies. Unable to locate the opponents or find their way back, the men inside are forced to passively endure the violence, rather than being able to efficiently retaliate or retreat to safety. As such, in *Lebanon* the main protagonists are victimized for their inability to actively engage an unseen enemy or to retreat to safety, rather than for the violence committed against other human beings. This frame makes the film articulate an exclusionary discourse of war that is vested in the implied necessity of fighting a largely invisible enemy.

The problem in *Lebanon* is not only that camera and microphone hardly ever provide access to the other—civilian or otherwise—but also the way the other, once it appears on-screen, is framed. For instance, when the camera catches sight of a Lebanese victim—an almost naked woman who mindlessly staggers through the rubble of her house in search of her children—she is not put into a position to articulate a competing frame of meaning and action that might serve to dislodge an underlying exclusionary and polarizing discourse of war. Rather, the victim appears as an object. The tank-scope camera zooms in on the woman and implicates the spectator in a voyeuristic perspective on the suffering other, before a benevolent Israeli soldier covers her with a blanket and leads her aside. The trauma of the tank crew in *Lebanon,* as such, appears not as a result of the violence they are forced to commit as soldiers, but is due to sufferings caused by an anonymized form of violence without agent that these soldiers are forced to witness.

Correspondingly, the only visible death of an innocent bystander directly inflicted by the main protagonists—a Lebanese chicken farmer approaching the tank in his car—is explained with reference to the previous inability of the tank's gunner to fire at an approaching vehicle that then killed one of his fellow soldiers. In this way, not the act of killing itself, but the inability to do so in situations where it is required becomes the core of the trauma of war. The questions whether killing the other really is a necessity, who commands the killing, and whether there are alternative ways of relating to the opponent remain unanswered and are, indeed, not even posed in Maoz's film.

In *Lebanon* the Israeli soldiers are "imagined as lost children, helpless victims trapped in a tank in hostile surroundings."[37] By means of this narrative frame, the violence unleashed by the Israeli forces appears justified from the outset with reference to an unambiguously violent imminent threat by an invisible, faceless, and voiceless Palestinian enemy. The Israeli soldiers apparently merely stumble into the conflict with no other intentions but to get home alive as soon as possible. Even though this notion might capture well the experiences that Israeli veterans recall from this particular war, exclusive focus on their individual psychology sets up an exclusionary frame that prevents the Palestinian other's perspective and subjectivity from emerging within the moral universe of the film. Besides functioning as objectified victim, the other remains an unequivocal threat, the mere existence of which frames all the experienced hardships and sufferings as ultimately born of necessity. Slavoj Žižek argues accordingly that Maoz's film "is ideology at its purest: the focus on the perpetrator's traumatic experience enables us to obliterate the entire ethico-political background of the conflict. . . . We are there, with our boys, identifying with their fear and anguish instead of questioning what they are doing."[38]

Also in *Beaufort* a biased distribution of camera and speech invites alignment to and allegiance with Israeli soldiers alone. Repeated shot/reverse shot sequences support dialogues between protagonists that provide subjective access to their individual life stories, political attitudes, and personal traits. These means provide familiarity with the men who are caught up in a bunker on Lebanese soil as the last remnants of an Israeli army about to retreat from southern Lebanon. In particular, in sequences where Israeli soldiers are killed or wounded, lingering shots strongly motivate allegiance with the surviving men, who try in vain to keep their comrades alive and who mourn their meaningless deaths. By these means an emotional and intellectual engagement with the Israeli main protagonists is systematically facilitated.

As in *Lebanon,* in Cedar's *Beaufort* trauma is inflicted by an invisible other that kills indiscriminately from a distance. Throughout the whole film, not one enemy appears on-screen—they are ubiquitously absent, constantly attacking from virtually everywhere, yet at the same time entirely inaccessible. The film never extends the frame to reveal the political rationale behind, or grievances underlying, the deployed violence. The viewer is predisposed to align and ally with the Israeli men enduring anonymized hardships of war.

In *Beaufort,* the experience of being targeted by a "totally invisible enemy" only develops into full-fledged trauma when the Israeli soldiers are prohibited from effectively retaliating.[39] Military command denies them permission to sweep the surrounding areas for the purpose of not jeopardizing the commencing Israeli disengagement from Lebanon. As such, rather than explaining the political rationale behind, and the historical context of, the Israeli retreat, *Beaufort* frames a politics of appeasement as a form of deceit or betrayal of the victimized Israeli trooper suffering on the ground without the required support by civilian and military authorities.

Yael Munk rightly asserts that *Beaufort* undermines key "military pedagogic values" centered on the will to die for the sake of a wider collective.[40] Through its focus on the ultimate meaninglessness of soldiers' suffering and death and its attention to the growing distance between the soldier on the ground and the military and political leadership, Cedar's film indeed challenges such key military norms and values. Munk, however, does not explain how the film's focus on individual traumatic abandonment can challenge the implied necessity to kill the enemy that is a constitutive element of the same military pedagogics. On the contrary, I argue that one major point made in *Beaufort* is that military life and ethos lose their meaning precisely when the soldiers' urge to confront the enemy on the battlefield is not met with corresponding orders from military command and political leadership.

In Cedar's film, retreat for the sake of appeasement becomes a source of trauma. The diplomatic and political restraints that force the military to avoid further bloodshed are presented as preventing the soldiers from doing a meaningful job and dying a meaningful death—the form of "abandonment" outlined by Raz Yosef.[41] As a consequence, within the discursive frames of *Beaufort,* it is not ingrained militarism and civilian casualties that appear as the core of the problem, but civilian restraints that prevent the military machinery from functioning properly when attacked by faceless enemies, and a retreat that renders the sacrifices on behalf of territorial extension meaningless.

In contrast to the two films discussed above, Folman's *Waltz with Bashir* seems to present a more complex picture of the First Lebanon War. According to Katrina Schlunke, the animated documentary that is centered on the individual war memories of an Israeli veteran puts considerable emphasis on the suffering other. Schlunke argues that *Waltz with Bashir* is "unreal enough to make the reality of death true while preserving space of what cannot be entirely known or shown—the death of others."[42] Indeed, the sudden intrusion of real-life footage of Palestinian victims of the Sabra and Shatila massacre into the drawn representation of often disparate and erratic individual recollections recounted by Israeli veterans constitutes "more than a formal capitulation to routine verité."[43] Rather, as I have argued in an earlier article, the photographic evidence presented at the end of Folman's film "connects contingent reconstructions to a concrete material basis . . . and adds a notion of necessity and verifiability to constructions of historical narratives."[44] Or, in Garrett Stewart's words: "Burst through the labors of animated reconstruction is the true archive of terror—and the final trope of recognition."[45] Indeed, in the end *Waltz with Bashir* provides a prominent place for the innocent Palestinian victim and acknowledges some form of tacit support of the massacre by the Israeli Defence Force. The Palestinian enemy, however, remains faceless and speechless throughout the whole narrative, which, similar to *Lebanon* and *Beaufort,* predominantly presents Israeli soldiers as the ultimate victims of the First Lebanon War.

Raz Yosef has pointed out that *Waltz with Bashir* can be criticized for not dealing "with the trauma of the Palestinian victim but, rather, with that of the Israeli bystander." As such, according to Yosef, Folman's film initiates a fundamental "reversal between perpetrator and victim" regarding the First Lebanon War.[46] Also Jonathan Murray accuses *Waltz with Bashir* of sidelining the Palestinian experience and of "psychologiz[ing] a complex political event": "[The] microcosmic sense of individual Israelis being involved but somehow not fully implicated in, accidental victims of rather than active vehicles for, the horrors of the Lebanon War preempts *Waltz with Bashir*'s climactic, self-exonerating depiction of the Sabra and Shatila massacres. These become the fundamental moral responsibility of someone else, whether the Phalangist militia or isolated individuals far higher up the Israeli chain of command than Folman and his comrades."[47]

Even though posing the question whether or not *Waltz with Bashir* authentically represents the role of Israeli ground forces in the Sabra and Shatila massacres appears fully legitimate, I argue that Yosef's and Murray's criticisms miss a crucial point. The real-life sequence at the end of Folman's film clearly frames the Palestinian other as the ultimate victim, a fact that Murray also reluctantly acknowledges, even though he doubts the director's intentionality.[48] What remains consistently excluded, however, is the alternative perspective of the Palestinian opponents—their competing rationale and frames of meaning that might explain and provide certain legitimacy to their actions and thereby undermine a hegemonic Israeli war discourse that is based on the constitutive exclusion of a confined or caricatured enemy-other.[49]

Similar to the films by Maoz and Cedar, *Waltz with Bashir* exclusively focalizes the events through the minds, eyes, and ears of Israeli soldiers and veterans. The camera almost exclusively provides access to their suffering, fears, pain, and hopes. In this way, the formal structure of engagement of Folman's film systematically invites alignment and allegiance with these protagonists and excludes access to an increasingly obscured other.

This pervasive invisibility of the Palestinian other can, to a certain extent, be explained with reference to the fact that *Waltz with Bashir* (similar to *Beaufort* and *Lebanon*) is about the individual traumatic memories of a group of Israeli soldiers and, as such, never aspired to provide a comprehensive framework for an understanding of the conflict and all involved groups and individuals. This seems to be a viable argument. The lack of attention to the enemy-other becomes palpable on more than one register, however. The main problem with *Waltz with Bashir* is not only a biased structure of engagement that precludes access to the alternative frames of meaning of the other as either victim or opponent, but the fact that Folman's film (again similar to *Beaufort* and *Lebanon*) consistently disconnects the traumatic experiences of Israeli soldiers from the suffering and dying Palestinian other.

Waltz with Bashir shows several atrocities willingly or unwillingly committed by Israeli soldiers, such as the indiscriminate aerial bombardment of housing estates, the killing of an unarmed Palestinian family approaching the soldiers in its Mercedes, and the toleration of Phalangist torture camps. However, apparently none of these events leaves a permanent mark on any of the soldiers presented in Folman's film. What brings the soldiers' "camera to break," to use the expression of one of the trauma experts interviewed by Folman, is not the death and suffering of the human (Palestinian) opponent, but dead or dying animals.

The whole story of a slow recollecting of suppressed traumatic war memories starts with the nightmare of dogs chasing a veteran of the Lebanon war in his dreams. Unable to kill human beings, the man had to shoot dogs during his assignment in Lebanon and is still haunted by the creatures in his dreams. On another occasion a war reporter loses his grip not because he witnessed grotesque torture, civilian deaths, or suffering children, but because of dying horses in the Beirut hippodrome. Not one soldier recalls truly traumatic experiences that are in any way connected to his direct involvement in killing or maiming other human beings—Palestinian or otherwise. Folman apparently reverts to generic narrative schemata and paradigm scenarios that resonate with a hegemonic war discourse. *Waltz with Bashir* frames the sad fact of civilian casualties as the ultimately necessary consequence, not of war as such, but of the acts of faceless opponents whose hostile intentions enforce, if not entirely justify, the violent acts carried out by traumatized Israeli soldiers. These soldiers and the veterans depicted in the film as such become "combatants with blood-free hands" and the ultimate victims of war.[50]

In the universe of all three films discussed here, the enemy emerges as ubiquitously absent—potentially anywhere, yet consistently deprived of concrete features, subjectivity, and humanity. The Israeli soldiers are predominantly presented as victims who are unintentionally caught up in a violent struggle with an invisible, hostile other that, through its actions, implies the necessity of harsh countermeasures for the purpose of mere survival. As a result, the violence inflicted by Israeli soldiers is implicitly justified, and dead or maimed Palestinian civilians appear as tragic collateral damage caused by a situation that is largely imposed upon the main protagonists by a hidden opponent or an agentless form of violence.

This particular way of presenting the underlying logic of war and violent conflict plays into and reinforces cognitive schemata and frames that predispose individual and collective engagements not only with diegetic, but also with real-world, enemies and opponents. In reducing the other to a mere threat and preventing access to the grievances and rational considerations underlying this enemy's performances, a politics of polarity and exclusion is implicitly enabled and facilitated. This politics perpetuates warfare in that it denies the other the recognition that would enable the emergence of nonviolent alternatives as viable means of conflict resolution. Rather, the ubiquitously absent enemy continues to implicitly justify massive violence as an allegedly reactive countermeasure to apparently imminent threats.

The pervasive absence of the enemy-other in the universes of the films discussed in the present essay prompts two additional reflections that have to be briefly acknowledged.[51] First, the absence of the other-as-character (which conditions its ubiquitous presence as faceless threat) leaves a discursive and cognitive empty slot that can be filled with preconceived ideas about the identity and intentions of this anonymized enemy. The formal properties of the films cue a form of engagement with the other that is almost entirely dependent on extradiegetic knowledge of this other whom the audience believes it already knows. As a result, established hegemonic understandings regarding the nature of the opponent and the conflict are implicitly activated and subsequently reinforced.

Second, as has already been acknowledged at an earlier stage in this essay, the three films never aspired to present a balanced account of the conflict that pays equal attention to all sides; they aim instead to present the often traumatic experiences and disparate memories of individual soldiers. As such, the ubiquitous absence of the other might reflect a peculiar psychology of soldiers in war, where the enemy in fact looms as an unknown, unseen specter. From this perspective, the fact that, for instance, *Waltz with Bashir* predominantly connects the traumatic nature of Israeli soldiers' war experiences with dead or dying animals (rather than suffering and dying humans) might be explained as the effect of processes of dehumanization and desubjectification of this enemy that, through propaganda and cognitive training, indeed reduce the enemy to the status of animals in the soldiers' minds.

Arguing in a similar vein but with the focus on the spectator, Gil Hochberg suggests that *Waltz with Bashir* and *Lebanon* cannot be treated as antiwar films simply because they show suffering and abandoned Israeli soldiers, but because they interrogate the audience's ways of seeing. According to him, Folman's and Maoz's films demand an "ethical spectatorship" that becomes aware of "the danger involved in the militarization of vision" and warns about "the relative ease with which the eye . . . can be manipulated and trained to see selectively." As such, both films articulate a critical stance toward war "within and not outside the principle of the spectacle."[52]

Though apparently viable positions, these views cannot account for the way Folman's and Maoz's films frame the soldiers' acts of violence, nor do they really provide a good explanation of why the killing of, for instance, a whole Palestinian family leaves a lesser impression on the minds of the young men depicted than the shooting of a number of dogs. To convincingly drive home the ideas of ideological priming of soldiers or of a demanded ethical spectatorship, a more thorough articulation of preceding propagandistic interventions and a clearer contextualization of the camera's implied gaze would have been necessary. As such, the allegedly realistic depictions of an ideologically biased mind-set or scopic regime might quickly revert and reproduce or reinforce the very cognitive and perceptive frames it purports to challenge or unveil.

Absent Bodies and Unarticulated Lives

In his study of different forms of militarism in Israel, Baruch Kimmerling distinguishes between a *force dimension*, a *cultural dimension*, and a *cognitive dimension* of the phenomenon. While a force dimension and a cultural dimension refer to periods in a given collective's history "when military rule directly or indirectly is established and imposed for a length of time," and "when the armed forces become essential to the social experience and collective identity," a cognitive dimension "suffuses both the structural and cultural state of mind of the collectivity."[53] Cognitive militarism is hard to detect. It is "liable to be reflected by . . . institutional or cultural expressions, yet the main expression is a *latent state-of-mind.*"[54] One consequence of this latency of a military mind-set and value system is that the issue hardly ever becomes subject to explicit debate, but rather tacitly influences politics and individual as well as collective attitudes, performances, and expressions.

In a recent dissertation, Noa Roei employs Kimmerling's concepts to describe "the ubiquitous and naturalized way in which militarism participates in Israeli art and visual culture." She uses the term "civilian militarism" to address "a cultural phenomenon in which conflict and war are understood as self-evident parts of everyday life" and that "locates war outside any constellation of political decision-making."[55] Roei identifies a pervasive militarism at the heart of Israeli culture and society that constitutes an elusive background of meaning that tacitly structures form and content of cultural expressions. As a consequence of this, the exceptional state of war becomes an implied normality that informs even cultural products that overtly attempt to challenge and subvert an ingrained culture of war.

The ubiquitous absence of the Palestinian other in the films discussed in the present essay can be seen as constituting another incident of such a civilian or cognitive militarism that pervades Israeli culture and society. In consistently excluding the opponents' competing perspectives, subjectivities, and conceptualizations, the cognitive schemata and paradigm scenarios that *Beaufort, Lebanon,* and *Waltz with Bashir* draw upon, activate, and reinforce tacitly predispose audiences toward an acceptance of violent means as ultimately necessary and imposed by an incomprehensible, dangerous enemy. Even though critical of an overt militarism and plump demonization, the formal properties of the three films still reinforce an ultimately belligerent discourse of conflict that constitutively denies the emergence of the other's competing subjectivity and point of view.

The spectator, though, is not determined by schemata and frames deployed in film or other cultural expressions. Rather, the overdetermined viewer actively navigates in a complex environment of supports and restraints that predispose conceptualizations, attitudes, and behavior at both an individual and a collective level. Paradigm scenarios, schemata, and frames do not enforce a particular originally unintended conduct but render certain alternatives for action or articulation slightly more attractive than others. In this way, general understandings pertaining to self, other, and the nature of their conflict that are tacitly implied in widely consumed expressions of popular culture influence real-life political decisions and performances. It is the objective of this contribution to exemplify such interconnections between cognitive schemata, textual frames, and political performances with reference to three supposedly critical Israeli war films.

Notes

1. See, for instance, Greg M. Smith, *Film Structure and the Emotion System* (Cambridge: Cambridge University Press, 2003); or Torben Grodal, *Embodied Visions: Evolution, Emotion, Culture, and Film* (Oxford: Oxford University Press, 2009).

2. See, for instance, the seminal studies by David Bordwell and Edward Branigan: David Bordwell, *Narration and the Fiction Film* (London: Routledge, 1985); and Edward Branigan, *Narrative Comprehension and Film* (London: Routledge, 1992).

3. Murray Smith, *Engaging Characters: Fiction, Emotion, and the Cinema* (Oxford:

Oxford University Press, 1995); Carl Plantinga, *Moving Viewers: American Film and the Spectator's Experience* (Berkeley: University of California Press, 2009); Margrethe Bruun-Vaage, "Fiction Film and the Varieties of Emphatic Engagement," *Midwest Studies in Philosophy* 34 (2010): 158–79.

4. Smith, *Engaging Characters,* 17.

5. Ibid. See, for instance, Holger Pötzsch, "Challenging the Border as Barrier: Liminality in Terrence Malick's 'The Thin Red Line,'" *Journal of Borderlands Studies* 25, no. 1 (2010): 67–80; Holger Pötzsch, "Border, Barriers, and Grievable Lives: The Discursive Production of Self and Other in Film and Other Audio-Visual Media," *Nordicom Review* 32, no. 2 (2011): 75–94, Holger Pötzsch, "Between Constitutive Presence and Subversive Absence: Self and Other in the Contemporary War Film" (PhD diss., University of Tromsø, 2012); and Holger Pötzsch, "Ubiquitously Absent Enemies: Character Engagement in the Contemporary War Film," *Nordicom Review* 34, no. 1 (2013): 125–44.

6. In a recent article, Carl Plantinga further elaborates Murray Smith's threefold distinction concerning audience engagement with characters: Carl Plantinga, "'I Follow the Rules and They All Loved You More': Moral Judgement and Attitudes toward Fictional Characters in Film," *Midwest Studies in Philosophy* 34 (2010): 34–51. In his article Plantinga distinguishes between eight "levels of 'pro' and 'con' affective and cognitive attitudes toward characters" (43). However, he takes over Smith's term *allegiance* to describe a "strong 'pro' stance [that is] extended through large portions of a narrative" (43). Since I am here predominantly interested in the ways through which allegiance to protagonists vicariously positions the viewer within the moral and discursive universes of these characters, I will refrain from introducing the additional dimensions of engagement suggested by Plantinga.

7. See, for instance, Pötzsch, "Challenging the Border," 71; or Pötzsch, "Ubiquitously Absent Enemies," 130–34.

8. Pötzsch, "Challenging the Border," 71.

9. Grodal, *Embodied Visions.*

10. See, for instance, Pötzsch, "Between Constitutive Absence and Subversive Presence: Self and Other in the Contemporary War Film" (PhD diss., University of Tromsø, 2012), 81–83.

11. Janet Staiger, *Perverse Spectators: The Practices of Film Reception* (New York: New York University Press, 2000).

12. Judith Butler, *Frames of War: When Is Life Grievable?* (London: Verso, 2009).

13. Arguably, not every war film univocally reproduces the core narrative of a good and righteous soldier-self engaged in an inevitably violent struggle against an incomprehensible and evil enemy-other. War movies such as *The Thin Red Line* (Terrence Malick, 1998), *Battle for Haditha* (Nick Broomfield, 2007), and *The Situation* (Philip Haas, 2006) deliberately play with the camera's and microphone's selective gaze and thereby dislodge established paradigm scenarios and cognitive schemata that frame the

other as ungrievable. For such "liminal" aspects of certain war films, see, for instance, Pötzsch, "Challenging the Border," 72–77; and Pötzsch, *Constitutive Absence*, 86–90.

14. Ella Shohat, *Israeli Cinema: East/West and the Politics of Representation* (Austin: University of Texas Press, 1989). For the three phases of Israeli war film, see in particular pages 53–103.

15. For a similar phrasing of the representation of war in Israeli cinema, see Raz Yosef, *Beyond Flesh: Queer Masculinities and Nationalism in Israeli Cinema* (New Brunswick, NJ: Rutgers University Press, 2004), in particular 48–83. In his study Yosef draws heavily on the thought of Ella Shohat, but he directs more attention to gender and masculinity. For a detailed study on the interrelations between popular Israeli cinema and Israeli society during the 1980s and 1990s, see Yosefa Loshitzky, *Identity Politics on the Israeli Screen* (Austin: University of Texas Press, 2001). She argues for a transition from "a 'politics of ideas' to a 'politics of identity'" that occurred during this period (xi). Loshitzky, however, directs little attention to the genre of the war film.

16. Raz Yosef, "Traces of War: Memory, Trauma, and the Archive in Joseph Cedar's 'Beaufort,'" *Cinema Journal* 50, no. 2 (2011): 61–83, quotation p. 62; Shohat, *Israeli Cinema*, 59.

17. Yosef, *Beyond Flesh*, 45; Benedict Andersen, *Imagined Communities: Reflections on the Origins and Spread of Nationalism* (London: Verso, 1983).

18. Drawing on an analysis of *Hill 24 Doesn't Answer* (*Giv'a 24 Eina Ona;* Dickinson, 1955), also Uri S. Cohen observes that classical Israeli war cinema sees war "through eyes beyond and above the existential condition of the individual" and does "not go beyond a symbolic treatment of . . . characters as an illustration of history." Uri S. Cohen, "From Hill to Hill: A Brief History of the Representation of War in Israeli Cinema," in *Israeli Cinema: Identities in Motion*, ed. Miri Talmon and Yaron Peleg (Austin: University of Texas Press, 2011), 46 and 47.

19. Judd Ne'eman, "The Empty Tomb in the Postmodern Pyramid: Israeli Cinema in the 1980s and 1990s," in *Documenting Israel: Proceedings of a Conference Held at Harvard University, May 10–12, 1993*, ed. Charles Berlin (Cambridge, MA: Harvard College Library, 1995), 121, 120.

20. Shohat, *Israeli Cinema*.

21. Ilan Avisar, "The National and the Popular in Israeli Cinema," *Shofar* 24, no. 1 (2005): 125–44; Cohen, "From Hill to Hill"; Yosef, "Traces of War."

22. Avisar, "The National and the Popular," 135.

23. Yosef, "Traces of War," 65–66. Yosef explicitly lists all the three films discussed in this essay as examples for this new introspective treatment of war.

24. Eran Kaplan, "From Hero to Victim: The Changing Image of the Israeli Soldier on Screen," in *Israeli Cinema: Identities in Motion*, ed. Miri Talmon and Yaron Peleg (Austin: University of Texas Press, 2011), 60, 59.

25. Yael Munk, "The Privatization of War Memories in Recent Israeli Cinema," in Talmon and Peleg, *Israeli Cinema*, 105.

26. Also earlier films, such as *Ricochets* (1982), *Fragments* (1989), *Cherry Season* (1991), and *Cup Final* (1991), have critically treated the First Lebanon War. Raz Yosef, however, observes that, in spite of their overtly critical and progressive thrust, all these films ultimately become "subservient to a pro-Israel 'liberal-humanist' ideological perspective . . . that purports to demonstrate the Israeli soldier's moral supremacy." Yosef, "Traces of War," 67. See also Nurith Gertz, "The Medium That Mistook Itself for a War: 'Cherry Seasons' in Comparison with 'Ricochets' and 'Cup Final,'" *Israel Studies* 4, no. 1 (1999): 153–65. For an illustrative comparison of *Beaufort* with the classical war narrative *Hill 24 Doesn't Answer* (1955), see Cohen, "From Hill to Hill." I argue that in spite of several important differences, also *Beaufort, Lebanon,* and *Waltz with Bashir* ultimately articulate a similar image of the inherently innocent and victimized Israeli soldier.

27. Yosef, "Traces of War," 62.

28. Raz Yosef, "War Fantasies: Memory, Trauma, and Ethics in Ari Folman's 'Waltz with Bashir,'" *Journal of Modern Jewish Studies* 9, no. 3 (2010): 311–26, quotation p. 313; Munk, "Privatization of War Memories," 97.

29. Ella Taylor, "Beaufort," *Village Voice,* January 8, 2008, villagevoice.com; Cohen, "From Hill to Hill," 50.

30. Walter Adiego, "In 'Lebanon' War Closes In," *San Francisco Chronicle,* August 20, 2010, sfgate.com.

31. Leonard Quart, "Dramatizing Traumatic Memories of War: An Interview with Samuel Maoz," *Cineaste* 35, no. 1 (2010): 34.

32. Yosef, "War Fantasies," 316; Yosef, "Traces of War," 66; Gil Hochberg, "Soldiers as Filmmakers: On the Prospect of 'Shooting War' and the Question of Ethical Spectatorship," *Screen* 54, no. 1 (2013): 44–61, quotations p. 56.

33. For a detailed study of the antiwar genre, see, for instance, Burkhard Röwekamp, *Antikriegsfilme: Zur Ästhetik, Geschichte und Theorie einer filmhistorischen Praxis* (Munich: Richard Boorberg, 2011). For interviews with the directors of *Beaufort, Lebanon,* and *Waltz with Bashir,* see Leonard Quart, "Surviving a Futile War: An Interview with Joseph Cedar," *Cineaste* 33, no. 2 (2008): 27–31; Quart, "Dramatizing Traumatic Memories of War," 34–37; and John Esther, "'Waltz with Bashir': An Interview with Ari Folman," *Cineaste* 34, no. 2 (2009): 67–69.

34. Yosef, "Traces of War," 68.

35. Ibid., 70.

36. Gil Hochberg, for instance, asserts that *Lebanon* "is a film about the hijacking of the eye by military . . . devices." Hochberg, "Soldiers as Filmmakers," 58.

37. Yosef, "War Fantasies," 324.

38. Slavoj Žižek, "Green Berets with a Human Face," *London Review of Books Blog,* March 22, 2010, lrb.co.uk/blog.

39. Cohen, "From Hill to Hill," 53.

40. Munk, "Privatization of War Memories," 98.

41. Yosef, "Traces of War," 70.

42. Katrina Schlunke, "Animated Documentary and the Scene of Death: Experiencing 'Waltz with Bashir,'" *South Atlantic Quarterly* 110, no. 4 (2011): 949–62, quotation p. 961.

43. Garrett Stewart, "Screen Memory in 'Waltz with Bashir,'" *Film Quarterly* 63, no. 3 (2010): 58–62, quotation p. 62. For an analysis of the use of animation for documentary filmmaking, see, for instance, Robert Moses, "'It's Fine as Long as You Draw, But Don't Film': 'Waltz with Bashir' and the Postmodern Function of Animated Documentary," *Visual Communication Quarterly* 18, no. 4 (2011): 223–35.

44. Holger Pötzsch, "Imag(in)ing Painful Pasts: Mimetic and Poetic Style in War Films," in *Ethics and Images of Pain*, ed. Asbjørn Grønstad and Henrik Gustafsson (London: Routledge, 2012), 185.

45. Stewart, "Screen Memory," 60.

46. Yosef, "War Fantasies," 322, 323.

47. Jonathan Murray, "Waltz with Bashir," *Cineaste* 34, no. 1 (2009): 65–68, quotation p. 68.

48. Murray writes that "the intensely moving eleventh-hour formal shift to live action puts *Waltz with Bashir* into proportion and perspective in a way perhaps not intended by its maker." Ibid., 68.

49. I wish by no means to imply a moral or ethical superiority of Palestinian perspectives and positions. Rather, I argue that a nonviolent approach to conflict resolution rests upon the acceptance of both opposing worldviews' ultimate validity and meaningfulness. This way the recognition of the Palestinian other would not provide a better frame of meaning, but only bring into motion again sedimented positions that are stabilized in and through the constitutive exclusion of the respective other. As also hegemonic bellicose Palestinian positions rest upon an exclusion (of the Israeli other), a truly inclusive discourse would undermine and subvert both mutually exclusive frameworks. I introduce the term liminality to conceptualize such a subversive in-between position. See Pötzsch, "Challenging the Border," 72–73; and *Constitutive Absence*, 86–90 and 174–76.

50. Murray, "Waltz with Bashir," 68.

51. I owe the following reflections to the insightful comments by David LaRocca on a draft version of the present essay.

52. Hochberg, "Soldiers as Filmmakers," 60, 46.

53. Baruch Kimmerling, "Patterns of Militarism in Israel," *Archives européennes de sociologie* 34 (1993): 196–223, quotations pp. 200, 202, 206.

54. Ibid., 206 (emphasis in original).

55. Noa Roei, "Shifting Sights: Civilian Militarism in Israeli Art and Visual Culture" (PhD diss., University of Amsterdam, 2012), 9, 11, 12.

General Patton and Private Ryan

The Conflicting Reality of War and Films about War

Andrew Fiala

In the opening scene of the film *Patton* (Shaffner, 1970), George C. Scott—who embodies the eponymous general—gives voice to the spirit of militaristic collectivism: "Now, an army is a team. It lives, eats, sleeps, fights as a team. This individuality stuff is a bunch of crap. The bilious bastards who wrote that stuff about individuality for the *Saturday Evening Post* don't know anything more about real battle than they do about fornicating."

Scott's Patton condemns individualism as a "bunch of crap," claiming that commentators on war do not know anything about "real battle." This points toward ontological, moral, and aesthetic questions. What is "real battle"? Should our moral evaluation of war focus on the individual or on the collective? And how do representations of war, such as war films, help us answer these questions?

Unfortunately, there are no clear answers to these sorts of questions. War contains a basic conflict between the individual and the collective.[1] The individual soldier is the one who fights and suffers. But the individual's experience is part of a much larger whole. Individual soldiers do matter morally—especially within the framework of Western liberal democracies. But war is a collective endeavor in which individuals are sacrificed for the larger whole. Human rights reside within autonomous individuals who deserve, in Kant's terms, to be respected as ends-in-themselves and not used or sacrificed in service to the collective. And yet, war creates a circumstance in which even liberal-democratic nations ask some individuals to sacrifice their individuality for the good of the whole.

This conflict in the morality and ontology of war is reflected in conflicting representations of war in war films. Some films emphasize the collective vantage point, while others emphasize the experience of the individual. And each approach can lay claim to being "realistic." These differing emphases show us the challenge of representing the reality of war; and they show us the challenge of thinking critically about the moral problem of war.

Realism and Representation

The term *realism* has multiple meanings. In discussions of the ethics of war, the "realist" perspective is focused on power and on national interests—it is oriented toward collective goods and public welfare. Realism tends to hold that there are no moral limits in warfare; rather, there are practical limits imposed by strategic needs and goals. Opposed to realism are both pacifism and the just-war tradition. While pacifists reject all wars, the just-war tradition permits wars to be fought within morally appropriate limits. These limits often focus on the value of individuality—both the individual soldier and the noncombatants caught up in the violence of war. We see this in the just-war tradition's deontological prohibitions against torture and rape, its respect for war conventions dealing with prisoners of war, and its ideal of noncombatant immunity. There are some parallels between discussion of realism in the ethics of war and the question of realism in representations of war, with the crucial question being the value we place upon the individual.

This essay touches upon the problem of judging the morality of war, arguing that this problem is related to the problem of representing the reality of war. There are several layers of complexity in trying to think about realism and representations of reality in war films.[2] We need to consider narrative structure and cinematic style. We also should consider the way that real life and art intersect—in terms of the material conditions and propaganda function of war films.

The problem of representation becomes apparent as we consider the question of whether Scott's Patton speech is "realistic." It is obvious that the iconic image of Scott's Patton (in riding breeches with a chest full of medals, standing in front of a huge American flag) represents an artistic interpretation. But Scott's Patton speech is supposed to be grounded in reality. The film is, after all, a film about a real person, thoroughly grounded in historical fact. The real General Patton did deliver a speech similar to the one that Scott re-created in his role. But the film represents an *interpretation* of this reality. Patton's actual speech was more colorful and crude than the one in the film: "An Army is a team. It lives, sleeps, eats, and fights as a team. This individual heroic stuff is pure horse shit. The bilious bastards who write that kind of stuff for the *Saturday Evening Post* don't know any more about real fighting under fire than they know about fucking!"[3] This shows us the problem of realism. Even this speech about the reality of fighting has been altered in the film. Indeed, there is a subtle comment in this speech about the very problem we are considering here: Patton himself is suspicious of journalists and filmmakers. So if we are going to understand war and "real fighting under fire," as Patton puts it, it is not clear that we can rely upon journalists and filmmakers.

And yet one could argue that it is the journalists and filmmakers who provide a distilled reality that is more easily comprehensible. One could also argue that a realistic war film should be focused on historical detail in documentary fashion, aiming at distilling the "truth." The idea behind "realism" in war films is that filmmakers are like historians, offering us an account of the truth of events—an idea that has been around since D. W. Griffith's *The Birth of a Nation* (1915). Steven Jay Rubin explains that as Griffith worked on the Civil War sequences in *Birth of a Nation,* he was obsessed with realism: "He strongly felt that such a desire to film the truth would increase the very popularity of films themselves. He predicted that filmmakers of the future would be able to teach history through the film medium, and that when it came to realism, audiences would not settle for less."[4]

There is an open question, however, about what it means to "film the truth," as Rubin puts it, especially the truth about war. Is the truth of war the struggle and suffering of the individual soldier; or is the truth of war the movement of armies and the general point of view?

The problem is that we are always struggling to connect our representations of things to the reality of these things. This is an aesthetic and epistemological problem. And it creates a problem for moral judgment. If we want to be able to judge whether a particular war (or wars in general) is good or bad, just or unjust, we need to be able to grasp the reality of war. But a careful analysis of the problem of representation as it manifests in war films reminds us that we should not be too hasty in thinking that we have actually grasped that reality. Indeed, our attempts to represent the truth of war are always already infused with values and judgments. Any moral judgment we would make should cautiously admit the difficulty of representation.

One problem of representation has to do with narrative structure. The typical narratives that we expect in film and in literature are focused on individuals. Even a film such as *Patton* traces out the living and dying of individual soldiers. Typical narratives focus on characters with names; they are not merely about armies and collectives. In ethics and in the narrative of war films, the individual matters. But war runs counter to individualism: it is a collective effort involving armies aimed toward defending public goods. In war, private individuals are viewed as mere parts of the larger whole.

The narrative focus on individualism reaches a zenith of sorts with *Saving Private Ryan* (Spielberg, 1998). Rubin argues that *Saving Private Ryan* changed the paradigm in terms of realism, with a special emphasis on the "realism" of the first-person perspective of the Normandy D-Day sequence. Moreover, the film's very plotline reverses Patton's collectivist ideal. In *Saving Private Ryan,* the army shifts its focus toward rescuing one individual soldier, Private Ryan. The general point of view—the point of view of someone like General Patton—is not focused on individual soldiers. And yet the private point of view—the point of the view of the individuals who fight—remains the most significant point of view for ethics and for storytelling on film. This is part of the reason that the narrative of *Saving Private Ryan* is so compelling: it fits with the value we place upon individuality. American audiences want the army, especially the *American* army, to be concerned with the well-being of individual soldiers. And yet, we recognize that Patton is probably right, that in war, individualism is, as Scott's Patton puts it, "a bunch of crap."

Another issue of representational realism has to do with the cinematography used in war films. *Saving Private Ryan*'s representational realism is seen in the D-Day sequence, which is said to accurately represent the actuality of the battle—at least as it was lived from the perspective of the individual soldier. But this idea of what is realistic is a matter of interpretation. Is a battle most realistically portrayed by the use of handheld cameras and first-person point of view (as in *Private Ryan*); or is a battle more realistically represented in a wide-angle aerial shot of troops of soldiers in combat that shows the movements of the collectives (as seen in several scenes in *Patton*)? This question points toward the moral question: What matters more, the individual's perspective or the more general perspective?

Realism in representation is connected to claims about historical accuracy. Hollywood war films are often grounded very firmly in the events, places, and individuals of actual history. Representational realism is also a matter of authenticity of the hardware and locales used in filming. In order to firm up the claim to being "realistic," filmmakers employ advisory experts from the military and obtain real military hardware to use in their films. To obtain access to hardware and expert advisers, filmmakers have to cooperate with the military. There is thus the risk of war films becoming propaganda. During the Second World War, war films were deliberately made and used as propaganda—both by American filmmakers and by the Nazis. While Leni Riefenstahl's *Triumph of the Will* (1935) is often singled out in this regard, the American military was also involved in producing its own propaganda films—such as the seven-film series *Why We Fight* (1942–1945); most of those films were directed by beloved American director Frank Capra, with animation provided by Disney Studios. Some of our most cherished studio war films also served a propaganda function: for example, Humphrey Bogart's 1942 classic *Casablanca* served a patriotic purpose and was approved by the Office of War Information's Bureau of Motion Pictures.[5]

It is not surprising that the military has been heavily involved in the war-film industry, since these films can serve as promilitary propaganda and as recruiting instruments. Lawrence Suid explains this in his book *Guts and Glory:* "Virtually all the military movies made up to the early 1960's received assistance from the armed services in their production.... Beginning with *Dr. Strangelove, Fail Safe,* and the other anti-bomb films of the mid-1960's and the growing protest against the Vietnam War, however, the traditional relationship came to an end and the armed services began to reject scripts which they believed contained negative portrayals of their men and activities."[6] As Suid indicates, the heroic narrative of military glory and self-sacrifice began to unravel with antiwar films in the 60s that either assert the importance of individuality against the cold indifference of the military machine or blatantly criticize the madness of war.

We've seen the idea of war-film propaganda parodied recently in Quentin Tarantino's *Inglourious Basterds* (2009), a film about war films. The climax of the film occurs at a movie theater that is premiering a typical Nazi propaganda film. At the premier, the Nazis are killed—including Hitler and the Nazi propaganda minister, Goebbels. The completely unrealistic nature of this film's story runs counter to its emotionally satisfying narrative. This is a reminder of a conflict between what we want in terms of a good story and what is realistic. *Saving Private Ryan* includes a similar sort of satisfying emotional content: the implausible narrative of saving Private Ryan is nonetheless emotionally satisfying and serves to reaffirm the idea that the individual-loving American forces are the good guys.

A key part of the propaganda function of a war film is its supposed "realism," at least in terms of the use of military hardware and insignia; historical locations; and actual names of officers, armies, and operations. Military advisers often provide advice aimed at making war films more realistic. It is important to note, however, that in the United States such advisers also offer advice to ensure that American soldiers are portrayed in a positive light. As David Robb has outlined in some detail, the Pentagon has long been involved in shaping and censoring the movies.[7] The "reality" that is portrayed in such films is thus a reality shaped by the needs and interest of the military. The military itself has been actively involved in filmmaking, for example, in *Act of Valor* (McCoy and Waugh, 2012), a film that was widely advertised as an "unprecedented blend of real-life heroism and original filmmaking which stars active-duty Navy SEALS." The film began as a short feature that was intended for recruiting purposes. It evolved into a full feature film, including a red-carpet release party that brought the Navy SEAL "actors" in the film to the New York premier in limousines.[8] The realism of such a film (in terms of its access to hardware and expert advisers) is touted as its virtue, even though this realism is utilized for obvious propaganda purposes. Of course, we should note that the realism of such a film is still an artistic product: crafted by producers and directors and edited for specific purposes.

In more recent years, a new genre of war films appears to provide the most realistic portrayal of war yet offered. This is found in the first-person videos shot by soldiers in the field that show up on YouTube and other places. We might think that videos made and posted by active-duty military personnel are the most realistic war films of all. Certainly these videos are realistic in terms of the personnel involved, the locations used, the hardware employed, and the immediacy of the events. With these videos we have active-duty personnel, at work in the field, recording themselves in action. While one might argue that these personal videos show us a new standard of realism, it is important to remember that even these videos are planned, staged, and edited. Indeed, one could argue that the presence of the camera and the knowledge that such videos will be broadcast on the Internet changes the behavior of those who are recorded—which presents a serious puzzle for any analysis of the "reality" of what is represented in these videos.

At any rate, these personal videos also often remind us of the moral ambiguities of war. The most controversial of these sorts of videos have shown U.S. Marines urinating on the dead bodies of people they have killed and flinging puppies off of cliffs. A focus of controversy in the trial of Bradley Manning (now Chelsea), an American soldier who released classified information to WikiLeaks and the media was a video entitled "Collateral Murder" in which an American Apache helicopter in Iraq killed eleven individuals including two journalists. Some argued that WikiLeaks had edited the video to make it look worse than it was—an issue that points back toward the question of truth and realism. At any rate, such videos remind us that the "reality" of war is not just the masculine prowess of Navy SEALs in action; it is also the malicious mischief of young men with guns. But of course, much of the "reality" of the soldier's daily life does not make it onto YouTube: we don't see a soldier's uneventful patrols or watch him lounging back at camp. The point to be noted here is that choices are made and a certain sort of "reality" is represented even in these first-person videos and cockpit camera recordings.

The General and the Private

The question of realism can be crystalized into the differing perspectives, narrative themes, and cinematographic approaches that we see in *Saving Private Ryan* and in *Patton*. The opening D-Day sequence of *Saving Private Ryan* is firmly rooted in the actual D-Day invasion. Moreover, the opening scene of *Patton* is firmly rooted in Patton's own speech about the reality of war. Patton maintains that war is in reality a collective effort. This reality is not best seen from the vantage point of the individual. However, in terms of the question of realism in depicting battle, many critics maintain that *Saving Private Ryan* takes the prize.[9] The realism of *Private Ryan* is found in the very fact that the film's most "realistic" sequences unfold from the vantage point of the individual. Realism in this sense is what is experienced by the very individuals that Patton says do not matter.

The reality of war, from Patton's perspective, is the mass movement of human groups—armies, brigades, and battalions—toward an objective that is also focused on collectives, that is, toward the defeat of the enemy army, as a whole. Individual soldiers have no importance here, except as parts of the whole. The fear, the pain, the sweat, the blood, and the experience of the individual soldier is not important from the standpoint of war as a collective endeavor aimed at a public good. Patton maintains that commentators who focus on individuality don't understand "real battle." A real battle is about the team, the platoon, the nation itself. From this perspective, the reality of a battle or a war is seen from above or from outside the battlefield itself. The spectator who hovers outside of the battle is able to understand the reality of the battle in a way that the individuals inside the battle themselves do not. To see the reality of a battle, one must view it from above, as Patton does in the first major battle scene of the film, sitting on a hilltop with binoculars watching tanks and men engage on a field below.

Such wide-angle shots and scenic vantage points are mainstays of Hollywood war films. These elevated angles appear to show us the reality of war in Patton's sense, as a movement of collectives. But a rival approach to realism in war films focuses on the point of view of the individual soldier. This approach was perfected in *Saving Private Ryan* in the famous D-Day sequence. Steven Spielberg's attempt to provide a realistic first-person point of view on the violence of war in the famous D-Day sequence was praised by veterans of the invasion as the most realistic portrayal of the war they had seen. Jeanine Basinger, for example, concluded that *Private Ryan* reached a high point in terms of "visual honesty," which refuted the "dishonesty" of previous war films.[10] The grueling first-person point of view of war's violence was viewed as a refutation of the Patton-esque point of view that looks at the collective and ignores the individual. It is interesting to note that the claim of realism was used to defend Spielberg's film against censorship and problems with ratings. The FCC decided to allow *Saving Private Ryan* to run on network television in 2005 because they thought its essential realism provided a defense against the charge that the movie was obscene—both because of its violence and because of its use of expletives, especially its twenty-one uses of the word *fuck*.[11]

The question of realism in war films has to do in part with the question of which perspective of war is the most realistic: the *Patton*-esque view from on high or the first-person vantage point of *Saving Private Ryan*. One wonders whom we should believe in deciding which approach is most realistic. Perhaps we should trust the veterans of D-Day who agreed that *Saving Private Ryan* provided the most realistic visual representation of the battle they had ever seen. But on the other hand, we might trust Patton's reputation as one of the most celebrated generals of the Second World War. His stature gives us a good reason to believe that he understands war better than the rest of us—that it really is about the brigades and battalions and not about the individuals. Furthermore, it may be that success in war requires the sort of perspective that Patton espouses. A successful general does need to look from above so he can see beyond the immediate suffering of the individuals under his command. But it may also be the case that this perspective is fundamentally immoral. After all, most modern liberal-democratic theories of ethics emphasize the idea of individual personality, the importance of individual rights, and the sacred value of autonomy. To win a war, individuals may have to be sacrificed in the way that Patton proposes. But it might be that such sacrifices are essentially immoral. In the end, we are left with a conflict of perspectives that cannot easily be resolved.

Hollywood war films are not primarily intended as philosophical texts focused on analysis of ethical questions. They are not treatises on just-war theory or ethics. While they may indeed contain philosophically interesting content and present critical perspectives, they are also products to be marketed. These films are primarily diversions, entertainment, propaganda, art, and vehicles for making vast sums of money. The controversy about the graphic realism of violence in *Saving Private Ryan* was not only about artistic vision and license; it was also a marketing ploy, as the controversy about the film helped to generate box-office receipts. And it is important to remember that films are interpretations made with the collaboration of a number of individuals. Films themselves are collective products, despite our tendency to focus on the individual efforts of screenwriters, actors, and directors. The words we hear in a film are the words of a scriptwriter or a team of scriptwriters, realized by the director in collaboration with the cinematographer, the actors, and the producer.

All of this reminds us that war films are artistic and technological productions that involve choices and interpretations—even when they record and present actual historical events. The truth is that war—like most other human endeavors worth thinking about—is so complex that claims about reality, truth, and morality may cease to make much sense. One feature of the complexity of war is that it is a public event involving world historical forces and massive movements of human beings, machinery, fuel, and capital. All the while, these events are carried out by individuals who live the reality of war in the first person, from within a limited subjective point of view.

Pro-War and Antiwar War Films

Saving Private Ryan and *Patton* are both patriotic, promilitary, pro-war films. And they remain crowd-pleasing favorites. *Patton* won the Academy Award for best picture in 1970 (and George C. Scott was offered the award for best actor—an award he refused to receive). A poll in the United Kingdom in 2009 rated *Saving Private Ryan* as the best war film of all time.[12] *Private Ryan* is a paean to "the greatest generation," many of whom died on the beaches of Normandy—as made clear in the maudlin retrospective view from the cemetery at Normandy that frames the film. Second World War veterans and supporters of the military are proud of the spirit of the film, despite the absurdity of its plotline. One of the virtues of *Saving Private Ryan* is supposed to be its realism: especially in the opening D-Day invasion sequence (reputed to have caused PTSD [post-traumatic stress disorder] flashbacks for some veterans who watched it). *Patton* also remains a favorite war film for militarists and American patriots, in part because Patton's hard-nosed spirit is celebrated for its rugged realism. Patton remains a model of the tough-guy, no-nonsense military commander whose unsentimental approach to the reality of war leads to victory.

Claims about realism remain central to the critical evaluation of war films. Films such as *The Hurt Locker* (Bigelow, 2008)—which received the Academy Award for Best Picture in 2009—have been panned by Iraq War veterans for lacking realism.[13] According to such critics, the problem with *The Hurt Locker* is that there is too much individualism among the soldiers, with soldiers working in small groups and sneaking off on their own to feed their "addiction" to adrenaline and war. On the other hand, *Patton* and *Saving Private Ryan* have both been heralded by veterans for being realistic. In 2008, Mark Brinkley of *Army Times* voted *Patton* as the second-best war movie of all time. Brinkley considered Stanley Kubrick's *Full Metal Jacket* (1987) the best war film of all time. *Full Metal Jacket* is "as real as it comes" according to Brinkley.[14]

For Brinkley, and for many others, what matters in a war film is the realistic nature of the film. Of course, as we have seen, there is a fundamental dispute at the heart of claims about "realism." For many critics, it appears that the "realism" of a war film is connected to its sense of collectivism. The common thread between *Patton* and *Full Metal Jacket* is the version of collectivism that occurs as the recruits are worn down in boot camp and formed into marines. But in *Full Metal Jacket* collectivism becomes darker, more sinister. *Full Metal Jacket* is clearly not a pro-war film (indeed the antimilitary message of the film becomes obvious when we interpret the film in conjunction with Kubrick's earlier *Dr. Strangelove*).[15] It is interesting that the *Army Times* author selected an antiwar film such as *Full Metal Jacket* for the honor of best war film: the film shows the sadism of boot camp, a murder-suicide in the barracks, and the madness of the war in Vietnam. Other recent films that routinely show up in top-ten lists of war movies include other seemingly antiwar films such as Terrence Malick's *The Thin Red Line* (1998) and Francis Ford Coppola's *Apocalypse Now* (1979). These are visually intriguing and intellectually provocative films, with realistic (and surrealistic) elements included. But *Patton*'s patriotic opening scene remains one of the most memorable scenes in war-movie history; and it would be hard to put *Patton* on the antiwar side of things, despite the fact that *Patton*'s opening speech, and most of the film, is so much at odds with the individualism of American liberal democracy. The film is also a patriotic celebration of what we might call "Americanism": a more nationalistic form of patriotism that runs counter to the individualism that is often typical of those who are critical of war. Patton's brand of patriotism is about sacrifice for the country and its ideals as a collective good. This sort of patriotism is closely connected with nationalism and with warrior values.[16]

On the other hand, antiwar critics may be repelled by Patton's collectivism. And it is possible to draw an antiwar conclusion from Patton—as Patton's callous indifference to his own soldiers is viewed as his tragic flaw. More explicitly antiwar films mock the patriotic collectivism embodied in Patton. Even *Saving Private Ryan* can be interpreted as concealing an antiwar message, especially in its opening sequence and in the death of the protagonist, Captain Miller (Tom Hanks). But while the film makes it clear that death is part of war, it appears to celebrate the sacrifices of ordinary soldiers, while showing that the Americans are the good guys insofar as they are willing to make these sacrifices in order to save the individual.

This discussion of divergent interpretations of *Patton* and *Private Ryan* reminds us that it is not so easy to define the difference between antiwar films and other war films. When asked whether *Apocalypse Now* was an antiwar film, Coppola—who won the Academy Award for the script he wrote for *Patton*—responded as follows: "All war movies are antiwar movies in that they describe horrible incidents and the most profound thing of all, to lose a young person."[17] There is some truth to the claim that all war movies are antiwar movies. War is a tragedy and movies about war cannot ignore the tragedy: the loss, suffering, and madness of war. But films such as *Patton* and *Private Ryan* emphasize the reasons that justify the tragedy of war.

It is also important to note that the historical context of war films matters. Films that focus on the Second World War tend to be pro-war films, since that was a supposedly good or just war. Vietnam war films—such as *Full Metal Jacket* and *Apocalypse Now*—are not so clearly patriotic or pro-war because the Vietnam war was not so easily viewed as a just war. We are still figuring out how best to represent the equally problematic wars in Iraq and Afghanistan. Of course, the justness of the Second World War can also be called into question. Allied forces in the Second World War were involved in atrocities, especially the fire-bombing of cities (Tokyo, Hamburg, and Dresden). While Japanese soldiers were fighting for the United States in Italy, their families were held in internment camps in California. While African American soldiers fought for freedom, their friends and families on the home front were being denied the very rights the soldiers were seeking to protect. The United States remains the only nation on earth to have used atomic weapons against civilian population centers—and the United States used these weapons twice on two different cities. Another "war film"—Errol Morris's documentary *The Fog of War* (2003)—makes this clear: Robert S. McNamara claims that if the United States had lost the war, Americans would have been accused of committing war crimes for their use of these terror bombing tactics.

Although *Saving Private Ryan* is not an antiwar film, it does represent in graphic and gruesome detail the "reality" of battle—at least as experienced in the first person on the beaches of Normandy. But it tends to frame this reality in a larger context, one in which war is seen as heroic and noble. The film does not criticize the notion that it is good for society to ask its sons (and daughters) to make such heroic sacrifices. One of the few commentators who has criticized the implicit patriotism and pro-war sentiment in *Private Ryan* is Howard Zinn—a radical historian and Second World War veteran.[18] Zinn recalls seeing the film with an audience that included many men his own age. The film prompted him to recall his own war experience, including friends who were killed in the war. Zinn maintains that *Private Ryan* is yet another example of military propaganda: war films being used to show that service in the cause of war is noble, just, and heroic. And Zinn points out—as mentioned above—that the United States was not entirely free from reproach in its conduct of the Second World War. Zinn goes on to contrast *Private Ryan* with *All Quiet on the Western Front* (Milestone, 1930), which is decidedly antiwar (as was the Erich Maria Remarque novel on which it was based). For Zinn, the power of *All Quiet on the Western Front* is that it not only shows the *horrors* of war, as *Private Ryan* clearly does, but that it also shows the *futility* of war.

Tim O'Brien and "True War Stories"

A poignant statement of the problem of representing the reality of war is found in the work of Tim O'Brien, a Vietnam veteran and popular novelist. O'Brien reminds us of the difficulty of telling the truth about war. In the chapter "How to Tell a True War Story" in *The Things They Carried,* O'Brien implies that the reality of war escapes attempts at understanding to such a degree that fiction may tell more truth about war than nonfiction—while nonfiction may present us with a lie. The stylized opening scene in *Patton* is a fictionalized interpretation, as is the D-Day invasion scene from *Private Ryan:* these are works of art. But from O'Brien's perspective, such fictions can represent deep truths, even conflicting truths. Indeed, the only truth of war that is not contestable may well be the claim that there are conflicting perspectives—the perspective of the individual soldier in the foxhole and the perspective of the general who is concerned with the entire war.

O'Brien claims that fiction and lies actually disclose truth. One significant lie is the very idea that there is a "reality" of war that is easily captured in words or images. If we recognize this, then it becomes very hard to think about the morality of war. O'Brien writes:

> A true war story is never moral. It does not instruct, nor encourage virtue, nor suggest models of proper human behavior, nor restrain men from doing the things they have always done. If a story seems moral, do not believe it. If at the end of a war story you feel uplifted, or if you feel that some small bit of rectitude has been salvaged from the larger waste, then you have been made the victim of a very old and terrible lie. There is no rectitude whatsoever. There is no virtue. As a first rule of thumb, therefore, you can tell a true war story by its absolute and uncompromising allegiance to obscenity and evil.[19]

A wide variety of literature and film shows us that war is so complex that it is difficult to represent and judge either its reality or its morality. Art and literature present us with "truth" in the complex sense of the lived experience of a reality that has so many multiple perspectives that no single word or image or scene can capture it. O'Brien suggests that art and literature must deal in fiction, hyperbole, metaphor, and lie in order to make this truth manifest. This is why it is difficult to assess literature and film from the perspective of truth and realism. Which war film provides the best, most accurate, truest, or more realistic representation of war? Is the truth found in the newsreels of the Second World War or in the first-person YouTube and cockpit videos from Iraq and Afghanistan? Or is there even more truth in the more deliberately fictional re-creations we find in mainstream cinema?

The problem of representation makes moral judgment about war that much more difficult. O'Brien's chapter "How to Tell a True War Story" contains a story about Rat Kiley's savage attack on a baby water buffalo. Kiley shoots the water buffalo in the knee, in the belly, in the butt, in the ribs, in the nose, and in the throat—leaving it alive throughout. How can we judge this action, if we do not know whether it is true or if we do not understand the truth that is being expressed in this fictional story?

From the perspective of the just-war tradition, it was wrong of Rat Kiley to slaughter the water buffalo—just as it was wrong for Corporal David Motari to throw a puppy off a cliff in Iraq in an infamous Iraq War first-person video. But such moral clarity evaporates, at least in some cases, when we dig into the "truth" of the matter. The viral video clip in which Motari throws the puppy off the cliff lasts only seventeen seconds. We don't see what happened before or after the puppy is thrown. Motari was discharged from the Marine Corps as a result of his behavior. But he did offer an explanation: his unit routinely disposed of stray animals by shooting them, since they could not bring them along on patrol. Motari protested that in the end there was little difference between killing the dog with a bullet, as was usually done, and killing the dog by flinging it off a cliff.[20] Of course, it is disturbing that the video shows Motari smiling and records some other Marines giggling as the puppy is thrown to its death. But Motari's explanation reminds us that moral judgment in war is complicated. Perhaps things are less complicated when considering the video of the marines urinating on the bodies of those they had killed; or when considering the cockpit video exposed by Bradley Manning. The actions in these videos seems to run counter to war convention and to principles of justice in war. But even here there is a question of how blame is to be distributed and whether what we are seeing fits within (and is justified by) a larger context. How are we to make sense of (and criticize) young men vaunting over the dead, when this has been part of war—and representations of war—since Achilles dragged Hector's body before Troy's walls? And how are we to make sense of (and criticize) collateral damage, which has often been much worse than what we've seen in the Apache cockpit video? Can we put ourselves in the place of these soldiers, caught up in a war they did not choose and thrown into battles they have no control over?

Individuals, Collectives, and the Moral Imagination

Film, literature, and art distill complexity. Representational arts work with our imaginations to allow us to see, grasp, and experience reality. But these representations always involve interpretations. Film, especially, is very good at reducing immense historical events, such as wars, and individual lives, such as Patton's, to a two- or three-hour highlight reel. But we should not forget that this process of distillation uses staged dialogue, emotionally leading music, cinematographic sleights of hand, and substantial editing. When the drama is produced effectively, we tend to forget that the film is a representation of a complicated reality. And this creates a problem for judgment.

We forget that supposedly "realistic" representations of war are re-presentations of reality that are guided by the director's choices, the cameraman's vantage point, the narratives contrived by screenwriters, and the interpretations of the actors. Even a first-person video, such as those from Iraq and Afghanistan, cut the viewer off from reality, offering only a limited representation of reality. This reminder about the problem of realism and verisimilitude in war films is important today, since very few Americans will ever experience war directly.[21] While the reality of military service is very far from the experience of most Americans, the traditional war film—now being supplemented by these first-person videos—provides a stand-in description of what war is like. But we must remember that such cinematic representations are always susceptible to manipulation and interpretation.

The conflict between the macroscopic or public view of war and the private experience of war's human subjects represents an aesthetic and epistemological problem. It is difficult to represent the reality of any social event in a way that does justice to both the public and the private elements involved. But the depth and breadth of this conflict between public and private, between objective and subjective points of view, becomes acute in attempts to represent war. It is exceedingly difficult to do justice to both perspectives on war. If one focuses on the private experience, one misses the public rationale and historical exigencies of war. But if one focuses on the grand historical scope of war, one misses its effects on the subjective individual. This problem has been recognized by scholars who have interpreted war films, such as Dana Polan, who focuses on Malick's *Thin Red Line,* along with *Saving Private Ryan, Full Metal Jacket,* and *Apocalypse Now.* Polan argues that the recent aesthetic trend in war films is one of incoherence: "In the recent combat film, unity—unity of form and content, of mission and meaning, of character and moral purpose—frequently comes undone." Polan concludes by noting that this difficulty in establishing unity and coherence is part of "modern cinema's ambitious and auspicious inability to find a way to recount war."[22] Perhaps the problem is that it is impossible to adequately represent both the public and the private elements in war: to see war as a public event that sweeps up individuals in its wake, while also doing justice to the lived experience of war for these individuals. What is discovered in the attempt to represent both perspectives is the inability to make sense of and recount war. Recognizing this inability is "auspicious" (to use Polan's term) because it indicates a greater sense of awareness and understanding, both about the phenomenon of war and about the limitations of art.

If we are going to judge war, we need to find a way to comprehend it. The process of moral comprehension is a function of what we might call "the moral imagination." One feature of the moral imagination is the ability to imagine oneself into the experience of another. Martha Nussbaum has indicated in a number of places the central importance of literature for stimulating the moral imagination. In her interpretation of Henry James, Nussbaum suggests that moral knowledge is a sort of perception: "It is seeing a complex, concrete reality in a highly lucid and richly responsive way; it is taking in what is there, with imagination and feeling."[23] In an interpretation of Nussbaum, Mark Johnson concludes that narrative is centrally important for moral education.[24] Nussbaum and Johnson emphasize the power of narrative to help us imagine good lives. They also recognize the importance of acknowledging irreducible complexity in moral decision making. A further feature of the moral imagination lies in the creation or expansion of empathy.[25] Jonathan Glover recounts how failures of imagination and deliberate hardness in the face of natural sympathy led to atrocities in the Second World War. He concludes: "Central to the moral imagination is seeing what is humanly important. When it is stimulated, there is a breakthrough of the human responses, otherwise deadened by such things as distance, tribalism, or ideology."[26] The problem that we have seen in this essay is that there are conflicting interpretations of "what is humanly important": Is it the individual perspective or the general perspective?

War usually occurs as a result of a failure of moral imagination: as human beings fail to find common ground. Unfortunately, our imaginations are fallible and limited. This essay has attempted to show that it is nearly impossible to fully imagine the reality of war. When we imagine war—in film, literature, or in the process of making moral evaluations—it is very difficult to imagine the totality of war. Should we emphasize the blood and brutality? Should we emphasize the public good and just-war rationales of war? Should we emphasize the strategy, the complexity of the machinery, and the organization of men that we see in war? Should we emphasize the heroism and camaraderie of the warriors? Or should we focus on the death, misery, and dehumanizing process of battle? The problem is that war is not one thing: it is both a collective event aimed at public goods and a very private activity in which individuals live, kill, and die.

If it is hard to fully represent the complexity of war in film, it may also be difficult to imagine oneself into the place of another, in any circumstance. While *Patton* provides us with the vantage point of the general concerned with the collective, it remains extremely difficult fully to imagine what it would be like to be General Patton and to make the sorts of decisions that the real Patton made. Who but an actual general or a president can really understand what it would be like to be responsible for millions of people in an effort of world-historical importance? While the opening sequence of *Saving Private Ryan* presents us with the first-person perspective of the individual soldier landing at Normandy, no film can ever fully represent the actuality of battle. Who but the soldier himself can ever understand what it is like to fight and die on a foreign beach? Furthermore, any attempt to imagine the reality of war would have to find a way to synthesize both perspectives. But when we attempt to combine these perspectives in our mind's eye, we see the challenge of fully comprehending the reality of war: the collective focus of war and the individual experience of battle cannot be fully synthesized. And thus, the problem of the war film reminds us of the problem that leads to war in the first place: our inability to fully represent or understand the complex reality of the human experience.

Notes

1. I examine the conflict between collectivism and individualism in war in *Public War, Private Conscience* (London: Continuum, 2010). I discuss the morality of war in *The Just War Myth* (Lanham, MD: Rowman and Littlefield, 2008). The present essay benefited greatly from the insights of Valerie Fiala, a film buff who guided my research on the topic.

2. There are a variety of issues that we cannot discuss here with regard to representation and realism in art and in film. These issues have been recognized at least since Walter Benjamin's 1936 essay "The Work of Art in the Age of Mechanical Reproduction," in Benjamin, *Illuminations* (New York: Harcourt Brace Jovanovich, 1969). For more recent discussions, see Stanley Cavell, *The World Viewed: Reflections on the Ontology of Film* (Cambridge, MA: Harvard University Press, 1979); or Lúcia Nagib, *World Cinema and the Ethics of Realism* (London: Continuum, 2011).

3. Charles M. Province, "The Famous Patton Speech," www.pattonhq.com/speech.html.

4. Steven Jay Rubin, *Combat Films: American Realism, 1945–2010* (Jefferson, NC: McFarland, 2011), 5.

5. See the "Bureau of Motion Pictures Report" on Casablanca's propaganda value at Digital History, www.digitalhistory.uh.edu.

6. Laurence H. Suid, *Guts and Glory: The Making of the American Military Image in Film* (Lexington: University Press of Kentucky, 2002), xii.

7. David L. Robb, *Operation Hollywood: How the Pentagon Shapes and Censors the Movies* (New York: Prometheus Books, 2004).

8. "In 'Act of Valor,' a Secret Military World, Approved for Public Viewing," *New York Times*, February 10, 2012.

9. See Keith Dromm, "Spielberg and Cinematic Realism," in *Steven Spielberg and Philosophy*, ed. Dean Kowalski (Lexington: University Press of Kentucky, 2008).

10. Jeanine Basinger, *The World War II Combat Film: Anatomy of a Genre* (Middletown, CT: Wesleyan University Press, 2003), 253.

11. See the 2005 transcript from the Federal Communications Commission (FCC) at http://transition.fcc.gov/eb/Orders/2005/FCC-05-23A1.html.

12. *Telegraph* (London), August 19, 2009, telegraph.co.uk.

13. See, for example, Matt Gallagher, "Why Vets Aren't Buying 'The Hurt Locker,'" *AOL News*, March 6, 2010, aolnews.com.

14. Mark C. Brinkley, "Our Top 10 Best Military Movies of All Time," *Army Times*, July 5, 2007, armytimes.com.

15. For a useful discussion of the complexity of *Full Metal Jacket* in the context of Kubrick's other work, see Bill Krohn, "Full Metal Jacket," www.visual-memory.co.uk/amk/doc/0104.html.

16. For discussion of patriotism and war, see Stephen Nathanson, *Patriotism, Morality, and Peace* (Lanham, MD: Rowman and Littlefield, 1993).

17. Rebecca Winters Keegan, "10 Questions for Francis Ford Coppola," *Time Magazine*, Aug. 14, 2006.

18. Howard Zinn, "Saving Private Ryan," in *Howard Zinn on War* (New York: Seven Stories Press, 2001); also see Albert Auster, "*Saving Private Ryan* and American Triumphalism," in Robert T. Eberwein, ed., *The War Film* (New Brunswick, NJ: Rutgers University Press, 2004).

19. Tim O'Brien, *The Things They Carried* (New York: Houghton Mifflin Harcourt, 2009), 65.

20. See Last Free Voice, http://lastfreevoice.wordpress.com/2008/06/13/david-motari/. I was unable to trace the original place where this explanation was posted, although several websites suggest that it began on Motari's now-defunct MySpace page. Some online commentators have argued that the Motari video was a hoax. But the story did appear in the mainstream press. And the Everett, Washington, newspaper, the *Herald*, published several articles on the topic, including an interview with David Motari's

mother; see Yoshiaki Nohara and Justin Arnold, "Monroe Mother Defends Son Kicked Out of Marines," heraldnet.com.

21. See the Pew Research Center report "The Military-Civilian Gap: Fewer Family Connections," November 23, 2011, pewsocialtrends.org.

22. Dana Polan, "Auteurism and War-teurism: Terrence Malick's War Movie," in *The War Film,* ed. Robert T. Eberwein (New Brunswick, NJ: Rutgers University Press, 2004), 55, 61.

23. Martha Nussbaum, *Poetic Justice: The Literary Imagination and Public Life* (Boston: Beacon Press, 1997), 152. Also see Cora Diamond, "Anything but Argument?" *Philosophical Investigations* 5, no. 1 (January 1982): 23–41.

24. Mark Johnson, *Moral Imagination: Implications of Cognitive Science for Ethics* (Chicago: University of Chicago Press, 1994). Also see Joseph H. Kupfer, "Film Criticism and Virtue Theory," in *Philosophy of Film and Motion Pictures: An Anthology,* ed. Jinhee Choi and Noël Carroll (London: Wiley, 2006), 335–46.

25. See Alex Neill, "Empathy and (Film) Fiction," in Choi and Carroll, *Philosophy of Film and Motion Pictures,* 247–59.

26. Jonathan Glover, *Humanity: A Moral History of the 20th Century* (New Haven, CT: Yale University Press, 1999), 408. Also John Paul Lederach, *The Moral Imagination: The Art and Soul of Building Peace* (Oxford: Oxford University Press, 2005). I have discussed the issue of "moral imagination" in Andrew Fiala, *Tolerance and the Ethical Life* (London: Continuum, 2005), where I use the term in a way that refers back to David Norton, *Imagination, Understanding, and the Virtue of Liberality* (Lanham, MD: Rowman and Littlefield, 1996); and Martin Buber, *The Knowledge of Man* (New York: Harper and Row, 1965).

The Work of Art in the Age of Embedded Journalism

Fiction versus Depiction in *Zero Dark Thirty*

K. L. Evans

Zero Dark Thirty, directed by Kathryn Bigelow and written by Mark Boal, takes its title from a military term for half-past midnight—that still, nocturnal hour in which Osama bin Laden's Pakistan compound was raided and robbed of its prize. To civilians, the term also implies that some people are awake while the rest of us sleep, that we are safeguarded by their sharp-eyed vigilance, and in Bigelow's film these silent soldiers get their day in the sun. "I was interested in putting the audience into the shoes of the men and women in the thick of this hunt," noted Bigelow, after she and Boal, a former freelance journalist, began investigating how bin Laden was finally tracked down. Her instinct lay in "giv[ing] people a glimpse at the dedication and courage and sacrifice they made."[1]

Already there is something of a puzzle, though, in Bigelow's description, since she aims to provide a truthful view of CIA field agents *and* to convincingly simulate the view from where they stand, to offer at-home audiences an accurate account of what these agents undergo. And what happens when a film switches back and forth between two radically different representational modes? Can it throw light on matters of moral, social, and political concern, as *Zero Dark Thirty* hopes to, when it brings together in one continuous narrative that method of representation associated with feature films (the work of art, an effort of the imagination) and the quasi-journalistic approach Bigelow uses to reconstruct a topical incident, a kind of aesthetic articulation of the film's opening promise that it has been "based on firsthand accounts of actual events"? How distorted is the "glimpse" *Zero Dark Thirty* presents when the film's expressive possibilities are not only located in its verisimilitude, but anchored by the background of an actual, recent event? Or when instead of looking *at* something, we are invited (by the real soundtrack of 9/11 panic that opens the film, for example, or by the view through night-vision lenses of the raid in Pakistan) to go through it?

These are questions made more germane in relation to mounting criticism that *Zero Dark Thirty* misrepresents an issue central to it: the CIA's use of what, in a chilling euphemism, it called "enhanced interrogation." In response to the charge from many quarters that *Zero Dark Thirty* misleadingly promotes the efficacy of torture (in that it encourages viewers to associate torture with the capture of Osama bin Laden), Bigelow and Boal insist that rather than come to any conclusion about what Bigelow calls "a part of the story we couldn't ignore," their film unsparingly portrays reality. "Depiction is not endorsement," Bigelow has quite fairly noted.[2] She also says, "What we were attempting is almost a journalistic approach to film," and that she wishes torture were "not part of our history. But it was."[3] However if Bigelow's view of herself as reluctant truth-teller has been largely accepted by film critics (the movie "is a cool, outwardly nonpartisan intelligence procedural," writes Manohla Dargis),[4] it has infuriated a cross-section of politicians, public officials, and newspersons, many of whom maintain that the filmmakers' commitment to just-the-facts journalism only highlights how far their film strays from real life.[5]

There is, in other words, an additional dimension to the rather significant business, given the film's success, the magnitude of its audience, of deciding whether *Zero Dark Thirty* excuses or excoriates torture; whether it champions the covert operations of the CIA or offers an unparalleled view of America's most celebrated display of force, the illegal invasion of Pakistan and the execution of an unarmed man. For while this film fully intends to operate at the level of reality, it is also determined to tell the truth, and for the makers of *Zero Dark Thirty,* we get closer to the truth as we increase our experiential limits. For screenwriter-producer Boal, "the real power of filmmaking is found at the intersection of investigation and imagination," where the combination of reporting and creativity "reaches further and pushes harder than traditional reporting or purely fictional storytelling on their own."[6] For director Bigelow, a film's truthfulness lies in its attention to visual and atmospheric detail and is earned by way of a filmmaker's heuristic use of her tools. As she puts it, "I've spent a fair amount of time thinking about what my aptitude is and I really think it's to explore and push the medium."[7] "Pushing the medium," for both Boal and Bigelow, means using innovative technology and a mixture of fiction and reportage to transform firsthand accounts into a firsthand experience for viewers—to "make the news behind the news more accessible, more visceral, more real."[8] By "more real," these filmmakers tacitly mean "more true." In this essay, then, I consider where *Zero Dark Thirty* alights in our oldest (and, increasingly, most misunderstood) philosophical dispute: Does knowledge derived from experience make it *more* or *less* possible to see rightly? The point is worth brooding over because the fact that this film locates itself firmly on one side of *this* dispute in effect decides the outcome of the other, however well each side assembles its arguments.

Virtual Experience

For *Zero Dark Thirty,* Kathryn Bigelow has explained, she "wanted a boots-on-the-ground experience."[9] To Bigelow this phrase describes what she wants viewers to feel in the way of direct and immediate participation—as if, if the events in the film are to be understood, they must be lived through. But Bigelow has also employed this phrase to fend off criticism about her film's fairness and historical accuracy, which suggests that for her it denotes more than her audience's heightened sense of involvement. Having "boots on the ground" also implies a different kind of access to reality—and in particular, a more varied, nuanced view, since it follows that where there are feet there are eyes, and where eyes, perspective more fluid and wide-ranging than a camera's limited scope. Wanting to put "boots on the ground" means offering audiences a chance to see naturalistically, that is to say, which is the basis for the audiences' feeling of complete involvement. For Bigelow the phrase is shorthand for the technical sophistication indispensable to her films' trademark verisimilitude (particularly since 2008's *The Hurt Locker,* for which she won an Oscar), a style of shooting that can involve running four camera crews simultaneously and editing hundreds of hours of footage in order to accommodate the multiple perspectives required by Bigelow's sophisticated approach to composition and montage. Offering multiple perspectives is important to Bigelow because "that's how we experience reality," she says, "by looking at the microcosm and the macrocosm simultaneously. The eye sees differently than the lens, but with multiple focal lengths and a muscular editorial style, the lens can give you that microcosm/macrocosm perspective, and that contributes to the feeling of total immersion."[10]

Certainly, as an opportunity to experience something—to feel immersed in the work of the CIA unit charged with finding bin Laden—*Zero Dark Thirty* resoundingly succeeds. Thanks largely to her shooting and editing approach, Bigelow is able to marshal a largely fruitless and fragmentary manhunt dragging out over a decade into a gripping psychological thriller. "It's all hurry up and wait, hurry up and wait," writes an enamored David Edelstein, naming it the best film of 2012.[11] And while "with ample reason, we often dismiss what comes out of the commercially minded dream factory of Hollywood as simplistic, candied, trivial," writes Frank Bruni, *Zero Dark Thirty* (like *Lincoln,* another contender in 2012's Oscar race) is "dedicated to the ethical ambiguities and messy compromises of governing—to the muck and stink that sometimes go into the effort of keeping this mighty country of ours intact and safe."[12] Few other celebrated critics have failed to admire what David Denby calls *Zero Dark Thirty*'s "radical realism," a phrase that simultaneously captures Bigelow's passion for plunging audiences into events in a way that feels "raw, immediate, and visceral," as Bigelow said about her celebrated work on *The Hurt Locker,* and her flair for assembling lifelike renderings of objectionable acts, unlikable people, and unkempt, uninspiring spaces.

"The virtue of *Zero Dark Thirty,*" writes Denby, "is that it pays close attention to the way that life does work"—which for Denby means that "it combines ruthlessness and humanity in a manner that is paradoxical and disconcerting and yet satisfying as art."[13] Denby's juxtaposition of "ruthlessness" and "humanity" presumably conveys the idea that what viewers see in this film isn't pretty; the CIA unit charged with finding bin Laden is not simply trying to prevent further attacks but is openly seeking revenge, and its methods for intelligence-gathering involve acts any viewer can recognize as immoral and even unlawful.[14] But the fact that we *do* see these acts—that we experience what CIA field agents chose or were required to experience, and that in addition to becoming onlookers at the torment and degradation American field agents inflict upon their captives, we are made privy to "the anger and the desperation; the terse, anxious exchanges among agents; the breathless chase through crowded Pakistani streets"—turns the film into a frank look at the fact or condition of being human.

On this point we should concentrate, then, since it constitutes in essence the defense Bigelow and Boal assemble in response to their critics: that rather than take sides over the question of what part "enhanced interrogation" played in the hunt to find bin Laden, the film takes a candid look at the lives of what Bigelow calls "ordinary Americans who fought bravely even as they *sometimes* crossed moral lines."[15] Though prior to the film's release some right-wing pundits thought it would bolster Obama's image in time for reelection, and following its release many left-leaning politicians and reporters have called the film dangerous and morally reprehensible, the filmmakers insist that *Zero Dark Thirty* "doesn't have an agenda, and it doesn't judge," as Bigelow told the *New Yorker*'s Dexter Filkins.[16] Or that if it does have an agenda, "it isn't a partisan agenda," as Mark Boal has said. "It's an agenda of trying to look behind the scenes at what went down."[17]

Even so, partly because "what went down" includes an unvarnished look inside the CIA's largely frustrating search for bin Laden, including what went on in the early years of the hunt at "black sites" (where the CIA's treatment of terror suspects has now been declared "torture" by the European Court of Human Rights in Strasbourg—the first time this has happened), and partly because the filmmakers got considerable cooperation from the CIA in the making of the film, the hope Boal once expressed for staying "above the political fray" has been unsuccessful.[18] The accusation to which Bigelow and Boal have, with reluctance, been compelled to respond, is that without flinching from the brutality or inhumanity of the CIA's use of torture, *Zero Dark Thirty* nevertheless portrays torture as something of a necessary option—as repellent but, on occasion, fruitful.

Enthusiasts of the film have generally agreed with Boal that on the subject of torture, "what the film does over the course of two hours is show the complexity of the debate."[19] Some have even pointed out that in the film, only misinformation is attained by torture, or that *Zero Dark Thirty* "does not present torture as the silver bullet that led to bin Laden," as Spencer Ackerman writes. Instead, "it presents torture as the ignorant alternative to that silver bullet."[20] Viewers suffer through a scene in which detained al-Qaeda operative Ammar (Reda Kateb) is subjected to emotional distress, naked humiliation, and waterboarding, but Manohla Dargis of the *New York Times* writes that "it is only later," *after* Ammar is tortured, when CIA agents Dan (Jason Clarke) and Maya (Jessica Chastain) "lie to Ammar, sit across from him at a table, talk to him like a human being and give him food and a cigarette, that he offers them a potential lead."[21]

And yet despite the film's many ambiguities, critics' impression of what the film sanctions is worth taking seriously if only because the narrative engine of Boal's detective story is kick-started by torture, as filmmaker Alex Gibney sagely points out, and because the film's viewers first hear the nickname of bin Laden's courier, Abu Ahmed al-Kuwaiti, from the lips of a CIA detainee, the composite character "Ammar." These rather mundane facts are significant because even viewers who agree with Dargis that the film actually questions the efficacies of torture still understand that there is *some* connection between the CIA's detention program and the discovery of the leading clue in the race to find bin Laden, some causative connection between torture and actionable intelligence, even if it is an unpredictable connection. Though what stays in the mind of a viewer like Dargis is the *fraught* connection between coercive interrogation methods and actionable intelligence, the fact is, a connection, however unreliable, has been established. In other words, even a careful viewer of the film (as opposed to a careless viewer like Joe Scarborough, the conservative host of MSNBC's show *Morning Joe,* who, as Jane Mayer points out, argued that the film's narrative, "whether you find it repugnant or not," shows that the CIA program was effective and "led to the couriers, that led, eventually, years later, to the killing of Osama bin Laden") is left with the feeling that torture was not just a part of the story of our interrogation program, but part of the story of bin Laden's capture; that torture played a vital if unpredictable part in the capture of the world's most wanted man.[22]

This is a considerable point because of what it makes incontestable: that in its narrative logic this dramatization of events contradicts the findings of the Senate Intelligence Committee's study of the CIA's Detention and Interrogation Program, which, following the examination of more than 6 million pages of records from the Intelligence Community, concludes that the CIA did *not* obtain its first clues about the identity of bin Ladin's courier from CIA detainees subjected to coercive interrogation techniques. That is, we do not need to decide how this film tells its story visually and tonally—we do not need to give it the close, careful reading it deserves—in order to say that the film accepts without question that the CIA's "enhanced interrogation techniques" played a role in enabling the agency to identify the courier who unwittingly led them to bin Laden. In this regard the filmmakers' vision goes against the information offered by dependable sources, for instance, the letter Leon Panetta, then director of the CIA, sent to Arizona senator John McCain shortly after bin Laden was killed, clearly stating, "We first learned about 'the facilitator/courier's nom de guerre' from a detainee not in the CIA's custody."[23]

It is for this reason that the film's sharpest critics don't object to the fact that the film *depicts* torture; rather they object to the *inadequacy* of its depiction. Jane Mayer, author of *The Dark Side,* argues that the film airbrushes the inexcusability of torture when Maya, the key CIA investigator into bin

Laden's whereabouts, "is shown standing mutely by when the detainee is strung up by ropes, stripped naked, and forced to crawl in a dog collar." Mayer points out, "In reality, when the CIA first subjected a detainee to incarceration in a coffin-size 'confinement box,' as is shown in the movie, an FBI agent present at the scene threw a fit, warned the CIA contractor proposing the plan that it was illegal, counterproductive, and reprehensible. The fight went all the way to the top of the Bush Administration."[24]

Then again, since *Zero Dark Thirty* really isn't about the crisis of conscience that rocked the top ranks of the U.S. government but about those whom Bigelow calls the ordinary Americans who sometimes cross moral lines, film director Alex Gibney's confusion over Maya's seeming unassailability seems more apposite: "Kathryn Bigelow must have been delighted when she discovered a female C.I.A. agent was at the heart of the hunt for bin Laden," Gibney writes.

> But compare Maya's infallibility in the film with the case of another female C.I.A. agent—a redhead, like Jessica Chastain—who . . . supervised the kidnapping and torture of a man named Khaled el-Masri in the C.I.A.'s "Salt Pit," a black site in Afghanistan. Despite a valid German passport, the agent insisted on his continued torment and incarceration (despite the protests of Condoleezza Rice) until it was finally revealed that the agent had mixed him up with another man named al-Masri. (Whoops, we tortured a man over a spelling mistake!) Without apology, he was then dropped on a lonely road in Albania to try to pick up the pieces of his life.[25]

Gibney then asks judiciously, "Where did we see this kind of cruel incompetence treated in *Zero Dark Thirty?*"[26] What Gibney's comparison highlights is not only the reprehensibility of the CIA's "detainee program," but its illogicality and confusedness. We might put it this way: given *Zero*'s journalistic approach, shouldn't the general senselessness of the program compete, visually, with its general repulsiveness?

The answer to this question, I think, returns us to the problem Bigelow runs into, logically and technically, when she tries simultaneously to construct a view of one of these largely anonymous agents and the view from where she stands. For as Bigelow reports, "I was thrilled" to discover that one of the key CIA agents was a young woman, "and it wasn't just the gender aspect, though it was kind of extraordinary to me to learn that there were women pivotal in this operation. But it was the opportunity to tell this story through somebody at the ground level, to put the audience in the shoes of somebody like that. The story is inherently dramatic."[27] Underlying Bigelow's notion that a story told from an individual's point of view is more dramatic is her assumption that the story's central character or medium for communication should be a person with whom a largely civilian audience can have a connection—and that in trying to imagine oneself living the life of a CIA operative, a female character (particularly one who can be played by an appealing actress like Jessica Chastain, whom David Denby describes as having "a slightly distraught look, a sudden smile, a warm-spirited responsiveness") feels more relatable than a male. Bigelow's interest in ordinary people doing extraordinary things is evidenced, at least, by her assertion that "Bin Laden wasn't defeated by superheroes zooming down from the sky; he was defeated by ordinary Americans who fought bravely even as they *sometimes* crossed moral lines, who labored greatly and intently, who gave all of themselves in both victory and defeat, in life and in death, for the defense of this nation."[28]

But if the connection the audience has with Maya is so crucial—if the particular function of this character is to let viewers into this story "at the ground level," or allow us to put ourselves in the shoes of someone facing these obstacles and responsibilities, then *as a good film critic,* and not just as a man of conscience, Alex Gibney is right to worry about the fact that Maya is never wrong and her unerring certainty is never questioned. Conflating the criticism of Mayer and Gibney, we might say that Maya's lack of objection to the use of waterboarding, for example, lends a stomach-turning quality to the scene in which she persuades representatives from the Defense Department to green-light the raid on the Abbottabad compound she believes is bin Laden's. Not that the filmmakers offer any sign that viewers ought to question Maya, who in this scene is positioned as the fail-safe champion of truth, daringly fighting bureaucratic number-crunchers. Maya's response to a query regarding her credentials or her relevance—the "Who are you?" that becomes the final expression of doubt about Maya's value, begun with her assignment to a dusty, unused desk in a dilapidated office and held like a high, painful note throughout the film—is meant to be triumphant: "I'm the motherfucker who brought you the house." Lurking behind Gibney's legitimate question about Maya's worrying infallibility, that is to say, is some concern that the source of this film's strength, the feeling of immersion it gives viewers, is also its greatest liability. That is because the world into which

Zero Dark Thirty's viewers are immersed is, largely, *Maya's* world—and by extension the world of CIA operatives—which is perhaps why there is no way to inject the (now legendary) failures of the CIA's "detainee program" into this drama.

Girl, Implanted

Filmmaker Alex Gibney's answer to the question of why, with so much evidence of so many failures—practical, legal, moral—of the CIA's "detainee program," there is so little evidence of it in the film, is that "Boal and Bigelow were seduced by their sources."[29] This is a common problem, he says, since those who are given extraordinary access are inclined to believe the persons granting the access. In this way Gibney contextualizes the worry some viewers have expressed about a screenplay based largely on the firsthand accounts of CIA operatives. As Peter Maass of the *Atlantic* most pointedly argues, "*Zero Dark Thirty* represents a new genre of embedded filmmaking that is the problematic offspring of the worrisome endeavor known as embedded journalism."[30]

Maass explains, "Embeds, officially begun during the invasion of Iraq, are deeply troubling because not every journalist or filmmaker can get these coveted invitations . . . and once you get one, you face the quandary of keeping a critical distance from sympathetic people whom you get to know and who are probably quite convincing. That's the reason the embed or special invitation exists; the government does its best to keep journalists, even friendly ones, away from disgruntled officials who have unflattering stories to tell." Maass doesn't fault Bigelow and Boal, since he "can't imagine any filmmaker or journalist saying 'no' to the kind of access they apparently received," nor can he "imagine many filmmakers or journalists, having gotten that access, writing a story or making a movie that would be less favorable to the CIA than *Zero Dark Thirty*." That is the nature of embedding, he writes: "It primes its targets (I mean, journalists and filmmakers) to create stories that are skewed in the government's favor. That is one reason, I think, the film presents torture as effective—the C.I.A. is ground zero of that unholy belief. If Boal and Bigelow had embedded at the FBI, whose agents have been critical of torture, their film would probably have a different message about waterboarding, sleep deprivation, and cramming a prisoner into a sealed box that's no bigger than an oven." Nevertheless, as a journalist who has on several occasions benefited from embedded or invitation-only reporting (and who would like to think that the stories he produced on those occasions were critical and worthwhile), Maass is less worried about the problems attached to getting special access ("let's be honest—similar omissions are committed every day by journalists, pundits, politicians and filmmakers, and we don't get terribly upset") than by what he calls "the government's skill, time and time again, for getting its story told so uncritically."[31] In a variation on this theme, Gibney writes that "there is nothing wrong with access per se," but that "what is concerning is the way that the C.I.A.—and other military agencies—grant selective access."[32]

Nevertheless, "access" is by nature selective, and it seems as though there is more to be gained by questioning these filmmakers' faith in what access *achieves,* their confidence that imagination combined with reporting "reaches further and pushes harder than traditional reporting or purely fictional storytelling on their own," than in discussing the problems inherent in selective access.

In her stoutly favorable review of the film for the *New York Times,* Manohla Dargis calls *Zero Dark Thirty* "a seamless weave of truth and drama."[33] But isn't it the case that so long as the film's audience is positioned to see through these agents' eyes, or feel ourselves in their shoes (to feel their frustration as al-Qaeda pulled off attacks in Saudi Arabia, Britain, and Pakistan; also to see "what went down" in agency-run "Black sites," or have a green-tinged night-vision of what it is like to move stealthily into the airless, cramped rooms of a family compound and shoot whoever is seen), our view *of* these agents—all that is encompassed by what Boal dismissively calls "purely fictional storytelling"—will necessarily be obscured? What Bigelow and Boal clearly believe is that the more closely we approximate what Maya sees, the better we will see Maya. However this idea is the source of much confusion in the film.

For one thing, what makes Maya so convincing—what allows her to be the point person in the film's fabrication of Operation Neptune's Spear, the May 1, 2011, Navy SEAL siege of bin Laden's hideout in Abbottabad, or what makes her the "motherfucker" who can tell the Defense Department when to strike—is, as one character says, "her conviction." Conviction about something as important as whom to detain and interrogate, or whose house to raid, ought to be based on the actionable intelligence garnered from what acting director of the CIA Michael J. Morell describes as information gathered from "the selfless commitment of hundreds" of analysts and officers.[34] And yet as an individual soldier, someone working at the ground level,

Maya's conviction is the product of what she sees and feels, the immediate knowledge that comes from her senses. About one detainee Maya notes that she has to see him with her own eyes in order to tell whether he is lying or not, and the message everywhere in the film is that Maya has authority precisely because she's done her *own* looking. We see her watching countless hours of taped "interviews" with detainees, torture sessions we know she can stand to see because the first and most important piece of information the film's audience has about Maya is that she is willing to watch Ammar being tortured. And it's because of all she has seen that viewers are supposed to trust her instincts: when Maya's fellow agent Dan accuses her of pushing a theory about Abu Ahmed al-Kuwaiti because she *feels* it to be true, Maya emphatically agrees, as if it were is a point of pride.

Of course, if we ever saw Maya be wrong about something—saw her torture the wrong person, perhaps—the foundation for her conviction could be subject to some examination, and the crudity of her experiential approach could be exposed. (In that case viewers might find themselves watching an ordinary American fighting bravely even as she sometimes crossed moral lines.) And yet because we do not see Maya guessing wrongly—in sum, because it *is* bin Laden's house that she eventually targets—the audience forgets that her methods never achieved more than her own personal certainty and that she might well have encountered a contradiction that would have brought the whole edifice of her thinking down in ruins. In the equation "CIA agent with ordinary powers of observation + superhuman dedication = bin Laden," that is to say, it must still be borne in mind that the rigor of the proof remains an illusion, so long as the premise is justified by the conclusion, or so long as the ends justify the means.

And yet I digress, since what matters to me is not really where Maya goes wrong but where filmmaking does, and I think this film goes off the rails when Bigelow and Boal carry out their belief that putting audiences in a scene helps them to understand something about it. What is interesting to me is how completely that notion falls apart in *Zero Dark Thirty*, despite the fact that the film is a stylistic masterwork. For what the film tries to bring into view in a truthful way is the existence of someone like Maya, the filmmakers' chosen representative for the small army of hard-to-see field agents whose sacrifices were perhaps more tangible than their accomplishments; yet the irony is that whatever truthful glimpse of Maya's life these filmmakers can contrive is constrained and ultimately *falsified* by what Bigelow calls her "responsibility to be faithful to the material," her hope of cleaving so closely to a field agent's experience that at-home viewers virtually undergo the same. Consequently, even as *Zero Dark Thirty* tries to provide a true account of what Steve Coll names "the most undigested trauma in American National life," all it in fact reveals is the vast difference between faithful accounts of experience—truths of the "I have been there and seen it" strain—and those glimpses of something we call reality for the reason that they are *not* limited to any particular perspective, no matter how close to the action. If a glimpse of reality is what we're after, I'm going to argue, we must go looking for it in fiction.[35]

Should we need proof that seeing what Maya sees doesn't help us see *her*, in any case, we have it. That is because catching a truthful glimpse of Maya's life ought to offer a truthful glimpse of the CIA's "detainee program," as the film's critics have intuited, and *that* this film does not do—and not because it fails to show the repulsiveness of "enhanced interrogation" (David Denby describes the film's most difficult scenes as "expertly done, without flinching from the horror of the acts and without exploitation") but because it fails to show what Alex Gibney calls the "lunacy" of it.[36]

In his review of the film for the *New York Times Review of Books,* Steve Coll describes that aspect of the program that did not surface in the film: namely, the way the agency enfolded "enhanced interrogation" into its ordinary bureaucratic or administrative activities. Coll recalls how "a partially declassified report prepared by the C.I.A.'s former inspector general, John Helgerson, indicates that physicians from the C.I.A.'s Office of Medical Services attended interrogation sessions and took prisoners' vital signs to assure they were healthy enough for the torture to continue. Agency officers typed out numbingly detailed cables and memos about the enhanced interrogation sessions, as the available outline of the Senate Intelligence Committee's classified investigation makes clear. Videotapes were recorded and logged." This, more than anything else, reveals the extent of the madness of the CIA's "detainee program," which is perhaps the reason the filmmakers chose to exclude it. As Coll notes, "This C.I.A. office routine might have been more shocking on screen than the clichéd physical abuse of prisoners that the filmmakers prefer."[37]

To this criticism we can imagine Mark Boal responding that one can't put in everything, as he did when he joked to an interviewer that some people seem to think a film "based on firsthand accounts" should resemble "a videotaped transcription of a six volume Senate report."[38] And yet there is something very shrewd about Coll's suggestion that witnessing American agents make brutalizing use of torture (as we have come to expect from watching television shows like *24* or *Homeland*) is finally less alarming than seeing "what the record shows about how regulated, lawyerly, and bureaucratized—how banal—torture apparently became at some of the C.I.A. black sites,"[39] and thus that this film exorcises from the narrative that which would *really* surprise and upset its viewers. For while the film's audience can observe Maya witnessing and even making use of torture in a way that is appalling (that is meant to appall, or to inspire us to question her choices, as we might question our own), we cannot see anything that would disrupt *this* narrative, this story about what Frank Bruni called "the muck and stink that sometimes go into the effort of keeping this mighty country of ours intact and safe." What Coll's point brings to light is that the audience for *Zero Dark Thirty* can't see something that *someone treated or acted upon in the film* can't see—which, of course, is precisely the trouble with a film wherein the audience's view of the world on-screen is identical to that of a subject in a scene.

For that reason it is not enough to make plain, as many excellent critics have done, why *Zero Dark Thirty*'s depiction of events is not a truthful one. Because the film's reviewers must finally decide whether this film is "satisfying as art," in Denby's phrase, we should also explicitly tie the film's limited or inadequate outlook to the filmmakers' choice of *narrative mode*—tie it, as I will now argue, to the fact that the preponderance of the film has been conceived from a special perspective, the view from the ground that is also the film's defining or driving force.

Rather than suggest that this film doesn't replicate reality, that is to say, to which criticism any filmmaker has only to shrug, and win the point, we should argue that ultimately it is Bigelow and Boal's underlying aesthetic, their championing of a "see for yourself" perspective, that makes inevitable the film's moral complacency. My argument is simply that this film's employment of a privileged point of view (which according to literary convention requires some complicity between the film's creators and its audience) extinguishes the imaginative viewpoint from which this film's subject matter can be fairly seen.

This is in effect a quarrel with the film's psychological realism, a mode of narration that is designed to "let the events talk," or in which a sophisticated creative apparatus (writer, director, multiple cameras, crew) works to remove without trace all signs of that creative apparatus in order to generate in viewers the sense that we are becoming acquainted with real people and real events. So, recalling that the criterion for "realness" in *Zero Dark Thirty* is whether people and events materialize convincingly as our focus shifts back and forth between minutiae and an overall view, or between what Bigelow calls the "microcosm" and the "macrocosm," what happens when filmmakers assume that so long as cameras can be made to function like eyes, filmgoers can confront the events of the film just as we would reality? Because this technique works well, as most viewers of *Zero Dark Thirty* will attest. However, when cameras are turned into eyes, the world viewed is governed or determined by the erection of a limit beyond which filmgoers cannot see *and which we also cannot feel.* That is because the viewing subject can't be conscious of itself as providing a limit. As Wittgenstein (abbreviating Schopenhauer) has noted, "the subject does not belong to the world: rather, it is a limit of the world."[40] Just as "nothing in the visual field allows you to infer that it is seen by an eye," as Wittgenstein explains, since the form of the visual field does not include awareness of the eye ("for the form of the visual field is surely not like this [in the text Wittgenstein includes an illustration—an eye-as-point-of-view with a loop extending outward from that position suggesting the range of its visual field, with the eye's status, as it were, inside the field]") to the viewing subject, the I/eye or solipsistic self "shrinks to a point without extension, and there remains the reality coordinated with it."[41]

With Wittgenstein's help we can better understand what is deceptive about a "boots-on-the-ground" view and thus what is deceptive about this film's realism. As we might now put it, realism is always realism *relative to the perspective* from which things appear, since as Bigelow explains, what makes objects appear visually real are cameras positioned to bring them in and out of focus. Technically, in order to give the impression of being real, the view must be circumscribed. Yet this distinctive or limited view must *feel* as if it exists independently from any individual mind, since from it an audience must have the impression that they may arrive at a proper grasp of the facts. Hence the significance to *Zero Dark Thirty* of cinematographer Grieg Fraser's "fluid but firm use of a handheld camera," as David Denby notes, "so that you feel pitched into the middle of things but also see clearly what you need to see."[42] The view in *Zero Dark Thirty* is from *somewhere,* in other words, since any realistic view has to have a source. And yet this source must be rubbed out since it is its effacement that allows audiences to feel like the view is impartial. That in sum is what this film teaches us about having special access or a privileged perspective. For in order to come off, the film must employ a particular point of view, even though the effectiveness or power of the film rests on the assumption that this view is disinterested and for that reason valid.

The filmmakers' choice of narrative point of view thus occasions a logical problem that can't be solved with tricky camera work. They have constructed a privileged viewpoint (the "boots-on-the-ground" view from which this story is shot and told) from which they can steal away, as it were, leaving viewers to confront the events of the film just as we would a slice of real life, only, of course, with the unshakable certainty of the adequacy of the vision of reality afforded us by this fictional point of view, one that is sadly lacking in *real* real life!

This point about the contradiction a privileged viewpoint creates is made by the philosopher Bernard Harrison, who in his earliest book of literary criticism points out that the "privileged viewpoint is, of course, merely the other side of the coin of authorial omniscience," or that for works of fiction that employ this viewpoint, "the reader knows 'the facts,' and knows that they are all relevant facts, and all the facts that *are* relevant, because they are the facts the author has chosen to lay before him."[43] Of interest to Harrison, accordingly, is the difference between works of fiction that employ a privileged viewpoint (and in this way count on a reader's complicity, or count on a reader to look the other way over the matter of the author's necessary self-effacement) and their opposite: fictional works that subvert this complicity between author and reader or in which it is essential that the reader does *not* enjoy any viewpoint guaranteed in advance to be the one from which everything can be revealed.

What Harrison's discussion calls to mind is that there are fiction writers who painstakingly avoid psychological realism and the privileged viewpoint on which it depends, not because they think there is no such thing as reality, but because they think reality can only ever be glimpsed by two or more points of view at once. About *reality* we should say that no one viewpoint ever feels wholly adequate as a basis from which to grasp what's going on. That is why fiction that hopes to offer glimpses of it usually employs the technique of ironically juxtaposing *contrasting* points of view, of "exposing actions simultaneously to being morally and psychologically construed from more than one direction." In this way whatever the reader manages to learn, about himself or others, he learns by having his preconceptions unsettled. He "must be kept off balance," writes Harrison, "so that, missing his footing in one viewpoint he will regain it again momentarily in another and so learn that perpetual motion of the imagination from which dispassionate moral judgment and understanding of others both grow."[44]

We might say, consequently, that only when *Zero Dark Thirty* does *not* strive to create in viewers the sense that we are becoming acquainted with real people and real events as we would in real life can it offer viewers this chance, since seeing something from more than one direction or in more than one moral register—looking at something from two or more points of view at once—is only possible in *fiction.* Only when the viewer is encouraged to look *at* what is happening on-screen and by an effort of imagination project herself into several viewpoints can we say she transcends the view she most comfortably occupies and in this way has the chance to glimpse (what Plato would call) reality and what Mark Boal means by "what went down."

Now, finally, we can begin to answer the question of whether *Zero Dark Thirty* is satisfying as art, and not simply find fault with the narrow bandwidth of facts it chooses to report. For as Alex Gibney has argued, what is most pernicious about *Zero Dark Thirty* is the way it conveys the views of a particular group of characters—Maya; Dan; the CIA counterterrorism's chief, nicknamed "the Wolf" (Fredric Lehne), who describes how his efforts have been undermined by the sissies in Congress; the Islamabad station chief (Kyle Chandler), who's a Bush administration functionary; an ambitious operative (Jennifer Ehle) who gets killed during an attack—as if they "[exist] in a vacuum," or as if, "for the tough-minded folks who had 'boots on the ground,' there was no other point of view." That's wrong, of course, but "by immersing us only in the world of the C.I.A.," writes Gibney, "Boal and Bigelow don't show us the perspective we need as viewers to see the lunacy of the C.I.A.'s 'detainee program.'" Gibney then points out something fundamental about film, which is that:

> If you want to reveal how tall a man is, you don't shoot him in limbo; you must show him in relation to others. Likewise, how can viewers of *Zero Dark Thirty* judge the CIA's record if they can't see how others were shocked by the cruelty, cowardice and stupidity of EITs [enhanced interrogation techniques]. In the film, long after the torture of "Ammar," an agent hands Maya a file folder with the real name of al-Kuwaiti. "If only I had this years ago," says Maya. Because Maya is the glamorous heroine of the film, we identify with her and wonder about the inefficiency of her colleagues. But where is the character who wonders if Maya had spent less time slapping

> detainees around and more time scanning actual evidence—as the FBI did—she might have got to bin Laden's courier much sooner.[45]

Here Gibney is not suggesting that Bigelow and Boal should have somehow put into the film everything that happened in life, but that they should have put in something that creates a perspective richer or more multidimensional than what Bigelow likes to think of as the "multiple perspective" created by that organ of vision, the human eye. In a film, or in something one has to look *at* in order to understand, perspective is achieved in the way Gibney describes: by contriving to show what someone does or says *in the context in which she does or says it.* If anyone in the scene in which Maya is handed the crucial file, for instance—another overlooked woman from another overlooked corner of the office, say—had offered a rueful smile at Maya's expression of annoyance, and Maya, by chance catching it, had looked momentarily mortified, then viewers of the film would be able to consider the consequences of human error in such situations without the pedestrian interruption of a blank screen with the caption "Human Error" printed on it. The filmmakers' decision to insert this weirdly depersonified signboard between this scene and the next leaves Maya's perfect record intact but the viewer's suspension of disbelief shaken. The very moment in which Bigelow and Boal want "what went down" to be indisputable or self-evident, that is to say, the moment when they want the "facts" they have assembled to "speak for themselves," as it were, is the moment in which the *filmmakers* must make an announcement.

In this kind of film, that kind of authorial interruption only highlights some shortcoming or shows that the filmmakers have not done their work properly. But more importantly, it further illustrates why these filmmakers' immersive techniques—their attempt to offer audiences the chance to virtually experience certain events for themselves—fail to accomplish what much "purely fictional storytelling" accomplishes just fine: the *ironically juxtaposed* points of view that continually unsettle viewers and mock our preconceptions.

Disruptive Filmmaking

If disrupting the viewer's moral complacency is the goal, we should conclude, immersion is not the means. But perhaps some of this film's supporters will object that the creators of *Zero Dark Thirty* do not attempt to encourage moral reflection. After all, in an oft-cited remark, Boal has called the film a "Rorschach test," by which he presumably means to suggest that he and Bigelow have not tried to force viewers to reflect upon what we are doing so much as measure our underlying emotional responses, particularly over issues about which we are reluctant to describe our thinking process openly. And yet given that these filmmakers have called "preposterous" the idea that their dark, intense portrayal of the killing of Osama bin Laden contains an argument for torture, noting that such criticisms amount to a gross misreading of the film, this suggestion about the film's neutral stance seems disingenuous.[46] It is out of keeping, at least, with what feels like Bigelow and Boal's more sincerely felt justification for the film: that it will help those who view it become good citizens. To encourage the opinion that these filmmakers *are* hoping to increase their audience's capacity for moral reflection, then, let's turn briefly to Mark Boal's description of *Zero Dark Thirty* as an example of "disruptive filmmaking," the topic of his keynote address at Loyola Marymount University's 2012 First Amendment Week.

"People talk about 'disruptive technology,'" Boal tells the audience of recent graduates, which "sounds like a bad thing, but disruptive technology isn't good or bad; it's what our society and our culture makes of it that matters. And from the wheel to the automobile, the signal fire to the iPhone, society has generally, if often slowly, found a way to bend disruptive innovation toward the greater good."[47] This was "really what we hoped to do with the disruptive filmmaking of *Zero Dark Thirty*," notes Boal. "To use this relatively new blend of current events and creativity to make the news behind the news more accessible, more visceral, more real." Careful not to forget the reason for his invitation, Boal then notes that "unlike newspaper reports or books or paintings, movies have a special power to put audiences right there—in the scene, in the center of the action, in interrogation cells, in the Pakistani hills. And by giving people a chance to virtually experience these events for themselves, we have a chance to do exactly what the First Amendment creates the space to do: to challenge people to be citizens, to understand and to confront the issues of our day, in our hearts and in our minds."[48]

Because Boal thinks of the film as disruptive and so in the long run illuminating, it is perhaps worth noting that precisely as more Americans virtually experience events like waterboarding, fewer Americans seem willing to denounce the practice. As Steve Coll writes, in the 2012 election campaign "Mitt Romney declared that he would revive the use of 'enhanced interrogation techniques.'" Coll also points out that "in public opinion polling, a bare majority of Americans opposes torturing prisoners in the struggle against terrorism" and that "public support for torture has risen significantly during the last several years, a change that the Stanford University intelligence scholar Amy Zegart has attributed in part to the influence of 'spy-themed entertainment.'"[49]

But never mind for now the discomfiting fact that realistically witnessing the brutality of torture seems to be making us feel more complacent, rather than more ashamed. What we must grapple with is the intuition that the radical realism of *Zero Dark Thirty*, its amplified ability to put audiences "in the scene," will produce citizens better able to understand and to confront the issues of our day; citizens better able to wisely tackle what Bigelow calls "the thorny subjects of our time."[50] For it is by pulling a viewer into the film—and through it to reality—that Bigelow and Boal think they draw him, as spectator and judge, into a complex imagined world in which he must actually exercise moral judgment. And yet as the work of Bernard Harrison has made clear, it is because the viewer is forced into active moral judgments *through being drawn into an elaborate fiction* that this method of pulling in a viewer may yield philosophical enlightenment.[51]

We can say with some certainty, at least, that what makes viewers more self-conscious *is not* the feeling that we're experiencing certain events for ourselves. We know that realistically witnessing the brutality of torture, for instance, doesn't make us more vocal as a nation about the necessity of more humane methods of interrogation. This is likely because watching one character torture another "means no more than deciding, on the basis of whatever subjective moral preferences you yourself happen to subscribe to, whether you like or dislike the way he carries on," writes Harrison, and when moral judgment is as arbitrary and subjective as this, a work of art "can be no more than, at most, a useful instrument for inculcating or reinforcing the moral prejudices" of those who encounter it.[52]

If that, finally, is what Boal means by calling *Zero Dark Thirty* a kind of Rorschach test, then he would not be too unhappy with the idea that his film does no more than impress on a viewer's mind what that viewer already believes. However, I do not think he would be satisfied with this conclusion. Nor do I think we should forget those scenes in the film that give credence to Bigelow's sense of herself as an artist trying to "shine a light on dark deeds," as she says, a task made harder "when those deeds are cloaked in layers of secrecy and government obfuscation." Because Bigelow is "very proud to be part of a Hollywood community that has made searing war films part of its cinematic tradition," as she says, I want to separate out my criticism of the film's narrative mode, its use of psychological realism (which in a truth-telling film ought to be avoided since it rests on the assumption that the viewer's viewpoint is valid), from what Bigelow rightly defends as an important history of filmmakers who have not "shied away from depicting the harsh realities of combat."[53]

For of course there is much in *Zero Dark Thirty* that indicates that these filmmakers *do* wish to subvert the complicity between the film's audience and any particular perspective, or which suggests that they do not think a viewer ought to enjoy the luxury of trusting her own view, and thus must be encouraged to entertain some misgivings about the viewpoint she is most naturally disposed to fall into. English professor Lennard Davis has, for example, found ample textual evidence supporting the interpretation that Maya (a name, as he points out, which means "illusion" in the Hindu religion) has all along been "caught in an illusion of her own making—whether it is the false hope that bin Laden's capture will change the world or whether it is that the procedures of the C.I.A. work well." As the film's ending makes clear, Davis notes, the mission was never to take bin Laden captive, as the White House claimed, but to kill him, "and the invasion of the cramped house filled with women and children is nothing short of depressing, including the wailing and begging of the women and crying children and the wanton slaughter of any male who comes into sight." Davis calls the final moment when bin Laden is shot "a non-moment, cinematically. We don't see what happens and there is no 'money-shot' of triumph. Rather the death is anti-climactic, mundane, and banal. Bin Laden ends with a bang without so much as a whimper, and since we've already been told that he is no longer in control of al Queda, the moment is so deflated as to be almost absurd." Moreover, when Maya enters the SEALs' base tent, Davis notes, SEALs whooping it up in the background and bin Laden's body bag on the table,

> Bigelow eschews any sense of glorification and heroism by marking Maya's entrance as the somber chord that chastens the SEALs. She walks over to the body bag, unzips it, looks down, and closes it up. We don't see Bin Laden's face as we are held at a middle-distance by the camera. The whole moment that the film has built up to is crafted as an ironic and deflationary shot. The film ends with Maya boarding a huge and empty transport plane, sitting alone and then

> sobbing. What heroic film do you know of that ends with the female protagonist weeping uncontrollably?[54]

However while Davis's reading of the film's ending is a fine one, it highlights the fact that the kind of scene that makes *Zero Dark Thirty* searing or affecting is precisely the kind of scene in which we are not in "the shoes of the men and women in the thick of this hunt" but in which we look at these men and women in a way (i.e., from *more than one direction*) that compels us to recognize that what we are confronting is not reality but fiction. Because rather than virtually experiencing what these characters are experiencing, an audience watching this scene is able to consider these characters as the planes and mirrors of transposed points of view turn and shift about them. In other words we learn something about bin Laden's death—what Americans hoped for from it, what we lost in our attempt to get it—by looking at the difference between the SEALs' reactions and Maya's when she gazes down onto her dead target.[55]

Thus, in thinking about where *Zero Dark Thirty* goes right, when it veers in the direction of "pure storytelling," I am inclined to suggest that what film captures best isn't "feeling," the way our earliest directors seemed to believe, and it isn't "thought," as Orson Wells astutely noted. It is in fact "character," since what filmmakers almost can't help but understand is that certain kinds of knowledge about characters—for example who Maya is, what her actions reveal about her, and so forth—are easier to convey through the juxtaposition of contradictory viewpoints than by creating an illusion of direct knowledge of a character's inner life. This naturally returns us to what the concept of character means in fiction, since, as Bernard Harrison points out, the concept is founded on the notion of the coherence of someone's speech and action *when seen from different viewpoints.*[56] Unless we are watching the kind of film in which viewers are let into the inner workings of a character's mind, that is to say—something that is usually done by means of a voice-over, and usually done badly—someone's character isn't something we discover by knowing what someone is thinking (who can tell?) but by the way other characters react to that person. It's by the way certain characters look and sound to *other characters* (whose opinions we learn to value or discount on the basis of the way, in relation, they look and sound, and so on), that viewers discover how to see them.

Consequently, it is all very well to find Maya weeping in *Zero Dark Thirty*'s closing moments, but part of what makes this scene frustrating, as well as intriguing, is how little viewers know about Maya by the film's final scene, and thus how many interpretations her crying allows. That, I would argue, is because the meticulous detail with which Bigelow puts her shots together does not generally extend to the relations between characters. Not until the film's final scenes does Bigelow spend any time trying to shift her audience's attention between *concordant and opposed viewpoints,* which is a shame not only because we consequently lack the materials to properly assess these characters but because this is the only means by which a film's audience can come to engage in self-reflection. The existence of multiple viewpoints is what breaks the spell in which a viewer's preconceptions are confirmed or reinforced, in other words, since the effort of projecting oneself imaginatively in several different directions makes it impossible to relax into the role of passive observer.[57]

Thus, in my view, one of *Zero Dark Thirty*'s most intellectually interesting moments occurs when, in Black Hawk helicopters, Navy SEALs journey across the mountains from the base in Afghanistan. For the scene, Bigelow's meticulous sound editor Paul Ottosson created what he calls the "stealth sound" that accompanies the helicopters, the cut-cut-cut noise Ottoson describes as "a cross between a cat purring and a quiet lawn mower,"[58] and David Denby notes that the journey "is conducted in darkness and quiet, like a sacred ritual."[59] And yet what sticks in my mind is the casual chatter of the Navy SEALs on the way to the raid. The scene centers on a young man who is listening to headphones.

> "Hey Justin," another SEAL asks, "What you listening to?"
> "Tony Robbins."
> "Tony Robbins, really?"
> "You should listen to it. I've got plans for after this. Big time. I want to talk to all you about it."

Some of the other SEALs then laugh amiably, perhaps at Justin's earnestness; his faith in the power of motivational speaking; his sweet, sad goals.

It is possible that this edifying bit of dialogue exists in the scene because somebody told Mark Boal that this is what the SEALs were talking about on the way to the raid—more proof that this movie's strength lies in its truthfulness, the key to which is authenticity. And yet what feels truthful about this scene is the juxtaposition between what a man like Justin is about to undertake—end lives because he has received that instruction, the basis for which will remain unknown to him—and his own trifling aspirations, his young man's desire to make his life and the lives of his friends better, somehow, coupled with his having selected for this transformation a pitiable or inadequate vehicle. What I mean to suggest is that we understand something about the scene that follows this one, in which the man shot might be the man sought, and might not, because of the way it plays against this scene, just as what we understand about Justin is made possible by the looks on his friends' faces when he speaks.

It is finally for this reason that I have tried to say why Bigelow and Boal are mistaken in their belief that fiction is enhanced by fact, or that if we want to see what went down we need a view from the ground. Because being in the story means seeing it from only one point of view, the real lesson is *how much further* "purely fictional storytelling" can go when it is not weighed down by a privileged point of view. For while David Denby has very usefully questioned the filmmakers' desire to simultaneously "claim the authority of fact and the freedom of fiction,"[60] as it turns out, what fiction offers isn't "freedom" but *perspective.* It's only by playing off one viewpoint against another that filmmakers can ever depict reality—including, naturally, the harsh realities of combat.

Notes

1. Brook Barnes, "As Enigmatic as Her Picture," an Interview with Kathryn Bigelow, *New York Times,* December 27, 2012, nytimes.com.

2. Kathryn Bigelow, "Kathryn Bigelow Addresses *Zero Dark Thirty* Torture Criticism," *Los Angeles Times,* January 15, 2013, latimes.com.

> Those of us who work in the arts know that depiction is not endorsement. If it was, no artist would be able to paint inhuman practices, no author could write about them, and no filmmaker could delve into the thorny subjects of our time. This is an important principle to stand up for, and it bears repeating. For confusing depiction with endorsement is the first step toward chilling any American artist's ability and right to shine a light on dark deeds, especially when those deeds are cloaked in layers of secrecy and government obfuscation. Indeed, I'm very proud to be part of a Hollywood community that has made searing war films part of its cinematic tradition. Clearly, none of those films would have been possible if directors from other eras had shied away from depicting the harsh realities of combat.

3. Dexter Filkins, "Bin Laden, the Movie," *New Yorker,* December 17, 2012, newyorker.com; and Steve Pond, "Kathryn Bigelow Denies *Zero Dark Thirty* Apologizes for Torture," *The Wrap,* December 16, 2012, thewrap.com.

4. Manohla Dargis, "By Any Means Necessary," *New York Times,* December 17, 2012, nytimes.com.

5. See, for example, Jane Mayer's eviscerating critique, "Zero Conscience in *Zero Dark Thirty,*" *New Yorker,* December 14, 2012, newyorker.com, in which she argues that "by the time millions of Americans have seen this movie, they will believe that, as Frank Bruni put it . . . 'No waterboarding, no bin Laden.'" Or see acting CIA chief Michael Morell's unusually outspoken criticism of the film as reported in an article by Scott Shane, "Acting C.I.A. Chief Critical of Film *Zero Dark Thirty,*" *New York Times,* December 22, 2012, nytimes.com.

6. For Mark Boal's remarks on "disruptive filmmaking," see Anthony Breznican, "*Zero Dark Thirty* Writer Mark Boal Says U.S. Torture Was 'Dead Wrong,'" *Entertainment Weekly,* February 7, 2013, insidemovies.ew.com.

7. Andrew Anthony, "Kathryn Bigelow: Drama Queen Who Captured Osama," *Guardian/Observer,* December 29, 2012, guardian.co.uk/the observer.

8. See Breznican, *Entertainment Weekly,* February 7, 2013, including an excerpt from Mark Boal's remarks as keynote speaker at the First Amendment Week at Loyola Marymount University.

9. Filkins, *New Yorker,* December 17, 2012.

10. Nick Dager, "Shooting *The Hurt Locker,*" *Digital Cinema Report,* February 12, 2010, digitalcinemareport.com.

11. David Edelstein, "The Year in Culture: Movies," *New York,* December 10, 2012, 50. The New York Film Critics Circle named the film best picture of 2012, and it was nominated for five Academy Awards, including one for the best picture of the year.

12. Frank Bruni, "Bin Laden, Torture, and Hollywood," *New York Times,* December 9, 2012, 3.

13. David Denby, "Dead Reckoning," *New Yorker,* December 24/31, 2012, 130.

14. As Jane Mayer has pointed out, practices regularly employed by America's brutal detention program—waterboarding, for example—are not just questioned by human-rights activists and civil-liberties lawyers but by many individuals "inside the F.B.I., the military, the Justice Department, and the C.I.A. itself, which eventually abandoned waterboarding because it feared, correctly, that the act constituted a war-crime." Mayer, *New Yorker,* December 14, 2012.

15. Barnes, *New York Times,* December 27, 2012.

16. Filkins, *New Yorker,* December 17, 2012.

17. Pond, *The Wrap,* December 16, 2012.

18. Boal notes, "Hopefully art or cinema can present a point of view that's a little above the political fray, but that doesn't mean the political narrative doesn't try to assert itself and pull you back in." Ibid.

19. Mayer, *New Yorker,* December 14, 2012.

20. Spencer Ackerman, *Wired,* quoted in Pond, *The Wrap,* December 16, 2012.

21. Manohla Dargis, *New York Times,* December 17, 2012, nytimes.com. On the

other hand, some careful critics find this argument misleading, since even on those occasions in the film in which actionable intelligence is obtained without torture, the threat of torture is ever present. Film director Alex Gibney writes, "Mark Boal has responded to critics by saying that, in the film, the actionable intelligence from Ammar was obtained 'over the civilized setting of a lunch.' But that's disingenuous. Because the conversation occurs after brutal torture, the implication is that Ammar provides information because he doesn't want to trade his hummus for a wet washcloth and a sojourn in a plywood box." Alex Gibney, "*Zero Dark Thirty*'s Wrong and Dangerous Conclusion," *Huffington Post,* May 3, 2013.

22. Mayer, *New Yorker,* December 14, 2012.

23. Ibid. As the *Washington Post*'s Greg Sargent first reported, Leon Panetta told John McCain that "no detainee in C.I.A. custody revealed the facilitator/courier's full true name or specific whereabouts." Senators Dianne Feinstein, chairman of the Senate Intelligence Committee, and Carl Levin, chairman of the Senate Armed Services Committee, have further undermined the film's version of events by noting in their own letter that "the original lead information had no connection to C.I.A. detainees." Sargent, *Washington Post,* May 16, 2011.

24. Mayer, *New Yorker,* December 14, 2012.

25. Gibney, *Huffington Post,* May 3, 2013.

26. Ibid.

27. Pond, *The Wrap,* December 16, 2012.

28. Denby, *New Yorker,* December 24/31; Bigelow, *Los Angeles Times,* January 15, 2013. Italics added.

29. Gibney, *Huffington Post,* May 3, 2013.

30. Peter Maass, "Don't Trust *Zero Dark Thirty,*" *Atlantic,* December 13, 2012, theatlantic.com.

31. Ibid.

32. Gibney, *Huffington Post,* May 3, 2013.

33. Dargis, *New York Times,* December 17, 2012.

34. Shane, *New York Times,* December 22, 2012.

35. Steve Coll, "Disturbing and Misleading," *New York Review of Books,* February 7, 2013, nybooks.com.

36. Denby, *New Yorker,* December 24/31.

37. Coll, *New York Review of Books,* February 7, 2013.

38. Breznican, *Entertainment Weekly,* February 7, 2013.

39. Coll, *New York Review of Books,* February 7, 2013.

40. Ludwig Wittgenstein, *Tractatus Logico-Philosophicus,* trans. G. E. M. Anscombe (Englewood Cliffs, NJ: Prentice Hall, 1953), 5.632.

41. See Wittgenstein's discussion of how solipsism coincides with pure realism or how it is not within the range of someone's experience to *feel the limits* of her experience. *Tractatus,* 5.5563–5.641.

42. Denby, *New Yorker,* December 24/31.

43. Bernard Harrison, *Henry Fielding's* Tom Jones: *The Novelist as Moral Philosopher* (London: Sussex University Press, 1975), 47, 46. Harrison's extraordinary insightfulness as a literary critic coupled with his history of having made highly original contributions to moral philosophy (from this first work through his recent book on anti-Semitism in the British press, *The Resurgence of Anti-Semitism: Jews, Israel, and Liberal Opinion* [2006]) makes him feel like the right critical voice to give this essay some intellectual backing.

44. Harrison, *Henry Fielding's* Tom Jones, 48.

45. Gibney, *Huffington Post,* May 3, 2013.

46. Then again, the analogy may be apt, for in fact many researchers have raised questions about the validity of the Rorschach technique. Under dispute are, for example, the objectivity of testers, the limited number of psychological conditions that it accurately diagnoses, the inability to replicate the test's norms, and the proliferation of the ten inkblot images, potentially invalidating the test for those who have been exposed to them.

47. "Disruptive technology" is a term coined by Harvard Business School professor Clayton Christensen to describe a new technology that unexpectedly displaces an established technology. In his 1997 best-selling book *The Innovator's Dilemma,* Christensen categorizes new technology as either sustaining or disruptive. Sustaining technology relies on incremental improvements to an already established technology. Disruptive technology lacks refinement, often has performance problems because it is new, appeals to a limited audience, and may not yet have a proven practical application, but because it inspires waves of innovation can make or break companies and markets.

48. Breznican, *Entertainment Weekly,* February 7, 2013.

49. See Coll, *New York Review of Books,* February 7, 2013. (Here lurks another entire essay on the important differences in the world of "spy-themed entertainment," for instance the difference between the pro-CIA vehicle *Zero Dark Thirty* and the anti-CIA vehicle the *Bourne* series.)

50. Bigelow, *Los Angeles Times,* January 15, 2013.

51. Harrison, *Henry Fielding's* Tom Jones, 56–57.

52. Ibid., 52.

53. Bigelow, *Los Angeles Times,* January 15, 2013.

54. Lennard Davis, "*Zero Dark Thirty:* The Politics of Art or Why All the Critics Are Wrong," *Huffington Post,* May 10, 2013.

55. This last sentence has been paraphrased from a point Harrison makes in *Henry Fielding's* Tom Jones, 45.

56. Ibid.

57. In this essay I had originally planned to compare the professed "fact and fiction" of *Zero Dark Thirty* with the "pure storytelling" of the 2009 film *District 9,* directed by Neill Blomkamp. Because of the limitations of space, I've had to leave out my discussion of the second film. This is a shame, since, for reasons I don't understand, *District 9* has received inadequate critical attention: of well-known American critics, only Anthony

Lane offered a fair summary of the film when, on its release, he noted that for an action-packed sci-fi thriller, "you don't feel bamboozled, fooled, or patronized by *District 9*, as you did by most of the summer blockbusters. You feel, winded, shaken, and shamed." "Only Human," *New Yorker*, September 14, 2009. Because I believe *District 9* offers an almost perfect example of the way a filmmaker might help an audience engage in self-reflection by shifting our attention between concordant and opposed viewpoints, I hope interested viewers will turn immediately to *District 9* for many fine examples of how audiences might come to know the worthlessness or merits of a character—like the film's protagonist, a nebishy civil servant named Wikus van der Merwe (Sharlto Copley)—by detailed reference to what he says and does in the context in which he says and does it. See, for example, the scene in which Wikus, newly appointed by his father-in-law to the position of Head Officer for the Department of Alien Affairs, travels by armed convoy into a township of segregated aliens (given the epithet "prawns") for the purpose of forcibly evicting them and interning them to even less hospitable environs. (For though *District 9* is both an alien film and a war film, it is also instinctively alive to the history of segregation in Blomkamp's native home of South Africa.) News cameras follow Wikus and his team, so it is to this imagined audience that Wikus spouts company propaganda ("What we try to do is engage with the prawn on behalf of MNU and on behalf of the humans") and assembles xenophobic accounts of the aliens' stupidity and uselessness. Thus *District 9*'s audience watches as Wikus straps on an armored vest and brags to his imagined news audience of the danger of his mission, even while he assures a black colleague accompanying him that there is really no need for this man to wear a vest, since he has not been brought one. The casuistical precision with which the scene is put together—Wikus's ingratiating comments to the news cameras; his falsely reassuring speech to his colleague; our view of the man's worried face—makes us doubt Wikus's scruples and leadership abilities as much as we doubt that the alien eviction is undertaken for humanitarian reasons. The comparison between *Zero Dark Thirty* and *District 9* is of particular interest since, as Anthony Lane notes, the audiences that have continued to gather for Blomkamp's film have been "lured by rumors of a hybrid—a writhing, snapping chunk of science fiction that looks and smells like fact." *District 9* looks and feels like a documentary, in other words, and this is what enhances its power as fiction and truth-telling.

58. Barnes, *New York Times*, December 27, 2012.

59. Denby, *New Yorker*, December 24/31.

60. Ibid.

Part 4

War, Nature, and the Absolute

Vernacular Metaphysics

On Terrence Malick's *The Thin Red Line*

Robert Pippin

The narrative conventions that make the Hollywood "war movie" a recognizable genre are among the most familiar, fixed, and predictable of any genre conventions, so much so that even variations or inversions of the conventions are just as familiar.[1] War movies from different wars are also all different, but the heart of the most familiar species of the war movie genre, the Hollywood World War II movie, almost always involves some sort of group dynamic, and that dynamic is broadly egalitarian. A cast is made up of colorful characters from various parts of the country and various social classes, thrown together in a combat unit and destined in the course of the movie to face some great test. Likable, wise-cracking minor characters are usually the first to die, increasing our emotional stake in the fate of the rest of the crew. There is some crusty "lifer," a sergeant or chief, who is inconceivable in any walk of life other than the military and who is usually a comic character, often a supposedly amusing alcoholic. No well-known war movie in the twentieth century is about a professional army or about mercenaries. World War II or Korea or Vietnam movies are naturally about a citizen's army of draftees or volunteers who yearn to return to their civilian lives, hate the army, but do their duty. Their memories of home (and sometimes what we see of their home life) and what they will do after the war are among the most frequent topics of conversation, are what sustains them, give what they do meaning (they are protecting "home"). Loyalty to their new friends, the revelation of the unique power of relationships forged in wartime, and great courage from unexpected characters are all familiar themes.[2]

As noted, the variations in the formulas are just as familiar. The most frequent violation of the straight "ordinary" or "democratic heroism" theme concerns ambitious and thereby corrupt career officers who see the war as a means of advancement and so are far more indifferent to the risks and suffering of their men than any humane perspective should tolerate. *Paths of Glory* is perhaps the most famous example of such a film.[3] (Sometimes, though, the ambition, while clear, is also linked to qualities of great military leadership on an epic scale, as in *Patton.*) Another variation or inversion, very prominent in Vietnam-era war films, concerns the pointlessness, even the absurdity, of the war itself, a meaningless project concocted by distant politicians, requiring enormous sacrifices for goals that no sane, ordinary soldier can possibly accept or even understand, with psychological costs that are incalculable. (*Apocalypse Now* can serve as the paradigm of such movies. The soldiers whistling the theme of "The Mickey Mouse Club" at the end of *Full Metal Jacket* could serve as well.) In both the formula and the variations, then, an underlying theme emerges: how (or whether) ordinary citizens of a commercial republic, whose daily lives involve no exposure to physical danger or violence, can come to be able to participate wholeheartedly in acts of nearly unimaginable ferocity, and how they can deal with the psychological trauma of constant death, often of buddies loved in a way not permitted to men in any other context, often for geopolitical purposes that seem pointless. An underlying, often implicit question is, What do men need to believe, what do they need to understand, to endure such an ordeal?

In all of Terrence Malick's seven films, various genre conventions of Hollywood movies like these are invoked and clearly structure much of the narration,[4] and this is especially true of his 1998 film, *The Thin Red Line,* which has many of the elements of a Hollywood World War II movie. But as in his other films, these genre conventions create expectations and suggest explanations that are then undermined, refused, left open, made to seem irrelevant, made mysterious, or even ironicized. The implication is unavoidable that, therefore, these conventions about motivation and value are no longer available and no longer credible; and the viewer has to struggle to find some point of orientation. This sense of being lost, once these conventions are invoked and then refused, is the main effect on any viewer and seems a major point of the film itself. Genre considerations can be said to provide a common or even a mythic structure of intelligibility in film, and in this genre, that means the narrative and even visual structure concern how we, as modern viewers of the movie, have come to understand war. War movies both purport to instruct us on how to understand war (and so sometimes raise questions like whether war is avoidable or evil or "natural") and rely on what are already assumed to be our settled conventions about the issue.

However, especially in this war movie, Malick's two quite dramatic technical innovations—his almost devout concentration on the visual beauty, magisterial indifference, and sublimity of the natural world, and the unusual meditative interior monologues, voice-overs by individual characters—violate not only genre conventions but many narrative, dramatic, and psychological elements of realist fiction films.[5] (They have also been intensely criticized.) Malick often composes his movies with contrasting and interlocking visualizations of, or visual embodiments of, or allegorical allusions to, or even visual contrasts with, voiced reflective meditations.[6] The visual narrative always seems to be inflected, in a number of different ways, by the content and tonality of these meditations (more than by requirements of the plot alone) and framed in some way by shots of the living, natural world that are for the most part not required by, and are often independent of, the plot. That is, to say the least, an unusual mode of filmic composition. It is a kind of genre for which there are few conventions except Malick's other films.[7]

There *is* of course a gripping war narrative in *The Thin Red Line,* driven by the planning for and anticipation of a horrific frontal assault on an entrenched position, followed by further attacks on Japanese positions, and the development of two sets of complex character relationships. But that narrative, and even much of the character conflict, while clearly important, can often seem subsidiary to Malick's novel compositional approach. Neither the narrative nor the character development bears the meaning of the film in the significant way that the visual compositions and their related voiced reflections do.[8] (At the most, one could say that the narrative and character developments are only one of the four main structuring elements of the film, along with the shots of nature, the voice-overs, and the music.)[9] The aim of this essay is to understand the relation between these narratological, visual, and psychological innovations and the thematic developments in the film, most of which concern that traditional war movie theme: how ordinary citizens of commercial republics can both come to participate in acts of extreme violence and come to understand in some way what they are doing, come to confront, much more vividly than they do in ordinary life, that they will kill other human beings and that they themselves may die.

There are two central pairs of characters in the film. The first sergeant, Welsh (Sean Penn), and the enigmatic, moody soldier Witt (Jim Caviezel) form the first pair. Lt. Colonel Tall (Nick Nolte, in an extraordinary, riveting performance) and Captain Staros (Elias Koteas) form the other. But we are given very little time or sufficient background or dialogue to know very much about these characters as individuals, and the other characters in the infantry company appear on-screen so randomly and disappear so quickly that none of the usual war-movie group dynamics that we expect can even begin. For a long time, it is completely impossible, even for someone who has read the novel, to link up characters with individual names. We do not, except for two isolated instances, get to see their home life, so there is little to fill out their characters.[10] The camera does not follow them for sufficient stretches of time for the normal association and identification to occur within the plot of the movie, and the central dramatic event of the film, the frontal assault up "Hill 210," held by the Japanese, is not photographed in a way that allows us to follow the action in the normal sense, anticipating what might happen or understanding very well who is at what risk and why. This difficulty of identifying individuals is also greatly compounded by the fact that that the spoken monologues are unattributed. Having almost everyone speak with a southern accent does not help either. We often do not know with any certainty who is speaking in the voice-overs, and so it is hard to place a monologue in the plot. Why some particular character would be thinking just *this* or *that, then* is as impossible to determine as who is speaking. This is uniquely disorienting, even more so than that so many characters look alike, especially when wearing their helmets. We are prevented from any normal psychological identification of the voices and so from any normal inference about the motives and implications of what is said. At one extreme point, we even hear one character's musings, a character named Train, voice "over" a kind of *visual* monologue clearly imagined by *another* character (Bell, Ben Chaplin's character) (32:34–33:12).

The result of this is the most radical departure from what could be called the main convention of war films: the creation of solidarity between men, a solidarity of such profundity that nothing in ordinary life (certainly not politics) comes close, and that is usually offered as an explanation for the acts of selfless heroism that we see.[11] There is no such solidarity here, and there is instead a great deal of emphasis on isolation, alienation from others, and loneliness.[12] (Welsh at one point insists that the best a man can do is "to make an island for himself" [2:38:50]. And we also hear Witt say: "War don't ennoble men. It turns 'em into dogs. Poisons the soul" [2:06:13].) War, the ever-present possibility of death and killing, forces on everyone the question of death, the unavoidable need to make some sense of it, to learn how to live with a possibility we easily ignore in daily life. And this pressure, we see, isolates everyone from everyone else, rather than creating a new community. (As the difficulty of tracking characters already suggests, however, such isolation, remarkably, does not in itself mean an *individualization.* The visual, voiced, and even psychological identities of characters can seem porous, shifting, and unstable, even though no new group unity is created. And since the voice-overs are unattributed by visual cues or anything else, the "thoughts" seem to float in logical space, as if they could "visit" any character or be shared by, be thought by, anyone.) When, near the end of the film, the new company commander (Bosche, played by George Clooney), does describe their group as a "family," the irony, his unknowingness, given what we have just seen for two hours, is almost unbearable, and in Welsh's voice-over, interspersed in the new captain's palaver, he thinks to himself, "Everything a lie; everything you hear, everything you see; they just keep coming, one after another; . . . they want you dead or in their lie" (2:37:21). More subtly, when Staros invokes the family image as he departs, relieved of command, he too says, "You are my sons, my dear sons; you'll live inside me now. I'll carry you wherever I go" (2:05:24). Here the tone is pathos, not irony. For he has *not* been able to act as their father, to "protect" them, defend them. He had to yield command to their true military father, Tall, and so he obviously needs to believe in a familial bond that was never actually possible.[13]

This profound isolation is a sense heightened by the most untraditional and controversial technique in the film, those reflective voice-overs that are not addressed to anyone and are in effect monologues. They thus bear some resemblance to dramatic monologues in stage plays, when a character says what he thinks out loud, to himself. But Malick's monologues are rarely tied to any specific event in the action, are not reflections about what one should do and why, do not provide information about a character's view of what has just happened or will happen. Even some dialogues are in effect, ironically, monologues: those between the Japanese and Americans, each speaking their own language, sometimes at length and in bizarre indifference to the obvious incomprehension of the other.[14] Welsh mentions the isolation theme several times in his monologues, especially when he describes us as mere "moving boxes," as if all shut up "inside," prevented from any real contact with an "outside" (2:38:16). And the dramatic action plays out such a theme. A character swears to a dying comrade that he will write the man's wife, then immediately recoils in horror from what he promised, saying he won't do it. A character, Storm, admits to Welsh, "I look at that boy dying, I don't feel nothing. I don't care about nothing any more" (2:09:54). And it is not irrelevant that Guadalcanal is an island. Witt, of course, is the great exception, but his love of the men and for Welsh seems independent of, prior to, even indifferent or resistant to, the experience of war, not inspired by it. (The war also creates an even vaster gulf between the Americans and the Japanese prisoners, whom the soldiers treat as animals or things. Again the great exception is Witt, and that again raises the question of the meaning of his role in the film, clearly the central one, the thematic center of the movie, however mysterious.)

Malick has also profoundly changed the narrative and characterization in James Jones's novel, all in ways that move the narration father away from any formula (or, one could even say, further away from mere narration).[15] Witt has been changed from a rather stupid Kentucky racist into a kind of meditative warrior and the spiritual center of the movie. Scenes that took many pages for Jones to fill out and motivate are dropped briefly into the film without development, as if sections of film that did explain them have been simply cut out. For example, in the film, on the ship before landing, we see a *very* brief couple of scenes in which a character, Doll, says he will steal a pistol, and we then see him doing it. The reasons for this desire and what it means, developed at length in the novel, are not given. We just see Doll later, using the pistol. (The same is true of the machine gun Welsh carries in the film.) We sense in the film only that *some* sort of standard moral constraint is already wearing away, but not why. Or, in the film, we know far too little about Sgt. Keck (Woody Harrelson's character) to understand the significance of his falling on a grenade to protect his men, after Keck accidentally pulled the pin and threw the pin, not the grenade. Sgt. McCrone (John Savage) goes mad in the assault after having lost his entire squad, and he begins to rave about how we are all dirt—but who is Sgt. McCrone, and why do we only know him in his madness?[16] Dale (Arie Verveen) desecrates bodies, stealing gold teeth, and torments a prisoner (as if the prisoner could understand English), but we know virtually nothing about Dale, and it is very difficult to identify him later when he sits alone, shirtless in the rain in obvious, intense psychological pain. Welsh is a deep cynic in the novel, convinced that the entire war is about "property," something he goes on about at great length. In the film, though, we only hear this once from Welsh. Mysteriously, and in a way unmotivated by anything we have seen, it is after he has risked nearly certain death in an act of great beneficence that has nothing to do with property. He rushes headlong into withering fire in order to get morphine to a dying soldier.[17] (Also, before a major assault, a soldier complains that he has stomach cramps and cannot proceed. His sergeant is about to force him to go when our supposed cynic, Welsh, again mysteriously, in a kind of gratuitous act of sympathy, allows the soldier, likely a cowardly malingerer, to return to the rear and sick bay.) Very famous movie stars, like John Travolta and Clooney, and relatively major stars, like John Cusack and Woody Harrelson, are briefly introduced only to disappear (thus defeating the predictability and familiarity that comes from the Hollywood star system). Major characters in the novel, like Fife (Adrien Brody), are also reduced to cameo roles in the film, and therewith one of the most important themes in the novel, one focused mostly on Fife and elaborated at length in the novel, physical homosexual love among the men, is eliminated.[18] All of this functions to interrupt any genre-based expectations about narrative and that great forward movement of Hollywood narratives we have become so used to in American films since the likes of Griffith and others discovered how to control and accelerate narrative pace. I want to say that all of this is quite deliberate and shifts our attention to the alternate compositional method alluded to above.

Moreover, and as already noted, in the most unusual departure, we learn whatever we do learn about these characters through the voice-overs, and what we learn is not at all standard psychological detail about their ordinary lives. The voiced monologues have a figurative, meditative, poetic form totally at odds with any war-movie convention. Indeed, it would be fair to say, now that Malick has released two other films, *The New World* and *The Tree of Life,* since his return to filmmaking with *The Thin Red Line,* that his use of these meditative voice-overs by individual characters, and the very sweeping philosophical and religious scope of these voice-overs (in effect asking what could the "whole" be within which these sorts of events could have any significance), have mostly divided audiences and critics. Some viewers (like me) clearly find them engrossing and successful, the key to the films' great distinctiveness; others find them pretentious, unmotivated in the film, and off-putting.

But the voice-overs also introduce a great deal of narrative and thematic tension into the film's visual narration, and if we begin by noticing these unusual tensions, we can better appreciate how the underlying theme of so many movies about twentieth century warfare is being addressed (and in a way negated) by Malick. I mean the large question: How is it possible for citizen soldiers of at least putatively pacific commercial republics to come to suffer the trauma and engage in the killing required by modern warfare, especially in foreign lands, far away from their own homes and families?[19] This is, of course, simply a question for any human being who must do what war requires, but Malick's focus on the Tall-Staros conflict, and the necessity for contemporary men to understand in some way what their predicament means, without a conventional appeal to "the mysteries of God's plan" (never an issue cited in the film; no character avows any conventional theodicy, apart from temptations to Manicheanism) or the protection of the nation (never mentioned in the film), gives the film its distinctive character.

I mean such things as the following. The film opens on a scene of Witt and another soldier in what appears to be a kind of peaceful island paradise of Melanesians, playing with children and swimming through beautiful, crystal clear ocean water. Several things are strange, though, upon reflection. Witt, throughout the film, avows a great love for C Company, volunteering to return to the fight after his exile into a medical support company. (In the novel he leaves and returns five times.) We see several times in the film that this avowal is quite genuine. But Witt at the beginning is, after all, AWOL. He has left the fight to others, abandoning them until he is caught and brought back in the brig.[20] He says he is "twice the man" Welsh is (12:30), and he clearly means in bravery and soldiering, but his (in effect) brief desertion (in battlefield conditions, yet) is never explained.[21] Still, the unremarked-on fact is very important. Whatever Witt's allegiance to his company is, it is not mediated by political, national, and military institutions. He is certainly not a hypocrite. He *does* love his comrades, but that love has little to do with their common institutional bond, and what Witt is led to do has nothing to do with anything like his duty to them.

Moreover, the Melanesian setting is ambiguous. Witt once remarks to a mother that the Melanesian children never fight. The mother corrects him, saying that the children *do* fight. This correction is a brief signal that all is not, in effect, what it seems, certainly not what it seems to Witt. (Not to mention the ominous crocodile at the very beginning.) Nor is this correction by the mother the first indication of some tension between what we see and what we come to understand. This scene occurs at the very beginning of the voice-overs, as we hear an overpowering, ominous organ chord (*Annum per Annum* by Arvo Pärt) and see that deadly-looking crocodile, see a huge tree and root and enveloping vine system "attacking" the tree, and hear an unattributed voice intone, "What's this war in the heart of nature? Why does nature vie with itself? The land contend with the sea. Is there an avenging power in nature? Not one power, but two?" (1:47–2:18).[22]

So now we come to one of the most startling facts about the film. Unless one has an *extremely* sensitive ear, it is almost impossible to realize that this voice we hear at the very beginning—by far the most frequent voice we will continually hear intone the most general reflections and questions about the meaning of war, killing, death, and the place of such violence in nature, and which will voice the last reflection we hear ("All things shining")—belongs *not* to Witt, an almost inescapable attribution on first hearing, but to a character we have barely caught a glimpse of: one Private Edward B. Train, played by John Dee Smith. We have only seen him briefly in the bathroom aboard ship. He tells Welsh how afraid he is, that he wants to own an automobile after the war, that "the only thing that's permanent is, is dying and the Lord," and that "this war ain't gonna be the end of me or you neither" (20:48–21:07). He is an unlikely candidate to be the one raising the large questions he does, to say the least. This is confirmed even more strongly when the film circles back to the very same Train at the end, in the landing craft heading back to the ship, and he again babbles away about how life just has to be better for him after all this suffering, that he is older now, not old, but older, and other such banalities. Yet again, as with narrative conventions, what we think we know about character cues and expressive possibilities are given no purchase or grip in the film, and we are, again, lost. It is not only very difficult to identify Train's voice; it is even more difficult to believe that he could voice such sentiments, could have such an inner life.

All this worry about a violent, warring nature is, nevertheless, in preparation for our being *visually* pulled immediately into the quite *contrary* romantic conventions of native innocence and a harmonious nature, as if, as in the post-Rousseauean convention, it is only the arrival of the civilized world that introduces brutality and violence into a naturally peaceful world (as if the forbidding destroyer belching black smoke is the human avatar of the crocodile). It is as if we hear what may be true (what *Train thinks may be true*), that a Manichean view is true: there is great beauty and harmony in nature, as well as great violence, chaos, and brutality, and there is no mediation or synthetic point of view possible. Yet we *see* what we are encouraged to think Witt believes or is trying to believe, that the Rousseauean convention is true, and that he has discovered the deeper truth about the possibility of natural beauty and true natural harmony. (But even in the opening, idyllic scenes, we hear Fauré's *Requiem* on the sound track as a kind of subtle counterpoint, reminding us that even so, however beautiful and innocent the scene we are seeing, the film will be about death, killing, and sorrow about death; the musical theme is sounded over a scene seemingly at odds with it.) Indeed, at the end of the film, we see a very different Melanesian village, more consistent with what we heard from Train, now with violent arguments among the tribe members; suspicious, wary children; disease; stacks of human skulls; and so a hint of cannibalism in the tribe, testifying again to how much of what *we originally see* depends on *what Witt thinks he sees* (or wants to see). There is no suggestion whatsoever that the village has been transformed by the invasion of the Japanese and Americans,[23] and the existence of the skulls is clearly designed to signal just that, that the violence in the tribe is long-standing, was there, but not seen by Witt (and so not by us). This is only the first indication of the many complicated relationships between what we see, what characters avow, and what other characters believe. (All of which is not even to mention the confusing elements of the next scene in the village. Witt looks around, obviously very sad, and we begin to see what appears to be his remembrance of the village as it was [as he thought it was] and we hear a voice-over begin to wonder what had happened to produce these divisions. But the voice is not Witt's, even though his is the face we see. It is Train's again [2:16:55–2:17:49]).

Welsh is the most cynical character in the film, deeply skeptical of the war itself (the whole thing is just for "property") and clearly very concerned that Witt's loyalty to the company and fearless dedication will get him killed, pointlessly. ("If you die, it's gonna be for nothing.") At one point, after he tells Witt that there is "just this world"—and this time is not contradicted by Witt, who only looks up to the moon—we see a hellish scene of wild dogs eating corpses of soldiers, as if to confirm Welsh's cynicism (1:22:23–1:23:44). But Welsh also clearly loves Witt, and so somewhat ironically embodies rather than confounds part of the war-movie formula. Even someone who thinks the war effort is corrupt and worthless *is* willing, almost gratuitously, despite himself, to take great risks for his comrades, and he is deeply concerned with Witt's fate. This is a mirror in effect to the fact that Witt, who is introduced to us in pacific scenes, is no pacifist at all (something we would clearly expect) but is willing to fight and kill with intensity and never questions the job of killing.[24]

Then there is the unusual story of Bell (Ben Chaplin), a soldier who had been an officer but who gave up his commission so he could spend time with his wife, before being shipped out again as a private. There are long, idyllic voiced-over scenes of Bell's memories of physical affection with his wife and his intense longing for a total union with her. (The prominent image is water, a figure for harmony, merger, and a common bond of life throughout the film, especially in the assault scenes, which the men must fight with inadequate water. This is another way in which the theme of isolation or aloneness is stressed, by emphasis on what is missing, the harmony symbolized by water, as when the men rest in the rear and swim naked together, joyously, in the ocean. The last battle scene, when Witt saves the company by sacrificing himself, takes place as the soldiers wade hip-deep in the waters of a river. Witt sends a badly injured soldier floating away on the water, as if he is returning him to a primal origin.)[25] We are led to believe that these memories are what sustain him, motivate him to get home, give his life some ultimate meaning, as if, if there is no national or "familial" community, there is at least a reliable romantic connection with others. But we then learn that these may be imaginative projections, romantic fantasies. He gets a devastating letter from his wife, suddenly asking for a divorce and even, in a sublimated moment of sheer, deep aggression, asking Bell to "help her leave him" (2:14:10). She has fallen in love with someone else.

So, while there are other voice-overs, these four are the most frequent: Train's Manichean reflections, Witt's concern with death and facing it calmly, Welsh's cynicism, and Bell's romantic idealism. And they all introduce various tensions: between what a character does and what he thinks; between the voice-over and what we see and hear; and among the voiceovers themselves, all of which are both integrated into and also somewhat independent of normal plot and character development and the war-movie conventions.

The most significant tension, though, occurs between Tall and Staros and is a more straightforward character conflict, the closest to a war-movie genre convention. That is, while we are set up, again by a standard convention, to see Staros as the caring humanist leader whose first concern is for his men and to see Tall as the egomaniacal careerist, the plot development is quite surprising—perhaps the biggest, though subtly presented, surprise in the film.[26] The Japanese are dug in on the top of a hill, in entrenched machine-gun positions that artillery cannot damage. The only option, Tall tells Staros, is a frontal assault. A flanking movement to the right would have to go through that thick, nearly impassable jungle and is not an option. Staros, agonized by the losses his company will suffer, nevertheless dutifully begins the attack. It is indeed horrific. His men are mercilessly cut down, and at a break in the action, Staros declines to attack further, telling Tall that it is simply suicidal. (He also explains, in a way that, even if we suspect Tall's careerism and are deeply sympathetic to Staros, we have to regard as oddly out of place, unusually squeamish and openly so, in a battlefield conversation. Staros says, "We had a man . . . his gut got shot out on the slope, sir. Created quite an upset" [1:05:36]. We can imagine Tall thinking: "Your men are *upset?*")

This amounts to a moment in the film very much like Witt's having gone AWOL; that is, a crucial ambiguity not much attended to by critics and commentators and another comforting convention denied to us. In short, the heart of *the* dramatic event in the film, the attack on Hill 210 by C-for-Charlie company, is in effect a mutiny under battlefield conditions by an officer, a refusal to fight on. What is *much* more surprising is that despite our expectations and identification with Staros the humanist, the Colonel turns out in the end to have been right; something quite extraordinary, given our invitation to regard Tall as not only heartless but, as is often the case in such movies and characters, incompetent.[27] Tall himself goes to the forward position, standing up bravely, not flinching when ordnance goes off, apologizing for the lack of water in the assault, and rallying the troops. The men have been able to make it to a ridge that the Japanese have mistakenly left unguarded, and one might argue that this is just a piece of luck that Tall could not have counted on, but the fact remains that Tall turned out to be right that a direct assault, if conducted with a full commitment, could succeed.[28] (Not to mention that he is right when he has to tell Staros: "This is not a court of law; this is a war" [1:08:20]. Bell finds an approach that allows a volunteer force to get close enough to the nests to attack and take them out, and the assault succeeds. Tall does not bring any charges against Staros, but he notes that Staros is not really suited to command ["You're too soft."] and sends him home. We are inclined by a kind of movie logic to be "for" Staros, but his question "Have you ever had anyone die in your arms, sir?" is maudlin and self-congratulatory [and is countered simply by a withering, incredulous stare by Tall] and we end up unsure what to think [1:56:50–1:59:45].) (There is, moreover, an ominous, growling music on the soundtrack that has been and will be a feature of the film for a while.) Tall is also earlier given a striking voice-over, again contra-type, creating a strange moment of sympathy: "Shut up in a tomb; can't lift the lid. Played a role I never conceived" (1:11:26–1:11:38). The isolation theme again: he is as trapped as the rest of them by what the war requires.[29]

We are not done with Tall, though. He has two more extremely important scenes, and after both, his status in the film, or our suggested judgment of him, is almost impossible to sort out. After the initial victory, he has a conversation with Captain Gaff (John Cusack), who led the seven-man team that made the initial breach. Gaff is quite worried about the state of the men. They are dehydrated and cannot, he thinks, press on. Tall thinks the men have momentum and spirit and so cannot wait around for water. "If some of the men pass out, well, hell, they'll just have to pass out," he says (1:41:11). Gaff, staring at Tall in an openly judgmental way, reminds Tall that this means some of the men could die. So we have our Staros moment again, as an attractive, humane character pleads for "the men." Tall stays both true to form as, on the one hand, a craven careerist, the man who could tell Staros that he must capture the objective because "the Admiral got up at dawn for this" (50:46). Here he tells Gaff that Gaff has no idea what it feels like to be passed over for a promotion, as if *that* is why the men must press on, and that death could just as easily occur from a sniper. And yet, on the other hand, he is also a ruthless and ultimately successful leader. (Tall's ambition is not great or world-historical, like Patton's; it is small-minded and bourgeois: he wants a promotion and respect. But this ambition is not unconnected with the military victory, and the implication seems to be that it, this self-serving, careerist ambition, is all that is left of ancient "spiritedness," *thymos,* the need for distinction, greatness, and glory. The same point is made by Travolta's preening, pompous officer at the beginning of the film.) This next assault *again* succeeds, and what happens again appears to justify Tall's willingness to press on. Yet the moment is personalized, too. Tall (who, throughout, in trying hard to persuade Gaff, is clearly trying to persuade himself) tells Gaff that Gaff is like a son to him and, in a way that silently speaks volumes about the powerful and complicated *attraction of war* to many of these modern "domesticated" men, asks Gaff if he knows what his, Tall's, son does. "My son is a bait salesman," Tall says (1:43:04). Not the usual way, in war movies, of referring to the home front. (It is clear that Gaff does not at all feel this familial bond, and so the image of the familial bond in war is undermined again.) And finally, in a way that complicates everything, Tall finally *does* send runners back for water, as if conceding Gaff's point. Again this confounding of genre and narrative and psychological expectations seems quite deliberate and thereby leaves us, to some extent, as "lost" as many of the main characters.

And then, after the scene where he relieves Staros of command, we see

Tall sitting alone (dramatically and sadly alone, one has to say), looking at the devastation and death around him. Nolte creates a powerful sense of futility and sadness in a silent, brief scene in which all Tall does is sigh, twice, and very movingly, and is in effect rehumanized for us yet again in his isolation and obvious self-doubt. We are not, therefore, allowed to mock or simply dismiss him. This is the last we see of him (2:00:52–2:01:40).

So both the voice-overs and the filmed scenes can often seem to take back with one hand what they have given with another, raising expectations and suggesting allegiances that are then undermined or called into some question. And this emerges as the underlying structure of the whole film. In the way negative theology is held to be itself a mode of knowledge about God, Malick's *negation* of narrative and character conventions, patterns of intelligibility, we might say, forces us to see things about the dramatic events and the characters and the visual images in a distinct way, in a kind of fresh strangeness, a strangeness echoed in the photography of nature, as we shall see.

For one thing, these unresolved tensions create an appropriate sense of mystery and bewilderment, and a lack of resolution one must simply learn to live with. One such mystery, a major one in the narrative, is the mystery of command itself, that some men will actually follow an order, get up and run straight toward a machine gun firing right at them. This is not a completely stable, clear-cut matter. Staros does not acknowledge the authority of Tall, and even Staros himself at one point has to ask, "Am I the captain or a goddamn private?" (48:47). They are of course afraid of the consequences of disobeying, but no war can be won, no assault successful, if that is the only motivation of those who attack. They must in some sense or other invest, ideally wholeheartedly, in the ends of the command. How that happens, how it can be sustained, is something our attention is drawn to several times in the film, especially in the opening charge when a young soldier must order two others to get up and run into almost certain death. They hesitate but then obey and are immediately killed.

For another, from what we have seen so far, we can say that Malick has again refused us two conventional ways of thinking about this willingness to face death. The politics of the world war are never invoked, and so the question—deeply interesting in itself and explored in different ways in many film genres—of the psychological bases of political and thereby military authority, is not raised.[30] And the idea that war creates an emotional bond of love that "takes over" in critical situations, that the men fight, even to the death, for each other, is also refused. We are not allowed to come to any coherent sense of what the group is, who is in it, how to identify and track individual characters, who even *likes* whom. The family image is invoked only to be undermined, and the deepest "connection" in the film, between Welsh and Witt, is fraught with distance and incomprehension.

In effect, the sense we get is that these men are caught up in some vast historical force sweeping them forward to a remote island in the South Pacific, so the issue for them is not how to get themselves to do what they are ordered to do. As we see several times in the assaults up the hill, there is no way out, no option for them. They look around and look forlornly at each other and realize that they have no choice but to go forward. Once they are engaged, the violence itself has its own dynamic. The more they fight, the more ferocious, even vicious they become, the more many of them like it. (Doll says: "I killed a man. Nobody can touch me for it" [52:59].)[31] Malick has largely de-emphasized what are traditionally understood to be "the psychological issues" (especially when compared with the novel, where they are quite prominent) and has concentrated on something else. I have claimed that Malick has not allowed the narrative line or even character conflict to carry the primary meaning or the primary significance of what we are seeing and that, while he realizes that an associative connection with the conventions of war movies is inevitable for the viewer, he also takes a number of steps to invert those expectations, frustrate them, ironicize them. This implies that we cannot "understand war" as we have; the expectation that we can understand it leads us to expect the genre conventions and then leads to our being lost when they fail us. This can be said to be about both the way movies have rendered human practices intelligible, the way they no longer can, and about the problem of the intelligibility of the events themselves.

To come to the basic issue: (a) Malick instead forces our attention predominantly on motion pictures of nature, framed and panned in a certain characteristic Malick-like way, and (b) he has interrupted any usual narrative flow with very frequent and occasionally difficult-to-attribute voice-overs. This de-emphasis on narrative meaning and the anticipation it creates (Who will do what to whom? Why? Do they know why? Are they self-deceived?) shifts our attention to two of the main frameworks Malick allows us for understanding the action we do see. That is, first, the kind of reflective interrogation of meaning, especially of death and killing, voiced in the interior monologues, and, second, what he is trying to achieve with photographic effect. And here, especially with the former issue, the voice-overs, he takes very great risks.

First, Malick is willing to frame the issue that he thinks is most pressing in the situation of war—the ever-present possibility of sudden death—in starkly simple and direct terms. As noted, the issue threading through the main voice-overs is not "What is this death of mine *for?* Is it worth the cost (for the nation, for my family)?" but "What does it mean in general for my life as a whole that I will die? What is it to live, to direct or lead a life, if it must be led under such a constant certitude?" And "Why, if death is such an evil, is there so much killing, violence?" The consolation we are led to believe the characters need is not political or social, but—and here any choice of a word will be inadequate or misleading—"philosophical" or metaphysical or religious. (I say "led to believe" because the issue depends yet again on the status of Train in the film, about whom we know almost nothing, and so depends on the status of his voice-overs.) But this invokes another set of conventions and another set of dangers for Malick.

For when a character in a film engages in what sounds like very general philosophical reflection, we expect the formulations to be equal to the difficulty of the subject matter, and we easily, unproblematically, assume that any such sympathetic character speaks for the maker of the film, the auteur. But we have already seen that what we see in *The Thin Red Line* is some sort of visual embodiment of or comment on or contrast with some aspects of a character's world, and this visual point of view is not necessarily stable, conceived in that way by the character speaking, and in no sense does it necessarily trump some other voiced point of view (and world), like Welsh's. (It is a very simple point but one that often seems lost in discussions of this film and *The Tree of Life.* No one speaks "for the movie," for the auteur; the characters speak for themselves.) What is even more striking is that Malick allows these characters to muse over what is happening to them in prose meditations that aspire to a kind of poetic expressiveness, yet strictly within the limitations and background of each character. The musings are not elevated to some sort of canonical status by an attempt to inflate the quality of the prose. When we hear Witt (Witt finally, and not his near-voice-twin, Train) at the beginning, after Train's introductory questions, we hear what appears to be an ordinary man straining the limits of his powers of expression.

> I remember my mother when she was dying. Looked all shrunk up and gray. I asked her if she was afraid. She just shook her head. I

> was afraid to touch the death I seen in her. . . . I heard people talk about immortality, but I ain't seen it. (4:11–4:44)
>
> I wondered how it'd be when I died. What it'd be like to know that this breath now was the last one you was ever gonna draw. I just hope I can meet it the same way she did. With the same . . . calm. 'Cause that's where it's hidden—the immortality I hadn't seen. (5:52–6:22)

The "death I seen in her," "immortality hidden in a moment"; the poor grammar and the like make clear we are hearing a *particular* voice, and this is true even when Witt struggles to use figurative language, evocative of Emerson. "Maybe all men got one big soul, that everybody's part of—all faces are the same man, one big self." Or "Everyone's lookin' for salvation by himself—each like a coal thrown from the fire" (36:31–37:22). The sense we get is that the war can be borne, endured (the prospect of our own death, so terribly heightened by war, can be borne or endured) if the questions addressed in the monologues can get some sort of purchase, can lead to some sort of presentiment about their resolution, but that must happen from the point of view of the ordinary men—men unused to violence and the presence of death, the bourgeoisie at war—who are forced to ask them. This point is relevant to something that Stanley Cavell sometimes says: that there can be no real "virtuosity" for true philosophy, as there is for mathematics or music. It must be something that in some way anyone does, can do (in their own way, of course, as in Emerson on individual genius). What these men need is not politics or love or real "fathers" or to become "a band of brothers," but some kind of vernacular speculative position, a vernacular orientation within the whole.

The issue of the content of these reflections, which in one way or another deal with the question of how death and killing can be understood and thereby, perhaps, endured, is linked to the unusual visual composition of the film. Our attention is sometimes drawn to photographed scenes of animal and plant life in a striking, meditative way. For the most part, there is no internal plot-related reason for editing in, at various points, shots of such organic life and sunlight. For the most part, we do not see establishing shots for any point of view and so do not see "what characters see" in the course of the narrative: the animals and plants perhaps as obstacles, threats, food, the uncanny, the frightening (for them). We do not much see them looking at what the camera is looking at. I've said that what we see often is related to a monologue we've heard, but this need not mean, from the point of view of the character *as such*, as if *this* thought of his could be captured by *this* visual. (Generally, these are not related to the plot, but some of the Manichean reflections of Train and the more nihilistic meditations of Welsh are framed in a montage of sublime and mysterious natural violence, as if a confirmation of the monologue: crocodiles, wild dogs, bats, dying birds.) But both the presence of the non-plot-driven photographs and the seriousness, even solemnity, of the attention to such objects (often heightened by the musical score) create a general expectation of a different kind of attention from the viewer, and the seriousness of the tone suggests much more than mere atmospherics. The effect of the sort of framing, attentiveness, and lingering over the living things is to alter *what it is* that we should actually attend to. It is not merely the objects we see when framed this way, but rather, given the lingering attention of the camera, if one can put it this way, the *objects-in-the-light-of-such-attention*, photographed as if *seen* in a mode of interrogative attention that, by its very intensity and independence from the plot, detaches the objects from any normal intercourse with viewers and allows some other dimension of meaningfulness (or some different sort of question about life) to emerge visually, and so it requires some other stance or attitude to be possible with regard to such a presence. To a large extent that suggested stance is similar in tone to the voice-overs: intensely interrogative and unresolved.

So, looked at this way, we do not see the mere beings ("one-dimensionally," one might say, to retrieve an older term), but we see them in the light of the question of what it is for them to be at all, especially to be alive, a presence that cannot be rightly captured as a discursive theme, but only in a kind of intimation or disclosure available to a visual art. There is a modern tradition in philosophical reflection on art that holds that artworks can be said to be the bearers of truth, but not as making any tacitly assertoric or even discursive claim, but rather as disclosive, and disclosive especially of a kind of truth unavailable discursively. (One could count Hegel, Schiller, Schelling, Schlegel, Schopenhauer, Nietzsche, Heidegger, and Merleau-Ponty as representative of this tradition.) And Malick's photography evokes such a tradition, in the way it resonates with the mute presence and strangeness of such beings, as well as with their silent, contrastive presence not only with narrative and dialogue, but with the inescapable threat of sudden nonbeing or death. But such a disclosure, intuitive and prediscursive, about "the thin red line" between life and death, the meaning of the title in the novel, also somehow announces its own unavailability for any determinate thinking, as if something is also being withheld or hidden from such discursive intelligibility, from what the voice-overs alone could make sense of.

In the film, this sense of "ontological attention" is often both insisted on and intensified by the emphasis on sunlight. We look up through the water to the sun; we pan up huge trees to the light; sunlight streaming through leaves pervades many of the scenes, as if to suggest that we are seeing not mere objects but objects *in their being illuminated* by this basic ontological question, prompted by their being at all. To emphasize this even more, in Witt's early memory of the bedroom in which his mother was dying, at the end the camera pans up to reveal, quite surprisingly, that there is no ceiling. The room is exposed to the sky and sun, and so we are first introduced to this sort of ontological trope: what it is to see everything, even death, in the light of this interrogation and wonder, in the light of the question of the meaning of their living presence, a question that does not, perhaps cannot, arise in our everyday dealings with such organisms. (The sunlight image returns at the end, in the last and ultimate conversation between Witt and Welsh on an old plantation. Witt looks up and again there is no full ceiling or roof. They are relatively "unprotected" from the imperative for this sort of attentiveness [2:20:53–2:22:54].)

Seeing matters this way allows us to say that the main structuring element in the organization of the film is then a kind of counterpoint between the primarily aesthetic (in the sense of sensible, intuitive, affective) interrogation of such an issue (the living nature within which death must make some sort of sense, must be confronted and borne) and the discursive interrogation carried on in the monologues. By implication, we sense too that we need both these modalities of intelligibility, even if they can be difficult to think together.

There is much to say about that counterpoint, but the relation to the main monologues also occasionally suggests another kind of question, at least for Train. Train *also* wants to know, and Welsh is sure that he does know, whether *what there is,* in whatever weighty sense in which the question of life can be said to be posed by the photography, *is good.* The question of a kind of natural theodicy emerges. Given what there is, especially the "war with itself" that is nature according to Train, and given the crushing human awareness of ever-impending death, given the need to kill to stay alive, and given that one needs some orienting attitude toward it all, especially when the primary issues are forced on one by war, what should that attitude be? *How* valuable is mere life?

The different possibilities—never really resolved, because everything remains suspended in an interrogative mode—that we are given in the film as responses to such a question are presented mostly in the dialogues between Witt and Welsh. A major focus of the contrast concerns the existence of "another world." The first extended exchange between them sets the terms of the contrast. Welsh says, "In this world . . . a man himself is nothing. And there ain't no world but this one." Witt counters, "You're wrong there, Top. I seen another world. Sometimes I think it was just . . . my imagination." Welsh responds, "We're living in a world that's blowing itself to hell as fast as everybody can arrange it. In a situation like that all a man can do is shut his eyes and let nothing touch him. Look out for himself" (12:42–13:47).

We already know that Witt is not talking about a separate world, heaven, or the afterlife. (Train's monologues [Train, who believes only in "dying and the Lord"] *are* often posed in the second person, as if to someone: "Who are you to live in all these many forms?" [30:51]. "This great evil. Where does it come from? Who's doin' this to us? Who's killin' us?" [1:50:33]. But even his inclinations seem pantheistic, even if Manichean, not transcendent.) The "immortality" Witt seeks is in *this* life, *in* his mother's calm acceptance of her own death, as if she has made some sense of it and so is at peace with it. It is as if he is saying that the interrogative framing of living nature that we see does (despite Welsh's skepticism that it does not) open some sort of possibility that can be realized, even if not discursively "justified." *Who can see what,* in these terms, is a frequent theme. After the last, and now touching, dialogue between Witt and Welsh, we hear another voice-over by Train that marks the arbitrariness of who can see anything in the light of whatever question a reflective attentiveness can raise. "One man looks at a dying bird and thinks there's nothing but unanswered pain. But death's got the final word. It's laughing at him. Another man sees that same bird, feels the glory. Feels something smiling through him" (2:23:13).

But things are hardly clear-cut even for Witt, who clearly aspires to a kind of goodness, and who even dies in an act of sacrifice, altruism. In a striking scene, he looks at the partially buried face of a Japanese soldier. (This immediately follows a dialogue with no visual place, a dialogue just heard, as if floating from nowhere, between Storm [John C. Reilly] and Fife, unattributed as such, about dead people. We are told that the dead are "no different than dead dogs, once you get used to the idea." And "We're meat, kid" [1:44:11–1:44:27].) We hear the imagined voice of the dead Japanese soldier, addressed to Witt as if a kind of indictment: "Are you righteous? Kind? Does your confidence lie in this? Are you loved by all? Know that I was, too. Do you imagine your sufferings will be less because you loved goodness? Truth?" (1:44:31–1:45:17). Whatever will be seen or not seen, it will not be redemptive, not be justifying in any sense, at least, that Train could recognize. This strange, imagined dialogue in effect rejects the whole premise of Train's speculative questions and makes it even less likely that Train's monologues, far and away the most frequent that we hear, are in any way representative of the film's point of view, if we can ever say that about any film, especially one by Malick.

Appropriately, all the monologues and dialogues never resolve anything, and we are left at the end with what amounts to two sorts of poems, or perhaps prayers, as if the artwork that is the film is a sort of poem or prayer. Welsh, after he yet again remarks that the only possible orientation in this world is to make oneself an island, nevertheless addresses a prayer or invocation to some "you," as if addressed to Witt, or what Witt saw, some dimension of meaning he envies: "If I never meet you in this life, let me feel the lack. A glance from your eyes, and my life will be yours" (2:39:05–2:39:24). This (again, revealingly, a glance, a *look*) is the most Welsh can manage, and we have seen enough of him to know it is nevertheless a considerable achievement, opened up by Witt.

After this, we find ourselves on a landing craft, leaving the war, and as we do, the language of a kind of thoughtless everyday, the world of the quotidian bourgeoisie, returns, as Train prattles on in a banal aspiration for a successful life. (In a last, visual emphasis on the lack of community, only Train is talking with someone. The hundreds of other men mill about silently for several minutes.) But we hear one last time what sort of reflection the experience of war has occasioned, at least for Train, whoever he is. Astonishingly, as one last refusal of what, conventionally, we think we know about "a character like Train," a simple country boy, afraid to die, his banal everyday voice blends seamlessly with the metaphysical "voice-over voice," one last time confounding our settled expectations of what is in or out of character for an individual. In an apostrophe to his own soul (or the World Soul),[32] Train says, "Where is it that we were together? Who were you that I lived with? Walked with? The brother. The friend. Darkness from light. Strife and love. Are they the workings of one mind? The features of the same face? Oh, my soul, let me be in you now. Look out through my eyes. Look out at the things you made. All things shining" (2:41:00–2:42:53).[33]

This apostrophe suggests a last inflection on the reflective nature of the moving picture we have just seen, as well as returning us to the concerns of the opening monologue. For we *have* been looking through the "eyes" of the film, and what is "made" in and by the film, but whether we can hear the question Train poses (*all* things shining, genuinely illuminated by the light of this reflective interrogation) seems a matter of grace, a dispensation of one's soul that one can only hope for, perhaps occasionally inspired by a work of art. Appropriately, the film closes with three silent images of life (more accurately, it ends with three photographs), no voice-over, no music; whatever is to be intelligible will be so (if it is) primarily visually: human, animal, and plant; three natives in canoes, two tropical birds, and a single somewhat forlorn but living plant, a leaf, growing out of a coconut in the water. Or, the film ends with the question of what it is that we "see," or can see; what it is that we have seen.

Notes

I am especially indebted to Richard Neer for his acute comments on an earlier draft, and I profited as well from conversations with Michael Fried, Dan Morgan, and Ralph Ubl and from a spirited discussion held after a presentation of a version of this paper at the University of Basel.

1. And there are several species. There is the "boot-camp transformation" movie; the "impossible objective" movie; the "prisoner-of-war" and the "escape" movie; the "daring, reckless fly-boy" movies: the "war as seen by children" movie; the "coming-of-age in war" movie, the "underground-resistance" movie; the "patriotic propaganda" movie, and so forth.

2. Since genres exist for the sake of variations, even in more traditional Hollywood war movies, this theme can have a kind of inverse presentation too. That is, the loyalty and love that grows between men can also be a great difficulty for the group's particular or national purpose. That is certainly the case for Staros (Elias Koteas), when he decides not to attack. A fine treatment, one might even say a study, of such a theme: Anthony Mann's 1957 *Men in War.*

3. An equally impressive example would be Robert Aldrich's *Attack!* (1956).

4. The "outlaw road" movie; the "social-class/romantic-triangle" movie; the "settlement/aboriginal" movie, the war movie, the coming-of-age movie.

5. There are few films for which George Wilson's apposite remarks about the perils

of heavy reliance on plot exposition alone in understanding the film are more appropriate. (However, there are certainly many Hollywood films for which the remarks are just as apposite, as Wilson shows better than anyone ever has. Malick is just making the issue exceptionally clear.) I mean remarks like these:

> Perhaps it is the confused idea that film is the most "direct and immediate" way of narrating a story which has led most viewers, professional and otherwise, to suppose that the requirements of plot exposition confine a film's significance . . . Viewers dispose their attention toward the "focus" of the story's ultimate resolution. They are perceptually set to follow the evolution of those plot conflicts that are marked out to be the subject of an audience's most immediate and engaged regard. Indeed, it is the normal goal of narrative strategies to make this temptation effectively irresistible.

George Wilson, *Narration in Light: Studies in Cinematic Point of View* (Baltimore: Johns Hopkins University Press, 1986), 10.

6. This takes up, in a different way, an important suggestion by Richard Neer in his fine piece on *The New World,* when he says, "More specifically, there is at any given moment in *The New World* a reciprocal relation between the narrative of discovery on the one hand, and the declaration of the film's own possibilities on the other." *nonsite* 2 (June 2011). This reciprocal relation assumes a number of different forms in *The Thin Red Line,* only some of which can be explored here.

7. One could make a case for the relevance of Kon Ichikawa's *Fires on the Plain* (1959). There are voice-overs in the film (more monologues than meditative) and non-narrative concentration on animals (insects, dogs, birds); and the visual emphasis on the emaciated state of the Japanese, the widespread insanity and desperation, is echoed in Malick's depiction of the Japanese on Guadalcanal.

8. It is fair to say that Malick's use of the voice-overs has changed over the course of his career. In the first two films, it is different from later experiments. In *Badlands,* Holly's commentary (Sissy Spacek's character) is largely *counterpoint,* dissociated from, rather than reflected in, the scenes we see. (We see murder; she wants to talk about what they ate.) In *Days of Heaven,* Linda's voice-over (Linda Manz's character) is both knowing and innocent at the same time. Her flat, almost affectless narration, rather than help to reveal the psychology of the characters, renders the drama more opaque and strange. After *The Thin Red Line,* John Smith's voiced musings (Colin Farrell's character) are more politically tinged but very much in character, not generally reflective, and Pocahontas's are more religious (in the vague sense of "spiritual"). In *The Tree of Life,* the technique is much more like that in *The Thin Red Line.* Malick is clearly experimenting with the right relation between what we might call being "inside" the (and our own) narration and "outside." And that is itself a complicated issue, because, while we need to believe that we can both inhabit an inside and also "step back" and assess things from "outside," there is obviously no "outside."

9. The intended meaning of the musical soundtrack is a very interesting issue in itself. After the Arvo Pärt opening chord, the idyllic scenes are accompanied, as if in

counterpart, by a requiem, Fauré's, but to add to the complexity, it is the "In Paradisum" section that we hear. A counterpoint choral song (and the chorus is something connected to the solidarity-isolation theme to appear shortly) is then heard ("The Prophecy from the Village of Kremnus"). Perhaps the most interesting piece of music, the title of which directly addresses the many interrogative moments in the film, is Charles Ives's "The Unanswered Question," played during and after the overrunning of the Japanese camp, perhaps the most violent sequence in the film.

10. The exceptions are Bell's memories of his wife and a brief memory by Witt of his mother's death and childhood. Both instances are dreamlike and do not contribute much to any standard psychological profile of a character.

11. A good example of the formation of such a cohesive group: the patriotic (and very British) Carol Reed wartime vehicle *The Immortal Battalion* (aka *The Way Ahead*) (1944). There is an especially explicit concentration here on the particular challenges of a citizen's army in democratic societies, although the tone is naïvely optimistic about the issue throughout.

12. This issue is one of the main themes of Michael Chion, *The Thin Red Line* (London: BFI, 2004).

13. In Welsh's first conversation with Witt, Welsh had already made clear that any such claim by Staros would have to be a fantasy. Welsh says, "This is C Company, of which I'm First Sergeant. I run this outfit. Captain Staros, he's the CO, but I'm the guy who runs it. Nobody's gonna foul that up" (11:53–12:01).

14. In a scene at the beginning of the campaign on the islands, the American troops pass by a Melanesian man, and neither side registers in the slightest the other's presence. Nothing in the film is dispositive about anything, however. Later we see a Melanesian man tenderly helping the American wounded.

15. A good summary of the relation between the novel and the film can be found in Stacy Peebles's "The Other World of War: Terrence Malick's Adaptation of *The Thin Red Line*," in Hannah Patterson, *The Cinema of Terrence Malick: Poetic Visions of America* (New York: Columbia University Press, 2007), 152–63.

16. The fact that the actor is John Savage suggests yet another intertextual reference, this time to Savage's character in *The Deer Hunter*.

17. The tenderness of the soldier's dying "good-bye" is one of the film's most poignant and effective small moments.

18. There is one very tender scene of a Japanese soldier cradling a comrade as if a lover, but nothing is made of it.

19. "Putatively pacific" because the American republic has so often been at war during its relatively short history. The traditional American war movie treats war as episodic and unusual, but here the voice-overs by Train elevate such violence and destruction to permanent metaphysical status. This is another reason why the narrative framework of the genre is invoked only to be refused.

20. The only commentators I have found who notice this odd fact are Leo Bersani

and Ulysse Dutoit, in their fine chapter on the film in their *Forms of Being: Cinema, Aesthetics, Subjectivity* (London: BFI, 2004), 124–78.

21. Not only are many characters in the film hard to identify and reidentify; it is also hard to connect what a character avows with what the character does, upsetting another important dimension of "movie logic." Witt loves Company C but is AWOL; Welsh seems a cynic and encourages selfishness but performs a genuinely heroic, altruistic act.

22. Throughout a great deal of the second half of the film, a low, humming musical undertone can be heard, occasionally accompanied by the sound of a clock ticking for long stretches, especially in battle scenes. I say "Manichean" here because the tonality is religious, and sometimes second-personal, but the reflection could certainly be understood in a Freudian way, as Freud in his late career came to realize that there might be a "death instinct," as well as eros, a duality for which there is no resolution or synthesis, just a constant struggle, much like the one Train is concerned about. This is something suggested by Bersani and Dutoit, *Forms of Being.*

23. As Bersani and Dutoit mistakenly surmise. Ibid., 157.

24. Insofar as a film as a whole can suggest or inspire allegiances, create sympathy, provoke aversion or disgust, one might say that at least this aspect of Witt's relation to war is echoed in the film as a whole, which is not an "antiwar" film at all. Or even a political film, for that matter. The national mission in fighting the Japanese, the "cause of freedom," and so forth are never mentioned.

25. "I drink you" (1:25:26) is Bell's closing apostrophe. Later, before he gets her letter, he writes her a kind of hymn to love. "Love. Where does it come from? Who lit this flame in us? No war can put it out, conquer it. I was a prisoner. You set me free" (2:08:26–2:09:17). As I am trying to show, the irony (here somewhat bitter) and the unexpected reversal of our standard expectations is not unique but runs through the film from beginning to end.

26. Besides the 1964 Hollywood film of Jones's novel, there is another film about the battle for Guadalcanal, Nicholas Ray's 1951 *The Flying Leathernecks.* There is the same sort of confrontation there between a very stern, by-the-book commander (who we suspect may be a martinet, a prig), played by John Wayne, and his "humanist" second-in-command, played by Robert Ryan. This dynamic plays out in the more formulaic way, as each comes to appreciate what is of value in the other. Wayne really cares deeply (we are allowed to see his home life and tenderness for his children); Ryan comes to understand the burdens of command: he must refuse help to his dying friend and brother-in-law in order to complete the mission. (In a way typical of Ray's films, there is a jolting, unsettling moment at the end of the film when Ryan and Wayne "bond" in a quasi-jocular, now very friendly way, totally at odds with the fact that the bond was built over the sacrifice by Ryan of his own brother-in-law. I am convinced that Malick is referring to and so commenting on this film [there is even the same sort of possibly malingering, reluctant warrior], just as I am that the ending scene of Witt racing through the jungle, a moving camera tracking him as the enemy closes in, is a comment of sorts on Elias's

running through the jungle, same camera motion, immediately preceding his death, in Oliver Stone's *Platoon* [1986], but I am not sure any of that can be proven. [Cf. Elias's comment in *Platoon,* "I love it here at night. The stars. Not good or bad. Just there."].)

27. There are plenty of war movies where the "hardness-softness" issue is prominent, something one might expect to be more important for citizen armies. A good example is Henry King's *Twelve O'Clock High* (1949), where the problem is given an official name, "Over-identification with the men." This is a pressing issue in the film, since part of Gregory Peck's job is to push the flyers as far as possible so command can learn how many continuous daylight precision bombing raids they can take before they crack.

28. This is not something as clear as it ought to be in discussions of the film. Critchley thinks that Tall has devised an alternative to a frontal assault, but the flanking movement Tall proposes is not the "flanking-through-the-jungle" that Staros wanted. (We never see the jungle.) It is another route up the hill itself, all of which is exposed to Japanese fire. There is simply a ridge not occupied by the enemy that the men can use to stage a small squad attack. Sinnebrink thinks that what Tall eventually orders was Staros's idea and Tall "takes it over" when he arrives. That is also incorrect. Staros wanted to avoid an attack up the hill altogether and to flank through the jungle. That is what Tall rejects. See Simon Critchley, "Calm: On Terrence Malick's *The Thin Red Line,*" *Film-Philosophy* 6, no. 48 (December 2002); and Robert Sinnerbrink, "A Heideggerian Cinema? On Terrence Malick's *The Thin Red Line,*" *Film-Philosophy* 10, no. 3 (December 2006): 26–37. Someone who gets it exactly right: Kaja Silverman, in her article "'All Things Shining,'" in *Loss: The Politics of Mourning,* ed. David L. Eng and David Kazanjian (Berkeley: University of California Press, 2003), 223–42, especially 327, 329.

29. There are also "religious" differences between Staros, presumably a Greek orthodox Christian (the character is Jewish in Jones's novel), who prays before the battle, "Let me not let You down. Let me not let down my men," and Tall, whose "religion" appears more ancient, more suited to a warrior, not a Christian; that is, for a believer for whom the equal and absolute value of human life makes war a complicated business. Tall invokes Homer, not Christianity (41:31). (Not that Tall's Greek ethos is genuine. The invocation is deeply ironic, given that Tall's only real motivation is careerist.)

30. This is something rightly stressed by Bersani and Dutoit, *Forms of Being.* They also note that this refusal is another indication of a lack of commonality in the enterprise of the war. Staros seems completely indifferent, given everything we see, to the strategic importance of Guadalcanal and what it might be "worth" in lives.

31. This is particularly vivid in the final attack on the Japanese position, staged as if the men had become seized with some collective insanity, shooting unarmed prisoners, looting, desecrating bodies.

32. This mode of address to a personalized soul might be an invocation of mystical literature, perhaps St. John of the Cross, where such a dialogue with one's soul is prominent.

33. This is, as Jacob Leigh has pointed out, a reference to Wordsworth's Prelude.

Tumult and peace, the darkness and the light—
Were all like workings of one mind, the features
Of the same face, blossoms upon one tree;
Characters of the great Apocalypse,
The types and symbols of Eternity,
Of first, and last, and midst, and without end.

Leigh, "Unanswered Questions: Vision and Experience in Terrence Malick's *The Thin Red Line*," *CineAction!* 62 (October 2013).

War and Its Fictional Recovery On-Screen

Narrative Management of Death in *The Big Red One* and *The Thin Red Line*

Elisabeth Bronfen

Recovering Life's Full Content in Wartime

Writing his timely thoughts on war and death one year after World War I began, Sigmund Freud notes how two things have aroused his deep sense of disillusionment: the low standards of morality shown by European nations supposedly guardians of humanist standards and the brutality shown by individual combatants who, as members of these highly civilized nations, were thought to be incapable of such inhuman behavior. Recognizing that more is required than a nostalgic lament for the loss of civilized culture, Freud shifts his attention to what he perceives to be an altered attitude toward death dictated by the outbreak of war. While we tend to exclude mortality from our quotidian calculations in times of peace, its ubiquitous presence can no longer be denied in wartime. "We are forced to believe in it," Freud states. "People really die." In addition, death can no longer be seen as a chance event, but must be perceived in relation to necessity. "To be sure," he continues, "it still seems a matter of chance whether a bullet hits this man or that; but a second bullet may well hit the survivor; and the accumulation of deaths puts an end to the impression of chance." Astonishing, however, is the conclusion he draws from the changed attitude toward death that war calls forth: "Life has, indeed, become interesting again; it has recovered its full content."[1]

His own stance as an analyst of both personal and collective psychic states regarding the more primitive, indeed barbaric, embrace of death retrieved in the face of war is fraught with ambivalence. After all, if being compelled to acknowledge mortality as an inevitable truth of human existence makes life recover its full content, then implicitly the exclusion of death from peace is based on an absence or loss. Furthermore, Freud introduces his astonishing claim by invoking the world of fiction as the site where in times of peace we find compensation for the denial of death civilized culture is predicated on. "There we still find people who know how to die—who, indeed, even manage to kill someone else," Freud contests. "There alone too the condition can be fulfilled which makes it possible for us to reconcile ourselves with death: namely, that behind all the vicissitudes of life we should still be able to preserve a life intact." The compensation fiction can afford, however, itself proves to be duplicitous. Fiction can give voice to the death we seek to deny with impunity, because it renders the knowledge of our mortality compatible with our need to believe in our own invincibility. "In the realm of fiction we find the plurality of lives which we need," Freud adds. "We die with the hero with whom we have identified ourselves; yet we survive him, and are ready to die again just as safely with another hero."[2]

If the world of fiction is the place where attitudes toward death, curtailed by civilized behavior, are preserved during times of peace, how does it correspond to the world of war that resuscitates these suppressed instincts? More importantly, how do films taking the ubiquitous presence of death in zones of war as their theme not only themselves recover the full content of life by lavishly putting death on display, but in so doing also reflect on their own fictionality? By aesthetically celebrating what civility censors, do they feed a barbaric destructive instinct of their own, or do they use the spectacle of death to reassert survival in the face of war's destruction, regarding both the heroes in the story and the way telling their tale assures their immortality in our collective image repertoire? I take Freud's equation between the world of fiction and the world of war as my theoretical point of departure for this essay in part because, when it comes to illustrating his claim that war unleashes unconscious instincts that civilization necessarily forbids, he offers a list of retrieved attitudes that dovetail with standard formulas of war-film narratives. War, he surmises, "compels us once more to be heroes who cannot believe in their own death; it stamps strangers as enemies, whose death is to be brought about or desired; it tells us to disregard the death of those we love."[3]

The conversation I propose between Freud's more generalized interpretation of death in war and Hollywood's imaginary reconceptualization of specific historic campaigns is one given by the films themselves. Both Freud's writings and the films by Samuel Fuller and Terrence Malick I will be discussing respond to the same onslaught of violence brought about by the global industrialized wars of the twentieth century, even if his psychoanalytic investigation precedes their cinematic reenactment. At the historical moment when this cultural shift took place, namely, the mass deaths of trench warfare unimaginable before World War I, Freud formulates the critical tropes that films could readily refigure when bringing the experience of death and survival during any of the subsequent wars back to the screen. By aligning the altered attitudes toward death in the vast war machinery of total mobilization with notions of regeneration through violence found in the fictional world of tragedy or melodrama, Freud offers a narrative template that allows filmmakers to endow their restaging of war with a similar pathos. Indeed, by foregrounding how the ability to kill in war is predicated on a leap into magical thinking that pits cruelty, brutality, and a disregard for the life of others against a trust in one's own invincibility, Freud emerges as the seminal theorist of the barbarism inhabiting civilized modernity. His thinking can fruitfully be brought to bear on films that reconceive war not only in terms of a systemic power struggle but also in relation to the psychic effects war calls forth in those killing and dying on the ground. Indeed, my point is that his writings inaugurate the stories interpreting war, which filmmakers since have come to appropriate and readapt to the cultural needs of their times.

It is worth recalling that the experience of World War I marks a seminal shift in Freud's conception of the psychic apparatus. If, while military conflict was still ongoing, he merely sought to explain the reemergence of a destructive impulse on the part of those caught in the gigantic machine of war, once the fighting was over, this concern prompted his theory of the death drive. Having witnessed the demise of the civilized world as he knew it, Freud found himself compelled to rethink the origins and motivations for psychic anguish, adding to his discussion of the vicissitudes and perversions of sexual drives a second, indeed more primary, psychic proclivity toward aggression and destruction. In the interim between the two world wars that came to characterize the twentieth century, he came to speculate that an eternal struggle between Eros and Thanatos subtends the psychic life of individuals as well as communities, which in times of war tips toward the latter. His claim is that while the erotic instinct seeks to preserve life and unite with others, the aggressive instinct seeks to kill and destroy, reducing life to its original condition of inanimate matter. For the conversation between Freud's conceptualization of death and war films I am proposing, it is particularly noteworthy that, in his exchange with Albert Einstein entitled "Why War?" taking place in 1932, he admits that his theory of a double instinct is "a kind of mythology." He can propose a "formula for *indirect* methods of combating war," because he unabashedly rethinks military struggle in terms of the world of fiction. "If willingness to engage in war is an effect of the destructive instinct," he suggests, "the most obvious plan will be to bring Eros, its antagonist, into play. Anything that encourages the growth of emotional ties between men must operate against war."[4]

In hindsight, one can only ruefully note how historical events shattered the fragile hope Freud gives voice to in his theory of instincts. The fact that he has nothing other than a mythological formula to offer may, however, also help explain the proximity of his prognosis to the stories with which Hollywood addresses the same issue. As Anton Kaes notes, it is as though Freud were writing about films he had never seen, yet whose visual language his own critical narratives unwittingly anticipate.[5] One might surmise that where Freud reflects on war by relating the attitudes toward death it calls forth to fiction, Hollywood films reconceptualize war by pitting the life of cinematic recapturing against the death of real war. The analogy between the world of war and the world of fiction they propose serves to contain death in the same way Freud's mythological theory of instincts does. The stories they bring to the screen recall the real war, putting on display attitudes about life and death unobtainable anywhere else. At the same time, in the spirit of Eros, war films recast into personalized stories of survival the ubiquity of destruction and with it the somber recognition that death cannot be denied, ultimately tipping the scales in favor of a protection of life.

Writing one year after the armistice that ended the Great War in Europe was signed, Freud came once more to link the psychic attitudes toward death it had evoked to a literary figure. Diagnosing the flight into illness some soldiers undertook in order to escape the horror of trench warfare, he speculates that shell shock may well be promoted by a "conflict in the ego between the soldier's old peaceful ego and his new warlike one." This struggle, he adds, "becomes acute as soon as the peace-ego realizes what danger it runs of losing its life owing to the rashness of its newly formed, parasitic double."[6] Freud thus locates a twofold mortal danger as the source for traumatic neurosis, splicing together the threat posed by an external enemy with the one attributed to an internal one. The outbreak of traumatic neurosis simply renders pathological the split between civilian and soldier that all fighting is predicated on. Disregarding the actual psychiatric value of this interpretation, decisive for my own discussion is that the figure Freud chooses to embody the intense anxiety that internal psychic conflict can provoke is one he unabashedly borrows from gothic fiction. In the stories Hollywood tells about real war on the ground, the rhetorical gesture of reduplication abounds.

Protecting Life at All Costs: *The Big Red One*

Indeed, the two films I will now turn to—Samuel Fuller's *The Big Red One* (1980) and Terrence Malick's *The Thin Red Line* (1998)—both draw on the figure of the uncanny double to externalize an inner conflict regarding death in war, ranging from psychic incapacitation, cynicism, and guilt to lethal self-expenditure and an erotic enjoyment of killing. The panoply of parasitic doublings they bring to the screen serves to explore the luck of survival, the fascination of transcending finitude, and the atonement made possible through self-sacrifice. Given the theatrical nature of this staging of psychic conflict, it is worth recalling Paul Fussell's observation that treating warfare as spectacle provides a psychic escape for the participant. By splitting off his "real self" from the one performing the perverse, cruel, and absurd acts required of a man in war, Fussell argues, the foot soldier can retain his conviction that the world is still a rational place.[7] What this experience of self-duplication borrows particularly from the world of gothic fiction is the way the double renders tangible a distinction between friendly and hostile versions of the self, even while its appearance also indicates that, in fantasy at least, the self is in doubt as to which is his true self.

For the war films under discussion, one can surmise that the doubling of the self provides psychic protection precisely when, in contrast to Freud's cases of traumatic war neurosis, rather than bringing about a flight into illness, it allows the soldier to remain engaged in military action. As a residue of magical thinking, these fictional doubles give voice to a seminal psychic ambivalence regarding death: If, in battle, I double myself, I may die, but the life of the part of me that has come to be split off might be protected.[8] While the double gives body to cruel and barbaric aspects of the self that men in war may wish to abnegate, it also assures their survival, if only in the cinematic recapture of their deeds. There is, therefore, a further dimension to the deployment of the double in Hollywood's war narratives.

It draws attention to a repetition of events, seemingly involuntary but having therapeutic effect. The hero, rather than merely accepting death in war as an inescapable necessity, gains the chance to repeat a previous action and thereby can determine his own destiny by consciously choosing death. Or, finding himself repeating a scene to which he was previously helplessly subjected, he can make a different choice and thus alter the previous fatal outcome. In either case, the restitution gained through repetition makes use of the same magical thinking regarding death that links the world of war to that of fiction. In both worlds, the deaths of others can be dealt with as negligible because they are not regarded as fellow human beings, while the designated heroes, in turn, can trust in their invincibility because in fantasy they, too, have transcended the laws of human finitude.

War films that self-consciously make use of the figure of the double, along with narrative repetition, reflect on the gesture of fictionalization that real soldiers tap into as a particularly viable means of psychic protection while on the ground in a war zone. When, as is the case in *The Big Red One,* a director uses his story about foot soldiers to retrace on-screen his own experiences of real war, he quite explicitly draws attention to the self-reflexive power of cinema. In Fuller's case, the doubling and interchanging autobiographical and fictional selves offer up a very specific implication of the world of war and the world of fiction. The uncanny recurrence of an event serves as a powerful protection of the ego's narcissism, transcoding the world of war into a personal fantasy revolving around a hero who is given a second chance to turn the senseless contingency of death in war into a meaningful psychic rite de passage. For this reason, *The Big Red One,* which took more than two decades to get made, uses repetition with a difference as its seminal rhetorical device to rework the anxiety of real war. As Fuller welds together memories of his experience during World War II with pathos formulas of cinematic war available to him, he both continues the autobiographical story that ended on V-Day 1945 and substitutes its horror with a restitutive story about the glory that survival affords.[9]

To signal that at issue is a return to some unfinished business in the past, the film begins with a title card explaining, "This is fictional life based on factual death." It then follows up its claim to facticity with a second title, superimposed over images of a battleground, shot in black and white: "France, November 1918." Enveloped by the clouds of smoke still lingering on after what will only later prove to have been a final battle, a lone man with a rifle is seen cautiously walking among the corpses strewn beneath a gigantic wooden sculpture of Christ on the Cross. The camera stays close to his feet as he probes the dead men to see whether anyone is still alive. We only recognize Lee Marvin's face once a shell-shocked horse has begun attacking him, kicking his rifle to pieces. Able to protect himself by hiding behind the Cross, he espies an enemy soldier, suddenly emerging from the heavy fog, his arms raised above his head, calling out, "Der Krieg ist vorbei, nicht schiessen" ("The war is over, don't shoot"). Fearing this to be nothing more than an old soldier's trick, Lee Marvin pulls his knife and stabs him. While he leaves the scene of death, the camera pans forward into one of the hollow eyes of the wooden Christ. The ants crawling out of the dark hole seem to animate the gaze of this sole witness to the killing. Only upon returning to his trench does Lee Marvin learn from his Captain that the armistice was signed four hours ago. In response to the look of quiet horror that begins to spread over his face, the Captain explains, "Well, you didn't know it was over," to which Lee Marvin can only tersely reply, "He did."[10]

This opening scene proves to be a founding moment in two ways. It inaugurates the sense of guilt that will return to haunt this foot soldier when, two and a half decades later, he once again finds himself fighting in France. At the same time, he gets the idea of using a single red stripe as the insignia for the First Infantry Division from the cap of the man he involuntarily murdered because, having gotten lost in the fog of war, he didn't know that peace had already set in. The visual sequencing, in turn, uses the strip of red cloth, initially the only bit of color in this scene of anagnorisis, as a transition to Lee Marvin's return to combat, now as a sergeant who remains nameless, leading a rifle squad in the First Platoon of I-Company. As the red stripe turns into the number 1 on a uniform badge, bringing with it full color to the screen, the narrator explains: "A quarter of a century later that piece of red cloth from the dead Hun's hat had become famous all over the world." Although Fuller was pressured by his producer to include this voice-over, it is, in fact, consistent with the strategy of repetition and doubling that his story of the foot soldier is grounded on. Gesturing toward a national repetition compulsion, the disembodied voice of Private Zab, who at this point in the film we have not yet seen, adds: "Twenty-four years later, the Big Red One was fighting the Krauts again."[11]

The voice-over serves as an acoustic double of Robert Carradine's performance of the director's wartime self. It focalizes the adventures of the Sergeant's rifle squad from the position of someone who we know from the start has survived to tell the tale. The postwar Zab often uses his streetwise commentary to endow meaning to the cruel butchery we see him and his wartime buddies implicated in. This acoustic double, however, also serves to split in two the personal perspective on a national repetition compulsion that *The Big Red One* recaptures on-screen. The film adroitly pits the visual charisma of Fuller's star, Lee Marvin, along with his laconic gravitas, against the playful banter of the four members of his squad, who will manage to survive the European Campaign by his side. His quiet gaze and war-seasoned wisdom serve not so much to contradict as to balance Zab's youthful black humor, regulating the attitudes toward life and death that these young men will obtain as they move from one battle scene to the next.

In his effort to give fictional life on-screen to his factual experience of death in real war, Fuller chooses two storytellers as a continuation of and substitution for his earlier wartime self. On the one hand, we find the disingenuous dogface, who, seeing himself as the Hemingway of the Bronx, wants to come out of combat with a war novel. On the other hand, we have the experienced soldier who has come up with a protective fiction to help himself live with the human cruelty and destruction war necessitates. The nameless sergeant's personal fiction, tacitly referring to the inaugural scene, initially comes up in a conversation with Private Griff (Mark Hamill) early on in the film. Compelled to defend himself against the charge of being a coward because he had been unable to shoot a French soldier during their landing in North Africa, Griff declared: "I can't murder anybody." Trusting in the force of his words to prevent neurotic incapacitation, the Sergeant gruffly retorts, "We don't murder, we kill." When Griff, as yet unwilling to accept any neat distinction that sanctions giving death to a person whose face he can see, challenges him that the two are, in fact, the same, the Sergeant counters deftly by reencoding the enemy as nonhuman: "You don't murder animals, you kill them."[12] For the Sergeant, this formula serves as a psychic protection against the brutality involved in treating strangers as lethal enemies. The killing required of him, he maintains, is compatible with his civilized notion of ethical behavior because he can split off the parasitic warlike double from its peacetime self with impunity.

Many months later, after they have moved into Germany, Griff, who by then has himself become a battle-seasoned foot soldier, will remind the Sergeant of the conversation they had in North Africa, prompting him to give the backstory to the personal fiction that allows him to stay sane in the world of war. The camera moves into a close-up of Fuller's star, Lee Marvin, so as to visually underscore the significance that the point the Sergeant is about to make has for Fuller's own cinematic recapturing of the European Campaign. "When the second hand of that watch calls the shot and the Kaiser picks up that pen and scratches his name on that paper then you gotta call it quits," he explains. The boys fall into a grave silence as he adds, almost as an afterthought, "Kill all the Huns you can before then, but never after, never."[13] The fact that he has fallen back into military lingo from World War I draws attention to the way his own guilt is the oblique force dictating his sense of justified killing. What psychically protects the hero of Fuller's war narrative isn't so much the denial of his own mortality as his insistence on an unequivocal difference between wartime and peacetime attitudes toward death. His peacelike morality does not find itself in conflict with the cruelty and barbarity required of him as a soldier because he lives by a story that keeps the two separate. Fuller's psychological point, however, is morally complex. His sergeant is invested in the distinction between killing and murder because at the end of World War I, he had come to discover that he had not quit in time. The decisive point is that although his crime occurred in a murky interzone between war and peace, rendering him legally innocent, the guilt he feels sheds light on what is necessary for the civilized self not to be in conflict with its parasitic wartime double. He must allocate murder and killing to two different psychic topographies, clearly demarcating the world of peacetime from the zone of war.

How much emotional protection the Sergeant's story about a watch, a piece of paper, and a pen affords becomes chillingly clear when, a few scenes later, he and his rifle squad enter a concentration camp in Czechoslovakia. Unprepared for the atrocities awaiting him inside the barracks, Griff finds himself moving beyond the killing sanctioned by war into an excessive desire to give death, bordering on madness. No longer does a conflict between his peacetime self and its warlike double threaten to incapacitate him. Rather, for the brief period of his neurotic breakdown, it is as though all sense of civilized behavior has vanished and he is completely consumed by his warlike self. Following a prison guard into the crematorium, he finds him hiding in one of the ovens. With an eerie smile on his face, Griff keeps firing his rifle long after he has killed his enemy, thus mirroring the senselessness of the camp's industrialized mass death by his own mechanical killing. Even the Sergeant's sober assurance, "I think you got him," does not put an end to the mindless automatism of the younger man's shooting. Only when his desire for death is fully satisfied does he, still grinning, stop firing his rifle.[14] To render the American squad leader's protective formula, "You don't murder animals, you kill them," more ambiguous, the film narrative also gives an individualized face to the enemy, casting Sgt. Schroeder as Lee Marvin's fanatic Nazi double. Although the two men treat each other as hostile strangers whenever their paths cross, this doubling is used to disclose a disturbing similarity in their attitude toward death. While we never see the American officer resort to quite the same merciless killing of everyone who interferes with his objectives, the film leaves no doubt that he, too, wouldn't hesitate to use lethal force were his command to be disobeyed.

One further instance of the use of doubling as a narrative strategy needs to be addressed. After they have crossed the border into Germany for the first time in October 1944, the Sergeant and his squad encounter a war correspondent reporting from one of the first German cities occupied by American troops. He is played by the director himself. As the real Samuel Fuller moves among the people who are resting outside in a sun-filled street, he asks them to smile and wave at his handheld camera. Under his direction, the black-and-white footage we see interpolated into the fictional narrative of *The Big Red One* (in a gesture imitating the inclusion of documentary footage in classic war films of the 1940s) captures images of postwar civility. Soldiers are sharing their food with children, some of whom are wearing their fathers' helmets and playing war games. Even the boy who raises his arm in a Hitler salute appears to be only a benign parody of his parents' lethal political passion.[15] In more than one sense, this scene taps into the duplicitous rhetoric of the double, functioning both as an assurance against destruction and as a harbinger of death. The war will not be over for another eight months. Once the nameless sergeant and his squad move on through Germany, the war games played by the children will once again regain a deadly reality. Furthermore, Fuller did, in fact, film a part of his real war experience, though his footage captured the liberation of the concentration camp at Falkenau, where his commanding officer forced German civilians to walk through the camp and witness the atrocities they had condoned.

The inclusion of this mock news footage, of course, reflects back on the other black-and-white sequence at the beginning of the film, as though, by analogy, we are to take Fuller's impersonation of a war correspondent as the second primal scene of *The Big Red One.* This leads me to surmise that, by including himself in his fictional revisitation of the scenes of factual death he experienced some thirty years earlier, Fuller seeks to expose his idiosyncratic equation between the world of war and that of fiction. On-screen he can revise his own past with impunity, shifting his role from the one facing real death on the battlefield to the one reporting about it. Looking through the protective lens of a camera, he is not, furthermore, capturing images of those who were exterminated in a concentration camp but of those who, at this point in the story at least, had managed to survive war's destruction. By explicitly drawing our attention to the fact that the smiles on the faces of civilians and soldiers alike are the product of his direction, Fuller discloses the sleight of hand at work when scenes of real death are brought back to fictional life on-screen. The cheer they embody screens the grim reality of war that precedes and follows upon this short interlude of a premature peace. Functioning as a double of both the factual death to which his film obliquely refers and its fictional reenactment on-screen, even while shown to be clearly distinct from both, this black-and-white footage uncovers the magical thinking any imaginary revisitation of war is predicated on. By conjoining the world of war with that of fiction, the wish Fuller's cinematic re-creation of a previous experience most satisfies is a trust in survival, over and against the grand-scale death of the real war.

That the denial of one's own mortality, which treating the world of war as fiction entails, also involves a degree of sadism toward others becomes equally clear in relation to the sorry fate of the squad's replacements. While resting among the rubble of an Italian village, Zab's voice-over explains: "By now we'd come to look at all replacements as dead men who temporarily had the use of their arms and legs. They came and went so fast and so regular that sometimes we didn't even get to know their names." By admitting that they avoided getting to know them, Zab gives voice to the way that, in order to protect himself against the cruel barbarity of war, the foot soldier disregards the death of those he would in peacetime hold dear. At the same time, his comment serves as a magical invocation. By treating these replacements as ghostly doubles who will die in their stead, the original members of the rifle squad mutually sustain the fiction of their own immortality. How deeply this narrative is indebted to the magical logic of an omnipotence of thought is, in turn, revealed when one of the replacements actually falls for Zab's mischievous tale. He confesses that down at battalion they are called the Sergeant's Four Horsemen because they alone seem to be immune to war's destructive force. He wonders whether this puts him at risk. What initially appears as playful banter turns uncanny when, a few minutes later, going to get some water, he is indeed the one who trips a mine and is wounded by the explosion.[16]

Most importantly, Fuller's multifaceted play with doubles converges on two scenes of involuntary repetition. While we see the Sergeant and his men cautiously approach the gigantic Christ on the Cross familiar to us from the first scene of the film, Zab's voice-over comments, "As we slogged through the hedgerows and across France, the Sergeant began keeping to himself. It was a little spooky. He kept ahead as if looking for some old ghost to rise up out of the mist." Indeed, having returned to the primal scene of his personal haunting, Lee Marvin finds himself once again walking among a group of enemy corpses. This time, however, hiding among the Panzer gunners are Schroeder's foot soldiers, merely pretending to be dead. Like a stage director, the Nazi officer has strategically placed live men around as well as inside the burning tank to feign a scene of ambush. Hiding behind the head of the wooden Christ, he is now using his radio to give instructions to his men, his objective being to lure an entire platoon of American troops into this theatrical death trap. The Sergeant, however, expecting to meet the specter of the man he should not have killed, is keenly in tune with an uncanny blurring between the living and the dead. Having climbed into the tank, he immediately notices that the badges of the men lying there are infantry and stabs them before they can signal to their commanding officer.

Once he has returned to his own dogfaces outside the tank, Lee Marvin is able to warn them that they are being watched by live people, staging a bushwhack. The camera moves into a close-up of each of their faces, now enveloped by the fog of war, to signal that at this point they are all looking for ghosts to rise up out of the mist, knowingly partaking in the fantasy that has been haunting their leader. After one of the Nazi soldiers breaks his sergeant's command and opens fire, the furious killing that sets in transforms false corpses into real ones. By transforming this theatrical scene back into the spectacle of real battle, the scene also puts an erotic enjoyment of killing on display. Lee Marvin, as devious at war games as his Nazi double, gets back into the tank while his men take cover behind it. The close-up shots of the machine gun he now directs at his enemy unambivalently cast it as a phallic instrument, unfurling an orgasm of destruction. Schroeder, in turn, is rendered impotent by Lee Marvin's prowess. No longer able to transmit any stage directions for fear of being discovered, he is reduced to watching the unexpected turn his ruse has taken. He will ultimately climb down from his hiding place and steal away into the sunset while his enemy's back is turned, hoping to kill him another day.

If *The Big Red One* discloses the eroticism involved in giving death to one's enemy, it also pits this lethal enjoyment against an equally resilient life drive. Almost immediately after the Sergeant has fired his last shot, a young Frenchman suddenly appears on the scene with his pregnant wife. In the same tank from which he had dispensed his lethal barrage, the Sergeant now directs his dogfaces in an operation whose aim is to protect life. The sequence ends as it began, with Zab's voice-over. Wryly taking note of the curious mutual implication of giving death and bringing forth life, which he and his squad performed that day, he explains, "We got a bunch of medals, not for delivering the kid, just for killing Krauts."[17] *The Big Red One* is grounded in a narrative resolution, therefore, that tips the scales decidedly in favor of survival. After having liberated the Czech concentration camp, Lee Marvin's Sergeant is once more lost in a psychic fog of war, as though in a dream state, when flyers declaring the fighting to be over are dropped over the forest his squad has been marching through all night. Suddenly a stranger approaches from behind, his arms raised above his head, calling out the same sentence as in the primal scene of the film: "Der Krieg ist vorbei." Instinctively, without waking up from his reverie, the Sergeant once again pulls his knife and stabs the man he takes to be his enemy. He does not have to wait long to discover that he has involuntarily repeated the same mistake.

The surviving members of his rifle team all simultaneously emerge from the fog of what is clearly more a psychic topography than a real one, asking him where he has been. From them he once again learns that the war has been over for four hours. When Griff, discovering the enemy soldier lying on the ground, repeats the same words the Captain had uttered in the opening scene, "You didn't know it was over," Lee Marvin can only helplessly repeat what he had said once before: "He did." This time, however, Fuller does not show his hero's anguish in a close-up. As though resigning himself to his terrible fate, Lee Marvin begins to walk away, back into the forest. Then Griff, who has tarried over the fallen body, calls out that Schroeder is, in fact, still alive. Only once the others rush back, does the camera move into close-ups, showing us in detail the significant reversal of the primal scene that has been haunting Fuller's hero.

In a final equation of the world of war with that of fiction, the nameless American Sergeant is given a second chance. With the same furor he previously exhibited when killing his enemies, he once more directs an operation, now aimed at giving life rather than death. His dogfaces help him dress and bandage the wound of his former enemy, burning the flyers whose headlines read "War is Over," so as to produce some light in this nocturnal scene. Repetition compulsion turns to luck; the destructive instinct, however, isn't obliterated. It is simply put to the service of the life drive. Lee Marvin, seeing that the German has finally begun to open his eyes, threatens him, "You're gonna live if I have to blow your brains out." Indeed, residues of an unhampered impulse to destroy move into peacetime along with the soldier resurrected from the dead. As we see the small band of brothers make their way through the foggy forest, Zab explains, "Saving the Kraut was the final joke of the whole goddamned war. We had more in common with him than with all our replacements who got killed whose names we never knew."[18] The decisive line of demarcation in Samuel Fuller's fictional revisitation of the war, we discover, was never between enemy and friend, but between the dead and those who manage to survive the grand-scale killing.

If *The Big Red One* ends by showing that, in the face of a death that will not be denied, life recovers its full content, the film's narrative equally foregrounds the way this compensation requires an act of fictionalization. It may be over the dead bodies of the many recruits that Fuller's nameless Sergeant can tell his tale of collective heroism and, in so doing, bestow belated meaning on contingent slaughter. Yet in the end, we have a story, a fictional resuscitation on-screen based on factual death in real battle. The film's narrative management is predicated on the mutual implication of a denial of death and an invincible trust in survival that Freud locates in the realm of fiction. As the film's implicit (and complicit) audience, we are able to die with each of the heroes with whom we choose to identify, yet, together with Lee Marvin and his band of brothers, we survive all the casualties, ready to die again just as safely in the next war film we watch. The closing sequence is so chilling precisely because it discloses heroism, and the denial of one's own death this is predicated on, as the stuff that dreams are made of in Hollywood. The bare facts of death, contingent and meaningless, are, in turn, exposed as the foundation and the untranscendible vanishing point of the film.

The Big Red One underscores how films about the world of war can be likened to collective dream work. I take the fact that the nameless Sergeant wakes up as from a haunted reverie once the other soldiers call out to him that the war is over to signify that, above and beyond historical reimagination, the film retrieves on-screen attitudes toward death that in their ordinary civil life the audience must necessarily repress.[19] Like the language of dreams, the aesthetic refiguration is what protects us, reworking an uncomfortable knowledge by self-consciously depicting war in terms of fiction. The film shares in the magical thinking the heroes have been shown to espouse, itself invested in the cathartic power of commemoration. Recapturing scenes of killing and barely escaping death on-screen is unabashedly conceived as an act of working through the destruction of life in the very world of war the film also invokes. Screening death is conceived as an apotropaic charm. Even while the cinematic image retrieves repressed attitudes toward death, celebrating both an unbridled killing of the enemy and a blind trust in one's own invincibility, it always already contains this death by presenting it from the start as part of the world of fiction.

The Big Red One self-consciously ends by reflecting back on its own act of narration. With the last shots of the film, we move to a final close-up of the nameless sergeant. Still carrying his wounded double on his shoulder, Lee Marvin has stopped walking and stands perfectly still in front of the camera, which captures him from a low angle. His grim look, eerily illuminated by a moving spotlight so that the left part of the face keeps falling into shadow, authorizes the final point Zab's spectral voice-over makes: "I'm gonna dedicate my book to those who shot but didn't get shot because it's about survivors and surviving is the only glory in war."[20] The Sergeant, we are to understand, is no longer in combat with his Nazi double. By keeping him alive, he has broken the spell of involuntary repetition. What this means for the national experience his individualized narrative has come to represent remains an open question. The face of the man who is walking into a world of renewed peace reflects light and shadow. The struggle between survival and death may be contained but not disbanded. The film, as such, recaptures the struggle, anticipating a future renewal of real death in war.[21]

Acknowledging Death's Glory: *The Thin Red Line*

In his cinematic reconception of the battle on Guadalcanal, where American troops fought from August 1942 through February 1943, Terrence Malick deploys narrative strategies of reduplication not only to treat war as a spectacle of aesthetic splendor, but also to bring into focus the division between a bodily and a spiritual presence in the world of military strife. Rather than valorizing the protection of life in the face of death and deploying narrative repetition to harness destruction, Malick explores modes of acknowledging death as a way of transcending the world of war. The glory he celebrates has less to do with the Homeric *kleos* of the *Iliad*, aimed at bestowing military honor on a valiant warrior, than with the apprehension of radiant light that is the mark of a spiritual survival beyond earthly finitude. The glory his foot soldier, Private Witt (Jim Caviezel), comes to discover in the war-riddled world of this South Pacific island serves as a double of the aesthetic immortality that characterizes Malick's own world of cinema.

The Thin Red Line begins not with a title card but with a narratorial comment, framing personalized scenes from the historical battle it gives fictional life to again on-screen. Superimposed on images of the tropical jungle, we hear Private Train asking: "What's this war in the heart of nature? Why does nature vie with itself, the land contend with the sea? Is there an avenging power in nature? Not one power, but two?"[22] That Malick should choose a voice-over as his way of entering into his story sets the tone for the complex play of doubling he takes both as his theme and his privileged mode of narration. Throughout the film, a disjunction between the images on the screen and the spoken text accompanying these rhetorically underscores the film's recasting of war as a quasi-mythic struggle between the forces of life and death. The voice of one character repeatedly contends with the visual presence of another, while flashbacks from past civilian life vie with the wartime present. That Train should introduce the theme of war in the form of a string of questions sets up a further premise of Malick's film. *The Thin Red Line* is to be understood as an open inquiry into how war came into being and why its destructive force persists, shedding cinematic light on a panoply of highly subjective experiences of its destructive force without offering any definitive answer.

Like conventional combat films, *The Thin Red Line* tracks the movement of a select group of foot soldiers, beginning with a beach landing and ending with the securing of an airfield, after which those who have survived the battles it took to fulfill this mission are shipped out to another island in the Pacific theater of war. Yet, with the first sequence, Malick also introduces his idiosyncratic touch to the standard narrative formula of the war film by drawing attention to the way different psychic topographies come to vie with each other in this fight over Guadalcanal.[23] Train's introductory questions, speaking to nature's fundamental conflict with itself, introduce a series of visual vignettes showing everyday life in a Melanesian village, existing outside yet parallel to the topography of war that the presence of Japanese and American troops has brought to their island. In the closing sequence of the film, after C-Company has moved on, the camera will tarry with this world, stringing together three images that mark ordinary life in the midst of wartime—villagers in their boats paddling into the rainforest, two colorful birds sitting on a tree branch, and a sprouting coconut plant growing out of the ocean close to the shoreline.

The film opens up a further psychic topography as it juxtaposes images of Private Witt watching the villagers bathing with his voice-over, recollecting: "I remember my mother when she was dying. Looked all shrunk up and gray. I asked her if she was afraid. She just shook her head. I was afraid to touch the death I seen in her. I couldn't find nothing beautiful or uplifting about her going back to God. I heard people talk about immortality but I ain't seen it." Though he is nominally speaking to Private Hoke, who has gone AWOL with him, the narrative includes a flashback of Witt at his mother's deathbed. As the spectral scene fades back into the present, Witt's voice-over continues, "I just hope I can meet it the same way she did. With the same . . . calm. 'Cause that's where it's hidden—the immortality I hadn't seen."[24] Malick's Guadalcanal thus emerges as a spectral site, where those dead or absent can be resuscitated in spirit, allowing his soldiers to exist both in the midst of and apart from the violent destruction surrounding them. Indeed, in the case of Witt, the division is not between a warlike and a peacetime self, but rather between his bodily presence on this war-torn island and his imaginary conception of a world beyond the finitude of his mortal existence.

Witt's emotional detachment from the world of war, which he sustains even after the patrol boat picks him up and brings him back to his platoon in C-Company, places him in a psychic topography between two deaths. As he recasts his experience of war in terms of a narrative pertaining to what he believes to be the most graceful attitude one can adopt toward one's own death, he straddles his mother's demise with an anticipation of his own. The doubling of the self he undertakes in fantasy is his idiosyncratic form of psychic protection. It allows him to treat ground warfare as merely the most extreme manifestation of a death whose necessity he has already come to recognize for himself. The fragility of life that war renders palpable calls forth a spiritual vigilance, bestowing on him glimpses of precisely the immortality he did not see at his mother's deathbed. He calls his visions sparks of light, which he is able to detect as much in the strange natural phenomena of the rainforest as in his fellow soldiers. At the same time, Malick self-consciously draws attention to the fact that the shining light his foot soldier experiences in the midst of war's barbarity stands to double the light emanating from the surface of the cinema screen from which the world of war he is recasting in terms of a struggle between factual demise and spiritual transcendence emerges.

The Thin Red Line keeps returning to Train's questions about how strife came into the world. When, late in the film, Witt revisits the Melanesian village, now because of his uniform more clearly marked as a stranger, the narrative once more juxtaposes his foot soldier's voice-over with vignettes of ordinary civilian life. "We were a family. How'd it break up and come apart so that now we're turned against each other, each standing in the other's light?" we are asked, as we see the villagers separate from the ongoing war yet reflect its spirit in the form of petty strifes. "How'd we lose the good that was given us, let it slip away, scattered, careless?" Train asks, "What's keeping us from reaching out, touching the glory?"[25] Malick's narrative framing of the historic battle for Guadalcanal recaptures war as a quasi-mythic story about how a destructive force, by virtue of intervening in an originary life-sustaining unity, prevents but also anticipates the achievement of glory's perfect happiness. Although this cinematic reimagination of the battle for Guadalcanal is refracted into a plethora of individualized perspectives, on an aesthetic level these separate experiences are all held together by the disembodied voice of Train. His meditations on what it might take to return to a state of spiritual glory punctuate the battalion's trek across the island. His commentary, doubling the battle action, keeps drawing our attention to the possibility of spiritual transcendence opened up by the fragility of existence that the nightmare of war renders manifest.

Although, among the foot soldiers fighting side by side in C-Company, the film presents a range of attitudes toward death obtainable in war, my discussion will focus on Private Witt, who, rather than denying his own mortality, is the one fully attentive to the death around him. Indeed, diametrically opposed to Fuller's heroes, the magical thinking he espouses allows him to recover a state of resplendence in death rather than blindly trust that death will not touch him. During a nocturnal conversation before battle, his squad leader tries to convince him that if he dies it will be for nothing. The silent gaze with which Witt responds signifies his insistence in trusting in the glory not of military feats but of an existence beyond earthly strife. Given his emotional detachment from the actual military campaign, he can staunchly maintain that war does not ennoble the soul but poisons it, but he is also the one whose focalization of the violence of battle most forcefully puts compassion on display. In *The Thin Red Line,* what blurs the boundary between enemies isn't the survival they share, but rather the soldiers' mutual vulnerability in the face of death.

In a scene preceding the attack on a Japanese village, we find Witt standing above the corpse of an enemy soldier with all but his face covered by dirt. He hears the stranger's spectral voice speaking to him through the fog emanating from the ground, as though in anticipation of the death about to come. "Do you imagine your sufferings will be less because you loved goodness? Truth?" the dead man asks.[26] By having this corpse speak, I take Malick to be suggesting that his own work as a director taps into the same magical thinking that allows his hero to reanimate the spirit of his enemy and, in so doing, break down the very distinctions between friend and foe, as well as life and death, upon which war is predicated. Furthermore, because Malick tampers with the temporal sequence of his narrative, the spectral conversation between Witt and the dead Japanese soldier introduces the attack on the village, though in the actual story line the conversation succeeds it. As such, the speaking corpse in fact frames our experience of the death the two embattled soldiers share. When, a few moments later, the Americans viciously charge through the village to kill all enemies in sight, the camera tarries not only with their casualties but also with those of the vanquished Japanese. In the pain and destruction they mutually inflict, they are not separate but welded together.

The glory with which Malick's aesthetic refiguration endows the spectacle of barbarity, most prominently by using Hans Zimmer's sublimely elegiac soundtrack as acoustic double for his resplendent images, calls for a sharing of life's fragility. Indeed, the compassion he insists on throughout *The Thin Red Line* is such that we are called upon to recognize the humanness of all those engaged in the grand-scale killing. Even while he reconceives the violence of war in terms of the cinema's fictionalizing visual splendor, Malick will not allow us to avert our gaze from the anguish of all those embroiled in the dispensing of death. In a particularly chilling narrative inset, we see another foot soldier, Private Dale, using a pair of pliers to rob a corpse of its gold teeth rather than helping the enemy soldier who is lying next to him, writhing in pain. So as to protect himself from the death he sees reflected in the other man's wounded body, he explains to the Japanese man in a language the other can't understand that he is already dead meat. The narrative returns to Dale in a subsequent scene, compelling our compassion where we would prefer to distance ourselves by judging him for his cruelty. We see him, as though overcome with a belated sense of guilt, sitting in the rain, sobbing uncontrollably, the voice of the dying Japanese soldier resounding in his head, until he throws away his war trophies in terror. The scene bespeaks a moment of poetic justice. The shivering may well be a symptom of malaria, with the tossing away of his spoils an indication that he suspects these may be the very source of his infection.[27]

By contrast, Train's sustained meditations on the agent behind a great evil that stole into the world, "killing us, robbing us of life and light," allow Malick to introduce the notion of self-expenditure as the most radical form of moving into glory. The mythical struggle between evil and light, which his sustained voice-over narration juxtaposes with the gruesome yet splendidly lit images of battle recaptured on the screen, opens up the possibility of a choice. It reintroduces the issue of ethical judgment. If the spirit of destruction is indelibly inscribed in worldly existence, material survival in war involves remaining in a dark world robbed of spiritual light. Giving in to death, in turn, becomes tantamount to embracing an act of transcendence; not as a glorification of war's destruction but as a move outside its parameters. In this quasi-mythic struggle between evil and light, the solitary act Witt undertakes, by which he will, after all, have made a difference in the midst of the military barbarity, is staged (in contrast to *The Big Red One*) not as an involuntary repetition, but as a conscious appropriation of his mother's calmness in the face of death.

During a reconnaissance mission, Witt comes up with a ruse to distract the Japanese troops, so that the other man on patrol with him has enough time to return to their battalion and warn it. Running through the jungle and making noises to suggest he is an entire platoon, Witt is successful in drawing the enemy to himself. As he emerges onto an open meadow, he finds himself completely surrounded. Recognizing the futility of escape, he hesitates until he has reached moral certainty. Then he raises his gun in the pathos gesture of self-sacrifice, willingly taking onto himself the death he, at this point, can no longer *not* choose. Immediately following the first gunshot, the narrative inserts an image of white light breaking through the leaves of the jungle as the dying man would have seen it from his position on the ground, before moving into a flashback to the beginning of the film. Witt is swimming beneath the surface of the ocean with the children from the Melanesian village. This visual doubling signifies the release of his soul from his mortal body. As we see him resurfacing into the white light above the water, we hear a second gunshot, while the camera lingers a few seconds longer with the children, who keep swimming.[28]

If, beginning with the opening sequence of the film, Witt has been portrayed as a man living in division with himself, his warlike self a double of the spiritual self, his actual demise amounts to a passage into the state of illumination he was touched by throughout. Sacrificing himself to preserve the lives of his comrades, he transcends the parameters of all earthly struggle between death and the protection of life. The calmness he has achieved in the face of his bodily demise opens him up to a world beyond all forces of mortal destruction, to the shining light that characterizes his aesthetically conceived realm of immortality.[29] Yet the concept of spiritual glory invoked by Train's voice-over, which Malick repeatedly uses as a narrative comment on Witt's psychic detachment, also functions as his directorial reflection on cinema as an aesthetic recapturing of the world of war, giving voice and image to an immortality of its own. If Witt is the character whose vigilance allows him to see a shining light in the midst of war's barbarity, this insight implicitly aligns him with the magic power of the camera.

In *The Thin Red Line* a sustained white light emerges as the seminal point of convergence between the world of war and the aesthetic realm of cinema. In the final sequence of the film, Malick's camera pans along the faces of the foot soldiers who, having survived the battle for Guadalcanal, are back on a landing craft that will take them to a new scene of war. The camera comes to rest in a medium shot of Private Train. He is pondering one last time the unifying force subtending but also transcending the world of war we have traversed with him. "Darkness and light, strife and love, are they the workings of one mind, the features of the same face?" he asks. As Malick's camera moves away from his face to focus on the backwash of the boat, leaving its white foam on the ocean's surface, his disembodied voice bespeaks the camera's power of transcendence, unfolding its own play of light in the face of worldly transience: "Oh, my soul, let me be in you now. Look out through my eyes. Look out at the things you made, all things shining."[30]

At the close of *The Big Red One,* Fuller's alter ego declares he will dedicate his war novel to those who survived, because that is the supreme glory of war. In the final moments of *The Thin Red Line,* Malick's voice-over narration draws our attention to the shining light on which his own cinematic recapturing of a world at strife with itself is grounded. In each case, the trust in immortality sustained in the face of the fragility of life, which battle renders so tangibly visible, is predicated on a passage of war into fiction. To recapture actual death in battle as fictional life on-screen involves a seminal ruse. In the face of an irretrievable loss, an assurance of imaginary survival is maintained. We have watched these men die, and yet on-screen they also survive. The point, of course, is not that in war people become fictional characters, but rather that, in order to psychically survive the atrocious madness of the battlefield, they conceive of themselves as such. In a similar manner, we, the audience, can protect ourselves from the real atrocity of war by recasting it in terms of coherence, pathos, and meaning that have always been the possession of fiction. The restitutive claim of war films requires this pact with the audience. Each of the films discussed straddles the disbelief in mortality that its heroes rely on with an acknowledgment of death's inevitability. Both turn the casualties of battle into stories by which to remember and honor the dead, and in so doing they contain this knowledge. They restrict death's strategic power by enveloping it in personalized stories, even while preserving its affective effect.

Notes

1. Sigmund Freud, "Thoughts for the Times on War and Death," in *The Standard Edition,* vol. 14 (London: Hogarth Press, 1957), 291.

2. Ibid.

3. Ibid., 299.

4. Sigmund Freud, "Why War?" in *The Standard Edition,* vol. 22 (London: Hogarth Press, 1964), 212.

5. In *Shell Shock Cinema: Weimar Culture and the Wounds of War* (Princeton, NJ: Princeton University Press, 2009), Anton Kaes reads Weimar cinema as reworking the collective cultural trauma of World War I in conjunction with the critical terms Freud developed to explain war neurosis and the cultural malaise of the postwar period. One might also note that by the 1950s, when the first of the war films I will discuss was made, Freud's psychoanalysis had become household knowledge, with film audiences as acquainted with his thinking as those writing, visually designing, and directing films.

6. Sigmund Freud, "Introduction to Psycho-Analysis and the War Neurosis" (1919), in *The Standard Edition,* vol. 17 (London: Hogarth Press, 1955), 209.

7. See Paul Fussell, *The Great War and Modern Memory* (Oxford: Oxford University Press, 1979), 192. One might add that the cinematic doubling at stake in recapturing war on-screen provides a similar psychic escape for the viewer. Fussell's chapter on war entertainment is focused on how Hollywood refigures the theatrical aspect of war in the musical genre.

8. As Freud notes, the experience of the uncanny is "in reality nothing new or alien, but something which is familiar and old-established in the mind and which has become alienated from it only through the process of repression." Reading this in conjunction with his thoughts on death and war, one might add that what is perceived as a

parasitic duplication of the peacetime ego is, in fact, a reembodiment of the more primitive destructive instinct that civilized behavior represses; see "The 'Uncanny'" (1919), in *The Standard Edition,* vol. 17 (London: Hogarth Press, 1955), 241.

9. Samuel Fuller, himself a foot soldier in the First Infantry Division in World War II who was decorated with a Silver Star for his military valor on D-Day, had been sent by Jack Warner on a trip to Europe in the late 1950s to scout locations for a film about his war experience. Not only did he have to wait until the late 1970s to have the film produced by Lorimar, but he had to accept a version cut down to two hours, with a music score he did not approve of. The reconstructed version, reedited by the film historian Richard Schickel with material found in the Warner Archives and based on the last version of Fuller's screenplay, was premiered at the Cannes Film Festival in 2004. It is dedicated to Samuel Fuller. See Samuel Fuller, *A Third Face: My Tale of Writing, Fighting, and Filmmaking* (New York: Applause Theatre & Cinema Books, 2002).

10. *The Big Red One: The Reconstruction* (Samuel Fuller, 2004), 1:24–5:39.

11. Ibid., 00:05:39–00:06:00.

12. Ibid., 00:15:50–00:16:08.

13. Ibid., 02:12:28–02:13–16.

14. Ibid., 2:24.59–2:29.20.

15. Ibid., 1:50:52–1:52:25.

16. Ibid., 47:23–49:35.

17. Ibid., 1:28:14–1:40–47.

18. Ibid., 2:36:04–2:39:33.

19. I take the concept of historical reimagination from Robert Burgoyne's insightful discussion of war's reenactment on-screen, in *Film Nation: Hollywood Looks at US History,* rev. ed. (Minneapolis: University of Minneapolis Press, 2010).

20. *The Big Red One,* 2:39:34–2:39:50.

21. It is noteworthy to recall that although Fuller had initially expected his World War II saga to come out at the same time as Zanuck's *The Longest Day,* production difficulties were such that it was not released until the war in Vietnam had been fought. Indeed, films recapturing this war in Southeast Asia came to overshadow *The Big Red One,* which initially failed at the box office and with many critics.

22. *The Thin Red Line* (Terrence Malick, 2000, The Criterion Collection), 1:58–2:28.

23. For a discussion of the classic combat film, see Jeanine Basinger's *The World War II Combat Film: Anatomy of a Genre* (Middletown, CT: Wesleyan University Press, 2003).

24. *The Thin Red Line,* 5:27–6:32.

25. Ibid., 2:15:07–2:18:00.

26. Ibid., 1:44:40–1:45:18.

27. Ibid., 2:06:22–2:07:20.

28. Ibid., 2:33:05–2:35:20.

29. For a Heideggarian reading of the film, from which I take the notion of an aesthetic realm of immortality, see Hubert Dreyfus and Camilo Salazar Prince, "*The Thin Red Line:* Dying without Demise, Demise without Dying," in a collection of essays on this film edited by David Davies, *The Thin Red Line* (London: Routledge, 2009).

30. *The Thin Red Line,* 2:42:03–2:42:56.

"Profoundly Unreconciled to Nature"

Ecstatic Truth and the Humanistic Sublime in Werner Herzog's War Films

David LaRocca

At the beginning of *The Romantic Sublime: Studies in the Structure and the Psychology of Transcendence,* Thomas Weiskel says "the essential claim of the sublime is that man can, in feeling and in speech, transcend the human," and as such, he concludes: "The humanistic sublime is an oxymoron."[1] In contradistinction, I suggest that selected works of Werner Herzog—principally, what may be called his war films—antagonize the oxymoronic status of this concept and yield instead an artful and arresting series of illustrations of the embattled term. Herzog's war films, as I will define and describe them, remove the contradiction by transforming our inherited impressions of the relationship between man, war, and nature. Though man at war, in the context of nature, may be the very epitome of the human on the verge of annihilation, the *representation* of this circumstance need not lead uniformly to transcendence. In short, instead of being the occasion to end or occlude or otherwise overcome the human, there are representations of war—as we find them in films by Herzog, images that illustrate his peculiar invocation of the sublime—that seem a better fit with the notion of the *humanistic* sublime. In part, the viability of a hybrid concept such as the humanistic sublime, much less its intellectual or emotive credibility, is supported by Herzog's frequently referenced and widely discussed notion of ecstatic truth, the description or definition of which continually involves the presence of the human. The concept of the sublime is familiar from Longinus to Kant to Lyotard, but Herzog's heterodox treatment of it is, as one might expect, not a conventional translation of the category, since far from aiming to transcend the human, Herzog endeavors to situate the human at the very limit of its experience, at that place where its presence in nature—or at war—is at once fantastical and dreamlike but nevertheless utterly authentic, a necessary part of an encounter and yet illusive, mirage-like, shimmering.

Moreover, and highly pertinent to those who wish to write about his work, Herzog does not make it easy to undertake a speculative or academic investigation of his films. He seems to have a very low opinion of such writing, and says so. In a string of controversies about the apparent resemblance of Herzog's *Bad Lieutenant: Port of Call–New Orleans* (2009) and Abel Ferrara's earlier *Bad Lieutenant* (1992), Herzog commented sardonically: "I'm sure some of the more pedantic practitioners of 'film studies' out there will be ecstatic to find a reference in my film to Ferrara's here and there. I call upon the theoreticians of cinema to go after this one. Go for it, losers."[2] Despite his occasionally barbed incitements and derisive pronouncements, however, there is a veritable and thriving industry of scholars trying, I suspect with good intentions and with obvious tremendous intellectual resources, to make sense of his work and make it available to a wide, and ever-widening, audience. A scholar might want, now and again, a little less begrudging acknowledgment from his subject, but then Herzog's contrariness may be part of the process of writing about his films—an obstruction that is, as so many are, generative. Or as Paul Cronin suggests less optimistically: Herzog's "work, in fact, seems almost to defy analysis, and I can't claim to have read any substantial piece of writing from an academic angle that sheds sustained, engrossing light on [Herzog's] films, or teaches me anything radically new about them."[3] Cronin's confident conclusion may be a mark of despair for the interested scholar hoping to make a worthwhile contribution to our thinking on Herzog's films, though perhaps Cronin's assessment can be treated as an invitation—hope against hope—to defy its principal implication, namely, that one should remain silent about the critical inheritance of Herzog's work.

Herzog's resistance or indifference to the analysis of his films might be taken up from the spirit in which he appears to create—a spirit more concerned with native apprehension, instinct, intuition, and the pulsing rhythms of a changing present than probing analysis, terminological definition, and taxonomical investigation. Because one of the central mantras underlying Herzog's advice at the Rogue Film School is the overly, almost comically emphasized repetition "read, read, read, read, read, read, read,

read, read, read, read, read, read," and because he is himself so well-read, it is hard to take his skepticism about academic theory and criticism as a justification for charging him with being anti-intellectual.[4] Rather, it would seem he simply does not like to look back, to rehearse what he has done, or to think much about his works' meaning or impact. Like Woody Allen, in this respect, he is already on to his next project. As Cronin notes in a preface to the second edition of *Herzog on Herzog*: "Werner is, after all, a man who by his own admission lives with as little personal reflection as possible. He just isn't interested. Intuition is a more powerful guiding light than analysis ever will be, and the new film has always taken precedence over talking about old work."[5] If Herzog's disinterest in theory is feigned (and given his apprenticeship to great books, there is reason to think so), we should enjoy its playful remonstrance to our research; but if it is genuine, this may mean we have work to do in his stead—despite his skepticism.

The attempt to write speculatively about Herzog's films is further complicated by those scholars who remain committed to the existing—well-researched, well-defended—theories of the sublime (for example, and most prominently, the romantic, tragic, transcendental, ironic, hysterical, apocalyptic, and abstract sublime, among other variations) and would thereby regard any effort to explore or give credence to the humanistic sublime as fruitless, another academic exercise, and an empty one at that. Countering dissent from the filmmaker and from aesthetic theorists, and trying to do so without being defensive, I suggest that there is something to be learned in both cases: either the humanistic sublime remains an oxymoron—and we can glean a view of the contradiction as it appears in Herzog's work—or Herzog's films do in fact offer some credibility to the notion and we come away with an unexpected incarnation and redemption of the concept. Despite Weiskel's expressed doubts about the viability of the humanistic sublime, I would like to hazard the effort to recover it and, through Herzog's war films, propose a case for its habilitation in the wider conversation about the cinematic and photographic representation of war. Hopefully I can make clear how Herzog's work puts in relief the degree to which the representation of war (in his films at least, and perhaps more generally in work by others) is uniquely suited to complement our postulated understanding of the humanistic sublime, since this kind of sublime is a phenomenon fundamentally defined by human agency and ecstatic potency, that is, experienced at the border of life and death, where one gets out of one state and into another.

Given the headiness of these claims and their antagonism to long-standing and highly regarded accounts in aesthetic theory, it behooves me to qualify my assertions with examples, to make evident the kinds of things I claim for Herzog's films—as well as draw support from Herzog's own appraisals; I will, for this reason, proceed inductively by a refractive analysis of some of Herzog's films and couple those remarks with Herzog's estimations of his aims and achievements. Fortunately for such inquiries, Herzog is, despite his expressed doubts about critical commentary, startlingly competent as an interpreter of his work—realizing a kind of self-awareness rarely glimpsed by even the finest creators of artworks, perhaps especially film. Consequently, the belief that Herzog does not look back, that he is averse to study and analysis, is amusingly undermined; a critic would be naïve, it seems, to believe Herzog does not do his homework—and occasionally our own. We are, for example, lucky to have between two covers Paul Cronin's editorial feat *Herzog on Herzog*, with which we might begin and almost end our pursuit of clarity on these matters. Cronin demonstrates the promise of Herzogian principles of truth through fabrication, evidence-based improvisation, and shrewd consolidation, by creating gripping intellectual and emotional arcs where there would otherwise be just notes or merely suggestions of them. Partly, then, I begin this essay with the hunch that while we have *a lot* of serious commentary by Herzog on his own work and an appreciable and growing secondary literature on his films, there are still things to ask after. Though Herzog has said a great deal and has said it with captivating intensity and dramatic poise, he has also—perhaps for that style and its regular coupling of profundity and ellipsis—provoked further thoughts and questions. So it is, then, importantly in the wake of a compendium such as *Herzog on Herzog* and other efforts to digest his reflections on critical terms, that I commence my own inquiry, as if both to get a better grasp of what I have read and to bring Herzog's comments into the company of other texts that might refract his meanings and methods in useful ways.

A Kind of Sublime for War and Its Representation

If we have sought a concept to engage or reflect or define our understanding—or more viscerally, our *feeling*—of war's visual representation (in photography and film), the humanistic sublime may be it. While the sublime in the romantic or transcendental sense is meant to suggest an experience that gets you out of your humanness, where you feel instead connected to the external, eternal, absolute, or atemporal, the humanistic sublime by contrast is informed by a return to, a remembrance of, or a reengagement with the human through an encounter with nature—that is, with limits, obstacles, the extremes of existence, fatality, mortality. And so war as a phenomenon would appear ultimately linked to the concept or experience of the humanistic sublime, since war is fundamentally an activity of humans at the edge (where dying is a moment-to-moment possibility and survival means not falling into the abyss, into nonexistence). War means continually, constantly living at the limit—a radical state of consciousness that, on this reading, prompts an awareness of the sublimity inherent in that mode of attention to the existential parameters of the human condition. Unlike the spectator of nature, as depicted in paintings by Caspar David Friedrich, the soldier at war is immersed in nature—has become part of its natural order, its rhythms, its logic.[6] Even a soldier's accomplices are "embedded." These soldiers, photographers, war correspondents, diplomats, spies, and bystanders are not dispassionately contemplating the vastness of high mountains, deep oceans, wide deserts, and interstellar space; they are, in the crushing immediacy of their hyperspecific condition, pushed up to the edge of their own lives. Am I breathing my final breaths? Is this the last thing I will see on earth? What lies ahead for me after I am killed? What happens to me if I survive? These are the kinds of questions that must ring in the head of the soldier firing shots or the photographer firing frames. This is the sublime as humans know it when at war; this is the humanistic sublime.

In Herzog's war films, the defining characteristics of war are placed in the context of nature—a commingling that comes to varying results in the genre. At times, the two forces become complementary, coalescing into a single entity (e.g., when nature itself becomes part of the conditions or obstacles of war—"Don't you understand? The jungle is the prison," says one inmate to another in a POW camp in *Rescue Dawn* [2006]). At other times the two forces are strikingly individuated (e.g., when nature is an ally in the midst of war—when the river becomes a means of escape).[7] Just as nature, like war, is possessed of beauty and terror, the conditions of either may save or savage a soldier's chances of survival.[8] Regardless of how the relation between war and nature occurs at any given moment, man (who has created war, but not nature) is pressed to the limits of his natural attributes—of physical and psychological strength. Since Herzog's depiction of war highlights a different parallel, a different braid—namely, the interwoven relationship between the factual and the fictitious, the documentary and the narrative, the found and the invented—his films become a space of encounter that accentuates how war is an activity that people choose to engage in or a process that humans find themselves in; in this respect, war is an event, while nature is a circumstance. For Herzog, going into nature and going "into" war are related—parallel initiatives—and Herzog's films, I suggest, show us how war is especially suited to revealing a humanistic sublime (whereas man's encounter with nature per se stirs the notion of the [romantic or transcendental] sublime we find in the lengthy, heavily theorized, and entrenched history of the concept), and this is owing to the fact that war is human-developed, human-invented. As Brad Prager has noted: "Building on Immanuel Kant's idea that 'the sublime is not to be sought in the things of nature, but in our ideas,' Herzog asserts that sublimity is an effect; its truths are located in the spectator, rather than on the screen."[9] The human encounter with war or nature on film, consequently, turns the viewer inward and inspires introspection. Nature remains, or in these films becomes, even more pronounced as different from the human.

As part of the human enterprise of representing war (often in the context of nature and its extremes), Herzog's radical—rogue—commitment to the conscious fabrication of cinema, even in documentary, underlies his stimulation of the humanistic sublime. For his films do not presume to be points or planes of direct access to war—as if the movie screen were a window onto a foreign, distant reality—but rather constantly remind viewers of a creator's intervention in the making of film (and, by implication, the making of war). Herzog's war films, while adroit and affecting, do not shirk the fact that war-as-the-viewer-comes-to-see-it is (also) made through the stylization of shots and their arrangement in the editing room—images often compellingly coupled with prominent music and Herzog's now-iconic voice-over. In this sense, war *remains* a human phenomenon (never wholly giving over to the war in nature, never presented as if from on high—as a view of war in absolute terms sub specie aeternitatis); neither do the films become part of what we think of as History, that is, as documents purporting to reveal unmediated facts and empirical data. Herzog's war films in effect, therefore, show Herzog's wars—what he wants of them as a subject for thinking about humanity, and as a prompt for humanity to think about itself.

In a late-eighties documentary by Peter Buchka entitled *To the Limit—And Then beyond It: The Ecstatic World of Filmmaker Werner Herzog* (1989), Herzog makes the following remark about an abiding purpose for inventing moving images: "I often get the feeling that the cinema should create an image of humanity. . . . There always should be an image of humanity. Who are we? What is our inner history?"[10] For Herzog the project of imaging the world as an outward sign of inner, human experience is profoundly linked to our notion of mortality, of limits. "Here I get the feeling," Herzog notes, "that if we truly want deeper insights into ourselves we can only do so if we step back to the very edge of things."[11] Or, as the case may be, step forward, as if to the threshold of an abyss. We see Herzog literally doing just that in *La Soufrière* (1977)—a documentary about "an inevitable disaster" that did not happen—when he steps up to the receding ledge of the erupting volcano and is thrown back by exploding chunks of molten rock. He cites this film as an example of a movement toward points of transition between the present and the absent, the human and the nonhuman: "Often in cinema, in the films that I make, it's only possible to obtain a truly deep insight when you push things to the outermost limits."[12] In *La Soufrière,* he is not after the volcano as a metaphor for something but rather is focused on the human insight the natural phenomenon makes possible through our introspection. We find this pursuit in Herzog's own quest to visit the active volcano (to dare himself to face nature when it is at odds with the presumed conditions for human survival) and, more intriguingly, in Herzog's curiosity to meet the one man among seventy-five thousand island inhabitants who did not evacuate. "And so I thought," Herzog recollects, "'This man is interesting.' His relationship to death is one that I don't know and one I find very interesting. Where is this guy? Let's go and find out."[13] Herzog's roving camera seeks the loner, and questions are asked of him. Instead of concluding that the stalwart should be dismissed for possessing an unsound mind, Herzog draws closer, recognizing in him an attribute he finds generally in so many of his subjects: "I believe that it is an existential mindset. This rebellion against situations that are too big for us to handle. It's a mindset that enables us to preserve the dignity of our existence."[14] The "too big for us to handle" is a sentiment that links Herzog's subject to the history of the sublime, especially to Kant and Schiller, who believed that the sublime was essential to our apprehension and expression of human dignity.[15] Instead of the customary notion that sober reason, detached calculation, and other attributes of refined judgment assure one's dignity, Herzog says that it is the "insanity or such eccentricity, or something so extraordinary"—found in so many of his film subjects and characters—that "is necessary to gain human dignity."[16]

In part, this description of Herzog's approach to the revelation of human dignity on film—often in the midst of circumstances that threaten the human as such—is caught up with what Grazia Paganelli, in her book

Ecstasy and Truth, calls "Herzog's tactile gaze." She says this unique attribute accounts for what we experience as his unmoored, interested camera (often achieved by delegating the machine to the hands of cinematographer and longtime collaborator Peter Zeitlinger).[17] As Herzog stated in his Minnesota Declaration that "*cinéma vérité* is devoid of *vérité*," we might say that in his films we never find a documentarian's search for truth as something to be captured in (or from) the world, but rather an artist's sense that truth is something illuminated by invention.[18] Challenging the tension between fact and fiction, between documentary and drama, Herzog's incitements are, in this respect, similar to work by Paolo and Vittorio Taviani (from *Padre Padrone* [1977] to *Caesar Must Die* [2012]), who invest their fiction work with certain documentary effects; the hybridizations of encountered and envisioned facts in the work of Abbas Kiarostami (most notably in *Close-Up* [1990]); and more recently the palpable incitements of Casey Affleck's scandalously staged *I'm Still Here* (2010). On the pretext and prevalence of such blending of found and made scenes, Kiarostami has remarked: "We can never get close to the truth except through lying."[19] Or, more tenderly, Hossain Sabzian (played by Hossain Sabzian), the protagonist of *Close-Up,* says, while he is on trial for impersonating a famous Iranian film director: "It looks like fraud from the outside." When Kiarostami asks him what he was doing, as part of a filmed cross-examination, Sabzian replies with heartbreaking sincerity what he believes amounts to a fitting and sufficient counterdescription of his inadvertent stunt: "I'm interested in art and film."[20] In Herzog's work, and especially prevalent in his war films, we find the particular manifestation of his designs in moments of connection (or fissure) between the human and the nonhuman. It is precisely at these cleaving points that Herzog replaces cinéma vérité with *cinema umano.* As he says: "My goal is to explore and chronicle the human condition and our states of mind, and cinema is my way of doing this. I don't make films using images only of clouds and trees; I work with human beings."[21] Herzog might endorse ersatz director Sabzian's aphorism that "nature is a mirror in which to study ourselves," and furthermore agree that when such attention is translated into art—into film—we are, in our best moments, able to convey what Sabzian calls an "inner reality" and what Herzog commonly refers to as our "inner landscapes."[22]

For the sake of assessing Herzog's interest in, even preoccupation with, moments of transition into and out of human embodiment and experience, his films could be described, in part, as myriad, layered approaches to finding the limits of the human shift to the other-than-human (call it death, or regard it as nature, the alien, or that which is beyond comprehension, for instance, as screened in *Lessons of Darkness* [1992], or earlier in *Fata Morgana* [1971]—which includes the physical detritus of war and the child-spoken chant "War is insane"). Paganelli claims, "There is no Herzog film that does not hide a sort of paradoxical nostalgia for what the world might have been before mankind, or else for what the world will be after it ends."[23] Similarly, Paul Cronin says of Herzog that "he's a primeval sophisticate, a man of extraordinary erudition who yearns nostalgically for a pre-literate, pre-electric existence (or, even, post-literate and post-electric), where the wisdom of the illiterate—those able to memorize stories and poems, and recite them free of all props—predominates."[24] Paganelli and Cronin point up a contradiction that also appears to be part of a productive tension at the heart of Herzog's imaginative initiatives in film. He seems inspired, at times possessed, by a vision of the pre- or posthuman, or of those very instances of intimacy and distance that define the human against all other forms, cosmic and terrestrial. We might then say that Herzog's interest in the "before" and "after" of humankind is actually an expression of his curiosity about the peculiar *presence* of the human "in between" the time-before and the time-after. Herzog has remarked: "I still like the shots at the beginning and ending [of *Where the Green Ants Dream* (1994)] very much, images as if from the end of the world."[25] Meanwhile, Stanley Cavell has noted the incongruous discovery that "nothing could be more human" than "the power of the motive to reject the human."[26] In part the impulse seems expressed in "the human drive to transcend itself, make itself inhuman."[27] Herzog's work offers a novel, unconventional interpretation of what Cavell calls one of "the most inescapably human of motivations"—"the drive to the inhuman."[28] For Herzog's visions are the very opposite of a nihilistic, cynical, ironic, or misanthropic wish to dwell on the nonexistence of the human; instead they are oriented to the use of the before and after *of* the human as an occasion to radicalize, revitalize, and reinvigorate our attention *to* the human. The viewer seems to be seeing something she could not presume to see: a time when humans are no longer or never were; Herzog presents a privileged—imagined, stylized—view of existence without human habitation and intervention, and thereby radicalizes one's own status as a human viewer. We occupy a viewpoint from nowhere and never—namely, the pre- and posthuman—and from there catch a glimpse of our own humanity (in the form of postulated nonexistence, before and after). Since the traditional philosophical reading of the sublime could be cited as support for Cavell's claims, it must remain intriguing for us that Herzog directs his representation of the sublime *toward* the human.

The Human at War in Nature

Perhaps the most striking difference between other sublimes and the humanistic sublime—and establishing the stakes of the difference—is found in the contrast between immanent and imagined danger. Of course, on some accounts, it is the very suggestion of real danger that the notion of sublimity seems to eviscerate (and on Weiskel's reading leads to the oxymoronic or contradictory status of a humanistic sublime). And yet that does not seem borne out by the representations of war we find in war films (and war photography). In case after case, representations of the human encounter with the destructive capacities of war—the threat of genuine annihilation—often coupled and compounded by the indifference of nature, suggest that some kind of sublimity is being experienced, is making itself known to the soldier or image-maker, or, in some instances, to the viewer of these images. Herzog's war films should be counted among those works that contribute meaningfully to our assessment not of referents (bullets and bombs) but of the *representations* of those real-world threats; these are films that revel in their artifice as a means for redressing our inurement to reality. Herzog's fictions and fabrications, then, bring us up against vital, terrestrial, existential facts that are somehow obscured by the ubiquity of undeniable (but unseen) peril. Consider Herzog's account of the relationship between *Little Dieter Needs to Fly* (a documentary [1997]) and *Rescue Dawn* (a feature [2006]) and between Dieter Dengler and the actor who would play Dengler (Christian Bale):

> Although with *Little Dieter* I made a distinction between "fact" and "truth," in many ways the film is the truth I was bound to for practical reasons at the time. I remember watching it for the first time with Dieter. The lights went up and he turned to me. "Werner," he said without missing a beat, "this is unfinished business." The story of Dieter and Duane was always one I wanted to tell, this unbelievable and beautiful tale of human friendship. But to do this you either need Duane himself or someone playing him, and a feature film seemed the only way of reaching the depths of these truths that remained

untouched by *Little Dieter.* In that respect, the two films complement each other nicely. Though *Rescue Dawn* came second, in its fact and spirit, it really came first, and the paradox is that *Little Dieter* was strongly influenced by a feature film that hadn't yet been made.[29]

If one compares Herzog's war films with Terrence Malick's *The Thin Red Line* (1998), one finds similar questions being asked ("What's this war in the heart of nature?" Private Train poses in the film's opening question). But Malick's more meditative interest in nature overtakes his reflections on war; the men behave as bugs, creatures-under-the-compulsion-of-orders that climb anonymous hills like ants and are killed in the name of achievements soon forgotten or forsaken. (In this way, Malick's view seems more Darwinian than Herzog's. Darwin made much of the metaphor of war in *The Origin of Species*—regularly referring to "battle within battle," how "the law of battle descends," how all species are engaged in "the great battle for life" and "the great and complex battle of life"—and he concludes his epochal book by suggesting that his labors are meant to explain the "war of nature").[30] The men in Malick's film go into nature to fight war, and nature goes on all around them, indifferently; something similar happens in *Come and See* (1985), Elem Klimov's haunting depiction of nature's ceaseless flow while men are caught up in war (for the most part, unconsciously absorbed by its conduct or anxiously trying to flee its hazards). Some soldiers in *The Thin Red Line*—such as Private Witt (Jim Caviezel) find peace, or illumination, from their awareness of nature, but Witt's enigmatic departure from the war still leaves him a casualty of combat. Herzog's craft or conjuring of ecstatic truth (through proficient modes of construction and manipulation), contrariwise, brings us back into the man-madeness of war, the humanistic quality of war in the *context* of nature. Urban warfare, or rural fights—in fields and battlefields—remain subject to a bevy of natural preconditions. Herzog's revelation of a humanistic sublime does not make us transcend ourselves—or the natural world—but brings us back to ourselves as human in nature.

Paul Virilio claims in *War and Cinema: The Logistics of Perception* that we inhabit an era increasingly defined by "a growing derealization of military engagement." As part of the "aesthetics of disappearance" and the "logistics of perception," this derealization entails a concomitant depersonalization and dehumanization of the agents of war, combatant and his foe alike.[31] Very far from the hand-to-hand conflicts that formerly defined military engagement—often creating an unsettling intimacy between combatants—

modern warfare is continually becoming more mechanized, accelerated, and anonymous.[32] In recent decades war films have regularly integrated the "active optics" of computer-imaging technology as part of the narrative of war-making.[33] But just as often, such films grapple with the human factor—as emotional and erring beings, and also as casualty-of-machine and victor-over-machine. We discover how war films, paralleling the derealization of military engagement, invert a viewer's sense of distance by personalizing and humanizing our relationship to conflict. While a Persian Gulf veteran may have only "seen combat" on a video screen from a thousand miles away from his target, in a narrative film we are given a dramatic, materialized representation of his life before and after the weapon's launch. We follow him to training camp and we escort him home after the war; the release of ordnance, proximately or at a distance, is just a portion of the story. Generally, then, war films are—and it seems always have been—a forum for humanizing war, even as war itself has become increasingly a matter of seeking the removal of humans altogether (not just as intended targets but as the agents who pursue those targets); the implementation of unmanned drones has become a signal feature of twenty-first-century combat, and it accounts for an ever-enlarging percentage of the total war apparatus. For this reason, in political and military speech, the use of the synecdoche "boots on the ground" has evolved into a euphemism for the least desirable course of action. In Virilio's phrase, the "ubiquitous orbital vision of enemy territory" would create the conditions in which a soldier, sailor, or airman never sees the enemy as a person but only as a display of visual information on a screen.[34] More eerily, the decision to "act" on the displayed information may at some point cease to be a human decision but instead itself become an electronic pulse generated by a computer's program.[35]

Far from being a remote, arcane, or otherwise antiquated academic subject (even if interesting in terms of intellectual history), the sublime is, in the present context, possessed of tremendous urgency primarily because war reminds us of the absolute—whether we are fighting in a war or watching one represented on-screen. In the history of the concept, the sublime is fundamentally caught up with our notion of limits—and more particularly, the vertiginous worry that we might exceed them, or already have exceeded them. Simon Morley has argued that Kant's notion of the sublime entailed a "negative experience of limits," which is to say, the sublime becomes "a way of talking about what happens when we are faced with something we do not have the capacity to understand or control—something excessive."[36] Morley continues:

> Behind Kant's discussion lay a keen sense of the independence of nature, whose sheer complexity and grandeur continuously exceeds any human ability to control or understand it. This sense of the sublime may be initiated by the terrifying aspects of nature such as Burke describes, or be provoked by an experience so complex that our inability to form a clear mental conception of it leads to a sense of the inadequacy of our imagination and of the vast gulf between that experience and the thoughts we have about it. We are made aware, Kant observed, that sometimes we cannot present to ourselves an account of an experience that is in any way coherent. We cannot encompass it by thinking, and so it remains indiscernible or unnameable, undecidable, indeterminate and unpresentable.[37]

And yet it is precisely because, for most noncombatants, war is real via the surrogate of war films (and photographs) that we recognize how these movies must constantly postulate a representation of the ineffable, must attempt to picture what otherwise would remain "indiscernible or unnameable, undecidable, indeterminate and unpresentable." Even though the execution of war may closely resemble the conditions of the classical romantic (or transcendental) sublime—a constant engagement with the excessive—I suggest we not lose sight of the categorical differences between the soldier and the cinema spectator. The soldier is at war, and always already in nature. So the kind of consciousness he or she will come to about the sublime—in the midst of combat—will not be a remote and ethereal sublime but a visceral, bloody sublime. And even the soldier in a command center—facing screens that erupt from deadly explosions half a world away—must be granted an encounter with the *effects* of military force that are of a different order from the staged versions we see in movies.

Homing in on one of the most astonishing and unprecedented displays of cruelty to humankind, Michael Berenbaum has said that "part of [the Holocaust's] attraction to filmmakers, part of its attraction to an audience is: you're touching the absolute as you come closer to the truth of the Holocaust. And part of the failure of film, if it fails, is not to touch that absolute, not to go to the extreme."[38] Touching or even approaching the absolute on film, in terms of Nazi crimes or the Jewish experience of suffering them, or more broadly in the experience of war-as-phenomenon (in battles from Thermopylae to Bunker Hill, or genocides from the Peloponnesian War to Rwanda), we may suggest that nearing hate, evil, oppression, and discrimination—or discovering their countermovements in love, goodness, respect, and dignity—stimulates our humanity, our conscience, and our moral sense. War is the space of radical mortality, or rather where its radicalness may be most keenly felt—as if to heighten consciousness about something that is persistently there, part of our moment-to-moment existence. An infantryman who lived through D-Day reports a sentiment familiar to many soldiers: war "gives you attitudes about life and death that are unattainable anywhere else."[39] As viewers of war films, therefore, we must feel the threat of our nonexistence by proxy—by association with some characters or disassociation from others. In this sense, going to see a war film is a choice to approach the absolute that reflects a desire to be moved into a space of radical consciousness about the reality and inevitability of death. For those who are receptive, the refined cinema projection would appear to grant truths vicariously. Yet, can war *films* give a viewer attitudes about life and death that are unattainable elsewhere? Do the lessons of war translate from the midnight battle to the matinee spectacle? We can at least point out that war films are unlike any genre or subgenre where the hero has many lives, leaves the firefight unscathed (perhaps only with a bloody scratch on a dirty cheek as a totem of his or her bravery), returns to fight another day, survives without psychic torment, carries on/out a mission without reproach or ethical perplexity, applies himself to the next assignment with certainty, and so forth. A war film and its variants, hybrids, and subgenres is fundamentally about living *one* life and thus risking an encounter with the ultimate, the absolute: death.[40] In this respect, at least, a war film can be said to represent war.

Maybe there is no humanistic sublime for Weiskel and his reading of nature, or for Kant and the mathematical sublime, but perhaps war—as the very definition of living at the brink of existential threat—is the appropriate place to speak of it. Because Herzog is attuned both to the romantic tradition and its representational corollaries (for example, in the paintings of Hercules Seghers and the plays of Georg Büchner) and to the creative nature of fabrication in documentary image-making, Herzog's work in the genre of war films seems especially poised, perhaps urgently and latently, to offer some real insight into the meaning—and nonparadoxical status—of the humanistic sublime.[41]

For the present investigation, I have narrowed the field of Herzog's scores of films to a few of what might be called his "war films"—those works that wear war more overtly on the surface of the film (e.g., the war in Vietnam and the Persian Gulf War). The very attribution of the moniker "war films" to some of his creations usefully complicates the genre as it finds expression in his other films: after all, war is the pretext, subtext, or even condition of filming in much of Herzog's oeuvre, whether in *Ballad of the Little Soldier* (1985) (pretext), *Fata Morgana* (subtext), or *Fitzcarraldo* (1982) and *Cobra Verde* (1987) (condition). I address three films from Herzog's vast catalogue—*Lessons of Darkness, Little Dieter Needs to Fly,* and *Rescue Dawn*—in an effort to analyze some ways in which these productions exemplify Herzog's representation of war and what that representation makes possible for us in thinking about the concept he refers to as "ecstatic truth." In these three depictions, Herzog—like Terrence Malick—seems to create a cinema in which the transcendence of the human is predicated on a hyperrealization of human consciousness: a going-beyond the human that requires a form of immanence. In this way, Herzog makes a substantive contribution to the history of aesthetics—reaching back as far as Longinus, who said, "In discourse we demand that which transcends the human"—by suggesting that a humanistic sublime is not an oxymoron but, perhaps, the highest and hardest kind of sublimity possible for human experience.[42] We might readily appreciate the values and virtues of the romantic sublime and the tragic sublime, especially as they are forms that have become familiar, almost banal in their ubiquitous invocation. But a humanistic sublime is another matter. It appears to be the least available to linguistic conceptualization and instead invites articulation in other media—and the visual, aural, and narrative power of film seems especially well positioned and capable (in the right hands) for just this kind of expression.[43] Not the expression of a preliterate naïf, but instead the creations of a well-read humanist who, nevertheless, wishes to challenge the tropes, logic, and narrative structures that philosophy and literature have bequeathed to cinema.

Ecstatic Truth as Heuristic for the Humanistic Sublime

Historically, the sublime has been discussed mainly in reference to natural phenomena and works of art. One of the many kinds of sublime objects that has drawn the attention of theorists—since the appearance of Friedrich Schiller's "On the Sublime" (1801), the first of many recoveries of Longinus's notion from antiquity—can be found in landscape painting, a perfect amalgam of nature and its representation. Though there are many definitions of the sublime, most describe a phenomenon that *exceeds* one's experience or ability to account for it—that either is unrepresentable (hence the daring of the romantic landscape painters such as C. D. Friedrich and Joseph Turner) or is unintelligible (hence the bravery of theorists trying to make the notion philosophically understandable and credible).

A contemporary appeal to the sublime typically might refer to an experience that eclipses one's expectations, that remains unaccountable or excessive in some way or another. But the notion of sublimity—from Longinus to Schiller through Burke into Kant and Hegel, and later Lyotard, Weiskel, and Žižek—preserves a close proximity to the experience of awe, terror, disorientation, and horror, and, as Simon Morley has noted, "something we cannot encompass by thinking, and so it remains indiscernible or unnameable, undecidable, indeterminate and unpresentable."[44] If this is our working definition of the, we might say generic, sublime, then it seems highly pertinent to draw our attention to the ways in which the phenomenon of war is sublime. Moreover, given this account of how war is sublime because it exceeds total comprehension (and in many cases even partial comprehension), consider filmmakers' attempts to represent these varied and difficult phenomena on film—bold efforts to confront the terrible facts of war by capturing and creating new conditions for thinking about its elusiveness—coupled with the extent to which war often elides the historian's and the artist's gifted renderings. In this respect, saying that "war is sublime" is both apodeictic and tautological; it is not a claim that stands in need of explanation.

Several of Herzog's most celebrated films were made in the midst of wars (*Fitzcarraldo,* for instance), some invoke war's ineluctable presence in our lives (*Fata Morgana*), and some are explicitly "war films," such as *Little Dieter Needs to Fly* (a documentary about Dieter Dengler), *Rescue Dawn* (a feature film version of Dengler's story), and *Lessons of Darkness* (a documentary addressing the Persian Gulf War and its aftermath). In the context of his war films, as adduced, I suggest that Herzog's notion of ecstatic truth helps us recognize a new (or newly recovered) kind of sublime—not the romantic, transcendental, tragic, apocalyptic, ironic, hysterical, or abstract sublime, as so many others have theorized, but instead, the humanistic sublime. If war films—like nature and paintings—invoke phenomena that outreach comprehension (and in many cases cause forms of post-traumatic stress disorder, depression, hysteria, and psychosis); and if war is so complex that it leaves us, as Fredric Jameson notes, with the "suspicion that war is unrepresentable";[45] then it would be highly useful to properly inherit a concept that might direct us to the things war films *do* make possible—for they are realities unto themselves, if not the realities they allude to. In the case of Herzog's war films, I contend it is precisely in that space of anxiety about the possibility of representing an unintelligible phenomenon such as war that the ecstatic truth becomes pertinent, for it emerges at the point where factual representation (that which corresponds to reality, or aligns with evidence, what Herzog calls the "accountant's truth") is given over to a representation that seeks to go beyond the given: to instead reveal truth through invention and fabrication. Importantly, since he is said to make documentaries, Herzog qualifies his documentary approach by eschewing its proximity to ethnography: "A film like *Wodaabe* [: *Herdsmen of the Sun* (1989)] can't really be considered ethnographic because it's stylized to such an extent that the audience is taken into the realm of the ecstatic."[46] The ecstatic truth emerges, then, not from facts per se but from their arrangement and distortion. This kind of truth subverts a wish or expectation for correspondence to reality (usually understood as outer, empirical, observable reality) and instead awakens an experience of *inner* reality. Hence the consecutive relationship between the representation of ecstatic truth and the achievement of a humanistic sublime—a sublime that is unapologetically a function of the human perception of its reality. War, like other extreme conditions, natural or otherwise, seems uniquely situated for rendering an experience of the humanistic sublime; and for those who do not undergo combat, the innovation and implementation of ecstatic truth may become an ally and agitator for experiencing this kind of rare but profound—and distinctly human—sublimity. With war films composed of ecstatic truth, the medium becomes an intermediary.

Precisely because Herzog departs from the actual, literal, or real elements of the experience of war—say, Dengler's first-person account of what happened, or evidence drawn from military or historical records as well as on-the-ground reports—Herzog is able to better express the *human* factor in war, to reveal what he calls our "inner landscapes."[47] By abstracting or poetizing the individual's experience, and for that matter the war's narrative in general, Herzog reaches for something, as Coleridge phrased it, at once "far higher and far inward,"[48] beyond the limits, namely, a work of art that in Herzog's words "intensifies" and "elevates" the human. In this way, the pursuit of the ecstatic truth—going beyond the facts of an individual's human experience—serves humanity, trying to summon it to a higher perception of itself, as Kant suggests, to a recognition of human dignity. Again, in Kant's view, "Man's dignity is the ground of the judgment that man himself is sublime."[49]

While Herzog has been criticized, for the most part playfully and occasionally with a measure of scandal, for his interventions in documentaries, including his war films, there is reason to believe that his instinct to subvert fact in favor of fantasy and dreams might, paradoxically, be a better way to represent the *realities* of war. At the end of Herzog's films, as a result of his fabrication and invention, we do not end up with abstractions and clichés but with concrete emotional and cognitive responses. Having been told lies, as it were, having let a war story become a science-fiction story, we are left with an unsettling sense that we are in a better place to speak of the *truth* of war: namely, how it is a truth that denies or exceeds direct representation. It is a truth, in the wake of Herzog's war films, that appears both conspicuously sublime and ineluctably human.

Presented with a film such as *Fitzcarraldo,* one may justifiably think Herzog's natural métier is the romantic sublime, but then that was not a story about a man's contemplation of nature but rather his engagement with it, his entanglement within it. And Les Blank and Maureen Gosling's enduring documentary *Burden of Dreams* (1982) even more surely returns us to the space of a different sublime: Herzog is not in awe of nature, but, paralleling his title character, he aims to contend with its fates and forces—to literally pull a ship over a jungle-laden mountain. Some scholars have selected yet another sublime to describe Herzog's work: Alan Singer, for instance, argues for an ironic sublime, despite Herzog's apparently genuine claim that he is incapable of understanding irony.[50]

What if we consider instead whether Herzog's work—by and large, or in particular instances—constitutes an attempt to generate the conditions for an experience of the humanistic sublime? Herzog himself has theorized—though he would likely resist the suggestion that he is theorizing—the prime impulse and achievement of his work as a search for what he calls "ecstatic truth." (We can ask, as Emerson does, "Is not the sublime felt in an analysis as well as in a creation?")[51] Like the humanistic sublime, ecstatic truth is a compact concept that needs elaborate glossing; in a speech entitled "On the Absolute, the Sublime, and Ecstatic Truth," Herzog describes the term this way:

The reason is simple and comes not from theoretical, but rather

> from practical, considerations. With this quotation [the opening intertitle of *Lessons of Darkness* featuring ersatz lines by Pascal] as a prefix I elevate [*erheben*] the spectator, before he has even seen the first frame, to a high level, from which to enter the film. And I, the author of the film, do not let him descend from this height until it is over. Only in this state of sublimity [*Erhabenheit*] does something deeper become possible, a kind of truth that is the enemy of the merely factual. Ecstatic truth, I call it.

Herzog's effort to prepare his audience by "elevating" its point of entry into the film is itself an expression of the customary ways of speaking about ecstasy.[52] Etymologically, *ekstasis* literally means "to take out or remove (*ek*) from the regular position or standing (*stasis*)" and bring into a different state (say, rapture) beyond ordinary perception. More figuratively, *ekstasis* can be understood as "bewilderment" and "amazement"; "distraction or disturbance of mind caused by shock"; or "displacement or derangement of the mind"; but perhaps most pointedly for our exploration with Herzog, it also means entering into a trance; (additionally, the word can be defined, as Weiskel does, as "transport," which makes it an uncanny conceptual sibling to the Greek meaning of metaphor [*metapherein*], "transfer"). Herzog has a long-standing interest in hypnotism and the nature of human physicality when a person is under a trance; for example, he had all the actors in *Heart of Glass* (1976) perform while under hypnosis.

The abiding interest in hypnosis, as Herzog has emphasized, is not theoretical but practical. The varieties of ecstasy as seen in his films—induced through meditation, music (usually with his frequent collaborators Popol Vuh and more recently Ernst Reijseger),[53] physical and bodily techniques, and athletic trial (e.g., in *The Great Ecstasy of the Woodcarver Steiner* [1974])—are meant to create access to a realm of truth otherwise inaccessible to us. What is readily accessible and widely prevalent, however, is what Herzog calls "the accountant's truth," a strict faith in the alignment of fact with observable reality—what philosophers regularly call a correspondence theory of truth. Ecstatic truth is, by contrast, a truth that emerges from fabrication, conflict, and obscurity. And it is precisely this kind of truth that we find in a *humanistic* sublime. The continual pressure to exceed the human—for example, (sky-jumper skier) Steiner's radical, literal, elevation beyond the normal plane of human existence—is transformed into the promise of a new moment of contact, that is, when he returns safely to the slope. Steiner leaves terra firma and we fathom those aerial moments of disconnection (intense, if terse, periods of tremendous mental concentration and physical exertion on his part). A viewer watches Steiner leap into another realm of existence, even *ex-istence*—living beyond his own humanness, if briefly. We behold this alien aerialist. Elevated to this degree, Steiner has left us; he has transcended the human while remaining human; from this height, we could say his humanness is enhanced—pushed to the very threshold of its destruction. After all, our view of Steiner aloft and his view of us may be his last—a radical, hovering final moment of his awareness as a human being. It is this flash of disruption in the continuity of the everyday—its accountant-truth-based human life—that creates the occasion for perceiving an ecstatic truth. Unlike a romantic sublime (of a Teutonic sort) that "concerns power and sets man and nature in desperate opposition," what I attribute to Herzog as a humanistic sublime makes nature (or Nature) the proper antagonist—and facilitator—of the human perception of ecstatic truth.[54] Without the grandeur of nature, humans would be less able to comprehend their condition, states of consciousness, and modes of revelation. Thus, at times Herzog's sublime may seem closer to a nineteenth century *English* romantic sublime "in which nature is not merely thrown over but appears as the medium through which the mind discovers and presents itself, in eddies of separation and reunion"—much as we see in Steiner's departure from earth and his return to earth.[55] And yet, Herzog does not employ nature for instrumental purposes—even if for the heightening of human consciousness—but instead focuses on the *human* situation within a natural setting. Nature, whether it is figured as the densely verdant Peruvian jungle or the bleached vastness of Antarctica, is secondary to man's scenario. Though the frigid winds howl on the other side of the tent in *Encounters at the End of the World* (2007), Herzog's primary focus is not on outward conditions but "inner landscapes"—the emotional, intellectual, moral, aesthetic, and psychological terrain of the remote human explorers. His question is not what they discover in the air, ice, and water but what they find in their own souls—a much more terrifying encounter.

Herzog, unlike so many of his contemporaries, has not become inured or immune to the allure of the sublime—treating it, as they often do, only with ironic detachment and modern condescension as a "moribund aesthetic."[56] But, almost as a traveler from the past, Herzog has retained "the obsession, so fundamental to the Romantic sublime, with natural infinitude."[57] As part of his inheritance, and *transformation*, of this tradition—reaching, as he does, to Longinus, Kant, and other thinkers of the sublime—Herzog advances the notion into a new medium, cinema, and locates in this form a way of relating the human to nature that other kinds of representation, from the poem to the novel, cannot, or have not. As a visual space of moving (in at least two senses of the word) representations, often accompanied by sound, the cinema screen suggests an alternate reality: and as such, the chance to perceive another world before us (brute reality as a phantasm) or within us (a dream or nightmare as a brute reality).

POW, POV: *Little Dieter Needs to Fly* and *Rescue Dawn*

Herzog seems to be trying to *represent* the humanistic sublime for the characters or subjects in his films (either as part of their experience retold in documentary or by means of dramatic reenactment)[58]—and it is a postulation in itself whether he succeeds at this—but I am seeking a further valence, namely, whether that representation stimulates an experience of the humanistic sublime in his viewers; might it be something only a POW or a soldier in combat can experience? Or can film—these films of Herzog's in particular—create conditions for us to perceive absolute, existential limits, and the sort of ecstatic truth Herzog claims the medium should avail? This second question underwrites my inquiry into those works of Herzog's that are most expressly part of the war-film genre; meanwhile, it could be asked of nearly all his films. So if Steiner needs to soar and Dieter needs to fly, what can be said for the heights a viewer may attain by encountering these purportedly sublime feats of human expression and exhibition? Film may be inherently revelatory of the sublime—since it is an interface between worlds—yet selected screened content appears to accentuate these moments of liminal engagement. A viewer comes face-to-face with a presence that is already no longer, as if it were absorbed by the medium itself and transcended itself. Does it matter, then, if the person we see is an actor or instead the person the actor portrays? And what if the historical figure, as it were, acts? We turn, then, to consider how ecstatic truth may emerge for an audience, in part, because of a confluence of these roles.

Herzog's documentary *Little Dieter Needs to Fly* participates in a sturdy subgenre of war films that could be defined by the aim to escape confinement or the protagonist's status as a prisoner of war. Most of the well-known representative examples of the subgenre are feature dramas—*Grand Illusion* (1937), *The Bridge on the River Kwai* (1957), *The Great Escape* (1963), *King*

Rat (1965), *The Dirty Dozen* (1967), *The Deer Hunter* (1978), and more recently, *Hart's War* (2002), *Defiance* (2008), *District 9* (Blomkamp, 2009), and *The Way Back* (2010); and for narrative similarity, though not war content, one also thinks of *Cool Hand Luke* (1967), *Papillon* (1973), *Escape from Alcatraz* (1979), and *The Shawshank Redemption* (1994). But *Little Dieter* is a documentary, and since Dieter Dengler is its subject, the viewer already knows he survived his ordeal, so the drama of the film will be how he did so and, perhaps—as we meet him in late maturity—how he has weathered the effects of being a POW in his life since emancipation. Almost a decade later, and five years after Dengler's death, Herzog staged a narrative feature, *Rescue Dawn,* starring Christian Bale as the shot-down navy pilot. The relationship between these two films is complicated, and complicating, because Herzog sees them as coextensive: not a documentary and a feature, but two dramatizations of a narrative told by Dengler. Herzog says: "We were very careful in the reenactment and stylization of Dieter's reality. He had to become an actor who is performing himself."[59] For Herzog, the camera does not bear witness to Dengler's story but rather contributes to its fabrication. Herzog continues:

> When we made *Little Dieter,* it was very clear to me that we were making a fiction film. But from the moment we realized that it would take so long to find the money and the actors, we decided to make a documentary, but a documentary that was both staged and stylized, with invented moments, but without touching the heart of the story. So the documentary came first, and then the fiction film *Rescue Dawn.* But in my mind, just like in the mind of Dieter Dengler, *Little Dieter* was always a fiction film. . . . In simple words, I could say that the documentary is a remake of the fiction film but, of course, neither is a remake of the other because they're so different. And yet they complement each other very well.[60]

Though *Little Dieter* would have to be a remake of *Rescue Dawn avant le lettre,* Herzog is drawing attention to the customary, one might say naïve, notion that documentary filmmaking is "more true" than fictitious narrative; or even more troublingly, that documentary filmmaking, by virtue of its form or the intention of its creators, provides unmediated access to the otherwise obfuscated and unreachable. A couple years after *Little Dieter,* Herzog stated in his "Minnesota Declaration" (a kind of send-up of Lars von

Trier's "Dogme 95" creed): "*Cinéma Vérité* is devoid of *vérité*."[61] So truth is on Herzog's mind—in this pair of films, as elsewhere—just not the kind of truth commonly associated with vérité: namely, a kind of revelation of reality, a secret disclosure of otherwise concealed things. No, Herzog's truth in *Little Dieter* and *Rescue Daw* is ecstatic. It is not, as he says, "the truth of accountants," but a collaboratively discovered mode of cinematic storytelling.[62] One does not point a camera in a certain direction to get a true picture of things; rather, one shoots in the direction of one's interest—encounters obstacles, finds false paths, collects unusable footage—and later, often much later, in editing, discovers or creates, as the case may be, lines of connection and affiliation. These are the assemblages that are more than the sum of parts; as such, they do not generate the truth of a referential realist, but a truth that emerges from within the film itself—and in relation to its viewers.

What is perhaps most illuminating about *Rescue Dawn* is its relationship to narrative invention and storytelling compared with *Little Dieter Needs to Fly*. The two films offer a clinic in different ways of telling "the same" story. Or rather, as Herzog has noted, the different approaches are complementary, and, one might add, mutually reinforcing. The constitutive elements of both films—montage and music, plotting and pacing, diegesis (as narration) and mimesis (as reanimation)—are variously, sometimes conversely, represented in the two works. Consider how *Rescue Dawn* begins with the same documentary aerial footage that *Little Dieter* begins with (footage of napalm being dropped from airplanes onto Southeast Asian villages and farms), yet this framing device comes to different effect when it is followed by after-the-fact documentary footage of a man who participated in such a campaign (*Little Dieter*), as compared to a dramatic visualization of a man training before-the-fact (*Rescue Dawn*). Both presentations of archival footage are offered without diegetic sound and are set to music. As such, the graphic footage frames the personal story to follow: this, we will learn, is a tale of a boy who was bombed and who grows up to find himself bombing others. As Dwayne (Steve Zahn) says after hearing Dieter's story about how he "needed to fly" upon seeing a pilot eye-to-eye while the latter laid waste to his beloved Bavarian town, "A guy tries to kill you and you want his job."[63]

The structure of the two films, among other things, highlights the nature of point of view (POV). In *Little Dieter,* we are meant to see and hear Dengler's experience narrated firsthand and reenacted by the man who underwent the trials he describes; in *Rescue Dawn,* without the presence of the historical Dieter Dengler (the realist referent of the action), the narrative takes on a more familiar chronological progression. Where the audience is addressed directly in *Little Dieter* (by Dengler), those same stories are consolidated in *Rescue Dawn* for the purposes of a dramatic representation by professional actors. Despite the shift in perspective (or POV), these two approaches, when they are both taken together—as a pair of complementary productions—require that spectators discover how the two films work back in time slowly, from documentary to fictional re-creation in an efficient, continuous fashion. In *Little Dieter*, we *begin* with a sixty-seven-year-old and end—hours later—in *Rescue Dawn* with him on board the carrier, at the beginning of his liberation. *Little Dieter*, structurally, may be said to possess three basic segments: (1) documentary footage of Dengler in the present day, living the life of a survivor; (2) Dengler retelling, recollecting, and recounting his experiences as a POW; and (3) Dengler returning to the site of his capture and incarceration—and going so far as to reenact the conditions he suffered, including torture. In *Rescue Dawn*—after the initial footage of aerial bombing (a sort of overture that links the documentary and the feature)—familiar narrative conventions take over and the film moves chronologically from Dengler as a child, to him entering the navy, shot down while flying, being taken prisoner, escaping, and finally being rescued. Taken together, however, *Little Dieter* and *Rescue Dawn* illuminate aspects of each other.

Where in *Little Dieter* we see a military training video coupled with Herzog's sardonic voice-over, in *Rescue Dawn* the documentary voice-from-above is replaced with Spook's (Toby Huss's) sarcastic diegetic commentary. When scenes in *Little Dieter*—such as when Dengler reenacts making a fire, or describes how he was tortured, or how to open handcuffs—are played beside scenes in *Rescue Dawn*, where these same narrated and reenacted elements are dramatized, we experience something crucial about the modes and effects of narrative invention. One almost understands this contrast as a proper gloss on the meaning of the filmic proviso here rendered as "Inspired by True Events in the Life of Dieter Dengler." The Latin origins of "inspired" come to mind as a way of understanding what we could possibly mean by "true." All events in a life, we could say, are true. Whatever happens is true. It is our telling about the events, though, that (even as the telling is part of life, and so reveals its own truth), "gives them breath"—and in the manner of that propulsion, we discover a new reality, a new perspective on facts. The facts that are "inspired," we are invited by Herzog to remember, are not the facts as we experience them. The inspired fact—the sort of fact that is a hybrid or mutation with fabrication—is the sort we can hope to experience something different with: not truth, but ecstatic truth.

War, for Herzog, is intimately bound up with questions of orientation and disorientation—hence the crucial role that POV plays in framing Herzog's subjects (in documentary work) or characters (in dramatic work). One might say generally that Herzog's films are preoccupied neither with personal romantic life nor even with personal identity, but with something more like the relationship between a human being and his knowledge of where he is or belongs. This existential outlook reveals itself, for example, by the interaction between the imprisoned Eugene's (Jeremy Davies) stitchwork on the back of his shirt that asks *Quo Vadis* and later, after the successful escape, the deliriously free Eugene pleading with others, "You tell me where to go. You tell me where to go," and asking rhetorically, "Where am I going to go? Where am I going to go?"[64] Similarly, soon after Dengler arrives in the prison camp and starts planning his escape, Dwayne points out something obvious but unseen: "The jungle is the prison. Don't you get that?"[65] War among men, we appear always to forget, is *also* always a war with nature—with its particular forces of menace and imposed disorientation. One may survive the bullet only to be eaten by the bear.

Illumination from *Lessons of Darkness*

The question of orientation arises early in *Lessons of Darkness,* where in Herzog's self-authored voice-over we hear, "The men appear to be trying to communicate with one another. Offering signals."[66] After a close study of *Little Dieter* and *Rescue Dawn,* however, we may appreciate how *Lessons of Darkness* offers yet another approach to the relationship between man and nature during war, namely, through the conceit of science fiction. There are no soldiers in *Lessons of Darkness,* though we hear stories about them and what they have done (e.g., testimonials about the tortures carried out by Iraqi soldiers). No battles are waged on-screen, unless the attempt to quell oil fires is a kind of battle; and even then, out of boredom or perversity, the oil wells are relit so the "battle" to extinguish them might continue. No injuries are inflicted on camera, and no deaths are shown. But above all—there is no protagonist. The film is largely comprised of long takes of landscapes: with ground-level views of men at work in oil fields ablaze and aerial shots (which Herzog achieved by hiring out a daring helicopter pilot) of the cityscape and surrounding land. How does this series of images amount to a representation of war? We are meant to believe that the city we see is one that existed in splendor before the war began, but we learn (from Herzog's confession) that the aerial views of Kuwait City were filmed *after* the war ended. This is not a city reconstructed after a calamitous war, but a city that survived it. Such a deception—achieved merely by redescribing or recontextualizing documentary footage—gives us another occasion of Herzog's method of transforming facts to give up a truth that would not otherwise obtain—that is, a truth he calls ecstatic, we presume, because it stands outside of or beside the given. Customarily we have a name for the kind of representation that is a redescription or fabrication: a lie. And yet, Herzog's filmic alterations are not aimed to deceive but to enlighten.

In *Lessons of Darkness,* among other works, Herzog aims to engender epiphanic effects through fiction. Though the images are themselves strictly documentary—in the sense that there *are* oil fires burning and men trying to snuff them out—the construction of the film undermines the apparent givenness of the action. Even the subjects of the documentary cannot be trusted to be speaking their own words, a violation of documentary conventions and "conventional realism" that Brigette Peucker has pointed out: "As in *Fata Morgana* (1969) and *The Great Ecstasy of the Woodcarver Steiner* (1973), *Lessons [of] Darkness* features frontal shots of war victims delivering scripted poetic monologues, one of which voices the recurrent Herzog theme of the insufficiency of language."[67] That is, the war victims speak Herzog's scripted lines, not their own narration of emotions and events; through ventriloquism he gives shape to their accounts. Furthermore, the added voice-over written and read by Herzog, along with the muted diegetic sound replaced with the presence of bold nondiegetic music by the likes of Richard Wagner, contributes to the chances that a viewer will be stimulated or provoked to have a view of things that are not there per se, and instead will be moved to a space of mirages, hypnosis, hallucinations, dreams, and nightmares.

As Herzog does not conform to visual and narrative conventions of documentary, so his use of music departs from the standard supporting or even explanatory role usually assigned or hoped for from such accompaniment. When he laid down the music for *Wodaabe: Herdsmen of the Sun,* he said playing the *Ave Maria* "creates a strange ecstasy" and "using that aria means the film isn't a 'documentary' about a specific African tribe, rather a story about beauty and desire."[68] Herzog tells us: "The music helps carry us out of the realm of what I call the accountant's truth, and without that specific recording, the images of this amazing and bizarre male beauty contest wouldn't touch us as deeply"—which is to say the film as a work of art would not have found its connection to the human phenomenon that Herzog aimed to represent.[69] In *Lessons of Darkness,* the prominent role of music is similarly affecting—from Arvo Pärt's *Stabat Mater* to Gustav Mahler's *Symphony No. 2,* from Prokofiev, Schubert, and Verdi (*Messa da Requiem*) to a range of works by Wagner (*Das Rheingold, Parsifal,* and *Götterdämmerung*). These are not works that naturally—that is, historically or contextually—align with the oil fields of Kuwait. And yet, it is precisely that discontinuity—that sense of unnatural juxtaposition—that awakens what might be described as an ecstatic apprehension of the unaltered footage.

The perception of our inner landscapes through encounters with Herzog's films—and their representations of outer landscapes—reinforces, uncannily, how inner landscapes are necessarily human. The interaction of these two kinds of landscapes, in Herzog's hands, informs our understanding of war—for example, how Herzog's films about war do not stylize violence and destruction but instead poetize them. Watching these films—*Little Dieter, Rescue Dawn,* and *Lessons of Darkness*—should not feel voyeuristic, masochistic, or cathartic, but instead should be occasions for contemplation and insight: generative of a true apocalypse (*apokaluptein,* to disclose, uncover, or reveal). A viewer should not, it seems, feel punished or frightened by Herzog's war films but illuminated by them: as if the words and images made these difficult elements apparent to us differently—not with gruesome depictions but with incitements that make the inner human experience (fear, awe, panic, grief) more available to us. "Has life without fire become unbearable for them?" Herzog asks in voice-over when we see the silent "creatures" relight the squelched shoots of vertically jetting oil; and in that question he shows us something singular about what might be going on inside those distant figures.[70] What are *they* thinking? Not surprisingly, though, such questions revert to the viewer, who must contend with her own inner landscapes—their concealment or disclosure.

Herzog reminds us that we are in need of asking ourselves: Why do we watch—or want to watch—war films? And part of our reply suggests that we want to *understand* something about the human experience of war in particular, and humanness more generally. This will not be achieved by spectacle, but instead by seeing the spectacular elements of the antispectacle: the brutality of torture, the shock of a murdered comrade, the pain of hunger, the contest between courage and despair, the desire to survive pursuit, and the preservation of will and hope in the face of grave and terrible odds that bend toward nonexistence. Herzog's technique, or habit, of recontextualizing documentary footage by reordering it, applying nondiegetic sound, using fanciful intertitles ("The War," "A Pilgrimage," "The Drying Up of the Source," "I am so tired of sighing; Lord, let it be night")[71] and mock-serious voice-overs (courting religious profundity and science-fiction fantasy), and so forth, is something he brings to war films from a lifetime doing other kinds of films. We might ask, then, what the features and characteristics of Herzog's creative practice contribute to the representation of war on film. One postulation—given the evidence of his work in *Lessons of Darkness*, *Little Dieter*, and *Rescue Dawn*—is that war films may be particularly suited to the expression, or should we say provocation, of ecstatic truth.

Is War Sublime?

If war is by definition dangerous, the romantic sublime is by definition that which induces fear but is not dangerous. And so, to survive war—to literally *live through* its mortifying terror—cannot be a sublime fact for combatant or civilian. Thus, no matter how much death a soldier or bystander sees, no matter how close he comes to his own extinction, surviving is not sublime because death is a genuine, even plausible, effect of military engagement: one may have approached the threshold of nonexistence and lived to say something (or remain silent) about it, but the precipice was not a fabrication, not a specter. And so the reality of war's danger, on this view, denies a combatant's claim to an experience of the sublime, humanistic or otherwise. If war experience cannot generate an apprehension of the sublime (as it is defined by Kant, for example), we may yet counter that war's *representation*—on film, among other places—can be sublime; by a frisson from genuinely felt effects, the cinema prevails over its apparent fakery. Of course, many representations of war on film suggest that *war* is sublime—from Private Witt's apotheosis in the remote jungle of a Pacific Island in *The Thin Red Line* to Swofford's (Jake Gyllenhaal's) apocalyptic oilfield phantasmagoria in *Jarhead* (2005). But these are *depictions* of soldiers apprehending aesthetic impressions of war's conditions; these are sublime visions produced for viewers.

Though the foregoing terminological or conceptual account would appear to deny a soldier on the front line an experience of the humanistic sublime, we may object from an appeal to common sense—for it would seem the person most in danger of losing his or her life is also the most capable of recognizing the quintessence of his or her humanity. Yet, in the history of the idea's reception, we find that Kant has described the "terrifying sublime" as something that can induce or activate or otherwise "move" us to feel fear—but *without danger.*[72] If this is so, then, as noted, the firsthand experience of war would be disqualified from summoning the sublime since those conditions are simply and straightforwardly full of danger. This is precisely why, for example, *we* may take Private Witt's experience in the jungle depicted in *The Thin Red Line* as sublime, and why he (or, more accurately, the soldier his performance is meant to conjure) cannot: he is in mortal danger and we are safe spectators. Partly this distinction is made on the basis of our lack of access to Witt's narration of his personal sacrifice; he cannot attest to a perception of sublimity after the fact, that is, after his death. We are then left to conjecture that *his* experience in the jungle is on a different register of embodied consciousness than that of the moviegoer watching *The Thin Red Line.* As a result, we are led to conclude that the representation of war (even combat) can be sublime for *viewers* since we are brought up close, face-to-face, with the force and effect of war—the bullets, the blood, the pain, the hunger, the longing, the loss—and yet are physically left as we were found. What has changed, or may have changed, is our understanding of war as a projected scene of strife and annihilation. We have, in short, been "moved" (in Kant's parlance); we find that our feel or feelings [*Gefühl*] for war has/have altered because of our intimacy with its representation on film; Kant cites one's experience of tragedy as stirring the person—allowing him to be "gently moved"—to feel "the dignity of his own nature."[73] Herzog's harrowing—terrifying—depictions of escape from a POW camp in *Little Dieter* and *Rescue Dawn* engage Kant's "terrifying sublime" (for the viewer) since we see the escapees summiting a mountain only to face a vast expanse of "inescapable" jungle: this is a moment of awe and terror for the viewer, one that agitates an awareness of one's deepest *human* nature. This insight is possible in part because, in Edmund Burke's description, one has experienced something "analogous to terror."[74]

Yet there is something suspicious about this attempt to read Kant's terrifying sublime in the context of war and war films, since it seems to miss or misrepresent what appears to be the genuine experience of *a* sublime that happens both for soldiers in combat (and prisoners of war) *and* those who look upon the representations of those experiences (as depicted on film, or as they are characterized in literature). We need, therefore, a way to speak about what the literal act of genuine danger (for soldiers) and the figurative acts of filmic representation (for viewers) stimulate. Perhaps the resolution is as simple as dividing Kant's terrifying sublime from the proposed humanistic sublime—to affirm, at last, that though they may share points of resemblance, they are distinct. As war so often brings its combatants to the boundary of (actual not imagined) nonexistence, so accomplished war films bring viewers to the (terrifying but not dangerous) point of contemplation of the humanistic sublime. For after all, it is the human encounter with its own limits—coming right up to the edge of ultimate and unredeemable erasure—that becomes the terrifying fact for the soldier. And the viewer might be said to participate in a recognition of this fact. The soldier lives a sort of perpetual death shudder, always aware that by the hand of another agent (usually another anonymous soldier, a manned vehicle or craft, an unmanned drone dropping ordnance, or a strategically placed improvised explosive device), or some other contingency (including "friendly fire"), he might not return home. The viewer becomes sensitive to or empathically aware of this life lived at the limit. The emotional or cognitive effect of these states of mind—at times trancelike, at other points dreamlike, at still others a sort of enhanced perspicacity—is a discernment of the grave nature of human corporeality. In effect, war films remind viewers that there may be no escape from the enemy, or no way to dodge the bullet once it has been released from its chamber. When a war film becomes an allegory for some kind of mortal struggle—to love, to live, to survive—it activates a viewer's sense of the humanistic sublime.

Herzog is known for films featuring nature prominently and has explicitly addressed his motivation for this representation as having to do with the affective presence of our natural condition—not, for example, to celebrate nature as such. In the documentary *To the Limit—And Then beyond It,* Herzog replied pointedly: "Someone once called me a nature lover. Just because I'd filmed in the rainforest or desert. But ultimately this is completely wrong. Actually I think that nature is stupid and obscene."[75] In his war films, for example, the presence of nature is highlighted almost as a third aspect of war (one's side, the enemy's side, and nature—variously for or against). Nature conceals the soldier from the enemy (camouflage) but may as easily leave him stranded and starving—exposed to the elements or the sights of enemy guns. And yet even with a robust focus on nature's role in human affairs—especially during wartime, Herzog's war films push the sublime in the direction of our consideration of human life, human dignity, and the peculiarity of humanity more generally (e.g., in relation with or opposition to nature).

One way to make these claims about the meaning and relevance of ecstatic truth more concrete is by considering Herzog's contempt for the blasé sentimentalism of generic pathos regarding nature. For instance, in *Conquest of the Useless,* Herzog's journal written during the making of *Fitzcarraldo,* he writes at odds with the customary, unqualified applause for nature and its workings: "In its all-encompassing, massive misery, of which it has no knowledge and no hint of a notion, the mighty jungle stood completely still for another night, which, however, true to its innermost nature, it did not let pass unused for incredible destruction, incredible strangulation."[76] He conveyed a similar sentiment in an articulate but apparently off-the-cuff soliloquy about the jungle featured in *Burden of Dreams:* "Nature here is vile and base. I wouldn't see anything erotical here. I would see fornication and asphyxiation and choking and fight for survival and growing and just rotting away. . . . Taking a close look at—at what's around us there—there is some sort of a harmony. It is the harmony of overwhelming and collective murder. And we in comparison to the articulate vileness and baseness and obscenity of all this jungle. . . . We have to get acquainted to this idea that there is no real harmony as we have conceived it."[77] Many years later in *Grizzly Man* (2005)—far from the jungle, in the midst of a vast arctic wilderness—Herzog offered another counternarrative (this time presented in voice-over) about nature, maintaining a strict antisentimental, anti-anthropomorphic relation to its form and features. Herzog no doubt is drawn to Treadwell's film footage because it contains "human ecstasies," but these are rude and rough effects of time spent in the unforgiving wilderness. Echoing his earlier remarks, Herzog says the fundamental characteristic of the universe is not "harmony but chaos, hostility, and murder." When Timothy Treadwell looks into the eyes of the grizzly, he sees a "friend," a cuddly teddy bear, even a "savior," but Herzog by contrast sees only an agent of death: "What haunts me," Herzog confides, "is that in all the faces of all the bears that Treadwell ever filmed, I discover no kinship, no understanding, no mercy. I see only the overwhelming indifference of nature. To me, there is no such thing as a secret world of the bears. And this blank stare speaks only of a half-bored interest in food."[78]

And yet, while Herzog continually reminds us of, and remains adamant about, the depravity and indifference of nature, he also amplifies our proximity to the strange fact of the human presence in nature. For example, in *Cave of Forgotten Dreams* (2010) the revelation of a man's handprint that includes a crooked pinky finger radically reinforces the particularity of this prehistoric man so much so that we are tempted to include him *in* human history. The man with the crooked finger is not an anonymous ancient cave dweller but comes alive as an instance of situated, individuated human consciousness and intentionality—and at that, offering a certain resonance with a contemporary notion of an independent installation artist or muralist. Suddenly the Chauvet painter is not a transitional figure between animal and human but human in fact, a proto-Michelangelo or -Giotto.

Our distance in time from the inhabitants of the Chauvet cave is collapsed in the moment we see its paintings or hold up our hands for comparison. Likewise, filmic depictions of war—ancient or not—draw us very intimately into its tremulous energy. Even as protected voyeurs we are, in a sense, subjecting ourselves to the extremes of human experience. By way of film, we go into combat by proxy—and yet (or for that reason) we walk out of combat unharmed. Still, we are not unaffected. The degree to which we are *moved*—in *feeling* and *understanding* in Kant's lexicon—registers the way ecstatic truth transforms our encounter with cinematic representations; they do have an effect—not the soldier's bloody or cognitive wound but the invitation to fathom his humanity, and ours. In Kant, we find the crucial link between the ability to experience the sublime and the ability to grasp human dignity.[79] In effect, an apprehension of sublimity is a sign of one's capacity to perceive the worth of human beings. Paradoxically, then, an encounter with a natural or "inhuman" landscape (whether it be a jungle or a mountain top, a vast ocean or an arctic expanse) can instigate a feeling of or for humanity. And the combat zone—a man-made condition, always immanent in some natural context, lying at one extreme of human creation—may be similarly generative of such recognition. For these reasons, I contend that Herzog's war films—and many of his other works of documentary and fiction—draw on the same insight: *Little Dieter* and *Rescue Dawn,* among others, are films that put the viewer in a position to experience the sublime by means of ecstatic truth *in order to* appreciate and apprehend the strangeness—and therefore the value—of human life.

The symbiotic connection between ecstatic truth and a perception of humanness (in its variability and peculiarity) is precisely why Herzog defiantly pursues the manifestation of truth through fabrication—instead of the presentation of truth through documentary pieces of evidence and the delivery of facts. Herzog is a poet-filmmaker who falsifies in order to give us truth, and in so doing he "consciously muddle[s] that classic distinction between narrative and non-narrative form";[80] he eschews the "accountant's truth" because it does not bring us face-to-face (as voyeurs, as adventurers, as rogues, as mortals) with the limits of experience—the very limits that become the conditions for the revelation of the humanistic sublime.

Sincere, not Cynical Images

Some viewers might take Herzog's solicitation for ecstatic truth as part of some quasi-mystical or pseudo-religious ambition. And in recent years, as Herzog's fame continues to spread and his persona becomes more prominent—especially in the form of voice-overs that may seem increasingly sententious—his work has become the subject of parody; as a result, speculation may rise whether *his own* films are parodic. It is precisely because Herzog does so much of his own voice-over that *he* is vulnerable to attack from those who hear his voice as an indication of parody or play. The empirical Herzog and the filmic Herzog coalesce in the sound of his voice—its particular tones, rhythms, accents, and so forth—so he leaves himself open to skeptical or cynical critics.

A viewer may wonder if, for example, in his films Herzog is satirizing religious experience. Is he playing a gag on a postmodern capitalist society that appears to have no fixed commitments to divine reality? Yet as early as *Fata Morgana*, then with the hypnotized actors of *Heart of Glass*, importantly in *Bells from the Deep: Faith and Superstition in Russia* (1993), and onward into the meditations present in more recent films such as *Cave of Forgotten Dreams*, *Happy People: A Year in the Taiga* (2010), and *Into the Abyss* (2011), Herzog has long appeared to be engaged in the attempt to conjure a kind of religious experience: where mirage or mysticism or hallucination gives rise to clarity, where facing the absurdities, incongruities, and enigmas present in nature and mortality, humans become their most vulnerable. (Of course, all the while fabricating the "documentary" material to suit the expression of ecstatic truth.) While fine scholars such Alan Singer have suggested that Herzog's is an "ironic sublime," I think there is good reason to resist what might be cynical readings of Herzog's work. That is not to say we must suppress or deny a sense of humor about his films, especially since they are often extremely funny. But our principal mode of engagement with them should not be undertaken as if these works were produced by Christopher

Guest (*This Is Spinal Tap!* [1984], *Waiting for Guffman* [1996], *Best in Show* [2000]) and other mockumentarians, but rather by a visionary whose grand schemes and interventions are meant to prompt our insight into human desires, human aspirations, and human dignity. Herzog's work should not, I think, be dismissed as pretentious art films nor as playful and sometimes caustic amusements about human folly, since their primary mode of address is the proximate experiences of human life as transformed through grand, alien, and uncanny figures, scenarios, and landscapes.

I can neither claim that Herzog intends the kinds of effects I describe nor prove that Herzog's films have these effects on viewers. But I think there is evidence that the accumulated body of his images entails that he does not set out to mock or otherwise satirize his subjects—whether they are people or landscapes. If Herzog wanted to ridicule his subjects, for example, he would aim for as much objectivity as possible; he would, in short and with sincerity, adopt the routine and rhetoric of cinéma vérité. Instead of revealing a genuine interest in what people say and do (even if he sometimes feeds them lines and directs their actions), he would instead set them up for exposure and embarrassment. We have seen this approach adopted in extremis by Sacha Baron Cohen (*Borat* [2006] and *Brüno* [2009]). While Herzog could surely mock the authentic or found nature of the people he finds, he goes radically in the other direction and boldly, willfully, provocatively flaunts the fabricated nature of his films. Take, for example, his stunt in *Bells from the Deep:* "I wanted to get shots of pilgrims crawling around on the ice trying to catch a glimpse of the lost city, but as there were no pilgrims around I hired two drunks from the next town and put them on the ice. One of them has his face right on the ice and looks like he is in very deep meditation. The accountant's truth: he was completely drunk and fell asleep, and we had to wake him at the end of the take."[81] But the ecstatic truth is wholly different: not a portrait of soporific inebriation but of men seeking the reality of myth, the power of faith. Consequently, and quite consequentially, by aiming to reveal ecstatic truth, Herzog makes his subjects, in effect, immune from satire. Since they are not on display—not there to give up the literal truth of the situation—they are no longer subjects who can be investigated. Instead, the films become imagined expressions, some version or vision that Herzog has invented.

When we look at Herzog's treatment of landscapes, the situation is the same. Whether drawing on the innovative Dutch painter Hercules Seghers, the German romantic tradition in painting, or the *Heimatfilm* tradition in Germany (e.g., as seen in *Heart of Glass* and *The Great Ecstasy of the Woodcarver Steiner*), Herzog creates images of landscapes that resist our condescension to them. The images of mountains, fog, mirages, jungles, deserts, rivers, oceans, ice, and caves are offered as invitations to make oneself available to them—trying, in effect, to see what can be seen; allowing oneself to be affected by them. In this respect, it is the image itself that is communicating, not Herzog-as-auteur. And it is precisely in that framing—of landscape directed to human perception and sentiment—that we may contemplate how filmed (that is, represented) landscapes may kindle the humanistic sublime in the viewer.

The Effects of Regressive Irony

Earlier I noted Herzog's self-described inability to understand irony. Whether or not this is true, there is a kind of irony that usefully contextualizes the achievements of Herzog's *films,* namely, an irony that is, in effect, suited for someone who is sincere in his effort to create and emphasize the image itself. Timothy Corrigan has called it "regressive irony."[82] I think there is good reason to appropriate Corrigan's attribution of regressive irony in Herzog's work as a way of explaining the effectiveness with which Herzog's images—expressed through his films—establish the conditions for an experience of the sublime in viewers, in particular the humanistic sublime I have described. "This kind of irony," Corrigan notes, "would align Herzog with other contemporary directors like Terrence Malick, Chantal Ackerman, or Nagisa Oshima who each in their very different ways have attempted to move beyond the literary irony of Godard and others using irony to reconstruct images as significance." According to Corrigan, Herzog and the others "juggle and undermine a variety of points of view, human and non-human alike, so that the stability of any perspective gives way to the indeterminate point of view of the physical image in and of itself" and thereby achieves the eponymous "regression": "Like the child's sense that the physical world is all an imagistic extension of self, this narrative and imagistic irony becomes a 'regression' in that the material presence of the image moves to usurp the symbolic, socially determined distinctions of any single perspective."[83] This is, to use Herzog's own description, not very French, and certainly not cynical. Herzog's work, instead, appears not only to court an anti-auteurist effect (by displacing the fantasy of the director-as-sole-creator with "intentions") but also to invoke and invite from the audience a kind of prelinguistic and prehistorical perspective—something that will situate the viewer at his or her "interpretive limits and capacity." As Corrigan continues, "the difficult irony implicit in this action is that it forces perceptual desire to confront its real object—the unsocialized acquisition of the world as material image, not language." When Corrigan describes the effect of regressive irony on the audience, he seems to presage the way Herzog's films create the conditions for an encounter with the humanistic sublime: regressive irony "works to place the spectator on the edge or at the brink of an acquisition of the world through images themselves."[84] Where the cinematic irony of the nouvelle vague and neorealists encouraged viewers to look away from the film to find meaning, Herzog wants the images themselves to captivate and hold the viewer's attention. *Fata Morgana* begins with airplanes landing on a tarmac serially. Depending on whether the regressive irony takes effect, a viewer will either become hypnotized by the images—and therefore availed of them so that the ecstatic truth or the humanistic sublime may dawn—or, instead, look around nervously wondering if he is the subject of a psychological experiment or a practical joke.

It is in the context of works that possess or court regressive irony that we can appreciate Herzog's oft-quoted comment that "film is not the art of scholars, but of illiterates."[85] The temptation is to read this as a critique of academics—perhaps to overlook that he says "of scholars" and *not* "for scholars," in effect to say cinema is not available for the kind of analysis scholars want to give it, or make of it. Yet Herzog does not claim that film is anti-intellectual, but that it has the capacity—when the images are powerful enough—to be *pre*-intellectual. That is, film—in its visceral, visual movements—has the power to summon primal, instinctive, intuitive truths. So when Herzog says, "We have to articulate ourselves, otherwise we would be cows in the field," he does not mean by way of linguistic invention, but instead by the fabrication of new images—images that might penetrate *through* our linguistic apparatus and the mass of "worn-out images" that surround, numb, and distract us.[86] Herzog is, as he says, perpetually "searching for a new grammar of images."[87]

Regressive irony offers a different relationship with and to spectacle. The film image is no longer a place to get lost, but a place to see something on its own terms. In that mood of availability to the visual, of exposure to the perceived image, one gains orientation, one is free to fear the rapture of imagistic possibilities and allow that influence to shape one's understanding of existence. With Herzog, the transformation of spectacle from a moment of distancing or distracting (that makes the phenomenon allergic or other than itself) into a moment of intimacy (where the viewer feels implicated, mesmerized, summoned, even seduced) can happen in scenes of oral storytelling such as when Dengler narrates his experience after his dear friend Dwayne was beheaded in front of him. Sitting on the bank of the Mekong River—no professional actor, no majestic landscape, and no computer-generated imagery in sight—Dengler tells his tale of coming to the limit, facing his own death, living on the very precipice of annihilation: "I couldn't care less if I would live or die. But then, later on there was this bear—this beautiful bear that was following me. It was circling me. . . . Of course I knew this bear was there: he was waiting to eat me. [Pausing, welling up] When I think about it, this bear meant death to me. It is really ironic that the only friend I had at the end was death."[88] Thus we have Dengler's bear and Treadwell's bear and Herzog's bear—all staring at us—and we have to know what to make of these encounters and these options for thinking. As spectators, the way we look at looking—in these parables of the face-to-face, or the face-to-film—is telling.

When Dengler calls his experience "ironic," it is a regressive irony—an irony that returns him to the fundamental gift of the extreme proximity to death he experienced eye-to-eye with the patient, hungry bear. As *Little Dieter* begins with an epigraph from Revelation 9:6, stating "And in those days shall men seek death, and shall not find it; and shall desire to die, and death shall flee from them," and as Herzog concludes the film paraphrasing Dengler—"Death did not want him"—Dengler's tale continually confronts the viewer with the fact of his survival.[89] That is a fact in the accountant's sense: he survived. But how he survived, and what it meant to see Dwayne beheaded, requires an orientation to the ecstatic truth. Dengler did not ask to be sent to the limit of human existence—neither to hallucinate, to see mirages, to have dreams, to suffer nightmares, nor to bleed, starve, and be tortured and humiliated—but his account of his ordeal, regardless of his intent, kindles a fundamental encounter with the humanistic sublime. The viewer is, in Dengler's company, changed from voyeur to vicarious victim. In the safety of our seats, we nevertheless have gone some distance toward ourselves—in our shared humanity—have seen and suffered, in our minds, the trial Dengler narrates.

What exactly is the meaning of the protracted reenactment of Dengler's captivity in a prisoner-of-war camp? Why did Herzog put Dengler through this revisitation, this reliving? Dengler clearly seems upset by the reenactment (it is, for him, "too close to home"), but for Herzog and his viewers, the return to the jungle—Dengler's presence, frame after frame—antagonizes his seemingly assured death in Laos. Just like the stockpiles of food in his California home, and the paintings of open doors, Dengler's very existence creates a mood of wonder in the audience. How is it possible to endure this kind of torture *and* survive it? The wonder is further intensified by a kind of bracketing that creates the illusion that having once survived, Dengler has forever survived; living becomes a transcendental achievement akin to resurrection. These are not phenomena that can fit into the accountant's ledger.

One instance of regressive irony that emerges when watching either *Little Dieter* or *Rescue Dawn,* but especially when they are seen in tandem, is the inversion of positions occupied by Dengler. When he was a child, perhaps five years old, he watched as his small Bavarian town was bombed. Dengler himself recounts the formative quality of this raid, especially seeing a pilot up close: "From that moment on, little Dieter needed to fly." His desire to fly seems to have obscured the fact—even to him, as he does not mention what seems to be a paradox or a complication worthy of note—that as a pilot himself, he has been sent to bomb small towns in Laos, home to small children looking out windows at fighter planes. Of course, Dengler only has a chance to unleash a few bombs before he is returned to his former, childhood status as under attack, this time as a combatant behind enemy lines, and soon after as a prisoner. Once again, the planes fly overhead and become a sight for fear and hope; once again, they are objects of threat and salvation. Dengler's authenticator name was "Rescue Dawn," a time of day associated with the natural sublime but also a state of affairs—the need for rescue—that reaches back to his childhood in Bavaria. Since Dengler survived four plane crashes *after* his escape from the Laotian camp, the theme and the structure of this relationship lingers throughout his mature life.[90]

Thinking of the empirical or historical Dengler and *Little Dieter* (as a vision or version of his story), we see how both of these bodies (one of a man, the other of a film) antagonize *Rescue Dawn,* the feature film made almost a decade later starring Hollywood star Christian Bale in the lead. We are familiar with the frequent announcement "based on a true story" (a disclosure meant to heighten the viewer's perception of referentiality—and authenticity) and yet with professional actors and modes of showing (instead of telling or narrating) Dengler's story, the filmic representation operates in an alternate register. *Rescue Dawn* reveals different attributes of Dengler's story: not his (true) experience, but instead the way in which fiction-*based-on*-fact is necessarily a kind of dream. Reenactment does not mean re-creation, but something more like an *invocation:* as if summoning a spirit, mood, or phantasm. Viewers do not see Dengler's life on-screen; they see an apparition of it. This is movie-watching as a willingness to be haunted.

The Dream of Humans

In a speech given after a screening of *Lessons of Darkness,* Herzog spoke in a Heideggerian vein about the nature of truth—yet with his films as illustrations, the sentiment of his remarks was directed to the nature of cinema as well:

> Nor is the Greek word for truth, *alêtheia,* simple to grasp. Etymologically speaking, it comes from the verb *lanthanein,* "to hide," and the related word *lêthos,* "the hidden," "the concealed." *A-lêtheia* is, therefore, a form of negation, a negative definition: it is the "not-hidden," the revealed, the truth. Thinking through language [*im sprachlichen Denken*], the Greeks meant, therefore, to define truth as an act of disclosure—a gesture related to the cinema, where an object is set into the light and then a latent, not yet visible image is conjured onto celluloid, where it first must be developed, then disclosed.[91]

Herzog's (purportedly unrehearsed, improvised) excursus suggests how the cinematic medium itself is a form of "disclosure" and thus a participant in or a condition for truth (*alêtheia*). If cinematic reality has been likened to a dream—that is, a conjuring trick humans have invented to entertain the senses beyond their limits, into the realm of the sublime—is it possible that truth itself is a human dream? And by relation, or implication, could the very notion of the *human* be part of this vision—a dream only humans can have, a kind of hallucination in itself?

Herzog has noted how the erosion of the foundations of civilization "means that human dignity has also been destroyed" and by extension "that people's dreams have been destroyed."[92] If we cannot dream, it would seem, we cannot be human (or at least humans with dignity). Herzog counters the destruction by invoking film, for cinema is "something that can make our dreams whole again."[93] Cinema may be an ephemeral trick of light, but it is also a substantive support to—even creator of—human dignity.

In film after film, and especially in his war films, Herzog appears to transcend the human in order to become cognizant of it, to create a cinema of dreams in which the human makes its appearance in the form of absence or eradication or threatened disappearance; one might go so far as to describe this approach as the mission of ecstatic truth. If literalness precludes a sense of irony, then it also seems to give rise to an awareness of human existence: what is literally there before us, as us. But direct approaches to the presiding state of affairs are compromised by habit, ritual, and the blindness that derives from familiarity. We often do not see what is always already before our eyes. Hence Herzog's turn to fiction, fabrication, dreams, as a means for attuning us to the peculiarity of the ordinary, including the brash but often occluded fact (and delayed promise) of eternal nonexistence. Among other topics or themes, Herzog has found that exploring life lived at the limits—such as we regularly encounter in war between humans, or war between man and nature—we are given dreams to consider, dreams that define and enrich human consciousness and identity. Herzog's dogged pursuit of limits, and those who share his passion for them, has given us filmic evidence for the manner in which the sublime is a way of amplifying, not diminishing, one's sense of humanness.

Herzog's films, including and especially his war films, direct us to our world, though often by making that world strange, or estranging it from us. After all, Herzog contends that "film is not analysis, it is agitation of mind."[94] We could at least say that an encounter with *Herzogian* cinema should not be sought as a confirmation of what we already know or believe, but instead faced as if addressing a foreign being, or entering an unfamiliar land. We become alienated. We become aliens. Herzog's methodology—liberated from any fastidious loyalty to the accountant's truth—invents worlds from the traumas and terrors that surround us. Searching for an exemplification of such invention, Herzog invokes the circus as the "one place left where you find artists."[95] Like a circus performer himself, Herzog challenges conventional (especially cinematically conventional) notions of narrative, genre, character, causation, and consecutive logic. If he is, then, a bit of a circus performer (an assignation he would likely feel complimented by and proud of), we might attend to the capacity his films possess for shining a spotlight on the exotic aspects of the everyday—often through acts of fabrication—holding up odd creations for our reflection, as we might encounter them at a circus. In the way we become caught up in the artifice of magic and science fiction, so we should, along these lines, also confirm our stupefaction in the human circumstance. By acts of artistry, Herzog creates new relationships to existing phenomena, to immanent life—seemingly weighing each moment with a freshly appointed transcendental significance (as if continuously on the verge of revealing how the trick was achieved and then denying us a glimpse behind the mystery). One may be justified in seeing such circuslike artistry-of-agitation-and-awe as part of his initiative to "create images"—since the prevailing images we live with are "tired," or we are tired of them. After all, these tired images do not stimulate our thinking about our human predicament but leave us complacent about it, or worse, indifferent to it.

Coming to a close, then, I can summarize what should be obvious by now, and hopefully also granted some measure of credibility: namely, that the aim of this investigation has been to find, by way of Herzog, a pathway for considering seriously, though without sanctimoniousness, the recovery and rehabilitation of the notion of the humanistic sublime, and therefore to resist Thomas Weiskel's dismissal of the term and its referents (noted at the outset of the essay). Though Herzog does not theorize as I have, he has articulated in several ways—in his films, in his writing, and in his remarks at sessions of the Rogue Film School—an approach to cinematic creation that would appear to lend itself, and offer credence to, the revitalized and even invigorated notion of the humanistic sublime.

Herzog being "profoundly unreconciled to nature" means that he continually figures the human as a measure apart from or allergic to total natural reality.[96] We exist in nature *differently* from natural things, perhaps strictly because we can fathom a conscious relation to—or alienation from—nature. Consequently, with Herzog's films, we discover at once the human capacity to perceive this lack of reconciliation—perpetually invoked as a version of the question "What's this war in nature?"—and to acknowledge this awareness as a point of human distinction from nature. The human is, then, simultaneously special and irrelevant. In the tension of this double status, we apprehend what animates Herzog's war films and confirms how the humanistic sublime is not just nonoxymoronic, but also profoundly salient.

Notes

I dedicate this essay, in loving memory, to two World War II veterans: U.S. Army Master Sergeant and Warrant Officer Earl C. LaRocca (1921–2010), a battalion sergeant major of the 78th Lightning Division and a recipient of the Bronze Star; and U.S.

Army Air Corps Staff Sergeant Nassea Hodge (1924–1992), held captive by Nazis as a prisoner of war at Stalag 398 Wels, Austria, and later a recipient of the Purple Heart.

1. Thomas Weiskel, *The Romantic Sublime: Studies in the Structure and the Psychology of Transcendence* (Baltimore: Johns Hopkins University Press, 1976), 3.

2. Werner Herzog, *Herzog on Herzog,* ed. Paul Cronin (New York: Faber and Faber, 2002; revised and expanded second edition, 2014, bearing the revised and expanded title *Werner Herzog: A Guide for the Perplexed: Conversations with Paul Cronin*). I cite both editions and indicate which version I draw from; in this case, the 2nd ed., chap. 1.

3. *Herzog on Herzog,* from the introduction to the 2nd ed.

4. From notes taken during Herzog's Rogue Film School, July 2010; see also *Herzog on Herzog,* 2nd ed., chap. 7.

5. *Herzog on Herzog,* 2nd ed., preface.

6. See, most famously, Caspar David Friedrich's *Wanderer above the Sea of Fog* (1818), but also *Woman before the Rising Sun (Woman before the Setting Sun)* (1818–1820) and *Moonrise (Two Men on the Shore)* (1835–1837).

7. See *Little Dieter Needs to Fly* (1997) and remarks by Dieter Dengler in his *Escape from Laos* (San Rafael, CA: Presidio Press, 1979). The notion of nature- or jungle-as-enemy appears in other war films, e.g., *The Pacific* (2010; E2: 00:01:35).

8. "For all its horror, you can't help but gape at the awful majesty of combat," Tim O'Brien writes in "How to Tell a True War Story": "You admire the fluid symmetries of troops on the move, the harmonies of sound and shape and proportion, the great sheets of metal-fire streaming down from a gunship, the illumination rounds, the white phosphorous, the purply orange glow of napalm, the rocket's red glare. . . . It's astonishing. It fills the eye. It commands you. You hate it, yes, but your eyes do not." But this "awful majesty" does not allow for a dispassionate or disinterested perspective; the "awe" of the "awful" is not in any way privileged or protected. The soldier may experience the penetrating effects of a firsthand reality, but the vitality of the impression must be linked with the very *real* threat to his life. Thus, this is an *awful* majesty, not a sublime one." Tim O'Brien, *The Things They Carried* (New York: Penguin, 1990), 87.

9. Brad Prager, "Werner Herzog's Companions: The Consolation of Images," in *A Companion to Werner Herzog,* ed. Brad Prager (Oxford: Wiley-Blackwell, 2012), 3.

10. *To the Limit—And Then Beyond It: The Ecstatic World of Filmmaker Werner Herzog* [*Bis ans Ende—und dann noch weiter: Die estatische Welt des Filmemachers Werner Herzog*] (Peter Buchka, 1989), 00:11:01.

11. Ibid., 00:11:31.

12. Ibid., 00:23:04.

13. *La Soufrière: Waiting for an Inevitable Disaster* (Werner Herzog, 1997).

14. *To the Limit,* 00:17:10.

15. See Immanuel Kant, *Observations on the Feeling of the Beautiful and Sublime,* trans. John T. Goldthwait (Berkeley: University of California Press, 1960, 1991); and Friedrich Schiller, *On the Sublime* (1801), trans. Julius Elias (New York: Ungar, 1966).

16. *To the Limit,* 00:22:40.

17. Grazia Paganelli, *Ecstasy and Truth* (Munich: Goethe Institut, 2010), 102.

18. Herzog, "Minnesota Declaration," in *Herzog on Herzog,* 1st ed., 301.

19. "Abbas Kiarostami: Biography," Zeitgeist Films: The Spirit of the Times, zeitgeistfilms.com.

20. *Close-Up* (Abbas Kiarostami, 1990).

21. *Herzog on Herzog,* 2nd ed., chap. 8.

22. *Close-Up.*

23. Paganelli, *Ecstasy and Truth,* 89.

24. *Herzog on Herzog,* 2nd ed., introduction.

25. Ibid., chap. 8.

26. Stanley Cavell, *The Claim of Reason: Wittgenstein, Skepticism, Morality, and Tragedy* (New York: Oxford University Press, 1979), 207.

27. Stanley Cavell, *This New Yet Unapproachable America* (Albuquerque: Living Batch Press, 1989), 57. See also Cavell, *Must We Mean What We Say?* (Cambridge: Cambridge University Press, 1969, 1979), 96; Cavell, *The Claim of Reason,* 206–7; and Cavell, *Emerson's Transcendental Etudes,* ed. David Justin Hodge (Stanford, CA: Stanford University Press, 2003), 23, 58, and especially 252–53n3.

28. James Conant, "An Interview with Stanley Cavell," in *The Senses of Stanley Cavell,* ed. Richard Fleming and Michael Payne (Cranbury, NJ: Associated University Presses, 1989), 50. See also Richard Eldridge, "Introduction: Between Acknowledgment and Avoidance," in *Stanley Cavell* (Cambridge: Cambridge University Press, 2003), 4; and Richard Eldridge and Bernie Rhie, eds., *Stanley Cavell and Literary Studies: Consequences of Skepticism* (New York: Continuum, 2011), 5.

29. *Herzog on Herzog,* 2nd ed., chap. 11.

30. Charles Darwin, *On the Origin of Species by Means of Natural Selection or the Preservation of Favoured Races in the Struggle for Life* (London: Grant Richards, 1902), 67, 71, 73, 80, 441.

31. Paul Virilio, *War and Cinema: The Logistics of Perception* (New York: Verso, 1989), 1, 5. Originally published in 1984.

32. Compare a contemporary war increasingly defined by aerial drone attacks (where virtual and real scenarios on-screen resemble one another) with the very urgent and undeniable fact of embodied immediacy in what may be called "traditional" combat, namely, the way this particular man is killing this other particular man—as presented, for example, in the stabbing scenes in *Saving Private Ryan* (Steven Spielberg, 1998) and *Coriolanus* (Ralph Fiennes, 2011); and similar agonizing intimacies in *All Quiet on the Western Front* (Lewis Milestone, 1930). The face-to-face nature of such combat is something that cinema has long been both focused on for dramatic purposes and uniquely successful in depicting.

33. Virilio, *War and Cinema,* 3.

34. Ibid., 2.

35. See Virilio, *War and Cinema;* Joshua Gooch's essay in this volume; and *Eagle Eye* (D. J. Caruso, 2008).

36. Simon Morley, ed., *The Sublime* (Cambridge, MA: MIT Press, with Whitechapel Gallery, 2010), 16.

37. Ibid., 16.

38. *Imaginary Witness: Hollywood and the Holocaust* (Daniel Anker, 2004), 01:28:04–29.

39. Paul Fussell, *The War* (Ken Burns, 2007), part 4, 00:15:08.

40. Science-fiction treatments of war, such as we find in *Source Code* (Jones, 2011) and *Oblivion* (Kosinski, 2013), have explored what it means to die once, often through the conceit of dying more than once—serially, in repetition. See also *Edge of Tomorrow* (Liman, 2014), the tagline for which is "Live. Die. Repeat."

41. See Werner Herzog's exhibit "Hearsay of the Soul" on Hercules Seghers, in the 2012 Whitney Bienniel, a work he created in collaboration with composer Ernst Reijseger. See also *Herzog on Herzog,* 1st ed., 136–37; and the short stories and plays of Georg Büchner, such as *Lenz* (1835) and *Woyzeck* (1837), in *Complete Plays, Lenz and Other Writings,* trans. John Reddick (New York: Penguin, 1993).

42. Longinus, *On the Sublime,* 36.3.

43. Along similar lines, Timothy Corrigan writes: "[Herzog's] characters, like his films, are again and again drawn to the powers of language as a vehicle for dramatizing, producing, and communicating their desires, but, at the same time, they are revolted, like Kaspar Hauser before Lord Stanhope, before language's murderously reductive properties." Timothy Corrigan, ed., *The Films of Werner Herzog* (New York: Methuen, 1986), 16.

44. Morley, *The Sublime,* 16.

45. Fredric Jameson, "War and Representation," in this volume.

46. *Herzog on Herzog,* 2nd ed., chap. 8.

47. *Herzog on Herzog,* 1st ed., 81, 136.

48. Samuel Taylor Coleridge, *Biographia Literaria; or, Biographical Sketches of My Literary Life and Opinions* (1817; New York: Leavitt, Lord, 1834), book 12, 144: "But in all ages there have been a few, who measuring and sounding the rivers of the vale at the feet of their furthest inaccessible falls have learned, that the sources must be far higher and far inward; a few, who even in the level streams have detected elements, which neither the vale itself nor the surrounding mountains contained or could supply."

49. Kant, *Observations,* 25.

50. Herzog remarks: "One aspect of who I am that might be important is the communication defect I have had since a young child. I am someone who takes everything very literally. I simply do not understand irony, a defect I have had ever since I was able to think independently. . . . I am just a complete fool. There are things in language that are common to almost everyone, but that are utterly lost on me. . . . And compared to other filmmakers—particularly the French, who are able to sit around their cafes waxing

eloquent about their work—I am like a Bavarian bullfrog just squatting there brooding. I have never been capable of discussing art with people. I just cannot cope with irony." *Herzog on Herzog,* 1st ed., 26–27. See also Alan Singer, "Comprehending Appearances: Werner Herzog's Ironic Sublime," in *The Films of Werner Herzog: Between Mirage and History,* ed. Timothy Corrigan (New York: Methuen, 1986), chap. 11.

51. Ralph Waldo Emerson, *Journals of Ralph Waldo Emerson,* ed. Edward Waldo Emerson and Waldo Emerson Forbes (Boston: Houghton Mifflin, 1911), vol. 5, 327.

52. Eschewing the theoretical or speculative—in favor of the strictly practical—announces his shift, his adjustment on the English romantic sublime. See, for example, in *Biographia Literaria,* where Coleridge writes: "For, as philosophy is neither a science of the reason or understanding only, nor merely a science of morals, but the science of BEING altogether, its primary ground can be neither merely speculative nor merely practical, but both in one" (book 12, 150).

53. See again the 2012 Whitney Bienniel collaboration between Reijseger and Herzog, "Hearsay of the Soul."

54. Weiskel, *Romantic Sublime,* 5.

55. Ibid., 6.

56. Ibid.

57. Ibid.

58. For more on reenactment in Herzog's work, see Eric Ames, "The Case of Herzog: Re-Opened," in *A Companion to Werner Herzog,* ed. Brad Prager (Oxford: Wiley-Blackwell, 2012), 393–415; and Ames, *Ferocious Reality: Documentary According to Werner Herzog* (Minneapolis: University of Minnesota Press, 2012).

59. Paganelli, *Ecstasy and Truth,* 112.

60. Ibid., 112–13.

61. Herzog, "Minnesota Declaration," in *Herzog on Herzog,* 1st ed., 301.

62. *Herzog on Herzog,* 1st ed., 301.

63. *Rescue Dawn,* 51:44.

64. Ibid., 1:24:40; cf. John 13:16.

65. *Rescue Dawn,* 39:30.

66. *Lessons of Darkness* (Werner Herzog, 1992).

67. Brigette Peucker, "Herzog and Auteurism: Performing Authenticity," in Prager, *Companion to Werner Herzog,* 36–37.

68. *Herzog on Herzog,* 2nd ed., chap. 8.

69. Ibid.

70. *Lessons of Darkness.*

71. These are selected intertitles from *Lessons of Darkness.*

72. Kant, *Observations,* 48–49, 53, 55.

73. Ibid., 52.

74. Edmund Burke, *A Philosophical Enquiry into the Origin of Our Ideas of the Sublime and Beautiful,* ed. Adam Phillips (Oxford: Oxford University Press, 1990), 36.

75. *To the Limit,* 00:45:11.

76. Werner Herzog, *Conquest of the Useless: Reflections from the Making of Fitzcarraldo,* trans. Krishna Winston (New York: Ecco, 2009), 251 (June 1, 1981); originally published as *Der Eroberung des Nutzlosen* (Carl Hanser Verlag, 2004).

77. *Burden of Dreams* (Les Blank, 1982).

78. *Grizzly Man* (Werner Herzog, 2005).

79. Kant, *Observations,* 60.

80. Timothy Corrigan, "Producing Herzog: From a Body of Images," in *Films of Werner Herzog,* 11.

81. *Herzog on Herzog,* 1st ed., 252.

82. Corrigan, *Films of Werner Herzog,* 16, passim 13–16.

83. Ibid., 14–15.

84. Ibid., 15–16.

85. Alan Greenberg, Herbert Achternbusch, and Werner Herzog, *Heart of Glass* (Munich: Skellig, 1976), 174.

86. *Burden of Dreams; Herzog on Herzog,* 1st ed., 66.

87. *Herzog on Herzog,* 2nd ed., chap. 7.

88. *Little Dieter,* 00:57:44.

89. Ibid., 01:05:00; 00:59:40.

90. *Rescue Dawn,* from the intertitle at the end of the film, 02:01:09.

91. Werner Herzog, "On the Absolute, the Sublime, and Ecstatic Truth," trans. Moira Weigel, bu.edu/arion/on-the-absolute-the-sublime-and-ecstatic-truth/.

92. *To the Limit,* 47:04.

93. Ibid., 50:24.

94. *Herzog on Herzog,* 1st ed., 139.

95. Ibid.

96. Herzog, *Conquest of the Useless,* 72 (July 3, 1980).

Acknowledgments

I begin with sincerest gratitude to all the contributors to this volume: their scholarly rigor, coupled with their inventive approaches to a solemn and sensitive topic, has yielded essays of remarkable depth, insight, and sophistication. As a fortunate consequence of their intrepid and compelling investigations, we now possess an invigorating new series of vital, perspicacious, and lasting reflections on war's representation on film. All of the participants have written previously on war or film, and many have generated indispensable works on war films. Needless to say, though it is a delight to express it nevertheless, I am immensely grateful for their generosity with their new work and willingness to share it with the readers of this book.

At the University Press of Kentucky, it is my pleasure to thank, once again, senior editor Anne Dean Dotson and the director of the press, Stephen M. Wrinn, both of whom provided crucial support and knowing guidance throughout the development and production process. Series editor Mark T. Conard has again encouraged work that explores the conditions and terms for philosophical scholarship on film; with extensive experience in the field, he has advocated for another session of dynamic criticism. Also at UPK, I was helpfully assisted by David Cobb, Bailey Johnson, Iris A. Law, Cameron Ludwick, Mack McCormick, Ashley Runyon, and Allison Webster; I am duly humbled by their care with this text.

I extend warm thanks to Fredric Jameson for graciously allowing "War and Representation" to be featured here, a work reprinted with permission from the copyright owner, the Modern Language Association of America, and originally published in *PMLA, Special Topic: War* 124, no. 5 (2009): 1532–47. I express the same grateful tidings to Robert Pippin for offering "Vernacular Metaphysics: On Terrence Malick's *The Thin Red Line*," which appeared in *Critical Inquiry* 39, no. 2 (Winter 2013): 247–75, and is published with permission of the author in the present volume.

I am very appreciative of the many esteemed scholars who offered constructive advice and productive liaising during the development of the volume, in particular: Mieke Bal, Elisabeth Bronfen, Rebecca M. Brown,

Giuliana Bruno, Thanassis Cambanis, Noël Carroll, Stanley Cavell, Timothy Corrigan, William Day, Henry T. Edmondson III, Ian M. Evans, Michael Fried, Tarleton Gillespie, Carolyn Korsmeyer, John Lachs, David Mikics, Lawrence Rhu, D. N. Rodowick, William Rothman, Vivian Sobchack, Garrett Stewart, Bernadette Wegenstein, and Guy Westwell.

Working with filmmakers—several of them with salient contributions to the genre of war films—has been a tremendous satisfaction, an honor, and intellectually enlightening.

I thank Werner Herzog for the invitation to attend Rogue Film School. I am especially grateful for his expansive and incisive reflections on the interrelationship between creating films and thinking about them. Moreover, Herzog's deceptively simple but piercingly profound dictum for filmmakers—"Read, read, read, read, read, read, read, read, read, read, read, read, read. . . . If you don't read, you will never be a filmmaker"—draws meaningful attention to the abiding consanguinity between film and philosophy, film and literature, film and religion, film and the imagination. Herzog's chosen metaphor for the spirit of rogue filmmaking—lock-picking—inspires unpretentious, adaptive, and occasionally transgressive solutions for the onward initiative to make moving images.

I also extend thanks to fellow participants at RFS in whose company I discovered more than a shared admiration for Herzog's work.

Antedating my engagement with Herzog, I was very fortunate to speak with Maureen Gosling (perennial Herzog and Les Blank collaborator), who generously shared remarks on her experiences making documentary films—including her perception that ideas anticipate and underwrite the technical realization of such work and its improvised development. I have Catherine DeSantis to thank for introducing me to Gosling, and for my first screening of *Fitzcarraldo.*

In matters of research, I am particularly obliged to Paul Cronin for extensive, deeply informed reflections on the history of war cinema, and principally for notes on the directorial work of John Huston and George Stevens Jr. and the cinematography of Janusz Kaminski; kindly allowing me access to the revised and expanded second edition of *Herzog on Herzog,* a forbearance that allowed me the privilege of citing from new and revised text ahead of its publication; generously sharing with me his unmatched knowledge of Werner Herzog's films and related Herzogiana; reading an earlier version of my essay on Herzog's war films (from his comments I gleaned many valuable cues and connections); welcoming me to his workshop on

Aristotle's *Poetics* and Alexander Mackendrick's craft of filmmaking at the City College of New York; and, regarding all this material, occasion, and otherwise, conversations with him were a pleasure and proved invaluable for giving shape and meaning to the essay I contribute to this volume and the project as a whole.

Owing to the propitious conditions of the Signet Society at Harvard, and in recent years the kind and continuing warm welcomes from Mark Hruby, I have benefited from numerous conversations with visiting artists, actors, writers, and filmmakers. For the present occasion, I thank Edward Zwick in particular for his informed and candid reminiscences on the experience of making films, some of them indelible war films; and Sanford R. Climan for directing my attention to several essential war films, and remarks on the work of, and working with, Michael Mann.

I appreciate the collaboration and mentorship of cinematographer Robert Elfstrom—from workshop to shooting in the field—and drew singular inspiration from his remarkable *Vietnam's Unseen War: Pictures from the Other Side;* director William Jersey, whose approach to filmmaking has been instrumental to my thinking on documentary films and attempts to make them, from his Academy Award–nominated *A Time for Burning* to *Eames: The Architect & the Painter;* and, more recently, director J. Mitchell Johnson for a fecund series of conversations about discerning a story and putting it on film. I also drew much from discussions with director Michael Wadleigh, whose critical acumen about the making and meaning of motion pictures remains for me a constructive agitation.

The composition of this volume coincided with my term as Fellow at the Moving Picture Institute in New York. I am grateful to the members of the foundation, especially Erin O'Connor and Maurice Black, for promoting worthwhile connections with other filmmakers, and to those filmmakers for thoughtful remarks and field-tested ideas about documentary practice and the art of war films.

I am indebted to the generosity and talent of filmmakers Tom Small and Angela Small of Joule Q, and James Fitzgerald Jr. of ColdWater Media.

With regard to the conspicuous interrelationship between war films and image-making in the context of war, I acknowledge with gratitude the participants of "War Photography," a conference held in Washington, D.C., October 30 through November 2, 2008, that I developed, convened, and directed for Liberty Fund. In addition to the invigorating proceedings, full of conducive remarks on the representation of war, I am grateful for follow-up conversations and correspondences in the intervening years with Joel Bettridge, Richard Deming, Nick Gillespie, Daniel Austin Green, Peter Mentzel, Michael Valdez Moses, and Alessandro Subrizi.

Photographers who helped me think through the relationship between the still and the moving image as it relates to the representation of war include Diane Bush (for comments on the interaction between photography and advocacy) and Donna Ferrato (especially her candid recollections of the life and work of Philip Jones Griffiths). John Opera has been a cherished interlocutor on photography for as long as I can remember believing it was important to have opinions on the subject, and he continues to inspire me through his thinking on the medium and the creation of his own work—an artistic practice so often conducted at the very limit of photography's domain and definition. A conversation over many years with Julian Hibbard, much of it undertaken in the context of his writing "'Why Don't You See Me, I'm Here': Haunting Visions of War in Elem Klimov's *Come and See*," has enriched my reading of that film both visually and narratively.

Also instrumental in drawing my attention to Klimov was Haaris Naqvi, who eloquently conveyed both his high estimation of *Come and See* and the reasons underlying his esteem.

Samuel A. Chambers shared useful, highly generative commentary on the relevance of television for thinking about film, especially in terms of seriality and seasons.

Despina Kakoudaki kindly allowed me to read an early draft of her manuscript "Reconfiguring the Narrative Form of War and the Hazards of the Soldier from *Sergeant York* to *The Hurt Locker*," a brilliant analysis that—like her captivating lectures on melodrama at Harvard—informed my approach here.

Mario von der Ruhr articulated lasting insights on *Of Gods and Men* and *Sophie Scholl: The Final Days* and has, himself, been an enduring source of meaningful support and salutary input.

I appreciate the positive assessment of the book proposal by two anonymous referees, invited by the press, whose endorsement inspired the excellent authors gathered here to fulfill their erudite experiments in reading war films. Two anonymous readers, also solicited by the press, offered helpful remarks on and enthusiastic endorsement of a draft of the manuscript—comments that improved the volume's structure and led to refinements of accuracy, style, and argument. And, in the phase just before production, Lois R. Crum copyedited the manuscript; in that capacity she became an aid to good grammar and refined expression and helped excise inadvertent errors while prompting meaningful revisions throughout the book.

While researching this volume, I have enjoyed the privilege of being Writer-in-Residence in the Frederick Lewis Allen Room at the New York Public Library, and I take this occasion to thank Jay Barksdale, once again, for facilitating the conditions for extended study and composition and for assisting with the Manhattan Research Libraries Initiative, which allowed me access to the resources of the Butler Library at Columbia University and the Bobst Library at New York University.

I am grateful to Roger Stephen Gilbert for arranging my appointment as Visiting Scholar in the Department of English at Cornell University, a position that emphatically aided the progress of research.

Though my debts to Andrew Fitz-Gibbon may have just begun, I delightedly take this chance to thank him, and colleagues, for welcoming me as Lecturer in the Department of Philosophy at the State University of New York College at Cortland.

Love to my brave wee ones, R. L. L. and S. C. L., from whom I learn continuously. *Voi siete doni dal cielo.*

For consistently transformative readings of films, and war films in particular, and morally substantive orientation to these works, and much else, I am devotedly beholden to Dr. K. L. E. LaRocca.

Appendix

The Multifarious Forms of War Films: A Taxonomy of Subgenres

Childhood and Coming-of-Age during Wartime: *Rome, Open City* (Rossellini, 1945), *The Diary of Anne Frank* (Stevens, 1959), *The Tin Drum* (Schlöndorff, 1979), *Ballad of the Little Soldier* (Herzog, 1984), *Racing with the Moon* (Benjamin, 1984), *Red Dawn* (Milius, 1984; Bradley, 2012), *Come and See* (Klimov, 1985), *Empire of the Sun* (Spielberg, 1987), *The Last Emperor* (Bertolucci, 1987), *Europa Europa* (Holland, 1990), *Anne Frank Remembered* (Blair, 1995), *Kundun* (Scorsese, 1997), *Life Is Beautiful* (Benigni, 1997), *Jakob the Liar* (Kassovitz, 1999), *Nowhere in Africa* (Link, 2001), *Miracle at St. Anna* (Lee, 2008), *The Reader* (Daldry, 2008), *Winter in Wartime* (Koolhoven, 2008), *The Courageous Heart of Irena Sendler* (Harrison, 2009), *The Hunger Games* (Ross, 2012), *War Witch* (Nguyen, 2012), *The Book Thief* (Percival, 2013), *How I Live Now* (Macdonald, 2013), *Lore* (Shortland, 2013)

Historical Drama (Including Elements of Re-creation or Reenactment): *The Birth of a Nation* (Griffith, 1915), *Battleship Potemkin* (Eisenstein, 1925), *Arsenal* (Dovzhenko, 1929), *All Quiet on the Western Front* (Milestone, 1930), *Bataan* (Garnett, 1943), *Battleground* (Wellman, 1949), *The Longest Day* (Zanuck et al., 1962), *The Dirty Dozen* (Aldrich, 1967), *The Big Red One* (Fuller, 1980), *Glory* (Zwick, 1989), *Gettysburg* (Maxwell, 1993), *Saving Private Ryan* (Spielberg, 1998), *Sophie Scholl: The Final Days* (Rothemund, 2005), *Into the Storm* (O'Sullivan, 2009), *The King's Speech* (Hooper, 2010), *Hyde Park on Hudson* (Michell, 2012), *Lincoln* (Spielberg, 2012), *Zero Dark Thirty* (Bigelow, 2012)

War Romance and Melodrama: *Wings* (Wellman, 1927), *A Farewell to Arms* (Borzage, 1932), *Gone with the Wind* (Fleming, 1939), *Casablanca* (Curtiz, 1942), *For Whom the Bell Tolls* (Wood, 1943), *To Have and Have Not* (Hawks, 1944), *A Matter of Life and Death* (Powell and Pressburger, 1946),

One Minute to Zero (Garnett, 1952), *From Here to Eternity* (Zinnemann, 1953), *The Quiet American* (Mankiewicz, 1958; Noyce, 2002), *Doctor Zhivago* (Lean, 1965), *Out of Africa* (Pollack, 1985), *Cinema Paradiso* (Tornatore, 1988), *The Unbearable Lightness of Being* (Kaufman, 1988), *The English Patient* (Minghella, 1996), *The End of the Affair* (Jordan, 1999), *Pearl Harbor* (Bay, 2001), *Cold Mountain* (Minghella, 2003), *A Very Long Engagement* (Jeunet, 2004), *Dresden* (Richter, 2006), *Atonement* (Wright, 2007), *The Reader* (Daldry, 2008), *Spring 1941* (Barbash, 2008), *Dear John* (Hallström, 2010), *The King's Speech* (Hooper, 2010), *The Flowers of War* (Zhang, 2011), *Hemingway & Gellhorn* (Kaufman, 2012), *A Promise* (Leconte, 2013), *Suite Française* (Dibb, 2014)

Serial Melodrama: *Foyle's War* (Horowitz, 2002–), *Downton Abbey* (Fellowes, 2010–), *Homeland* (Gordon and Gansa, 2011–), *Parade's End* (White, 2012), *Generation War* (Kadelbach, 2013)

Serial Combat: *Band of Brothers* (Frankel and Salomon, 2001), *Generation Kill* (White et al., 2008), *The Pacific* (Podeswa et al., 2010)

Ancient Battle: *Spartacus* (Kubrick, 1960), *Gladiator* (Scott, 2000), *Alexander* (Stone, 2004), *Troy* (Petersen, 2004), *300* (Snyder, 2006), *The Last Legion* (Lefler, 2007), *Red Cliff* (Woo, 2008), *Centurion* (Marshall, 2010), *Prince of Persia: The Sands of Time* (Newell, 2010), *The Eagle* (Macdonald, 2011), *300: Rise of an Empire* (Murro, 2014); television series: *Rome* (Apted et al., 2005–2007), *Spartacus* (DeKnight, 2010–2013)

Medieval: *The Passion of Joan of Arc* (Dreyer, 1928), *Alexander Nevsky* (Eisenstein, 1938), *The Seventh Seal* (Bergman, 1957), *Camelot* (Logan, 1967), *Robin Hood: Prince of Thieves* (Reynolds, 1991), *Braveheart* (Gibson, 1995), *The Messenger: The Story of Joan of Arc* (Besson, 1999), *The 13th Warrior* (McTiernan and Crichton, 1999), *King Arthur* (Fuqua, 2004), *Kingdom of Heaven* (Scott, 2005), *Tristan + Isolde* (Reynolds, 2006), *Robin Hood* (Scott, 2010), *Season of the Witch* (Sena, 2011)

Shakespeare: *Henry V* (Olivier, 1944), *Julius Caesar* (Mankiewicz, 1953), *Richard III* (Olivier, 1955), *Henry V* (Branagh, 1989), *Richard III* (Loncraine, 1995), *Titus* (Taymor, 1999), *Coriolanus* (Fiennes, 2011), *The Hollow Crown* series (Gould, 2012)

Religious Drama or Epic: *Intolerance* (Griffith, 1916), *Quo Vadis* (LeRoy, 1951), *The Ten Commandments* (DeMille, 1956), *Ben-Hur* (Wyler, 1959), *King of Kings* (Ray, 1961), *The Greatest Story Ever Told* (Stevens, 1965), *The Message* (Akkad, 1976), *The Mahabharata* (Brook, 1989), *The Passion of the Christ* (Gibson, 2004), *Kingdom of Heaven* (Scott, 2005), *Of Gods and Men* (Beauvois, 2010), *Exodus: Gods and Kings* (Scott, 2014), *Noah* (Aronofsky, 2014)

Dictatorships and Totalitarian Regimes: *Napoleon* (Gance, 1927), *Duck Soup* (McCarey, 1933), *Triumph of the Will* (Riefenstahl, 1935), *The Great Dictator* (Chaplin, 1940), *You Nazty Spy!* (White, 1940), *To Be or Not to Be* (Lubitsch, 1942; Johnson, 1983), *Herr Meets Hare* (Freleng, 1945), *The King and I* (Lang, 1956), *Bananas* (Allen, 1971), *Sleeper* (Allen, 1973), *Brazil* (Gilliam, 1975), *Mephisto* (Szabó, 1981), *1984* (Radford, 1984), *Kiss of the Spider Woman* (Babenco, 1985), *The Last Emperor* (Bertolucci, 1987), *Romero* (Duigan, 1989), *Richard III* (Loncraine, 1995), *Kundun* (Scorsese, 1997), *Fidel* (Attwood, 2002), *Kamchatka* (Piñeyro, 2002), *Max* (Meyjes, 2002), *Downfall* (Hirschbiegel, 2004), *Team America: World Police* (Parker, 2004), *The Last King of Scotland* (Macdonald, 2006), *The Wave* (Gansel, 2008), *Dzi Croquettes* (Alvarez, 2009), *Inglourious Basterds* (Tarantino, 2009), *The Devil's Double* (Tamahori, 2011), *The Dictator* (Charles, 2012), *The Hunger Games* (Ross, 2012), *The Grand Budapest Hotel* (Anderson, 2014); and television series: *Mussolini: The Untold Story* (Graham, 1985), *Mussolini and I* (Negrin, 1985), *Stalin* (Passer, 1992), *Napoléon* (Simoneau, 2002), *House of Saddam* (Holmes and O'Hanlon, 2008)

Wars of Revolution/Insurrection/Independence: *Lawrence of Arabia* (Lean, 1962), *The Battle of Algiers* (Pontecorvo, 1966), *Red Dawn* (Milius, 1984; Bradley, 2012), *The Unbearable Lightness of Being* (Kaufman, 1988), *In the Name of the Father* (Sheridan, 1993), *Braveheart* (Gibson, 1995), *Michael Collins* (Jordan, 1996), *The Patriot* (Emmerich, 2000), *The Wind That Shakes the Barley* (Loach, 2006), *Che: Part One* and *Che: Part Two* (Soderbergh, 2008), *Of Gods and Men* (Beauvois, 2010), *Robin Hood* (Scott, 2010); television series: *John Adams* (Hooper, 2008)

American Revolution: *The Last of the Mohicans* (Tourneur, 1920; Mann, 1992), *America* (Griffith, 1924), *Drums along the Mohawk* (Ford, 1939), *The Patriot* (Emmerich, 2000); television series: *John Adams* (Hooper, 2008)

Civil War: *The Birth of a Nation* (Griffith, 1915), *The General* (Keaton and Bruckman, 1926), *Gone with the Wind* (Fleming, 1939), *The Red Badge of Courage* (Huston, 1951), *Shenandoah* (McLagen, 1965), *The Outlaw Josey Wales* (Eastwood, 1976), *Glory* (Zwick, 1989), *Dances with Wolves* (Kostner, 1990), *Ride with the Devil* (Lee, 1999), *Cold Mountain* (Minghella, 2003), *Gods and Generals* (Maxwell, 2003), *The Last Samurai* (Zwick, 2003), *Lincoln* (Spielberg, 2012)

World War I: *Hearts of the World* (Griffith, 1918), *The Big Parade* (Vidor, 1925), *Wings* (Wellman, 1927), *Four Sons* (Ford, 1928), *All Quiet on the Western Front* (Milestone, 1930), *Sergeant York* (Hawks, 1941), *The African Queen* (Huston, 1951), *Paths of Glory* (Kubrick, 1957), *Lawrence of Arabia* (David Lean, 1962), *Gallipoli* (Weir, 1981), *Legends of the Fall* (Zwick, 1994), *A Very Long Engagement* (Jeunet, 2004), *Merry Christmas* (Carion, 2005), *Flyboys* (Bill, 2006), *The Red Baron* (Müllerschön, 2008), *The White Ribbon* (Haneke, 2009), *War Horse* (Spielberg, 2011), *Battle Ground* (Earl and Powers, 2013)

World War II (Combat, Holocaust, and Home Front): *Foreign Correspondent* (Hitchcock, 1940), *The Great Dictator* (Chaplin, 1940), *The Battle of Midway* (Ford, 1942), *In Which We Serve* (Lean and Coward, 1942), *Mrs. Miniver* (Wyler, 1942), *Went the Day Well?* (Cavalcanti, 1942), *Fires Were Started* (Jennings, 1943), *Guadalcanal Diary* (Seiler, 1943), *Days of Glory* (Tourneur, 1944; Bouchareb, 2006), *The Memphis Belle* (Wyler, 1944), *Ministry of Fear* (Lang, 1944), *Thirty Seconds over Tokyo* (LeRoy, 1944), *They Were Expendable* (Ford, 1945), *A Walk in the Sun* (Milestone, 1945), *The Best Years of Our Lives* (Wyler, 1946), *Battleground* (Wellman, 1949), *Sands of Iwo Jima* (Dwan, 1949), *Twelve O'Clock High* (King, 1949), *From Here to Eternity* (Zinnemann, 1953), *A Generation* (Wajda, 1955), *To Hell and Back* (Hibbs, 1955), *Kanal* (Wajda, 1956), *Ashes and Diamonds* (Wajda, 1958), *Run Silent, Run Deep* (Wise, 1958), *Ballad of a Soldier* (Chukhray, 1959), *The Guns of Navarone* (Thompson, 1961), *Judgment at Nuremberg* (Kramer, 1961), *The Longest Day* (Zanuck et al., 1962), *The Train* (Frankenheimer, 1964), *Where Eagles Dare* (Hutton, 1968), *Army of Shadows* (Melville, 1969), *Patton* (Schaffner, 1970), *Cross of Iron* (Peckinpah, 1977), *MacArthur* (Sargent, 1977), *Soldier of Orange* (Verhoeven, 1977), *The Inglorious Bastards* (Castellari, 1978), *The Last Metro* (Truffaut, 1980), *Das Boot* (Petersen, 1981), *Sophie's Choice* (Pakula, 1982), *The Keep* (Mann, 1983), *Come and*

See (Klimov, 1985), *Europa/Zentropa* (Trier, 1991), *A Midnight Clear* (Gordon, 1992), *Schindler's List* (Spielberg, 1993), *Stalingrad* (Vilsmaier, 1993; Bondarchuk, 2013), *The English Patient* (Minghella, 1996), *Life Is Beautiful* (Benigni, 1997), *Saving Private Ryan* (Spielberg, 1998), *The Thin Red Line* (Malick, 1998), *U-571* (Mostow, 2000), *Conspiracy* (Pierson, 2001), *The Pianist* (Polanski, 2002), *Windtalkers* (Woo, 2002), *Saints and Soldiers* (Little, 2003), *The Good German* (Soderbergh, 2006), *Defiance* (Zwick, 2008), *Valkyrie* (Singer, 2008), *Inglourious Basterds* (Tarantino, 2009), *Sarah's Key* (Paquet-Brenner, 2010), *In Darkness* (Holland, 2011), *Emperor* (Webber, 2012), *Into the White* (Næss, 2012), *Red Tails* (Lucas, 2012), *The Monuments Men* (Clooney, 2013), *Fury* (Ayer, 2014)

Korean War (Combat and Home Front): *Fixed Bayonets!* (Fuller, 1951), *I Want You* (Robson, 1951), *Korea Patrol* (Nosseck, 1951), *The Steel Helmet* (Fuller, 1951), *Submarine Command* (Farrow, 1951), *Japanese War Bride* (Vidor, 1952), *One Minute to Zero* (Garnett, 1952), *Retreat, Hell!* (Lewis, 1952), *Battle Circus* (Brooks, 1953), *Cease Fire* (Crump, 1953), *Take the High Ground!* (Brooks, 1953), *The Bridges of Toko-Ri* (Robson, 1954), *Prisoner of War* (Marton, 1954), *The Rack* (Laven, 1956), *Battle Hymn* (Sirk, 1957), *Men in War* (Mann, 1957), *Sayonara* (Logan, 1957), *Pork Chop Hill* (Milestone, 1959), *All the Young Men* (Bartlett, 1960), *Marines, Let's Go* (Walsh, 1961), *The Manchurian Candidate* (Frankenheimer, 1962; Demme, 2004), *War Hunt* (Sanders, 1962), *War Is Hell* (Topper, 1963), *The Young and the Brave* (Lyon, 1963), *M*A*S*H* (Altman, 1970), *MacArthur* (Sargent, 1977), *Big Fish* (Burton, 2003); and the television series *Mad Men* (Weiner, 2007–2015)

Vietnam War (Combat and Home Front): *The Green Berets* (Wayne, 1968), *Taxi Driver* (Scorsese, 1976), *Heroes* (Kagan, 1977), *The Boys in Company C* (Furie, 1978), *Coming Home* (Ashby, 1978), *The Deer Hunter* (Cimino, 1978), *Apocalypse Now* (Coppola, 1979), *Hair* (Forman, 1979), *The War at Home* (Silber, 1979), *First Blood* (Kotcheff, 1982), *Rambo: First Blood Part II* (Cosmatos, 1985), *Platoon* (Stone, 1986), *Full Metal Jacket* (Kubrick, 1987), *Good Morning, Vietnam* (Levinson, 1987), *Hamburger Hill* (Irvin, 1987), *The Hanoi Hilton* (Chetwynd, 1987), *Born on the Fourth of July* (Stone, 1989), *Casualties of War* (De Palma, 1989), *Jacknife* (Jones, 1989), *Jacob's Ladder* (Lyne, 1990), *JFK* (Stone, 1991), *Heaven & Earth* (Stone, 1993), *Forrest Gump* (Zemekis, 1994), *Dead Presidents* (Hughes, 1995), *Little Dieter Needs* *to Fly* (Herzog, 1997), *We Were Soldiers* (Wallace, 2002), *Rescue Dawn* (Herzog, 2006)

Persian Gulf War, Iraq War, and Military Actions in the Middle East and Africa (Combat and Home Front): *Lessons of Darkness* (Herzog, 1992), *Courage under Fire* (Zwick, 1996), *Bravo Two Zero* (Clegg, 1999), *Three Kings* (Russell, 1999), *Rules of Engagement* (Friedkin, 2000), *Black Hawk Down* (Scott, 2001), *Live from Baghdad* (Jackson, 2002), *Jarhead* (Mendes, 2005), *In the Valley of Elah* (Haggis, 2007), *The Kingdom* (Berg, 2007), *Redacted* (De Palma, 2007), *Body of Lies* (Scott, 2008), *The Hurt Locker* (Bigelow, 2008), *Stop-Loss* (Peirce, 2008), *The Messenger* (Moverman, 2009), *The A-Team* (Carnahan, 2010), *Fair Game* (Liman, 2010), *Green Zone* (Greengrass, 2010), *Return* (Johnson, 2011), *The Boys of Abu Ghraib* (Moran, 2013), *The Patrol* (Petch, 2013); and the television series *Generation Kill* (White, 2008)

War in Afghanistan: *The Living Daylights* (Glen, 1987), *Rambo III* (MacDonald, 1988), *The Beast of War* (Reynolds, 1998), *Kandahar* (Makhmalbaf, 2001), *At Five in the Afternoon* (Makhmalbaf, 2003), *Osama* (Barmak, 2003), *Brothers* (Bier, 2004; Sheridan, 2009), *Fahrenheit 9/11* (Moore, 2004), *Enemies of Happiness* (Mulvad, 2006), *Kabul Express* (Khan, 2006), *Road to Guantanamo* (Whitecross and Winterbottom, 2006), *Charlie Wilson's War* (Nichols, 2007), *The Kite Runner* (Forster, 2007), *Lions for Lambs* (Redford, 2007), *Taxi to the Dark Side* (Gibney, 2007), *Iron Man* (Favreau, 2008), *Watchmen* (Snyder, 2009), *Armadillo* (Pedersen, 2010), *Essential Killing* (Skolimowski, 2010), *The Oath* (Poitras, 2010), *Restrepo* (Hetherington and Junger, 2010), *The Tillman Story* (Bar-Lev, 2010), *Afghan Luke* (Clattenburg, 2011), *Hell and Back Again* (Dennis, 2011), *Source Code* (Jones, 2011), *Where Soldiers Come From* (Courtney, 2011), *Zero Dark Thirty* (Bigelow, 2012), *Dirty Wars* (Rowley, 2013), *Lone Survivor* (Berg, 2013), *1,000 Times Good Night* (Poppe, 2013), *The Patrol* (Petch, 2013), *White House Down* (Emmerich, 2013), *Jack Ryan: Shadow Recruit* (Branagh, 2014)

Westerns (Related to the Civil War): *The Battle at Elderbrush Gulch* (Griffith, 1914), *Geronimo* (Sloane, 1940), *They Died with Their Boots On* (Walsh, 1941), *Fort Apache* (Ford, 1948), *Rio Grande* (Ford, 1950), *Bugles in the Afternoon* (Rowland, 1952), *The Savage* (Marshall, 1952), *Escape from Fort Bravo* (Sturges, 1953), *Apache* (Aldrich, 1954), *Sitting Bull* (Salkow, 1954),

Taza, Son of Cochise (Sirk, 1954), *Chief Crazy Horse* (Sherman, 1955), *The Searchers* (Ford, 1956), *Run of the Arrow* (Fuller, 1957), *The True Story of Jesse James* (Ray, 1957), *How the West Was Won* (Ford, 1962), *Dances with Wolves* (Costner, 1990)

Mercenary: *Flying Tigers* (Miller, 1942), *For Whom the Bell Tolls* (Wood, 1942), *Hell and High Water* (Fuller, 1954), *Seven Samurai* (Kurosawa, 1954), *Soldier of Fortune* (Dmytryk, 1955), *Bandido* (Fleischer, 1956), *The Magnificent Seven* (Sturges, 1960), *The Professionals* (Brooks, 1966), *Duck, You Sucker* (Leone, 1971), *The Last Valley* (Clavell, 1971), *The Wild Geese* (McLaglen, 1978), *The Dogs of War* (Irvin, 1980), *The Empire Strikes Back* (Kershner, 1980), *Flesh + Blood* (Verhoeven, 1985), *Men of War* (Lang, 1994), *Ronin* (Frankenheimer, 1998), *Blood Diamond* (Zwick, 2006), *Rambo* (Stallone, 2008), *The Expendables* series (Stallone, 2008–2014), *The Dark Knight Rises* (Nolan, 2012)

Samurai (Depicting Japan's Edo Period, 1603–1868): *Yôjimbô* (Kurosawa, 1961), *Sanjurô* (Kurosawa, 1962), *Zatoichi* films (Misumi et al., 1962–1989)

Pulp War/Western: *Indiana Jones* series (Spielberg, 1981–2008)

Modern Western/Terrorism: *Die Hard* series (McTiernan et al., 1988–2013)

Cold War: *The Quiet American* (Mankiewicz, 1958; Noyce, 2002), *The Manchurian Candidate* (Frankenheimer, 1962; Demme, 2004), *Dr. Strangelove or: How I Learned to Stop Worrying and Love the Bomb* (Kubrick, 1964), *Stripes* (Reitman, 1981), *First Blood* (Kotcheff, 1982) and *Rambo* series (1982–2008), *The Right Stuff* (Kaufman, 1983), *WarGames* (Badham, 1983), *Red Dawn* (Milius, 1984), *Rocky IV* (Stallone, 1985), *White Nights* (Hackford, 1985), *Top Gun* (Scott, 1986), *The Hunt for Red October* (McTiernan, 1990), *JFK* (Stone, 1991), *Blue Sky* (Richardson, 1994), *Apollo 13* (Howard, 1995), *Crimson Tide* (Scott, 1995), *Thirteen Days* (Donaldson, 2000), *Buffalo Soldiers* (Jordan, 2001), *Confessions of a Dangerous Mind* (Clooney, 2002), *K-19: The Widowmaker* (Bigelow, 2002), *Good Bye Lenin!* (Becker, 2003), *Miracle* (O'Connor, 2004), *Good Night, and Good Luck* (Clooney, 2005), *The Good German* (Soderbergh, 2006), *The Good Shepherd* (De Niro, 2006), *The Lives of Others* (von Donnersmarck, 2006), *Watchmen* (2009), *Salt* (Noyce, 2010), *Tinker Tailor Soldier Spy* (Alfredson, 2011), *X-Men First Class* (Vaughn, 2011), *Ginger and Rosa* (Potter, 2012), *Phantom* (Robinson, 2013)

European Post–Cold War: *The Peacemaker* (Leder, 1997), *The Perfect Circle* (Kenovic, 1997), *Welcome to Sarajevo* (Winterbottom, 1997), *Savior* (Antonijevic, 1998), *Behind Enemy Lines* (Moore, 2001), *No Man's Land* (Tanovic, 2001), *The Whistleblower* (Kondracki, 2010), *In the Land of Blood and Honey* (Jolie, 2011)

Clandestine/Covert/Intelligence/Espionage/Black Ops: *The Third Man* (Reed, 1949), Jack Ryan series (McTiernan et al., 1990–2013), *Bourne* series (Liman et al., 2002–2012), *Munich* (Spielberg, 2005), *Rendition* (Hood, 2007), *Body of Lies* (Scott, 2008), *The Debt* (Madden, 2010), *Fair Game* (Liman, 2010), *Green Zone* (Greengrass, 2010), *Hanna* (Wright, 2011), *Tinker Tailor Soldier Spy* (Alfredson, 2011), *Argo* (Affleck, 2012), *Seal Team Six* (Stockwell, 2012), *Zero Dark Thirty* (Bigelow, 2012)

Terrorist Threats to the U.S. Presidency: *JFK* (Stone, 1991), *In the Line of Fire* (Petersen, 1993), *Independence Day* (Emmerich, 1996), *Air Force One* (Petersen, 1997), *X2* (Singer, 2003), *Vantage Point* (Travis, 2008), *Lincoln* (Spielberg, 2012), *Olympus Has Fallen* (Fuqua, 2013), *White House Down* (Emmerich, 2013)

War on Terror (Including Biowar and Cyberwar): *WarGames* (Badham, 1983), *Dirty War* (Percival, 2004), *Déjà Vu* (Scott, 2006), *World Trade Center* (Stone, 2006), *Rendition* (Hood, 2007), *Eagle Eye* (Caruso, 2008), *Source Code* (Jones, 2011), *Lone Survivor* (Berg, 2013), *A Most Wanted Man* (Corbijn, 2014)

Domestic Terrorism and Terrorist Networks: *The Battle of Algiers* (Pontecorvo, 1966), *The Day of the Jackal* (Zinnemann, 1973), *Running on Empty* (Lumet, 1988), *Under Siege* (Davis, 1992), *In the Name of the Father* (Sheridan, 1993), *Michael Collins* (Jordan, 1996), *The Siege* (Zwick, 1998), *Fight Club* (Fincher, 1999), *Munich* (Spielberg, 2005), *Syriana* (Gaghan, 2005), *V for Vendetta* (Wachowski brothers, 2005), *United 93* (Greengrass, 2006), *The Wind That Shakes the Barley* (Loach, 2006), *World Trade Center* (Stone, 2006), *The Kingdom* (Berg, 2007), *A Mighty Heart* (Winterbottom, 2007), *The Baader Meinhof Complex* (Edel, 2008), *Four Lions* (Morris, 2010), *Of Gods and Men* (Beauvois, 2010), *Argo* (Affleck, 2012), *The Company You Keep* (Redford, 2012), *A Hijacking* (Lindholm, 2012), *Captain Phillips* (Greengrass, 2013)

Home Front (Including Deployment and Returning from War): In most cases, these films shift our attention from combat to the cognitive effects and emotional traces of the battlefield, and therefore many of the works explore notions of memory, trauma, and orientation.
Miracle of Morgan's Creek (Sturges, 1944), *The Best Years of Our Lives* (Wyler, 1946), *Home of the Brave* (Robson, 1949), *I Want You* (Robson, 1951), *The Searchers* (Ford, 1956), *Alice's Restaurant* (Penn, 1969), *Medium Cool* (Wexler, 1969), *Taxi Driver* (Scorsese, 1976), *The Deer Hunter* (Cimino, 1978), *First Blood* (Kotcheff, 1982) and *Rambo* series (1982–2008), *Gardens of Stone* (Coppola, 1987), *Born on the Fourth of July* (Stone, 1989), *Casualties of War* (De Palma, 1989), *Jacknife* (Jones, 1989), *Jacob's Ladder* (Lyne, 1990), *Dogfight* (Savoca, 1991), *JFK* (Stone, 1991), *Heaven & Earth* (Stone, 1993), *Forrest Gump* (Zemekis, 1994), *Dead Presidents* (Hughes, 1995), *Little Dieter Needs to Fly* (Herzog, 1997), *Code Unknown: Incomplete Tales of Several Journeys* (Haneke, 2000), *Tigerland* (Schumacher, 2000), *Pearl Harbor* (Bay, 2001), *Brothers* (Bier, 2004; Sheridan, 2009), *Lord of War* (Niccol, 2005), *Déjà Vu* (Scott, 2006), *Home of the Brave* (Winkler, 2006), *The Messenger* (Moverman, 2009), *Taking Chance* (Katz, 2009), *Return* (Johnson, 2011), *Warrior* (O'Connor, 2011), *The Lucky One* (Hicks, 2012), *The Master* (Anderson, 2012)

Journalists and Photojournalists (Features, Documentaries, and Series): *The Story of G.I. Joe* (Wellman, 1945), *The Quiet American* (Mankiewicz, 1958; Noyce, 2002), *Medium Cool* (Wexler, 1969), *The Year of Living Dangerously* (Weir, 1982), *The Killing Fields* (Joffé, 1984), *Full Metal Jacket* (Kubrick, 1987), *The Unbearable Lightness of Being* (Kaufman, 1988), *84 Charlie MoPic* (Duncan, 1989), *Welcome to Sarajevo* (Winterbottom, 1997), *War Photographer* (Frei, 2001), *Gunner Palace* (Epperlein and Tucker, 2004), *The War Tapes* (Scranton, 2006), *The Devil Came on Horseback* (Stern and Sundberg, 2007), *Pictures from a Revolution* (Meiselas, Rogers, and Guzzetti, 2007), *Blood Trail* (Parry, 2008; later re-released as *Shooting Robert King,* 2012), *Generation Kill* (White, 2008), *Triage* (Tanovic, 2009), *Armadillo* (Metz, 2010), *The Bang Bang Club* (Silver, 2010), *Restrepo* (Hetherington and Junger, 2010), *Hannah Arendt* (von Trotta, 2012), *Witness* (Frankham and Omeish, 2012), *1,000 Times Good Night* (Poppe, 2013)

Documentary: *Triumph of the Will* (Riefenstahl, 1935), *China Strikes Back* (Dunham, 1937), *The Spanish Earth* (Ivens, 1937), *The Four Hundred Million* (Ivens, 1939), *Baptism of Fire* (Feuertaufe, 1940), *Yellow Caesar* (Cavalcanti,

1940), *Victory in the West* (Hippler, 1941), *Day of War* (Slutsky, 1942), *Listen to Britain* (Jennings, 1942), *Desert Victory* (Boulting, 1943), *Stalingrad* (Varlamov, 1943), *The True Glory* (Kanin and Reed, 1945), *Cameraman at the Front* (Sushinsky and Slavinskaya, 1946), *Night and Fog* (Resnais, 1955), *Black Fox: The Rise of Adolf Hitler* (Stoumen, 1962), *Hearts and Minds* (Davis, 1974), *The War at Home* (Silber, 1979), *Genocide* (Schwartzmann, 1981), *Ballad of the Little Soldier* (Herzog, 1984), *Shoah* (Lanzmann, 1985), *Sherman's March* (McElwee, 1986), *Dear America: Letters Home from Vietnam* (Couturié, 1987), *Hotel Terminus* (Ophuls, 1988), *Anne Frank Remembered* (Blair, 1995), *The Last Days* (Moll, 1998), *One Day in September* (McDonald, 1999), *Occupation: Dreamland* (Olds and Scott, 2005), *Iraq for Sale: The War Profiteers* (Greenwald, 2006), *Iraq in Fragments* (Longley, 2006), *My Country, My Country* (Poitras, 2006), *The Rape of Europa* (Berge, 2006), *Section 60 Arlington National Cemetery* (Alpert and O'Neill, 2008), *Worse Than War* (DeWitt, 2009), *The Battle for Marjah* (Wonke, 2010), *The Oath* (Poitras, 2010), *The Tillman Story* (Bar-Lev, 2010), *The War You Don't See* (Lowery and Pilger, 2010), *5 Broken Cameras* (Burnat and Davidi, 2011), *The Act of Killing* (Oppenheimer, 2012), *Dirty Wars* (Rowley, 2013), *The Last of the Unjust* (Lanzmann, 2013), *Manhunt* (Barker, 2013)

On Policy: *Why We Fight* series (Capra, 1942–1945), *Steal This Movie!* (Greenwald, 2000), *The Weather Underground* (Green and Siegel, 2002), *The Fog of War* (Morris, 2003), *Fahrenheit 9/11* (Moore, 2004), *Why We Fight* (Jarecki, 2005), *No End in Sight* (Ferguson, 2007), *Standard Operating Procedure* (Morris, 2008), *The Gatekeepers* (Moreh, 2012), *The Invisible War* (Dick, 2012), *Dirty Wars* (Rowley, 2013), *The Unknown Known* (Morris, 2013), *We Steal Secrets: The Story of WikiLeaks* (Gibney, 2013)

On Mental Health: *Let There Be Light* (Huston, 1946), *Mind Zone: Therapists behind the Front Lines* (Haaken, 2011)

With Fictional Elements and Reenactments: *The Battle of San Pietro* (Huston, 1945), *Lessons of Darkness* (Herzog, 1992), *Little Dieter Needs to Fly* (Herzog, 1997), *Standard Operating Procedure* (Morris, 2008)

Faux Documentary: *C.S.A.: Confederate States of America* (Willmott, 2004), *Redacted* (De Palma, 2007), *District 9* (Blomkamp, 2009)

Depictions of Race: *The Eternal Jew* (Hippler, 1940), *The Negro Soldier* (Heisler, 1944)

Serial or Episodic: *The Civil War* (Burns, 1990), *The War* (Burns, 2007), *Witness* (Mann, 2012; episodes: *Juarez, Libya, Rio,* and *South Sudan*)

Class/Race Conflict, e.g., Drafting Minorities, the Poor, and Immigrants into War: *All the Young Men* (Bartlett, 1960), *Glory* (Zwick, 1989), *Tuskegee Airmen* (Markowitz, 1995), *Men of Honor* (Tillman, 2000), *Gangs of New York* (Scorsese, 2002), *Hart's War* (Hoblit, 2002), *The Last Samurai* (Zwick, 2003), *Blood Diamond* (Zwick, 2006), *Days of Glory* (Bouchareb, 2006), *District 9* (Blomkamp, 2009), *Lincoln* (Spielberg, 2012), *Red Tails* (Lucas, 2012)

Gender Conflict: *Alien* (Scott, 1979), *Private Benjamin* (Zieff, 1980), *Aliens* (Cameron, 1986), *A Few Good Men* (Reiner, 1992), *Courage under Fire* (Zwick, 1996), *G.I. Jane* (Scott, 1997), *Starship Troopers* (Verhoeven, 1997), *Sky Captain and the World of Tomorrow* (Conran, 2004), *Avatar* (Cameron, 2009), *Salt* (Noyce, 2010), *Return* (Johnson, 2011)

Courtroom and War Trials: *The Passion of Joan of Arc* (Dreyer, 1928), *The Caine Mutiny* (Dymtryk, 1954), *The Rack* (Laven, 1956), *Paths of Glory* (Kubrick, 1957), *Judgment at Nuremberg* (Kramer, 1961), *King and Country* (Losey, 1964), *Breaker Morant* (Beresford, 1980), *A Few Good Men* (Reiner, 1992), *Rules of Engagement* (Friedkin, 2000), *Hart's War* (Hoblit, 2002), *Sophie Scholl: The Final Days* (Rothemund, 2005), *The Reader* (Daldry, 2008), *Shaurya* (Khan, 2008), *Melvilasom* (Dasan, 2011)

Prisoner of War/Escape: *Grand Illusion* (Renoir, 1937), *The Wooden Horse* (Lee, 1950), *Stalag 17* (Wilder, 1953), *Prisoner of War* (Marton, 1954), *The Rack* (Laven, 1956), *The Bridge on the River Kwai* (Lean, 1957), *The Manchurian Candidate* (Frankenheimer, 1962; Demmer, 2004), *The Great Escape* (Sturges, 1963), *The Young and the Brave* (Lyon, 1963), *King Rat* (Forbes, 1965), *Hell in the Pacific* (Boorman, 1968), *Papillon* (Schaffner, 1973), *Escape to Victory* (Huston, 1981), *Missing in Action* (Zito, 1984), *Rambo: First Blood Part II* (Cosmatos, 1985), *The Hanoi Hilton* (Chetwynd, 1987), *Little Dieter Needs to Fly* (Herzog, 1997), *To End All Wars* (Cunningham, 2001), *Hart's War* (Hoblit, 2002), *Rescue Dawn* (Herzog, 2006), *The Counterfeiters* (Ruzowitzky, 2007), *Defiance* (Zwick, 2008), *District 9* (Blomkamp, 2009), *Essential Killing* (Skolimowski, 2010), *The Way Back* (Weir, 2010), *Elysium* (Blomkamp, 2013), *The Railway Man* (Teplitzky, 2013), *Unbroken* (Jolie, 2014)

Military Science Fiction: *The Day the Earth Stood Still* (Wise, 1951), *Star Trek* series (1966–1969), *Star Wars* series (Lucas et al., 1977–2015), *Alien* series

(Scott et al., 1979–1997), *Predator* (McTiernan, 1987), *Independence Day* (Emmerich, 1996), *Starship Troopers* (Verhoeven, 1997), *War of the Worlds* (Spielberg, 2005), *Avatar* (Cameron, 2009), *Star Trek* (Abrams, 2009), *Battle: Los Angeles* (Liebesman, 2011), *Battleship* (Berg, 2012), *Elysium* (Blomkamp, 2013), *Pacific Rim* (Del Toro, 2013), *Star Trek into Darkness* (Abrams, 2013)

Military Science Fiction and Cognition/Artificial Intelligence: *Star Wars* series (Lucas et al., 1977–2015), *Blade Runner* (Scott, 1982), *The Terminator* series (Cameron, 1984–2015), *The Matrix* (Wachowski brothers, 1999), *Planet of the Apes* series (Burton et al., 2001–2014), *Battlestar Galactica* (Moore et al., 2004–2009), *Déjà Vu* (Scott, 2006), *Gamer* (Neveldine and Taylor, 2009), *Source Code* (Jones, 2011), *Prometheus* (Scott, 2012), *Edge of Tomorrow* (Liman, 2014), *RoboCop* (Padilha, 2014)

Space Western: *Star Wars* (Lucas, 1977), *Firefly* (Whedon, 2002), *Serenity* (Whedon, 2005), *Avatar* (Cameron, 2009), *Cowboys & Aliens* (Favreau, 2011)

Fantasy: *Slaughterhouse-Five* (Roy Hill, 1972), *The Lord of the Rings* series (Jackson, 2001–2003), *Pan's Labyrinth* (Del Toro, 2006), *Clash of the Titans* (Leterrier, 2010), *The Hobbit* series (Jackson, 2012–2014), *Wrath of the Titans* (Liebesman, 2012), *47 Ronin* (Rinsch, 2013)

Environmental/Intergalactic Disaster: *Mad Max* series (Miller et al., 1979–2014), *Armageddon* (Bay, 1998), *The Day after Tomorrow* (Emmerich, 2004), *2012* (Emmerich, 2009)

Alien Invasion: *War of the Worlds* (Spielberg, 2005), *AVPR: Aliens vs. Predator Requiem* (Strause brothers, 2007), *Transformers* (Bay, 2007), *District 9* (Blomkamp, 2009), *Battle: Los Angeles* (Liebesman, 2011), *Cowboys & Aliens* (Favreau, 2011), *Super 8* (Abrams, 2011), *Battleship* (Berg, 2012), *Ender's Game* (Hood, 2013), *Oblivion* (Kosinski, 2013), *Pacific Rim* (Del Toro, 2013)

Virus Pandemic: *Outbreak* (Petersen, 1995), *28 Days Later* (Boyle, 2002), *The Invasion* (Hirschbiegel, 2007), *Contagion* (Soderbergh, 2011), *World War Z* (Forster, 2013)

Postapocalyptic and Dystopian (Including Body Seizure, Vampires, and Zombies): *The Omega Man* (Sagal, 1971), *Alien* series (Scott et al., 1979–1997), *Mad Max* series (Miller et al., 1979–2014), *I Am Legend* (Lawrence, 2007), *The Twilight Saga* series (Hardwicke et al., 2008–2012), *The Road* (Hillcoat, 2009), *Prometheus* (Scott, 2012), *World War Z* (Forster, 2013)

Comic Book Adaptation and Animation: *Titan A. E.* (Bluth and Goldman, 2000), *300* (Snyder, 2006), *Watchmen* (Snyder, 2009), all the films under the aegis of Hasbro (*G.I. Joe* series, *Transformers* series, and *Battleship*), Marvel (*Spider-Man, X-Men, Captain America, Iron Man, Thor, The Incredible Hulk*), and DC (*Superman* series, *Batman* series, and the Batman *Dark Knight* trilogy)

War Comedy, Parody, and Satire: *Shoulder Arms* (Chaplin, 1918), *The General* (Keaton and Bruckman, 1926), *Duck Soup* (McCarey, 1933), *The Great Dictator* (Chaplin, 1940), *You Nazty Spy!* (White, 1940), *To Be or Not to Be* (Lubitsch, 1942; Johnson, 1983), *The Life and Death of Colonel Blimp* (Powell and Pressburger, 1943), *Herr Meets Hare* (Freleng, 1945), *I Was a Male War Bride* (Hawks, 1949), *One, Two, Three* (Wilder, 1961), *Dr. Strangelove* (Kubrick, 1964), *Alice's Restaurant* (Penn, 1969), *Catch-22* (Nichols, 1970), *Kelly's Heroes* (Hutton, 1970), *M*A*S*H* (Altman, 1970), *Bananas* (Allen, 1971), *Sleeper* (Allen, 1973), *Love and Death* (Allen, 1975), *Monty Python and the Holy Grail* (Gilliam and Jones, 1975), *Hair* (Forman, 1979), *Private Benjamin* (Zieff, 1980), *Stripes* (Reitman, 1981), *Good Morning, Vietnam* (Levinson, 1987), *Indiana Jones and the Last Crusade* (Spielberg, 1989), *Forrest Gump* (Zemekis, 1994), *Mars Attacks!* (Burton, 1996), *The Big Lebowski* (Coen brothers, 1998), *Three Kings* (Russell, 1999), *Team America: World Police* (Parker, 2004), *Tropic Thunder* (Stiller, 2008), *Inglourious Basterds* (Tarantino, 2009), *The Men Who Stare at Goats* (Heslov, 2009), *The Dictator* (Charles, 2012), *Django Unchained* (Tarantino, 2012), *The Grand Budapest Hotel* (Anderson, 2014)

Contributors

Inger S. B. Brodey is the Bank of America Distinguished Term Professor at the University of North Carolina at Chapel Hill, as well as Associate Professor in the Department of English and Comparative Literature; she is also affiliated with both Asian Studies and Global Studies. She has served as Director of the Comparative Literature Program and as Director of the Global Cinema Minor. She has won national awards for her scholarship, including a Mellon Fellowship in the Humanities and a DAAD Fellowship. At UNC-CH, she received a Tanner Award and a Chapman Family award for distinguished undergraduate teaching of courses including "Global Jane Austen," "Cowboys, Samurai, Rebels," "Approaches to Comparative Literature," "Rhetorics of Silence," and "Literature and Landscape." Brodey's other publications place Jane Austen and her eighteenth-century contemporaries within broader contexts, such as British political philosophy, English landscape gardening, and German and Japanese literary traditions; she is working on a study of representations of Jane Austen in Asia. She published a translation of a work by Natsume Sôseki, who was one of Japan's foremost novelists: *Rediscovering Natsume Soseki* (Global Oriental, 2000). Brodey's book on landscape gardening and the history of the novel, focusing on the novels of Sterne, Goethe, and Austen—*Ruined by Design: Novels and Gardens in the Culture of Sensibility* (Routledge, 2008)—won the Best Book Award from the South Atlantic Modern Language Association in 2009 and was reissued in paperback in 2012. She has published in the *U.S.-Japan Women's Journal* on the relationship between cowboys and samurai in film and has received funding from the Earhart Foundation to complete a book-length comparison of cowboys and samurai in film.

Elisabeth Bronfen is Professor of English and American Studies at the University of Zurich, Switzerland, and the author of *Specters of War: Hollywood's Engagement with Military Conflict* (Rutgers University Press, 2012). Other books include *Over Her Dead Body: Death, Femininity, and the Aesthetic* (Manchester University Press, 1992); a collection of essays, *Death and Representation*, coedited with Sarah W. Goodwin (Johns Hopkins University

Press, 1993); *The Knotted Subject: Hysteria and Its Discontents* (Princeton University Press, 1998); *Home in Hollywood: The Imaginary Geography of Cinema* (Columbia University Press, 2004); *Die Diva: Eine Geschichte der Bewunderung* (Schirmer und Mosel, 2002), about the importance of the diva in celebrity culture; and most recently, a book on the cultural history of the night, *Night Passages: Philosophy, Literature, and Film* (Columbia University Press, 2013).

Robert Burgoyne is Professor and Chair in Film Studies at the University of St. Andrews. His work centers on historical representation and film, with a particular emphasis on questions of memory and emotion. In addition to *The Hollywood Historical Film* (Blackwell, 2008), *Film Nation: Hollywood Looks at U.S. History* (University of Minnesota Press, revised edition, 2010), and *The Epic Film in World Culture* (Routledge, 2011), recent publications include "Abstraction and Embodiment in the War Film: *Paradise Now* and *The Hurt Locker*," *Journal of War & Culture Studies* (2012); and "Generational Memory and Affect in *Letters from Iwo Jima*," in *A Companion to Historical Film*, ed. R. A. Rosenstone and C. Parvulescu (Blackwell, 2013). Currently he is working on the representation of war in film and photography.

K. L. Evans is the author of *Whale!* (University of Minnesota Press, 2003) and is in the final stages of her latest manuscript, *Realism without Empiricism in Melville's* Moby-Dick. She was formerly Associate Professor of Philosophy and Literature at Yeshiva University's Stern College for Women in New York City, and before that Assistant Professor of English at the University of Redlands, California. Recent publications include "Why the *Tractatus*, like the Old Testament, Is 'Nothing but a Book,'" in *Wittgenstein Reading*, ed. Sascha Bru, Wolfgang Huemer, and Daniel Steuer (De Gruyter, 2013); "While Reading Wittgenstein," in *Stanley Cavell, Literature, and Criticism*, ed. James Loxley and Andrew Taylor (Manchester University Press, 2012); "A Rest from Reason: Wittgenstein, Drury, and the Difference between Madness and Religion," *Philosophy*, 2010; and "A Machine for Becoming Decent," *Denver Quarterly*, 2008. She contributed an essay on *Adaptation* to *The Philosophy of Charlie Kaufman* (University Press of Kentucky, 2011) and an essay on *A Serious Man* to *The Philosophy of the Coen Brothers* (University Press of Kentucky, 2012, updated edition).

Andrew Fiala is Professor of Philosophy, Chair of the Philosophy Department, and Director of the Ethics Center at California State University, Fresno. He is the author of a number of books and articles on ethics, war and peace, religion, and political philosophy, including *Practical Pacifism* (Algora, 2004), *Tolerance and the Ethical Life* (Continuum, 2005), and *The Just War Myth* (Rowman and Littlefield, 2008); his newest book is *Against Religions, Wars, and States: Enlightenment Atheism, Just War Pacifism, and Liberal-Democratic Anarchism* (Rowman and Littlefield, 2013). Forthcoming work includes coauthoring (with Barbara MacKinnon) an extensively revised 8th edition of *Ethics: Theory and Contemporary Issues* (Cengage, 2014). Fiala is coeditor of the journal *Philosophy in the Contemporary World,* and he writes a column on religion and ethics for the *Fresno Bee.*

Joshua Gooch is Assistant Professor of English at D'Youville College in Buffalo, New York. He has published in *Widescreen, LIT: Literature Interpretation Theory, Texas Studies in Literature and Language, Cinema Journal,* and the *Iowa Journal of Cultural Studies;* his essays include "Militants and Cinema: Digital Attempts to Make the Multitude in *Hunger, Che, Public Enemies*" and "'Making a Go of It': Paternity and Prohibition in the Films of Wes Anderson." He is currently at work on a monograph about service work and the Victorian novel.

Garry L. Hagberg is James H. Ottaway Jr. Professor of Philosophy and Aesthetics at Bard College. He is author of *Describing Ourselves: Wittgenstein and Autobiographical Consciousness* (Oxford University Press, 2008), *Art as Language: Wittgenstein, Meaning, and Aesthetic Theory* (Cornell University Press, 1995), and *Meaning and Interpretation: Wittgenstein, Henry James, and Literary Knowledge* (Cornell University Press, 1994); editor of *Art and Ethical Criticism* (Blackwell, 2008); and coeditor of *The Blackwell Companion to the Philosophy of Literature* (Blackwell, 2009). He is also author of about 50 articles and 35 reviews, review-essays, and art catalogue essays; he wrote an essay on *Being John Malkovich* for *The Philosophy of Charlie Kaufman* (University Press of Kentucky, 2011). Hagberg has contributed to philosophical journals such as *Philosophy, Mind,* and *Philosophical Quarterly;* specialized journals such as the *British Journal of Aesthetics,* the *Journal of Aesthetics and Art Criticism,* the *Journal of Aesthetic Education, Philosophy and Literature,* and *Ethics;* journals in the Wittgensteinian tradition such as *Philosophical Investigations* and *Wittgenstein-Studien;* literary journals such as *New Literary History, Poetics Today,* the *Henry James Review,* and the *New Novel Review;* reference works such as *The Encyclopedia of Aesthetics, The Encyclopedia of the Essay, The Encyclopedia of Life-Writing,* and *The Blackwell Companion to Art Theory;* and numerous edited collections. He is editor of the journal *Philosophy and Literature* and serves on the editorial board of the *Journal of Aesthetics and Art Criticism.* He has also served the American Society for Aesthetics as National Program Chair, Trustee, and guest-editor of its journal (for a special issue on Improvisation in the Arts); and he serves on the executive committee of the British Society for Aesthetics, Oxford.

Burke Hilsabeck is Visiting Assistant Professor of Cinema Studies at Oberlin College. His writing has appeared in *Senses of Cinema,* the *Kenyon Review,* and *LOLA,* among other places. He is currently preparing a book on slapstick film comedy and modernism, which explores the surprisingly theoretical work of the slapstick cinema. Hilsabeck argues that the films of comedians from Mack Sennett and Buster Keaton to the Marx Brothers and Jerry Lewis articulate the "accidental specificity" of the Hollywood film—not the self-conscious specificity of high modernist artworks, but the transitory and intermedial identity of vernacular modernity.

Fredric Jameson is William A. Lane Jr. Professor of Comparative Literature and Professor of Romance Studies at Duke University. He previously taught at Harvard, Yale, and the University of California. He is the author of *Postmodernism, or, The Cultural Logic of Late Capitalism* (Duke University Press, 1991), which won the MLA Lowell Award; *Seeds of Time* (Columbia University Press, 1994), *Brecht and Method* (Verso, 1998), *The Cultural Turn* (Verso, 1998), and *A Singular Modernity* (Verso, 2002). His recent works include *Archaeologies of the Future* (Verso, 2005), *The Modernist Papers* (Verso, 2007), *Valences of the Dialectic* (Verso, 2009), *The Hegel Variations* (Verso, 2010), and most recently *Representing Capital* (Verso, 2011). His most frequently taught courses deal with modernism, Third World literature and cinema, Marx and Freud, Jean-Paul Sartre, the modern French novel and cinema, and the Frankfurt School. Among his ongoing concerns are the need to analyze literature as an encoding of political and social imperatives, and the interpretation of modernist and postmodernist assumptions through a rethinking of Marxist methodology. He received the 2008 Holberg Prize for his scholarship.

David LaRocca is Visiting Assistant Professor in the Cinema Department at Binghamton University, and was Visiting Assistant Professor of Philosophy at the College of Cortland, Lecturer in Screen Studies at Ithaca College, and Visiting Scholar in English at Cornell University. Author of *On Emerson* (Wadsworth, 2003) and *Emerson's English Traits and the Natural History of Metaphor* (Bloomsbury, 2013), he is editor of Stanley Cavell's *Emerson's Transcendental Etudes* (Stanford University Press, 2003), *Estimating Emerson: An Anthology of Criticism from Carlyle to Cavell* (Bloomsbury, 2013), *The Phiosopohy of Documentary Films: Image, Sound, Fiction, Truth* (Rowman & Littlefield, 2017), and another title in the Philosophy of Popular Culture Series—*The Philosophy of Charlie Kaufman* (University Press of Kentucky, 2011). He has contributed to other volumes in the same series, including essays on *Malcolm X* for *The Philosophy of Spike Lee* (2011), on *True Grit* for *The Philosophy of the Coen Brothers* (updated edition, 2012), on *Ed Wood* for *The Philosophy of Tim Burton* (2014), and on *The Insider* for *The Philosophy of Michael Mann* (2014). LaRocca studied philosophy, film, rhetoric, and religion at SUNY–Buffalo, the University of California–Berkeley, Vanderbilt, and Harvard. He served as Harvard's Sinclair Kennedy Travelling Fellow in the United Kingdom and as Scholar-in-Residence at Liberty Fund and was a participant in a National Endowment for the Humanities Institute. His journal articles on film include "The Limits of Instruction: Pedagogical Remarks on Lars von Trier's *The Five Obstructions*" (2009) and "A Desperate Education: Reading *Walden* in *All That Heaven Allows*" (2004), both in *Film and Philosophy;* journal articles on photography include "The False Pretender: Deleuze, Sherman, and the Status of Simulacra" in the *Journal of Aesthetics and Art Criticism* (2011) and "Still, Standing: Anonymous Desire and Unarticulated Threat in Julian Hibbard's *The Noir A-Z*" in *Afterimage* (2011); and he wrote the introduction to Takashi Homma's book of photographs, *New Waves: 2000–2013* (Longhouse Projects, 2013). LaRocca directed *Brunello Cucinelli: A New Philosophy of Clothes* (a Fine Print Film Production, 2013), which was an official selection of the New York City International Film Festival, made documentary films with Academy Award–nominated director William Jersey and master cinematographer Robert Elfstrom, and attended Werner Herzog's Rogue Film School. For more information, please contact DavidLaRocca@Post.Harvard.Edu or visit www.DavidLaRocca.org.

Stacey Peebles is Assistant Professor of English and Director of Film Studies at Centre College in Danville, Kentucky. She is the author of *Wel-*

come to the Suck: Narrating the American Soldier's Experience in Iraq (Cornell University Press, 2011) and has two books forthcoming: the anthology *Violence in Literature* (Salem Press) and a monograph tentatively titled *Cormac McCarthy and Performance* (University of Texas Press). She is also editor of the *Cormac McCarthy Journal*. Her other publications include articles about McCarthy's fiction and the film adaptations of his work, the special effects used in war films, and Terrence Malick.

Robert Pippin is the Evelyn Stefansson Nef Distinguished Service Professor in the John U. Nef Committee on Social Thought, the Department of Philosophy, and the College at the University of Chicago and author of *Hollywood Westerns and American Myth: The Importance of Howard Hawks and John Ford for Political Philosophy* (Yale University Press, 2010). A continuous draw for prestigious endowed lectures and the recipient of numerous academic awards, honors, and prizes, Pippin works primarily on the modern German philosophical tradition, with a concentration on Kant and Hegel. In addition, he has published on issues in theories of modernity, political philosophy, theories of self-consciousness, the nature of conceptual change, and the problem of freedom. He is interested in a number of interdisciplinary issues, especially those that involve the relation between philosophy and literature, and has published a book on Henry James and articles on Proust, modern art, and contemporary film. He is currently finishing a book on Hegel's practical philosophy and is at work on a book about political psychology in American film. He is the author of more than one hundred scholarly articles and a dozen books, including *Hegel's Idealism: The Satisfactions of Self-Consciousness* (Cambridge University Press, 1989).

Holger Pötzsch is Associate Professor in Media and Documentation Studies at the Department of Culture and Literature at Tromsø University (UiT), where he is associated with the Border Culture research group. Pötzsch holds an M.A. in Peace and Conflict Studies and a Ph.D. in Media and Documentation Studies. His field of research includes audiovisual representations of war (in particular the war film and computer games), film and cultural memory, digital media and politics, and the interrelation between processes of bordering, technology, and popular culture. In his dissertation, "Between Constitutive Absence and Subversive Presence: Self and Other in the Contemporary War Film," he focused on the productive and disruptive potentials of shared locations and border-crossing characters in Hollywood war films and applied a combination of cognitive film theory with a postfoundational discourse theoretical approach to reception. Recent work includes "*Black Hawk Down:* Film zwischen Reflektion und Konstruktion gesellschaftlicher Wirklichkeit," *International Review of Education* 55 (2009); "Challenging the Border as Barrier: Liminality in Terrence Malick's *The Thin Red Line,*" *Journal for Borderlands Studies* 25, no. 1 (2010); "Renegotiating Difficult Pasts: Two Documentary Dramas on Bloody Sunday, Derry 1972," *Memory Studies* 5, no. 2 (2012); and "Beyond Mimesis: War, Memory, and History in Clint Eastwood's *Flags of Our Fathers,*" in *Eastwood's Iwo Jima: A Critical Engagement with* Flags of our Fathers *and* Letters from Iwo Jima, ed. Anne Gjelsvik and Rikke Schubart (Wallflower Press, 2013).

Lawrence F. Rhu holds the William Joseph Todd Chair in the Italian Renaissance at the University of South Carolina, where he teaches English and comparative literature. He has written two books, *Stanley Cavell's American Dream* (Fordham University Press, 2006) and *The Genesis of Tasso's Narrative Theory* (Wayne State University Press, 1993), and numerous articles, mainly on Shakespeare and Renaissance literature. His edition of *The Winter's Tale* recently appeared in the Evans Shakespeare Editions from Cengage.

Garrett Stewart is James O. Freedman Professor of Letters at the University of Iowa and the author of two books on film, *Between Film and Screen: Modernism's Photo Synthesis* (University of Chicago Press, 2000) and *Framed Time: Toward a Postfilmic Cinema* (University of Chicago Press, 2007), and many volumes on narrative fiction and visual media. He has written about current war films in recent articles for *Film Quarterly,* including "Digital Fatigue" (Summer 2009). His essay in the current volume builds on the analytic mode of "narratography" developed in his *Framed Time* and pursued in a forthcoming study called *Closed Circuits: Screening Narrative Surveillance* (University of Chicago Press).

INDEX

The Philosophy of Popular Culture

The books published in the Philosophy of Popular Culture series will illuminate and explore philosophical themes and ideas that occur in popular culture. The goal of this series is to demonstrate how philosophical inquiry has been reinvigorated by increased scholarly interest in the intersection of popular culture and philosophy, as well as to explore through philosophical analysis beloved modes of entertainment, such as movies, TV shows, and music. Philosophical concepts will be made accessible to the general reader through examples in popular culture. This series seeks to publish both established and emerging scholars who will engage a major area of popular culture for philosophical interpretation and examine the philosophical underpinnings of its themes. Eschewing ephemeral trends of philosophical and cultural theory, authors will establish and elaborate on connections between traditional philosophical ideas from important thinkers and the ever-expanding world of popular culture.

Series Editor

Mark T. Conard, Marymount Manhattan College, NY

Books in the Series

The Philosophy of Stanley Kubrick, edited by Jerold J. Abrams
The Philosophy of Ang Lee, edited by Robert Arp, Adam Barkman, and James McRae
Football and Philosophy, edited by Michael W. Austin
Tennis and Philosophy, edited by David Baggett
The Philosophy of J. J. Abrams, edited by Patricia Brace and Robert Arp
The Philosophy of Film Noir, edited by Mark T. Conard
The Philosophy of Martin Scorsese, edited by Mark T. Conard
The Philosophy of Neo-Noir, edited by Mark T. Conard
The Philosophy of Spike Lee, edited by Mark T. Conard
The Philosophy of the Coen Brothers, edited by Mark T. Conard
The Philosophy of David Lynch, edited by William J. Devlin and Shai Biderman

The Philosophy of the Beats, edited by Sharin N. Elkholy
The Philosophy of Horror, edited by Thomas Fahy
The Philosophy of The X-Files, edited by Dean A. Kowalski
Steven Spielberg and Philosophy, edited by Dean A. Kowalski
The Philosophy of Joss Whedon, edited by Dean A. Kowalski and S. Evan Kreider
The Philosophy of Charlie Kaufman, edited by David LaRocca
The Philosophy of War Films, edited by David LaRocca
The Philosophy of Clint Eastwood, edited by Richard T. McClelland and Brian B. Clayton
The Philosophy of Tim Burton, edited by Jennifer L. McMahon
The Philosophy of the Western, edited by Jennifer L. McMahon and B. Steve Csaki
The Philosophy of Steven Soderbergh, edited by R. Barton Palmer and Steven M. Sanders
The Olympics and Philosophy, edited by Heather L. Reid and Michael W. Austin
The Philosophy of David Cronenberg, edited by Simon Riches
The Philosophy of Science Fiction Film, edited by Steven Sanders
The Philosophy of TV Noir, edited by Steven Sanders and Aeon J. Skoble
The Philosophy of Michael Mann, edited by Steven Sanders, Aeon J. Skoble, and R. Barton Palmer
The Philosophy of Sherlock Holmes, edited by Philip Tallon and David Baggett
Basketball and Philosophy, edited by Jerry L. Walls and Gregory Bassham
Golf and Philosophy, edited by Andy Wible